Nissan Pathfinder Automotive Repair Manual

by Jeff Killingsworth and John H Haynes

Member of the Guild of Motoring Writers

Models covered:

Nissan Pathfinder - 2005 through 2014

Does not include information specific to hybrid models

ABCDE
FGHIJ
KLMNO
PQRST

Haynes Publishing Group
Sparkford Nr Yeovil
Somerset BA22 7JJ England

Haynes North America, Inc
861 Lawrence Drive
Newbury Park
California 91320 USA

Acknowledgements

Technical writers who contributed to this project include John Wegmann and Bob Henderson.

© **Haynes North America, Inc. 2015**

With permission from J.H. Haynes & Co. Ltd.

A book in the Haynes Automotive Repair Manual Series

Printed in the U.S.A.

ISBN-13: 978-1-62092-145-6
ISBN-10: 1-62092-145-6

Library of Congress Control Number: 2015940176

Contents

Introductory pages

About this manual	0-5
Introduction	0-5
Vehicle identification numbers	0-6
Recall information	0-7
Buying parts	0-10
Maintenance techniques, tools and working facilities	0-11
Jacking and towing	0-18
Booster battery (jump) starting	0-19
Automotive chemicals and lubricants	0-20
Conversion factors	0-21
Fraction/decimal/millimeter equivalents	0-22
Safety first!	0-23
Troubleshooting	0-24

Chapter 1
Tune-up and routine maintenance — 1-1

Chapter 2 Part A
V6 engines — 2A-1

Chapter 2 Part B
V8 engine — 2B-1

Chapter 2 Part C
General engine overhaul procedures — 2C-1

Chapter 3
Cooling, heating and air conditioning systems — 3-1

Chapter 4
Fuel and exhaust systems — 4-1

Chapter 5
Engine electrical systems — 5-1

Chapter 6
Emissions and engine control systems — 6-1

Chapter 7 Part A
Automatic transmission/transaxle — 7A-1

Chapter 7 Part B
Transfer case - 2012 and earlier models — 7B-1

Chapter 7 Part C
Transfer case - 2013 and later models — 7C-1

Chapter 8
Driveline — 8-1

Chapter 9
Brakes — 9-1

Chapter 10
Suspension and steering systems — 10-1

Chapter 11
Body — 11-1

Chapter 12
Chassis electrical system — 12-1

Wiring diagrams — 12-19

Index — IND-1

Haynes photographer and mechanic with a 2008 Nissan Pathfinder

About this manual

Its purpose

The purpose of this manual is to help you get the best value from your vehicle. It can do so in several ways. It can help you decide what work must be done, even if you choose to have it done by a dealer service department or a repair shop; it provides information and procedures for routine maintenance and servicing; and it offers diagnostic and repair procedures to follow when trouble occurs.

We hope you use the manual to tackle the work yourself. For many simpler jobs, doing it yourself may be quicker than arranging an appointment to get the vehicle into a shop and making the trips to leave it and pick it up. More importantly, a lot of money can be saved by avoiding the expense the shop must pass on to you to cover its labor and overhead costs. An added benefit is the sense of satisfaction and accomplishment that you feel after doing the job yourself.

Using the manual

The manual is divided into Chapters. Each Chapter is divided into numbered Sections, which are headed in bold type between horizontal lines. Each Section consists of consecutively numbered paragraphs.

The reference numbers used in illustration captions pinpoint the pertinent Section and the Step within that Section. That is, illustration 3.2 means the illustration refers to Section 3 and Step (or paragraph) 2 within that Section.

Procedures, once described in the text, are not normally repeated. When it's necessary to refer to another Chapter, the reference will be given as Chapter and Section number. Cross references given without use of the word "Chapter" apply to Sections and/or paragraphs in the same Chapter. For example, "see Section 8" means in the same Chapter.

References to the left or right side of the vehicle assume you are sitting in the driver's seat, facing forward.

Even though we have prepared this manual with extreme care, neither the publisher nor the author can accept responsibility for any errors in, or omissions from, the information given.

NOTE

A **Note** provides information necessary to properly complete a procedure or information which will make the procedure easier to understand.

CAUTION

A **Caution** provides a special procedure or special steps which must be taken while completing the procedure where the Caution is found. Not heeding a Caution can result in damage to the assembly being worked on.

WARNING

A **Warning** provides a special procedure or special steps which must be taken while completing the procedure where the Warning is found. Not heeding a Warning can result in personal injury.

Introduction

2012 and earlier models are equipped with either a 4.0L V6 or 5.6L V8 engine. 2013 and later models are only available with a 3.5L V6 engine. All models are equipped with a sequential multi-port electronic fuel injection system.

2012 and earlier models are of body-on-frame construction with a longitudinally mounted engine and transmission. 2013 and later models are of steel uni-body construction with a transversely mounted engine and transaxle.

On 2012 and earlier models, the engine transmits power to the rear wheels through a 5-speed automatic transmission via a driveshaft and and rear driveaxles. On 2013 and later models, the engine transmits power to the front wheels through a continuously variable automatic transaxle (CVT) via independent driveaxles.

All-Wheel Drive (AWD) is available as an option. On 2012 and earlier AWD models, the front wheels are also propelled by way of a transfer case, driveshaft and two front driveaxles. On 2013 and later models AWD models, the rear wheels are also propelled by way of a transfer case, driveshaft, rear differential and two rear driveaxles.

All models are equipped with four-wheel independent suspension. The rack-and-pinion steering unit is mounted behind the engine. Power assist is standard on all models; 2012 and earlier models utilize a belt-driven hydraulic power steering pump, while 2013 and later models are equipped with an electric motor-driven hydraulic power steering pump.

All models are equipped with power assisted front and rear disc brakes. An anti-lock braking system is standard equipment on all models.

Vehicle identification numbers

Modifications are a continuing and unpublicized process in vehicle manufacturing. Since spare parts manuals and lists are compiled on a numerical basis, the individual vehicle numbers are essential to correctly identify the component required.

Vehicle Identification Number (VIN)

This very important identification number is located on a plate attached to the dashboard inside the windshield on the driver's side of the vehicle (see illustration). The VIN also appears on the Vehicle Certificate of Title and Registration. It contains information such as where and when the vehicle was manufactured, the model year and the body style.
VIN engine and model year codes

Two particularly important pieces of information found in the VIN are the engine code and the model year code. Counting from the left, the engine code letter designation is the 4th character and the model year code designation is the 10th character.

On the models covered by this manual the engine codes are:

A VQ40DE 4.0L DOHC V6
   (2005 through 2012 models)
B VK56DE 5.6L DOHC V8
   (2008 through 2012 models)
A VQ35DE 3.5L DOHC V6
   (2013 and later models)

On the models covered by this manual the model year codes are:

Code	Year
5	2005
6	2006
7	2007
8	2008
9	2009
A	2010
B	2011
C	2012
D	2013
E	2014

Manufacturer's Certification Regulation label

The manufacturer's Certification Regulation label is attached to the driver's side door post (see illustration). The label contains the name of the manufacturer, the month and year of production, the Gross Vehicle Weight Rating (GVWR), the Gross Axle Weight Rating (GAWR) and the certification statement.

Engine identification number

On 4.0L V6 engine models, the engine code number is located at the left end (driver's side) of the engine under the a/c compressor (see illustration). On 3.5L V6 engines, the engine code number is located at the left end (driver's side) of the engine, just above the transaxle bellhousing. On 5.6L V8 engines, the engine code number is located at the front of the engine block on a machined surface just behind the water pump (see illustration).

Transmission/Transaxle identification number

On 2012 and earlier models, the transmission identification number is stamped on

The Vehicle Identification Number (VIN) is visible through the driver's side of the windshield

The Manufacturer's Certification label is affixed to the driver's side door post

The Engine Identification Number is stamped on the left end (driver's side) of the engine block (under the a/c compressor) - 4.0L V6 engine model shown

Engine identification number - V8 models

The transmission ID number is located on a tag mounted to the side of the transmission, near the shift cable - 2012 and earlier models shown

The Vehicle Emissions Control Information (VECI) label is located on the underside of the hood

top of the bellhousing **(see illustration)**. On 2013 and later models, the transaxle identification number is stamped on top of the bellhousing.

Vehicle Emissions Control Information (VECI) label

The emissions control information label is found on the bottom side of the hood. This label contains information on the emissions control equipment installed on the vehicle **(see illustration)**.

Recall information

Vehicle recalls are carried out by the manufacturer in the rare event of a possible safety-related defect. The vehicle's registered owner is contacted at the address on file at the Department of Motor Vehicles and given the details of the recall. Remedial work is carried out free of charge at a dealer service department.

If you are the new owner of a used vehicle which was subject to a recall and you want to be sure that the work has been carried out, it's best to contact a dealer service department and ask about your individual vehicle - you'll need to furnish them your Vehicle Identification Number (VIN).

The table below is based on information provided by the National Highway Traffic Safety Administration (NHTSA), the body which oversees vehicle recalls in the United States. The recall database is updated constantly. For the latest information on vehicle recalls, check the NHTSA website at www.nhtsa.gov, www.safercar.gov, or call the NHTSA hotline at 1-888-327-4236.

Recall date	Recall campaign number	Model(s) affected	Concern
DEC 29, 2008	08V690000	2005, 2006, 2007, 2008, 2009 Pathfinder	On some models operated in areas of the country which use heavy concentrations of road salt in the winter, a mixture of snow/water and salt can enter into the front Crash Zone Sensor (CZS) housing. This issue could result in the non-deployment of the driver and passenger front airbags in a crash, increasing the risk of personal injury.
MAR 03, 2010	10V075000	2006, 2008 Pathfinder	On some models, the molded fuel tank shells can deform, causing the fuel sender float arm to contact an embossment molded into the tank shell, causing the instrument panel fuel gauge to show that the vehicle has approximately one quarter tank when the fuel tank is empty. This could cause the vehicle to run out of gas and stall in traffic, increasing the risk of a crash.

Recall date	Recall campaign number	Model(s) affected	Concern
MAR 24, 2010	10V115000	2010 Pathfinder	On some models, the fasteners securing the passenger front airbag module, and the steering shaft positioning bracket, may not have been tightened to the proper torque specification. In the event of a crash, the passenger front airbag deployment trajectory might be affected. The fasteners could possibly come out of the steering column positioning bracket increasing the risk of a crash.
MAY 14, 2010	10V208000	2010 Pathfinder	On some models, the lower control link assembly has two cylindrical collars forming the inboard attachment points to the chassis. Due to an improper welding process some collars may contain welds that do not meet strength specifications. If the collar weld separates, the vehicle handling will deteriorate, possibly resulting in a vehicle crash.
MAY 20, 2010	10E019000	2005, 2006, 2007, 2008, 2009, 2010 Pathfinder	On some models, certain front and rear lower links (sold as replacement parts for model year 2005 through 2010 vehicles) were subjected to an improper welding process, and some collars may contain welds that do not meet strength specifications. If the collar weld separates, the vehicle handling will deteriorate, possibly resulting in a vehicle crash.
SEP 10, 2010	10V401000	2008, 2009 Pathfinder	On some models equipped with a Garmin NUVI model 750 navigation system, the batteries contained in the affected GPS units can overheat. Overheated batteries could result in a fire.
OCT 28, 2010	10V517000	2005, 2006 Pathfinder	On some models, the Intelligent Power Distribution Module (IPDM) assembly contains an Engine Control Module (ECM) relay that has a diode for electrical current noise reduction. The ECM relay may allow silicon vapor to form and, over time, the silicon evaporates from the diode molding, causing silicon oxide to develop on the ECM relay contact due to arcing. This could cause engine stalling, increasing the risk of a crash.
DEC 19, 2011	11V592000	2011, 2012 Pathfinder	On some models, some of the bolts that connect the engine oil cooler and the engine oil filter to the engine may have been manufactured to below specification strength. As a result, the bolt may break at the oil filter attachment point and cause an engine oil leak. If there is an engine oil leak, the engine oil pressure would drop and the engine could seize, increasing the risk of a crash.
SEP 20, 2012	12V462000	2012 Pathfinder	Some models may have been equipped with front wheel hubs that may not meet the design hardness specifications. A wheel hub that was manufactured below hardness specification may wear prematurely and eventually crack. If the vehicle is driven in this condition, the wheel hub may break, possibly resulting in a vehicle crash.

Recall date	Recall campaign number	Model(s) affected	Concern
OCT 17, 2013	13V445000	2013, 2014 Pathfinder	On some models, during light braking on rough roads, the antilock brake system (ABS) brake pressure output software may lead to an increase in stopping distance. The increased stopping distance may increase the risk of a crash.
SEP 26, 2013	13V456000	2014 Pathfinder	On some models with Almond interiors only, the instrument panel tear seam on the passenger frontal airbag was incorrectly cut on the back side of the instrument panel, which could cause the airbag to not deploy properly. In the event of a crash necessitating deployment of the passenger's frontal airbag, the improper airbag deployment may increase the risk of personal injury.
MAR 25, 2014	14V138000	2013, 2014 Pathfinder	On some models, the Occupant Classification System (OCS) software may incorrectly classify the passenger seat as empty, when it is occupied by an adult. If the OCS does not detect an adult occupant in the passenger seat, the passenger airbag would be deactivated. Failure of the passenger airbag to deploy during a crash (where deployment is warranted) could increase the risk of injury to the passenger.
MAR 26, 2014	14V142000	2013 Pathfinder	On some models equipped with a continuously variable transmission (CVT), the internal oil cooler (ITOC) hose may detach from the cooler due to inadequate clamping force, allowing transmission fluid to leak. The loss of transmission fluid could cause the transmission to function improperly and the vehicle to stop accelerating, increasing the risk of a crash.
MAY 02, 2014	14V229000	2014 Pathfinder	On some models, the right side wheels may have one lug nut each that was not properly tightened. If the lug nut becomes loose from not being properly tightened, it may fall off, allowing the other lug nuts to become loose, possibly resulting in a wheel separation, and increasing the risk of a crash.

Buying parts

Replacement parts are available from many sources, which generally fall into one of two categories - authorized dealer parts departments and independent retail auto parts stores. Our advice concerning these parts is as follows:

Retail auto parts stores: Good auto parts stores will stock frequently needed components which wear out relatively fast, such as clutch components, exhaust systems, brake parts, tune-up parts, etc. These stores often supply new or reconditioned parts on an exchange basis, which can save a considerable amount of money. Discount auto parts stores are often very good places to buy materials and parts needed for general vehicle maintenance such as oil, grease, filters, spark plugs, belts, touch-up paint, bulbs, etc. They also usually sell tools and general accessories, have convenient hours, charge lower prices and can often be found not far from home.

Authorized dealer parts department: This is the best source for parts which are unique to the vehicle and not generally available elsewhere (such as major engine parts, transmission parts, trim pieces, etc.).

Warranty information: If the vehicle is still covered under warranty, be sure that any replacement parts purchased - regardless of the source - do not invalidate the warranty!

To be sure of obtaining the correct parts, have engine and chassis numbers available and, if possible, take the old parts along for positive identification.

Maintenance techniques, tools and working facilities

Maintenance techniques

There are a number of techniques involved in maintenance and repair that will be referred to throughout this manual. Application of these techniques will enable the home mechanic to be more efficient, better organized and capable of performing the various tasks properly, which will ensure that the repair job is thorough and complete.

Fasteners

Fasteners are nuts, bolts, studs and screws used to hold two or more parts together. There are a few things to keep in mind when working with fasteners. Almost all of them use a locking device of some type, either a lockwasher, locknut, locking tab or thread adhesive. All threaded fasteners should be clean and straight, with undamaged threads and undamaged corners on the hex head where the wrench fits. Develop the habit of replacing all damaged nuts and bolts with new ones. Special locknuts with nylon or fiber inserts can only be used once. If they are removed, they lose their locking ability and must be replaced with new ones.

Rusted nuts and bolts should be treated with a penetrating fluid to ease removal and prevent breakage. Some mechanics use turpentine in a spout-type oil can, which works quite well. After applying the rust penetrant, let it work for a few minutes before trying to loosen the nut or bolt. Badly rusted fasteners may have to be chiseled or sawed off or removed with a special nut breaker, available at tool stores.

If a bolt or stud breaks off in an assembly, it can be drilled and removed with a special tool commonly available for this purpose. Most automotive machine shops can perform this task, as well as other repair procedures, such as the repair of threaded holes that have been stripped out.

Flat washers and lockwashers, when removed from an assembly, should always be replaced exactly as removed. Replace any damaged washers with new ones. Never use a lockwasher on any soft metal surface (such as aluminum), thin sheet metal or plastic.

Fastener sizes

For a number of reasons, automobile manufacturers are making wider and wider use of metric fasteners. Therefore, it is important to be able to tell the difference between standard (sometimes called U.S. or SAE) and metric hardware, since they cannot be interchanged.

All bolts, whether standard or metric, are sized according to diameter, thread pitch and length. For example, a standard 1/2 - 13 x 1 bolt is 1/2 inch in diameter, has 13 threads per inch and is 1 inch long. An M12 - 1.75 x 25 metric bolt is 12 mm in diameter, has a thread pitch of 1.75 mm (the distance between threads) and is 25 mm long. The two bolts are nearly identical, and easily confused, but they are not interchangeable.

In addition to the differences in diameter, thread pitch and length, metric and standard bolts can also be distinguished by examining the bolt heads. To begin with, the distance across the flats on a standard bolt head is measured in inches, while the same dimension on a metric bolt is sized in millimeters (the same is true for nuts). As a result, a standard wrench should not be used on a metric bolt and a metric wrench should not be used on a standard bolt. Also, most standard bolts have slashes radiating out from the center of the head to denote the grade or strength of the bolt, which is an indication of the amount of torque that can be applied to it. The greater the number of slashes, the greater the strength of the bolt. Grades 0 through 5 are commonly used on automobiles. Metric bolts have a property class (grade) number, rather than a slash, molded into their heads to indicate bolt strength. In this case, the higher the number, the stronger the bolt. Property class numbers 8.8, 9.8 and 10.9 are commonly used on automobiles.

Strength markings can also be used to distinguish standard hex nuts from metric hex nuts. Many standard nuts have dots stamped into one side, while metric nuts are marked with a number. The greater the number of

dots, or the higher the number, the greater the strength of the nut.

Metric studs are also marked on their ends according to property class (grade). Larger studs are numbered (the same as metric bolts), while smaller studs carry a geometric code to denote grade.

It should be noted that many fasteners, especially Grades 0 through 2, have no distinguishing marks on them. When such is the case, the only way to determine whether it is standard or metric is to measure the thread pitch or compare it to a known fastener of the same size.

Standard fasteners are often referred to as SAE, as opposed to metric. However, it should be noted that SAE technically refers to a non-metric fine thread fastener only. Coarse thread non-metric fasteners are referred to as USS sizes.

Since fasteners of the same size (both standard and metric) may have different

strength ratings, be sure to reinstall any bolts, studs or nuts removed from your vehicle in their original locations. Also, when replacing a fastener with a new one, make sure that the new one has a strength rating equal to or greater than the original.

Tightening sequences and procedures

Most threaded fasteners should be tightened to a specific torque value (torque is the twisting force applied to a threaded component such as a nut or bolt). Overtightening the fastener can weaken it and cause it to break, while undertightening can cause it to eventually come loose. Bolts, screws and studs, depending on the material they are made of and their thread diameters, have specific torque values, many of which are noted in the Specifications at the beginning of each Chapter. Be sure to follow the torque recommen-

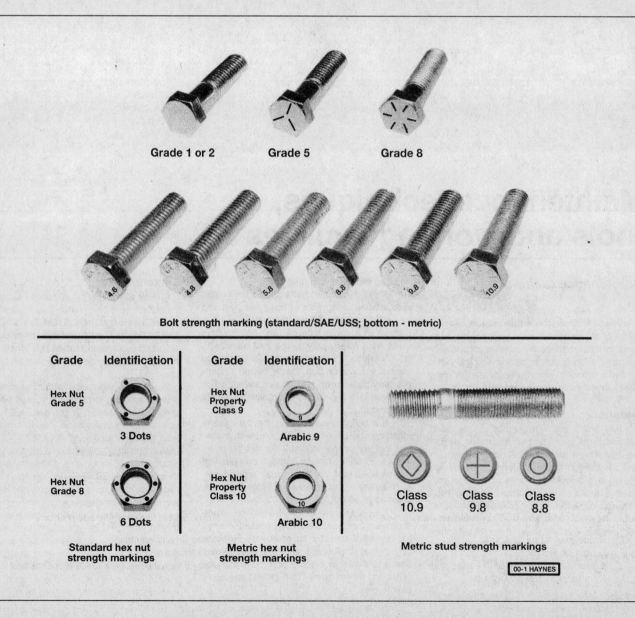

Grade 1 or 2   Grade 5   Grade 8

Bolt strength marking (standard/SAE/USS; bottom - metric)

Grade	Identification		Grade	Identification
Hex Nut Grade 5	3 Dots		Hex Nut Property Class 9	Arabic 9
Hex Nut Grade 8	6 Dots		Hex Nut Property Class 10	Arabic 10

Standard hex nut strength markings

Metric hex nut strength markings

Class 10.9   Class 9.8   Class 8.8

Metric stud strength markings

00-1 HAYNES

dations closely. For fasteners not assigned a specific torque, a general torque value chart is presented here as a guide. These torque values are for dry (unlubricated) fasteners threaded into steel or cast iron (not aluminum). As was previously mentioned, the size and grade of a fastener determine the amount of torque that can safely be applied to it. The figures listed here are approximate for Grade 2 and Grade 3 fasteners. Higher grades can tolerate higher torque values.

Fasteners laid out in a pattern, such as cylinder head bolts, oil pan bolts, differential cover bolts, etc., must be loosened or tightened in sequence to avoid warping the component. This sequence will normally be shown in the appropriate Chapter. If a specific pattern is not given, the following procedures can be used to prevent warping.

Initially, the bolts or nuts should be assembled finger-tight only. Next, they should be tightened one full turn each, in a criss-cross or diagonal pattern. After each one has been tightened one full turn, return to the first one and tighten them all one-half turn, following the same pattern. Finally, tighten each of them one-quarter turn at a time until each fastener has been tightened to the proper torque. To loosen and remove the fasteners, the procedure would be reversed.

Metric thread sizes

	Ft-lbs	Nm
M-6	6 to 9	9 to 12
M-8	14 to 21	19 to 28
M-10	28 to 40	38 to 54
M-12	50 to 71	68 to 96
M-14	80 to 140	109 to 154

Pipe thread sizes

	Ft-lbs	Nm
1/8	5 to 8	7 to 10
1/4	12 to 18	17 to 24
3/8	22 to 33	30 to 44
1/2	25 to 35	34 to 47

U.S. thread sizes

	Ft-lbs	Nm
1/4 - 20	6 to 9	9 to 12
5/16 - 18	12 to 18	17 to 24
5/16 - 24	14 to 20	19 to 27
3/8 - 16	22 to 32	30 to 43
3/8 - 24	27 to 38	37 to 51
7/16 - 14	40 to 55	55 to 74
7/16 - 20	40 to 60	55 to 81
1/2 - 13	55 to 80	75 to 108

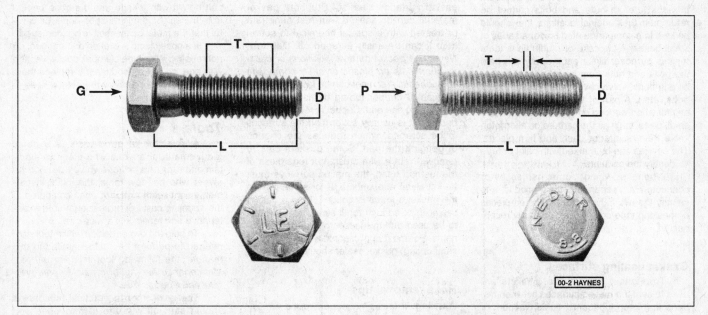

Standard (SAE and USS) bolt dimensions/grade marks

G   Grade marks (bolt strength)
L   Length (in inches)
T   Thread pitch (number of threads per inch)
D   Nominal diameter (in inches)

Metric bolt dimensions/grade marks

P   Property class (bolt strength)
L   Length (in millimeters)
T   Thread pitch (distance between threads in millimeters)
D   Diameter

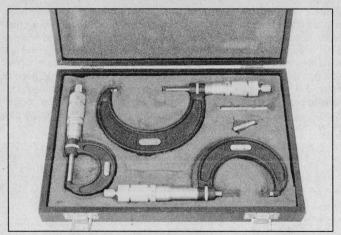

Micrometer set

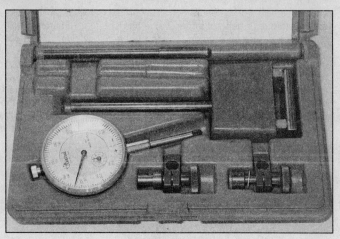

Dial indicator set

Component disassembly

Component disassembly should be done with care and purpose to help ensure that the parts go back together properly. Always keep track of the sequence in which parts are removed. Make note of special characteristics or marks on parts that can be installed more than one way, such as a grooved thrust washer on a shaft. It is a good idea to lay the disassembled parts out on a clean surface in the order that they were removed. It may also be helpful to make sketches or take instant photos of components before removal.

When removing fasteners from a component, keep track of their locations. Sometimes threading a bolt back in a part, or putting the washers and nut back on a stud, can prevent mix-ups later. If nuts and bolts cannot be returned to their original locations, they should be kept in a compartmented box or a series of small boxes. A cupcake or muffin tin is ideal for this purpose, since each cavity can hold the bolts and nuts from a particular area (i.e. oil pan bolts, valve cover bolts, engine mount bolts, etc.). A pan of this type is especially helpful when working on assemblies with very small parts, such as the carburetor, alternator, valve train or interior dash and trim pieces. The cavities can be marked with paint or tape to identify the contents.

Whenever wiring looms, harnesses or connectors are separated, it is a good idea to identify the two halves with numbered pieces of masking tape so they can be easily reconnected.

Gasket sealing surfaces

Throughout any vehicle, gaskets are used to seal the mating surfaces between two parts and keep lubricants, fluids, vacuum or pressure contained in an assembly.

Many times these gaskets are coated with a liquid or paste-type gasket sealing compound before assembly. Age, heat and pressure can sometimes cause the two parts to stick together so tightly that they are very difficult to separate. Often, the assembly can

be loosened by striking it with a soft-face hammer near the mating surfaces. A regular hammer can be used if a block of wood is placed between the hammer and the part. Do not hammer on cast parts or parts that could be easily damaged. With any particularly stubborn part, always recheck to make sure that every fastener has been removed.

Avoid using a screwdriver or bar to pry apart an assembly, as they can easily mar the gasket sealing surfaces of the parts, which must remain smooth. If prying is absolutely necessary, use an old broom handle, but keep in mind that extra clean up will be necessary if the wood splinters.

After the parts are separated, the old gasket must be carefully scraped off and the gasket surfaces cleaned. Stubborn gasket material can be soaked with rust penetrant or treated with a special chemical to soften it so it can be easily scraped off. **Caution:** *Never use gasket removal solutions or caustic chemicals on plastic or other composite components.* A scraper can be fashioned from a piece of copper tubing by flattening and sharpening one end. Copper is recommended because it is usually softer than the surfaces to be scraped, which reduces the chance of gouging the part. Some gaskets can be removed with a wire brush, but regardless of the method used, the mating surfaces must be left clean and smooth. If for some reason the gasket surface is gouged, then a gasket sealer thick enough to fill scratches will have to be used during reassembly of the components. For most applications, a non-drying (or semi-drying) gasket sealer should be used.

Hose removal tips

Warning: *If the vehicle is equipped with air conditioning, do not disconnect any of the A/C hoses without first having the system depressurized by a dealer service department or a service station.*

Hose removal precautions closely parallel gasket removal precautions. Avoid scratching or gouging the surface that the

hose mates against or the connection may leak. This is especially true for radiator hoses. Because of various chemical reactions, the rubber in hoses can bond itself to the metal spigot that the hose fits over. To remove a hose, first loosen the hose clamps that secure it to the spigot. Then, with slip-joint pliers, grab the hose at the clamp and rotate it around the spigot. Work it back and forth until it is completely free, then pull it off. Silicone or other lubricants will ease removal if they can be applied between the hose and the outside of the spigot. Apply the same lubricant to the inside of the hose and the outside of the spigot to simplify installation.

As a last resort (and if the hose is to be replaced with a new one anyway), the rubber can be slit with a knife and the hose peeled from the spigot. If this must be done, be careful that the metal connection is not damaged.

If a hose clamp is broken or damaged, do not reuse it. Wire-type clamps usually weaken with age, so it is a good idea to replace them with screw-type clamps whenever a hose is removed.

Tools

A selection of good tools is a basic requirement for anyone who plans to maintain and repair his or her own vehicle. For the owner who has few tools, the initial investment might seem high, but when compared to the spiraling costs of professional auto maintenance and repair, it is a wise one.

To help the owner decide which tools are needed to perform the tasks detailed in this manual, the following tool lists are offered: *Maintenance and minor repair, Repair/overhaul* and *Special*.

The newcomer to practical mechanics should start off with the *maintenance and minor repair* tool kit, which is adequate for the simpler jobs performed on a vehicle. Then, as confidence and experience grow, the owner can tackle more difficult tasks, buying additional tools as they are needed. Eventually the basic kit will be expanded into the *repair and overhaul* tool set. Over a period of time, the

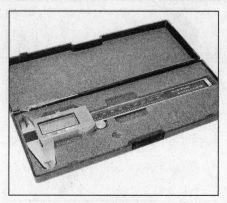

Dial caliper

Hand-operated vacuum pump

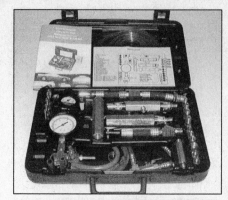

Fuel pressure gauge set

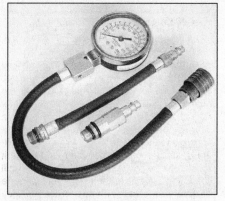

Compression gauge with spark plug hole adapter

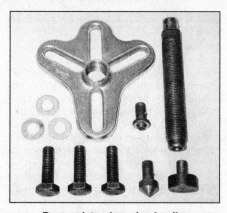

Damper/steering wheel puller

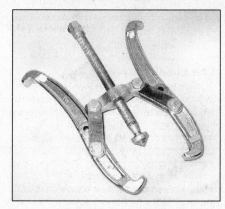

General purpose puller

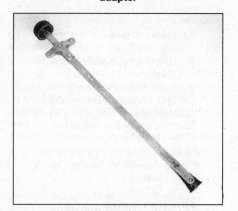

Hydraulic lifter removal tool

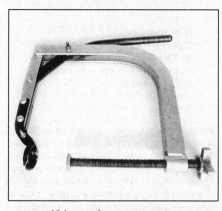

Valve spring compressor

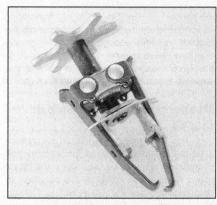

Valve spring compressor

Ridge reamer

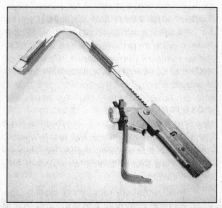

Piston ring groove cleaning tool

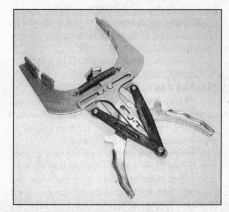

Ring removal/installation tool

Ring compressor

Cylinder hone

Brake hold-down spring tool

Torque angle gauge

Clutch plate alignment tool

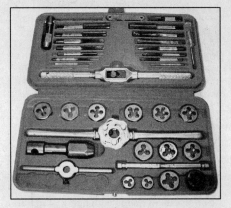

Tap and die set

experienced do-it-yourselfer will assemble a tool set complete enough for most repair and overhaul procedures and will add tools from the special category when it is felt that the expense is justified by the frequency of use.

Maintenance and minor repair tool kit

The tools in this list should be considered the minimum required for performance of routine maintenance, servicing and minor repair work. We recommend the purchase of combination wrenches (box-end and open-end combined in one wrench). While more expensive than open end wrenches, they offer the advantages of both types of wrench.

Combination wrench set (1/4-inch to
   1 inch or 6 mm to 19 mm)
Adjustable wrench, 8 inch
Spark plug wrench with rubber insert
Spark plug gap adjusting tool
Feeler gauge set
Brake bleeder wrench
Standard screwdriver (5/16-inch x
   6 inch)
Phillips screwdriver (No. 2 x 6 inch)
Combination pliers - 6 inch
Hacksaw and assortment of blades
Tire pressure gauge
Grease gun
Oil can
Fine emery cloth

Wire brush
Battery post and cable cleaning tool
Oil filter wrench
Funnel (medium size)
Safety goggles
Jackstands (2)
Drain pan

Note: If basic tune-ups are going to be part of routine maintenance, it will be necessary to purchase a good quality stroboscopic timing light and combination tachometer/dwell meter. Although they are included in the list of special tools, it is mentioned here because they are absolutely necessary for tuning most vehicles properly.

Repair and overhaul tool set

These tools are essential for anyone who plans to perform major repairs and are in addition to those in the maintenance and minor repair tool kit. Included is a comprehensive set of sockets which, though expensive, are invaluable because of their versatility, especially when various extensions and drives are available. We recommend the 1/2-inch drive over the 3/8-inch drive. Although the larger drive is bulky and more expensive, it has the capacity of accepting a very wide range of large sockets. Ideally, however, the mechanic should have a 3/8-inch drive set and a 1/2-inch drive set.

Socket set(s)
Reversible ratchet

Extension - 10 inch
Universal joint
Torque wrench (same size drive as
   sockets)
Ball peen hammer - 8 ounce
Soft-face hammer (plastic/rubber)
Standard screwdriver (1/4-inch x 6 inch)
Standard screwdriver (stubby -
   5/16-inch)
Phillips screwdriver (No. 3 x 8 inch)
Phillips screwdriver (stubby - No. 2)
Pliers - vise grip
Pliers - lineman's
Pliers - needle nose
Pliers - snap-ring (internal and external)
Cold chisel - 1/2-inch
Scribe
Scraper (made from flattened copper
   tubing)
Centerpunch
Pin punches (1/16, 1/8, 3/16-inch)
Steel rule/straightedge - 12 inch
Allen wrench set (1/8 to 3/8-inch or
   4 mm to 10 mm)
A selection of files
Wire brush (large)
Jackstands (second set)
Jack (scissor or hydraulic type)

Note: Another tool which is often useful is an electric drill with a chuck capacity of 3/8-inch and a set of good quality drill bits.

Special tools

The tools in this list include those which are not used regularly, are expensive to buy, or which need to be used in accordance with their manufacturer's instructions. Unless these tools will be used frequently, it is not very economical to purchase many of them. A consideration would be to split the cost and use between yourself and a friend or friends. In addition, most of these tools can be obtained from a tool rental shop on a temporary basis.

This list primarily contains only those tools and instruments widely available to the public, and not those special tools produced by the vehicle manufacturer for distribution to dealer service departments. Occasionally, references to the manufacturer's special tools are included in the text of this manual. Generally, an alternative method of doing the job without the special tool is offered. However, sometimes there is no alternative to their use. Where this is the case, and the tool cannot be purchased or borrowed, the work should be turned over to the dealer service department or an automotive repair shop.

Valve spring compressor
Piston ring groove cleaning tool
Piston ring compressor
Piston ring installation tool
Cylinder compression gauge
Cylinder ridge reamer
Cylinder surfacing hone
Cylinder bore gauge
Micrometers and/or dial calipers
Hydraulic lifter removal tool
Balljoint separator
Universal-type puller
Impact screwdriver
Dial indicator set
Stroboscopic timing light (inductive pick-up)
Hand operated vacuum/pressure pump
Tachometer/dwell meter
Universal electrical multimeter
Cable hoist
Brake spring removal and installation tools
Floor jack

Buying tools

For the do-it-yourselfer who is just starting to get involved in vehicle maintenance and repair, there are a number of options available when purchasing tools. If maintenance and minor repair is the extent of the work to be done, the purchase of individual tools is satisfactory. If, on the other hand, extensive work is planned, it would be a good idea to purchase a modest tool set from one of the large retail chain stores. A set can usually be bought at a substantial savings over the individual tool prices, and they often come with a tool box. As additional tools are needed, add-on sets, individual tools and a larger tool box can be purchased to expand the tool selection. Building a tool set gradually allows the cost of the

tools to be spread over a longer period of time and gives the mechanic the freedom to choose only those tools that will actually be used.

Tool stores will often be the only source of some of the special tools that are needed, but regardless of where tools are bought, try to avoid cheap ones, especially when buying screwdrivers and sockets, because they won't last very long. The expense involved in replacing cheap tools will eventually be greater than the initial cost of quality tools.

Care and maintenance of tools

Good tools are expensive, so it makes sense to treat them with respect. Keep them clean and in usable condition and store them properly when not in use. Always wipe off any dirt, grease or metal chips before putting them away. Never leave tools lying around in the work area. Upon completion of a job, always check closely under the hood for tools that may have been left there so they won't get lost during a test drive.

Some tools, such as screwdrivers, pliers, wrenches and sockets, can be hung on a panel mounted on the garage or workshop wall, while others should be kept in a tool box or tray. Measuring instruments, gauges, meters, etc. must be carefully stored where they cannot be damaged by weather or impact from other tools.

When tools are used with care and stored properly, they will last a very long time. Even with the best of care, though, tools will wear out if used frequently. When a tool is damaged or worn out, replace it. Subsequent jobs will be safer and more enjoyable if you do.

How to repair damaged threads

Sometimes, the internal threads of a nut or bolt hole can become stripped, usually from overtightening. Stripping threads is an all-too-common occurrence, especially when working with aluminum parts, because aluminum is so soft that it easily strips out.

Usually, external or internal threads are only partially stripped. After they've been cleaned up with a tap or die, they'll still work. Sometimes, however, threads are badly damaged. When this happens, you've got three choices:

1) *Drill and tap the hole to the next suitable oversize and install a larger diameter bolt, screw or stud.*
2) *Drill and tap the hole to accept a threaded plug, then drill and tap the plug to the original screw size. You can also buy a plug already threaded to the original size. Then you simply drill a hole to the specified size, then run the threaded plug into the hole with a bolt and jam nut. Once the plug is fully seated, remove the jam nut and bolt.*
3) *The third method uses a patented thread repair kit like Heli-Coil or Slimsert. These easy-to-use kits are designed to repair damaged threads in straight-through holes and blind holes. Both are available as kits which can handle a variety of sizes and thread patterns. Drill the hole, then tap it with the special included tap. Install the Heli-Coil and the hole is back to its original diameter and thread pitch.*

Regardless of which method you use, be sure to proceed calmly and carefully. A little impatience or carelessness during one of these relatively simple procedures can ruin your whole day's work and cost you a bundle if you wreck an expensive part.

Working facilities

Not to be overlooked when discussing tools is the workshop. If anything more than routine maintenance is to be carried out, some sort of suitable work area is essential.

It is understood, and appreciated, that many home mechanics do not have a good workshop or garage available, and end up removing an engine or doing major repairs outside. It is recommended, however, that the overhaul or repair be completed under the cover of a roof.

A clean, flat workbench or table of comfortable working height is an absolute necessity. The workbench should be equipped with a vise that has a jaw opening of at least four inches.

As mentioned previously, some clean, dry storage space is also required for tools, as well as the lubricants, fluids, cleaning solvents, etc. which soon become necessary.

Sometimes waste oil and fluids, drained from the engine or cooling system during normal maintenance or repairs, present a disposal problem. To avoid pouring them on the ground or into a sewage system, pour the used fluids into large containers, seal them with caps and take them to an authorized disposal site or recycling center. Plastic jugs, such as old antifreeze containers, are ideal for this purpose.

Always keep a supply of old newspapers and clean rags available. Old towels are excellent for mopping up spills. Many mechanics use rolls of paper towels for most work because they are readily available and disposable. To help keep the area under the vehicle clean, a large cardboard box can be cut open and flattened to protect the garage or shop floor.

Whenever working over a painted surface, such as when leaning over a fender to service something under the hood, always cover it with an old blanket or bedspread to protect the finish. Vinyl covered pads, made especially for this purpose, are available at auto parts stores.

Jacking and towing

Jacking

Warning: *The jack supplied with the vehicle should only be used for changing a tire or placing jackstands under the frame. Never work under the vehicle or start the engine while this jack is being used as the only means of support.*

1 The vehicle should be on level ground. Place the shift lever in Park. Block the wheel diagonally opposite the wheel being changed. Set the parking brake.

2 Remove the spare tire and jack from stowage. Remove the wheel cover and trim ring (if so equipped) with the tapered end of the lug nut wrench by inserting and twisting the handle and then prying against the back of the wheel cover. Loosen the wheel lug nuts about 1/4-to-1/2 turn each.

3 Place the scissors-type jack under the vehicle in the indicated position. There is a front and rear jacking point on each side of the vehicle **(see illustrations)**.

4 Turn the jack handle clockwise until the tire clears the ground. Remove the lug nuts and pull the wheel off. Replace it with the spare.

5 Install the lug nuts with the beveled edges facing in. Tighten them snugly. Don't attempt to tighten them completely until the vehicle is lowered or it could slip off the jack. Turn the jack handle counterclockwise to lower the vehicle. Remove the jack and tighten the lug nuts in a diagonal pattern.

6 Install the cover (and trim ring, if used) and be sure it's snapped into place all the way around.

7 Stow the tire, jack and wrench. Unblock the wheels.

Towing

8 Two-wheel drive models should be towed with the front (drive) wheels off the ground. If they can't be raised, place them on a dolly. The intelligent key must be in its slot in the instrument panel and the starter button display must be in the ACC position to unlock the steering column lock.

9 All-wheel drive models must be towed with all four wheels off the ground. A sling-type tow truck cannot be used, as body damage will result. The best way to tow the vehicle is with a flat-bed car carrier.

10 Equipment specifically designed for towing should be used. It should be attached to the main structural members of the vehicle, not the bumpers or brackets.

11 Safety is a major consideration when towing and all applicable state and local laws must be obeyed. A safety chain system must be used at all times.

Jacking locations (under the frame rails, below the stamped arrows) - 2012 and earlier models

On 2013 and later models the jack fits over the rocker panel flange (there are two jacking points on each side of the vehicle, indicated by a notch in the rocker panel flange)

Booster battery (jump) starting

1   Observe the following precautions when using a booster battery to start a vehicle:
Before connecting the booster battery, make sure the ignition switch is in the Off position.
Turn off the lights, heater and other electrical loads.
Your eyes should be shielded. Safety goggles are a good idea.
Make sure the booster battery is the same voltage as the dead one in the vehicle.
The two vehicles MUST NOT TOUCH each other.
Make sure the transmission is in Park (automatic).

2   Connect the red jumper cable to the positive (+) terminals of each battery.

3   Connect one end of the black cable to the negative (-) terminal of the booster battery. The other end of this cable should be connected to a good ground on the engine block (see illustration). Make sure the cable will not come into contact with the fan, drivebelts or other moving parts of the engine.

4   Start the engine using the booster battery, then, with the engine running at idle speed, disconnect the jumper cables in the reverse order of connection.

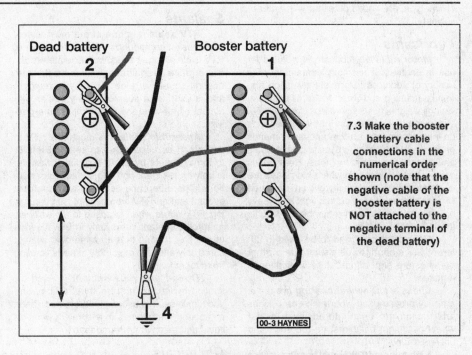

7.3 Make the booster battery cable connections in the numerical order shown (note that the negative cable of the booster battery is NOT attached to the negative terminal of the dead battery)

Automotive chemicals and lubricants

A number of automotive chemicals and lubricants are available for use during vehicle maintenance and repair. They include a wide variety of products ranging from cleaning solvents and degreasers to lubricants and protective sprays for rubber, plastic and vinyl.

Cleaners

Carburetor cleaner and choke cleaner is a strong solvent for gum, varnish and carbon. Most carburetor cleaners leave a dry-type lubricant film which will not harden or gum up. Because of this film it is not recommended for use on electrical components.

Brake system cleaner is used to remove brake dust, grease and brake fluid from the brake system, where clean surfaces are absolutely necessary. It leaves no residue and often eliminates brake squeal caused by contaminants.

Electrical cleaner removes oxidation, corrosion and carbon deposits from electrical contacts, restoring full current flow. It can also be used to clean spark plugs, carburetor jets, voltage regulators and other parts where an oil-free surface is desired.

Demoisturants remove water and moisture from electrical components such as alternators, voltage regulators, electrical connectors and fuse blocks. They are non-conductive and non-corrosive.

Degreasers are heavy-duty solvents used to remove grease from the outside of the engine and from chassis components. They can be sprayed or brushed on and, depending on the type, are rinsed off either with water or solvent.

Lubricants

Motor oil is the lubricant formulated for use in engines. It normally contains a wide variety of additives to prevent corrosion and reduce foaming and wear. Motor oil comes in various weights (viscosity ratings) from 0 to 50. The recommended weight of the oil depends on the season, temperature and the demands on the engine. Light oil is used in cold climates and under light load conditions. Heavy oil is used in hot climates and where high loads are encountered. Multi-viscosity oils are designed to have characteristics of both light and heavy oils and are available in a number of weights from 0W-20 to 20W-50.

Gear oil is designed to be used in differentials, manual transmissions and other areas where high-temperature lubrication is required.

Chassis and wheel bearing grease is a heavy grease used where increased loads and friction are encountered, such as for wheel bearings, balljoints, tie-rod ends and universal joints.

High-temperature wheel bearing grease is designed to withstand the extreme temperatures encountered by wheel bearings in disc brake equipped vehicles. It usually contains molybdenum disulfide (moly), which is a dry-type lubricant.

White grease is a heavy grease for metal-to-metal applications where water is a problem. White grease stays soft under both low and high temperatures (usually from -100 to +190-degrees F), and will not wash off or dilute in the presence of water.

Assembly lube is a special extreme pressure lubricant, usually containing moly, used to lubricate high-load parts (such as main and rod bearings and cam lobes) for initial start-up of a new engine. The assembly lube lubricates the parts without being squeezed out or washed away until the engine oiling system begins to function.

Silicone lubricants are used to protect rubber, plastic, vinyl and nylon parts.

Graphite lubricants are used where oils cannot be used due to contamination problems, such as in locks. The dry graphite will lubricate metal parts while remaining uncontaminated by dirt, water, oil or acids. It is electrically conductive and will not foul electrical contacts in locks such as the ignition switch.

Moly penetrants loosen and lubricate frozen, rusted and corroded fasteners and prevent future rusting or freezing.

Heat-sink grease is a special electrically non-conductive grease that is used for mounting electronic ignition modules where it is essential that heat is transferred away from the module.

Sealants

RTV sealant is one of the most widely used gasket compounds. Made from silicone, RTV is air curing, it seals, bonds, waterproofs, fills surface irregularities, remains flexible, doesn't shrink, is relatively easy to remove, and is used as a supplementary sealer with almost all low and medium temperature gaskets.

Anaerobic sealant is much like RTV in that it can be used either to seal gaskets or to form gaskets by itself. It remains flexible, is solvent resistant and fills surface imperfections. The difference between an anaerobic sealant and an RTV-type sealant is in the curing. RTV cures when exposed to air, while an anaerobic sealant cures only in the absence of air. This means that an anaerobic sealant cures only after the assembly of parts, sealing them together.

Thread and pipe sealant is used for sealing hydraulic and pneumatic fittings and vacuum lines. It is usually made from a Teflon compound, and comes in a spray, a paint-on liquid and as a wrap-around tape.

Chemicals

Anti-seize compound prevents seizing, galling, cold welding, rust and corrosion in fasteners. High-temperature ant-seize, usually made with copper and graphite lubricants, is used for exhaust system and exhaust manifold bolts.

Anaerobic locking compounds are used to keep fasteners from vibrating or working loose and cure only after installation, in the absence of air. Medium strength locking compound is used for small nuts, bolts and screws that may be removed later. High-strength locking compound is for large nuts, bolts and studs which aren't removed on a regular basis.

Oil additives range from viscosity index improvers to chemical treatments that claim to reduce internal engine friction. It should be noted that most oil manufacturers caution against using additives with their oils.

Gas additives perform several functions, depending on their chemical makeup. They usually contain solvents that help dissolve gum and varnish that build up on carburetor, fuel injection and intake parts. They also serve to break down carbon deposits that form on the inside surfaces of the combustion chambers. Some additives contain upper cylinder lubricants for valves and piston rings, and others contain chemicals to remove condensation from the gas tank.

Miscellaneous

Brake fluid is specially formulated hydraulic fluid that can withstand the heat and pressure encountered in brake systems. Care must be taken so this fluid does not come in contact with painted surfaces or plastics. An opened container should always be resealed to prevent contamination by water or dirt.

Weatherstrip adhesive is used to bond weatherstripping around doors, windows and trunk lids. It is sometimes used to attach trim pieces.

Undercoating is a petroleum-based, tar-like substance that is designed to protect metal surfaces on the underside of the vehicle from corrosion. It also acts as a sound-deadening agent by insulating the bottom of the vehicle.

Waxes and polishes are used to help protect painted and plated surfaces from the weather. Different types of paint may require the use of different types of wax and polish. Some polishes utilize a chemical or abrasive cleaner to help remove the top layer of oxidized (dull) paint on older vehicles. In recent years many non-wax polishes that contain a wide variety of chemicals such as polymers and silicones have been introduced. These non-wax polishes are usually easier to apply and last longer than conventional waxes and polishes.

Conversion factors

Length (distance)

Inches (in)	X	25.4	= Millimeters (mm)	X 0.0394	= Inches (in)
Feet (ft)	X	0.305	= Meters (m)	X 3.281	= Feet (ft)
Miles	X	1.609	= Kilometers (km)	X 0.621	= Miles

Volume (capacity)

Cubic inches (cu in; in³)	X	16.387	= Cubic centimeters (cc; cm³)	X 0.061	= Cubic inches (cu in; in³)
Imperial pints (Imp pt)	X	0.568	= Liters (l)	X 1.76	= Imperial pints (Imp pt)
Imperial quarts (Imp qt)	X	1.137	= Liters (l)	X 0.88	= Imperial quarts (Imp qt)
Imperial quarts (Imp qt)	X	1.201	= US quarts (US qt)	X 0.833	= Imperial quarts (Imp qt)
US quarts (US qt)	X	0.946	= Liters (l)	X 1.057	= US quarts (US qt)
Imperial gallons (Imp gal)	X	4.546	= Liters (l)	X 0.22	= Imperial gallons (Imp gal)
Imperial gallons (Imp gal)	X	1.201	= US gallons (US gal)	X 0.833	= Imperial gallons (Imp gal)
US gallons (US gal)	X	3.785	= Liters (l)	X 0.264	= US gallons (US gal)

Mass (weight)

Ounces (oz)	X	28.35	= Grams (g)	X 0.035	= Ounces (oz)
Pounds (lb)	X	0.454	= Kilograms (kg)	X 2.205	= Pounds (lb)

Force

Ounces-force (ozf; oz)	X	0.278	= Newtons (N)	X 3.6	= Ounces-force (ozf; oz)
Pounds-force (lbf; lb)	X	4.448	= Newtons (N)	X 0.225	= Pounds-force (lbf; lb)
Newtons (N)	X	0.1	= Kilograms-force (kgf; kg)	X 9.81	= Newtons (N)

Pressure

Pounds-force per square inch (psi; lbf/in²; lb/in²)	X	0.070	= Kilograms-force per square centimeter (kgf/cm²; kg/cm²)	X 14.223	= Pounds-force per square inch (psi; lbf/in²; lb/in²)
Pounds-force per square inch (psi; lbf/in²; lb/in²)	X	0.068	= Atmospheres (atm)	X 14.696	= Pounds-force per square inch (psi; lbf/in²; lb/in²)
Pounds-force per square inch (psi; lbf/in²; lb/in²)	X	0.069	= Bars	X 14.5	= Pounds-force per square inch (psi; lbf/in²; lb/in²)
Pounds-force per square inch (psi; lbf/in²; lb/in²)	X	6.895	= Kilopascals (kPa)	X 0.145	= Pounds-force per square inch (psi; lbf/in²; lb/in²)
Kilopascals (kPa)	X	0.01	= Kilograms-force per square centimeter (kgf/cm²; kg/cm²)	X 98.1	= Kilopascals (kPa)

Torque (moment of force)

Pounds-force inches (lbf in; lb in)	X	1.152	= Kilograms-force centimeter (kgf cm; kg cm)	X 0.868	= Pounds-force inches (lbf in; lb in)
Pounds-force inches (lbf in; lb in)	X	0.113	= Newton meters (Nm)	X 8.85	= Pounds-force inches (lbf in; lb in)
Pounds-force inches (lbf in; lb in)	X	0.083	= Pounds-force feet (lbf ft; lb ft)	X 12	= Pounds-force inches (lbf in; lb in)
Pounds-force feet (lbf ft; lb ft)	X	0.138	= Kilograms-force meters (kgf m; kg m)	X 7.233	= Pounds-force feet (lbf ft; lb ft)
Pounds-force feet (lbf ft; lb ft)	X	1.356	= Newton meters (Nm)	X 0.738	= Pounds-force feet (lbf ft; lb ft)
Newton meters (Nm)	X	0.102	= Kilograms-force meters (kgf m; kg m)	X 9.804	= Newton meters (Nm)

Vacuum

Inches mercury (in. Hg)	X	3.377	= Kilopascals (kPa)	X 0.2961	= Inches mercury
Inches mercury (in. Hg)	X	25.4	= Millimeters mercury (mm Hg)	X 0.0394	= Inches mercury

Power

Horsepower (hp)	X	745.7	= Watts (W)	X 0.0013	= Horsepower (hp)

Velocity (speed)

Miles per hour (miles/hr; mph)	X	1.609	= Kilometers per hour (km/hr; kph)	X 0.621	= Miles per hour (miles/hr; mph)

Fuel consumption*

Miles per gallon, Imperial (mpg)	X	0.354	= Kilometers per liter (km/l)	X 2.825	= Miles per gallon, Imperial (mpg)
Miles per gallon, US (mpg)	X	0.425	= Kilometers per liter (km/l)	X 2.352	= Miles per gallon, US (mpg)

Temperature

Degrees Fahrenheit = (°C x 1.8) + 32   Degrees Celsius (Degrees Centigrade; °C) = (°F - 32) x 0.56

*It is common practice to convert from miles per gallon (mpg) to liters/100 kilometers (l/100km), where mpg (Imperial) x l/100 km = 282 and mpg (US) x l/100 km = 235

DECIMALS to MILLIMETERS

Decimal	mm	Decimal	mm
0.001	0.0254	0.500	12.7000
0.002	0.0508	0.510	12.9540
0.003	0.0762	0.520	13.2080
0.004	0.1016	0.530	13.4620
0.005	0.1270	0.540	13.7160
0.006	0.1524	0.550	13.9700
0.007	0.1778	0.560	14.2240
0.008	0.2032	0.570	14.4780
0.009	0.2286	0.580	14.7320
		0.590	14.9860
0.010	0.2540		
0.020	0.5080		
0.030	0.7620		
0.040	1.0160	0.600	15.2400
0.050	1.2700	0.610	15.4940
0.060	1.5240	0.620	15.7480
0.070	1.7780	0.630	16.0020
0.080	2.0320	0.640	16.2560
0.090	2.2860	0.650	16.5100
		0.660	16.7640
0.100	2.5400	0.670	17.0180
0.110	2.7940	0.680	17.2720
0.120	3.0480	0.690	17.5260
0.130	3.3020		
0.140	3.5560		
0.150	3.8100		
0.160	4.0640	0.700	17.7800
0.170	4.3180	0.710	18.0340
0.180	4.5720	0.720	18.2880
0.190	4.8260	0.730	18.5420
		0.740	18.7960
0.200	5.0800	0.750	19.0500
0.210	5.3340	0.760	19.3040
0.220	5.5880	0.770	19.5580
0.230	5.8420	0.780	19.8120
0.240	6.0960	0.790	20.0660
0.250	6.3500		
0.260	6.6040		
0.270	6.8580	0.800	20.3200
0.280	7.1120	0.810	20.5740
0.290	7.3660	0.820	21.8280
		0.830	21.0820
0.300	7.6200	0.840	21.3360
0.310	7.8740	0.850	21.5900
0.320	8.1280	0.860	21.8440
0.330	8.3820	0.870	22.0980
0.340	8.6360	0.880	22.3520
0.350	8.8900	0.890	22.6060
0.360	9.1440		
0.370	9.3980		
0.380	9.6520		
0.390	9.9060		
		0.900	22.8600
0.400	10.1600	0.910	23.1140
0.410	10.4140	0.920	23.3680
0.420	10.6680	0.930	23.6220
0.430	10.9220	0.940	23.8760
0.440	11.1760	0.950	24.1300
0.450	11.4300	0.960	24.3840
0.460	11.6840	0.970	24.6380
0.470	11.9380	0.980	24.8920
0.480	12.1920	0.990	25.1460
0.490	12.4460	1.000	25.4000

FRACTIONS to DECIMALS to MILLIMETERS

Fraction	Decimal	mm	Fraction	Decimal	mm
1/64	0.0156	0.3969	33/64	0.5156	13.0969
1/32	0.0312	0.7938	17/32	0.5312	13.4938
3/64	0.0469	1.1906	35/64	0.5469	13.8906
1/16	0.0625	1.5875	9/16	0.5625	14.2875
5/64	0.0781	1.9844	37/64	0.5781	14.6844
3/32	0.0938	2.3812	19/32	0.5938	15.0812
7/64	0.1094	2.7781	39/64	0.6094	15.4781
1/8	0.1250	3.1750	5/8	0.6250	15.8750
9/64	0.1406	3.5719	41/64	0.6406	16.2719
5/32	0.1562	3.9688	21/32	0.6562	16.6688
11/64	0.1719	4.3656	43/64	0.6719	17.0656
3/16	0.1875	4.7625	11/16	0.6875	17.4625
13/64	0.2031	5.1594	45/64	0.7031	17.8594
7/32	0.2188	5.5562	23/32	0.7188	18.2562
15/64	0.2344	5.9531	47/64	0.7344	18.6531
1/4	0.2500	6.3500	3/4	0.7500	19.0500
17/64	0.2656	6.7469	49/64	0.7656	19.4469
9/32	0.2812	7.1438	25/32	0.7812	19.8438
19/64	0.2969	7.5406	51/64	0.7969	20.2406
5/16	0.3125	7.9375	13/16	0.8125	20.6375
21/64	0.3281	8.3344	53/64	0.8281	21.0344
11/32	0.3438	8.7312	27/32	0.8438	21.4312
23/64	0.3594	9.1281	55/64	0.8594	21.8281
3/8	0.3750	9.5250	7/8	0.8750	22.2250
25/64	0.3906	9.9219	57/64	0.8906	22.6219
13/32	0.4062	10.3188	29/32	0.9062	23.0188
27/64	0.4219	10.7156	59/64	0.9219	23.4156
7/16	0.4375	11.1125	15/16	0.9375	23.8125
29/64	0.4531	11.5094	61/64	0.9531	24.2094
15/32	0.4688	11.9062	31/32	0.9688	24.6062
31/64	0.4844	12.3031	63/64	0.9844	25.0031
1/2	0.5000	12.7000	1	1.0000	25.4000

Safety first!

Regardless of how enthusiastic you may be about getting on with the job at hand, take the time to ensure that your safety is not jeopardized. A moment's lack of attention can result in an accident, as can failure to observe certain simple safety precautions. The possibility of an accident will always exist, and the following points should not be considered a comprehensive list of all dangers. Rather, they are intended to make you aware of the risks and to encourage a safety conscious approach to all work you carry out on your vehicle.

Essential DOs and DON'Ts

DON'T rely on a jack when working under the vehicle. Always use approved jackstands to support the weight of the vehicle and place them under the recommended lift or support points.

DON'T attempt to loosen extremely tight fasteners (i.e. wheel lug nuts) while the vehicle is on a jack - it may fall.

DON'T start the engine without first making sure that the transmission is in Neutral (or Park where applicable) and the parking brake is set.

DON'T remove the radiator cap from a hot cooling system - let it cool or cover it with a cloth and release the pressure gradually.

DON'T attempt to drain the engine oil until you are sure it has cooled to the point that it will not burn you.

DON'T touch any part of the engine or exhaust system until it has cooled sufficiently to avoid burns.

DON'T siphon toxic liquids such as gasoline, antifreeze and brake fluid by mouth, or allow them to remain on your skin.

DON'T inhale brake lining dust - it is potentially hazardous (see *Asbestos* below).

DON'T allow spilled oil or grease to remain on the floor - wipe it up before someone slips on it.

DON'T use loose fitting wrenches or other tools which may slip and cause injury.

DON'T push on wrenches when loosening or tightening nuts or bolts. Always try to pull the wrench toward you. If the situation calls for pushing the wrench away, push with an open hand to avoid scraped knuckles if the wrench should slip.

DON'T attempt to lift a heavy component alone - get someone to help you.

DON'T rush or take unsafe shortcuts to finish a job.

DON'T allow children or animals in or around the vehicle while you are working on it.

DO wear eye protection when using power tools such as a drill, sander, bench grinder, etc. and when working under a vehicle.

DO keep loose clothing and long hair well out of the way of moving parts.

DO make sure that any hoist used has a safe working load rating adequate for the job.

DO get someone to check on you periodically when working alone on a vehicle.

DO carry out work in a logical sequence and make sure that everything is correctly assembled and tightened.

DO keep chemicals and fluids tightly capped and out of the reach of children and pets.

DO remember that your vehicle's safety affects that of yourself and others. If in doubt on any point, get professional advice.

Steering, suspension and brakes

These systems are essential to driving safety, so make sure you have a qualified shop or individual check your work. Also, compressed suspension springs can cause injury if released suddenly - be sure to use a spring compressor.

Airbags

Airbags are explosive devices that can **CAUSE** injury if they deploy while you're working on the vehicle. Follow the manufacturer's instructions to disable the airbag whenever you're working in the vicinity of airbag components.

Asbestos

Certain friction, insulating, sealing, and other products - such as brake linings, brake bands, clutch linings, torque converters, gaskets, etc. - may contain asbestos or other hazardous friction material. Extreme care must be taken to avoid inhalation of dust from such products, since it is hazardous to health. If in doubt, assume that they do contain asbestos.

Fire

Remember at all times that gasoline is highly flammable. Never smoke or have any kind of open flame around when working on a vehicle. But the risk does not end there. A spark caused by an electrical short circuit, by two metal surfaces contacting each other, or even by static electricity built up in your body under certain conditions, can ignite gasoline vapors, which in a confined space are highly explosive. Do not, under any circumstances, use gasoline for cleaning parts. Use an approved safety solvent.

Always disconnect the battery ground (-) cable at the battery before working on any part of the fuel system or electrical system. Never risk spilling fuel on a hot engine or exhaust component. It is strongly recommended that a fire extinguisher suitable for use on fuel and electrical fires be kept handy in the garage or workshop at all times. Never try to extinguish a fuel or electrical fire with water.

Fumes

Certain fumes are highly toxic and can quickly cause unconsciousness and even death if inhaled to any extent. Gasoline vapor falls into this category, as do the vapors from some cleaning solvents. Any draining or pouring of such volatile fluids should be done in a well ventilated area.

When using cleaning fluids and solvents, read the instructions on the container carefully. Never use materials from unmarked containers.

Never run the engine in an enclosed space, such as a garage. Exhaust fumes contain carbon monoxide, which is extremely poisonous. If you need to run the engine, always do so in the open air, or at least have the rear of the vehicle outside the work area.

The battery

Never create a spark or allow a bare light bulb near a battery. They normally give off a certain amount of hydrogen gas, which is highly explosive.

Always disconnect the battery ground (-) cable at the battery before working on the fuel or electrical systems.

If possible, loosen the filler caps or cover when charging the battery from an external source (this does not apply to sealed or maintenance-free batteries). Do not charge at an excessive rate or the battery may burst.

Take care when adding water to a non maintenance-free battery and when carrying a battery. The electrolyte, even when diluted, is very corrosive and should not be allowed to contact clothing or skin.

Always wear eye protection when cleaning the battery to prevent the caustic deposits from entering your eyes.

Household current

When using an electric power tool, inspection light, etc., which operates on household current, always make sure that the tool is correctly connected to its plug and that, where necessary, it is properly grounded. Do not use such items in damp conditions and, again, do not create a spark or apply excessive heat in the vicinity of fuel or fuel vapor.

Secondary ignition system voltage

A severe electric shock can result from touching certain parts of the ignition system (such as the spark plug wires) when the engine is running or being cranked, particularly if components are damp or the insulation is defective. In the case of an electronic ignition system, the secondary system voltage is much higher and could prove fatal.

Hydrofluoric acid

This extremely corrosive acid is formed when certain types of synthetic rubber, found in some O-rings, oil seals, fuel hoses, etc. are exposed to temperatures above 750-degrees F (400-degrees C). The rubber changes into a charred or sticky substance containing the acid. *Once formed, the acid remains dangerous for years. If it gets onto the skin, it may be necessary to amputate the limb concerned.*

When dealing with a vehicle which has suffered a fire, or with components salvaged from such a vehicle, wear protective gloves and discard them after use.

Troubleshooting

Contents

Symptom	Section
Engine and performance	
Engine backfires	15
Engine continues to run after switching off	18
Engine hard to start when cold	3
Engine hard to start when hot	4
Engine lacks power	14
Engine lopes while idling or idles erratically	8
Engine misses at idle speed	9
Engine misses throughout driving speed range	10
Engine will not rotate when attempting to start	1
Engine rotates but will not start	2
Engine runs with oil pressure light on	17
Engine stalls	13
Engine starts but stops immediately	6
Engine stumbles on acceleration	11
Engine surges while holding accelerator steady	12
Oil puddle under engine	7
Pinging or knocking engine sounds during acceleration or uphill..	16
Starter motor noisy or excessively rough in engagement	5
Engine electrical system	
Battery will not hold a charge	19
Voltage warning light fails to come on when key is turned on	21
Voltage warning light fails to go out	20
Fuel system	
Excessive fuel consumption	22
Fuel leakage and/or fuel odor	23
Cooling system	
Coolant loss	28
External coolant leakage	26
Internal coolant leakage	27
Overcooling	25
Overheating	24
Poor coolant circulation	29
Automatic transaxle	
Engine will start in gears other than Park or Neutral	33
Fluid leakage	30
General shift mechanism problems	32
Transaxle fluid brown or has a burned smell	31
Transaxle slips, is noisy or has no drive in forward or reverse gears	34
Driveaxles	
Clicking noise in turns	35
Knock or clunk when accelerating after coasting	36
Shudder or vibration during acceleration	37

Symptom	Section
Driveshaft	
Knock or clunk when transmission is under initial load (just after transmission is put into gear)	39
Leaks at front of driveshaft	38
Metallic grating sound consistent with vehicle speed	40
Scraping noise	42
Vibration	41
Rear differential	
Knocking sound when starting or shifting gears	44
Noise - same when in drive as when vehicle is coasting	43
Noise when turning	45
Oil leaks	47
Vibration	46
Brakes	
Brake pedal feels spongy when depressed	55
Brake pedal travels to the floor with little resistance	56
Brake roughness or chatter (pedal pulsates)	50
Dragging brakes	53
Excessive brake pedal travel	52
Excessive pedal effort required to stop vehicle	51
Grabbing or uneven braking action	54
Noise (grinding or high-pitched squeal) when the brakes are applied	49
Parking brake does not hold	57
Vehicle pulls to one side during braking	48
Suspension and steering systems	
Abnormal noise at the front end	64
Abnormal or excessive tire wear	59
Cupped tires	69
Erratic steering when braking	66
Excessive pitching and/or rolling around corners or during braking	67
Excessive play or looseness in steering system	73
Excessive tire wear on inside edge	71
Excessive tire wear on outside edge	70
Hard steering	62
Rattling or clicking noise in steering gear	74
Shimmy, shake or vibration	61
Steering wheel does not return to center position correctly	63
Suspension bottoms	68
Tire tread worn in one place	72
Wander or poor steering stability	65
Wheel makes a thumping noise	60
Vehicle pulls to one side	58

Engine and performance

1 Engine will not rotate when attempting to start

1 Battery terminal connections loose or corroded (Chapter 1).
2 Battery discharged or faulty (Chapter 1).
3 Automatic transaxle not completely engaged in Park (Chapter 7A or 7B).
4 Broken, loose or disconnected wiring in the starting circuit (Chapters 5 and 12).
5 Starter motor pinion jammed in driveplate ring gear (Chapter 5).
6 Starter solenoid faulty (Chapter 5).
7 Starter motor faulty (Chapter 5).
8 Ignition switch faulty (Chapter 12).
9 Neutral start switch faulty (Chapter 7A).
10 Starter pinion or driveplate teeth worn or broken (Chapter 5).
11 Faulty Body Control Module (BCM) or Intelligent Power Distribution Module (IPDM) (see Chapter 12).

2 Engine rotates but will not start

1 Fuel tank empty.
2 Battery discharged (engine rotates slowly) (Chapter 5).
3 Battery terminal connections loose or corroded (Chapter 1).
4 Leaking fuel injector(s), fuel pump, pressure regulator, etc. (Chapter 4).
5 Fuel not reaching fuel injection system (Chapter 4).
6 Ignition system problem (Chapter 5).
7 Worn, faulty or incorrectly gapped spark plugs (Chapter 1).

3 Engine hard to start when cold

1 Battery discharged or low (Chapter 1).
2 Fuel system malfunctioning (Chapter 4).
3 Emissions or engine control system malfunctioning (Chapter 6).

4 Engine hard to start when hot

1 Air filter clogged (Chapter 1).
2 Fuel not reaching the fuel injection system (Chapter 4).
3 Corroded battery connections, especially ground (Chapter 1).
4 Emissions or engine control system malfunctioning (Chapter 6).

5 Starter motor noisy or excessively rough in engagement

1 Pinion or driveplate gear teeth worn or broken (Chapter 5).
2 Starter motor mounting bolts loose (Chapter 5).

6 Engine starts but stops immediately

1 Insufficient fuel reaching the fuel injectors (Chapter 4).
2 Vacuum leak at the gasket between the intake manifold/plenum and throttle body (Chapters 1 and 4).
3 Restricted exhaust system (most likely the catalytic converter) (Chapters 4 and 6).

7 Oil puddle under engine

1 Oil pan gasket and/or oil pan drain bolt seal leaking (Chapters 1 and 2A or 2B).
2 Oil pressure sending unit leaking (Chapter 2A).
3 Valve cover gaskets leaking (Chapter 2A or 2B).
4 Engine oil seals leaking (Chapter 2A or 2B).

8 Engine lopes while idling or idles erratically

1 Vacuum leakage (Chapter 4).
2 Plugged PCV valve (Chapter 6).
3 Air filter clogged (Chapter 1).
4 Fuel pump not delivering sufficient fuel to the fuel injection system (Chapter 4).
5 Leaking head gasket (Chapter 2A).
6 Camshaft lobes worn (Chapter 2A).

9 Engine misses at idle speed

1 Spark plugs worn or not gapped properly (Chapter 1).
2 Faulty ignition coil(s) (Chapter 5).
3 Vacuum leaks (Chapters 1 and 4).
4 Uneven or low compression (Chapter 2C).
5 Problem with the fuel injection system (Chapter 4).

10 Engine misses throughout driving speed range

1 Fuel filter clogged and/or impurities in the fuel system (Chapters 1 and 4).
2 Low fuel pressure (Chapter 4).
3 Faulty or incorrectly gapped spark plugs (Chapter 1).
4 Faulty emission system components (Chapter 6).
5 Low or uneven cylinder compression pressures (Chapter 2C).
6 Weak or faulty ignition coil(s) (Chapter 5).
7 Vacuum leak in fuel injection system, intake manifold or vacuum hoses (Chapter 4).

11 Engine stumbles on acceleration

1 Spark plugs fouled (Chapter 1).
2 Problem with the fuel injection system (Chapter 4).
3 Fuel filter clogged (Chapter 1).
4 Intake manifold air leak (Chapter 4).

12 Engine surges while holding accelerator steady

1 Intake air leak (Chapter 4).
2 Fuel pump faulty (Chapter 4).
3 Loose fuel injector harness connections (Chapter 4).
4 Defective PCM (Chapter 6).

13 Engine stalls

1 Fuel filter clogged and/or water and impurities in the fuel system (Chapters 1 and 4).
2 Faulty emissions system or engine control system components (Chapter 6).
3 Faulty or incorrectly gapped spark plugs (Chapter 1).
4 Vacuum leak in the intake manifold or vacuum hoses (Chapter 4).

14 Engine lacks power

1 Faulty or incorrectly gapped spark plugs (Chapter 1).
2 Restricted exhaust system (most likely the catalytic converter) (Chapters 4 and 6).
3 Fuel injection system malfunctioning (Chapter 4).
4 Faulty coil(s) (Chapter 5).
5 Brakes binding (Chapter 1).
6 Automatic transaxle fluid level incorrect (Chapter 1).
7 Fuel filter clogged and/or impurities in the fuel system (Chapter 1).
8 Emission control system not functioning properly (Chapter 6).
9 Low or uneven cylinder compression pressures (Chapter 2C).

15 Engine backfires

1 Emissions system not functioning properly (Chapter 6).
2 Fuel injection system malfunctioning (Chapter 4).
3 Vacuum leak at fuel injectors, intake manifold or vacuum hoses (Chapter 4).
4 Valves sticking (Chapter 2A or 2B).

16 Pinging or knocking engine sounds during acceleration or uphill

1 Incorrect grade of fuel.
2 Fuel injection system malfunctioning (Chapter 4).
3 Improper or damaged spark plugs or wires (Chapter 1).
4 Worn or damaged ignition components (Chapter 5).
5 Faulty emissions system (Chapter 6).
6 Vacuum leak (Chapter 4).

17 Engine runs with oil pressure light on

1 Low oil level (Chapter 1).
2 Short in wiring circuit (Chapter 12).
3 Faulty oil pressure sender (Chapter 2C).
4 Oil viscosity too low or oil diluted.
5 Worn engine bearings and/or oil pump (Chapter 2A or 2B).

18 Engine continues to run after switching off

Faulty ignition switch (Chapter 12), Powertrain Control Module (PCM) (Chapter 6), or Body Control Module (BCM).

Engine electrical system

19 Battery will not hold a charge

1 Drivebelt worn or tensioner defective (Chapter 1).
2 Battery terminals loose or corroded (Chapter 1).
3 Alternator not charging properly (Chapter 5).
4 Loose, broken or faulty wiring in the charging circuit (Chapter 5).
5 Short in vehicle wiring (Chapters 5 and 12).
6 Internally defective battery (Chapters 1 and 5).

20 Voltage warning light fails to go out

1 Faulty alternator or charging circuit (Chapter 5).
2 Drivebelt worn or tensioner defective (Chapter 1).
3 Alternator voltage regulator inoperative (Chapter 5).

21 Voltage warning light fails to come on when key is turned on

1 Warning light bulb defective (Chapter 12).
2 Fault in the printed circuit, dash wiring or bulb holder (Chapter 12).

Fuel system

22 Excessive fuel consumption

1 Dirty or clogged air filter element (Chapter 1).
2 Emissions system not functioning properly (Chapter 6).
3 Fuel injection system malfunctioning (Chapter 4).
4 Low tire pressure or incorrect tire size (Chapter 1).

23 Fuel leakage and/or fuel odor

1 Leak in a fuel feed or vent line (Chapter 4).
2 Tank overfilled.
3 Evaporative emissions control canister defective (Chapters 1 and 6).
4 Fuel injector seals faulty (Chapter 4).

Cooling system

24 Overheating

1 Insufficient coolant in system (Chapter 1).
2 Drivebelt worn or tensioner defective (Chapter 1).
3 Radiator core blocked or grille restricted (Chapter 3).
4 Thermostat faulty (Chapter 3).
5 Electric cooling fan blades broken or cracked (Chapter 3).
6 Radiator cap not maintaining proper pressure (Chapter 3).

25 Overcooling

Incorrect (opening temperature too low) or faulty thermostat (Chapter 3).

26 External coolant leakage

1 Deteriorated/damaged hoses or loose clamps (Chapters 1 and 3).
2 Water pump seal defective (Chapters 1 and 3).
3 Leakage from radiator core (Chapter 3).
4 Engine drain or water jacket core plugs leaking.

27 Internal coolant leakage

1 Leaking cylinder head gasket (Chapter 2A or 2B).
2 Cracked cylinder bore or cylinder head (Chapter 2A or 2B).

28 Coolant loss

1 Too much coolant in system (Chapter 1).
2 Coolant boiling away because of overheating (Chapter 3).
3 Internal or external leakage (Chapter 3).
4 Faulty radiator cap (Chapter 3).

29 Poor coolant circulation

1 Inoperative water pump (Chapter 3).
2 Restriction in cooling system (Chapters 1 and 3).
3 Drivebelt worn or tensioner defective (Chapter 1).
4 Thermostat sticking (Chapter 3).

Automatic transaxle

30 Fluid leakage

1 Automatic transmission fluid (2012 and earlier models) is a deep red color. CVT fluid (2013 and later models) is a light green to amber color. Fluid leaks should not be confused with engine oil, which can easily be blown by airflow to the transaxle.
2 To pinpoint a leak, first remove all built-up dirt and grime from the transaxle housing with degreasing agents and/or steam cleaning. Drive the vehicle at low speeds so air flow will not blow the leak far from its source. Raise the vehicle and determine where the leak is coming from. Common areas of leakage are:

  a) *Fluid pan*
  b) *Fill plug*
  c) *Fluid cooler lines*
  d) *Transmission Speed Sensor(s) (Chapter 6)*

31 Transaxle fluid brown or has a burned smell

Transaxle overheated. Change fluid (Chapter 1).

32 General shift mechanism problems

1   Chapter 7A deals with checking and adjusting the shift cable on automatic transaxles. Common problems which may be attributed to a poorly adjusted cable are:
a Engine starting in gears other than Park or Neutral.
b Indicator on shifter pointing to a gear other than the one actually being used.
c Vehicle moves when in Park.

33 Engine will start in gears other than Park or Neutral

Transmission range switch malfunctioning (Chapter 6).

34 Transaxle slips, is noisy or has no drive in forward or reverse gears

1   There are many probable causes for the above problems, but the home mechanic should be concerned with only one possibility - fluid level. Before taking the vehicle to a repair shop, check the level and condition of the fluid as described in Chapter 1.
2   Correct the fluid level as necessary or change the fluid and filter if needed. If the problem persists, have a professional diagnose the probable cause.

Driveaxles

35 Clicking noise in turns

Worn or damaged outer CV joint. Check for cut or damaged boots (Chapter 1). Repair as necessary (Chapter 8).

36 Knock or clunk when accelerating after coasting

Worn or damaged CV joint. Check for cut or damaged boots (Chapter 1). Repair as necessary (Chapter 8).

37 Shudder or vibration during acceleration

Worn or damaged CV joints. Repair or replace as necessary (Chapter 8).

Driveshaft

38 Leaks at front of driveshaft

Defective transfer case seal.

39 Knock or clunk when transmission is under initial load (just after transmission is put into gear)

1   Loose or disconnected rear suspension components. Check all mounting bolts and bushings (Chapter 10).
2   Loose driveshaft bolts. Inspect all bolts and nuts and tighten them securely.
3   Worn or damaged universal joint bearings.
4   Worn sleeve yoke and mainshaft spline.

40 Metallic grating sound consistent with vehicle speed

1   Pronounced wear in the universal joint bearings. Replace driveshaft.
2   Worn center support bearing. Replace driveshaft.

41 Vibration

Note: Before blaming the driveshaft, make sure the tires are perfectly balanced and perform the following test.
3   Install a tachometer inside the vehicle to monitor engine speed as the vehicle is driven. Drive the vehicle and note the engine speed at which the vibration (roughness) is most pronounced. Now shift the transmission to a different gear and bring the engine speed to the same point.
4   If the vibration occurs at the same engine speed (rpm) regardless of which gear the transmission is in, the driveshaft is NOT at fault since the driveshaft speed varies.
5   If the vibration decreases or is eliminated when the transmission is in a different gear at the same engine speed, refer to the following probable causes:
a) Bent or dented driveshaft. Inspect and replace as necessary.
b) Undercoating or built-up dirt, etc. on the driveshaft. Clean the shaft thoroughly.
c) Worn universal joint bearings. Replace the driveshaft.

d) Driveshaft and/or companion flange out of balance. Check for missing weights on the shaft. Remove driveshaft and reinstall 180-degrees from original position, then recheck. Have the driveshaft balanced if problem persists.
e) Loose driveshaft mounting bolts/nuts.
f) Worn center support bearing. Replace the driveshaft.
g) Worn transfer case rear bushing.

42 Scraping noise

Make sure there is nothing, such as an exhaust heat shield or safety loop, rubbing on the driveshaft.

Rear differential

43 Noise - same when in drive as when vehicle is coasting

1   Road noise. No corrective action available.
2   Tire noise. Inspect tires and check tire pressures (Chapter 1).
3   Hub bearings worn or damaged (Chapter 10).
4   Insufficient differential oil (Chapter 1).
5   Defective differential.

44 Knocking sound when starting or shifting gears

Worn differential.

45 Noise when turning

Worn differential.

46 Vibration

See probable causes under Driveshaft. Proceed under the guidelines listed for the driveshaft. If the problem persists, check the rear hub bearings by raising the rear of the vehicle and spinning the wheels by hand. Listen for evidence of rough (noisy) bearings. Remove and inspect.

47 Oil leaks

1   Pinion oil seal damaged.
2   Driveaxle oil seals damaged.
3   Loose filler or drain plug on differential (Chapter 1).
4   Clogged or damaged breather on differential.

Brakes

48   Vehicle pulls to one side during braking

1   Incorrect tire pressures (Chapter 1).
2   Front end out of alignment (have the front end aligned).
3   Unmatched tires on same axle.
4   Restricted brake lines or hoses (Chapter 9).
5   Sticking caliper piston (Chapter 9).
6   Loose suspension parts (Chapter 10).
7   Contaminated brake pad material (Chapter 9).
8   Excessive wear of brake pad material or disc on one side.

49   Noise (grinding or high-pitched squeal) when the brakes are applied

Disc brake pads worn out. Replace pads with new ones immediately (Chapter 9).

50   Brake roughness or chatter (pedal pulsates)

1   Excessive brake disc lateral runout (Chapter 9).
2   Parallelism of disc not within specifications (Chapter 9).
3   Uneven pad wear caused by caliper not sliding due to improper clearance or dirt (Chapter 9).
4   Defective brake disc (Chapter 9).

51   Excessive pedal effort required to stop vehicle

1   Malfunctioning power brake booster (Chapter 9).
2   Partial system failure (Chapter 9).
3   Excessively worn pads (Chapter 9).
4   One or more caliper pistons seized or sticking (Chapter 9).
5   Brake pads contaminated with oil or grease (Chapter 9).
6   New pads installed and not yet seated. It will take a while for the new material to seat.

52   Excessive brake pedal travel

1   Partial brake system failure (Chapter 9).
2   Insufficient fluid in master cylinder (Chapters 1 and 9).
3   Air trapped in system (Chapter 9).
4   Faulty master cylinder (Chapter 9).

53   Dragging brakes

1   Master cylinder pistons not returning correctly (Chapter 9).
2   Restricted brake lines or hoses (Chapters 1 and 9).
3   Incorrect parking brake adjustment (Chapter 9).
4   Defective brake calipers (Chapter 9).

54   Grabbing or uneven braking action

1   Malfunction of proportioning valve (Chapter 9).
2   Contaminated brake linings (Chapter 9).

55   Brake pedal feels spongy when depressed

1   Air in hydraulic lines (Chapter 9).
2   Master cylinder mounting bolts loose (Chapter 9).
3   Master cylinder defective (Chapter 9).

56   Brake pedal travels to the floor with little resistance

Little or no fluid in the master cylinder reservoir caused by leaking caliper, or loose, damaged or disconnected brake lines (Chapter 9).

57   Parking brake does not hold

Parking brake improperly adjusted (Chapter 9).

Suspension and steering systems

58   Vehicle pulls to one side

1   Mismatched or uneven tires.
2   Broken or sagging springs (Chapter 10).
3   Wheel alignment incorrect.
4   Front brake dragging (Chapter 9).

59   Abnormal or excessive tire wear

1   Wheel alignment incorrect.
2   Sagging or broken springs (Chapter 10).
3   Tire out-of-balance.
4   Worn strut or shock absorber (Chapter 10).
5   Overloaded vehicle.
6   Tires not rotated regularly.

60   Wheel makes a thumping noise

1   Blister or bump on tire.
2   Improper strut or shock absorber action (Chapter 10).

61   Shimmy, shake or vibration

1   Tire or wheel out-of-balance or out-of-round.
2   Worn wheel bearings (Chapter 10).
3   Worn tie-rod ends (Chapter 10).
4   Worn balljoints (Chapter 10).
5   Excessive wheel runout.
6   Blister or bump on tire.

62   Hard steering

1   Worn balljoints or tie-rod ends (Chapter 10).
2   Front wheel alignment incorrect (Chapter 10).
3   Low tire pressure(s) (Chapter 1).

63   Steering wheel does not return to center position correctly

1   Worn balljoints or tie-rod ends (Chapter 10).
2   Binding in steering column (Chapter 10).
3   Defective steering gear assembly (Chapter 10).
4   Front wheel alignment problem.

64   Abnormal noise at the front end

1   Worn balljoints or tie-rod ends (Chapter 1).
2   Loose upper strut mount (Chapter 10).
3   Worn tie-rod ends (Chapter 10).
4   Loose stabilizer bar (Chapter 10).
5   Loose wheel lug nuts (Chapter 1).
6   Loose suspension bolts (Chapter 10).

65   Wander or poor steering stability

1   Mismatched or uneven tires.
2   Worn balljoints or tie-rod ends.
3   Worn struts or shock absorbers (Chapter 10).
4   Loose stabilizer bar (Chapter 10).
5   Broken or sagging springs (Chapter 10).
6   Front wheel alignment incorrect.

66   Erratic steering when braking

1   Wheel bearings worn (Chapter 10).
2   Broken or sagging springs (Chapter 10).
3   Leaking brake caliper (Chapter 9).
4   Warped brake discs (Chapter 9).
5   Wheel alignment incorrect.

67 Excessive pitching and/or rolling around corners or during braking

1 Loose stabilizer bar (Chapter 10).
2 Worn struts/shock absorbers or mounts (Chapter 10).
3 Broken or sagging springs (Chapter 10).
4 Overloaded vehicle.

68 Suspension bottoms

1 Overloaded vehicle.
2 Worn struts or shock absorbers (Chapter 10).
3 Sagging springs (Chapter 10).

69 Cupped tires

1 Wheel alignment incorrect (Chapter 10).
2 Worn struts or shock absorbers (Chapter 10).
3 Hub bearings worn (Chapter 10).

4 Excessive tire or wheel runout.
5 Worn balljoints (Chapter 10).

70 Excessive tire wear on outside edge

1 Inflation pressures incorrect (Chapter 1).
2 Excessive speed in turns.
3 Wheel alignment incorrect (excessive toe-in or positive camber). Have professionally aligned.
4 Suspension arm bent (Chapter 10).

71 Excessive tire wear on inside edge

1 Inflation pressures incorrect (Chapter 1).
2 Wheel alignment incorrect (toe-out or excessive negative camber). Have professionally aligned.
3 Loose or damaged steering components (Chapter 10).

72 Tire tread worn in one place

1 Tires out-of-balance.
2 Damaged wheel. Inspect and replace if necessary.
3 Defective tire (Chapter 1).

73 Excessive play or looseness in steering system

1 Hub bearings worn (Chapter 10).
2 Tie-rod end loose or worn (Chapter 10).
3 Steering gear loose (Chapter 10).

74 Rattling or clicking noise in steering gear

1 Steering gear mounting bolts loose (Chapter 10).
2 Steering gear defective (Chapter 10).

Notes

Chapter 1
Tune-up and routine maintenance

Contents

	Section
Air filter check and replacement	20
Automatic transmission/transaxle fluid change	28
Automatic transmission/transaxle fluid level check	7
Battery check, maintenance and charging	10
Brake check	18
Cabin air filter replacement	19
Cooling system check	13
Cooling system servicing (draining, flushing and refilling)	26
Differential lubricant change	30
Driveaxle boot check	24
Drivebelt check and replacement	11
Engine oil and oil filter change	8
Evaporative emissions control system check	27
Exhaust system check	23
Fluid level checks	4
Front differential lubricant level check	15
Fuel system check	21

	Section
Introduction	2
Maintenance reminder indicator resetting procedure	32
Maintenance schedule	1
Positive Crankcase Ventilation (PCV) valve check and replacement	29
Power steering fluid level check	6
Rear differential lubricant level check	16
Spark plug check and replacement	25
Steering and suspension check	22
Tire and tire pressure checks	5
Tire rotation	14
Tune-up general information	3
Transfer case lubricant change	31
Transfer case lubricant level check	17
Underhood hose check and replacement	12
Windshield wiper blade inspection and replacement	9

Specifications

Recommended lubricants and fluids

Note: *Listed here are manufacturer recommendations at the time this manual was written. Manufacturers occasionally upgrade their fluid and lubricant specifications, so check with your local auto parts store for current recommendations.*

Engine oil
  Type API "certified for gasoline engines"
  Viscosity .... SAE 5W-30
Engine coolant
  2010 and earlier models .... 50/50 mixture of Genuine Nissan Long life antifreeze coolant and distilled or demineralized water

  2011 and later models .... 50/50 mixture of Genuine Nissan Long life antifreeze coolant (blue) and distilled or demineralized water

Fuel Unleaded gasoline, minimum 91 RON octane
Automatic transmission fluid
  2007 and earlier models .... Nissan Matic J automatic transmission fluid
  2008 through 2012 models .... Nissan Matic S automatic transmission fluid
Automatic transaxle fluid (2013 and later models) .... Nissan CVT fluid NS-3* ONLY
Brake fluid .... DOT 3 brake fluid
Power steering fluid .... Nissan PSF or DEXRON VI automatic transmission fluid
Front differential lubricant (2012 and earlier AWD models) .... Nissan differential oil hypoid super GL-5, 80W-90
Rear differential lubricant
  2012 and earlier models .... Nissan synthetic gear oil GL-5, 75W-90
  2013 and later AWD models .... Nissan differential oil hypoid super semi-synthetic GL-5, 75W-90
Transfer case lubricant (AWD models)
  2012 and earlier models .... Nissan Matic D automatic transmission fluid
  2013 and later models .... API GL-5 SAE 80W-90 hypoid gear lubricant

Use of conventional transmission fluid will damage the transaxle and void the warranty according to the manufacturer.

Capacities*

Engine oil (including filter)

3.5L V6 engines	5.1 quarts	4.8 liters
4.0L V6 engines	5.4 quarts	5.1 liters
5.6L V8 engines	6.9 quarts	6.5 liters

Coolant (including reservoir tank)

2012 and earlier models

Without rear air conditioning	11 quarts	10.2 liters
With rear air conditioning	14 quarts	13.4 liters
2013 and later models	11.2 quarts	10.6 liters

Automatic transmission

V6 engines	10.9 quarts	10.3 liters
V8 engines	11.2 quarts	10.6 liters
Automatic transaxle** (2013 and later models)	9.3 quarts	8.8 liters

Differential

2012 and earlier models

Front (AWD)	7/8 quart	0.5 liter
Rear	1-1/2 quarts	1.4 liters
2013 and later models (AWD)	1/2 quart	0.5 liter

Transfer case

2012 and earlier models

ATX14B	3-1/8 quarts	3.0 liters
TX15B	2-1/8 quarts	2.0 liters
2013 and later models	5/8 pint	0.3 liters

Note: *All capacities approximate. Add as necessary to bring up to appropriate level.*

Note: **The best way to determine the amount of fluid to add during a routine fluid change is to measure the amount drained. Additionally, on 2007 and earlier models, the fluid changing procedure will require 30 to 50-percent more fluid than what is listed here (see Section 28).*

Ignition system

Spark plugs

Type

2012 and earlier models	NGK DILFR5A-11
2013 and later models	Denso FXE22HR-11
Gap	0.043 inch (1.1 mm)

Firing order

V6 engines	1-2-3-4-5-6
V8 engines	1-8-7-3-6-5-4-2

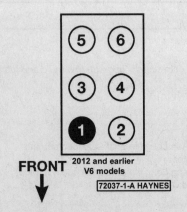

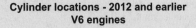

FRONT

Cylinder locations - 2012 and earlier V6 engines

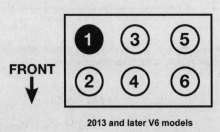

2013 and later V6 models

Cylinder locations - 2013 and later V6 engines

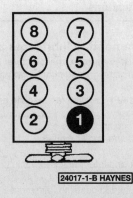

Cylinder locations - V8 engines

Valve clearance (engine cold)
Intake valves.. 0.010 to 0.013 inch (0.25 to 0.33 mm)
Exhaust valves .... 0.011 to 0.015 inch (0.28 to 0.38 mm)

Cooling system
Thermostat starts to open.. 176 to 183 degrees F (80 to 84 degrees C)

Brakes
Disc brake pad lining thickness (minimum) .... 0.079 inch (2.01 mm)
Brake disc minimum thickness .... See Chapter 9
Brake pedal height and freeplay.. See Chapter 9
Parking brake adjustment... See Chapter 9

Suspension and steering
Steering wheel freeplay limit.. 0 to 1.38 inches (35.05 mm)
Balljoint allowable movement 0

Torque specifications	Ft-lbs (unless otherwise indicated)	Nm

Note: *One foot-pound (ft-lb) of torque is equivalent to 12 inch-pounds (in-lbs) of torque. Torque values below approximately 15 foot-pounds are expressed in inch-pounds, because most foot-pound torque wrenches are not accurate at these smaller values.*

	Ft-lbs	Nm
Engine oil drain plug	25	34
Engine block coolant drain plug	46	62
Engine block heater*		
2012 and earlier models	54	73
2013 and later models	29	39
Automatic transmission drain plug (2012 and earlier models)	26	35
Automatic transaxle drain plug (2013 and later models)	25	34
Automatic transaxle fluid check/fill plug (2013 and later models)	89 in-lbs	10
Drivebelt tensioner		
Tensioner pulley mounting bolt		
2012 and earlier V6 models	41	56
2012 and earlier V8 models	18	24
2013 and later V6 models	18	24
Tensioner bracket mounting bolts	18	24
Idler pulley mounting bolts	26	35
Idler pulley bracket bolts	80 in-lbs	9
Rear differential drain and fill plugs	26	35
Spark plugs	18	24
Transfer case drain and fill plugs	26	35
Differential drain and fill plugs	26	35
Wheel lug nuts		
2012 and earlier models	98	133
2013 and later models	83	113

* *Canadian models*

Engine compartment components - 2012 and earlier models

1	Brake fluid reservoir	5	Automatic transmission fluid dipstick	9	Engine coolant reservoir
2	Air filter housing	6	Engine oil filler cap	10	Windshield washer fluid reservoir
3	Underhood fuse/relay block	7	Engine oil dipstick	11	Power steering fluid reservoir
4	Battery	8	Radiator cap		

Engine compartment components - 2013 and later models

1	Brake fluid reservoir	5	Radiator cap	8	Engine coolant reservoir
2	Air filter housing	6	Engine oil filler cap	9	Windshield washer fluid reservoir
3	Underhood fuse/relay block	7	Engine oil dipstick (not visible)	10	Power steering fluid reservoir
4	Battery				

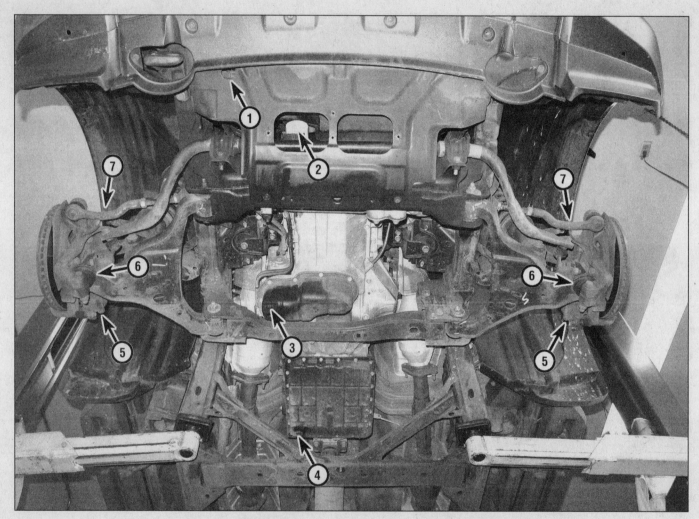

Engine compartment underside components - 2012 and earlier 2WD models

1	Radiator drain plug	4	Transmission drain plug	6	Lower balljoint
2	Engine oil filter	5	Brake caliper	7	Tie-rod end
3	Engine oil drain plug				

Rear underside components - 2012 and earlier models

1 Muffler	4 Lower balljoint	7 Universal joint
2 Exhaust system hanger	5 Driveaxle boot	8 Differential drain plug
3 EVAP system canister	6 Fuel tank	

1 Maintenance schedule

The maintenance intervals in this manual are provided with the assumption that you, not the dealer, will be doing the work. These are the minimum maintenance intervals recommended by the factory for vehicles that are driven daily. If you wish to keep your vehicle in peak condition at all times, you may wish to perform some of these procedures even more often. Because frequent maintenance enhances the efficiency, performance and resale value of your car, we encourage you to do so. If you drive in dusty areas, tow a trailer, idle or drive at low speeds for extended periods or drive for short distances (less than four miles) in below freezing temperatures, shorter intervals are also recommended.

When your vehicle is new, it should be serviced by a factory authorized dealer service department to protect the factory warranty. In many cases, the initial maintenance check is done at no cost to the owner.

Every 250 miles or weekly, whichever comes first

Check the engine oil level (Section 4)
Check the engine coolant level (Section 4)
Check the windshield washer fluid level (Section 4)
Check the battery electrolyte (Section 4)
Check the brake fluid level (Section 4)
Check the tires and tire pressures (Section 5)

Every 3000 miles or 3 months, whichever comes first

All items listed above plus:
Check the power steering fluid level (Section 6)
Check the automatic transaxle fluid level (Section 7)
Change the engine oil and oil filter (Section 8)

Every 7500 miles or 6 months, whichever comes first

All items listed above plus:
Inspect and replace if necessary the windshield wiper blades (Section 9)
Check and service the battery (Section 10)
Check the engine drivebelt (Section 11)
Inspect and replace if necessary all underhood hoses (Section 12)
Check the cooling system (Section 13)
Rotate the tires (Section 14)

Every 15,000 miles or 12 months, whichever comes first

All items listed above plus:
Check the differential lubricant level (Section 15 and 16)
Check the transfer case lubricant (Section 17)
Inspect the brake system (Section 18)*
Replace the cabin air filter (Section 19)
Check the air filter element (Section 20)
Inspect the fuel system (Section 21)
Inspect the suspension and steering components (Section 22)
Inspect the exhaust system (Section 23)
Check the driveaxle boots (Section 24)

Every 30,000 miles or 24 months, whichever comes first

All items listed above plus:
Replace the air filter (Section 20)
Service the cooling system (drain, flush and refill) (Section 26)
Inspect the evaporative emissions control system (Section 27)
Check and replace if necessary the PCV valve (Section 29)

Every 60,000 miles or 48 months, whichever comes first

All items listed above plus:
Change the automatic transaxle fluid (Section 28)**
Change the differential lubricant (Section 30)
Change the transfer case lubricant (Section 31)
Check (and adjust if noisy) the valve clearance (Chapter 2A or 2B)

Every 105,000 miles or 72 months, whichever comes first

Replace the spark plugs (Section 25)

* This item is affected by "severe" operating conditions as described below. If your vehicle is operated under "severe" conditions, perform all maintenance indicated with an asterisk (*) at half the indicated intervals. Severe conditions are indicated if you mainly operate your vehicle under one or more of the following conditions:
   a) Operating in dusty areas
   b) Towing a trailer
   c) Idling for extended periods and/or low speed operation
   d) Operating when outside temperatures remain below freezing and when most trips are less than 4 miles

** If operated under one or more of the following conditions, change the automatic transmission fluid and differential lubricant every 30,000 miles:
   a) In heavy city traffic where outside temperature regularly reaches 90-degrees F (32-degrees C) or higher
   b) In hilly or mountainous terrain
   c) Frequent trailer pulling

2   Introduction

1   This Chapter is designed to help the home mechanic maintain the Nissan Pathfinder for peak performance, economy, safety and long life.

2   Included in this Chapter is a master maintenance schedule, followed by Sections dealing specifically with each item on the schedule. Visual checks, adjustments, component replacement and other helpful items are included. Refer to the accompanying illustrations of the engine compartment and the underside of the vehicle for the location of various components.

3   Servicing your vehicle in accordance with the mileage/time maintenance schedule and the following Sections will provide it with a planned maintenance program that should result in a long and reliable service life. This is a comprehensive plan, so maintaining some items but not others at the specified service intervals will not produce the same results.

4   As you service your vehicle, you will discover that many of the procedures can, and should, be grouped together because of the nature of the particular procedure you're performing or because of the close proximity of two otherwise unrelated components to one another.

5   For example, if the vehicle is raised for any reason, you should inspect the exhaust, suspension, steering and fuel systems while you're under the vehicle. When you're rotating the tires, it makes good sense to check the brakes and wheel bearings since the wheels are already removed.

6   Finally, let's suppose you have to borrow or rent a torque wrench. Even if you only need to tighten the spark plugs, you might as well check the torque of as many critical fasteners as time allows.

7   The first step of this maintenance program is to prepare yourself before the actual work begins. Read through all Sections pertinent to the procedures you're planning to do, then make a list of and gather together all the parts and tools you will need to do the job. If it looks as if you might run into problems during a particular segment of some procedure, seek advice from your local auto parts stores or dealer service department.

3   Tune-up general information

1   The term tune-up is used in this manual to represent a combination of individual operations rather than one specific procedure.

2   If, from the time the vehicle is new, the routine maintenance schedule is followed closely and frequent checks are made of fluid levels and high wear items, as suggested throughout this manual, the engine will be kept in relatively good running condition and the need for additional work will be minimized.

3   More likely than not, however, there will be times when the engine is running poorly due to lack of regular maintenance. This is even more likely if a used vehicle, which has not received regular and frequent maintenance checks, is purchased. In such cases, an engine tune-up will be needed outside of the regular routine maintenance intervals.

4   The first step in any tune-up or engine diagnosis to help correct a poor running engine would be a cylinder compression check. A check of the engine compression (see Chapter 2C) will give valuable information regarding the overall performance of many internal components and should be used as a basis for tune-up and repair procedures. If, for instance, a compression check indicates serious internal engine wear, a conventional tune-up will not help the running condition of the engine and would be a waste of time and money.

5   The following series of operations are those most often needed to bring a generally poor running engine back into a proper state of tune.

Minor tune-up

Check all engine related fluids (Section 4)
Clean, inspect and test the battery
   (Section 10)
Check the drivebelts (Section 11)
Check all underhood hoses (Section 12)
Check the cooling system (Section 13)
Check the air filter (Section 20)

Major tune-up

All items listed under Minor tune-up, plus. . .
Replace the spark plugs (Section 25)
Replace the air filter (Section 20)
Check the fuel system (Section 21)
Check the charging system (Chapter 5)
Check the ignition system (Chapter 5)

4   Fluid level checks (every 250 miles or weekly)

1   Fluids are an essential part of the lubrication, cooling, brake, clutch and other systems. Because these fluids gradually become depleted and/or contaminated during normal operation of the vehicle, they must be periodically replenished. See *Recommended lubricants and fluids* and *Capacities* in this Chapter's Specifications before adding fluid to any of the following components.

Note: *The vehicle must be on level ground before fluid levels can be checked.*

Engine oil

2   The engine oil level is checked with a dipstick located at the front of the engine **(see illustration)**.

3   The oil level should be checked before the vehicle has been driven, or about 5 minutes after the engine has been shut off. If the oil is checked immediately after driving the vehicle, some of the oil will remain in the upper engine components, producing an inaccurate reading on the dipstick.

4   Pull the dipstick out and wipe all the oil from the end with a clean rag or paper towel. Insert the clean dipstick all the way back in and pull it out again. Observe the oil at the end of the dipstick; the level should be between the L and H marks **(see illustration)**.

5   It takes about one quart of oil to raise the level from the L mark to the H mark on the dipstick. Do not allow the level to drop below the L mark or oil starvation may cause engine damage. On the other hand, overfilling the engine (adding oil above the H mark) may cause oil fouled spark plugs, oil leaks or oil seal failures.

6   Wipe the area around the filler cap, then remove the cap from the valve cover to add oil. Use a funnel to prevent spills. After adding the oil, install the filler cap hand tight. Start the engine and look carefully for any small leaks around the oil filter or drain plug. Stop the engine and check the oil level again after it has had sufficient time to drain from the upper block and cylinder head galleys.

7   Checking the oil level is an important preventive maintenance step. A continually dropping oil level indicates oil leakage through damaged seals, from loose connections, or past worn rings or valve guides. If the oil looks milky in color or has water droplets in it, a cyl-

4.2 Engine oil dipstick is located close to the oil filler cap - early V6 models shown, other models similar

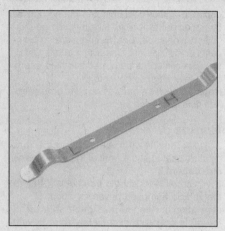

4.4 The oil level should be at or near the H mark - if it isn't, add enough oil to bring the level to near the H mark

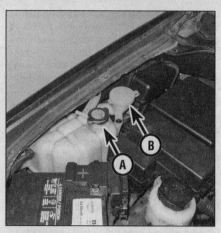

4.8 Don't confuse the engine coolant reservoir (A) with the windshield washer fluid reservoir (B)

4.17 The brake fluid level should be kept between the MIN and MAX marks on the translucent plastic reservoir

inder head gasket may be leaking. The cylinder head should be checked immediately. The condition of the oil should also be checked. Each time you check the oil level, slide your thumb and index finger up the dipstick before wiping off the oil. If you see small dirt or metal particles clinging to the dipstick, the oil should be changed (see Section 8).

Engine coolant

Warning: *Do not allow antifreeze to come in contact with your skin or painted surfaces of the vehicle. Flush contaminated areas immediately with plenty of water. Don't store new coolant or leave old coolant lying around where it's accessible to children or pets - they're attracted by its sweet smell and may drink it. Ingestion of even a small amount of coolant can be fatal! Wipe up garage floor and drip pan spills immediately. Keep antifreeze containers covered and repair cooling system leaks as soon as they're noticed.*

8   All vehicles covered by this manual are equipped with a pressurized coolant recovery system. A white coolant reservoir, located on the right side of the engine compartment, is connected by a hose to the base of the coolant filler cap **(see illustration)**. If the coolant gets too hot during engine operation, coolant can escape through the relief valve in the filler cap, then through a connecting hose into the reservoir. As the engine cools, the coolant is automatically drawn back into the cooling system to maintain the correct level.

9   The coolant level should be checked regularly. It must be between the MAX and MIN lines on the tank. The level will vary with the temperature of the engine. When the engine is cold, the coolant level should be at or slightly above the MIN mark on the tank. Once the engine has warmed up, the level should be at or near the MAX mark. If it isn't, allow the fluid in the tank to cool, then remove the cap from the reservoir and add coolant to bring the level up to the MAX line. Use only ethylene/glycol type coolant and water in the mixture

ratio recommended by your owner's manual. Do not use supplemental inhibitor additives. If only a small amount of coolant is required to bring the system up to the proper level, water can be used. However, repeated additions of water will dilute the recommended antifreeze and water solution. In order to maintain the proper ratio of antifreeze and water, it is advisable to top up the coolant level with the correct mixture. Refer to your owner's manual for the recommended ratio.

10   If the coolant level drops within a short time after replenishment, there may be a leak in the system. Inspect the radiator, hoses, engine coolant filler cap, drain plugs, air bleeder plugs and water pump. If no leak is evident, have the radiator cap pressure tested by your dealer.

Warning: *Never remove the radiator cap or the coolant reservoir cap when the engine is running or has just been shut down, because the cooling system is hot. Escaping steam and scalding liquid could cause serious injury.*

11   If it is necessary to open the radiator cap, wait until the system has cooled completely, then wrap a thick cloth around the cap and slowly unscrew it. If any steam escapes, wait until the system has cooled further, then remove the cap.

12   When checking the coolant level, always note its condition. It should be relatively clear. If it is brown or rust colored, the system should be drained, flushed and refilled. Even if the coolant appears to be normal, the corrosion inhibitors wear out with use, so it must be replaced at the specified intervals.

13   Do not allow antifreeze to come in contact with your skin or painted surfaces of the vehicle. Flush contacted areas immediately with plenty of water.

Windshield washer fluid

14   Fluid for the windshield washer system is stored in a plastic reservoir which is located on the right side of the engine compartment, adjacent to the coolant reservoir **(see illustra-**

tion 4.8). In milder climates, plain water can be used to top up the reservoir, but the reservoir should be kept no more than two-thirds full to allow for expansion should the water freeze. In colder climates, the use of a specially designed windshield washer fluid, available at your dealer and any auto parts store, will help lower the freezing point of the fluid. Mix the solution with water in accordance with the manufacturer's directions on the container. Do not use regular antifreeze, it will damage the vehicle's paint.

Battery electrolyte

15   On models not equipped with a sealed battery, check the electrolyte level of all six battery cells. It must be between the upper and lower levels. If the level is low, remove the filler/vent cap and add distilled water. Install and securely re-tighten the cap.

Caution: *Overfilling the cells may cause electrolyte to spill over during periods of heavy charging, causing corrosion or damage.*

Brake fluid

16   The brake master cylinder is mounted on the front of the power booster unit in the engine compartment. On 2013 and later models the fluid reservoir for the master cylinder is mounted on a bracket, inboard of the air filter housing.

17   To check the fluid level of the brake master cylinder, simply look at the marks on the reservoir **(see illustration)**. The level should be between the MIN and MAX marks.

18   If the level is low, wipe the top of the reservoir cover with a clean rag to prevent contamination of the brake system before lifting the cover.

19   Add only the specified brake fluid to the brake reservoir (refer to Recommended lubricants and fluids in this Chapter's Specifications or your owner's manual). Mixing different types of brake fluid can damage the system. Fill the brake master cylinder reservoir only to the MAX line.

Warning: *Use caution when filling the reservoir - brake fluid can harm your eyes and damage painted surfaces. Do not use brake fluid that has been opened for more than one year or has been left open. Brake fluid absorbs moisture from the air. Excess moisture can cause a dangerous loss of braking.*

20   While the reservoir cap is removed, inspect the master cylinder reservoir for contamination. If deposits, dirt particles or water droplets are present, the system should be drained and refilled.

21   After filling the reservoir to the proper level, make sure the lid is properly seated to prevent fluid leakage and/or system pressure loss.

22   The fluid in the brake master cylinder will drop slightly as the brake pads at each wheel wear down during normal operation. If the master cylinder requires repeated replenishing to keep it at the proper level, this is an indication of leakage in the brake system, which should be corrected immediately. If the brake system shows any indication of leakage, check all brake lines and connections, along with the calipers and booster (see Section 18).

23   If, upon checking the brake cylinder fluid level, you discover it empty or nearly empty, the system should be thoroughly checked for leaks, repaired if any are found, then bled (see Chapter 9).

5   Tire and tire pressure checks (every 250 miles or weekly)

1   Periodic inspection of the tires may spare you from the inconvenience of being stranded with a flat tire. It can also provide you with vital information regarding possible problems in the steering and suspension systems before major damage occurs.

2   Normal tread wear can be monitored with a simple, inexpensive device known as a tread depth indicator (see illustration). When the tread depth reaches the specified minimum, replace the tire(s).

3   Note any abnormal tread wear (see illustration). Tread pattern irregularities such as cupping, flat spots and more wear on one side than the other are indications of front end alignment and/or balance problems. If any of these conditions are noted, take the vehicle to a tire shop or service station to correct the problem.

4   Look closely for cuts, punctures and

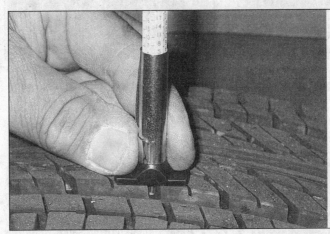

5.2 A tire tread depth indicator should be used to monitor tire wear - they are available at auto parts stores and service stations and cost very little

UNDERINFLATION

CUPPING

Cupping may be caused by:
- Underinflation and/or mechanical irregularities such as out-of-balance condition of wheel and/or tire, and bent or damaged wheel.
- Loose or worn steering tie-rod or steering idler arm.
- Loose, damaged or worn front suspension parts.

OVERINFLATION

INCORRECT TOE-IN OR EXTREME CAMBER

FEATHERING DUE TO MISALIGNMENT

5.3 This chart will help you determine the condition of your tires, the probable cause(s) of abnormal wear and the corrective action necessary

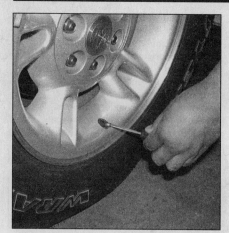

5.4a If a tire loses air on a steady basis, check the valve core first to make sure it's snug (special inexpensive wrenches are commonly available at auto parts stores)

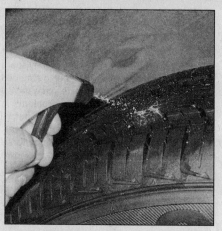

5.4b If the valve core is tight, raise the corner of the vehicle with the low tire and spray a soapy water solution onto the tread as the tire is turned slowly - slow leaks will cause small bubbles to appear

5.8 To extend the life of your tires, check the air pressure at least once a week with an accurate gauge (don't forget the spare!)

6.1 The power steering fluid reservoir is mounted on the passenger's side of the engine compartment

embedded nails or tacks. Sometimes a tire will hold its air pressure for a short time or leak down very slowly even after a nail has embedded itself into the tread. If a slow leak persists, check the valve stem core to make sure it is tight **(see illustration)**. Examine the tread for an object that may have embedded itself into the tire or for a plug that may have begun to leak (radial tire punctures are repaired with a plug that is installed in a puncture). If a puncture is suspected, it can be easily verified by spraying a solution of soapy water onto the puncture area **(see illustration)**. The soapy solution will bubble if there is a leak. Unless the puncture is inordinately large, a tire shop or gas station can usually repair the punctured tire.

5   Carefully inspect the inner sidewall of each tire for evidence of brake fluid leakage. If you see any, inspect the brakes immediately.

6   Correct tire air pressure adds miles to the lifespan of the tires, improves mileage and enhances overall ride quality. Tire pressure cannot be accurately estimated by look-

ing at a tire, particularly if it is a radial. A tire pressure gauge is therefore essential. Keep an accurate gauge in the glove box. The pressure gauges fitted to the nozzles of air hoses at gas stations are often inaccurate.

7   Always check tire pressure when the tires are cold. "Cold" in this case, means the vehicle has not been driven over a mile in the three hours preceding a tire pressure check. A pressure rise of four to eight pounds is not uncommon once the tires are warm.

8   Unscrew the valve cap protruding from the wheel or hubcap and push the gauge firmly onto the valve **(see illustration)**. Note the reading on the gauge and compare this figure to the recommended tire pressure shown on the tire placard on the left door. Be sure to reinstall the valve cap to keep dirt and moisture out of the valve stem mechanism. Check all four tires and, if necessary, add enough air to bring them up to the recommended pressure levels.

9   Don't forget to keep the spare tire inflated to the specified pressure (consult your owner's manual). Note that the air pressure specified for the compact spare is significantly higher than the pressure of the regular tires.

---

6   Power steering fluid level check (every 3000 miles or 3 months)

1   To check the fluid level in the reservoir, simply look at the MIN and MAX on the side of the reservoir **(see illustration)**. The level should be within the specified distance from the maximum fill line. Use the HOT range at fluid temperatures of 122 to 176 degrees F. Use the COLD range at fluid temperatures of 32 to 86 degrees F. At no time should the fluid level drop below the minimum mark on the reservoir.

2   If additional fluid is required, use a clean rag to wipe off the reservoir cap and area

around the cap. This will prevent any foreign matter from entering the reservoir during the check.

3   Unscrew the top cap and pour the specified type directly into the reservoir, using a funnel to prevent spills. Install the cap and tighten securely.

4   If the reservoir requires frequent fluid additions, all power steering hoses, hose connections, the power steering pump and the rack and pinion assembly should be carefully checked for leaks

---

7   Automatic transmission/ transaxle fluid level check (every 3000 miles or 3 months)

2012 and earlier models

1   The level of the automatic transmission/ transaxle fluid should be carefully maintained. Low fluid level can lead to slipping or loss of drive, while overfilling can cause foaming, loss of fluid and transaxle damage.

2   The fluid level should only be checked when the transmission is hot (at its normal operating temperature). If the vehicle has just been driven over 10 miles (15 miles in a frigid climate), and the fluid temperature is 160 to 175-degrees F, the transmission is hot.

Caution: *If the vehicle has just been driven for a long time at high speed or in city traffic in hot weather, or if it has been pulling a trailer, an accurate fluid level reading cannot be obtained. Allow the fluid to cool down for about 30 minutes.*

3   If the vehicle has not been driven, park the vehicle on level ground, set the parking brake, then start the engine and bring it to operating temperature. While the engine is idling, depress the brake pedal and move the selector lever through all the gear ranges, beginning and ending in Park.

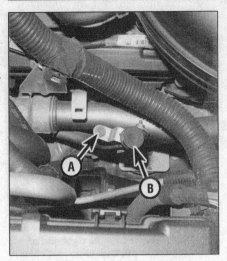

7.4a Remove the bolt (A) securing the automatic transmission dipstick (B) to its tube, then pull out the dipstick

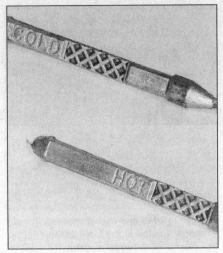

7.4b The automatic transmission fluid can be checked when at normal operating temperature using the HOT range (cross-hatched area), or before the transmission is fully warmed-up by using the COLD range

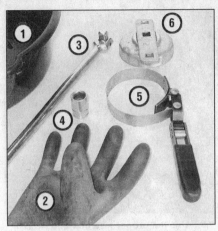

8.2 These tools are required when changing the engine oil and filter

1   *Drain pan - It should be fairly shallow in depth, but wide in order to prevent spills*
2   *Rubber gloves - When removing the drain plug and filter, it is inevitable that you will get oil on your hands (the gloves will prevent burns)*
3   *Breaker bar - Sometimes the oil drain plug is pretty tight and a long breaker bar is needed to loosen it*
4   *Socket - To be used with the breaker bar or a ratchet (must be the correct size to fit the drain plug)*
5   *Filter wrench - This is a metal band-type wrench, which requires clearance around the filter to be effective*
6   *Filter wrench - This type fits on the bottom of the filter and can be turned with a ratchet or breaker bar (different size wrenches are available for different types of filters)*

4   With the engine still idling, remove the dipstick from its tube **(see illustration)**. Check the level of the fluid on the dipstick **(see illustration)** and note its condition.

5   Wipe the fluid from the dipstick with a clean lint-free rag and reinsert it back into the filler tube until the cap seats.

6   Pull the dipstick out again and note the fluid level. If the level is at the low side of the range, add the specified automatic transmission fluid (see this Chapter's Specifications 0) through the dipstick tube with a funnel.

7   Add just enough of the recommended fluid to fill the transmission to the proper level. Once the fluid level is correct, reinstall the dipstick and the securing bolt.

8   The condition of the fluid should also be checked along with the level. If the fluid at the end of the dipstick is black or a dark reddish brown color, or if it emits a burned smell, the fluid should be changed (see Section 28). If you are in doubt about the condition of the fluid, purchase some new fluid and compare the two for color and smell.

2013 and later models

Warning: *This procedure is potentially dangerous and is best left to a professional shop with a safe lifting apparatus. The vehicle must be kept level while being safely raised high enough for access to the check plug on the transaxle.*

Caution: *These models use a special fluid designed specifically for the Nissan CVT transaxle. Don't use another fluid or damage may occur and the warranty may be voided. See this Chapter's Specifications 0 for the proper fluid type.*

Note: *Routine checks of the transaxle fluid level on these models is not necessary; this procedure should be used only when refilling*

the transaxle after the fluid has been drained, unless an obvious leak has been detected.

Note: *It is recommended to monitor the temperature of the CVT fluid with a scan tool, performing this procedure when the temperature of the fluid is between 95 and 113 degrees F (35 to 45 degrees C).*

Note: *A special adapter (tool no. KV311039S0 or equivalent) is necessary for this procedure.*

9   With the vehicle raised and safely supported, start the engine and move the shift lever through all the gear ranges, pausing five seconds in each range, ending in Park. Allow the engine to idle during this procedure.

10   Locate the check/fill plug on the transaxle **(see illustration 28.11)**.

11   Place a container under the check/fill plug and remove it. Install special adapter tool no. KV311039S0 (or equivalent) into the hole. Connect a hose to the adapter.

12   Using a fluid pump, add approximately 1/2-quart of the specified fluid (see this Chapter's Specifications 0) to the transaxle. Detach the hose from the adapter and see if any fluid drains out. If it does, allow it to drain until it stops.

13   If fluid does not drain out, repeat Step 12 until it does.

14   Reinstall the check/fil plug with a new O-ring and tighten it to the torque listed in this Chapter's Specifications.

---

8   Engine oil and oil filter change (every 3000 miles or 3 months)

---

1   Frequent oil changes are the best preventive maintenance the home mechanic can give the engine, because aging oil becomes diluted and contaminated, which leads to premature engine wear.

2   Make sure that you have all the necessary tools before you begin this procedure **(see illustration)**. You should also have plenty of rags or newspapers handy for mopping up any spills.

3   Park the vehicle on a level spot. Start the engine and allow it to reach its normal operating temperature. Warm oil and contaminates will flow out more easily. Turn off the engine when it's warmed up. Remove the filler cap from the valve cover.

4   Raise the vehicle and support it securely on jackstands. Remove the under-vehicle splash shield.

Warning: *To avoid personal injury, never get beneath the vehicle when it is supported by only by a jack. The jack provided with your vehicle is designed solely for raising the vehicle to remove and replace the wheels. Always use jackstands to support the vehicle when it becomes necessary to place your body underneath the vehicle.*

5   Being careful not to touch the hot exhaust components, place the drain pan under the drain plug in the bottom of the pan

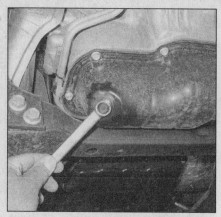

8.5 Use the proper size box-end wrench or socket to remove the oil drain plug and avoid rounding it off

8.10a On 2012 and earlier models, the oil filter is located at the front of the engine (V6 model shown)

8.10b On 2013 and later models the oil filter is located on the right end of the engine

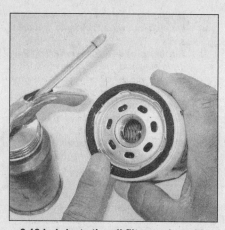

8.12 Lubricate the oil filter gasket with clean engine oil before installing the filter

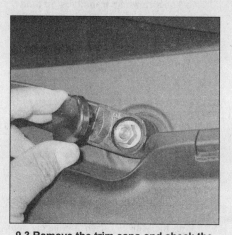

9.3 Remove the trim caps and check the tightness of the wiper arm retaining nuts

and remove the plug **(see illustration)**. Discard the washer. A new one must be used during installation. You may want to wear gloves while unscrewing the plug the final few turns if the engine is really hot.

6   Allow the old oil to drain into the pan. It may be necessary to move the pan farther under the engine as the oil flow slows to a trickle. Inspect the old oil for the presence of metal shavings and chips.

7   After all the oil has drained, wipe off the drain plug with a clean rag. Even minute metal particles clinging to the plug would immediately contaminate the new oil.

8   Clean the area around the drain plug opening, install a new washer, reinstall the plug and tighten it to the torque listed in this Chapter's Specifications.

9   Move the drain pan into position under the oil filter.

10   Loosen the oil filter by turning it counterclockwise with the filter wrench **(see illustrations)**. Any standard filter wrench should work. Once the filter is loose, use your hands to unscrew it from the oil cooler. Just as the filter is detached from the block, immediately tilt the open end up to prevent the oil inside the filter from spilling out.

Warning: *The engine exhaust manifold may still be hot, so be careful.*

11   With a clean rag, wipe off the oil filter mounting surface. Make sure that none of the old gasket remains stuck to the mounting surface. It can be removed with a scraper if necessary.

12   Compare the old filter with the new one to make sure they are the same type. Smear some engine oil on the rubber gasket of the new filter and screw it into place **(see illustration)**. Because over-tightening the filter will damage the gasket, do not use a filter wrench to tighten the filter. Most filter manufacturers recommend tightening the filter by hand only. Normally they should be tightened 2/3-turn after the gasket contacts the filter adapter/oil cooler, but be sure to follow the directions on the filter or container.

13   Remove all tools, rags, etc. from under the vehicle, being careful not to spill the oil in the drain pan, then lower the vehicle.

14   Remove the filler cap and add new oil to the engine. Use a spout or funnel to prevent oil from spilling onto the top of the engine. Pour four quarts of fresh oil into the engine. Wait a few minutes to allow the oil to drain into the pan, then check the level on the oil

dipstick (see Section 4). If the oil level is at or near the H mark, install the filler cap hand tight, start the engine and allow the new oil to circulate.

15   Allow the engine to run for about a minute. While the engine is running, look under the vehicle and check for leaks at the oil pan drain plug and around the oil filter. If either is leaking, stop the engine and tighten the plug or filter slightly.

16   Wait a few minutes to allow the oil to trickle down into the pan, then recheck the level on the dipstick and, if necessary, add enough oil to bring the level to the H mark.

17   During the first few trips after an oil change, make it a point to check frequently for leaks and proper oil level.

18   The old oil drained from the engine cannot be reused in its present state and should be disposed of. Check with your local auto parts store, disposal facility or environmental agency to see if they will accept the oil for recycling. After the oil has cooled it can be drained into a container (capped plastic jugs, topped bottles, milk cartons, etc.) for transport to one of these disposal sites. Don't dispose of the oil by pouring it on the ground or down a drain!

9   Windshield wiper blade inspection and replacement (every 7500 miles or 6 months)

1   The windshield wiper and blade assembly should be inspected periodically for damage, loose components and cracked or worn blade elements.

2   Road film can build up on the wiper blades and affect their efficiency, so they should be washed regularly with a mild detergent solution.

3   The action of the wiping mechanism can loosen bolts, nuts and fasteners, so they should be checked and tightened, as necessary **(see illustration)**, at the same time the wiper blades are checked.

9.5 Press on the release tab and push the blade assembly down out of the hook in the arm

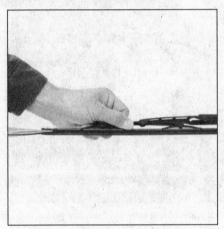

9.6 Use needle-nose pliers to compress the rubber element, then slide the element out. Slide the new element in and lock the blade assembly fingers into the notches of the wiper element

4   If the wiper blade elements are cracked, worn or warped, or no longer clean adequately, they should be replaced with new ones.

5   Lift the arm assembly away from the glass for clearance, press on the release lever, then slide the wiper blade assembly out of the hook in the end of the arm **(see illustration)**.

6   Use needle-nose pliers to compress the blade element, then slide the element out of the frame and discard it **(see illustration)**.

7   Installation is the reverse of removal.

10 Battery check, maintenance and charging (every 7500 miles or 6 months)

Warning: *Certain precautions must be followed when checking and servicing the bat-*

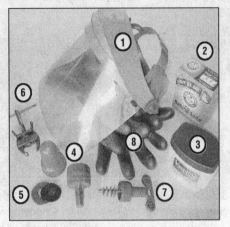

10.1 Tools and materials required for battery maintenance

1   **Face shield/safety goggles** - *When removing corrosion with a brush, the acidic particles can easily fly up into your eyes*
2   **Baking soda** - *A solution of baking soda and water can be used to neutralize corrosion*
3   **Petroleum jelly** - *A layer of this on the battery posts will help prevent corrosion*
4   **Battery post/cable cleaner** - *This wire brush cleaning tool will remove all traces of corrosion from the battery posts and cable clamps*
5   **Treated felt washers** - *Placing one of these on each post, directly under the cable clamps, will help prevent corrosion*
6   **Puller** - *Sometimes the cable clamps are very difficult to pull off the posts, even after the nut/bolt has been completely loosened. This tool pulls the clamp straight up and off the post without damage*
7   **Battery post/cable cleaner** - *Here is another cleaning tool that is a slightly different version of Number 4 above, but it does the same thing*
8   **Rubber gloves** - *Another safety item to consider when servicing the battery; remember that's acid inside the battery!*

tery. Hydrogen gas, which is highly flammable, is always present in the battery cells, so keep lighted tobacco and all other open flames and sparks away from the battery. The electrolyte inside the battery is actually dilute sulfuric acid, which will cause injury if splashed on your skin or in your eyes. It will also ruin clothes and painted surfaces. When removing the battery cables, always detach the negative cable first and hook it up last!

1   A routine preventive maintenance program for the battery in your vehicle is the only way to ensure quick and reliable starts. But before performing any battery maintenance, make sure that you have the proper equipment necessary to work safely around the battery **(see illustration)**.

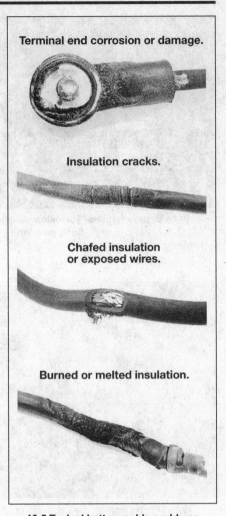

Terminal end corrosion or damage.

Insulation cracks.

Chafed insulation or exposed wires.

Burned or melted insulation.

10.5 Typical battery cable problems

2   There are also several precautions that should be taken whenever battery maintenance is performed. Before servicing the battery, always turn the engine and all accessories off and disconnect the the negative battery cable (see Chapter 5).

3   The battery produces hydrogen gas, which is both flammable and explosive. Never create a spark, smoke or light a match around the battery. Always charge the battery in a ventilated area.

4   Electrolyte contains poisonous and corrosive sulfuric acid. Do not allow it to get in your eyes, on your skin or on your clothes. Never ingest it. Wear protective safety glasses when working near the battery. Keep children away from the battery.

5   Note the external condition of the battery. If the positive terminal and cable clamp on your vehicle's battery is equipped with a rubber protector, make sure it isn't torn or damaged. It should completely cover the terminal. Look for any corroded or loose connections, cracks in the case or cover or loose hold-down clamps. Also check the entire length of each cable for cracks and frayed conductors **(see illustration)**.

10.6a Battery terminal corrosion usually appears as light, fluffy powder

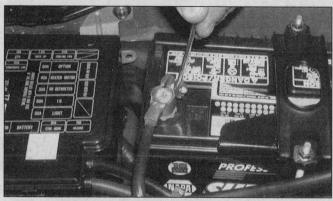

10.6b Removing a cable from the battery post with a wrench - sometimes special battery pliers are required for this procedure if corrosion has caused deterioration of the nut hex (always remove the ground cable first and hook it up last!)

10.7a When cleaning the cable clamps, all corrosion must be removed

10.7b Use the other side of the tool to clean the posts

6   If corrosion, which looks like white, fluffy deposits **(see illustration)** is evident, particularly around the terminals, the battery should be removed for cleaning. Loosen the cable clamp bolts with a wrench, being careful to remove the ground cable first, and slide them off the terminals **(see illustration)**. Then disconnect the hold-down clamp bolt and nut, remove the clamp and lift the battery from the engine compartment.

7   Clean the cable clamps thoroughly with a battery brush or a terminal cleaner and a solution of warm water and baking soda **(see illustration)**. Wash the terminals and the top of the battery case with the same solution but make sure that the solution doesn't get into the battery. When cleaning the cables, terminals and battery top, wear safety goggles and rubber gloves to prevent any solution from coming in contact with your eyes or hands. Wear old clothes too - even diluted, sulfuric acid splashed onto clothes will burn holes in them. If the terminals have been extensively corroded, clean them up with a terminal cleaner **(see illustration)**. Thoroughly wash all cleaned areas with plain water.

8   Make sure the battery tray is in good condition and the hold-down clamp bolt or nut

is tight. If the battery is removed from the tray, make sure no parts remain in the bottom of the tray when the battery is reinstalled. When reinstalling the hold-down clamp bolt or nut, do not over-tighten it.

9   Information on removing and installing the battery can be found in Chapter 5. Information on jump starting can be found at the front of this manual. For more detailed battery checking procedures, refer to the Haynes Automotive Electrical Manual.

Cleaning

10   Corrosion on the hold-down components, battery case and surrounding areas can be removed with a solution of water and baking soda. Thoroughly rinse all cleaned areas with plain water.

11   Any metal parts of the vehicle damaged by corrosion should be covered with a zinc-based primer, then painted.

Charging

Warning: *When batteries are being charged, hydrogen gas, which is very explosive and flammable, is produced. Do not smoke or allow open flames near a charging or a recently*

charged battery. Wear eye protection when near the battery during charging. Also, make sure the charger is unplugged before connecting or disconnecting the battery from the charger.

12   Slow-rate charging is the best way to restore a battery that's discharged to the point where it will not start the engine. It's also a good way to maintain the battery charge in a vehicle that's only driven a few miles between starts. Maintaining the battery charge is particularly important in the winter when the battery must work harder to start the engine and electrical accessories that drain the battery are in greater use.

13   It's best to use a one or two-amp battery charger (sometimes called a "trickle" charger). They are the safest and put the least strain on the battery. They are also the least expensive. For a faster charge, you can use a higher amperage charger, but don't use one rated more than 1/10th the amp/hour rating of the battery. Rapid boost charges that claim to restore the power of the battery in one to two hours are hardest on the battery and can damage batteries not in good condition. This type of charging should only be used in emergency situations.

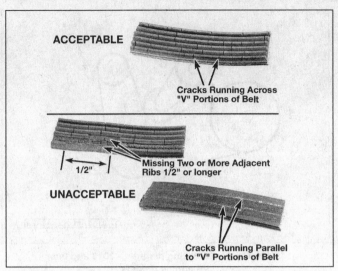

11.3 Here are some of the more common problems associated with drivebelts (check the belt very carefully to prevent an untimely breakdown)

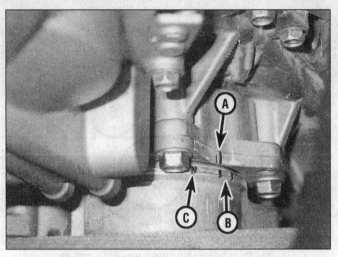

11.4 Observe the scale on the belt tensioner; if the maximum wear mark is aligned with the stationary mark, replace the belt

A   *Stationary mark*   C   *Wear limit mark*
B   *New belt range*

11.8a Use a socket and ratchet or breaker bar to rotate the tensioner counterclockwise far enough to remove the drivebelt, then slowly release the tensioner (V8 model shown)

11.8b On some models a square-drive tool is required to rotate the tensioner to remove the drivebelt (4.0L V6 model shown)

14   The average time necessary to charge a battery should be listed in the instructions that come with the charger. As a general rule, a trickle charger will charge a battery in 12 to 16 hours.

11   Drivebelt check (every 7500 miles or 6 months) and replacement

Check

1   These models use a serpentine drive-belt with a tensioner (automatic adjuster). The good condition and proper tension of the belt is critical to the operation of the engine. Because of their composition and the high stresses to which they are subjected, drivebelts stretch and deteriorate as they get older. They must therefore be periodically inspected.

2   The serpentine drivebelt transmits power to all the accessories.
3   With the engine off, open the hood and locate the drivebelt. With a flashlight, check the belt for separation of the adhesive rubber on both sides of the core, core separation from the belt side, a severed core, separation of the ribs from the adhesive rubber, cracking or separation of the ribs, and torn or worn ribs or cracks in the inner ridges of the ribs **(see illustration)**. Also check for fraying and glazing, which gives the belt a shiny appearance. Both sides of the belt should be inspected, which means you will have to twist the belt to check the underside. Use your fingers to feel the belt where you can't see it. If any of the above conditions are evident, replace the belt (see Steps 5 through 10).
Note: *On 2012 and earlier models, air intake duct removal will help with viewing and accessing the drivebelt (see Chapter 4)*

4   Check the drivebelt indicator for excessive stretch **(see illustration)**. If the drivebelt indicator is out of limit, replace the drivebelt (see Steps 5 through 10).

Drivebelt replacement

5   Disconnect the cable from the negative terminal of the battery (see Chapter 5).
6   2012 and earlier models: Remove the air intake duct between the air filter housing and the throttle body (see Chapter 4).
7   2013 and later models: Loosen the right front wheel lug nuts. Raise the vehicle and support it securely on jackstands. Remove the wheel and the inner fender splash shield.
8   Rotate the belt tensioner counterclockwise using a wrench, ratchet and socket or a breaker bar to release tension on the drivebelt **(see illustrations)**.
9   Remove the drivebelt from the tensioner and all accessories.

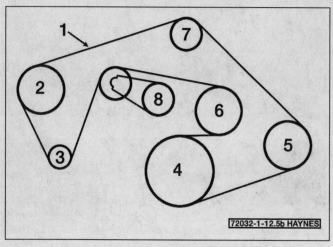

**11.10a Drivebelt routing diagram - 2012 and earlier
V6 engine models**

1 Drivebelt	5 Air conditioning compressor
2 Power steering pump	6 Cooling fan pulley
3 Alternator	7 Idler pulley
4 Crankshaft pulley	8 Tensioner

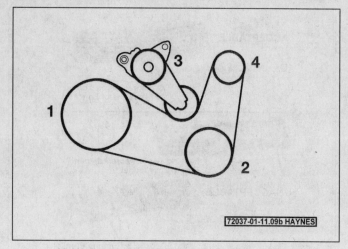

**11.10b Drivebelt routing diagram - 2013 and later
V6 engine models**

1 Crankshaft pulley	3 Tensioner
2 Air conditioning compressor pulley	4 Alternator

10   Install the new drivebelt, making sure that it's properly routed **(see illustrations)**.
11   Reconnect the battery and perform the necessary re-learn procedures (see Chapter 5).

Tensioner and idler pulley replacement

12   Remove the drivebelt (see Steps 5 through 8).
13   Remove the drivebelt tensioner mounting bolts and remove the tensioner.
14   Remove the idler pulley bolt and the idler pulley.
15   Installation is the reverse of removal. Tighten the tensioner and idler pulley mounting fasteners to the torque listed in this Chapter's Specifications.

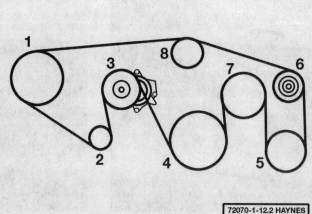

11.10c Drivebelt routing diagram - V8 engine models

1   Power steering pump
2   Alternator
3   Tensioner
4   Crankshaft pulley
5   Air conditioning compressor or idler pulley
6   Idler pulley
7   Water pump
8   Idler pulley

12   Underhood hose check and replacement (every 7500 miles or 6 months)

Caution: *Replacement of air conditioning hoses must be left to a dealer service department or air conditioning shop that has the equipment to depressurize the system safely. Never remove air conditioning components or hoses until the system has been depressurized.*

General

1   High temperatures in the engine compartment can cause the deterioration of the rubber and plastic hoses used for engine, accessory and emission systems operation. Periodic inspection should be made for cracks, loose clamps, material hardening and leaks.
2   Information specific to the cooling system hoses can be found in Section 13.

3   Some, but not all, hoses are secured to the fittings with clamps. Where clamps are used, check to be sure they haven't lost their tension, allowing the hose to leak. If clamps aren't used, make sure the hose has not expanded and/or hardened where it slips over the fitting, allowing it to leak.

Vacuum hoses

4   It's quite common for vacuum hoses, especially those in the emissions system, to be color coded or identified by colored stripes molded into them. Various systems require hoses with different wall thickness, collapse resistance and temperature resistance. When replacing hoses, be sure the new ones are made of the same material.
5   Often the only effective way to check a hose is to remove it completely from the vehicle. If more than one hose is removed, label the hoses and fittings to ensure correct installation.
6   When checking vacuum hoses, be sure

to include any plastic T-fittings in the check. Inspect the fittings for cracks and the hose where it fits over the fitting for distortion, which could cause leakage.
7   A small piece of vacuum hose (1/4-inch inside diameter) can be used as a stethoscope to detect vacuum leaks. Hold one end of the hose to your ear and probe around vacuum hoses and fittings, listening for the hissing sound characteristic of a vacuum leak.
Warning: *When probing with the vacuum hose stethoscope, be very careful not to come into contact with moving engine components such as the drivebelts, cooling fan, etc.*

Fuel hose

Warning: *Gasoline is flammable, so take extra precautions when you work on any part of the fuel system. Don't smoke or allow open flames or bare light bulbs near the work area, and don't work in a garage where a gas-type appliance (such as a water heater or clothes dryer) is present. Since fuel is carcinogenic,*

Check for a chafed area that could fail prematurely.

Check for a soft area indicating the hose has deteriorated inside.

Overtightening the clamp on a hardened hose will damage the hose and cause a leak.

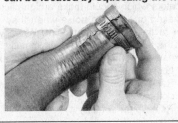

Check each hose for swelling and oil-soaked ends. Cracks and breaks can be located by squeezing the hose.

13.4 Hoses, like drivebelts, have a habit of failing at the worst possible time - to prevent the inconvenience of a blown radiator or heater hose, inspect them carefully as shown here

wear fuel-resistant gloves when there's a possibility of being exposed to fuel, and, if you spill any fuel on your skin, rinse it off immediately with soap and water. Mop up any spills immediately and do not store fuel-soaked rags where they could ignite. The fuel system is under constant pressure, so, if any fuel lines are to be disconnected, the fuel pressure in the system must be relieved first (see Chapter 4). When you perform any kind of work on the fuel system, wear safety glasses and have a Class B type fire extinguisher on hand.

8   Check all flexible fuel lines for deterioration and chafing. Check especially for cracks in areas where the hose bends and just before fittings, such as where the fuel line attaches to the fuel rail.

9   If any fuel lines are to be disconnected, be prepared to catch spilled fuel.

Warning: Your vehicle is equipped with fuel injection and you must relieve the fuel system pressure before servicing the fuel lines. Refer

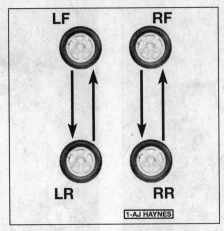

14.2 The recommended tire rotation pattern for these vehicles

to Chapter 4 for the fuel system pressure relief procedure.

10   When replacing a hose, use only hose that is specifically designed for your fuel injection system.

11   Some fuel lines use quick-connect fittings, which require a special tool to disconnect. See Chapter 4 for more information on these types of fittings.

Metal lines

12   Sections of metal line are often used for fuel line between the fuel pump and carburetor or fuel injection unit. Check carefully to be sure the line has not been bent or crimped and that cracks have not started in the line.

13   If a section of metal fuel line must be replaced, only seamless steel tubing should be used, since copper and aluminum tubing don't have the strength necessary to withstand normal engine vibration.

14   Check the metal brake lines where they enter the master cylinder and brake proportioning unit (if used) for cracks in the lines or loose fittings. Any sign of brake fluid leakage calls for an immediate thorough inspection of the brake system.

13   Cooling system check (every 7500 miles or 6 months)

1   Many major engine failures can be attributed to a faulty cooling system. If the vehicle is equipped with an automatic transaxle, the cooling system also cools the transaxle fluid and thus plays an important role in prolonging transaxle life.

2   The cooling system should be checked with the engine cold. Do this before the vehicle is driven for the day or after the engine has been shut off for at least three hours.

3   Remove the radiator cap by turning it to the left until it reaches a stop. If you hear a hissing sound (indicating there is still pressure in the system), wait until it stops. Press down on the cap with the palm of your hand

and continue turning to the left until the cap can be removed. Thoroughly clean the cap, inside and out, with clean water. Also clean the filler neck on the radiator. All traces of corrosion should be removed. The coolant inside the radiator should be relatively transparent. If it's rust colored, the system should be drained and refilled (see Section 26). If the coolant level isn't up to the top, add additional antifreeze/coolant mixture (see Section 4).

4   Carefully check the large upper and lower radiator hoses along with the smaller diameter heater hoses which run from the engine to the firewall. Inspect each hose along its entire length, replacing any hose which is cracked, swollen or shows signs of deterioration. Cracks may become more apparent if the hose is squeezed **(see illustration)**. Regardless of condition, it's a good idea to replace hoses with new ones every two years.

5   Make sure that all hose connections are tight. A leak in the cooling system will usually show up as white or rust colored deposits on the areas adjoining the leak. If wire-type clamps are used at the ends of the hoses, it may be a good idea to replace them with more secure screw-type clamps.

6   Use compressed air or a soft brush to remove bugs, leaves, etc. from the front of the radiator or air conditioning condenser. Be careful not to damage the delicate cooling fins or cut yourself on them.

7   Every other inspection, or at the first indication of cooling system problems, have the cap and system pressure tested. If you don't have a pressure tester, most gas stations and repair shops will do this for a minimal charge.

14   Tire rotation (every 7500 miles or 6 months)

1   The tires should be rotated at the specified intervals and whenever uneven wear is noticed. Since the vehicle will be raised and the tires removed anyway, check the brakes (see Section 18) at this time.

2   Radial tires must be rotated in a specific pattern **(see illustration)**.

3   Refer to the information in Chapter 0, Section 8 for the proper procedures to follow when raising the vehicle and changing a tire. If the brakes are to be checked, do not apply the parking brake as stated. Make sure the tires are blocked to prevent the vehicle from rolling.

4   Preferably, the entire vehicle should be raised at the same time. This can be done on a hoist or by jacking up each corner and then lowering the vehicle onto jackstands placed under the frame rails. Always use four jackstands and make sure the vehicle is firmly supported.

5   After rotation, check and adjust the tire pressures as necessary and tighten the lug nuts to the torque specified in this Chapter's Specifications 0.

6   For further information on the wheels and tires, refer to Chapter 10.

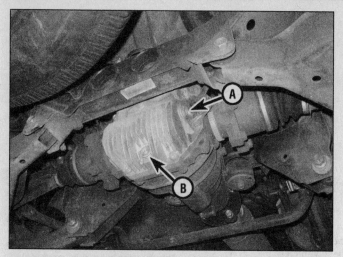

16.2 Rear differential check/filler plug (A) and drain plug (B) - 2012 and earlier models shown, later models similar

17.2 Transfer case filler plug (A), drain plug on ATX14B transfer cases (B), and approximate drain plug location on TX15B transfer cases (C) (2012 and earlier models)

15   Front differential lubricant level check (2012 and earlier AWD models) (every 15,000 miles or 12 months)

1   Raise the vehicle and support it securely on jackstands. The vehicle should be as level as possible to ensure an accurate check.
2   Remove the plug from the filler hole in the differential. Discard the washer. A new one should be used during installation.
3   The lubricant should be up to the bottom of the filler hole. Check the level by inserting your finger into the fill hole. If low, use a pump or squeeze bottle to add the lubricant listed in this Chapter's Specifications 0 until it just starts to run out of the hole.
4   Place a new sealing washer on the fill plug. Install the plug in the filler hole and tighten it to the torque listed in this Chapter's Specifications.

16   Rear differential lubricant level check (every 15,000 miles or 12 months)

Note: *This procedure applies to all 2012 and earlier models and 2013 and later AWD models.*
1   Raise the vehicle and support it securely on jackstands. The vehicle should be as level as possible to ensure an accurate check.
2   Remove the plug from the filler hole **(see illustration)**. Discard the washer. A new one should be used during installation.
3   The lubricant level should be up to the bottom of the filler hole. Check the level by inserting your finger into the fill hole. If low, use a pump or squeeze bottle to add the lubricant listed in this Chapter's Specifications until it just starts to run out of the opening.
4   Using a new sealing washer, install the plug in the filler hole and tighten it to the torque listed in this Chapter's Specifications.

17   Transfer case lubricant level check (AWD models) (every 15,000 miles or 12 months)

1   Raise the vehicle and support it securely on jackstands. The vehicle should be as level as possible to ensure an accurate check.
2   Remove the plug from the filler hole in the transfer case **(see illustration)**. Discard the washer. A new one should be used during installation.
Note: *On 2013 and later models the check/fill plug is located on the right side of the transfer case, facing the rear of the vehicle.*
3   The lubricant should be up to the bottom of the filler hole. Check the level by inserting your finger into the fill hole. If low, use a pump or squeeze bottle to add the lubricant listed in this Chapter's Specifications 0 until it just starts to run out of the hole.
4   Place a new sealing washer on the fill plug. Install the plug in the filler hole and tighten it to the torque listed in this Chapter's Specifications.

18   Brake check (every 15,000 miles or 12 months)

Warning: *The dust created by the brake system is harmful to your health. Never blow it out with compressed air and don't inhale any of it. An approved filtering mask should be worn when working on the brakes. Do not, under any circumstances, use petroleum-based solvents to clean brake parts. Use brake system cleaner only! Try to use non-asbestos replacement parts whenever possible.*
Note: *For detailed photographs of the brake system, refer to Chapter 9.*
1   In addition to the specified intervals, the brakes should be inspected every time the wheels are removed or whenever a defect is suspected. Any of the following symptoms

could indicate a potential brake system defect: The vehicle pulls to one side when the brake pedal is depressed; the brakes make squealing or dragging noises when applied; brake pedal travel is excessive; the pedal pulsates; brake fluid leaks, usually onto the inside of the tire or wheel.
2   The disc brake pads have built-in wear indicators which should make a high pitched squealing or scraping noise when they are worn to the replacement point. When you hear this noise, replace the pads immediately or expensive damage to the discs can result.
3   Loosen the wheel lug nuts.
4   Raise the vehicle and place it securely on jackstands.
5   Remove the wheels.

Disc brakes
6   There is an outer brake pad and an inner pad. Both must be checked for wear.
7   Measure the thickness of the outer pad at each end of the caliper and the inner pad through the inspection hole in the caliper body **(see illustrations)**. Compare the measurement with the limit given in this Chapter's Specifications ; if any brake pad thickness is less than specified, all brake pads must be replaced (see Chapter 9).
Note: *Keep in mind that the lining material is bonded to a metal backing plate and the metal portion is not included in this measurement.*
8   If it is difficult to determine the exact thickness of the remaining pad material by the above method, or if you are at all concerned about the condition of the pads, remove the caliper(s), then remove the pads from the calipers for further inspection (see Chapter 9).
9   Once the pads are removed from the calipers, clean them with brake cleaner and re-measure them with a ruler or a vernier caliper.
10   Measure the disc thickness with a micrometer to make sure that it still has service life remaining. If any disc is thinner than the specified minimum thickness listed in

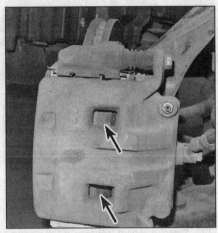

18.7a You will find an inspection hole like this in each caliper through which you can view the thickness of remaining friction material for the inner pad

18.7b Check the thickness of the outer pad material, too

18.11 Check along the brake hoses and at each fitting for deterioration and cracks

the Chapter 9 Specifications, replace it (see Chapter 9). Even if the disc has service life remaining, check its condition. Look for scoring, gouging and burned spots. If these conditions exist, remove the disc and have it resurfaced (see Chapter 9).

11 Before installing the wheels, check all brake lines and hoses for damage, wear, deformation, cracks, corrosion, leakage, bends and twists, particularly in the vicinity of the rubber hoses at the calipers **(see illustration)**. Check the clamps for tightness and the connections for leakage. Make sure that all hoses and lines are clear of sharp edges, moving parts and the exhaust system. If any of the above conditions are noted, repair, reroute or replace the lines and/or fittings as necessary (see Chapter 9).

Power brake booster

12 Sit in the driver's seat and perform the following sequence of tests:
13 With the brake fully depressed, start the engine - the pedal should move down a little when the engine starts.
14 With the engine running, depress the brake pedal several times - the travel distance should not change.
15 Depress the brake, stop the engine and hold the pedal in for about 30 seconds - the pedal should neither sink nor rise.
16 Restart the engine, run it for about a minute and turn it off. Then firmly depress the brake several times - the pedal travel should decrease with each application.
17 If your brakes do not operate as described above when the preceding tests are performed, the brake booster is either in need of repair or has failed. Refer to Chapter 9 for the removal procedure.

Parking brake

18 Apply the parking brake with a normal amount of force and count the number of clicks. The adjustment should be within the specified

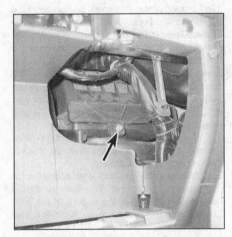

19.2 Cabin air filter cover fastener

number of clicks listed in the Chapter 9 Specifications. If you hear more or fewer clicks, adjust the parking brake (see Chapter 9).
19 An alternative method of checking the parking brake is to park the vehicle on a steep hill with the parking brake set and the transaxle in Neutral (be sure to stay in the vehicle during this check!). If the parking brake cannot prevent the vehicle from rolling, it is in need of adjustment (see Chapter 9).

---

19 Cabin air filter replacement (every 15,000 miles or 12 months)

2012 and earlier models

1 Remove the glove box and allow it to hang by the stop cord (see Chapter 11, Section 24).
2 On 2009 and earlier models, remove the filter cover fastener and cover (see illustration).

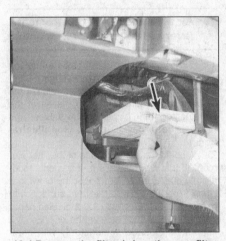

19.4 Remove the filter (when the new filter is inserted properly, the air flow indicator arrows should be pointed down)

3 On 2010 through 2012 models, lift up on the locking tab at the top center of the cover housing, then pull the cover downwards and off of the housing.
4 Slide the cabin air filter from the housing **(see illustration)**.
5 Installation is the reverse of removal. Note any directional arrows printed on the filter **(see illustration 19.4)**.

2013 and later models

6 On these models the filter is located on the passenger's side of the instrument panel, towards the center console.
7 Remove the instrument panel lower trim panel (see Chapter 11, Section 24).
8 Depress the locking tab at the end of the cover and remove the cover.
9 Slide the cabin air filter down and out from the housing.
10 Installation is the reverse of removal. Note any directional arrows printed on the filter.

20.1a Release the clips. . .

20.1b. . . then separate the air filter housing and remove the filter (2012 earlier models shown, later models similar)

22.1 Steering wheel freeplay is the amount of travel between an initial steering input and the point at which the front wheels begin to turn (indicated by a slight resistance)

20   Air filter check and replacement (every 30,000 miles or 24 months)

1   The air filter is located inside a housing at the left (driver's) side of the engine compartment. To remove the air filter, release the spring clips securing the two halves of the housing together, separate the halves, and remove the air filter element **(see illustrations)**.

2   Inspect the outer surface of the filter element. If it is dirty, replace it. If it is only moderately dusty, it can be reused by blowing it clean from the back to the front surface with compressed air. Because it is a pleated paper type filter, it cannot be washed or oiled. If it cannot be cleaned satisfactorily with compressed air, discard and replace it. While the cover is off, be careful not to drop anything down into the housing.

Caution: *Never drive the vehicle with the air filter removed. Excessive engine wear could result and backfiring could even cause a fire under the hood.*

3   Wipe out the inside of the air filter housing.

4   Place the new filter into the housing, making sure it seats properly.

5   Reassemble the housing halves and snap the clips into place.

21   Fuel system check (every 15,000 miles or 12 months)

Warning: *Gasoline is extremely flammable, so take extra precautions when you work on any part of the fuel system. Don't smoke or allow open flames or bare light bulbs near the work area, and don't work in a garage where a gas-type appliance (such as a water heater or clothes dryer) is present. Since gasoline is carcinogenic, wear fuel-resistant gloves when there's a possibility of being exposed to fuel, and, if you spill any fuel on your skin, rinse*

it off immediately with soap and water. Mop up any spills immediately and do not store fuel-soaked rags where they could ignite. The fuel system is under constant pressure, so, if any fuel lines are to be disconnected, the fuel pressure in the system must be relieved first (see Chapter 4 for more information). When you perform any kind of work on the fuel system, wear safety glasses and have a Class B type fire extinguisher on hand.

1   If you smell gasoline while driving or after the vehicle has been sitting in the sun, inspect the fuel system immediately.

2   Remove the gas cap and inspect it for damage and corrosion. The gasket should have an unbroken sealing imprint. If the gasket is damaged or corroded, remove it and install a new one.

3   Inspect the fuel feed and return lines for cracks. Make sure the threaded flare nut type connectors (which secure the metal fuel lines to the fuel injection system) and the clamps (which secure the hoses to the in-line fuel filter) are tight.

4   Since some components of the fuel system - the fuel tank and part of the fuel feed and return lines, for example - are underneath the vehicle, they can be inspected more easily with the vehicle raised on a hoist. If that's not possible, raise the vehicle and support it securely on jackstands.

5   With the vehicle raised and safely supported, inspect the gas tank and filler neck for punctures, cracks and other damage. The connection between the filler neck and the tank is particularly critical. Sometimes a rubber filler neck will leak because of loose clamps or deteriorated rubber. These are problems a home mechanic can usually rectify.

Warning: *Do not, under any circumstances, try to repair a fuel tank (except rubber components). A welding torch or any open flame can easily cause fuel vapors inside the tank to explode.*

6   Carefully check all rubber hoses and metal lines leading away from the fuel tank.

Check for loose connections, deteriorated hoses, crimped lines and other damage. Carefully inspect the lines from the tank to the fuel injection system. Repair or replace damaged sections as necessary (see Chapter 4).

22   Steering and suspension check (every 15,000 miles or 12 months)

Note: *For detailed illustrations of the steering and suspension components, refer to Chapter 10.*

With the wheels on the ground

1   With the vehicle stopped and the front wheels pointed straight ahead, rock the steering wheel gently back and forth. If freeplay **(see illustration)** is greater than listed in this Chapter's Specifications, a front wheel bearing, main shaft yoke, intermediate shaft yoke, lower arm balljoint or steering system joint is worn or the steering gear is out of adjustment or broken. Refer to Chapter 10 for the appropriate repair procedure.

2   Other symptoms, such as excessive vehicle body movement over rough roads, swaying (leaning) around corners and binding as the steering wheel is turned, may indicate faulty steering and/or suspension components.

3   Check the shock absorbers by pushing down and releasing the vehicle several times at each corner. If the vehicle does not come back to a level position within one or two bounces, the shocks/struts are worn and must be replaced. When bouncing the vehicle up and down, listen for squeaks and noises from the suspension components.

Under the vehicle

4   Raise the vehicle with a floor jack and support it securely on jackstands.

5   Check the tires for irregular wear patterns and proper inflation. See Section 5 for

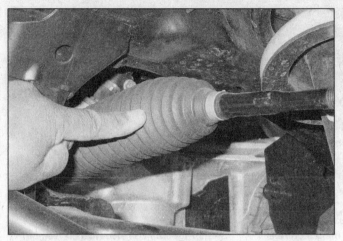

22.6a Check the steering gear boots for cracks and leaking steering fluid

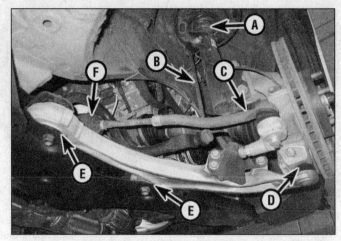

22.6b Front suspension and steering components (2013 and later models shown, earlier models similar)

A Strut/coil spring assembly	D Control arm balljoint
B Stabilizer bar link	E Control arm bushings
C Tie-rod end	F Steering gear boot

23.2a Inspect all exhaust hangers for deterioration

23.2b Inspect all the flange joints for signs of exhaust gas leaking

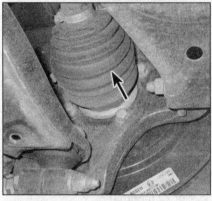

24.2 Check the driveaxle boots for cracks or leaking grease

information regarding tire wear.

6   Inspect the universal joint between the steering shaft and the steering gear housing. Check the steering gear housing for fluid leakage. Make sure that the boots are not damaged and that the boot clamps are not loose **(see illustration)**. Check the tie-rod ends for excessive play. Look for loose bolts, broken or disconnected parts and deteriorated rubber bushings on all suspension and steering components **(see illustration)**. While an assistant turns the steering wheel from side to side, check the steering components for free movement, chafing and binding. If the steering components do not seem to be reacting with the movement of the steering wheel, try to determine where the slack is located.

7   Check the balljoints by moving each lower arm up and down with a prybar to ensure that its balljoint has no play. If any balljoint does have play, replace it (see Chapter 10).

8   Inspect the balljoint boots for damage and leaking grease. Replace the balljoints with new ones if they are damaged (see Chapter 10).

23   Exhaust system check (every 15,000 miles or 12 months)

1   With the engine cold (at least three hours after the vehicle has been driven), check the complete exhaust system from its starting point at the engine to the end of the tailpipe. This should be done on a hoist where unrestricted access is available.

2   Check the pipes and connections for evidence of leaks, severe corrosion or damage **(see illustrations)**. Make sure that all brackets and hangers are in good condition and tight.

3   At the same time, inspect the underside of the body for holes, corrosion, open seams, etc. which may allow exhaust gases to enter the passenger compartment. Seal all body openings with silicone or body putty.

4   Rattles and other noises can often be traced to the exhaust system, especially the mounts and hangers. Try to move the pipes,

muffler and catalytic converter. If the components can come in contact with the body or suspension parts, secure the exhaust system with new mounts.

5   Check the running condition of the engine by inspecting inside the end of the tailpipe. The exhaust deposits here are an indication of engine state-of-tune. If the pipe is black and sooty or coated with white deposits, the engine is in need of a tune-up, including a thorough fuel system inspection.

24   Driveaxle boot check (every 15,000 miles or 12 months)

1   The driveaxle boots are very important because they prevent dirt, water and foreign material from entering and damaging the constant velocity (CV) joints.

2   Inspect the boots for tears and cracks as well as loose clamps **(see illustration)**. If there is any evidence of cracks or leaking lubricant, they must be replaced (see Chapter 8).

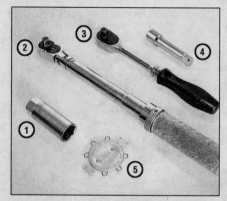

25.1 Tools required for changing spark plugs

1   *Spark plug socket - This will have special padding inside to protect the spark plug porcelain insulator*
2   *Torque wrench - Although not mandatory, use of this tool is the best way to ensure that the plugs are tightened properly*
3   *Ratchet - Standard hand tool to fit the plug socket*
4   *Extension - Depending on model and accessories, you may need special extensions and universal joints to reach one or more of the plugs*
5   *Spark plug gap gauge - This gauge for checking the gap comes in a variety of styles. Make sure the gap for your engine is included*

25   Spark plug check and replacement (every 105,000 miles or 72 months)

1   Spark plug replacement requires a spark plug socket and extension which fits onto a ratchet. This socket is lined with a rubber grommet to protect the porcelain insulator of the spark plug and to hold the plug while you remove it. You will also need a wire-type feeler gauge to check and adjust the spark plug gap and a torque wrench to tighten the new plugs to the specified torque **(see illustration)**.
2   If you are replacing the plugs, purchase the new plugs, adjust them to the proper gap, then replace each plug one at a time.
3   Inspect each of the new plugs for defects. If there are any signs of cracks in the porcelain insulator of a plug, don't use it.
4   Check the electrode gaps of the new plugs. Check the gap by inserting the wire gauge of the proper thickness between the electrodes at the tip of the plug **(see illustration)**. The gap between the electrodes should be identical to that listed in this Chapter's Specifications. If the gap is incorrect, the manufacturer recommends replacing the spark plug with a new one (rather than adjusting it).
5   If the side electrode is not exactly over

25.4 Spark plug manufacturers recommend using a wire-type gauge when checking the gap - if the wire does not slide between the electrodes with a slight drag, adjustment is required. Caution: Do not force the gauge into the gap - the platinum or iridium coating could be scraped off

25.8 Use a spark plug socket with a ratchet and an extension to remove the spark plugs

the center electrode, use the notched adjuster to align them.
Caution: *If the gap of a new plug must be adjusted, bend only the base of the ground electrode - do not touch the tip.*

Removal

6   On 2013 and later models, remove the upper intake manifold for access to the rear bank spark plugs (see Chapter 2A).
7   Disconnect the ignition coil electrical connectors and remove the mounting bolts (see illustration). Pull up on the coil/boot assembly using a twisting motion, and remove the ignition coils.
8   Remove the spark plugs with a spark plug socket **(see illustration)**.
9   Whether you are replacing the plugs at this time or intend to reuse the old plugs,

25.7 Ignition coil electrical connector (A) and mounting bolt (B)

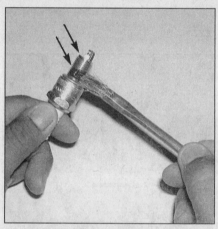

25.10 Apply a coat of anti-seize compound to the spark plug threads, being careful not to get any near the lower threads

compare each old spark plug to those shown in the photos located on the inside back cover of this book to determine the overall running condition of the engine.

Installation

10   Prior to installation, apply a coat of anti-seize compound to the plug threads **(see illustration)**.
11   It's often difficult to insert spark plugs into their holes without cross-threading them. To avoid this possibility, fit a short piece of snug-fitting rubber hose over the end of the spark plug **(see illustration)**. The flexible hose acts as a universal joint to help align the plug with the plug hole. Should the plug begin to cross-thread, the hose will slip on the spark plug, preventing thread damage. Tighten the plug to the torque listed in this Chapter's Specifications.
12   Follow the above procedure for the remaining spark plugs.
13   After replacing all the plugs, install the ignition coils (see Chapter 5) and the upper intake manifold (see Chapter 2A).

25.11 A length of snug-fitting rubber hose will save time and prevent damaged threads when installing the spark plugs

26.5 The radiator drain fitting is located at the bottom of the radiator

26.6a Right-side engine block drain plug - 4.0L V6

26.6b Left-side engine block drain plug - 4.0L V6

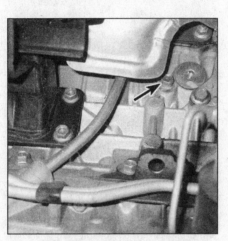

26.6c Right-side cylinder bank drain plug - 5.6L V8

26.6d Detach this hose from the engine oil cooler to drain the coolant from the left cylinder bank (5.6L V8)

26 Cooling system servicing (draining, flushing and refilling) (every 30,000 miles or 24 months)

Warning: *Do not allow engine coolant (antifreeze) to come in contact with your skin or painted surfaces of the vehicle. Rinse off spills immediately with plenty of water. Antifreeze is highly toxic if ingested. Never leave antifreeze laying around in an open container or in puddles on the floor; children and pets are attracted by it's sweet smell and may drink it. Check with local authorities about disposing of used antifreeze. Many communities have collection centers which will see that antifreeze is disposed of safely.*

1   Periodically, the cooling system should be drained, flushed and refilled to replenish the antifreeze mixture and prevent formation of rust and corrosion, which can impair the performance of the cooling system and cause engine damage. When the cooling system is serviced, all hoses and the radiator cap should be checked and replaced if necessary.

Draining

2   Apply the parking brake and block the wheels. If the vehicle has just been driven, wait several hours to allow the engine to cool down before beginning this procedure.

3   Remove the radiator cap.

4   On 2012 and earlier models, turn the ignition switch ON but do not start the engine. Set the temperature control all the way to HOT or to the highest temperature setting. Wait for 10 seconds and then turn the ignition switch off.

5   Move a large container under the radiator drain to catch the coolant. Using a large screwdriver, open the radiator drain plug and direct the coolant into the container **(see illustration)**.

6   After the coolant stops flowing out of the radiator, move the container under the engine block drain plug(s) **(see illustrations)**. Remove the plug(s) and allow the coolant in the block to drain. Discard any sealing washers and obtain new ones.

Note: *Canadian models use a block heater instead of a drain plug. Note the position of*

the plug and connector, and then remove the connector before removing the heater.

7   While the coolant is draining, check the condition of the radiator hoses, heater hoses and clamps (see Section 12).

8   Replace any damaged clamps or hoses (see Chapter 3).

Flushing

9   Fill the cooling system with clean water, following the Refilling procedure (see Steps 16 through 23).

10   Start the engine and allow it to reach normal operating temperature, then rev up the engine a few times.

11   Turn the engine off and allow it to cool completely, then drain the system as described earlier.

12   Repeat Steps 9 through 11 until the water being drained is free of contaminants.

13   Remove the overflow hose from the coolant recovery reservoir. Drain the reservoir and flush it with clean water, then reconnect the hose.

14   In severe cases of contamination or clog-

28.5 Location of the automatic transmission fluid drain plug

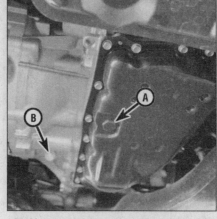

28.11 Automatic transaxle drain plug (A) and check/fill plug (B)

ging of the radiator, remove the radiator (see Chapter 3) and have a radiator repair facility clean and repair it if necessary.

15   Many deposits can be removed by the chemical action of a cleaner available at auto parts stores. Follow the procedure outlined in the manufacturer's instructions.

Note: *When the coolant is regularly drained and the system refilled with the correct anti-freeze/water mixture, there should be no need to use chemical cleaners or descalers.*

Refilling

16   Close and tighten the radiator drain.

17   Clean all sealant from the threads of the engine block drain plugs, or block heater if used. Install and tighten the engine block drain plug(s). Use new sealing washers where applicable and apply thread sealer to the engine block plugs (that don't use a sealing washer) or block heater threads. Tighten the drain plug(s). If a block heater is used, tighten it to the torque listed in this Chapter's Specifications 0.

18   Make sure the heater temperature control is in the maximum heat position.

19   On 2013 and later models, disconnect the uppermost heater hose at the firewall to bleed the system as it is being filled.

20   Slowly refill the radiator with the coolant listed in this Chapter's Specifications 0 until it flows from the disconnected heater hose, then reattach the hose and install the hose clamp. Continue adding coolant until the level reaches the lip on the radiator filler neck. Add coolant to the reservoir up to the lower mark.

21   Install the radiator cap and run the engine in a well-ventilated area until the thermostat opens (coolant will begin flowing through the radiator and the upper radiator hose will become hot).

22   Rev the engine to approximately 3000 rpm for ten seconds, then let it idle; do this a few times.

23   Turn the engine off and let it cool. Add more coolant mixture to bring the level back up to the lip on the radiator filler neck.

24   Squeeze the upper radiator hose to expel air, then add more coolant mixture if necessary. Replace the radiator cap.

25   Start the engine, allow it to reach normal operating temperature and check for leaks.

27   Evaporative emissions control system check (every 30,000 miles or 24 months)

1   The function of the evaporative emissions control system is to draw fuel vapors from the gas tank and fuel system, store them in a charcoal canister, then burn them during normal engine operation.

2   The most common symptom of a fault in the evaporative emissions system is a strong fuel odor in the engine compartment. If a fuel odor is detected, inspect the charcoal canister, located at the front of the engine compartment. Check the canister and all hoses for damage and deterioration.

3   The evaporative emissions control system is explained in more detail in Chapter 6.

28   Automatic transmission/ transaxle fluid change (every 30,000 miles or 24 months)

1   At the specified intervals, the transmission fluid should be drained and replaced. Since the fluid will remain hot long after driving, perform this procedure only after the engine has cooled down completely.

2   Before beginning work, purchase the specified transmission fluid (see *Recommended lubricants and fluids* in this Chapter's Specifications).

3   Other tools necessary for this job include a floor jack, jackstands to support the vehicle in a raised position, a drain pan capable of holding at least eight quarts, newspapers and clean rags.

4   Raise the vehicle and support it securely on jackstands.

2012 and earlier models

5   Place the drain pan underneath the transmission pan **(see illustration)**. Remove the drain plug and allow the fluid to drain, then reinsert the plug and tighten it to the torque listed in this Chapter's Specifications 0. Measure the amount of fluid drained (the same amount will be added to the transmission later, assuming that the fluid level was correct to begin with).

6   Lower the vehicle and add the specified type of automatic transmission fluid (the same amount that was drained in Step 5) through the filler tube.

7   With the transmission in Park and the parking brake set, run the engine at a fast idle, but don't race it.

8   Move the gear selector through each range and back to Park, then let the engine idle for a few minutes. Check the fluid level. It may be low. Add enough fluid to bring the level the COLD range on the dipstick. Be careful not to overfill.

9   Check under the vehicle for leaks during the first few trips. Check the fluid level again when the transmission is hot (see Section 7).

10   If desired, repeat Steps 4 through 8 once to flush any contaminated fluid from the torque converter and transmission cooler.

2013 and later models

Warning: *This procedure is potentially dangerous and is best left to a professional shop with a safe lifting apparatus. The vehicle must be kept level while being safely raised high enough for access to the check plug on the transaxle.*

Warning: *Wear safety glasses and gloves during this procedure - the transaxle fluid will be very hot and could burn if contact is made with the skin or eyes.*

Caution: *These models use a special fluid designed specifically for the Nissan CVT transaxle. Don't use another fluid or damage may occur and the warranty may be voided. See this Chapter's Specifications 0 for the proper fluid type.*

Caution: *It is critical that the transaxle fluid temperature be less the 104-degrees F when replacing the fluid. It is highly recommended to use a scan tool connected to the data connector; follow the prompts on the scanner to read the actual fluid temperature.*

Note: *A special adapter (tool no. KV311039S0 or equivalent) is necessary for this procedure.*

11   Place the drain pan under the fluid pan drain plug. While the fluid is at the appropriate temperature, remove the drain plug from the transaxle oil pan and allow the fluid to drain **(see illustration)**.

12   Place the drain pan under the check/fill plug and remove it. Install special adapter tool no. KV311039S0 (or equivalent) into the hole. Connect a fluid charger hose to the adapter.

13   Pump approximately 3-1/8 quarts of the specified fluid into the transaxle, then, as quickly as possible, remove the adapter tool and hose, and install the check plug.

14   Lower the vehicle, then start the engine

29.1a The PCV valve is located on the end of the passenger's side valve cover - (2012 and earlier V6 models)

29.1b The PCV valve (A) is at the rear of the engine, and the PCV fresh air hose (B) is at the front - (2013 and later V6 models)

and allow it to idle. Apply the brake and shift through all the gears, making sure to stay in each gear approximately 5 seconds.

15   Using the scan tool, verify the transaxle fluid temperature is at the appropriate temperature. If the temperature is correct, stop the engine. Raise the vehicle and support it securely on jackstands.

16   Remove the drain plug and drain the transaxle fluid.

17   Repeat Steps 12 through 17.

18   Once all the fluid has drained out, install the drain plug into the oil pan and tighten it to the torque listed in this Chapter's Specifications.

19   Thread special tool KV311039S0 (or equivalent) into the check/fill plug hole, then push the charger hose onto the tool.

20   Pump approximately 3-1/8 quarts of the specified fluid into the transaxle, then as quickly as possible remove the adapter tool and hose, and install the check/fill plug.

21   Lower the vehicle, then start the engine and allow it to idle. Apply the brake and shift through all the gears, making sure to stay in each gear approximately 5 seconds.

22   Using the scan tool, verify the transaxle fluid temperature is between 95-to-113-degrees F. If the temperature is correct, stop the engine. Raise the vehicle and support it securely on jackstands.

23   With the engine idling, remove the check/fill plug and verify that transaxle fluid drips out.

24   Allow the fluid to drain out until there is only a drip remaining, then install a new sealing gasket to the check plug. Tighten the plug to the torque listed in this Chapter's Specifications.

25   If no fluid drains out, install the special tool KV311039S0 (or equivalent) and add 1/2 quart of fluid. Allow the fluid to drain out; if no fluid drains out, add an additional 1/2 quart of fluid. Keep repeating this procedure until fluid pours out and turns to a drip. Install a new sealing gasket to the check/fill plug and

29.1c PCV valve locations (V8 models)

tighten it to the torque listed in this Chapter's Specifications.

29   Positive Crankcase Ventilation (PCV) valve check and replacement (every 30,000 miles or 24 months)

1   Remove the engine cover, if equipped, then locate the PCV valve on the valve cover (see illustrations).

2   Disconnect the hose, then remove the PCV valve.

3   With the engine idling at normal operating temperature, place your finger over the end of the valve. If there's no vacuum at the valve, check for a plugged hose or valve. Replace any plugged or deteriorated hoses.

4   When purchasing a replacement PCV valve, make sure it's for your particular vehicle and engine size. Compare the old valve with the new one to make sure they're the same.

5   Installation is the reverse of removal.

30   Differential lubricant change (every 60,000 miles or 48 months)

Note: *This procedure applies to the front (AWD models) and rear differential(s) 2012 and earlier models, and 2013 and later AWD models.*
Note: *This procedure should be performed after the vehicle has been driven so the lubricant will be warm and therefore will flow out of the differential easily.*

1   Raise the vehicle and support it securely on jackstands. Move a drain pan, rags, newspapers, new copper washers for the drain and fill plugs, and wrenches under the vehicle.

2   Remove the fill plug (see Section 16), then remove the drain plug and allow the fluid to drain into the pan. Clean and reinstall the drain plug, using a new copper washer. Tighten the plug to the torque listed in this Chapter's Specifications.

3   Using a hand pump, syringe or squeeze bottle, fill the differential housing with the specified lubricant until it's level with the bot-

tom of the fill plug hole.

4   Clean and reinstall the fill plug, using a new copper washer. Tighten the plug to the torque listed in this Chapter's Specifications.

5   Drive the vehicle a short distance, check for leaks and recheck the lubricant level.

---

31   Transfer case lubricant change (AWD models) (every 60,000 miles or 48 months)

Note: *This procedure should be performed after the vehicle has been driven so the lubricant will be warm and therefore will flow out of the transfer case easily.*

1   Raise the vehicle and support it securely on jackstands. Move a drain pan, rags, news-papers, copper plug washers and wrenches under the vehicle.

2   Remove the fill plug (see Section 17), then remove the drain plug and allow the fluid to drain into the pan. Use a new washer, clean the drain bolt threads and then reinstall the drain plug. Tighten the plug to the torque listed in this Chapter's Specifications using a new copper washer.

3   Using a hand pump, syringe or squeeze bottle, fill the transfer case with the specified lubricant until it's level with the bottom of the fill plug hole.

4   Clean and reinstall the fill plug. Tighten the plug to the torque listed in this Chapter's Specifications using a new copper washer.

5   Drive the vehicle a short distance, check for leaks and recheck the lubricant level.

---

32   Maintenance reminder indicator resetting procedure (2013 and later models)

Note: *On these models up to four reminders can be programmed; the reset process is the same for all four.*

1   Using the multi-function controller on the display, choose the item you'd like to reset, them press the ENTER button.

2   Reset the driving distance.

3   Set the mileage interval.

4   Using the multi-function controller, select the Interval Reminder key, then push the ENTER button.

5   Press the BACK button to return to Maintenance Info.

Chapter 2 Part A V6 engines

Contents

	Section
Camshafts and lifters - removal, inspection and installation.........	8
Crankshaft front oil seal - replacement.................................	13
Crankshaft pulley - removal and installation...........................	12
Cylinder head - removal and installation	11
Driveplate - removal and installation	17
Engine mounts - check and replacement	19
Engine oil cooler and oil filter adapter - general information and replacement	16
Exhaust manifold - removal, inspection and installation...............	10
General information	1

	Section
Intake manifold - removal and installation	9
Oil pans - removal and installation	14
Oil pump - removal, inspection and installation	15
Rear main oil seal - replacement......................................	18
Repair operations possible with the engine in the vehicle............	2
Timing chain and sprockets - removal, inspection and installation	7
Top Dead Center (TDC) for number one piston - locating............	3
Valve clearance check and adjustment	5
Valve covers - removal and installation	4
Valve springs, retainers and seals - replacement......................	6

Specifications

General

Displacement	
3.5L	213 cubic inches
4.0L	241 cubic inches
Designation	
3.5L	VQ35DE
4.0L	VQ40DE
Bore	3.760 inches (95.5 mm)
Stroke	
3.5L	3.205 inches (81.4 mm)
4.0L	3.622 inches (92.0 mm)
Cylinder numbers (front to rear)	
Bank 1	1-3-5
Bank 2	2-4-6
Firing order	1-2-3-4-5-6

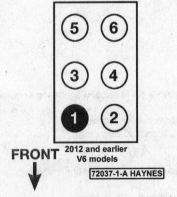

FRONT 2012 and earlier V6 models

72037-1-A HAYNES

Cylinder location diagram - 2012 and earlier models

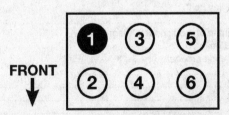

FRONT

2013 and later V6 models

72015-1-specs HAYNES

Cylinder location diagram - 2013 and later models

Camshaft

Camshaft endplay
- Standard.. 0.0045 to 0.0074 inch (0.114 to 0.188 mm)
- Limit .... 0.0094 inch (0.239 mm)

Camshaft journal diameter
- No. 1 .... 1.0211 to 1.0218 inches (25.936 to 25.954 mm)
- No. 2 through 4 .... 0.9230 to 0.9238 inch (23.444 to 23.465 mm

Camshaft bearing inside diameter
- No. 1 .... 1.0236 to 1.0244 inches (26.000 to 26.020 mm)
- No. 2 through 4 .... 0.9252 to 0.9260 inch (23.500 to 23.520 mm)

Bearing oil clearance
- No. 1 .... 0.0018 to 0.0034 inch (0.046 to 0.086 mm)
- No. 2 through 4 .... 0.0014 to 0.0030 inch (0.036 to 0.076 mm)
- Service limit... 0.0047 inch (0.019 mm)

Runout limit... 0.0020 inch maximum (0.051 mm maximum)
Camshaft sprocket runout limit..................................... 0.0059 inches (0.15 mm)

Lobe height
- 2012 and earlier models
  - Intake... 1.7900 to 1.7821 inches (45.465 to 45.265 mm)
  - Exhaust.. 1.7746 to 1.7667 inches (45.075 to 44.875 mm)
- 2013 and later models
  - Intake... 1.7978 to 1.7904 inches (45.665 to 45.475 mm)
  - Exhaust.. 1.7982 to 1.7907 inches (45.675 to 45.485 mm)

Exhaust manifold

Maximum allowable warpage .... 0.012 inch (0.305 mm)

Intake manifold, lower

Maximum allowable warpage, upper surface .... 0.004 inch (0.102 mm)

Valve clearance (cold)

Intake .... 0.010 to 0.013 inch (0.254 to 0.330 mm)
Exhaust .... 0.011 to 0.015 inch (0.280 to 0.381 mm)

Oil pump

Outer gear-to-body clearance....................................... 0.0045 to 0.0102 inch (0.114 to 0.259 mm)
Rotor tip tooth clearance .... 0.0071 inch maximum (0.180 mm maximum)
Inner gear-to-housing side clearance .... 0.0012 to 0.0028 inch (0.030 to 0.071 mm)
Outer gear-to-housing side clearance .... 0.0020 to 0.0043 inch (0.051 to 0.109 mm)
Inner rotor hub-to-housing clearance .... 0.0018 to 0.0036 inch (0.046 to 0.091 mm)
Regulator valve clearance .... 0.0010 to 0.0028 inch (0.025 to 0.070 mm)

Torque specifications

Note: *One foot-pound (ft-lb) of torque is equivalent to 12 inch-pounds (in-lbs) of torque. Torque values below approximately 15 ft-lbs are expressed in inch-pounds, since most foot-pound torque wrenches are not accurate at these smaller values.*

	Ft-lbs (unless otherwise indicated)	Nm
Camshaft sprocket bolts*	76	103
Camshaft bearing cap bolts**		
Step 1 (bolts 7 through 10)	17 in-lbs	2
Step 2 (bolts 1 through 6)	17 in-lbs	2
Step 3 (all bolts)	52 in-lbs	6
Step 4 (bolts 1 through 6)	96 in-lbs	11
Crankshaft pulley bolt*		
Step 1	32	43
Step 2 Tighten an additional 90-degrees		
Cylinder head bolts*,**,***		
2012 and earlier models		
Step 1	72	98
Step 2	Loosen completely (in reverse of tightening sequence)	
Step 3	29	39
Step 4	Tighten an additional 90-degrees	
Step 5	Tighten an additional 90-degrees	
2013 and later models		
Step 1	72	98
Step 2	Loosen completely (in reverse of tightening sequence)	
Step 3	29	39
Step 4	Tighten an additional 103-degrees	
Step 5	Tighten an additional 103-degrees	

Torque specifications (continued)

Note: *One foot-pound (ft-lb) of torque is equivalent to 12 inch-pounds (in-lbs) of torque. Torque values below approximately 15 ft-lbs are expressed in inch-pounds, since most foot-pound torque wrenches are not accurate at these smaller values.*

	Ft-lbs (unless otherwise indicated)	Nm
Valve cover bolts**		
Step 1 17 in-lbs	2	
Step 2 74 in-lbs	8	
Driveplate bolts*	65	88
Exhaust manifold nuts**,***	23	31
Intake manifold collector (upper intake manifold)		
Nuts and bolts	97 in-lbs	11
Studs	61 in-lbs	7
Intake manifold (lower intake manifold)**		
2012 and earlier models		
Nuts step 1	65 in-lbs	7.4
Nuts step 2	21	29
Studs	97 in-lbs	11
2013 and later models		
Nuts step 1	65 in-lbs	7.4
Nuts step 2	19	25.5
Studs	95.5 in-lbs	10.8
Oil cooler connector bolt	36	49
Oil pan bolts		
Upper (aluminum) oil pan**	16.5	22
Lower (steel) oil pan		
2012 and earlier models	80 in-lbs	9
2013 and later models	78 in-lbs	8.8
Oil pan-to-transmission/transaxle	37	50
Oil pan drain plug	25	34
Oil pan rear cover mounting plate		
2012 and earlier models	80 in-lbs	9
2013 and later models	62 in-lbs	7
Oil pick-up tube mounting bolts	16	22
Oil pressure switch	97 in-lbs	11
Oil pump cover screws	61 in-lbs	7
Oil pressure regulator plug		
2012 and earlier models	36	49
2013 and later models	40	54
*Front timing chain cover bolts***		
2012 and earlier models		
6 mm	112 in-lbs	12.7
10 mm	41	55
2013 and later models		
6 mm	112 in-lbs	12.7
8 mm	21	28.4
*Rear timing chain cover bolts***		
2012 and earlier		
20 mm (bolt position 1, 2, 3, 6, 7, 8, 9, 10)	112 in-lbs	12.7
16 mm (bolt position 4, 5, 11)	112 in-lbs	12.7
16 mm (bolt position 12 through 26)	133 in-lbs	15
2013 and later models	112 in-lbs	12.7
Intake valve timing (IVT) control cover bolts		
2012 and earlier models	100 in-lbs	11.3
2013 and later models	85 in-lbs	9.6
Upper timing chain guide(s) bolts	72 in-lbs	8.1
Main timing chain tensioner mounting bolt	72 in-lbs	8.1
Timing chain tensioner cover bolts	96 in-lbs	11
Water pump cover bolts	96 in-lbs	11
Main timing chain guide pivot bolt		
2012 and earlier models	106 in-lbs	12
2013 and later models	139 in-lbs	15.7
Secondary timing chain tensioner bolts	75 in-lbs	8.5
Rear main oil seal retainer bolts	78 in-lbs	9

*Lubricate fastener threads and heads with clean engine oil prior to installation
**Tighten fasteners in the proper sequence. See procedure for diagrams
***Bolts must be replaced with NEW ones

1   General information

1   This Part of Chapter 2 is devoted to in-vehicle repair procedures for the 3.5L and 4.0L Dual Overhead Camshaft (DOHC) V6 engines. Information concerning engine removal and installation and engine overhaul can be found in Chapter 2C.

2   The following repair procedures are based on the assumption that the engine is installed in the vehicle. If the engine has been removed from the vehicle and mounted on a stand, many of the steps outlined in this Part of Chapter 2 will not apply.

Note: *The engines on 2013 and later models are transversely mounted; the left (driver's) side of the engine is referred to as the front side, while the right (passenger's) side is referred to as the rear side.*

2   Repair operations possible with the engine in the vehicle

1   Many major repair operations can be accomplished without removing the engine from the vehicle.

2   Clean the engine compartment and the exterior of the engine with some type of degreaser before any work is done. It will make the job easier and help keep dirt out of the internal areas of the engine.

3   Depending on the components involved, it may be helpful to remove the hood to improve access to the engine as repairs are performed (see Chapter 11). Cover the fenders to prevent damage to the paint. Special pads are available, but an old bedspread or blanket will also work.

4   If vacuum, exhaust, oil or coolant leaks develop, indicating a need for gasket or seal replacement, the repairs can generally be made with the engine in the vehicle. The intake and exhaust manifold gaskets and the crankshaft front oil seal are accessible with the engine in place. On 2012 and earlier models the rear main oil seal is also replaceable with the engine in place.

5   Some exterior engine components, such as the intake and exhaust manifolds, the lower oil pan, the water pump (see Chapter 3), the starter motor, the alternator (see Chapter 5) and the fuel system components (see Chapter 4) can be removed for replacement with the engine in place.

6   On 2013 and later models, the upper oil pan, oil pump and cylinder heads can't be removed without first removing the engine (see Chapter 2C).

3   Top Dead Center (TDC) for number one piston - locating

1   Top Dead Center (TDC) is the highest point in the cylinder that each piston reaches as it travels up-and-down when the crank-

3.8 Align the TDC notch on the crankshaft pulley with the pointer on the timing chain cover - the TDC notch is the one farthest to the left when facing the front of the engine

1   TDC mark
2   10-degrees BTDC
3   15-degrees BTDC

shaft turns. Each piston reaches TDC on the compression stroke and again on the exhaust stroke, but TDC generally refers to piston position on the compression stroke.

2   Positioning the number one piston at TDC is an essential part of many procedures, such as camshaft and timing chain removal.

3   Before beginning this procedure, place the transmission in Neutral and apply the parking brake or block the rear wheels. Disconnect the cable from the negative terminal of the battery (see Chapter 5) and remove the spark plugs (see Chapter 1).

4   Install a compression pressure gauge in the number one spark plug hole (see Chapter 2C, Section 3). It should be a gauge with a screw-in fitting and a hose at least six inches long.

5   2013 and later models: Loosen the right front wheel lug nuts. Raise the front of the vehicle and support it securely on jackstands. Remove the wheel and the inner fender splash shield (see Chapter 11).

6   Using a socket and long breaker bar or ratchet, rotate the crankshaft clockwise while observing for pressure on the compression gauge. The moment the gauge shows pressure indicates that the number one cylinder has begun the compression stroke.

7   Once the compression stroke has begun, TDC for the compression stroke is reached by bringing the piston to the top of the cylinder.

8   Continue turning the crankshaft until the TDC notch in the crankshaft damper is aligned with the pointer on the timing chain cover (see illustration). At this point, the number one cylinder is at TDC on the compression stroke. If the marks are aligned but there was no compression, the piston was on the exhaust stroke. Continue rotating the crankshaft 360-degrees (1-turn).

9   After the number one piston has been positioned at TDC on the compression stroke, TDC for any of the remaining cylinders can be located by turning the crankshaft 120-degrees and following the firing order (see this Chapter's Specifications). For example, rotating the engine 120-degrees past TDC No. 1 will put

the engine at TDC compression for cylinder No. 2.

4   Valve covers - removal and installation

Note: *The engines on 2013 and later models are transversely mounted; the left (driver's) side of the engine is referred to as the front side, while the right (passenger's) side is referred to as the rear side.*

Removal

1   Disconnect the cable from the negative terminal of the battery (see Chapter 5).

2   Remove the engine cover fasteners, then pull up to disconnect the cover from its mounts.

3   Remove the air inlet duct (see Chapter 4).

4   Remove the Camshaft Position (CMP) sensor(s) (see Chapter 6).

Left (front) valve cover

5   Remove the blow-by hose from the valve cover.

6   On 2012 and earlier models, disconnect the electrical connector from the intake valve timing control solenoid and remove the valve (see Chapter 6).

Right (rear) valve cover

7   Remove the upper intake manifold (see Section 9).

All valve covers

8   Remove the ignition coils from the cover to be removed (see Chapter 5).

9   Detach the PCV hose and any wiring which would interfere with valve cover removal.

10   Remove the valve cover bolts and washers in several steps in the reverse order of the tightening sequence (see illustration 4.17a or 4.17b).

11   Remove the valve cover.

Note: *If the cover is stuck to the cylinder head, bump one end with a block of wood and a* *hammer to jar it loose. If that doesn't work, try to slip a flexible putty knife between the cylinder head and cover to break the gasket seal. Don't pry at the cover-to-cylinder head joint or damage to the sealing surfaces may occur (leading to oil leaks in the future).*

Installation

12   The mating surfaces of each cylinder head and valve cover must be perfectly clean when the covers are installed. Use a gasket scraper to remove all traces of sealant and old gasket material, then clean the mating surfaces with brake system cleaner.

13   If necessary, clean the bolt threads with a wire wheel to remove any corrosion. Make sure the threaded holes in the cylinder head are clean - run a tap into them to remove corrosion and restore damaged threads.

14   Replace the spark plug tube seals (see illustration).

15   Apply a thin coat of RTV sealant to the cover groove and to the corners on the front camshaft journal cap, then position the gasket inside the cover and allow the sealant to set up so the gasket adheres to the cover. If the sealant isn't allowed to set, the gasket may fall out of the cover as it's installed on the engine.

16   Carefully position the cover on the cylinder head and install the bolts.

17   Tighten the bolts, in sequence (see illustrations), to the torque steps listed in this Chapter's Specifications.

18   The remainder of installation is the

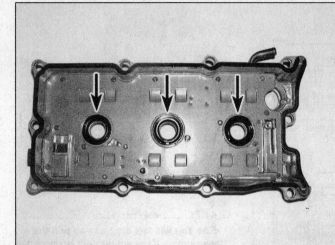

4.14 Install new spark plug tube seals into the valve cover

4.17a Valve cover bolt

reverse of removal.

19   Reconnect the battery and perform the necessary re-learn procedures (see Chapter 5).

5   Valve clearance check and adjustment

Note: *The manufacturer recommends checking and, if necessary, adjusting the valve clearance after replacement of the camshaft(s) or other valve-related parts, or if the valve train is making excessive noise.*

Note: *The illustrations in this Section are of 2013 and later models, which are transversely mounted. The procedure and valve designation are the same for 2012 and earlier models. To orient the illustrations for 2012 and earlier models, reference the arrow identifying the front of the engine to identify the correct locations for the valves to be adjusted.*

1   Disconnect the cable from the negative terminal of the battery (see Chapter 5).

2   Remove the valve covers (see Section 4).

3   Remove the spark plugs (see Chapter 1).

4   Position the number 1 piston at TDC on the compression stroke and align the timing marks (see Section 3).

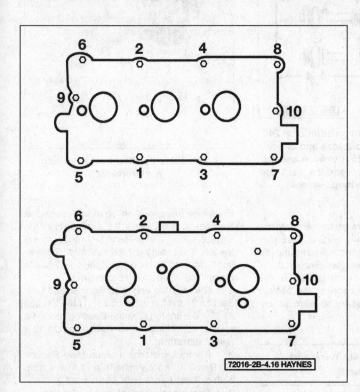

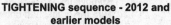

TIGHTENING sequence - 2012 and earlier models

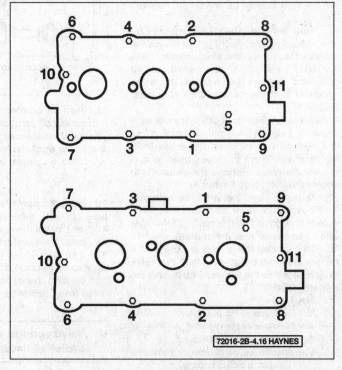

4.17b Valve cover bolt TIGHTENING sequence - 2013 and later models

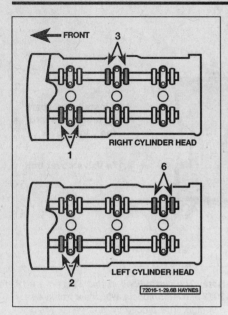

5.5a When the no. 1 piston is at TDC on the compression stroke, the valve clearance for the no. 1 and no. 6 cylinder intake valves and the no. 2 and no. 3 cylinder exhaust valves can be measured

5.5b You will feel drag as you pull the feeler gauge if the adjustment is correct

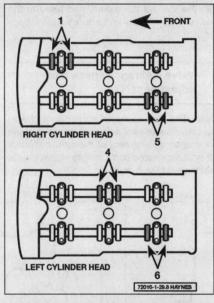

5.7 Turn the crankshaft an additional 240 degrees (2/3 turn) clockwise and check the valve clearances for the no. 4 and no. 5 cylinder intake valves, and the no. 1 and no. 6 cylinder exhaust valves

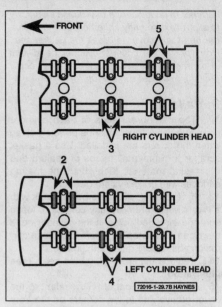

5.6 Turn the crankshaft 240 degrees (2/3 turn) clockwise and check the valve clearances for the no. 2 and no. 3 cylinder intake valves, and the no. 4 and no. 5 cylinder exhaust valves

5.9 Measure the lifter thickness with a micrometer

5   Measure the clearance of the indicated valves with a feeler gauge (see illustrations). Record each measurement and compare your measurements with the desired valve clearance found in this Chapter's Specifications 0 . Note which are out of specification; this data will be used later to determine the required lifter.

6   Turn the crankshaft 240 degrees (2/3 turn). Measure and record the clearances of the indicated valves (see illustration).

7   Rotate the crankshaft an additional 240 (2/3-turn) degrees and perform the same operation for the remaining valves (see illustration).

8   These engines don't use valve adjusting shims. If a clearance is out of specification, the lifter must be replaced with a new lifter that has a different thickness head to correct the clearance. Remove the camshafts to access the lifters (see Section 8).

9   Mark the lifters that are to be replaced, and record which valve they came from. Measure the thickness of the center of the lifter with a micrometer (see illustration).

10   To calculate the correct thickness of a replacement lifter that will place the valve clearance within the specified value, use the following formula:

$N = T + A - V$

N = thickness of the new lifter
T = thickness of the old lifter
A = valve clearance measured
V = desired valve clearance (see this Chapter's Specifications)

11   Select a lifter with a thickness as close as possible to the valve clearance calculated. Lifters are marked on the underside as to their size.

12   Mark the new lifters as to their destination, lubricate them with engine assembly lube and install them. After replacing the lifters, install the camshaft(s) (see Section 8).

13   The remainder of installation is the reverse of removal. Reconnect the battery and perform the necessary re-learn procedures (see Chapter 5).

6   Valve springs, retainers and seals - replacement

Note: Broken valve springs and defective valve stem seals can be replaced without removing the cylinder heads. Two special tools and a compressed air source are normally required

to perform this operation, so read through this Section carefully. Verify the availability of the correct spring compressor before beginning the job. If you can't get the special tools, then you'll have to remove the heads and use a clamp type valve spring compressor

1   Remove the upper intake manifold (see Section 9) and the valve cover(s) (see Section 4). If you want to leave the head on, obtain a special on-vehicle valve spring compressor (see illustration).

2   Remove the timing chain (see Section 7). Remove the camshafts and lifters from both cylinder heads (see Section 11).

3   Remove the spark plugs (see Chapter 1).

4   Turn the crankshaft until the piston in the affected cylinder is at Top Dead Center (see Section 3). If you're replacing all of the valve

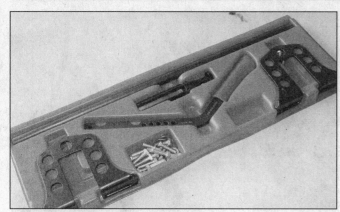

6.1 Here's an example of the special valve spring compressor that must be used to avoid having to remove the head

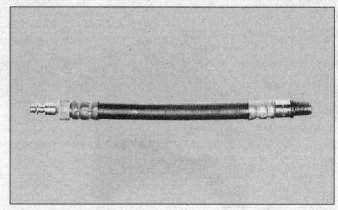

6.5 Thread the air hose adapter into the spark plug hole - adapters are commonly available from auto parts stores

6.7a Compress the valve spring enough to release the valve stem locks. . .

6.7b. . . and lift them out with a magnet or needle-nose pliers

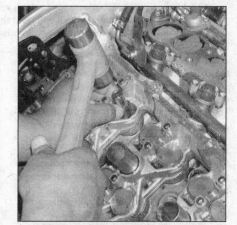

6.15 Using a deep socket and hammer, gently tap the new seals onto the valve guide only until seated

stem seals, begin with cylinder number one and work on the valves for one cylinder at a time. Move from cylinder-to-cylinder following the firing order sequence, turning the crankshaft 120-degrees to bring the next cylinder to TDC (see this Chapter's Specifications).

5   Thread a long adapter into the spark plug hole and connect an air hose from a compressed air source to it **(see illustration)**. Most auto parts stores can supply the air hose adapter.

Note: *Because of the length of the spark plug tubes, it will be necessary to use a long spark plug adapter with a length of hose attached (as used on many cylinder compression gauges), utilizing a quick-disconnect fitting to hook to your air source.*

6   Apply compressed air to the cylinder.

Warning: *The piston may be forced down by the compressed air, causing the crankshaft to turn suddenly. If the wrench used when positioning the number one piston at TDC is still attached to the bolt in the crankshaft nose, it could cause damage or injury when the crankshaft moves.*

7   Stuff shop rags into the cylinder head holes around the valves to prevent parts and tools from falling into the engine, then use a

valve spring compressor to compress the spring **(see illustrations)**. Remove the valve stem locks with small needle-nose pliers or a magnet.

Note: *The valves should be held in place by the air pressure. If the valve faces or seats are in poor condition, leaks may prevent air pressure from retaining the valves. If the valves cannot hold air, the cylinder head should be removed for a valve job at a machine shop.*

8   Remove the spring retainer and valve spring, then remove the valve stem seal.

9   Wrap a rubber band or tape around the top of the valve stem so the valve won't fall into the combustion chamber, then release the air pressure.

10   Remove the spark plug tubes if necessary. Use pliers to grab the tubes and pull them out.

11   Inspect the valve stem for damage. Rotate the valve in the guide and check the end for eccentric movement, which would indicate that the valve is bent.

12   Move the valve up-and-down in the guide and make sure it doesn't bind. If the valve stem binds, either the valve is bent or the guide is damaged. In either case, the cylinder head will have to be removed for repair.

13   If removed, reinstall the spark plug tubes as follows:

a) *Remove any sealant on the cylinder head.*

b) *Apply high-strength locking sealant within 0.47 in (12 mm) from the edge of the side of the tube to be installed into the head.*

c) *Install the tube so its height is 1.5 to 1.539 inches (38.1 to 39.1 mm). Be careful not to damage the tubes during installation.*

d) *Wipe off excess sealant from the cylinder head.*

e) *Follow the sealant manufacturer's curing time recommendations before continuing with the installation.*

14   Reapply air pressure to the cylinder to retain the valve in the closed position, then remove the tape or rubber band from the valve stem.

15   Lubricate the valve stems with engine oil and install the new valve stem seals. Valve stem seals can be installed with a special tool, or a deep socket and hammer - tap the seal only until seated **(see illustration)**.

16   Install the valve spring in position over the valve, with the more closely-wound spring

6.17 Apply a small dab of grease to each valve stem lock as shown here before installation - it will hold them in place on the valve stem as the spring is released

7.23 Insert a screwdriver into the notch at the top of the timing cover and pry the front timing cover off the engine

coils and the paint mark toward the cylinder head.

17   Install the valve spring retainer. Compress the valve springs and carefully position the valve stem locks in the groove. Apply a small dab of grease to the inside of each valve stem lock to hold it in place **(see illustration)**.

18   Remove the force from the spring tool and make sure the valve stem locks are seated.

19   Disconnect the air hose and remove the adapter from the spark plug hole.

20   When all of the seals to be replaced have been replaced, position the crankshaft at TDC **(see illustration 3.8)**.

21   Install the camshafts and lifters (see Section 8), then install the timing chain (see Section 7).

22   Install the valve covers (see Section 4).

23   Install the spark plugs (see Chapter 1), ignition coils (see Chapter 5) and the upper intake manifold (see Section 9).

24   Start and run the engine, then check for oil leaks and unusual sounds coming from the valve cover area.

---

7   Timing chain and sprockets - removal, inspection and installation

Warning: *The engine must be completely cool before beginning this procedure.*

Caution: *The timing system is complex. Severe engine damage will occur if you make any mistakes. Do not attempt this procedure unless you are highly experienced with this type of repair. If you are at all unsure of your abilities, consult an expert. Double-check all your work and be sure everything is correct before you attempt to start the engine.*

Removal

1   Remove the engine cover(s).

2   Disconnect the cable from the negative terminal of the battery (see Chapter 5).

3   2013 and later models: Remove the cowl cover and lower cowl (see Chapter 11).

4   Remove the air inlet duct.

5   Block the rear wheels and set the parking brake. On 2013 and later models, loosen the right front wheel lug nuts. On all models, raise the front of the vehicle and support it securely on jackstands. Remove the under-vehicle splash shield. On 2013 and later models, remove the wheel and the right inner fender splash shield (see Chapter 11).

6   Drain the cooling system, the power steering fluid and the engine oil (see Chapter 1). Remove the power steering fluid reservoir.

7   Remove the radiator and cooling fan assembly (see Chapter 3). On 2013 and later models, also remove the coolant reservoir.

8   2013 and later models: Remove the battery tray and support bracket (see Chapter 5).

9   2013 and later models: Remove the upper intake manifold (see Section 9).

10   2013 and later models: Remove the valve covers (see Section 4) and the dipstick.

11   Position the number one piston at TDC on the compression stroke (see Section 3).

12   Remove the drivebelt (see Chapter 1).

13   Remove the power steering pump (see Chapter 10).

14   Remove the alternator and its bracket (see Chapter 5).

15   Remove the air conditioning compressor mounting bolts and secure the compressor out of the way (see Chapter 3).

Warning: *The air conditioning system is under high pressure - do not disconnect the refrigerant lines.*

16   Remove the crankshaft pulley (see Section 12).

Note: *Don't allow the crankshaft to rotate during removal of the pulley. If the crankshaft moves, the number one piston will no longer be at TDC.*

17   2012 and earlier models: Detach the coolant hose from the oil cooler, then detach the water bypass pipe from the timing chain cover.

18   Disconnect the wiring from the oil pressure switch and the intake valve timing (IVT) control wiring harness (see Chapter 6). Label and disconnect any other interfering wiring and hoses.

19   Remove the bolts from the IVT covers in the reverse of the tightening sequence **(see illustration 7.46c)**. Pull the covers straight off so they disengage from the intake camshaft sprocket actuator assemblies.

20   Remove the drivebelt tensioner (see Chapter 1). Remove the air conditioning idler pulley and its bracket.

21   2013 and earlier models: Remove the lower oil pan (see Section 14).

22   Remove the two bolts in the front of the upper oil pan that secure the timing chain cover.

23   Remove the front timing chain cover bolts in several steps in the reverse of the tightening sequence (see illustration 7.45b). Pry the cover off using the slots at the top of the cover **(see illustration)**. Note that various types and sizes of bolts are used. Mark each bolt or make a sketch to ensure they are reinstalled in their original locations.

24   Remove the O-ring below each intake camshaft sprocket.

25   Confirm that the No. 1 piston is still at TDC on the compression stroke by verifying that the intake and exhaust camshaft lobes on the No. 1 cylinder are pointing upward **(see illustration)**.

26   Relieve tension on the primary timing chain. Depress the primary tensioner inward and lock it into place by inserting a suitable stopper pin into the hole on the front of the tensioner **(see illustration)**.

Note: *This engine utilizes three timing chains. The primary timing chain runs around the crankshaft sprocket, the water pump and two intake camshaft sprockets. This chain synchronizes the valve timing with the crankshaft and pistons, while two secondary timing chains run*

7.25 Verify that cylinder no. 1 is at TDC on the compression stroke by confirming that the intake and exhaust camshaft lobes on cylinder no. 1 are pointing upward

7.26 An ordinary paper clip can be straightened and used to lock the timing chain tensioner(s) in place

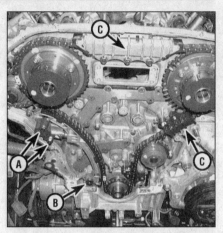

7.27 Primary timing chain tensioner mounting bolts (A), tensioner arm/chain guide pivot bolt (B) and upper chain guides (C)

7.28a Bend two paper clips so that they're long enough to protrude out past the camshaft sprocket once they're installed. . .

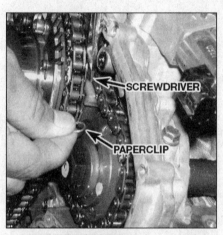

7.28b. . . then depress the secondary tensioners with a screwdriver and lock them in place by inserting a paper clip into the hole on the side of each tensioner - note that the secondary tensioner on the right bank points downward, while the secondary tensioner on the left bank points upward

7.29 Hold the lug on the camshaft with a wrench to keep it from rotating as the sprocket bolts are loosened

around the rear of the intake sprockets and separate exhaust camshaft sprockets to synchronize the intake and exhaust camshafts.

27   Remove the primary timing chain tensioner, the tensioner pivot arm/chain guide and the upper timing chain guides from the primary timing chain (see illustration).

28   Depress the secondary timing chain tensioners and lock the tensioners in place by inserting a suitable stopper pin into the hole on the front of each tensioner (see illustrations).

29   Remove the camshaft sprocket bolts (see illustration).

30   Disengage the primary timing chain from the teeth on the chain sprockets and remove it from the engine.

31   Mark the camshaft sprockets with either an R or L to indicate the right or left side, then remove the camshaft sprockets and the secondary timing chains from the engine. Don't mix the sprockets up. They must be installed on the same camshaft from which they were removed (see illustration).

Caution: The intake camshaft sprockets are

7.31 Note that the left intake camshaft sprocket has a sensor ring which is fastened to the front of the sprocket - be extremely careful not to damage or place a magnetic object of any kind near the sensor ring or a no start condition may occur

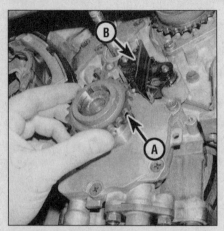

7.32 Crankshaft sprocket (A) and the lower chain guide (B - the mark on the chain guide must face up when reinstalling)

7.34a Examine the chain guides for deep grooves and excessive wear - replace them if necessary

7.34b Secondary timing chain tensioner(s) mounting bolts (A). Replace the O-ring (B) before reinstalling the front camshaft bearing cap

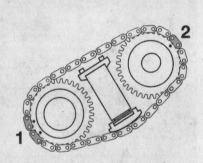

Rear cylinder bank

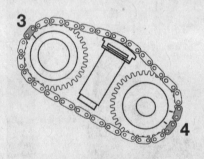

Front cylinder bank

72016-2B-6.34 HAYNES

7.38 Secondary timing chain alignment details

1   *Rear cylinder bank exhaust camshaft sprocket: Align the two colored links with the two round marks*
2   *Rear cylinder bank intake camshaft sprocket: Align the single colored link with the single round mark (mark is on the backside of sprocket)*
3   *Front cylinder bank intake camshaft sprocket: Align the single colored link with the single oval mark (mark is on the backside of sprocket)*
4   *Front cylinder bank exhaust camshaft sprocket: Align the two colored links with the two oval marks*

identified by the variable valve timing actuator and sensor ring which is fastened to the front of the sprocket. Be extremely careful not to damage or place a magnetic object of any kind near the sensor ring or a no start condition may occur after installation. Do not disassemble the variable valve timing actuator assembly from the intake camshaft sprocket for any reason.

32   Remove the crankshaft sprocket and the lower timing chain guide **(see illustration)**.

33   To remove the rear timing chain cover (necessary only if you're removing either cylinder head, the upper oil pan or the engine block), see Section 11.

Inspection

34   Inspect the camshaft, water pump and crankshaft sprockets for wear on the teeth and keyways. Inspect the chains for cracks or excessive wear of the rollers. Inspect the facing of the chain guides and the secondary timing chain tensioners for excessive wear **(see illustrations)**.

Note: *If the secondary timing chain tensioners*

need to be replaced, remove the front camshaft bearing cap to allow access to the secondary tensioner bolts (see illustration).

Installation

Caution: *Before starting the engine, carefully rotate the crankshaft by hand through at least two full revolutions using a socket and breaker bar on the crankshaft pulley bolt. If you feel any resistance, STOP! There is something wrong - most likely, valves are hitting the pistons. You must find the problem before proceeding.*

35   If you removed the rear timing chain cover, install it now (see Section 11).

36   Install the crankshaft sprocket and the lower timing chain guide with the mark facing up **(see illustration 7.32)**. If the secondary tensioners were removed, reinstall them and tighten the bolts to the torque listed in this Chapter's Specifications 0 and make sure the tensioner spring is locked in place.

37   Verify that you have the correct timing chains for your vehicle by counting the number of links each chain has and comparing the new chains with the old chains. Also compare

the position of the colored links in the new chains with the position of the colored links in the old chains.

38   Make sure the camshafts are positioned with the dowels on the exhaust camshafts in the 12 o'clock position in relation to the top of the cylinder head mating surface; the intake camshafts must be positioned with the small diameter dowel pin hole in the 12 o'clock position in relation to the top of the cylinder head mating surface. Install the secondary timing chains and sprocket assemblies on the camshafts with the timing marks aligned as shown **(see illustration)**. Install the camshaft sprocket bolts hand tight.

39   Reconfirm that the secondary camshaft sprocket timing marks are aligned correctly with the colored links on the secondary timing chains, and remove the stopper pins from the secondary chain tensioners.

40   Install the primary timing chain onto the engine by looping the chain around the crankshaft sprocket and aligning the orange colored chain link with the mark on the crankshaft sprocket. Place the chain around the

7.40a The orange colored link on the timing chain aligns with the mark on the crankshaft sprocket

7.40b The pink colored links on the primary timing chain align with the marks on the intake camshaft sprockets

water pump sprocket and finally around the primary camshaft sprockets, making sure the pink colored links align with their respective marks on the sprockets **(see illustrations)**.

Note: *It may be necessary to rotate the camshafts slightly in order to align the pink colored chain links with the marks on the intake camshaft sprockets.*

41 Install the upper timing chain guides tighten the bolts to the torque listed in this Chapter's Specifications 0. Install the primary tensioner arm/chain guide and the timing chain tensioner assembly **(see illustration 7.27)**. Tighten the main tensioner bolts to the torque listed in this Chapter's Specifications 0 .Reconfirm that the No. 1 piston is still at TDC on the compression stroke and that the timing marks on the camshaft and crankshaft sprockets are aligned with the colored links on the chain, then remove the stopper pin from the primary timing chain tensioner.

42 Lubricate the camshaft sprocket bolt heads and threads with clean engine oil and tighten them to the torque listed in this Chapter's Specifications.

43 Remove all traces of old sealant from the timing chain cover, the cover bolts and the rear cover bolt holes.

44 Install new O-rings in the variable valve timing oil control orifice of the rear timing cover **(see illustration)**.

45 Apply a 1/8-inch bead of RTV sealant to the timing chain cover sealing surfaces **(see illustration)**. Place the timing chain cover in position on the engine and install the bolts in their original locations. Tighten the bolts, in sequence **(see illustration)**, to the torque listed in this Chapter's Specifications.

Note: *It will also be necessary to install the air conditioning compressor bracket in order to tighten the bolts in the proper sequence.*

46 Install new O-rings in the IVT orifices of

7.44 Install new O-rings at the indicated area on the right and left side of the rear timing chain case

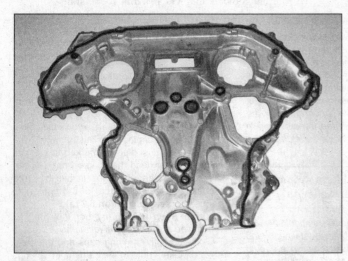

7.45a Apply RTV sealant to the timing chain cover at the areas shown - wipe off any excess sealant

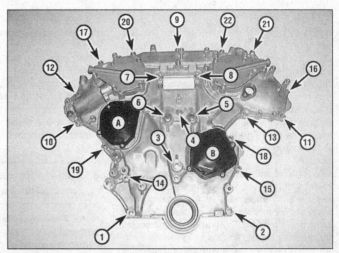

7.45b Front timing chain cover bolt TIGHTENING sequence. (A) is the primary timing chain cover and (B) is the water pump cover; neither of these covers need be removed during this procedure unless they are leaking

7.46a Install new O-rings in both of the IVT orifices on the front timing chain cover

7.46b Apply a light film of engine oil to the new O-rings and install them in the groove on the IVT actuator covers, then apply a 1/8-inch bead of RTV sealant to the indicated areas

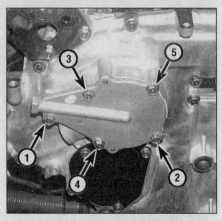

7.46c IVT cover bolt TIGHTENING sequence

8.4 The camshaft bearing caps should be marked with a number and letter stamp or a marker to ensure correct reinstallation

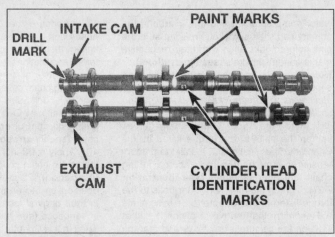

8.5 Each camshaft is marked with either an L for left (front) cylinder, or an R for right (rear) cylinder - paint marks between the number 1 and number 2 journals indicate that it is an intake camshaft, while paint marks between the number 3 and number 4 journals indicate that it is an exhaust camshaft

the front timing chain cover and on the IVT actuator covers. Then apply a 1/8-inch bead of RTV sealant to the sealing surface of the variable valve timing actuator covers **(see illustrations)**. Place the IVT covers in position over the dowels on the front timing cover and install the bolts in their original locations. Following the recommended tightening sequence **(see illustration)**, tighten the bolts to the torque listed in this Chapter's Specifications.

47   The remainder of installation is the reverse of removal. Follow the sealant manufacturer's recommendations for assembly and sealant curing times. Allow all sealant to fully cure per the manufacturer's recommendations before adding fluids.

48   Fill the crankcase with oil and install a new filter (see Chapter 1). Refill the cooling system and the power steering system. (see Chapter 1)

49   Reconnect the battery and perform the necessary re-learn procedures (see Chapter 5).
Note: *Timing chain noise may be apparent after performing this procedure. This noise is normal and should only last until the air has bled out of the high pressure chamber of the primary timing chain tensioner. If after several minutes the noise is still apparent, run the engine at 3,000 rpm with the transmission in Neutral or Park until the noise subsides.*

8   Camshafts and lifters - removal, inspection and installation

Note: *The camshafts and lifters should always be thoroughly inspected before installation, and camshaft endplay and valve clearance should always be checked prior to camshaft removal.*

Removal

1   Remove the timing chains and camshaft

sprockets (see Section 7).

2   Remove the camshaft position sensor brackets.

3   Mark each camshaft so it can be installed in its original position.

4   Mark the camshaft bearing caps from 1 to 4, and with an "I" or an "E," to indicate intake or exhaust. Also mark arrows indicating the front of the engine (see illustration). All the components must also be marked to indicate which cylinder head they came from. Loosen the camshaft bearing caps in two or three steps, in the reverse order of the tightening sequence **(see illustration 8.21a)**.
Caution: *Keep the caps in order; they must be reinstalled in their original locations.*

5   Remove the bearing caps and the camshafts. Make a note of the camshaft markings to ensure correct installation **(see illustration)**.
Note: *The intake camshaft has a drill spot on the side of the sprocket mounting flange.*

8.6 The lifters and shims can be stored in individually marked plastic bags or a divided box as shown

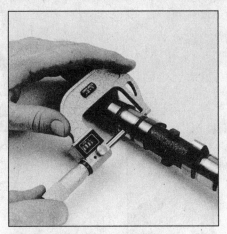

8.8a Measure each journal diameter with a micrometer - if any journal measures less than the specified limit, replace the camshaft

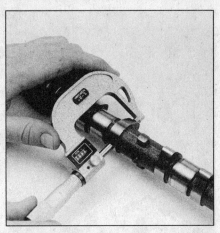

8.8b Measure the lobe heights - if any lobe height is less than the minimum listed in this Chapter's Specifications, replace the camshaft

8.12a Place a strip of Plastigage under each camshaft bearing cap and tighten the caps to Specifications

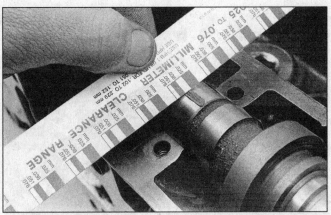

8.12b Compare the width of the crushed Plastigage to the scale on the envelope to determine the oil clearance

6   Remove the lifters from the cylinder head **(see illustration)**.
Caution: *Keep the lifters in order; they must be reinstalled in their original locations.*

Inspection

7   Visually examine the camshaft lobes, journals, bearing caps and lifters. Check for score marks, pitting and evidence of overheating (blue, discolored areas). If wear is excessive or damage is evident, the component will have to be replaced.

8   Using a micrometer, measure camshaft journal diameter and lobe height **(see illustrations)** , and compare your measurements to this Chapter's Specifications. If the lobe height is less than the minimum allowable, the camshaft is worn and must be replaced.

9   Check the camshaft runout by placing the camshaft back into the cylinder head and set up a dial indicator on the center journal. Zero the dial indicator. Turn the camshaft slowly and note the dial indicator readings. If the measured runout exceeds the runout listed in this Chapter's Specifications, replace

the camshaft. While using the dial indicator, also measure the camshaft sprocket runout. Place the dial indicator against the sprocket and slowly rotate it. If runout exceeds the limit listed in this Chapter's Specifications, replace it.

10   Also, while the camshaft is sitting in the cylinder head, check the endplay. Install the bearing caps and tighten them securely. Mount a dial indicator with the plunger of the dial indicator in line with and touching the end of the camshaft. Gently pry the camshaft fully toward the gauge, zero the gauge, then pry the camshaft fully away from the gauge and note the gauge reading. If the measured endplay is at or beyond the service limit listed in this Chapter's Specifications, replace the camshaft and check the endplay again. If the endplay is still excessive, replace the cylinder head.

11   Inspect each lifter for scuffing and score marks.

12   Check the oil clearance for each camshaft journal as follows **(see illustrations)**:
Caution: *Don't turn the camshaft while the*

Plastigage is in place.

a) *Clean the bearing caps and the camshaft journals with brake system cleaner.*

b) *Carefully lay the camshafts in place in the cylinder head. DON'T use any lubrication.*

c) *Lay a strip of Plastigage on each journal.*

d) *Install the bearing caps with the arrows pointing toward the front (timing chain end) of the engine.*

e) *Tighten the bolts, in sequence, to the torque listed in this Chapter's Specifications.*

f) *Remove the bolts, in sequence, and detach the bearing caps.*

g) *Compare the width of the crushed Plastigage (at its widest point) to the scale on the Plastigage envelope.*

If the clearance is greater than listed in this Chapter's Specifications, replace the camshaft and/or cylinder head.

13   Scrape off the Plastigage with your fingernail or the edge of a credit card - don't scratch or nick the journals or bearing caps.

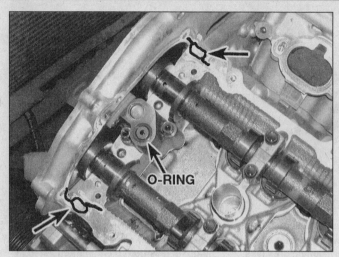

8.19a Apply RTV sealant to the cylinder head at the areas shown and install the secondary tensioner O-ring(s) - wipe off any excess sealant

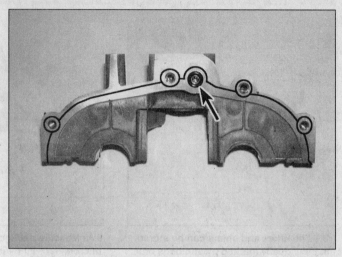

8.19b Apply a small dab of grease to the IVT oil control orifice O-ring to hold it in place on the No. 1 bearing cap, then apply RTV sealant to the areas shown

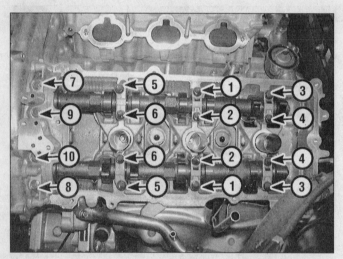

8.21a Camshaft bearing cap TIGHTENING sequence (front cylinder head shown, rear identical)

8.21b Tighten the rear timing cover-to-No. 1 bearing cap bolts

Installation

14   Remove all old RTV sealant from the bolts and the front bearing caps.

15   Set the number one piston at TDC if it has been moved.

16   Lubricate the lifters with clean engine oil, then install the lifters into their original locations.

17   Apply moly-based engine assembly lubricant to the camshaft lobes and journals.

18   Install the exhaust camshafts in their original positions with the dowel pins facing up (12 o'clock in relation to the cylinder head mating surface) and inline with the cylinder bank. The small dowel hole in the end of each intake camshaft should also be facing up.

19   Apply a bead of RTV sealant to the sealing surfaces of the No. 1 bearing cap(s) and the cylinder head. Install new O-rings on the secondary timing chain tensioner(s) and the IVT oil control orifice on the No. 1 bearing cap(s) **(see illustrations)**.

20   Install the bearing caps and bolts and tighten them hand tight. The stamp marks on the bearing caps should be in order.

21   Tighten the bearing cap bolts, in sequence **(see illustration)**, to the torque listed in this Chapter's Specifications, then tighten the rear timing cover-to-No. 1 bearing cap bolts **(see illustration)**.

22   Check the protrusion of the front bearing caps in front of the cylinder head front surface. The front bearing cap should be close to 0.0055 inch behind the front face of the cylinder head. If it isn't, remove and reinstall the camshaft and caps, then check again.

23   Install the camshaft sprockets and timing chain (see Section 7). Hold the camshafts with a suitable wrench as you tighten the sprocket bolts to the specified torque.

24   The remainder of installation is the reverse of removal. If any part of the valve train was replaced, check and adjust the valve clearance (see Section 5).

25   Reconnect the battery and perform the necessary re-learn procedures (see Chapter 5).

9   Intake manifold - removal and installation

Warning: *The engine must be completely cool before beginning this procedure.*

Upper intake manifold

1   If you are removing the upper intake manifold to remove the fuel rail and/or lower intake manifold, relieve the fuel system pressure (see Chapter 4).

2   Disconnect the cable from the negative battery terminal (see Chapter 5). Remove the engine cover and, if you're working on a 2013 and later model, the cowl cover and lower cowl (see Chapter 11).

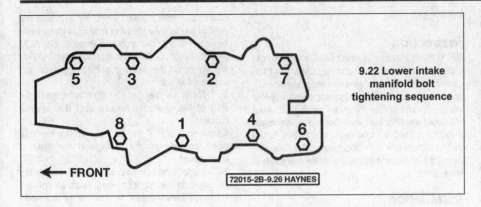

9.22 Lower intake manifold bolt tightening sequence

10.12 Exhaust manifold heat shield fasteners

3   Clamp-off the coolant hoses connected to the throttle body, then disconnect them from the throttle body. Be prepared to catch and clean up any spilled coolant.

4   Remove the air intake duct (see Chapter 4).

5   Disconnect the electrical connector from the throttle body and remove the throttle body (see Chapter 4).

6   Label and disconnect the following items:
PCV hose (between the upper intake manifold and rear valve cover)
All vacuum lines connected to the upper and lower manifolds

7   Detach and remove the following components:
   EVAP canister purge solenoid
   VIAS control solenoid valve and vacuum tank
   Power steering hose bracket
   Upper intake manifold support bracket

8   Loosen the upper intake manifold mounting fasteners a little at a time to prevent distortion, then remove the upper intake manifold. The upper intake manifold assembly consists of two parts: the upper intake (connects the throttle body to the plenum) and the plenum/intake manifold runners (lower part of the upper intake manifold). If you're replacing either of these parts of the upper intake manifold assembly, remove the fasteners that secure the intake to the plenum, again loosening the fasteners a little at a time to prevent distortion. If you're replacing the plenum/intake manifold runners, also remove the power valve fasteners, a little at a time to prevent distortion. Cover all engine openings to keep anything from falling into the engine.

9   Clean the mounting surfaces of the upper intake manifold and, if removed, the mounting surfaces of the intake and/or the power valve mounting surfaces. Carefully remove all traces of old gasket material and/or sealant. At this time, also check the studs for damage. If damaged, remove them and install new ones. Tighten the studs to the torque listed in this Chapter's Specifications.

10   Install new gaskets and reassemble the upper intake manifold assembly (if disassembled). Install the upper intake manifold assembly and tighten the fasteners gradually and evenly, a little at a time, to the torque listed in this Chapter's Specifications.

Note: *When tightening the upper intake manifold mounting fasteners, start with the center bolts and work your way out towards the ends.*

11   The remainder of installation is the reverse of removal. Check the coolant level, adding some if necessary (see Chapter 1).

12   Reconnect the battery and perform the necessary re-learn procedures (see Chapter 5).

Lower intake manifold

13   Relieve the fuel pressure (see Chapter 4).

14   Remove the upper intake manifold (see Steps 1 through 8).

15   Remove the fuel rail and injectors (see Chapter 4).

16   Label and detach any remaining hoses which would interfere with the removal of the lower intake manifold.

17   Loosen the manifold bolts in the reverse of the tightening sequence **(see illustration 9.22)**.

18   Remove the manifold. The manifold will probably be stuck to the cylinder heads and force may be required to break the gasket seal. Cover all engine openings to keep anything from falling into the engine.

Caution: *Don't pry between the manifold and the heads or damage to the gasket sealing surfaces may occur, leading to vacuum leaks.*

19   Carefully use a scraper to remove all traces of old gasket material and sealant from the manifold and cylinder heads, then clean the mating surfaces with brake system cleaner. At this time, also check the studs for damage. If damaged, remove them and install new ones. Tighten the studs to the torque listed in this Chapter's Specifications.

20   Use a precision straightedge and a feeler gauge to check the flatness of the top surface of the manifold. Compare your measurement to that listed in this Chapter's Specifications. If it's excessive, replace the manifold.

21   Install new gaskets, then position the lower manifold on the engine. Make sure the gaskets and manifolds are aligned over the studs in the cylinder heads and install the bolts.

22   Tighten the nuts/bolts in several steps, in sequence **(see illustration)**, to the torque listed in this Chapter's Specifications.

23   The remainder of installation is the reverse of removal. Refer to Steps 9 through 11 to install

the upper intake manifold.

24   Reconnect the battery and perform the necessary re-learn procedures (see Chapter 5).

10   Exhaust manifold - removal, inspection and installation

Warning: *The engine must be completely cool before beginning this procedure.*

Removal

1   Remove the engine cover.

2   Disconnect the cable from the negative terminal of the battery (see Chapter 5).

2012 and earlier models

Left (driver's) side

3   Remove the air filter housing (see Chapter 4).

4   Raise the front of the vehicle and support it securely on jackstands. Remove the under-vehicle splash shield and the inner fender splash shield (see Chapter 11).

5   Drain the engine coolant to a level lower than that of the heater pipe at the left cylinder head (see Chapter 1).

6   Remove the exhaust manifold heat shield (see illustration 10.12).

7   Remove the left-side catalytic converter (see Chapter 6).

8   Remove the dipstick and the dipstick tube.

9   Detach the coolant hose from the coolant pipe along the left cylinder head, then remove the pipe.

10   Loosen the exhaust manifold nuts, a little at a time and starting with the outer nuts, then remove them and detach the manifold from the cylinder head.

Right (passenger's) side

11   Raise the front of the vehicle and support it securely on jackstands. Remove the under-vehicle splash shield and the inner fender splash shield (see Chapter 11).

12   Remove the exhaust manifold seat shield **(see illustration)**.

13   Remove the right-side catalytic converter (see Chapter 6).

Note: *Depending on your tool selection, it might be necessary to remove the heat shield from the firewall to give you adequate working room.*

14   Remove the bolt securing the automatic transmission fluid tube, then position the tube out of the way.

15   Loosen the exhaust manifold nuts, a little at a time and starting with the outer nuts, then remove them and detach the manifold from the cylinder head.

2013 and later models

Rear cylinder bank

16   Remove the cowl cover and the lower cowl (see Chapter 11).

17   If you're working on an AWD model, loosen the right-front wheel lug nuts.

18   Raise the front of the vehicle and support it securely on jackstands. Remove the under-vehicle splash shield.

19   Remove the front part of the exhaust system **(see illustration)**.

AWD models

20   Remove the right-front wheel and the inner fender splash shield (see Chapter 11).

21   Remove the driveshaft and the right-front driveaxle (see Chapter 8).

All models

22   Remove the upstream and downstream oxygen sensors (see Chapter 6).

23   Support the rear part of the engine/transaxle assembly and remove the rear engine mounting bracket/insulator.

24   Remove the exhaust manifold and catalyst heat shields.

25   Remove the catalyst-to-exhaust manifold bolts first, then remove the nut, and detach the catalyst from the manifold.

26   Loosen the exhaust manifold nuts, a little at a time and starting with the outer nuts, then remove them and detach the manifold from the cylinder head.

Front cylinder bank

27   Remove the air filter housing and duct (see Chapter 4).

28   Remove the battery and the battery tray (see Chapter 5).

29   Loosen the front wheel lug nuts, then raise the front of the vehicle and support it securely on jackstands. Remove the wheels and the inner fender splash shields (see Chapter 11).

30   Remove the under-vehicle splash shield.

31   Remove the cooling fan assembly and the radiator (see Chapter 3).

32   Support the engine/transaxle assembly and remove the front engine mounting bracket/insulator.

33   Remove the catalyst-to-exhaust manifold bolts first, then remove the nut, and detach the catalyst from the manifold.

34   Loosen the exhaust manifold nuts, a little at a time and starting with the outer nuts, then remove them and detach the manifold from the cylinder head.

Inspection

35   Use a scraper to remove all traces of old gasket material and carbon deposits from the manifold and cylinder head mating surfaces.

36   Use a precision straightedge and a feeler gauge to check the flatness of the exhaust manifold sealing surface. Compare the measurement to the maximum allowable listed in this Chapter's Specifications. Replace the manifold or have it surfaced if the warpage is excessive.

Installation

37   Position the new exhaust manifold gasket, with the arrow on the gasket pointing up, over the studs on the cylinder head.

38   Install the manifold and thread the mounting nuts/bolts into place.

39   Tighten the nuts/bolts a little at a time, working from the center outwards, to the torque listed in this Chapter's Specifications. Once all of the nuts have been tightened, repeat the tightening sequence.

40   Reinstall the remaining parts in the reverse order of removal.

41   Refill the cooling system, if drained (see Chapter 1).

42   Reconnect the battery and perform the necessary re-learn procedures (see Chapter 5).

---

11   Cylinder head - removal and installation

Warning: *The engine must be completely cool before beginning this procedure*

2012 and earlier models

Removal

Note: *This procedure applies to either cylinder head.*

1   Drain the coolant (see Chapter 1).

2   Remove the camshafts (see Section 8).

3   Remove the intake manifold (see Section 9) and the exhaust manifold (see Section 10).

4   On AWD models, remove the front differential (see Chapter 8).

5   Remove the coolant outlet assembly (the metal pipe that carries coolant between the cylinder heads).

6   On 2013 and later models, if you're removing the front cylinder head, remove the coolant hose between the radiator and the coolant inlet, then remove the coolant inlet and thermostat assembly (see Chapter 3).

7   Remove the lower and upper oil pans (see Section 14).

8   Remove the rear timing chain cover bolts in the reverse of the tightening sequence **(see illustration 11.28d)**.

Caution: *If the rear cover is stuck to a cylinder head or the engine block, try to knock it loose with a dead blow hammer and a block*

of wood. If that doesn't work, try to break the gasket sealant by slipping a flexible putty knife between the cover and the engine. Do NOT pry off the cover or you might damage the timing cover or the sealing surfaces, which will cause oil leaks.

9   Remove the old O-rings from the front end of the cylinder heads and the engine block.

Caution: *Even if you're only removing one head, replace all the O-rings in the front of each head.*

10   Label and remove any remaining items attached to the cylinder head, such as coolant fittings, tubes, cables, hoses, wires or brackets.

11   Using a breaker bar and the appropriate sized Allen-head socket, loosen the cylinder head bolts in 1/4-turn increments until they can be removed by hand. Loosen the bolts in the reverse of the tightening sequence **(see illustration 11.25)** to avoid warping or cracking the head. Obtain new head bolts for installation.

12   Lift the cylinder head off the engine block. If it's stuck, very carefully pry up at a casting protrusion, beyond the gasket surface **(see illustration)**.

13   Remove all external components from the head to allow for thorough cleaning and inspection.

Installation

14   The mating surfaces of the cylinder head and block must be perfectly clean when the head is installed.

15   Use a gasket scraper to remove all traces of carbon and old gasket material from the cylinder head and engine block, then clean the mating surfaces with brake system cleaner **(see illustration)**. If there's oil on the mating surfaces when the head is installed, the gasket may not seal correctly and leaks could develop.

16   When working on the block, stuff the cylinders with clean shop rags to keep out debris. Use a vacuum cleaner to remove material that falls into the cylinders.

17   Check the block and head mating surfaces for nicks, deep scratches and other damage. If damage is slight, it can be removed with a file; if it's excessive, machining may be the only alternative.

18   Use a tap of the correct size to chase the threads in the head bolt holes, then clean the holes with compressed air - make sure that nothing remains in the holes.

Warning: *Wear eye protection when using compressed air!*

19   Use a straight edge to check the cylinder head at several places for warpage. The allowable limit for warpage is 0.004 inches (0.1 mm). If warpage exceeds the limit, replace the head. Also check the head gasket, intake and exhaust manifold surfaces to make sure they are within the warpage limit.

20   Install the components that were removed from the head.

21   Position the new cylinder head gasket

10.19 Mounting fasteners for the front portion of the exhaust system (2013 and later models)

11.12 Pry on a casting protrusion to break the head loose

11.15 Carefully remove all traces of old gasket material from the sealing surfaces

11.25 Cylinder head bolt TIGHTENING sequence

over the dowel pins on the block, noting which direction on the gasket faces up.

22 Set the camshaft so the No. 1 piston is set to TDC (see Section 3).

23 Carefully set the head on the block without disturbing the gasket.

24 Before installing the new head bolts, apply a small amount of clean engine oil to the threads and hardened washers (if equipped). The chamfered side of the washers must face the bolt heads.

25 Install the NEW cylinder head bolts and tighten them finger tight. Tighten the bolts, in sequence **(see illustration)**, to the torque steps listed in this Chapter's Specifications.

26 After installing the cylinder head, measure the distance between the front end faces of the block and the heads. The standard distance is 0.555 to 0.587 inches (14.1 to 14.9 mm). If the distance is greater than listed, remove and reinstall the cylinder head that is out of specification.

Note: *The manufacturer does not indicate to*

measure this dimension on 2013 and later models.

27 Remove all traces of old sealant from the rear timing chain cover and the cover bolts.

28 Apply a bead of RTV sealant to the rear timing cover sealing surfaces **(see illustration)**. Install new O-rings in the front of the engine block and in the variable valve timing

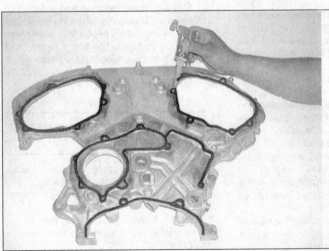

11.28a Apply RTV sealant to the rear timing chain cover at the areas shown - wipe off any excess sealant

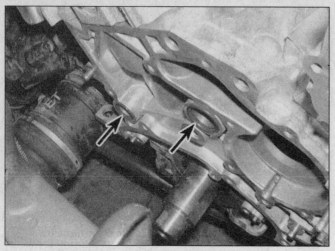

11.28b Install new O-rings in the front of the engine block. . .

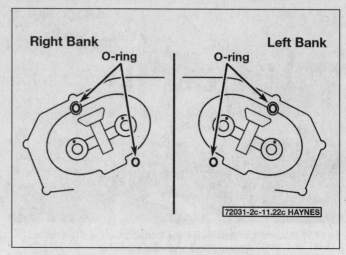

11.28c . . . and in the variable valve timing oil control orifices in the cylinder head

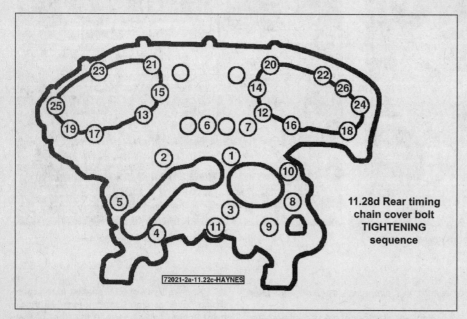

11.28d Rear timing chain cover bolt TIGHTENING sequence

oil control orifices in the cylinder head **(see illustrations)**. Place the rear timing chain cover in position over the dowels on the engine and install the bolts in their original locations. Tighten the bolts, in sequence **(see illustration)** to the torque listed in this Chapter's Specifications.

29   Install the camshafts (see Section 8), then install the timing chains and sprockets (see Section 7). The remainder of installation is the reverse of removal. If any part of the valve train was replaced, check and adjust the valve clearance (see Section 5).

30   Refill the cooling system and engine oil, and install a new oil filter (see Chapter 1).

31   Reconnect the battery and perform the necessary re-learn procedures (see Chapter 5).

32   Start the engine and check for oil and coolant leaks.

2013 and later models

33   Cylinder head removal and installation on these models requires removing the engine from the vehicle (see Chapter 2C). Other than that, the procedure is the same as for 2012 and earlier models, ignoring the steps which do not apply because the engine is out of the vehicle.

12   Crankshaft pulley - removal and installation

1   Disconnect the cable from the negative terminal of the battery (see Chapter 5).
2   Block the rear wheels and set the parking brake.
3   On 2012 and earlier models, remove the engine cooling fan, if necessary for clearance (see Chapter 3)

4   On 2013 and later models, loosen the right front wheel lug nuts.
5   Raise the front of the vehicle and support it securely on jackstands. On 2013 and later models, remove the right front wheel and the inner fender splash shield (see Chapter 11).
6   On 2012 and earlier models, remove the under-vehicle splash shield.
7   Remove the drivebelt (see Chapter 1).
8   Remove the starter (see Chapter 5) and lock the driveplate using a large screwdriver.
9   Attempt to slide the pulley off the crankshaft. If it is stuck, loosen the crankshaft pulley bolt until there is a 3/8 inch (10 mm) gap between the bolt head and the pulley, then use a three-jaw puller, with the claws of the puller engaging the hub of the pulley (NOT the outer diameter) and the puller screw bearing on the crankshaft pulley bolt head, to break the pulley loose.
10   To install the crankshaft pulley, align the pulley groove with the key on the crankshaft and slide the pulley onto the crankshaft.
11   Apply engine oil to the underside of the crankshaft pulley bolt head and to the threads, install the bolt and tighten it to the torque listed in this Chapter's Specifications.
12   The remainder of installation is the reverse of removal.
13   Reconnect the battery and perform the necessary re-learn procedures (see Chapter 5).

13   Crankshaft front oil seal - replacement

1   Remove the crankshaft pulley (see Section 12).
2   Carefully pry the seal out of the cover with a seal removal tool or a large screwdriver **(see illustration)**.
Caution: *Be careful not to scratch, gouge or distort the area that the seal fits into or an oil*

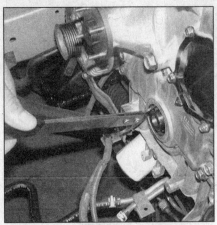

13.2 Pry the seal out very carefully with a seal removal tool or screwdriver, being careful not to nick or gouge the seal bore or the crankshaft

13.4 Use a large socket, seal driver or large-diameter pipe to drive the new seal into the cover

14.28 Insert a flathead screwdriver or small pry bar into the notch on the side of the oil pan to break it loose - be careful not to damage the sealing surfaces!

leak will develop.

3   Clean the bore to remove any old seal material and corrosion. Position the new seal in the bore with the seal lip (usually the side with the spring) facing IN (toward the engine). A small amount of oil applied to the outer edge of the new seal will make installation easier.

4   Drive the seal into the bore with a large socket and hammer **(see illustration)**. Select a socket that's the same outside diameter as the seal and make sure the new seal is pressed into place until it's flush with the face of the case.

5   Check the surface of the damper that the oil seal rides on. If the surface has been grooved from long-time contact with the seal, the new seal will leak. Replace the crankshaft pulley.

6   Lubricate the seal lips with engine oil and reinstall the crankshaft pulley. Apply clean engine oil to the crankshaft pulley retaining bolt head and threads, install the bolt and tighten it to the torque listed in this Chapter's Specifications.

7   The remainder of installation is the reverse of removal. Run the engine and check for oil leaks.

14   Oil pans - removal and installation

Lower oil pan

1   Raise the front of the vehicle and support it securely on jackstands.

2   Remove the under-vehicle splash shield.

3   Drain the engine oil (see Chapter 1).

4   Loosen the lower oil pan bolts in a criss-cross pattern, then remove them.

5   Use a soft-face hammer to bump the side of the oil pan to break it loose. If that doesn't work, tap a putty knife or other thin tool between the upper and lower oil pans. Remove the lower oil pan.

6   Clean all remnants of RTV sealant from the sealing surfaces. Wipe the surfaces with lacquer thinner to remove all traces of oil. Clean the strainer on the oil pick-up tube.

7   Check the lower steel oil pan flange for distortion, particularly around the bolt holes. If necessary, place the pan on a wood block and use a hammer to flatten and restore the gasket surface.

8   Apply a bead of RTV sealant around the steel oil pan flange and install the steel oil pan.

9   Tighten the oil pan fasteners in several steps, in a criss-cross pattern, to the torque listed in this Chapter's Specifications.

10   The remainder of installation is the reverse of removal. Wait the time recommended by the RTV sealant manufacturer to allow the sealant to fully cure before refilling the engine oil (see Chapter 1).

Upper oil pan

2012 and earlier models

Removal

Warning: *The engine must be cool before beginning this procedure.*

11   Remove the engine cover.

12   Remove the air filter housing (see Chapter 4).

13   Remove the lower oil pan (see Steps 1 through 5).

14   Drain the engine coolant (see Chapter 1).

15   Remove the oil dipstick tube fastener and dipstick tube.

16   On 4WD models, remove the front drive-axles and differential (see Chapter 8).

17   Unbolt the front stabilizer bar brackets and move the bar out of the way (see Chapter 10).

18   Detach the intermediate shaft from the steering gear, then remove the steering gear mounting bolts and move it out of the way (see Chapter 10).

19   Remove the front crossmember.

20   Unbolt the automatic transmission fluid cooler tube brackets.

21   Remove the oil filter (see Chapter 1).

22   Remove the oil cooler (see Section 16).

23   Remove the oil pick-up tube fasteners and remove the oil pick-up tube.

24   Disconnect and remove the oil pressure switch.

25   Remove the transmission-to-upper oil pan bolts.

26   Remove the rear cover plate fasteners and plate.

27   Remove the upper oil pan bolts in the reverse of the tightening sequence (see illustration 14.35a or 14.35b).

28   Insert a pry tool into the notch in the oil pan top rail and use it to break the oil pan loose **(see illustration)**. Remove the upper oil pan.

29   Remove the O-rings from the block and the oil pump housing.

30   Remove the gaskets from the front timing cover and the rear seal retainer.

Installation

31   Use a scraper to remove all traces of old gasket material and sealant from the upper aluminum section of the oil pan, the lower steel pan and the engine block. Clean the mating surfaces with brake system cleaner. Clean the strainer on the oil pick-up tube

Caution: *Be careful not to scratch or gouge the gasket surface of the block or oil pan. A leak could develop after the repairs have been completed.*

32   Make sure the threaded bolt holes in the block and aluminum section of the oil pan are clean.

33   Apply a bead of RTV sealant to the ends of the timing chain cover gasket and the rear oil seal retainer gasket, then place the gaskets in position on the oil pan. Apply a bead of RTV sealant around the upper aluminum oil pan flange.

Note: *The oil pan must be installed within 15 minutes once the sealant has been applied.*

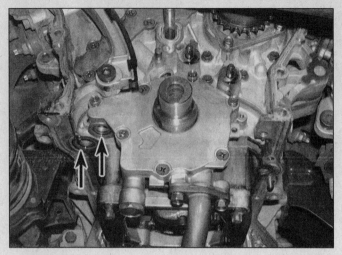

14.34 Install new O-rings in the block and the oil pump housing

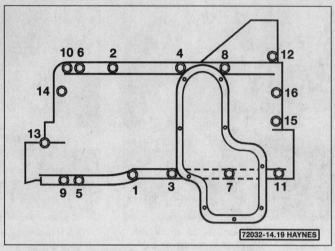

14.35a Upper (aluminum) oil pan bolt TIGHTENING sequence -
2012 and earlier models

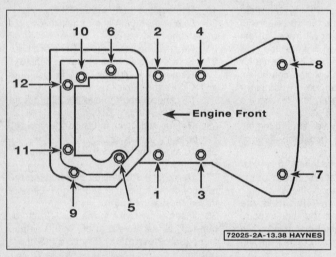

14.35b Upper (aluminum) oil pan bolt TIGHTENING sequence -
2013 and later models

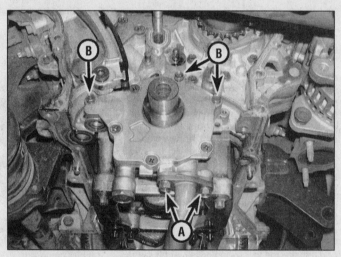

15.3 Oil strainer mounting bolts (A) and oil pump housing
retaining bolts (B)

34   Install new O-rings in the engine block and the oil pump body **(see illustration)**.

35   Carefully position the upper (aluminum) section of the oil pan on the engine block and install the bolts. Tighten the fasteners in three or four steps, in sequence **(see illustrations)**, to the torque listed in this Chapter's Specifications.

36   Install the oil pick-up tube, using a new O-ring, and tighten the mounting bolts to the torque listed in this Chapter's Specifications.

37   Install the oil pan-to-transmission mounting bolts and tighten to the torque listed in this Chapter's Specifications 0.

38   The remainder of installation is the reverse of removal. Install a new oil filter (see Chapter 1). Wait the time specified by the RTV sealant manufacturer to allow the sealant to fully cure before refilling the engine with coolant and engine oil (see Chapter 1).

2013 and later models

39   Upper oil pan removal and installation on these models requires removing the engine from the vehicle (see Chapter 2C). Other than that, the procedure is the same as for 2012 and earlier models, ignoring the steps which do not apply because the engine is out of the vehicle.

15   Oil pump - removal, inspection and installation

Removal

1   Remove the oil pans (see Section 14).

2   Remove the primary timing chain and the crankshaft sprocket (see Section 7).

Note: *It is not necessary to remove the cam-*

shaft sprockets, the camshaft sprocket bolts, the secondary timing chains or the primary timing chain tensioner pivot arm/chain guide during this procedure. Pivot the tensioner arm/ chain guide over to the left side to allow removal of the oil pump housing.

3   Remove the oil strainer-to-oil pump bolts from the lower section of the oil pump and separate the strainer from the pump. Remove the oil pump-to-engine block bolts **(see illustration)**.

4   Gently pry the oil pump housing outward enough to clear the dowel pins on the engine block and remove it from the engine.

Inspection

5   Use a large Phillips screwdriver to remove the screws holding the front cover on the oil pump housing **(see illustration)**.

15.5 Remove the screws and lift off the cover

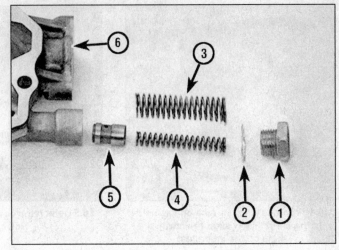

15.7 Oil pressure relief valve components

1	Plug	4	Inner spring (if equipped)
2	Washer	5	Relief valve
3	Outer spring	6	Oil pump housing

15.8a Use feeler gauges to measure the rotor tooth tip clearance. . .

15.8b. . . and the outer gear-to-body clearance

15.8c Measure the housing-to-gear side clearance with a straightedge and feeler gauge - measure above the inner rotor (A) and above the outer rotor (B)

6   Clean all components with solvent, then inspect them for wear and damage.

7   Remove the oil pressure regulator cap, washer, spring(s) and valve **(see illustration)**. Check the oil pressure regulator valve sliding surface and valve spring. If either the spring or the valve is damaged, they must be replaced as a set. Measure the regulator valve clearance by measuring the outside diameter of the relief valve and subtracting that amount from the inside diameter of the valve opening in the housing. If the clearance exceeds the amount listed in this Chapter's Specifications , replace the pump. Reassemble the oil pressure regulator and tighten the plug to the torque listed in this Chapter's Specifications.

8   Check the clearance of the following oil pump components with a feeler gauge **(see illustrations)** and compare the measure-

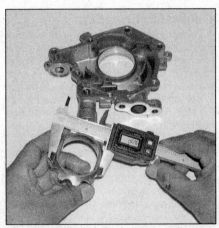

15.8d Use calipers to measure the diameter of the inner rotor ridge (the part of the inner rotor that rides in the pump body). . .

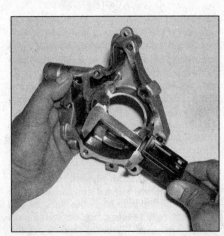

15.8e. . . and subtract the inner rotor ridge diameter from the opening in the pump body where the inner rotor rides to obtain the inner rotor ridge-to-housing clearance

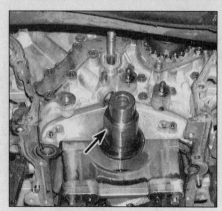

15.11 There is a flat surface on each side of the crankshaft - align them with the flats on the inner gear

16.5 Detach the coolant hoses from the oil cooler

16.6 Remove the oil cooler connector bolt

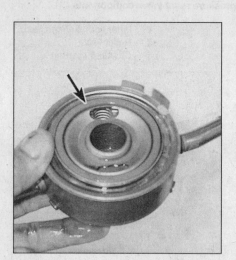

16.8 Install a new O-ring into the groove in the oil cooler

17.4 Hold a lever against a casting protrusion on the engine block or place a screwdriver through a hole in the driveplate to hold the driveplate while the mounting bolts are removed - note the painted marks made at the crank and driveplate for alignment

ments to the clearance listed in this Chapter's Specifications:

   a) *Rotor tooth tip clearance*
   b) *Outer gear-to-body clearance*
   c) *Inner gear-to-housing side clearance*
   d) *Outer gear-to-housing side clearance*
   e) *Inner rotor hub-to-housing clearance*

9   If any clearance is excessive, replace the entire oil pump assembly.
10   Assemble the oil pump and tighten the screws securely. Install the oil pressure regulator valve, spring and washer, then tighten the oil pressure regulator valve cap.
Note: *Pack the pump with grease to prime it.*

Installation

11   Installation is the reverse of removal. Use new gaskets (where applicable) on all disassembled parts. Align the flats on the crankshaft **(see illustration)** with the flats on the oil pump gear. Tighten all fasteners to the torque listed in this Chapter's Specifications.
Note: *Before installing the oil pan, replace the O-rings on the oil pump housing and engine block (see illustration 14.34).*

16   Engine oil cooler and oil filter adapter - general information and replacement

General information

1   These engines are equipped with a combination oil cooler/oil filter adapter that is mounted to the right end of the oil pan. The oil cooler/oil filter adapter also incorporates an oil pressure relief valve, which redirects oil flow to bypass the oil cooler when pressures are too high. The oil cooler has two hoses connecting the cooler to the engine.

Replacement

Warning: *The engine must be completely cool before performing this procedure.*
2   On 2013 and later models, loosen the right-front wheel lug nuts.
3   Raise the front of the vehicle and support it securely on jackstands. On 2012 and earlier models, remove the under-vehicle splash shield. On 2013 and later models, remove the wheel and the inner fender splash shield (see Chapter 11).

4   Drain the cooling system (see Chapter 1).
5   Place rags under the cooler to catch oil and coolant spillage. Detach the hose clamps and disconnect the inlet and outlet hoses from the oil cooler **(see illustration)**.
6   Remove the oil filter and the oil cooler connector bolt **(see illustration)**, then remove the oil cooler and O-ring from the adapter or oil pan.
7   Check the oil cooler for cracks. Also check that the cooler isn't clogged by blowing through the coolant inlet. Check the cooler relief valve for movement, cracks or breaks by pushing on the ball. If damaged, the relief valve can be replaced by prying it out of the cooler. Install a new relief valve by tapping it into place.
8   Lubricate the new oil cooler O-ring with engine oil. Install the O-ring in the groove on the oil cooler **(see illustration)**.
9   Clean all contact surfaces and position the oil cooler onto the adapter (2012 and earlier models) or oil pan (2013 and later models) and install the connector bolt.
10   Tighten the oil cooler connector bolt to the torque listed in this Chapter's Specifications. Do not overtighten.
11   Connect the coolant hoses to the cooler and install the clamps. Install a new oil filter, change the engine oil and refill the cooling system (see Chapter 1).

17   Driveplate - removal and installation

1   2012 and earlier models: Remove the transmission (see Chapter 7A).
2   2013 and later models: Remove the engine/transaxle assembly (see Chapter 2C), then separate the transaxle from the engine (see Chapter 7A).
3   Make alignment marks on the driveplate and crankshaft to ensure correct alignment during reinstallation.
4   Remove the driveplate-to-crankshaft bolts. Hold the driveplate with a prybar or wedge a screwdriver into the ring gear teeth to prevent the crankshaft from turning **(see illustration)**.

18.2 Pry the seal out very carefully with a seal removal tool or screwdriver - if the crankshaft is damaged, the new seal will leak!

18.4 If you don't have a seal installation tool, you can use a blunt tool to carefully work the seal into the bore, evenly and squarely

5   Remove the reinforcement plate and the driveplate from the crankshaft. Since the driveplate is fairly heavy, be sure to support it while removing the last bolt.

6   Clean the driveplate and inspect the it for cracks. Also make sure the signal plate is not loose. Check for cracked and broken ring gear teeth or a loose ring gear. Lay the driveplate on a flat surface and use a straightedge to check for warpage.

Caution: *Don't lay the driveplate on the signal plate side, and keep magnetized material away from the signal plate.*

7   Clean and inspect the mating surfaces of the driveplate and the crankshaft. If the crankshaft rear main oil seal is leaking, replace it before reinstalling the driveplate (see Section 18).

8   Position the driveplate against the crankshaft with the signal plate side facing the engine, and aligning the marks made during removal. Note that some engines have an alignment dowel or staggered bolt holes to ensure correct installation. Before installing the bolts, apply engine oil to the bolt threads and head. Install the reinforcement plate with its rounded or beveled edge against the driveplate.

9   Tighten the bolts to the torque listed in this Chapter's Specifications using the method described in Step 4 to prevent the crankshaft from turning

10   The remainder of installation is the reverse of the removal.

18   Rear main oil seal - replacement

1   Remove the driveplate (see Section 17).

2012 and earlier models

2   Carefully pry the old seal out with a seal removal tool or screwdriver **(see illustration)**.

3   Remove all old sealant from the rear of the engine. Clean the surfaces with brake system cleaner.

4   Apply engine oil to the crankshaft seal journal and the lip of the new seal. Preferably, a seal installation tool should be used to press the new seal into place. If the proper seal installation tool is not available, use a large socket, a section of pipe or a blunt tool to drive the seal into place **(see illustration)**. The lip is stiff, so carefully work it onto the seal journal of the crankshaft. Don't rush it or you may damage the seal.

Note: *Universal seal installation tools are available at many auto parts stores.*

Note: *Install the seal squarely and only until flush with the back of the seal retainer, no further.*

5   The remainder of installation is the reverse of removal.

2013 and later models

6   Remove the upper oil pan (see Section 14).

7   Remove the bolts from the rear seal retainer. Tap the retainer sideways with a plastic hammer to break the seal and remove it. Discard the seal/retainer assembly - it must be replaced with a new one.

8   Remove all old sealant from the rear of the engine and the upper oil pan. Clean the surfaces with brake system cleaner.

9   Apply a bead of RTV sealant to the sealing surface of the new retainer.

10   A special seal installation tool is recommended for use when installing the seal and retainer assembly. It attaches to the crankshaft and guides the lip of the seal up and onto the rear main journal. If the tool cannot be obtained, a substitute can be made from a plastic water bottle; slit the bottle and so it can fit snugly over the end of the crankshaft. Lubricate the seal and the tool with clean engine oil then slide the seal over the tool and onto the crankshaft.

11   Tighten the retainer bolts to the torque listed in this Chapter's Specifications.

12   The remainder of installation is the reverse of removal.

19   Engine mounts - check and replacement

1   2012 and earlier models: There are two engine mounts and one transmission mount installed on the vehicles covered by this manual. The two engine mounts are located on the passenger and driver's side of the vehicle, attached to the engine block and to each frame rail. The transmission mount is mounted to the rear of the transmission and the transmission crossmember. Refer to Chapter 7A for the transmission mount replacement procedure.

2   2013 and later models: There are three engine mounts and one transaxle mount. The engine mounts are located on the passenger's side of the vehicle and on the front and rear side of the engine block. The transaxle mount is bolted to the left side of the transaxle.

Check

3   During the check, the engine must be raised slightly to remove the weight from the mounts.

4   Raise the vehicle and support it securely on jackstands (unless you're checking the right-side mount on a 2013 or later model). Support the engine from above using an engine hoist.

5   Check the mounts to see if the rubber is cracked, hardened or separated from the bushing in the center of the mount.

6   Check for relative movement between the mounts and the engine or frame (use a large screwdriver or prybar to attempt to move the mounts). If movement is noted, lower the engine and tighten the mount fasteners.

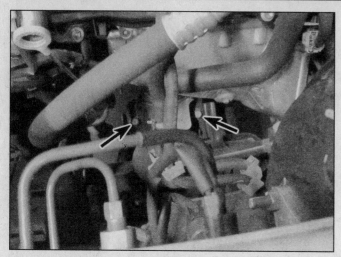

19.9 Engine mount-to-chassis bracket bolts (left side shown, right side similar).

19.12 Lower engine mount bolt

Replacement

2012 and earlier models

7   Disconnect the cable from the negative terminal of the battery (see Chapter 5), set the parking brake and block the rear wheels.

8   If you're removing the left-side engine mount, remove the air filter housing (see Chapter 4).

9   Remove the engine mount-to-chassis bracket bolts **(see illustration)**.

10   Raise the front of the vehicle and support it securely on jackstands.

11   Support the engine from above with an engine hoist.

Caution: *Do not use a jack under the oil pan to support the entire weight of the engine or the oil pump pick-up could be damaged.*

12   Remove the lower engine mount-to-bracket bolt **(see illustration)**.

13   Raise the engine slightly and remove the mount from between its brackets.

14   Installation is the reverse of the removal procedure.

2013 and later models

15   If you're replacing a front or rear engine mount, raise the front of the vehicle and sup-

port it securely on jackstands. Remove the splash shields from under the vehicle.

16   Attach an engine hoist to the engine/transaxle.

Caution: *Do not use a jack under the oil pan to support the entire weight of the engine or the oil pump pick-up could be damaged.*

17   Remove the engine mount-to-chassis fasteners.

18   Remove the engine mount-to-bracket nut.

19   Raise the engine slightly until the engine mount can be removed from the vehicle.

20   Installation is the reverse of removal.

Chapter 2 Part B   V8 engine

Contents

	Section
Camshafts and lifters - removal, inspection and installation	8
Crankshaft front oil seal - replacement	13
Crankshaft pulley - removal and installation	12
Cylinder head - removal and installation	11
Driveplate - removal and installation	17
Engine mounts - check and replacement	19
Engine oil cooler - general information, removal and installation	16
Exhaust manifolds - removal and installation	10
General information	1
Intake manifold - removal and installation	9

	Section
Oil pans - removal and installation	14
Oil pump - removal, inspection and installation	15
Rear main oil seal - replacement	18
Repair operations possible with the engine in the vehicle	2
Timing chains and sprockets - removal, inspection and installation	7
Top Dead Center (TDC) for number one piston - locating	3
Valve clearance - check and adjustment	5
Valve covers - removal and installation	4
Valve springs, retainers and seals - replacement	6

Specifications

General

Engine designation	VK56DE
Displacement	338.80 cubic inches
Bore 3.86 inches	98 mm
Stroke 3.62 inches	92 mm
Cylinder numbers (front to rear)	
Right (passenger's side)	2-4-6-8
Left (driver's side)	1-3-5-7
Firing order	1-8-7-3-6-5-4-2
Cylinder head warpage limit	0.004 inch (0.1 mm)

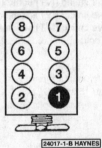

24017-1-B HAYNES

Cylinder location diagram

Camshaft and lifters

Thrust clearance (endplay)	0.0045 to 0.0074 inch (0.114 to 0.188 mm)
Camshaft runout	0.0008 inch (0.02 mm)
Camshaft bearing inside diameter	1.0236 to 1.0244 inches (26.000 to 26.020 mm)
Journal diameter	1.0217 to 1.0224 inches (25.951 to 25.969 mm)
Journal oil clearance	0.0012 to 0.0028 inch (0.030 to 0.071 mm)
Lobe height	
Intake	1.7663 to 1.7738 inches (44.864 to 45.055 mm)
Exhaust	1.7746 to 1.7821 inches (45.075 to 45.265 mm)
Lobe wear limit (all)	0.0008 inch (0.02 mm)
Lifter outside diameter	1.3377 to 1.3381 inches (33.978 to 33.988 mm)
Lifter bore diameter	1.3386 to 1.3392 inches (34.000 to 34.016 mm)
Lifter oil clearance	0.0005 to 0.0015 inch (0.013 to 0.038 mm)
Sprocket runout	less than 0.0059 inch (0.15 mm)

Valve clearance (cold)

Intake 0.010 to 0.013 inch	0.25 to 0.33 mm
Exhaust 0.011 to 0.015 inch	0.28 to 0.38 mm

Oil pump

Outer rotor-to-pump body clearance	0.0045 to 0.0079 inch (0.114 to 0.201 mm)
Inner rotor-to-outer rotor tip clearance (maximum)	0.0071 inch (0.180 mm)
Inner rotor flange-to-pump body clearance	0.0018 to 0.0036 inch (0.046 to 0.091 mm)
Inner rotor side clearance	0.0012 to 0.0028 inch (0.030 to 0.071 mm)
Outer rotor side clearance	0.0012 to 0.0035 inch (0.030 to 0.089 mm)
Regulator valve-to-oil pump body clearance	0.0016 to 0.0038 inch (0.040 to 0.097 mm)

Torque specifications

Note: One foot-pound (ft-lb) of torque is equivalent to 12 inch-pounds (in-lbs) of torque. Torque values below approximately 15 ft-lbs are expressed in inch-pounds, since most foot-pound torque wrenches are not accurate at these smaller values.

	Ft-lbs (unless otherwise indicated)	Nm
Camshaft bearing caps		
Step 1, bolts 9 through 12	17 in-lbs	2
Step 2, bolts 1 through 8	17 in-lbs	2
Step 3, all bolts (in sequence)	52 in-lbs	6
Step 4, all bolts (in sequence)	92 in-lbs	10
Camshaft sprocket bolts		
Intake	76	103
Exhaust*	112	152
Crankshaft pulley-to-crankshaft bolt**		
Step 1	69	94
Step 2	Tighten an additional 90-degrees	
Cylinder head bolts (in sequence)**, ***		
Step 1	33	45
Step 2	Tighten an additional 70-degrees	
Step 3	Loosen all bolts in the reverse order of tightening sequence	
Step 4	33	45
Step 5	Tighten an additional 60-degrees	
Step 6	Tighten an additional 60-degrees	
Drivebelt idler pulley bolt	26	35
Driveplate bolts	65	88
Engine mount		
Insulator bolt	65	88
Mount bracket-to-engine block bolts	36	49
Insulator-to-frame bolts	65	88
Exhaust manifold-to-cylinder head fasteners	25	34
Intake manifold-to-cylinder head bolts	73 in-lbs	8
Intake valve timing (IVT) control solenoid covers	97 in-lbs	11
Intake valve timing (IVT) position solenoid sensor	80 in-lbs	9
Intake valve timing (IVT) solenoid	88 in-lbs	10
Oil cooler bolt	36	49
Oil pan bolts		
Lower (steel) pan	80 in-lbs	9
Upper (aluminum) pan		
Bolts 15 and 16	80 in-lbs	9
All remaining bolts	16	22
Oil pick-up tube/strainer	16	22
Oil pump		
Mounting bolts	96 in-lbs	11
Cover screws	61 in-lbs	7
Pressure regulator valve cap	40	53
Timing chain tensioner bolts	61 in-lbs	7
Timing chain tension and slack guide bolts	144 in-lbs	16
Timing chain cover bolts	96 in-lbs	11
Valve cover bolts		
Step 1	17 in-lbs	2
Step 2	73 in-lbs	8

* Apply engine oil to the bolt threads.
**Apply engine oil to the bot threads and the bolt seating surface.
***Use new fasteners during installation.

1 General information

1   This Part of Chapter 2 is devoted to in-vehicle repair procedures for the 5.6L Dual Overhead Camshaft (DOHC) V8 engine. Information concerning engine removal, installation and overhaul can be found in Chapter 2C.

2   Most of the following repair procedures are based on the assumption that the engine is installed in the vehicle. If the engine has been removed from the vehicle and mounted on a stand, many of the steps outlined in this Part of Chapter 2 will not apply.

2 Repair operations possible with the engine in the vehicle

Note: *Many major repair operations can be accomplished only by removing the engine from the vehicle.*

1   Clean the engine compartment and the exterior of the engine with some type of degreaser before any work is done. It will make the job easier and help keep dirt out of the internal areas of the engine.

2   Depending on the components involved, it may be helpful to remove the hood to improve access to the engine as repairs are performed (see Chapter 11). Cover the fenders to prevent damage to the paint. Special pads are available, but an old bedspread or blanket will also work.

3   If vacuum, exhaust, oil or coolant leaks develop, indicating a need for gasket or seal replacement, the repairs can generally be made with the engine in the vehicle. The intake and exhaust manifold gaskets are accessible with the engine in place, but the upper oil pan gasket and cylinder head gaskets can't be replaced with the engine in the vehicle.

4   Exterior engine components, such as the intake manifolds (see Section 9) and exhaust manifolds (see Section 10), the water pump (see Chapter 3), the starter motor, the alternator (see Chapter 5) and the fuel system components (see Chapter 4) can be removed for repair with the engine in place. Removal of the camshafts and lifters (see Section 8) can be accomplished with the engine in the vehicle.

5   Since the cylinder heads cannot be removed without pulling the engine, valve servicing also requires the engine to be removed from the vehicle. On 2010 and earlier models, replacement of the timing chains and sprockets is also possible only with the engine out of the vehicle.

3 Top Dead Center (TDC) for number one piston - locating

1   Top Dead Center (TDC) is the highest point in the cylinder that each piston reaches as it travels up the cylinder bore. Each piston reaches TDC on the compression stroke and again on the exhaust stroke, but TDC generally refers to piston position on the compression stroke.

2   Positioning the piston(s) at TDC is an essential part of many procedures such as valve clearance checking, and camshaft and timing chain/sprocket removal.

3   Before beginning this procedure, place the transmission/transaxle in Park and apply the parking brake or block the rear wheels. Disconnect the cable from the negative terminal of the battery (see Chapter 5).

4   Install a compression pressure gauge in the number one spark plug hole (see Chapter 2C). It should be a gauge with a screw-in fitting and a hose at least six inches long.

5   Using a socket and long breaker bar or ratchet, rotate the crankshaft clockwise while observing for pressure on the compression gauge. The moment the gauge shows pressure indicates that the number one cylinder has begun the compression stroke.

6   Once the compression stroke has begun, TDC for the compression stroke is reached by bringing the piston to the top of the cylinder.

7   Continue turning the crankshaft until the TDC notch in the crankshaft damper (the only notch that is not painted) is aligned with the pointer on the front cover **(see illustration)**. At this point, the number one cylinder is at TDC on the compression stroke. If the marks are aligned but there was no compression, the piston was on the exhaust stroke. Continue rotating the crankshaft 360-degrees (1-turn).

8   After the number one piston has been positioned at TDC on the compression stroke, TDC for any of the remaining cylinders can be located by turning the crankshaft 90-degrees and following the firing order (see this Chapter's Specifications 0). Rotating the engine 90-degrees past TDC no. 1 will put the engine at TDC compression for cylinder no. 8, another 90 degrees puts cylinder no. 7 at TDC, etc.

4 Valve covers - removal and installation

Removal

1   Disconnect the cable from the negative terminal of the battery (see Chapter 5).

2   Remove the fasteners at the front of the engine cover, and remove the cover **(see illustration)**.

3   Disconnect the PCV hose from the PCV valve in each valve cover.

4   Remove the ignition coils from the valve cover (see Chapter 5). If both valve covers are being removed, remove all eight coils.

5   If you're removing the left valve cover, remove the air filter housing cover for access (see Chapter 4).

6   Detach any wiring or hoses which would interfere with valve cover removal **(see illustration)**.

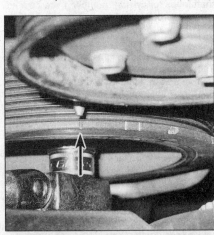

3.7 Align the TDC notch on the crankshaft pulley with the pointer on the timing chain cover - the TDC notch is the one farthest to the left when facing the front of the engine, and is typically the line without color

4.2 Engine cover fastener locations

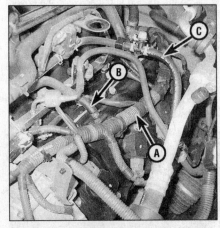

4.6 Disconnect the main harness (A) and the PCV hose (B), then the EVAP purge control solenoid hose (C)

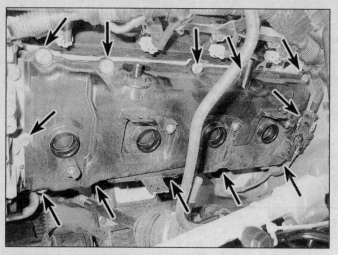

4.7 Remove the valve cover bolts

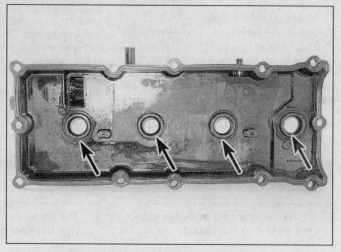

4.11 Install new spark plug tube seals if they're cracked or hardened

7   Remove the valve cover bolts in several steps and in a criss-cross pattern **(see illustration)**.

8   Detach the valve cover and remove the gaskets. Discard the old gaskets. New ones must be used during installation.

Note: *If the cover is stuck to the cylinder head, bump one end with a block of wood and a hammer to jar it loose. If that doesn't work, try to slip a flexible putty knife between the cylinder head and cover to break the gasket seal. Don't pry at the cover-to-cylinder head joint or damage to the sealing surfaces may occur (leading to oil leaks in the future).*

Installation

9   The mating surfaces of each cylinder head and valve cover must be perfectly clean when the covers are installed. Use a gasket scraper to remove all traces of sealant and old gasket material, then clean the mating surfaces with brake cleaner. If there's sealant or oil on the mating surfaces when the cover is installed, oil leaks may develop.

4.12 Apply a thin line of RTV around the gasket groove and press in the new valve cover gasket

10   If necessary, clean the bolt threads with a wire wheel to remove any corrosion. Make sure the threaded holes in the cylinder head are clean.

11   Inspect and replace, if necessary, the spark plug tube seals **(see illustration)**.

12   The valve cover gaskets should be mated to the covers before the covers are installed. Apply a thin coat of RTV sealant to the cover groove and to the corners on the front camshaft journal cap, then position the gasket inside the cover and allow the sealant to set up so the gasket adheres to the cover **(see illustration)**. If the sealant isn't allowed to set, the gasket may fall out of the cover as it's installed on the engine.

13   Carefully position the cover on the cylinder head and install the bolts.

14   Tighten the bolts, in two steps, to the torque listed in this Chapter's Specifications. Start with the bolts in the center of the cover and work outwards in a criss-cross pattern.

15   The remainder of installation is the reverse of removal.

5.5 At TDC for number one cylinder, the intake and exhaust lobes for that cylinder will be pointing outward

16   Start the engine and check for oil leaks.

---

5   Valve clearance - check and adjustment

Note: *The manufacturer recommends checking and, if necessary, adjusting the valve clearance after replacement of the camshaft(s) or other valve-related parts, or if the valve train is making excessive noise.*

1   Disconnect the cable from the negative terminal of the battery (see Chapter 5).

2   Remove the spark plugs (see Chapter 1).

3   Position the number 1 piston at TDC on the compression stroke and align the timing marks (see Section 3).

4   Remove the valve covers (see Section 4).

5   Check that the intake and exhaust camshaft lobes for cylinder number 1 are pointed toward the outside of the cylinder head **(see illustration)**.

6   Measure the clearance of the indicated valves with a feeler gauge **(see illustrations)**. Record each measurement and compare your measurements with the desired valve clearance found in this Chapter's Specifications. Note which are out of specification, as this data will be used later to determine the required replacement lifters.

7   Turn the crankshaft 270 degrees (3/4-turn) clockwise to place cylinder number 3 at TDC. Measure and record the clearances of the indicated valves **(see illustration)**.

8   Turn the crankshaft 90-degrees clockwise (TDC for cylinder number 6). Measure and record the clearances of the indicated valves **(see illustration)**.

9   If a lifter is out of specification, it must be replaced with a new one that has a different thickness head to correct the clearance. Remove the camshafts to access the lifters (see Section 8).

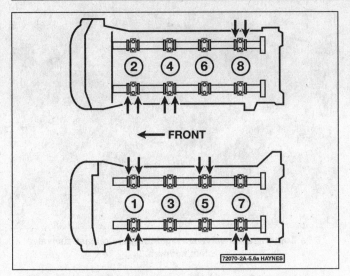

5.6a When the no. 1 piston is at TDC on the compression stroke, the intake valve clearance for the no. 1, no. 2, no. 4 and no. 5 cylinders can be measured, and the exhaust clearance for cylinders no. 1, no. 7 and no. 8 can also be measured

5.6b Measure the clearance for each valve with a feeler gauge of the specified thickness - if the clearance is correct, you should feel a slight drag on the gauge as you pull it out

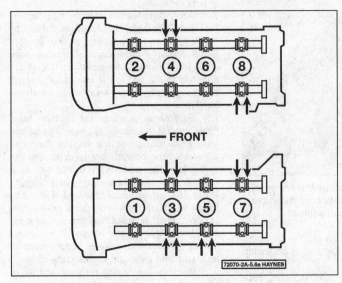

5.7 Turn the crankshaft 270-degrees clockwise (achieving TDC for cylinder no. 3) and check the intake valve clearances for the no. 3, no. 7 and no. 8 cylinders; the exhaust valve clearances can be checked at cylinders no. 3, no. 4 and no. 5

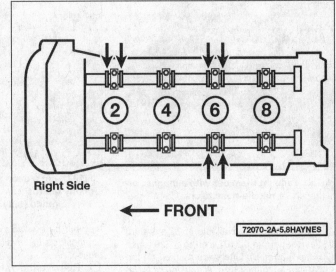

5.8 Turn the crankshaft 90-degrees (1/4-turn) clockwise and check the intake and exhaust valve clearances for cylinder no. 6, and the cylinder no. 2 exhaust valve clearances

10   Mark the lifters that are to be replaced, and record which valve they came from. Use a micrometer to measure the thickness of the lifter in the center, making sure the measurement is precise and on the center projection on the underside of the lifter (see illustration).

11   To calculate the correct thickness for a replacement lifter that will place the valve clearance within the specified value, use the following formula:

$N = R + (M1 - M2)$
N = thickness of new lifter
R = thickness of old lifter
$M1$ = measured valve clearance
$M2$ = standard valve clearance

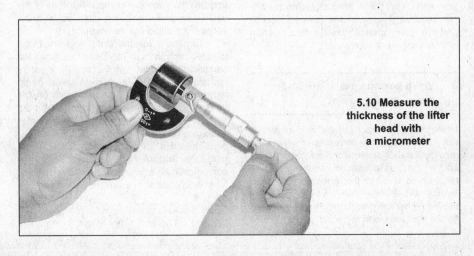

5.10 Measure the thickness of the lifter head with a micrometer

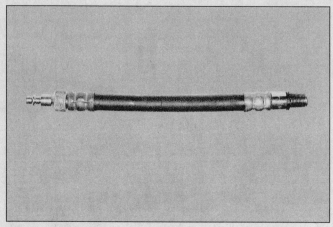

**6.5 The air hose adapter threads into the spark plug hole -
adapters are commonly available from auto parts stores**

**6.7a Compress the valve spring enough to release the valve
stem keepers. . .**

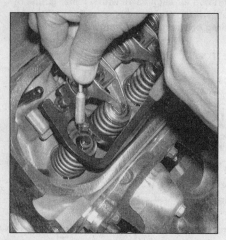

**6.7b. . . and lift them out with a magnet or
needle-nose pliers**

**6.13 Using a deep socket and hammer,
gently tap the new seals onto the valve
guide (only until seated)**

12   New lifters are available in 25 standard thicknesses, from 0.3102 inch to 0.3291 inch (7.88 to 8.36 mm). Lifters are marked on the underside as to their size. A marking of N788 on the underside of the lifter indicates a thickness value of 0.3102 inch (7.88 mm).

13   Mark the new lifters as to their destination, lubricate them with engine assembly lube and install them. After replacing the lifters, reinstall the camshafts (see Section 8) and the timing chains (see Section 7), then re-check the valve clearances.

**6   Valve springs, retainers and
      seals - replacement**

Note: *Broken valve springs and defective valve stem seals can be replaced without removing the cylinder heads. Two special tools and a compressed air source are normally required to perform this operation, so read through this Section carefully. The universal shaft-type valve spring compressor required for the tight valve spring pockets of this vehicle*

may not be available at all tool rental yards, so check on the availability before beginning the job.

1   Remove the valve cover(s) (see Section 4).

2   Remove the camshafts and lifters from the affected cylinder head (see Section 8).

3   Remove the spark plug from the cylinder that has the defective component. If all of the valve stem seals are being replaced, all of the spark plugs should be removed.

4   Turn the crankshaft until the piston in the affected cylinder is at Top Dead Center on the compression stroke (see Section 3). If you're replacing all of the valve stem seals, begin with cylinder number one and work on the valves for one cylinder at a time. Move from cylinder-to-cylinder following the firing order sequence (see this Chapter's Specifications).

5   Thread a long adapter into the spark plug hole and connect an air hose from a compressed air source to it **(see illustration)**. Most auto parts stores can supply the air hose adapter.

Note: *Because of the length of the spark plug tubes, it will be necessary to use a long spark*

plug adapter with a length of hose attached (as used on many cylinder compression gauges), utilizing a quick-disconnect fitting to hook to your air source.

6   Apply compressed air to the cylinder. **Warning:** *The piston may be forced down by the compressed air, causing the crankshaft to turn suddenly. If the wrench used when positioning the number one piston at TDC is still attached to the bolt in the crankshaft nose, it could cause damage or injury when the crankshaft moves.*

7   Stuff shop rags into the cylinder head holes around the valves to prevent parts and tools from falling into the engine, then use a valve spring compressor to compress the spring **(see illustrations)**. Remove the keepers with small needle-nose pliers or a magnet. **Note:** *The valves should be held in place by the air pressure. If the valve faces or seats are in poor condition, leaks may prevent air pressure from retaining the valves. If the valves cannot hold air, the cylinder head should be removed for a valve job at a machine shop.*

8   Remove the spring retainer and valve spring, then remove the valve stem seal.

9   Wrap a rubber band or tape around the top of the valve stem so the valve won't fall into the combustion chamber, then release the air pressure.

10   Inspect the valve stem for damage. Rotate the valve in the guide and check the end for eccentric movement, which would indicate that the valve is bent.

11   Move the valve up-and-down in the guide and make sure it doesn't bind. If the valve stem binds, either the valve is bent or the guide is damaged. In either case, the cylinder head will have to be removed for repair.

12   Reapply air pressure to the cylinder to retain the valve in the closed position, then remove the tape or rubber band from the valve stem.

13   Lubricate the valve stems with engine oil and install new valve stem seals. Valve stem seals can be installed with a special tool, or a deep socket and hammer - tap the seal only until seated **(see illustration)**.

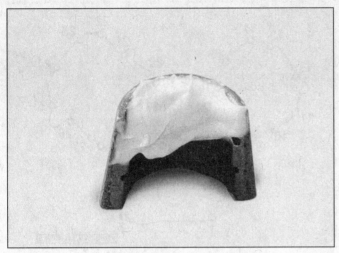

6.15 Apply a small dab of grease to each keeper as shown here before installation - it will hold them in place on the valve stem as the spring is released

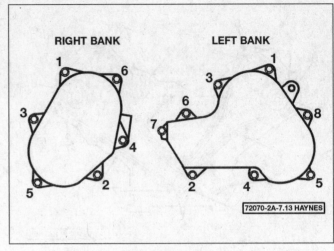

7.14 Upper timing chain covers - loosening and tightening sequence

14   Install the valve spring in position over the valve, with the more closely-wound spring coils and the paint mark toward the cylinder head.

15   Install the valve spring retainer. Compress the valve springs and carefully position the keepers in the groove. Apply a small dab of grease to the inside of each keeper to hold it in place **(see illustration)**.

16   Remove the pressure from the spring tool and make sure the keepers are seated.

17   Disconnect the air hose and remove the adapter from the spark plug hole.

18   Install the camshafts and lifters (see Section 8), then connect the cam sprockets and timing chain (see Section 7).

19   Install the valve covers (see Section 4).

20   Install the spark plug(s) (see Chapter 1) and ignition coils (see Chapter 5).

21   Start and run the engine, then check for oil leaks and unusual sounds coming from the valve cover area.

7   Timing chains and sprockets - removal, inspection and installation

Note: *Timing chain removal and installation on these engines is a difficult procedure for the home mechanic. Great care must be taken to mark the relationship of all parts before disassembly, the length of various bolts and their locations must be noted, and instant or digital photos should be taken for reference as you proceed.*

Removal

Caution: *The timing system is complex. Severe engine damage will occur if you make any mistakes. Do not attempt this procedure unless you are highly experienced with this type of repair. If you are at all unsure of your abilities, consult an expert. Double-check all*

your work and be sure everything is correct before you attempt to start the engine.

Note: *On 2010 and earlier models, the manufacturer states that the engine must be removed from the vehicle to perform this procedure (see Chapter 2C). Make sure you have all the proper equipment and tools before beginning.*

1   Relieve the fuel system pressure (see Chapter 4).

2   Remove the engine cover (see illustration 4.2).

3   Remove the spark plugs (see Chapter 1). Position the number 1 piston at TDC on the compression stroke (see Section 3).

4   Disconnect the cable from the negative terminal of the battery (see Chapter 5).

5   Remove the drivebelt and tensioner (see Chapter 1) and the idler pulley brackets.

6   Disconnect and remove the camshaft position sensor (see Chapter 6).

7   Drain the cooling system and the engine oil (see Chapter 1). Remove the upper and lower radiator hoses, the engine cooling fans and the radiator (see Chapter 3).

8   On 2010 and earlier models, remove the engine (see Chapter 2C).

9   Remove the crankshaft pulley (see Section 12).

Note: *Don't allow the crankshaft to rotate during removal of the pulley. If the crankshaft moves, the number one piston will no longer be at TDC.*

10   Remove the intake manifold (see Section 9) and the valve covers (see Section 4).

11   Remove the thermostat housing and the water hose (see Chapter 3).

12   Remove the upper and lower oil pans (see Section 14), and the oil pump strainer.

13   Remove the Intake Valve Timing (IVT) control position sensors and solenoids (see Chapter 6).

14   Remove the bolts securing the upper timing chain covers (one at the front of each cylinder head) in sequence **(see illustration)**.

Note: *Use a seal cutter to cut the liquid gasket during this procedure.*

15   Remove the front timing chain cover bolts in the reverse of the tightening sequence (see illustration 7.36). Note that three lengths of bolts are used. They must be reinstalled in their original locations. Mark each bolt or make a sketch to ensure they are reinstalled in their original locations. Carefully pry the timing chain cover off the engine, prying only against casting protrusions or the small cutouts provided for this purpose.

Note: *Use a seal cutter to cut the liquid gasket during this procedure.*

16   Slide the oil pump drive spacer from the front of the crankshaft, then remove the oil pump (see Section 15).

17   Confirm that the number one piston is still at TDC on the compression stroke by verifying that the intake and exhaust camshaft lobes on the number one cylinder are pointing outward towards the edge of the cylinder head (see illustration 5.5).

18   Relieve tension on the left timing chain tensioner by squeezing the two clips on the tensioner while pushing the plunger into the tensioner body, then insert a holding pin (a large paper clip will work). Remove the tensioner.

Caution: *Use care when handling a tensioner while the plunger is secured by the pin. If the pin slips out, your fingers could be injured by the sudden release of the plunger.*

19   Remove the left-hand tensioner guide and slack guide, keeping track of the bolts used.

20   Remove the left-hand timing chain and crankshaft sprocket.

21   Remove the left intake and exhaust camshaft sprockets, using a wrench to hold the hex portion of the camshaft while loosening the sprocket bolt.

Caution: *Do not allow the camshafts to rotate at all during this procedure.*

22   Repeat Steps 17 through 21 for the right-

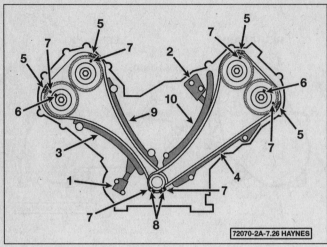

7.27 Timing chain details

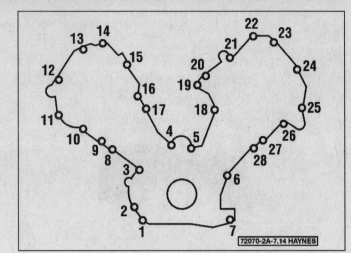

7.36 Front timing chain cover bolt tightening sequence

1   Right chain tensioner
2   Left chain tensioner
3   Right chain slack guide
4   Left chain tensioner guide
5   Copper colored chain links
6   Dowel pins
7   Identification marks
    (align with colored chain
    links)
8   Gold or yellow colored
    chain links
9   Right chain tensioner guide
10 Left chain slack guide

hand tensioner, chain and sprockets. Mark each camshaft sprocket with its location - left or right, intake or exhaust. Do not mix up the sprockets; they must be reinstalled in their original locations. Also mark the camshafts with their location, such as "LI" for left intake and "LE" for left exhaust.

Inspection

23   Inspect the camshaft and crankshaft sprockets for wear on the teeth and keyways. Inspect the chains for cracks or excessive wear of the rollers. Inspect the facing of the chain guides for excessive wear.

Installation

Caution: *Before starting the engine, carefully rotate the crankshaft by hand through at least two full revolutions (use a socket and breaker bar on the crankshaft pulley center bolt). If you feel anyresistance, STOP! There is something wrong -most likely, valves are contacting the pistons. You must find the problem before proceeding. Check your work and see if any updated repair information is available.*
24   Verify that you have the correct timing chains for your vehicle by counting the number of links each chain has and comparing the new chains with the old chains. Also compare the position of the colored links in the new chains with the position of the colored links in the old chains.
25   Install the crankshaft sprocket for the right timing chain, with the flange closest to the engine, followed by the crankshaft sprocket for the left timing chain, with its flange facing the end of the crankshaft. The keyway in the crankshaft should still be at a 45-degree angle from the 12 o'clock position, pointing up

towards the center of the left (driver's side) cylinder head.
26   Install the camshaft sprockets, then tighten the bolts to the torque listed in this Chapter's Specifications. Hold the camshafts with a wrench placed on the hex portion of the shafts.
Caution: *Don't allow the camshafts to turn at all when tightening the bolts.*
27   Install the timing chain for the right cylinder bank, aligning the copper-colored marks with the alignment marks on the camshaft sprockets, and the gold or yellow-colored marks with the alignment mark on the inner crankshaft sprocket **(see illustration)**.
Note: *It may be necessary to rotate the camshafts slightly to align the copper-colored chain links with the marks on the camshaft sprockets.*
28   Install the right-side slack guide, tension guide and chain tensioner in their original positions. Tighten the mounting fasteners to the torque listed in this Chapter's Specifications. If the chain tensioner cover was removed, apply RTV sealant around the cover and install the bolts securely.
29   Make sure the colored links are still aligned with their corresponding marks on the sprockets, then remove the holding pin from the timing chain tensioner.
30   Repeat Steps 26 through 28 to install the timing chain for the left cylinder bank.
31   Install the oil pump (see Section 15).
32   Install the oil pump drive spacer, with the front mark (a small triangle) facing out, and the keyway aligned with the crankshaft Woodruff key.
Note: *If the spacer won't slide into place, rotate the inner rotor of the oil pump as neces-*

sary to achieve alignment.
33   Remove all traces of old sealant from the front timing chain cover, the cover bolts and the rear cover bolt holes.
34   Install new O-rings wherever they were used originally, on the block and/or the back of the timing covers. Lubricate the O-rings with clean engine oil before pushing them into their recesses.
35   The front oil seal should also be replaced at this time. Use a seal removal tool to pull the seal out of the cover. Then, lubricate the seal with new engine oil and use a seal driver or suitably sized socket to install a new front oil seal into the front cover.
36   Apply a 1/8-inch (3 mm) diameter bead of RTV sealant to the timing cover sealing surfaces. Place the timing chain cover in position on the engine and install the bolts in their original locations. Tighten the bolts, in sequence **(see illustration)**, to the torque listed in this Chapter's Specifications. After tightening to the specified torque, re-tighten a second time to the specified torque.
Note: *Failure to tighten to the specified torque a second time can result in leaks.*
Note: *Wipe off excessive sealant and then follow the sealant manufacturer's recommendations for assembly and sealant curing times. Allow all sealant to fully cure before starting the engine.*
37   Install RTV sealant to the Intake Valve Timing (IVT) control solenoid covers and install the bolts in a criss-cross pattern and tighten them to the torque listed in this Chapter's Specifications 0. If the IVT solenoids or valves were removed, install them (see Chapter 6).
38   Install the upper timing chain covers,

8.11 The camshaft bearing caps should be marked with a number and letter to ensure correct reinstallation

8.12 Front camshaft bearing cap details (left side shown, right side similar)

A   Timing chain cover-to-front camshaft bearing cap bolts (lower bolt not visible; vicinity given)
B   Front camshaft bearing cap-to-cylinder head bolts

and tighten the bolts, in sequence (see illustration 7.13), to the torque listed in this Chapter's Specifications.
39   Install the crankshaft pulley, tightening the bolt to the torque listed in this Chapter's Specifications.
40   Turn the engine over by hand at least two revolutions (clockwise) to make sure the engine rotates freely. If you feel any resistance, STOP and find out why.
41   Install a new oil filter (see Chapter 1), then reinstall the engine, if removed (see Chapter 2C).
42   Refill the crankcase with oil and the cooling system with coolant (see Chapter 1).
43   Start the engine and check for leaks.

8   Camshafts and lifters - removal, inspection and installation

Removal

1   Disconnect the cable from the negative terminal of the battery (see Chapter 5).
2   Remove the valve covers (see Section 4).
3   Position the number 1 piston at TDC on the compression stroke (see Section 3).
4   Disconnect and remove the camshaft position sensor (see Chapter 6).
5   Disconnect and remove the Intake Valve Timing (IVT) control solenoid and the sensor (see Chapter 6) from the IVT cover. Then, remove the bolts securing the cover in a criss-cross pattern and in several steps and remove the cover. It might be necessary to cut the RTV sealant with a gasket remover. Be careful not to damage the mating surfaces.
6   Remove the upper timing chain covers (see Section 7).
7   Mark the relationship of the timing chains to the marks on the camshaft sprockets. The

8.14a Pull straight up to remove each lifter

locations of the camshaft sprocket marks are shown in illustration 7.26.
8   Retract and remove the left timing chain tensioner (see Section 7).
9   At the lower right of the main timing cover, remove the bolts and the cover providing access to remove the right chain tensioner. There isn't much room behind the cover to retract and pin this tensioner, so you may have to remove it by unbolting it and angling it out with the plunger extended.
10   Unbolt the camshaft sprockets from the camshafts (see Section 7). Mark each sprocket before removal so you don't mix up the sprockets. Disengage the camshaft sprockets from the timing chains and remove them.
Caution: Do not allow the camshafts to rotate at all during this procedure.
Caution: Don't let the timing chains fall down into the timing chain cover. Support them with wire.
11   Mark the positions of the camshaft bearing caps, and with an "I" or an "E," to indicate

8.14b The lifters can be stored in individually marked plastic bags or a divided box as shown

intake or exhaust. Also mark arrows indicating the front of the engine (see illustration). Loosen the camshaft bearing caps in two or three steps, in the reverse of the tightening sequence (see illustration 8.26).
Caution: Keep the caps in order; they must be reinstalled in their original locations.
12   Remove the timing chain cover-to-front camshaft bearing cap bolts (see illustration). Remove the front camshaft bearing cap-to-cylinder head bolts, in the reverse of the tightening sequence (see illustration 8.26). These caps will be stuck to the RTV sealant, so carefully use a plastic hammer to knock them loose.
13   Remove the camshafts. Mark them or store them separately so they can be returned to their original locations.
14   Remove the lifters from the cylinder head, keeping track of where they were installed (see illustrations).
Caution: Keep the lifters in order; they must be reinstalled in their original locations.

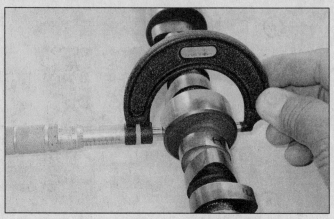

8.16 Measure each journal diameter with a micrometer - if any journal measures less than the specified limit, replace the camshaft

8.17 Measure the lobe heights on each camshaft - if any lobe height is less than the specified allowable minimum, replace that camshaft

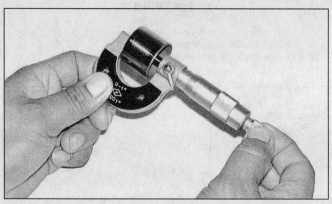

8.20 Measure the diameter of each lifter and compare it to Specifications

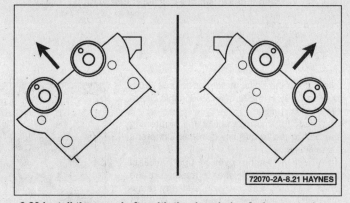

72070-2A-8.21 HAYNES

8.23 Install the camshafts with the dowel pins facing up and at a 90-degree angle to the cylinder head surface

Inspection

15   With the camshafts removed, visually check the camshaft bearing surfaces in the cylinder head for pitting, score marks, galling and abnormal wear. If the bearing surfaces are damaged, the cylinder head may have to be replaced.

16   Measure the outside diameter of each camshaft bearing journal and record your measurements **(see illustration)**. Then measure the inside diameter of each corresponding camshaft bearing and record the measurements. Subtract each cam journal outside diameter from its respective cam bearing bore inside diameter to determine the oil clearance for each bearing. Compare the results to the specified journal-to-bearing clearance. If any of the measurements fall outside the standard specified wear limits listed in this Chapter's Specifications, replace the camshaft and/or the cylinder head.

17   Using a micrometer, measure the height of each camshaft lobe **(see illustration)**. Compare your measurements with this Chapter's Specifications. If the height for any one lobe is less than the specified minimum, replace the camshaft.

18   Check the camshaft runout by placing the camshaft back into the cylinder head and

set up a dial indicator on the center journal. Zero the dial indicator. Turn the camshaft slowly and note the dial indicator readings. If the measured runout exceeds the runout listed in this Chapter's Specifications, replace the camshaft. Also use the dial indicator to check the camshaft sprocket runout. If runout exceeds the amount listed in this Chapter's Specifications, replace the sprocket.

19   Also, while the camshaft is sitting in the cylinder head, check the endplay. Install the bearing caps and tighten them securely. Mount a dial indicator with the plunger of the dial indicator in line with and touching the end of the camshaft. Gently pry the camshaft fully toward the gauge, zero the gauge, then pry the camshaft fully away from the gauge and note the gauge reading. If the measured endplay is at or beyond the service limit listed in this Chapter's Specification, replace the camshaft and check the endplay again. If the endplay is still excessive, replace the cylinder head.

20   Inspect each lifter for scuffing and score marks. Measure the outside diameter of each lifter **(see illustration)** and the corresponding lifter bore inside diameter. Subtract the lifter diameter from the lifter bore diameter to determine the oil clearance. Compare it to this

Chapter's Specifications. If the oil clearance is excessive, a new cylinder head and/or new lifters will be required.

Installation

21   Lubricate the lifters with clean engine oil and install them in their original locations.

22   Apply camshaft installation lubricant to the camshaft lobes and journals.

23   Install the camshafts in their original positions with the dowel pins facing up (180-degrees from the cylinder head mating surface) and in line with the cylinder bank **(see illustration)**.

24   Apply a bead of RTV sealant to the sealing surfaces of the front camshaft bearing caps and where they mate with the timing chain covers.

25   Install the bearing caps and bolts and the front cover-to-bearing cap bolts and tighten them hand tight.

26   Tighten the bearing cap bolts in several steps, to the torque listed in this Chapter's Specifications , using the proper tightening sequence **(see illustration)**. Then tighten the front cover-to-bearing cap bolts to the torque listed in this Chapter's Specifications 0. Carefully wipe up any excessive sealant once the caps are installed.

27   Engage the timing chains with the cam-

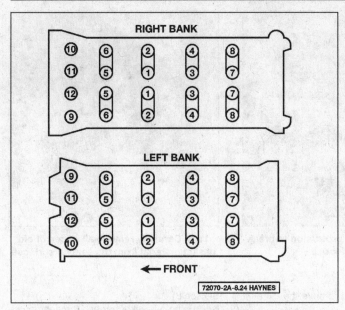

8.26 Camshaft bearing cap bolt TIGHTENING sequence

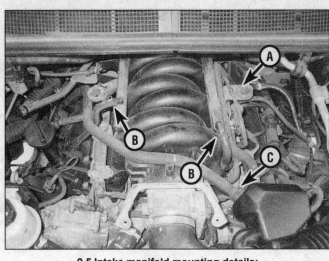

9.5 Intake manifold mounting details:

A   EVAP purge control solenoid
B   PCV hoses
C   Hose to the intake air resonator

9.7 Remove the intake manifold bolts (left side shown)

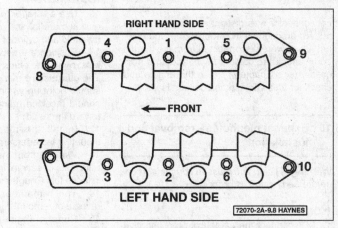

9.9 Intake manifold bolt TIGHTENING sequence

shaft sprockets, aligning the marks made in Step 5, being careful not to let the chain drop down into the timing chain cover. Install the camshaft sprocket bolts, tightening them to the torque listed in this Chapter's Specifications while preventing the camshafts from turning by holding them with a wrench placed on the hex portion of the shaft.

Caution: *Do not allow the camshafts to rotate at all during this procedure.*

28   The remainder of installation is the reverse of removal. If any part of the valve train was replaced, check and adjust the valve clearance (see Section 5).

9   Intake manifold - removal and installation

Warning: *Wait until the engine is completely cool before beginning this procedure.*

Note: *Disconnecting the electrical connector at the throttle body and later reconnecting it will*

cause the engine management system to require the throttle valve closed position relearn procedure to be performed (see Chapter 5). To avoid having to perform this procedure during removal or installation of the plenum, you can unbolt the throttle body from the plenum with the connector in place and set the throttle body aside carefully.

1   Relieve the fuel system pressure (see Chapter 4). With the engine cool, partially drain the coolant (see Chapter 1).

2   Disconnect the cable from the negative terminal of the battery (see Chapter 5).

3   Remove the air intake duct (see Chapter 4) and the engine cover **(see illustration 4.2)**.

4   Remove the throttle body, then remove the fuel rails and fuel injectors (see Chapter 4).

Warning: *If you're removing the throttle body completely, wait until the engine is completely cool, then pinch-off the coolant hoses leading to the throttle body before disconnecting them.*

5   Label and disconnect any hoses and harnesses that may be attached to the intake manifold **(see illustration)**. See the Note at the beginning of this Section.

6   Remove the fuel injectors and fuel rail (see Chapter 4).

7   Loosen and remove the intake manifold fasteners **(see illustration)** in the reverse of the tightening sequence **(see illustration 9.9)** and remove the manifold.

8   Clean the mounting surfaces of the intake manifold and the ports on the cylinder heads with brake system cleaner, removing all traces of the old gasket material or sealant. Install new gaskets on the intake manifold and position the manifold on the engine. There are eight individual gaskets for the manifold, one for each intake port.

9   Tighten the fasteners in several steps, in sequence **(see illustration)**, to the torque listed in this Chapter's Specifications.

10   The remainder of installation is the reverse of removal. If the throttle body electri-

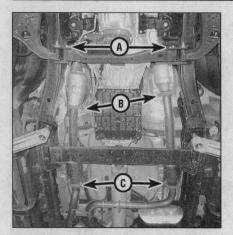

10.4 Exhaust manifold removal details

A   Front crossmember fasteners
B   Front exhaust pipe-to-catalytic
     converter flanges
C   Front exhaust pipe-to-rear exhaust
     pipe flanges

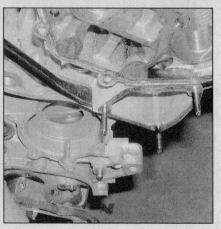

**11.7 Pry on a casting protrusion to break
the head loose**

**11.10 Carefully remove all traces of old
gasket material from the sealing surfaces**

cal connector was disconnected, perform the
relearn procedures in Chapter 5 . If the coolant hoses were disconnected from the throttle
body, check the coolant level, adding if necessary (see Chapter 1). Run the engine and
check for fuel, vacuum and coolant leaks.

---

10 Exhaust manifolds - removal and installation

Warning: *The engine must be completely cool
before beginning this procedure.*

Removal

1   Disconnect the cable from the negative
terminal of the battery (see Chapter 5). Disconnect the oxygen sensor electrical connector(s),
located at the rear of the valve cover(s).
2   Block the rear wheels and set the parking brake. Loosen the front wheel lug nuts.
3   Raise the front of the vehicle and support it securely on jackstands. Remove the
wheels, under-vehicle splash shield and the
fenderwell liners (see Chapter 11).
4   Apply penetrating oil to the exhaust fasteners and allow it to soak in. Remove the
front exhaust pipe(s) **(see illustration)**. If you
can't move the center and rear exhaust pipes
to the rear far enough to allow removal of the
front pipes, they will have to be removed.
5   Remove the oxygen sensor(s) (see
Chapter 6).
6   Support the engine from above and
remove the engine mount insulators and
brackets (see Section 19).
7   If you're removing the right-side exhaust
manifold, remove the dipstick and dipstick
tube.
8   Unbolt the exhaust heat shields from the
exhaust manifolds.
9   Remove the manifold-to-cylinder head

mounting fasteners and remove the exhaust
manifold.

Installation

10   Use a scraper to remove all traces of old
gasket material and carbon deposits from the
manifold and cylinder head mating surfaces.
11   Position the new exhaust manifold gaskets over the studs on the cylinder head.
The gaskets are marked with an arrow which
should point up when installed. The marking
should face the manifold side (outward, not
toward the head).
12   Install the manifold and thread the
mounting fasteners into place.
13   Working from the center out, tighten the
nuts/bolts in several increments, to the torque
listed in this Chapter's Specifications.
14   The remainder of installation is the
reverse of removal.
15   Run the engine and check for exhaust
leaks.

---

11 Cylinder head - removal and installation

Warning: *The engine must be completely cool
before beginning this procedure.*
Note: *The engine must be removed from the
vehicle for the following procedure. Make sure
you have the proper tools and equipment before beginning.*

Removal

1   Remove the timing chains and sprockets
(see Section 7).
Caution: *Be careful not to disturb the crankshaft from TDC on the compression stroke of
the No. 1 cylinder during the remainder of this
procedure.*
2   Remove the intake and exhaust manifolds (see Sections 9 and 10).
3   Remove the upper and lower oil pans
(see Section 14).
4   Remove the timing chain (see Section 7).
5   Remove the camshafts and lifters (see

Section 8).
6   Using a breaker bar and the appropriate
sized Allen-head socket, loosen the cylinder
head bolts in 1/4-turn increments until they
can be removed by hand. Loosen the bolts in
the reverse of the tightening sequence (see
illustration 11.18) to avoid warping or cracking
the head. Discard the bolts and obtain new
ones for reassembly.
7   Lift the cylinder head off the engine
block. If it's stuck, very carefully pry up at a
casting protrusion, beyond the gasket surface
(see illustration).
8   Remove all external components from
the head to allow for thorough cleaning and
inspection.

Installation

9   The mating surfaces of the cylinder head
and block must be perfectly clean when the
head is installed.
10   Use a gasket scraper to remove all
traces of carbon and old gasket material from
the cylinder head and engine block, then
clean the mating surfaces with brake system
cleaner **(see illustration)**. If there's oil on the
mating surfaces when the head is installed,
the gasket may not seal correctly and leaks
could develop. When working on the block,
stuff the cylinders with clean shop rags to
keep out debris. Use a vacuum cleaner to
remove material that falls into the cylinders.
11   Check the block and head mating surfaces for nicks, deep scratches and other
damage. If damage is slight, it can be removed
with a file; if it's excessive, machining may be
the only alternative.
12   Use a tap of the correct size to chase the
threads in the head bolt holes, then clean the
holes with compressed air to make sure that
nothing remains in the holes.
Warning: *Wear eye protection when using
compressed air!*
13   Check the gasket surface on the head,
and the intake and exhaust manifold surfaces
for any signs of damage, corrosion, cracks
or surface irregularities. Use a straight edge

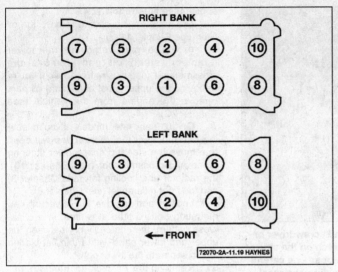

11.18 Cylinder head bolt TIGHTENING sequence

12.4 Lower splash shield mounting fasteners

to check for cylinder warpage. If warpage is beyond the amount listed in this Chapter's Specifications, replace the head.

14 Install any components that were removed from the head.

15 Position the new cylinder head gasket over the dowel pins on the block, noting which side of the gasket faces up.

16 Carefully set the head on the block without disturbing the gasket.

17 Before installing the NEW cylinder head bolts, apply a small amount of clean engine oil to the threads and the underside of the bolt heads.

18 Install the cylinder head bolts and tighten them finger tight. Tighten all the bolts, in sequence **(see illustration)**, to the torque steps listed in this Chapter's Specifications.

19 Remove all traces of old sealant from the rear timing chain cover and the cover bolts.

20 Apply a bead of RTV sealant to the timing chain cover sealing surfaces on the block and heads. Install new O-rings in the front of the engine block and timing chain covers.

21 Install the camshafts (see Section 8), then install the timing chains and sprockets (see Section 7). The remainder of installation is the reverse of removal. If any part of the valve train was replaced, check and adjust the valve clearance (see Section 5).

22 After the engine has been installed, change the engine oil filter, then add oil and coolant (see Chapter 1).

23 Start the engine and check for oil and coolant leaks.

12 Crankshaft pulley - removal and installation

1 Disconnect the cable from the negative terminal of the battery (see Chapter 5).

2 Block the rear wheels and set the parking brake. Drain the cooling system (see Chapter 1).

13.2 Pry the seal out very carefully with a seal removal tool or screwdriver, being careful not to nick or gouge the seal bore or the crankshaft

3 Raise the front of the vehicle and support it securely on jackstands.

4 Remove the lower splash shield if equipped **(see illustration)**.

5 Remove the engine cooling fan and fan shroud (see Chapter 3).

6 Remove the drivebelt (see Chapter 1).

7 Remove the starter and have an assistant wedge a large screwdriver into the ring gear teeth to prevent the engine from rotating. Unscrew the crankshaft pulley bolt.

8 Make alignment marks to help with installation, then remove the pulley. If the pulley is difficult to remove, use a puller that bolts to the hub of the pulley to remove it. The proper spacer should be used between the puller screw and the end of the crankshaft to prevent damage to the crankshaft.

Caution: *DO NOT use a puller with jaws that grip around the outside of the crankshaft pulley or damage to the pulley will occur.*

Note: *Depending on the length of puller you have, it may also be necessary to remove the radiator to gain sufficient clearance to use the puller.*

9 To install the crankshaft pulley, align the

pulley groove with the key on the crankshaft and slide the pulley onto the crankshaft.

10 Apply engine oil to the the crankshaft pulley retaining bolt threads and seating area and tighten it to the torque listed in this Chapter's Specifications.

11 The remainder of installation is the reverse of removal.

13 Crankshaft front oil seal - replacement

1 Remove the crankshaft pulley (see Section 12).

2 Carefully pry the seal out of the cover with a seal removal tool or a large screwdriver **(see illustration)**.

Caution: *Be careful not to scratch, gouge or distort the area that the seal fits into or an oil leak will develop.*

3 Clean the bore to remove any old seal material and corrosion. Position the new seal in the bore with the seal lip (usually the side with the spring) facing IN (toward the engine).

13.4 Use a seal driver to drive the new seal into the cover

14.13 Insert a flat-head screwdriver or small prybar into the notch on the side of the oil pan to break it loose - be careful not to damage the sealing surfaces!

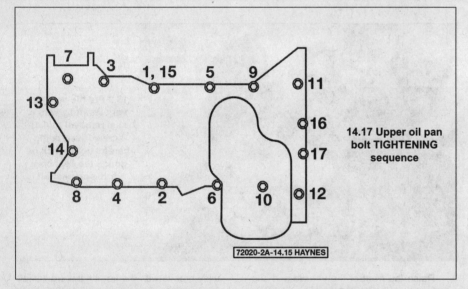

14.17 Upper oil pan bolt TIGHTENING sequence

72020-2A-14.15 HAYNES

A small amount of oil applied to the outer edge and inner lip of the new seal will make installation easier.

4 Drive the seal into the bore with a seal driver or a large socket and hammer until it's completely seated **(see illustration)**. Select a socket that's the same outside diameter as the seal, and make sure the new seal is pressed into place until it bottoms against the cover flange.

5 Check the surface of the crankshaft pulley that the oil seal rides on. If the surface has been grooved from long-time contact with the seal, the crankshaft pulley should be replaced.

6 Lubricate the seal lips with engine oil and reinstall the crankshaft pulley. Apply engine oil to the crankshaft pulley retaining bolt threads and tighten it to the torque listed in this Chapter's Specifications.

7 The remainder of installation is the reverse of the removal. Run the engine and check for oil leaks.

14 Oil pans - removal and installation

Warning: *The engine must be completely cool before beginning this procedure.*
Note: *On 2010 and earlier models, the engine must be removed from the vehicle to remove the upper (cast aluminum) oil pan. If you are just removing the lower (stamped steel) oil pan, ignore the steps which don't apply. On 2011 and 2012 models, the upper pan can be removed without removing the engine but it is easier and faster to remove the engine.*

Removal

1 Disconnect the cable from the negative terminal of the battery (see Chapter 5).
2 Set the parking brake and block the rear wheels.
3 Raise the front of the vehicle and support it securely on jackstands.
4 Remove the splash shields under the

engine **(see illustration 12.4)**.
5 Drain the engine oil and remove the oil filter (see Chapter 1).
6 If you're only removing the lower (stamped steel) oil pan, remove the crossmember (see illustration 10.4). If you're removing the upper (cast aluminum) oil pan, remove the engine from the vehicle (see Chapter 2C).
7 On 2012 and later models, if you're leaving the engine in the vehicle, you will need to remove the steering gear, power steering pump and crossmember (see Chapter 10), the radiator and cooling fan (see Chapter 3) and the front differential (see Chapter 8).
8 Loosen and remove the lower oil pan mounting bolts a little at a time, in a criss-cross pattern, then carefully pry between the upper and lower pans with a thin flat-bladed tool to separate the lower pan.
9 Remove the oil pick-up tube/strainer from the upper oil pan.
10 To remove the upper pan (also referred to as the lower block support), disconnect the hoses and remove the oil cooler (see Section 16).
11 Remove the engine oil dipstick, the dipstick tube and the oil pump screen (accessible once the lower pan is removed).
12 Remove the upper pan mounting bolts in the reverse of the tightening sequence **(see illustration 14.17)**.
13 To loosen the upper oil pan from the block, wedge a flat head screwdriver or thin prybar into the notches on the side of the oil pan, being careful not to damage the sealing surfaces of the oil pan or engine block **(see illustration)**.

Installation

14 Use a scraper to remove all traces of old gasket material and sealant from the upper aluminum section of the oil pan, the lower steel pan and the engine block. Clean the mating surfaces with brake cleaner.
Caution: *Be careful not to scratch or gouge the gasket surface of the block or oil pan. A leak could develop after the repairs have been completed.*
15 Make sure the threaded bolt holes in the block and aluminum section of the oil pan are clean.
16 Apply a bead of RTV sealant to the ends of the timing chain cover and the rear oil seal retainer. Install new O-rings at the front cover and oil pump, lubricated with engine oil. Apply a bead of RTV sealant around the upper aluminum oil pan flange.
Note: *Once the sealant has been applied, the oil pan must be installed within 15 minutes.*
17 Carefully position the upper aluminum oil pan on the engine block and install the bolts. Tighten the fasteners in three or four steps, in sequence **(see illustration)**, to the torque listed in this Chapter's Specifications.
18 Reinstall the oil pick-up tube/strainer and tighten the bolts to the torque listed in this Chapter's Specifications. Reinstall any upper pan bolts that were accessible only with the

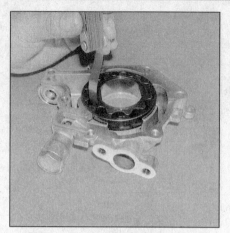

15.7a Use feeler gauges to measure the rotor tooth tip clearance. . .

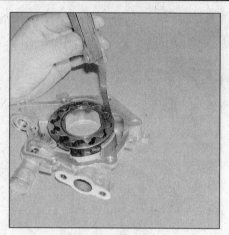

15.7b. . . and the outer rotor-to-body clearance

15.7c Measure the cover-to-rotor end clearance with a straightedge and feeler gauge - measure above the inner rotor (A) and above the outer rotor (B)

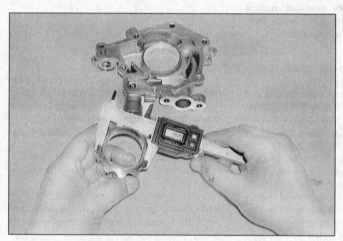

15.7d Use calipers to measure the diameter of the inner rotor ridge (the part of the inner rotor that rides in the pump body). . .

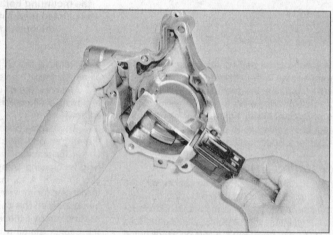

15.7e. . . and subtract the inner rotor ridge diameter from the opening in the pump body where the inner rotor rides to obtain the inner rotor ridge-to-body clearance

lower pan removed.

19   Check the lower steel oil pan flange for distortion, particularly around the bolt holes. If necessary, place the pan on a wood block and use a hammer to flatten and restore the gasket surface.

20   Apply a bead of RTV sealant around the lower oil pan flange and install the pan. Tighten the fasteners a little at a time, in a criss-cross pattern, to the torque listed in this Chapter's Specifications.

Note: *Once the sealant has been applied, the oil pan must be installed within 15 minutes.*

21   The remainder of installation is the reverse of removal. Install a new oil filter (see Chapter 1) and wait at least one hour before adding oil.

15   Oil pump - removal, inspection and installation

Note: *On 2009 and earlier models, the engine must be removed for this procedure (see Chapter 2C). On 2010 and later models, the*

oil pump can be removed without removing the engine.

Removal

1   On 2009 and earlier models, remove the engine (see Chapter 2C).

2   Remove the timing chain covers (see Section 7) and the oil pans (see Section 14).

3   Slide the oil pump drive spacer from the crankshaft. If the pump is to be disassembled, use a large Phillips screwdriver to loosen (but not remove) the oil pump cover screws.

4   Remove the oil pump mounting bolts and detach the pump from the engine.

Inspection

5   Remove the screws and pump cover, then lift out the rotors. Clean all components with solvent, then inspect them for wear and damage.

6   Remove the oil pressure regulator cap, washer, spring(s) and valve. Check the oil pressure regulator valve sliding surface and valve spring. If either the spring or the valve is damaged, they must be replaced as a set.

7   Check the clearance of the oil pump components **(see illustrations)** and compare the measurements to the clearance listed in this Chapter's Specifications. If any clearance is excessive, replace the entire oil pump as an assembly.

8   Check the regulator valve clearance by removing the regulator plug and removing the spring and the valve. Measure the valve hole inner diameter and the outside diameter of the valve. Subtract the valve measurement from the hole diameter. If the regulator valve-to-oil pump cover clearance is greater than the amount listed in this Chapter's Specifications , then measure the specification using a new valve. If a new valve doesn't correct the specification, then a new oil pump will be needed. Lubricate the valve and spring with clean engine oil and install it into the pump body and tighten the cap to the torque listed in this Chapter's Specifications.

9   Lubricate the oil pump rotors with clean engine oil, then install them in the pump body with the marks facing out. Pack the voids in the pump with petroleum jelly to prime it.

16.5 Remove the oil cooler mounting bolt

17.3 Hold a lever against a casting protrusion on the engine block or place a screwdriver through a hole in the driveplate to hold the driveplate while the mounting bolts are removed - note the painted marks made at the crank and driveplate for alignment

18.2 Pry the seal out very carefully with a seal removal tool or screwdriver - if the crankshaft is damaged, the new seal will leak!

Install the cover and tighten the screws to the torque listed in this Chapter's Specifications.

10   Lubricate the pressure regulator valve with clean engine oil. Install the valve, spring and washer, then tighten the oil pressure regulator valve cap to the torque listed in this Chapter's Specifications.

Installation

11   Install the oil pump drive spacer, with the front mark (a small triangle) facing out, and the keyway aligned with the crankshaft Woodruff key. Install the oil pump, aligning the flats on the inner rotor with the flats on the oil pump drive spacer. You may have to rotate the inner rotor slightly to align the flats. Install the oil pump bolts and tighten them to the torque listed in this Chapter's Specifications.

12   The remainder of installation is the reverse of removal.

16   Engine oil cooler - general information, removal and installation

General information

1   These engines are provided extra cooling by an oil cooler, which is incorporated into an adapter mounted at the front of the oil pan. The oil cooler has two hoses connecting the cooler to the engine, where oil temperature is lowered by the engine coolant.

Removal and installation

Warning: *The engine must be completely cool before beginning this procedure.*

2   Drain the engine oil and the cooling system (see Chapter 1).

3   Mark the hoses, then detach the hose clamps and remove the inlet and outlet hoses from the oil cooler.

4   Remove the oil filter from the oil cooler assembly (see Chapter 1).

5   Unscrew the oil cooler retaining bolt and remove the oil cooler and O-rings **(see illustration).**

6   Thoroughly clean the mating surfaces of the oil pan and the oil cooler. Check the oil cooler for cracks. Check the cooler for clogging by blowing compressed air through the coolant inlet. Also, inspect the relief valve in the cooler for movement, cracks and breaks by pushing on the ball. If replacement is necessary, remove the valve by prying it out of the cooler. Install a new valve by tapping it into place.

7   Lubricate the new oil cooler O-ring with clean engine oil. Install the O-ring in the groove on the oil cooler. Remove the relief valve from the oil pan and install a new one.

8   Position the oil cooler onto the aluminum oil pan, so that the casting tab on the cooler aligns between the two tabs on the pan, then install the retaining bolt.

9   Tighten the oil cooler retaining bolt to the torque listed in this Chapter's Specifications.

10   Connect the oil cooler hoses and install a new oil filter. Refill the cooling system with the proper type and mixture of antifreeze, and the engine with the proper type and amount of oil (see Chapter 1), then run the engine and check for leaks. Turn off the engine for five minutes and check the oil and coolant levels, adding fluids if necessary.

17   Driveplate - removal and installation

1   Raise the vehicle and support it securely on jackstands, then remove the transmission (see Chapter 7A).

2   Make alignment marks on the driveplate and crankshaft to ensure correct alignment

during reinstallation.

3   Remove the driveplate-to-crankshaft bolts **(see illustration).** If the crankshaft turns, hold the driveplate with a prybar or wedge a screwdriver into the ring gear teeth.

4   Remove the reinforcement plate and the driveplate from the crankshaft.

Caution: *Don't lay the driveplate on the signal plate side, and keep magnetized material away from the signal plate.*

5   Check for cracked and broken ring gear teeth or a loose ring gear. Lay the driveplate on a flat surface and use a straightedge to check for warpage.

6   Clean and inspect the mating surfaces of the driveplate and the crankshaft. If the rear seal is leaking, replace it before reinstalling the driveplate (see Section 18).

7   Position the driveplate against the crankshaft with the signal plate side facing the engine, and aligning the marks made during removal. Note that some engines have an alignment dowel or staggered bolt holes to ensure correct installation. Before installing the bolts, apply engine oil to the bolt threads and head. Install the reinforcement plate with its rounded or beveled edge against the driveplate.

8   Tighten the driveplate bolts to the torque listed in this Chapter's Specifications 0 using the method described in Step 3 to prevent the crankshaft from turning.

9   The remainder of installation is the reverse of the removal.

18   Rear main oil seal - replacement

1   Remove the driveplate (see Section 17).

2   Carefully pry the old seal out with a seal removal tool or screwdriver **(see illustration).**

3   Apply engine oil to the crankshaft seal journal and the lip of the new seal. Prefer-

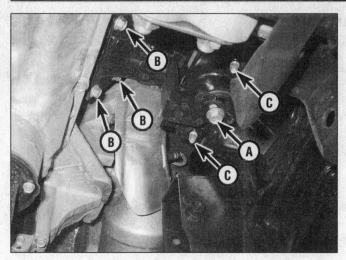

19.8 Engine mount details

19.9a Engine mount insulator-to-frame bolts - right side

A   Engine mount insulator bolt
B   Mount bracket-to-engine block bolts (three of four shown here)
C   Mount insulator-to-frame bolts (access from above)

ably, a seal installation tool should be used to press the new seal into place. The lip is stiff, so carefully work it onto the seal journal of the crankshaft. Don't rush it or you may damage the seal.

Note: *Install the seal squarely and only until flush with the back of the seal retainer, no further.*

4   The remainder of installation is the reverse of removal.

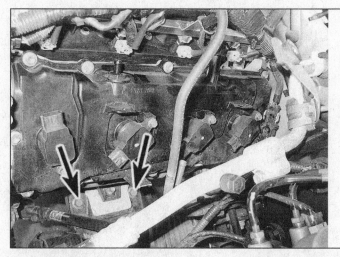

19.9b Engine mount insulator-to-frame bolts - left side

19   Engine mounts - check and replacement

1   There are two engine mounts and one transmission mount installed on the vehicles covered by this manual. The two engine mounts are located on the passenger and driver's side of the vehicle, attached to the engine block and to each frame rail. The transmission mount is mounted to the rear of the transmission and the transmission crossmember. Refer to Chapter 7A for the transmission mount replacement procedure.

Check

2   During the check, the engine must be raised slightly to remove the weight from the mounts.

3   Raise the vehicle and support it securely on jackstands. Support the engine/transmission from above using a hoist or three bar support fixture.

4   Check the mounts to see if the rubber is cracked, hardened or separated from the

bushing in the center of the mount.

5   Check for relative movement between the mounts and the engine or frame (use a large screwdriver or prybar to attempt to move the mounts). If movement is noted, lower the engine and tighten the mount fasteners.

Replacement

6   Disconnect the cable from the negative terminal of the battery (see Chapter 5), set the parking brake and block the rear wheels.

7   Raise the front of the vehicle and support it securely on jackstands. Remove the splash shields from under the vehicle.

8   With the engine supported from above with a hoist or three-bar engine support, raise the engine just enough to take the weight off

the mounts. Remove the engine mount insulator bolt and the engine mount bracket bolts from below **(see illustration)**.

9   Working in the engine compartment, remove the two upper engine mount insulator-to-frame bolts **(see illustrations)**.

10   Removing the air filter housing will make access to the left side bolts easier (see Chapter 4).

11   Installation is the reverse of removal. Make sure the metal heat shield is in place between the insulator and the engine bracket. Apply thread locking compound to the mount nuts before installing them, then tighten them to the torque listed in this Chapter's Specifications.

Notes

Chapter 2 Part C
General engine overhaul procedures

Contents

	Section		Section
Crankshaft - removal and installation	10	Engine removal - methods and precautions	6
Cylinder compression check	3	General information - engine overhaul	1
Engine - removal and installation	7	Initial start-up and break-in after overhaul	12
Engine overhaul - disassembly sequence	8	Oil pressure check	2
Engine overhaul - reassembly sequence	11	Pistons and connecting rods - removal and installation	9
Engine rebuilding alternatives	5	Vacuum gauge diagnostic checks	4

Specifications

General

Engine designation	
3.5L V6	VQ35DE
4.0L V6	VQ40DE
5.6L V8	VK56DE
Displacement	
3.5L V6	213 cubic inches
4.0L V6	241.30 cubic inches
5.6L V8	338.80 cubic inches
Compression ratio	
3.5L V6	10.3:1
4.0L V6	9.7:1
5.6L V8	9.8:1
Cylinder compression pressure	
Standard	185 psi (1275 kPa)
Minimum	142 psi (979 kPa)
Maximum variation between cylinders	14 psi (97 kPa)
Oil pressure (normal, warm engine)	
At idle	14 psi (97 kPa)
At 2000 rpm	43 psi (296 kPa)

Torque specifications* Ft-lbs (unless otherwise indicated) Nm

Note: *One foot-pound (ft-lb) of torque is equivalent to 12 inch-pounds (in-lbs) of torque. Torque values below approximately 15 ft-lbs are expressed in inch-pounds, since most foot-pound torque wrenches are not accurate at these smaller values.*

	Ft-lbs (unless otherwise indicated)	Nm
Engine lifting bracket bolts..	21	28
Connecting rod cap bolts**,***		
3.5L and 4.0L engines		
Step 1	168 in-lbs	19
Step 2	Tighten an additional 90 degrees	
5.6L engines		
Step 1	132 in-lbs	15
Step 2	Tighten an additional 90 degrees	
Main bearing cap bolts (lower crankcase-to-block)**,***		
3.5L engines		
Step 1	26	35
Step 2	Tighten an additional 90 degrees	
4.0L engines		
Step 1, bolts 17 - 24..	16	22
Step 2, bolts 1-16 (after rear seal is installed)	26	35
Step 3, bolts 1-16...	Tighten an additional 90 degrees	
5.6L engines		
Step 1, bolts 1-10..	29	39
Step 2, bolts 11-20..	22	30
Step 3, bolts 1-10..	Tighten an additional 40 degrees	
Step 4, bolts 11-20..	Tighten an additional 30 degrees	
Step 5, Side bolts 21-30	36	49

Refer to Chapter 2A or 2B for additional torque specifications.
**Use new bolts during installation.*
***Apply engine oil to the bolt head and threads before installation.*

1 General information - engine overhaul

1   Included in this portion of Chapter 2 are general information and diagnostic testing procedures for determining the overall mechanical condition of your engine.

2   The information ranges from advice concerning preparation for an overhaul and the purchase of replacement parts and/or components to detailed, step-by-step procedures covering removal and installation.

3   The following Sections have been written to help you determine whether your engine needs to be overhauled and how to remove and install it once you've determined it needs to be rebuilt. For information concerning in-vehicle engine repair, see Chapter 2A or 2B .

4   The Specifications included in this Part are general in nature and include only those necessary for testing the oil pressure and engine compression, and bottom-end torque specifications. Refer to Chapter 2A or 2B for additional engine Specifications.

5   It's not always easy to determine when, or if, an engine should be completely overhauled, because a number of factors must be considered.

6   High mileage is not necessarily an indication that an overhaul is needed, while low mileage doesn't preclude the need for an overhaul. Frequency of servicing is probably the most important consideration. An engine that's had regular and frequent oil and filter changes, as well as other required maintenance, will most likely give many thousands of miles of reliable service. Conversely, a neglected engine may require an overhaul very early in its service life.

7   Excessive oil consumption is an indication that piston rings, valve seals and/or valve guides are in need of attention. Make sure that oil leaks aren't responsible before deciding that the rings and/or guides are bad. Perform a cylinder compression check to determine the extent of the work required (see Section 3). Also, check the vacuum readings under various conditions (see Section 4).

8   Check the oil pressure with a gauge installed in place of the oil pressure sending unit and compare it to this Chapter's Specifications (see Section 2). If it's extremely low, the bearings and/or oil pump are probably worn out.

9   Loss of power, rough running, knocking or metallic engine noises, excessive valve train noise and high fuel consumption rates may also point to the need for an overhaul, especially if they're all present at the same time. If a complete tune-up doesn't remedy the situation, major mechanical work is the only solution.

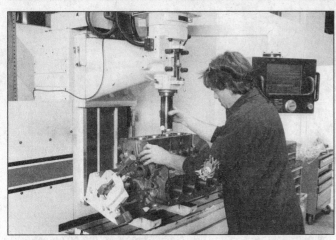

1.10a An engine block being bored. An engine rebuilder will use special machinery to recondition the cylinder bores

1.10b If the cylinders are bored, the machine shop will normally hone the engine on a machine like this

10   An engine overhaul involves restoring the internal parts to the specifications of a new engine. During an overhaul, the piston rings are replaced and the cylinder walls are reconditioned (rebored and/or honed) **(see illustrations)**. If a rebore is done by an automotive machine shop, new oversize pistons will also be installed. The main bearings, connecting rod bearings and camshaft bearings are generally replaced with new ones and, if necessary, the crankshaft may be reground to restore the journals **(see illustration)**. Generally, the valves are serviced as well, since they're usually in less-than-perfect condition at this point. While the engine is being overhauled, other components, such as the distributor, starter and alternator, can be rebuilt as well. The end result should be similar to a new engine that will give many trouble free miles.

Note: *Critical cooling system components such as the hoses, drivebelts, thermostat and water pump should be replaced with new parts when an engine is overhauled. The radiator should be checked carefully to ensure that it isn't clogged or leaking (see Chapter 3). If you purchase a rebuilt engine or short block,*

some rebuilders will not warranty their engines unless the radiator has been professionally flushed. Also, we don't recommend overhauling the oil pump - always install a new one when an engine is rebuilt.

11   Overhauling the internal components on today's engines is a difficult and time-consuming task which requires a significant amount of specialty tools and is best left to a professional engine rebuilder **(see illustrations)**. A competent engine rebuilder will handle the inspection of your old parts and offer advice concerning the reconditioning or replacement of the original engine, never purchase parts or have machine work done on other components until the block has been thoroughly inspected by a professional machine shop. As a general rule, time is the primary cost of an overhaul, especially since the vehicle may be tied up for a minimum of two weeks or more. Be aware that some engine builders only have the capability to rebuild the engine you bring them while other rebuilders have a large inventory of rebuilt exchange engines in stock. Also be aware that many machine shops could take as much as two weeks time

1.10c A crankshaft having a main bearing journal ground

to completely rebuild your engine depending on shop workload. Sometimes it makes more sense to simply exchange your engine for another engine that's already rebuilt to save time.

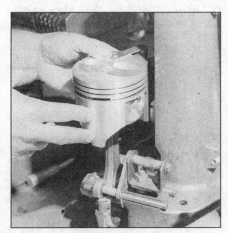

1.11a A machinist checks for a bent connecting rod, using specialized equipment

1.11b A bore gauge being used to check the main bearing bore

1.11c Uneven piston wear like this indicates a bent connecting rod

2.2a On 3.5L engines, the oil pressure sending unit is located at the right end of the engine, below the crankshaft pulley

2.2b On 4.0L engines, the oil pressure sending unit is located on the right-front corner of the upper oil pan

2.2c On 5.6L engines, the oil pressure sending unit is located at the left-front of the aluminum oil pan, near the oil filter

2   Oil pressure check

1   Low engine oil pressure can be a sign of an engine in need of rebuilding. A low oil pressure indicator (often called an "idiot light") is not a test of the oiling system. Such indicators only come on when the oil pressure is dangerously low. Even a factory oil pressure gauge in the instrument panel is only a relative indication, although much better for driver information than a warning light. A better test is with a mechanical (not electrical) oil pressure gauge.
2   Locate the oil pressure sending unit **(see illustrations)**.
3   Disconnect the electrical connector, unscrew and remove the oil pressure sending unit and screw in the hose for your oil pressure gauge. If necessary, install an adapter fitting. Use Teflon tape or thread sealant on the threads of the adapter and/or the fitting on the end of your gauge's hose.
4   Connect an accurate tachometer to the engine, according to the tachometer manufacturer's instructions.
5   Check the oil pressure with the engine running (normal operating temperature) at the specified engine speed, and compare it to this Chapter's Specifications. If it's extremely low, the bearings and/or oil pump are probably worn out.

3   Cylinder compression check

1   A compression check will tell you what mechanical condition the upper end of your engine (pistons, rings, valves, head gaskets) is in. Specifically, it can tell you if the compression is down due to leakage caused by worn piston rings, defective valves and seats or a blown head gasket.
Note: *The engine must be at normal operating temperature and the battery must be fully charged for this check.*
2   Begin by cleaning the area around the spark plugs before you remove them (compressed air should be used, if available). The idea is to prevent dirt from getting into the cylinders as the compression check is being done.
3   Remove the ignition coils (see Chapter 5). Disable the fuel pump by removing the fuel pump fuse (see Chapter 4, Section 2).
Note: *If you only need to get a general idea of the condition of the engine, it's easier to test the compression only on the left bank of cylinders (2012 and earlier models) or front bank of cylinders (2013 and later models). This eliminates having to remove the upper intake manifold and other components for access to the spark plugs on the other cylinder bank. If a problem is suspected after testing the more accessible bank, perform the test on the other cylinders as well.*
4   Remove all of the spark plugs (see Chapter 1).
5   Block the throttle wide open.
6   Install a compression gauge in the spark plug hole **(see illustration)**.
7   Crank the engine over at least seven compression strokes and watch the gauge.

3.6 Use a compression gauge with a threaded fitting for the spark plug hole, not the type that requires hand force to maintain the seal

The compression should build up quickly in a healthy engine. Low compression on the first stroke, followed by gradually increasing pressure on successive strokes, indicates worn piston rings. A low compression reading on the first stroke, which doesn't build up during successive strokes, indicates leaking valves or a blown head gasket (a cracked head could also be the cause). Deposits on the undersides of the valve heads can also cause low compression. Record the highest gauge reading obtained.
8   Repeat the procedure for the remaining cylinders and compare the results to this Chapter's Specifications.
9   Add some engine oil (about three squirts from a plunger-type oil can) to each cylinder, through the spark plug hole, and repeat the test.
10   If the compression increases after the oil is added, the piston rings are definitely worn. If the compression doesn't increase significantly, the leakage is occurring at the valves or head gasket. Leakage past the valves may be caused by burned valve seats and/or faces or warped, cracked or bent valves.
11   If two adjacent cylinders have equally low compression, there's a strong possibility that the head gasket between them is blown. The appearance of coolant in the combustion chambers or the crankcase would verify this condition.
12   If one cylinder is slightly lower than the others, and the engine has a slightly rough idle, a worn lobe on the camshaft could be the cause.
13   If the compression is unusually high, the combustion chambers are probably coated with carbon deposits. If that's the case, the cylinder head(s) should be removed and decarbonized.
14   If compression is way down or varies greatly between cylinders, it's a good idea to have a leak-down test performed by an automotive repair shop. This test will pinpoint exactly where the leakage is occurring and how severe it is.

4.4 A simple vacuum gauge can be handy in diagnosing engine condition and performance - be sure to connect it to intake manifold vacuum (not "ported" vacuum)

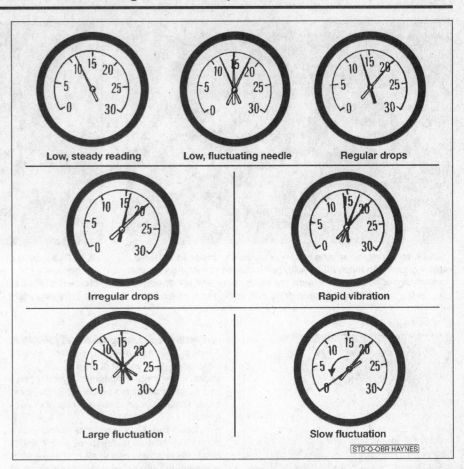

4.6 Typical vacuum gauge readings

4 Vacuum gauge diagnostic checks

1   A vacuum gauge provides inexpensive but valuable information about what is going on in the engine. You can check for worn rings or cylinder walls, leaking head or intake manifold gaskets, incorrect carburetor adjustments, restricted exhaust, stuck or burned valves, weak valve springs, improper ignition or valve timing and ignition problems.

2   Unfortunately, vacuum gauge readings are easy to misinterpret, so they should be used in conjunction with other tests to confirm the diagnosis.

3   Both the absolute readings and the rate of needle movement are important for accurate interpretation. Most gauges measure vacuum in inches of mercury (in-Hg). The following references to vacuum assume the diagnosis is being performed at sea level. As elevation increases (or atmospheric pressure decreases), the reading will decrease. For every 1,000 foot increase in elevation above approximately 2,000 feet, the gauge readings will decrease about one inch of mercury.

4   Connect the vacuum gauge directly to an intake manifold vacuum source, not to ported (throttle body) vacuum **(see illustration)**. Be sure no hoses are left disconnected during the test or false readings will result.

5   Before you begin the test, allow the engine to warm up completely. Block the wheels and set the parking brake. With the transaxle in Park, start the engine and allow it to run at normal idle speed.

Warning: *Keep your hands and the vacuum gauge clear of the fans.*

6   Read the vacuum gauge; an average, healthy engine should normally produce about 17 to 22 in-Hg with a fairly steady needle **(see illustration)**. Refer to the following vacuum gauge readings and what they indicate about the engine's condition:

7   A low, steady reading usually indicates a leaking gasket between the intake manifold and cylinder head(s) or throttle body, a leaky vacuum hose, late ignition timing or incorrect camshaft timing. Check ignition timing with a timing light and eliminate all other possible causes, utilizing the tests provided in this Chapter before you remove the timing chain cover to check the timing marks.

8   If the reading is three to eight inches below normal and it fluctuates at that low reading, suspect an intake manifold gasket leak at an intake port or a faulty fuel injector.

9   If the needle has regular drops of about two-to-four inches at a steady rate, the valves are probably leaking. Perform a compression check or leak-down test to confirm this.

10   An irregular drop or down-flick of the needle can be caused by a sticking valve or an ignition misfire. Perform a compression check or leak-down test and read the spark plugs.

11   A rapid vibration of about four in-Hg vibration at idle combined with exhaust smoke indicates worn valve guides. Perform a leakdown test to confirm this. If the rapid vibration occurs with an increase in engine speed, check for a leaking intake manifold gasket or head gasket, weak valve springs, burned valves or ignition misfire.

12   A slight fluctuation, say one inch up and down, may mean ignition problems. Check all the usual tune-up items and, if necessary, run the engine on an ignition analyzer.

13   If there is a large fluctuation, perform a compression or leak-down test to look for a weak or dead cylinder or a blown head gasket.

14   If the needle moves slowly through a wide range, check for a clogged PCV system, incorrect idle fuel mixture, throttle body or intake manifold gasket leaks.

15   Check for a slow return after revving the engine by quickly snapping the throttle open until the engine reaches about 2,500 rpm and let it shut. Normally the reading should drop to near zero, rise above normal idle reading (about 5 in-Hg over) and then return to the previous idle reading. If the vacuum returns slowly and doesn't peak when the throttle is snapped shut, the rings may be worn. If there is a long delay, look for a restricted exhaust system (often the muffler or catalytic converter). An easy way to check this is to temporarily disconnect the exhaust ahead of the suspected part and redo the test.

5 Engine rebuilding alternatives

1   The do-it-yourselfer is faced with a number of options when purchasing a rebuilt engine. The major considerations are cost, warranty, parts availability and the time required for the rebuilder to complete the proj-

6.4a After tightly wrapping water-vulnerable components, use a spray cleaner on everything, with particular concentration on the greasiest areas, usually around the valve cover and lower edges of the block. If one section dries out, apply more cleaner

6.4b Depending on how dirty the engine is, let the cleaner soak in according to the directions and then hose off the grime and cleaner. Get the rinse water down into every area you can get at; then dry important components with a hair dryer or paper towels

6.6 Get an engine stand sturdy enough to firmly support the engine while you're working on it. Stay away from three-wheeled models; they have a tendency to tip over more easily, so get a four-wheeled unit

ect. The decision to replace the engine block, piston/connecting rod assemblies and crankshaft depends on the final inspection results of your engine. Only then can you make a cost effective decision whether to have your engine overhauled or simply purchase an exchange engine for your vehicle.

2   Some of the rebuilding alternatives include:

3   **Individual parts** - If the inspection procedures reveal that the engine block and most engine components are in reusable condition, purchasing individual parts and having a rebuilder rebuild your engine may be the most economical alternative. The block, crankshaft and piston/connecting rod assemblies should all be inspected carefully by a machine shop first.

4   **Short block** - A short block consists of an engine block with a crankshaft and piston/

connecting rod assemblies already installed. All new bearings are incorporated and all clearances will be correct. The existing camshafts, valve train components, cylinder head and external parts can be bolted to the short block with little or no machine shop work necessary.

5   **Long block** - A long block consists of a short block plus an oil pump, oil pan, cylinder head, valve cover, camshaft and valve train components, timing sprockets and chain or gears and timing cover. All components are installed with new bearings, seals and gaskets incorporated throughout. The installation of manifolds and external parts is all that's necessary.

6   **Low mileage used engines** - Some companies now offer low mileage used engines which is a very cost effective way to get your vehicle up and running again. These engines often come from vehicles which have been in totaled in accidents or come from other countries which have a higher vehicle turn over rate. A low mileage used engine also usually has a similar warranty like the newly remanufactured engines.

7   Give careful thought to which alternative is best for you and discuss the situation with local automotive machine shops, auto parts dealers and experienced rebuilders before ordering or purchasing replacement parts.

6   Engine removal - methods and precautions

1   If you've decided that an engine must be removed for overhaul or major repair work, several preliminary steps should be taken. Read all removal and installation procedures carefully prior to committing to this job.

2   Locating a suitable place to work is extremely important. Adequate work space, along with storage space for the vehicle, will

be needed. If a shop or garage isn't available, at the very least a flat, level, clean work surface made of concrete or asphalt is required.

3   On 2012 and earlier models, the engine is removed by lifting it out of the engine compartment. This will require an engine hoist. On 2013 and later models the engine is removed by lowering it to the floor, along with the transaxle, then raising the vehicle sufficiently to slide the assembly out; this will require a vehicle hoist as well as an engine hoist. Make sure the hoist is rated in excess of the combined weight of the engine and transaxle. Safety is of primary importance, considering the potential hazards involved in removing the engine from the vehicle.

4   Cleaning the engine compartment and engine before beginning the removal procedure will help keep tools clean and organized **(see illustrations)**.

5   If you're a novice at engine removal, get at least one helper. One person cannot easily do all the things you need to do to remove a big heavy engine and transaxle assembly from the engine compartment. Also helpful is to seek advice and assistance from someone who's experienced in engine removal.

6   Plan the operation ahead of time. Arrange for or obtain all of the tools and equipment you'll need prior to beginning the job **(see illustration)**. Some of the equipment necessary to perform engine removal and installation safely and with relative ease are (in addition to a vehicle hoist [2013 and later models] and an engine hoist) a heavy duty floor jack (preferably fitted with a transmission jack head adapter), complete sets of wrenches and sockets as described in the front of this manual, wooden blocks, plenty of rags and cleaning solvent for mopping up spilled oil, coolant and gasoline.

7   Plan for the vehicle to be out of use for quite a while. A machine shop can do the work that is beyond the scope of the home mechanic. Machine shops often have a busy

schedule, so before removing the engine, consult the shop for an estimate of how long it will take to rebuild or repair the components that may need work.

---

7 Engine - removal and installation

Warning: *Gasoline is extremely flammable, so take extra precautions when you work on any part of the fuel system. Don't smoke or allow open flames or bare light bulbs near the work area, and don't work in a garage where a gas-type appliance (such as a water heater or clothes dryer) is present. Since gasoline is carcinogenic, wear fuel-resistant gloves when there's a possibility of being exposed to fuel, and, if you spill any fuel on your skin, rinse it off immediately with soap and water. Mop up any spills immediately and do not store fuel-soaked rags where they could ignite. The fuel system is under constant pressure, so, if any fuel lines are to be disconnected, the fuel pressure in the system must be relieved first (see Chapter 4). When you perform any kind of work on the fuel system, wear safety glasses and have a Class B type fire extinguisher on hand.*

Warning: *The engine must be completely cool before beginning this procedure.*

Note: *Label both ends of all electrical connectors and hoses and make notes or take photos showing their routing and all the locations of clamps and ties. This will help with reassembly and installation.*

2012 and earlier models

Removal

1   Have the air conditioning system discharged by an automotive air conditioning technician.

2   Park the vehicle squarely on a hard, level surface. Point the wheels straight ahead. Remove the hood (see Chapter 11).

3   Relieve the fuel system pressure (see Chapter 4), then disconnect the cables from the negative and positive battery terminals (see Chapter 5).

4   Remove the engine cover.

5   Remove the air filter housing and the intake air duct (see Chapter 4).

6   Remove the drivebelt (see Chapter 1).

7   Detach the fuel line from the fuel rail (see Chapter 4).

8   Remove the PCV hose(s) (see Chapter 6).

9   Label and remove all vacuum lines between the engine and the firewall (or other components in the engine compartment) **(see illustration)**. Masking tape and/or a touch-up paint applicator work well for marking items. Disconnect the main engine harness connectors at the PCM, and disconnect the engine harness from the underhood fuse/relay box. Look over the engine and engine compartment carefully to locate any ground wires attached to the engine or engine compartment.

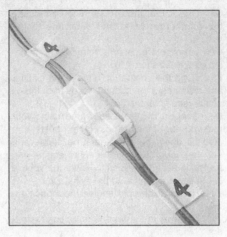

7.9 Label both ends of each wire or hose connection before disconnecting them

10   Loosen the front wheel lug nuts, then raise the front of the vehicle and support it securely on jackstands. Remove the wheels and the inner fender splash shields (see Chapter 11). Also remove the under-vehicle splash shield.

11   Drain the cooling system (see Chapter 1) and disconnect the heater hoses at the firewall.

12   Drain the engine oil and remove the oil filter (see Chapter 1).

13   Remove the radiator grille (see Chapter 11).

14   Remove the bumper cover (see Chapter 11) and the bumper beam.

15   Remove the radiator, shroud and engine cooling fans (see Chapter 3). Also remove the heater hoses and the coolant reservoir.

16   Detach the hood release cable from the hood latch, then remove the radiator support.

17   Remove the air conditioning compressor and the condenser (see Chapter 3).

18   Remove the alternator (see Chapter 5).

19   Remove the power steering fluid reservoir and power steering pump, without disconnecting the hoses, and tie them out of the way (see Chapter 10).

20   Remove the catalytic converters (see Chapter 6).

21   If you're working on an all-wheel drive model, remove the front differential (see Chapter 8).

22   Unbolt the transmission cooler line support brackets from the engine.

23   Disconnect the engine block heater, if equipped.

24   Disconnect the crankshaft position sensor electrical connector (see Chapter 6).

25   Remove the starter (see Chapter 5).

26   Remove the torque converter-to-driveplate bolts (see Chapter 7A).

27   Attach an engine hoist to the engine lifting brackets and raise it just enough to take weight off of the engine mounts. If no brackets are present, check with a Nissan dealer parts department to see if you can order them. Alternatively, attach the lifting chains or straps

to substantial parts of the engine, such as threaded holes in the cylinder heads, one at the left-rear and one at the right-front.

Caution: *Make sure the lifting mounts or hoist chains don't apply any force to the valve covers.*

28   Support the transmission with a floor jack; preferably one with a transmission adapter head. Remove the transmission-to-engine bolts.

29   Make sure nothing else is connected between the engine and the vehicle.

30   Remove the engine mount fasteners, then raise the engine slowly out of the vehicle. An assistant to guide the engine out is very helpful.

31   Remove the driveplate and mount the engine on an engine stand.

Installation

32   Installation is the reverse of removal, noting the following points:

a) *Check the engine/transmission mounts. If they're worn or damaged, replace them.*

b) *After lowering the engine into place, attach the transmission to the engine following the procedure described in Chapter 7A.*

c) *Add coolant, oil, power steering and transmission fluids as needed (see Chapter 1).*

d) *Reconnect tha battery and perform the necessary re-learn procedures (see Chapter 5).*

e) *Run the engine and check for proper operation and leaks. Shut off the engine and recheck fluid levels.*

f) *Have the air conditioning system recharged and leak tested by the shop that discharged it.*

2013 and later models

Note: *Engine removal on these vehicles is a difficult job, especially for the do-it-yourselfer working at home. The manufacturer states that the engine and transaxle have to be removed as a unit from the bottom of the vehicle, not the top. With a floor jack and jackstands, it can't be raised high enough or supported safely enough for the engine/transaxle to slide out from underneath. The manufacturer recommends that removal of the engine/transaxle only be performed with a frame-contact type hoist.*

Note: *During this procedure you'll have to adjust the height of the vehicle with the vehicle hoist to perform certain operations.*

Removal

33   Park the vehicle on a vehicle hoist, loosen the front wheel lug nuts, then raise the hoist arms to contact the jacking points on each side of the vehicle. Remove the front wheels.

34   Removing the hood (see Chapter 11) will make it easier to work on the vehicle, but isn't necessary. Relieve the fuel pressure (see Chapter 4).

35   Disconnect the cable from the negative terminal of the battery (see Chapter 5).

36   Drain the engine coolant (see Chapter 1) and the power steering fluid (see Chapter 10).

37   Remove the engine cover and the inner fender splash shields (see Chapter 11).

38   Remove the air filter housing and the air ducts (see Chapter 4).

39   Remove the battery and the battery tray (see Chapter 5).

40   Remove the drivebelt (see Chapter 1).

41   Remove the radiator and the coolant reservoir tank (see Chapter 3).

42   Remove the wiper motor (see Chapter 12) and the cowl top extension.

43   Drain the transmission/transaxle fluid (see Chapter 1).

44   Disconnect all of the main engine compartment wiring harnesses, including those at the Transmission Control Module (TCM) and the Engine Control Module (ECM).

45   Remove the battery support bracket along with the TCM and the ECM.

46   Unbolt the brake master cylinder reservoir bracket and secure the reservoir out of the way.

47   Disconnect both heater hoses, the EVAP hose and the fuel supply hose. Plug all open ends to prevent contamination.

48   Disconnect the shift cable from the transaxle.

49   Disconnect the brake booster vacuum hose from the engine.

50   Disconnect any ground cables or straps between the chassis and the engine or transaxle.

51   Remove the air conditioning compressor mounting bolts, but leave the refrigerant hoses attached. Move the compressor out of the way and secure it in place with wire.

52   Disconnect the power steering suction hoses from the reservoir and plug the ends.

53   Disconnect the transmission/transaxle cooler hoses from the radiator.

54   Remove the starter motor (see Chapter 5).

55   Remove the front driveaxles (see Chapter 8).

56   Remove the air deflector.

57   Remove the front section of exhaust pipe.

58   On AWD models, remove the driveshaft (see Chapter 8).

59   Disconnect the steering shaft from the steering gear (see Chapter 10).

60   Disconnect the stabilizer bar links from the stabilizer bar (see Chapter 10).

61   Separate the control arms from the steering knuckles (see Chapter 10).

62   Disconnect the power steering lines from the steering gear.

63   Remove the inspection cover from the rear of the upper oil pan. Remove the bolts from the torque converter, turning the crankshaft with a wrench to access all of them (see Chapter 7A).

64   Remove the transaxle bolts from the lower back side of the upper oil pan.

65   Remove the Crankshaft Position (CKP) sensor (see Chapter 6).

66   Check that there is nothing connecting the engine/transaxle and subframe to the vehicle.

67   Label and disconnect anything remaining (see illustration 7.9).

68   Drain the engine oil, remove the oil filter and disconnect the coolant hoses from the oil cooler (see Chapter 1).

69   Support the front subframe using four jackstands. Other kinds of supports can also be used, but they must be stable and secure enough to hold the entire engine and transaxle assembly. Slightly lower the vehicle to put some weight onto the jackstands.

70   Remove the right engine mount assembly.

71   Remove the subframe mounting fasteners.

72   Slowly raise the vehicle using the hoist, making sure that nothing interferes and nothing is still attached between the powertrain and the vehicle. Continue raising it until there is enough clearance above the engine to attach an engine hoist.

73   Roll an engine hoist into position and attach it to the engine with a couple pieces of heavy-duty chain (an engine support fixture could be used instead). If the engine is equipped with lifting brackets, use them. If not, you'll have obtain lifting brackets (special part numbers that you'll have to order from a dealer parts department), or fasten the chain to some substantial part of the engine - one that is strong enough to take the weight, but in a location that will provide good balance. If you're attaching the chain to a stud on the engine, or are using a bolt passing through the chain and into a threaded hole, place a washer between the nut or bolt head and the chain, and tighten the nut or bolt securely. Take up the slack in the chain, but don't lift the engine.

Warning: *DO NOT place any part of your body under the engine when it's supported only by a hoist or other lifting device.*

74   Remove the power steering pump assembly including the hoses and brackets.

75   Disconnect the vacuum hoses from the engine mounts (if so equipped).

76   Lift the engine assembly slightly with the hoist. Remove the rear torque rod and its bracket. Remove the other engine mounts.

77   Lift the engine/transaxle assembly to separate it from the subframe.

78   Remove the exhaust manifolds (see Chapter 2A).

79   On AWD models, remove the transfer case (see Chapter 8).

80   Remove the engine-to-transaxle bolts, then separate the two. Set the engine and the transaxle on wood blocks to avoid tipping and possible damage. Mount the engine on an engine stand using the hoist if necessary.

Installation

81   Installation is the reverse of removal, noting these points:

a) *Check the engine and transaxle mounts. If they're worn or damaged, replace them.*

b) *Attach the transaxle to the engine (see Chapter 7A).*

c) *Tighten the subframe mounting bolts to the torque listed in the Chapter 10 Specifications.*

d) *Tighten the wheel lug nuts to the torque listed in the Chapter 1 Specifications. Tighten the driveaxle/hub nuts to the torque listed in the Chapter 8 Specifications. Tighten the steering and suspension fasteners to the torque listed in the Chapter 10 Specifications.*

e) *Refill the engine coolant, engine oil, power steering fluid and transaxle fluid (see Chapter 1).*

f) *Reconnect the battery and perform the necessary re-learn procedures (see Chapter 5).*

g) *Run the engine and check for proper operation and leaks. Shut off the engine and recheck fluid levels.*

8   Engine overhaul - disassembly sequence

1   It's much easier to remove the external components if it's mounted on a portable engine stand. A stand can often be rented quite cheaply from an equipment rental yard. Before the engine is mounted on a stand, the driveplate should be removed from the engine.

2   If a stand isn't available, it's possible to remove the external engine components with it blocked up on the floor. Be extra careful not to tip or drop the engine when working without a stand.

3   If you're going to obtain a rebuilt engine, all external components must come off first, to be transferred to the replacement engine. These components include:

- *Driveplate*
- *Ignition coils and wiring harnesses*
- *Emissions-related components*
- *Engine mounts and mount brackets*
- *Intake/exhaust manifolds*
- *Fuel injection components*
- *Oil filter and oil cooler*
- *Spark plugs*
- *Thermostat and housing assembly*
- *Water pump*

Note: *When removing the external components from the engine, pay close attention to details that may be helpful or important during installation. Note the installed position of gaskets, seals, spacers, pins, brackets, washers, bolts and other small items.*

4   If you're going to obtain a short block (assembled engine block, crankshaft, pistons and connecting rods), then remove the timing chain, cylinder head, oil pan, oil pump pick-up tube, oil pump and water pump from your engine so that you can turn in your old short block to the rebuilder as a core. See Section 5 for additional information regarding the different possibilities to be considered.

9.1 Before you try to remove the pistons, use a ridge reamer to remove the raised material (ridge) from the top of the cylinders

9.3 Checking the connecting rod endplay (side clearance)

9.4 If the connecting rods or caps are not marked, use permanent ink or paint to mark the caps to the rods by cylinder number (for example, this would be number 4 cylinder connecting rod)

9 Pistons and connecting rods - removal and installation

Removal

Note: *Prior to removing the piston/connecting rod assemblies, remove the cylinder head and oil pan (see Chapter 2A or 2B).*

1   Use your fingernail to feel if a ridge has formed at the upper limit of ring travel (about 1/4-inch down from the top of each cylinder). If carbon deposits or cylinder wear have produced ridges, they must be completely removed with a special tool **(see illustration)**. Follow the manufacturer's instructions provided with the tool. Failure to remove the ridges before attempting to remove the piston/connecting rod assemblies may result in piston breakage.

2   After the cylinder ridges have been removed, turn the engine so the crankshaft is facing up.

3   Before the main bearing cap assembly and connecting rods are removed, check the connecting rod endplay with feeler gauges. Slide them between the first connecting rod and the crankshaft throw until the play is removed **(see illustration)**. Repeat this procedure for each connecting rod. The endplay is equal to the thickness of the feeler gauge(s). Check with an automotive machine shop for the endplay service limit (a typical endplay should measure between 0.005 to 0.015 inch [0.127 to 0.381 mm]). If the play exceeds the service limit, new connecting rods will be required. If new rods (or a new crankshaft) are installed, the endplay may fall under the minimum allowable. If it does, the rods will have to be machined to restore it. If necessary, consult an automotive machine shop for advice.

4   Check the connecting rods and caps for identification marks. If they aren't plainly marked, use paint or marker **(see illustra-**

9.13 Install the piston ring into the cylinder then push it down into position using a piston so the ring will be square in the cylinder

tion) to clearly identify each rod and cap (1, 2, 3, etc., depending on the cylinder they're associated with). Do not interchange the rod caps. Install the exact same rod cap onto the same connecting rod.
Caution: *Do not use a hammer and punch to mark the connecting rods or they may be damaged.*

5   Loosen each of the connecting rod cap bolts 1/2-turn at a time until they can be removed by hand. Obtain new connecting rod bolts (but save the old ones for the oil clearance check).

6   Remove the number one connecting rod cap and bearing insert. Don't drop the bearing insert out of the cap.

7   Remove the bearing insert and push the connecting rod/piston assembly out through the top of the engine. Use a wooden or plastic hammer handle to push on the upper bearing surface in the connecting rod. If resistance is felt, double-check to make sure that all of the ridge was removed from the cylinder.

8   Repeat the procedure for the remaining cylinders.

9   After removal, reassemble the connecting rod caps and bearing inserts in their

respective connecting rods and install the cap bolts finger tight. Leaving the old bearing inserts in place until reassembly will help prevent the connecting rod bearing surfaces from being accidentally nicked or gouged.

10   The pistons and connecting rods are now ready for inspection and overhaul at an automotive machine shop.

Piston ring installation

11   Before installing the new piston rings, the ring end gaps must be checked. It's assumed that the piston ring side clearance has been checked and verified correct.

12   Lay out the piston/connecting rod assemblies and the new ring sets so the ring sets will be matched with the same piston and cylinder during the end gap measurement and engine assembly.

13   Insert the top (number one) ring into the first cylinder and square it up with the cylinder walls by pushing it in with the top of the piston **(see illustration)**. The ring should be near the bottom of the cylinder, at the lower limit of ring travel.

14   To measure the end gap, slip feeler gauges between the ends of the ring until a

ENGINE BEARING ANALYSIS

Debris

Babbitt bearing embedded with debris from machinings

Microscopic detail of debris

Microscopic detail of gouges

Overplated copper alloy bearing gouged by cast iron debris

Aluminum bearing embedded with glass beads

Microscopic detail of glass beads

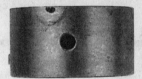

Damaged lining caused by dirt left on the bearing back

Misassembly

Result of a lower half assembled as an upper - blocking the oil flow

Excessive oil clearance is indicated by a short contact arc

Polished and oil-stained backs are a result of a poor fit in the housing bore

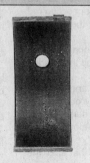

Result of a wrong, reversed, or shifted cap

Overloading

Damage from excessive idling which resulted in an oil film unable to support the load imposed

Damaged upper connecting rod bearings caused by engine lugging; the lower main bearings (not shown) were similarly affected

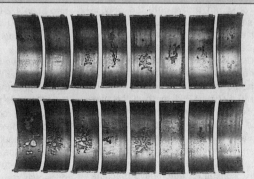

The damage shown in these upper and lower connecting rod bearings was caused by engine operation at a higher-than-rated speed under load

Misalignment

A warped crankshaft caused this pattern of severe wear in the center, diminishing toward the ends

A poorly finished crankshaft caused the equally spaced scoring shown

A tapered housing bore caused the damage along one edge of this pair

A bent connecting rod led to the damage in the "V" pattern

Lubrication

Result of dry start: The bearings on the left, farthest from the oil pump, show more damage

Result of a low oil supply or oil starvation

Severe wear as a result of inadequate oil clearance

Corrosion

Microscopic detail of corrosion

Corrosion is an acid attack on the bearing lining generally caused by inadequate maintenance, extremely hot or cold operation, or inferior oils or fuels

Microscopic detail of cavitation

Example of cavitation - a surface erosion caused by pressure changes in the oil film

Damage from excessive thrust or insufficient axial clearance

Bearing affected by oil dilution caused by excessive blow-by or a rich mixture

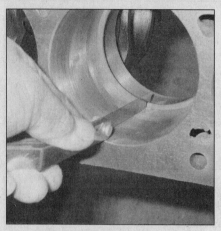

9.14 With the ring square in the cylinder, measure the ring end gap with a feeler gauge

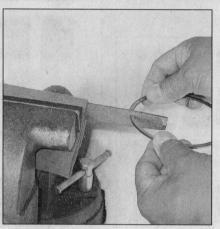

9.15 If the ring end gap is too small, clamp a file in a vise as shown and file the piston ring ends - be sure to remove all raised material

9.19a Installing the spacer/expander in the oil ring groove

9.19b DO NOT use a piston ring installation tool when installing the oil control side rails

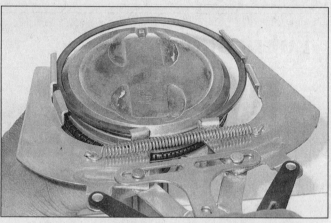

9.22 Use a piston ring installation tool to install the compression rings - on some engines the number two compression ring has a directional mark that must face toward the top of the piston

gauge equal to the gap width is found (see illustration). The feeler gauge should slide between the ring ends with a slight amount of drag. A typical ring gap should fall between 0.010 and 0.020 inch (0.25 to 0.50 mm) for compression rings and up to 0.030 inch (0.76 mm) for the oil ring steel rails. If the gap is larger or smaller than specified, double-check to make sure you have the correct rings before proceeding.

15 If the gap is too small, it must be enlarged or the ring ends may come in contact with each other during engine operation, which can cause serious damage to the engine. If necessary, increase the end gaps by filing the ring ends very carefully with a fine file. Mount the file in a vise equipped with soft jaws, slip the ring over the file with the ends contacting the file face and slowly move the ring to remove material from the ends. When performing this operation, file only by pushing the ring from the outside end of the file towards the vise (see illustration).

16 Excess end gap isn't critical unless it's greater than 0.040 inch (1.01 mm). Again,

double-check to make sure you have the correct ring type.

17 Repeat the procedure for each ring that will be installed in the first cylinder and for each ring in the remaining cylinders. Remember to keep rings, pistons and cylinders matched up.

18 Once the ring end gaps have been checked/corrected, the rings can be installed on the pistons.

19 The oil control ring (lowest one on the piston) is usually installed first. It's composed of three separate components. Slip the spacer/expander into the groove (see illustration). If an anti-rotation tang is used, make sure it's inserted into the drilled hole in the ring groove. Next, install the lower side rail in the same manner (see illustration). Don't use a piston ring installation tool on the oil ring side rails, as they may be damaged. Instead, place one end of the side rail into the groove between the spacer/expander and the ring land, hold it firmly in place and slide a finger around the piston while pushing the rail into the groove. Finally, install the upper side rail.

20 After the three oil ring components have been installed, check to make sure that both the upper and lower side rails can be rotated smoothly inside the ring grooves.

21 The number two (middle) ring is installed next. It's usually stamped with a mark which must face up, toward the top of the piston. Do not mix up the top and middle rings, as they have different cross-sections.

Note: *Always follow the instructions printed on the ring package or box - different manufacturers may require different approaches.*

22 Use a piston ring installation tool and make sure the identification mark is facing the top of the piston, then slip the ring into the middle groove on the piston (see illustration). Don't expand the ring any more than necessary to slide it over the piston.

Note: *Be careful not to confuse the number one and number two rings.*

23 Install the number one (top) ring in the same manner.

24 Repeat the procedure for the remaining pistons and rings.

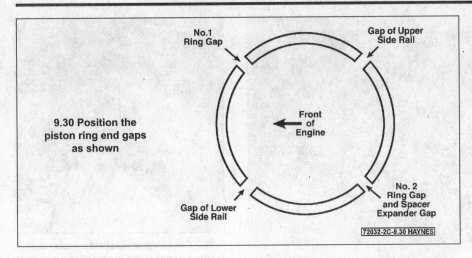

9.30 Position the piston ring end gaps as shown

No.1 Ring Gap

Gap of Upper Side Rail

Front of Engine

Gap of Lower Side Rail

No. 2 Ring Gap and Spacer Expander Gap

72032-2C-9.30 HAYNES

9.35 Use a plastic or wooden hammer handle to push the piston into the cylinder

Installation

25 Before installing the piston/connecting rod assemblies, the cylinder walls must be perfectly clean, the top edge of each cylinder bore must be chamfered, and the crankshaft must be in place.

26 Remove the cap from the end of the number one connecting rod (refer to the marks made during removal). Remove the original bearing inserts and wipe the bearing surfaces of the connecting rod and cap with a clean, lint-free cloth. They must be kept spotlessly clean.

Connecting rod bearing oil clearance check

27 Clean the back side of the new upper bearing insert, then lay it in place in the connecting rod.

28 Make sure the tab on the bearing fits into the recess in the rod. Don't hammer the bearing insert into place and be very careful not to nick or gouge the bearing face. Don't lubricate the bearing at this time.

29 Clean the back side of the other bearing insert and install it in the rod cap. Again, make sure the tab on the bearing fits into the recess in the cap, and don't apply any lubricant. It's critically important that the mating surfaces of the bearing and connecting rod are perfectly clean and oil free when they're assembled.

30 Position the piston ring gaps at the intervals around the piston as shown **(see illustration)**.

31 Lubricate the piston and rings with clean engine oil and attach a piston ring compressor to the piston. Leave the skirt protruding about 1/4-inch to guide the piston into the cylinder. The rings must be compressed until they're flush with the piston.

32 Rotate the crankshaft until the number one connecting rod journal is at Bottom Dead Center (BDC) and apply a liberal coat of engine oil to the cylinder walls.

33 With the "front" mark (letter F or arrow) on the piston facing the front (timing chain end) of the engine, gently insert the piston/ connecting rod assembly into the number one cylinder bore and rest the bottom edge of the ring compressor on the engine block.

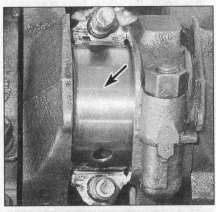

9.37 Place Plastigage on each connecting rod bearing journal parallel to the crankshaft centerline

Note: *Some engines have a letter "F" marking on the side of the piston near the piston pin, others have an arrow, an "F" or a dimple or groove on the top of the piston. All of these are marks that indicate the front of the piston.*

34 Tap the top edge of the ring compressor to make sure it's contacting the block around its entire circumference.

35 Gently tap on the top of the piston with the end of a wooden or plastic hammer handle **(see illustration)** while guiding the end of the connecting rod into place on the crankshaft journal. The piston rings may try to pop out of the ring compressor just before entering the cylinder bore, so keep some downward pressure on the ring compressor. Work slowly, and if any resistance is felt as the piston enters the cylinder, stop immediately. Find out what's hanging up and fix it before proceeding. Do not, for any reason, force the piston into the cylinder - you might break a ring and/or the piston.

36 Once the piston/connecting rod assembly is installed, the connecting rod bearing oil clearance must be checked before the rod cap is permanently installed.

37 Cut a piece of the appropriate size Plastigage slightly shorter than the width of the connecting rod bearing and lay it in place on the

9.41 Use the scale on the Plastigage package to determine the bearing oil clearance - be sure to measure the widest part of the Plastigage and use the correct scale; it comes with both standard and metric scales

number one connecting rod journal, parallel with the journal axis **(see illustration)**.

38 Clean the connecting rod cap bearing face and install the rod cap. Make sure the mating mark on the cap is on the same side as the mark on the connecting rod (see illustration 9.4).

39 Install the old rod bolts at this time and tighten them to the torque listed in this Chapter's Specifications. DO NOT rotate the crankshaft at any time during this operation.

Note: *Use a thin-wall socket to avoid erroneous torque readings that can result if the socket is wedged between the rod cap and the bolt or nut. If the socket tends to wedge itself between the fastener and the cap, lift up on it slightly until it no longer contacts the cap.*

40 Remove the fasteners and detach the rod cap, being very careful not to disturb the Plastigage. Discard the cap bolts at this time as they cannot be reused.

Note: *You MUST use new connecting rod bolts.*

41 Compare the width of the crushed Plastigage to the scale printed on the Plastigage envelope to obtain the oil clearance **(see illustration)**. The connecting rod bearing

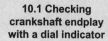

10.1 Checking crankshaft endplay with a dial indicator

10.3 Checking crankshaft endplay with feeler gauges at the thrust bearing journal

oil clearance is usually about 0.001 to 0.002 inch. Consult an automotive machine shop for the clearance specified for the rod bearings on your engine.

42　If the clearance is not as specified, the bearing inserts may be the wrong size (which means different ones will be required). Before deciding that different inserts are needed, make sure that no dirt or oil was between the bearing inserts and the connecting rod or cap when the clearance was measured. Also, recheck the journal diameter. If the Plastigage was wider at one end than the other, the journal may be tapered. If the clearance still exceeds the limit specified, the bearing will have to be replaced with an undersize bearing.

Caution: *When installing a new crankshaft, always use a standard size bearing.*

Final installation

43　Carefully scrape all traces of the Plastigage material off the rod journal and/or bearing face. Be very careful not to scratch the bearing - use your fingernail or the edge of a plastic card.

44　Make sure the bearing faces are perfectly clean, then apply a uniform layer of clean moly-base grease or engine assembly lube to both of them. You'll have to push the piston into the cylinder to expose the face of the bearing insert in the connecting rod.

45　Slide the connecting rod back into place on the journal, install the rod cap, install the new bolts and tighten them to the torque listed in this Chapter's Specifications.

Note: *You MUST install new connecting rod bolts.*

46　Repeat the entire procedure for the remaining pistons/connecting rods.

47　The important points to remember are:

a)　*Keep the back sides of the bearing inserts and the insides of the connecting rods and caps perfectly clean when assembling them.*

b)　*Make sure you have the correct piston/ rod assembly for each cylinder.*

c)　*The mark on the piston must face the front (timing chain end) of the engine.*

d)　*Lubricate the cylinder walls liberally with clean oil.*

e)　*Lubricate the bearing faces when installing the rod caps after the oil clearance has been checked.*

48　After all the piston/connecting rod assemblies have been correctly installed, rotate the crankshaft a number of times by hand to check for any obvious binding.

49　As a final step, check the connecting rod endplay again. If it was correct before disassembly and the original crankshaft and rods were reinstalled, it should still be correct. If new rods or a new crankshaft were installed, the endplay may be inadequate. If so, the rods will have to be removed and taken to an automotive machine shop for machining.

10　Crankshaft - removal and installation

Removal

Note: *The crankshaft can be removed only after the engine has been removed from the vehicle. It's assumed that the driveplate, crankshaft pulley, timing chain, oil pan, oil pump, oil filter and piston/connecting rod assemblies have already been removed. The rear main oil seal retainer must be unbolted and separated from the block before proceeding with crankshaft removal.*

1　Before the crankshaft is removed, measure the endplay. Mount a dial indicator with the indicator in line with and touching the end of the crankshaft (see illustration).

2　Pry the crankshaft all the way to the rear and zero the dial indicator. Next, pry the crankshaft to the front as far as possible and check the reading on the dial indicator. The distance traveled is the endplay. A typical crankshaft endplay will fall between 0.0055 to 0.018 inch (0.14 to 0.30 mm). If it is greater than that, check the crankshaft thrust washer/ bearing assembly surfaces for wear after it's removed. If no wear is evident, new main bearings should correct the endplay. Refer to Step 18 for the location of the thrust washer/ bearing assembly.

3　If a dial indicator isn't available, feeler gauges can be used. Gently pry the crank-

shaft all the way to the front of the engine. Slip feeler gauges between the crankshaft and the front face of the thrust bearing or washer to determine the clearance **(see illustration)**.

3.5L engines

4　Loosen the main bearing cap/main bearing beam bolts 1/4-turn at a time each, until they can be removed by hand. Obtain new main bearing cap bolts (but save the old ones for the oil clearance check).

5　Remove the main bearing beam, noting the arrow pointing to the front of the engine. Gently tap the main bearing caps assembly with a soft-face hammer around the perimeter of the assembly. Pull the main bearing caps straight up and off the cylinder block. Try not to drop the bearing inserts if they come out with the assembly.

4.0L engines

6　Loosen the main bearing cap/bedplate bolts 1/4 turn at a time each, until they can be removed by hand.

7　Gently tap the main bearing caps/bedplate assembly with a soft-face hammer around the perimeter of the assembly. Pull the main bearing cap/bedplate assembly straight up and off the cylinder block. Try not to drop the inserts if they come out with the assembly.

Caution: *The bedplate has built-in pry points; don't pry anywhere else or damage to the bedplate will occur.*

5.6L engines

8　Loosen the main bearing cap and block side-bolts 1/4-turn at a time each, until they can be removed by hand, following the opposite of the tightening sequence (see illustration 10.26). Loosen bolts 30 to 21 first, then bolts 20 to 11, and lastly 10 through 1.

9　Gently tap the main bearing caps with a soft-face hammer to loosen the caps. Pull the main bearing caps straight up and off the cylinder block one at a time. Try not to drop the bearing inserts if they come out with the assembly.

All models

10 Carefully lift the crankshaft out of the engine. It may be a good idea to have an assistant available, since the crankshaft is quite heavy and awkward to handle. With the bearing inserts in place inside the engine block and main bearing caps, reinstall the main bearing caps and main bearing beam onto the engine block and tighten the bolts finger tight. Make sure you install the main bearing main bearing beam assembly with the arrow facing the front of the engine.

Installation

11 Crankshaft installation is the first step in engine reassembly. It's assumed at this point that the engine block and crankshaft have been cleaned, inspected and repaired or reconditioned.
12 Position the engine block with the bottom facing up.
13 Remove the mounting bolts and lift off the main bearing caps.
14 If they're still in place, remove the original bearing inserts from the block and from the main bearing caps. Wipe the bearing surfaces of the block and main bearing caps with a clean, lint-free cloth. They must be kept spotlessly clean. This is critical for determining the correct bearing oil clearance.

Main bearing oil clearance check

15 Without mixing them up, clean the back sides of the new upper main bearing inserts (with grooves and oil holes) and lay one in each main bearing saddle in the block. Each upper bearing has an oil groove and oil hole in it. Clean the back sides of the lower main bearing inserts and lay them in the corresponding location in the main bearing cap. Make sure the tab on the bearing insert fits into the recess in the block or main bearing cap. The upper bearings with the oil holes are installed into the engine block while the lower bearings without the oil holes are installed in the caps.
Caution: *The oil holes in the block must line*

10.18 Insert the thrust washer into the machined surface between the crankshaft and the upper bearing saddle, then rotate it down into the block until it's flush with the parting line on the main bearing saddle - make sure the oil grooves on the thrust washer face the crankshaft

up with the oil holes in the upper bearing inserts.
Caution: *Do not hammer the bearing insert into place and don't nick or gouge the bearing faces. DO NOT apply any lubrication at this time.*
16 Clean the faces of the bearing inserts in the block and the crankshaft main bearing journals with a clean, lint-free cloth.
Note: *The backs of all bearings and the surfaces in which they are installed must be kept clean and free of oil at all times.*
17 Check or clean the oil holes in the crankshaft, as any dirt here can go only one way - straight through the new bearings.
18 Once you're certain the crankshaft is clean, carefully lay it in position in the block, which should be oriented on the engine stand to have the bottom side Up. Lube and insert the thrust washers on each side of journal 3 **(see illustration)**. The thrust washers must be installed in the correct journal.
Note: *Install the thrust washers with the groove in the thrust washer facing the crankshaft and*

10.21 Place the Plastigage onto the crankshaft bearing journal as shown

the smooth sides facing the main bearing saddle. Thrust washers are also installed along with the 3 main bearing cap.
19 Before the crankshaft can be permanently installed, the main bearing oil clearance must be checked.
20 Cut several strips of the appropriate size of Plastigage. They must be slightly shorter than the width of the main bearing journal.
21 Place one piece on each crankshaft main bearing journal, parallel with the journal axis as shown **(see illustration)**.
22 Clean the faces of the bearing inserts in the main bearing caps (3.5L and 5.6L engines) or bedplate assembly (4.0L engines). Hold the bearing inserts in place and install the assembly onto the crankshaft and cylinder block **(see illustrations)**. DO NOT disturb the Plastigage. Make sure you install the main bearing cap assembly with the arrows facing the front (timing chain end) of the engine. Install the main bearing beam over the caps.
23 Apply clean engine oil to all bolt threads

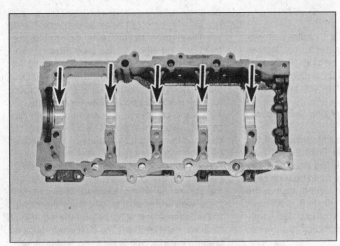

10.22a On 4.0L engines, the bearings are inserted into the corresponding saddles in the bedplate (typical bedplate shown). . .

10.22b. . . then the bedplate is set over the crankshaft onto the dowels of the engine block

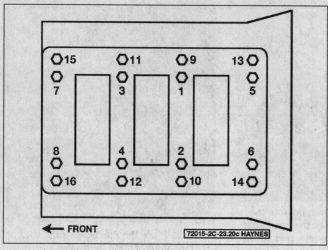

10.24 Main bearing cap/support beam bolt tightening sequence (3.5L engines)

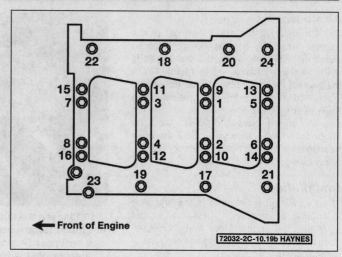

10.25 Main bearing cap/bedplate bolt tightening sequence (4.0L engines)

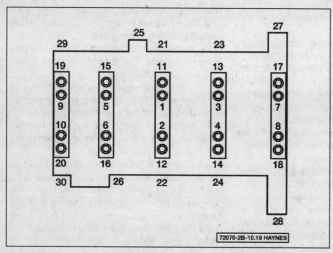

10.26 Main bearing cap and block side-bolt tightening sequence (5.6L engines)

10.28 Use the scale on the Plastigage package to determine the bearing oil clearance - be sure to measure the widest part of the Plastigage and use the correct scale; it comes with both standard and metric scales

prior to installation, then install all bolts finger-tight.

24   3.5L engines: Tighten the main bearing cap bolts in several steps, in sequence (see illustration), to the torque listed in this Chapter's Specifications. DO NOT rotate the crankshaft at any time during this operation.
Note: *Use the old bolts at this time (not the new ones).*

25   4.0L engines: Tighten the main bearing caps/bedplate assembly bolts in several steps, in sequence (see illustration), to the torque listed in this Chapter's Specifications. DO NOT rotate the crankshaft at any time during this operation.
Note: *Use the old bolts at this time (not the new ones).*

26   5.6L engines: Tighten main bearing cap and block side-bolts (see illustration)

to the torque listed in this Chapter's Specifications, in the following sequence: Tighten bolts 1 through 10 first, then bolts 11 through 20, and finally, side-bolts 21 through 30. DO NOT rotate the crankshaft at any time during this operation.
Note: *Use the old bolts at this time (not the new ones).*

27   Remove the bolts in the reverse of the tightening sequence (see illustration 10.24, 10.25 or 10.26). Remove the main bearing beam, then carefully lift the main bearing caps straight up from the block. Do not disturb the Plastigage or rotate the crankshaft. If the main bearing caps are difficult to remove, tap gently from side-to-side with a soft-face hammer to loosen it.

28   Compare the width of the crushed Plasti-gage on each journal to the scale printed on

the Plastigage envelope to determine the main bearing oil clearance (see illustration). A typical main bearing oil clearance should fall between 0.0014 to 0026 inch (0.035 to 0.065 mm). Check with an automotive machine shop for the clearance specified for your engine.

29   If the clearance is not as specified, the bearing inserts may be the wrong size (which means different ones will be required). Before deciding if different inserts are needed, make sure that no dirt or oil was between the bearing inserts and the cap assembly or block when the clearance was measured. If the Plasti-gage was wider at one end than the other, the crankshaft journal may be tapered. If the clearance still exceeds the limit specified, the bearing insert(s) will have to be replaced with an undersize bearing insert(s).
Caution: *When installing a brand new crank-*

shaft, always install a standard bearing insert set.

30   Carefully scrape all traces of the Plasti-gage material off the main bearing journals and/or the bearing insert faces. Remove all residue from the oil holes. Use your fingernail or the edge of a plastic card - don't nick or scratch the bearing faces.

Final installation

31   Carefully lift the crankshaft out of the cylinder block.

32   Clean the bearing insert faces in the cylinder block, then apply a thin, uniform layer of moly-base grease or engine assembly lube to each of the bearing surfaces that contact the crankshaft. Coat the thrust faces as well as the journal face of the thrust washers.

33   Make sure the crankshaft journals are clean, then lay the crankshaft back in place in the cylinder block.

34   Clean the bearing insert faces and then apply the same lubricant to them. Clean the engine block thoroughly. The surfaces must be free of oil residue. Install the thrust washers. The grooves on the thrust washers face outward, away from the bearing.

35   On 4.0L engines, apply a 3.5 mm bead of RTV sealant or equivalent to the bedplate sealing area on the block.

36   Install each main bearing cap, then install the support beam.

Note: *The arrow on the main bearing beam must point toward the front of the engine and it must be visible when looking at the bottom of the engine.*

37   Prior to installation, apply clean engine oil to the new bolt threads, wiping off any excess, then install all bolts finger-tight.

Note: *The main bearing cap bolts MUST be replaced with new ones.*

38   Tighten the main bearing cap bolts, in sequence **(see illustration 10.24, 10.25 or 10.26)**, to the torque listed in this Chapter's Specifications.

39   Recheck crankshaft endplay with a feeler gauge or a dial indicator. The endplay should be correct if the crankshaft thrust faces aren't worn or damaged and if new bearings have been installed.

40   Rotate the crankshaft a number of times by hand to check for any obvious binding. It should rotate with a running torque of 50 in-lbs or less. If the running torque is too high, identify and correct the problem at this time.

41   Install the new rear main oil seal and retainer (see Chapter 2A or 2B).

11   Engine overhaul - reassembly sequence

1   Before beginning engine reassembly, make sure you have all the necessary new parts, gaskets and seals as well as the following items on hand:

> Common hand tools
> A 1/2-inch drive torque wrench
> New engine oil
> Oil filter
> Gasket sealant
> Thread locking compound

2   If you obtained a short block it will be necessary to install the cylinder head, the oil pump and pick-up tube, the oil pan, the water pump, the timing chain and timing cover, and the valve cover (see Chapter 2A or 2B). In order to save time and avoid problems, the external components must be installed in the following general order:

> Thermostat and housing cover
> Water pump
> Intake and exhaust manifolds
> Fuel injection components
> Emission control components
> Spark plugs
> Ignition coils
> Oil filter and oil cooler
> Engine mounts and mount brackets
> Driveplate

12   Initial start-up and break-in after overhaul

Warning: *Have a fire extinguisher handy when starting the engine for the first time.*

1   Once the engine has been installed in the vehicle, double-check the engine oil and coolant levels.

2   With the spark plugs out of the engine and the fuel pump disabled (see Chapter 4, Section 2), crank the engine until oil pressure registers on the gauge or the light goes out.

3   Install the spark plugs and ignition coils, and reinstall the fuel pump fuse.

4   Start the engine. It may take a few moments for the fuel system to build up pressure, but the engine should start without a great deal of effort.

5   After the engine starts, it should be allowed to warm up to normal operating temperature. While the engine is warming up, make a thorough check for fuel, oil and coolant leaks.

6   Shut the engine off and recheck the engine oil and coolant levels.

7   Drive the vehicle to an area with minimum traffic, accelerate from 30 to 50 mph, then allow the vehicle to slow to 30 mph with the throttle closed. Repeat the procedure 10 or 12 times. This will load the piston rings and cause them to seat properly against the cylinder walls. Check again for oil and coolant leaks.

8   Drive the vehicle gently for the first 500 miles (no sustained high speeds) and keep a constant check on the oil level. It is not unusual for an engine to use oil during the break-in period.

9   At approximately 500 to 600 miles, change the oil and filter.

10   For the next few hundred miles, drive the vehicle normally. Do not pamper it or abuse it.

11   After 2000 miles, change the oil and filter again and consider the engine broken in.

COMMON ENGINE OVERHAUL TERMS

B

Backlash - The amount of play between two parts. Usually refers to how much one gear can be moved back and forth without moving the gear with which it's meshed.

Bearing Caps - The caps held in place by nuts or bolts which, in turn, hold the bearing surface. This space is for lubricating oil to enter.

Bearing clearance - The amount of space left between shaft and bearing surface. This space is for lubricating oil to enter.

Bearing crush - The additional height which is purposely manufactured into each bearing half to ensure complete contact of the bearing back with the housing bore when the engine is assembled.

Bearing knock - The noise created by movement of a part in a loose or worn bearing.

Blueprinting - Dismantling an engine and reassembling it to EXACT specifications.

Bore - An engine cylinder, or any cylindrical hole; also used to describe the process of enlarging or accurately refinishing a hole with a cutting tool, as to bore an engine cylinder. The bore size is the diameter of the hole.

Boring - Renewing the cylinders by cutting them out to a specified size. A boring bar is used to make the cut.

Bottom end - A term which refers collectively to the engine block, crankshaft, main bearings and the big ends of the connecting rods.

Break-in - The period of operation between installation of new or rebuilt parts and time in which parts are worn to the correct fit. Driving at reduced and varying speed for a specified mileage to permit parts to wear to the correct fit.

Bushing - A one-piece sleeve placed in a bore to serve as a bearing surface for shaft, piston pin, etc. Usually replaceable.

C

Camshaft - The shaft in the engine, on which a series of lobes are located for operating the valve mechanisms. The camshaft is driven by gears or sprockets and a timing chain. Usually referred to simply as the cam.

Carbon - Hard, or soft, black deposits found in combustion chamber, on plugs, under rings, on and under valve heads.

Cast iron - An alloy of iron and more than two percent carbon, used for engine blocks and heads because it's relatively inexpensive and easy to mold into complex shapes.

Chamfer - To bevel across (or a bevel on) the sharp edge of an object.

Chase - To repair damaged threads with a tap or die.

Combustion chamber - The space between the piston and the cylinder head, with the piston at top dead center, in which air-fuel mixture is burned.

Compression ratio - The relationship between cylinder volume (clearance volume) when the piston is at top dead center and cylinder volume when the piston is at bottom dead center.

Connecting rod - The rod that connects the crank on the crankshaft with the piston. Sometimes called a con rod.

Connecting rod cap - The part of the connecting rod assembly that attaches the rod to the crankpin.

Core plug - Soft metal plug used to plug the casting holes for the coolant passages in the block.

Crankcase - The lower part of the engine in which the crankshaft rotates; includes the lower section of the cylinder block and the oil pan.

Crank kit - A reground or reconditioned crankshaft and new main and connecting rod bearings.

Crankpin - The part of a crankshaft to which a connecting rod is attached.

Crankshaft - The main rotating member, or shaft, running the length of the crankcase, with offset throws to which the connecting rods are attached; changes the reciprocating motion of the pistons into rotating motion.

Cylinder sleeve - A replaceable sleeve, or liner, pressed into the cylinder block to form the cylinder bore.

D

Deburring - Removing the burrs (rough edges or areas) from a bearing.

Deglazer - A tool, rotated by an electric motor, used to remove glaze from cylinder walls so a new set of rings will seat.

E

Endplay - The amount of lengthwise movement between two parts. As applied to a crankshaft, the distance that the crankshaft can move forward and back in the cylinder block.

F

Face - A machinist's term that refers to removing metal from the end of a shaft or the face of a larger part, such as a flywheel.

Fatigue - A breakdown of material through a large number of loading and unloading cycles. The first signs are cracks followed shortly by breaks.

Feeler gauge - A thin strip of hardened steel, ground to an exact thickness, used to check clearances between parts.

Free height - The unloaded length or height of a spring.

Freeplay - The looseness in a linkage, or an assembly of parts, between the initial application of force and actual movement. Usually perceived as slop or slight delay.

Freeze plug - See Core plug.

G

Gallery - A large passage in the block that forms a reservoir for engine oil pressure.

Glaze - The very smooth, glassy finish that develops on cylinder walls while an engine is in service.

H

Heli-Coil - A rethreading device used when threads are worn or damaged. The device is installed in a retapped hole to reduce the thread size to the original size.

I

Installed height - The spring's measured length or height, as installed on the cylinder head. Installed height is measured from the spring seat to the underside of the spring retainer.

J

Journal - The surface of a rotating shaft which turns in a bearing.

K

Keeper - The split lock that holds the valve spring retainer in position on the valve stem.

Key - A small piece of metal inserted into matching grooves machined into two parts fitted together - such as a gear pressed onto a shaft - which prevents slippage between the two parts.

Knock - The heavy metallic engine sound, produced in the combustion chamber as a result of abnormal combustion - usually detonation. Knock is usually caused by a loose or worn bearing. Also referred to as detonation, pinging and spark knock. Connecting rod or main bearing knocks are created by too much oil clearance or insufficient lubrication.

L

Lands - The portions of metal between the piston ring grooves.

Lapping the valves - Grinding a valve face and its seat together with lapping compound.

Lash - The amount of free motion in a gear train, between gears, or in a mechanical assembly, that occurs before movement can begin. Usually refers to the lash in a valve train.

Lifter - The part that rides against the cam to transfer motion to the rest of the valve train.

M

Machining - The process of using a machine to remove metal from a metal part.

Main bearings - The plain, or babbit, bearings that support the crankshaft.

Main bearing caps - The cast iron caps, bolted to the bottom of the block, that support the main bearings.

O

O.D. - Outside diameter.

Oil gallery - A pipe or drilled passageway in the engine used to carry engine oil from one area to another.

Oil ring - The lower ring, or rings, of a piston; designed to prevent excessive amounts of oil from working up the cylinder walls and into the combustion chamber. Also called an oil-control ring.

Oil seal - A seal which keeps oil from leaking out of a compartment. Usually refers to a dynamic seal around a rotating shaft or other moving part.

O-ring - A type of sealing ring made of a special rubberlike material; in use, the O-ring is compressed into a groove to provide the sealing action.

Overhaul - To completely disassemble a unit, clean and inspect all parts, reassemble it with the original or new parts and make all adjustments necessary for proper operation.

P

Pilot bearing - A small bearing installed in the center of the flywheel (or the rear end of the crankshaft) to support the front end of the input shaft of the transmission.

Pip mark - A little dot or indentation which indicates the top side of a compression ring.

Piston - The cylindrical part, attached to the connecting rod, that moves up and down in the cylinder as the crankshaft rotates. When the fuel charge is fired, the piston transfers the force of the explosion to the connecting rod, then to the crankshaft.

Piston pin (or wrist pin) - The cylindrical and usually hollow steel pin that passes through the piston. The piston pin fastens the piston to the upper end of the connecting rod.

Piston ring - The split ring fitted to the groove in a piston. The ring contacts the sides of the ring groove and also rubs against the cylinder wall, thus sealing space between piston and wall. There are two types of rings: Compression rings seal the compression pressure in the combustion chamber; oil rings scrape excessive oil off the cylinder wall.

Piston ring groove - The slots or grooves cut in piston heads to hold piston rings in position.

Piston skirt - The portion of the piston below the rings and the piston pin hole.

Plastigage - A thin strip of plastic thread, available in different sizes, used for measuring clearances. For example, a strip of plastigage is laid across a bearing journal and mashed as parts are assembled. Then parts are disassembled and the width of the strip is measured to determine clearance between journal and bearing. Commonly used to measure crankshaft main-bearing and connecting rod bearing clearances.

Press-fit - A tight fit between two parts that requires pressure to force the parts together. Also referred to as drive, or force, fit.

Prussian blue - A blue pigment; in solution, useful in determining the area of contact between two surfaces. Prussian blue is commonly used to determine the width and location of the contact area between the valve face and the valve seat.

R

Race (bearing) - The inner or outer ring that provides a contact surface for balls or rollers in bearing.

Ream - To size, enlarge or smooth a hole by using a round cutting tool with fluted edges.

Ring job - The process of reconditioning the cylinders and installing new rings.

Runout - Wobble. The amount a shaft rotates out-of-true.

S

Saddle - The upper main bearing seat.

Scored - Scratched or grooved, as a cylinder wall may be scored by abrasive particles moved up and down by the piston rings.

Scuffing - A type of wear in which there's a transfer of material between parts moving against each other; shows up as pits or grooves in the mating surfaces.

Seat - The surface upon which another part rests or seats. For example, the valve seat is the matched surface upon which the valve face rests. Also used to refer to wearing into a good fit; for example, piston rings seat after a few miles of driving.

Short block - An engine block complete with crankshaft and piston and, usually, camshaft assemblies.

Static balance - The balance of an object while it's stationary.

Step - The wear on the lower portion of a ring land caused by excessive side and back-clearance. The height of the step indicates the ring's extra side clearance and the length of the step projecting from the back wall of the groove represents the ring's back clearance.

Stroke - The distance the piston moves when traveling from top dead center to bottom dead center, or from bottom dead center to top dead center.

Stud - A metal rod with threads on both ends.

T

Tang - A lip on the end of a plain bearing used to align the bearing during assembly.

Tap - To cut threads in a hole. Also refers to the fluted tool used to cut threads.

Taper - A gradual reduction in the width of a shaft or hole; in an engine cylinder, taper usually takes the form of uneven wear, more pronounced at the top than at the bottom.

Throws - The offset portions of the crankshaft to which the connecting rods are affixed.

Thrust bearing - The main bearing that has thrust faces to prevent excessive endplay, or forward and backward movement of the crankshaft.

Thrust washer - A bronze or hardened steel washer placed between two moving parts. The washer prevents longitudinal movement and provides a bearing surface for thrust surfaces of parts.

Tolerance - The amount of variation permitted from an exact size of measurement. Actual amount from smallest acceptable dimension to largest acceptable dimension.

U

Umbrella - An oil deflector placed near the valve tip to throw oil from the valve stem area.

Undercut - A machined groove below the normal surface.

Undersize bearings - Smaller diameter bearings used with re-ground crankshaft journals.

V

Valve grinding - Refacing a valve in a valve-refacing machine.

Valve train - The valve-operating mechanism of an engine; includes all components from the camshaft to the valve.

Vibration damper - A cylindrical weight attached to the front of the crankshaft to minimize torsional vibration (the twist-untwist actions of the crankshaft caused by the cylinder firing impulses). Also called a harmonic balancer.

W

Water jacket - The spaces around the cylinders, between the inner and outer shells of the cylinder block or head, through which coolant circulates.

Web - A supporting structure across a cavity.

Woodruff key - A key with a radiused backside (viewed from the side).

Notes

Chapter 3
Cooling, heating and air conditioning systems

Contents

	Section		Section
Air conditioning compressor - removal and installation	11	Heater and air conditioning control assembly - removal and installation	9
Air conditioning condenser - removal and installation	12	Heater core - removal and installation	10
Air conditioning and heating system - check and maintenance	3	Radiator and coolant reservoir - removal and installation	6
Air conditioning receiver-drier - removal and installation	13	Thermostat - removal and installation	4
Blower motor - removal and installation	8	Troubleshooting	2
Engine cooling fans - replacement	5	Water pump - replacement	7
General information	1		

Specifications

General

Radiator cap pressure rating	Refer to pressure specification on cap
Cooling system capacity	See Chapter 1
Refrigerant type	R-134a
Refrigerant capacity	Refer to "Air Conditioner" label in the engine compartment

Torque specifications

Ft-lbs (unless otherwise indicated)   **Nm**

Note: *One foot-pound (ft-lb) of torque is equivalent to 12 inch-pounds (in-lbs) of torque. Torque values below approximately 15 foot-pounds are expressed in inch-pounds, because most foot-pound torque wrenches are not accurate at these smaller values.*

	Ft-lbs (unless otherwise indicated)	Nm
Compressor mounting bolts		
2012 and earlier models		
V6 engines	23	31
V8 engines	45	61
2013 and later models	Not available	
Thermostat housing bolts		
V6 engines	80 in-lbs	9
V8 engines	15	20
Water pump cover bolts (V6 engines)	96 in-lbs	11
Water pump bolts		
V6 engines	85 in-lbs	9.5
V8 engines	18	24
Coolant drain plug		
2012 and earlier V6	87 in-lbs	9.8
2013 and later V6	108 in-lbs	12.3
Engine block heater (Canadian models)	29	39

2.2 The cooling system pressure tester is connected in place of the pressure cap, then pumped up to pressurize the system

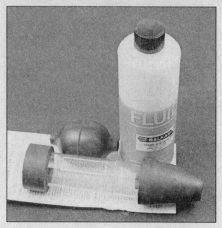

2.5a The combustion leak detector consists of a bulb, syringe and test fluid

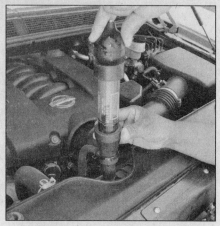

2.5b Place the tester over the cooling system filler neck and use the bulb to draw a sample into the tester

1   General information

Warning: *Do not allow antifreeze to come in contact with your skin or painted surfaces of the vehicle. Rinse off spills immediately with plenty of water. Antifreeze is highly toxic if ingested. Never leave antifreeze lying around in an open container or in puddles on the floor; children and pets are attracted by its sweet smell and may drink it. Check with local authorities about disposing of used antifreeze. Many communities have collection centers which will see that antifreeze is disposed of safely. Never dump used antifreeze on the ground or pour it into drains.*

Engine cooling system

1   All modern vehicles employ a pressurized engine cooling system with thermostatically controlled coolant circulation. The cooling system consists of a radiator, an expansion tank or coolant reservoir, a pressure cap (located on the expansion tank or radiator), a thermostat, a cooling fan, and a water pump.

2   The water pump circulates coolant through the engine. The coolant flows around each cylinder and around the intake and exhaust ports, near the spark plug areas and in close proximity to the exhaust valve guides.

3   A thermostat controls engine coolant temperature. During warm up, the closed thermostat prevents coolant from circulating through the radiator. As the engine nears normal operating temperature, the thermostat opens and allows hot coolant to travel through the radiator, where it's cooled before returning to the engine.

Heating system

4   The heating system consists of a blower fan and heater core located in a housing under the dash, the hoses connecting the heater core to the engine cooling system and the heater/air conditioning control head on the dashboard. Hot engine coolant is circulated through the heater core. When the heater mode is activated, a flap door in the housing opens to expose the heater core to the passenger compartment through air ducts. A fan switch on the control head activates the blower motor, which forces air through the core, heating the air.

Air conditioning system

5   The air conditioning system consists of a condenser mounted in front of the radiator, an evaporator mounted adjacent to the heater core, a compressor mounted on the engine, a receiver-drier or accumulator and the plumbing connecting all of the above components.

6   A blower fan forces the warmer air of the passenger compartment through the evaporator core (sort of a radiator-in-reverse), transferring the heat from the air to the refrigerant. The liquid refrigerant boils off into low pressure vapor, taking the heat with it when it leaves the evaporator.

2   Troubleshooting

Coolant leaks

1   A coolant leak can develop anywhere in the cooling system, but the most common causes are:

a) A loose or weak hose clamp
b) A defective hose
c) A faulty pressure cap
d) A damaged radiator
e) A bad heater core
f) A faulty water pump
g) A leaking gasket at any joint that carries coolant

2   Coolant leaks aren't always easy to find. Sometimes they can only be detected when the cooling system is under pressure. Here's where a cooling system pressure tester comes in handy. After the engine has cooled completely, the tester is attached in place of the pressure cap, then pumped up to the pressure value equal to that of the pressure cap rating **(see illustration)**. Now, leaks that only exist when the engine is fully warmed up will become apparent. The tester can be left connected to locate a nagging slow leak.

Coolant level drops, but no external leaks

3   If you find it necessary to keep adding coolant, but there are no external leaks, the probable causes include:

a) A blown head gasket
b) A leaking intake manifold gasket (only on engines that have coolant passages in the manifold)
c) A cracked cylinder head or cylinder block

4   Any of the above problems will also usually result in contamination of the engine oil, which will cause it to take on a milkshake-like appearance. A bad head gasket or cracked head or block can also result in engine oil contaminating the cooling system.

5   Combustion leak detectors (also known as block testers) are available at most auto parts stores. These work by detecting exhaust gases in the cooling system, which indicates a compression leak from a cylinder into the coolant. The tester consists of a large bulb-type syringe and bottle of test fluid **(see illustration)**. A measured amount of the fluid is added to the syringe. The syringe is placed over the cooling system filler neck and, with the engine running, the bulb is squeezed and a sample of the gases present in the cooling system are drawn up through the test fluid **(see illustration)**. If any combustion gases are present in the sample taken, the test fluid will change color.

6   If the test indicates combustion gas is present in the cooling system, you can be sure that the engine has a blown head gasket or a crack in the cylinder head or block, and will require disassembly to repair.

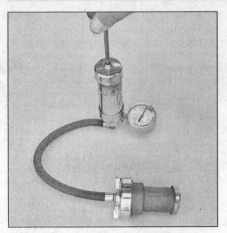

2.8 Checking the cooling system pressure cap with a cooling system pressure tester

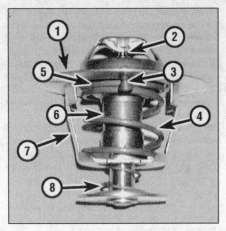

2.10 Typical thermostat:

1	Flange	5	Valve seat
2	Piston	6	Valve
3	Jiggle valve	7	Frame
4	Main coil spring	8	Secondary coil spring

2.28 The water pump weep hole is generally located on the underside of the pump

Pressure cap

Warning: *Wait until the engine is completely cool before beginning this check.*

7   The cooling system is sealed by a spring-loaded cap, which raises the boiling point of the coolant. If the cap's seal or spring are worn out, the coolant can boil and escape past the cap. With the engine completely cool, remove the cap and check the seal; if it's cracked, hardened or deteriorated in any way, replace it with a new one.

8   Even if the seal is good, the spring might not be; this can be checked with a cooling system pressure tester **(see illustration)**. If the cap can't hold a pressure within approximately 1-1/2 lbs of its rated pressure (which is marked on the cap), replace it with a new one.

9   The cap is also equipped with a vacuum relief spring. When the engine cools off, a vacuum is created in the cooling system. The vacuum relief spring allows air back into the system, which will equalize the pressure and prevent damage to the radiator (the radiator tanks could collapse if the vacuum is great enough). If, after turning the engine off and allowing it to cool down you notice any of the cooling system hoses collapsing, replace the pressure cap with a new one.

Thermostat

10   Before assuming the thermostat **(see illustration)** is responsible for a cooling system problem, check the coolant level (see Chapter 1), drivebelt tension (see Chapter 1) and temperature gauge (or light) operation.

11   If the engine takes a long time to warm up (as indicated by the temperature gauge or heater operation), the thermostat is probably stuck open. Replace the thermostat with a new one.

12   If the engine runs hot or overheats, a thorough test of the thermostat should be performed.

13   Definitive testing of the thermostat can only be made when it is removed from the vehicle. If the thermostat is stuck in the open position at room temperature, it is faulty and must be replaced.

Caution: *Do not drive the vehicle without a thermostat. The computer may stay in open loop and emissions and fuel economy will suffer.*

14   To test a thermostat, suspend the (closed) thermostat on a length of string or wire in a pot of cold water.

15   Heat the water on a stove while observing thermostat. The thermostat should fully open before the water boils.

16   If the thermostat doesn't open and close as specified, or sticks in any position, replace it.

Cooling fan

Electric cooling fan

17   If the engine is overheating and the cooling fan is not coming on when the engine temperature rises to an excessive level, unplug the fan motor electrical connector(s) and connect the motor directly to the battery with fused jumper wires. If the fan motor doesn't come on, replace the motor.

18   If the radiator fan motor is okay, but it isn't coming on when the engine gets hot, the fan relay might be defective. A relay is used to control a circuit by turning it on and off in response to a control decision by the Powertrain Control Module (PCM). These control circuits are fairly complex, and checking them should be left to a qualified automotive technician. Sometimes, the control system can be fixed by simply identifying and replacing a bad relay.

19   Locate the fan relays in the engine compartment fuse/relay box.

20   Test the relay (see Chapter 12).

21   If the relay is okay, check all wiring and connections to the fan motor. Refer to the wiring diagrams at the end of Chapter 12. If no obvious problems are found, the problem could be the Engine Coolant Temperature (ECT) sensor or the Powertrain Control Module (PCM). Have the cooling fan system and circuit diagnosed by a dealer service department or repair shop with the proper diagnostic equipment.

Note: *These models are equipped with a cooling fan motor resistor. Have the resistor checked if the fan motor does not respond to the speed variations signaled by the PCM.*

Belt-driven cooling fan

22   Disconnect the cable from the negative terminal of the battery and rock the fan back and forth by hand to check for excessive bearing play.

23   With the engine cold (and not running), turn the fan blades by hand. The fan should turn freely.

24   Visually inspect for substantial fluid leakage from the clutch assembly. If problems are noted, replace the clutch assembly.

25   With the engine completely warmed up, turn off the ignition switch and disconnect the negative battery cable from the battery. Turn the fan by hand. Some drag should be evident. If the fan turns easily, replace the fan clutch.

Water pump

26   A failure in the water pump can cause serious engine damage due to overheating.

Drivebelt-driven water pump

27   There are two ways to check the operation of the water pump while it's installed on the engine. If the pump is found to be defective, it should be replaced with a new or rebuilt unit.

28   Water pumps are equipped with weep (or vent) holes **(see illustration)**. If a failure occurs in the pump seal, coolant will leak from the hole.

29   If the water pump shaft bearings fail, there may be a howling sound at the pump while it's running. Shaft wear can be felt with

the drivebelt removed if the water pump pulley is rocked up and down (with the engine off). Don't mistake drivebelt slippage, which causes a squealing sound, for water pump bearing failure.

Timing chain or timing belt-driven water pump

30   Water pumps driven by the timing chain or timing belt are located underneath the timing chain or timing belt cover.
31   Checking the water pump is limited because of where it is located. However, some basic checks can be made before deciding to remove the water pump. If the pump is found to be defective, it should be replaced with a new or rebuilt unit.
32   One sign that the water pump may be failing is that the heater (climate control) may not work well. Warm the engine to normal operating temperature, confirm that the coolant level is correct, then run the heater and check for hot air coming from the ducts.
33   Check for noises coming from the water pump area. If the water pump impeller shaft or bearings are failing, there may be a howling sound at the pump while the engine is running. **Note:** Be careful not to mistake drivebelt noise (squealing) for water pump bearing or shaft failure.
34   It you suspect water pump failure due to noise, wear can be confirmed by feeling for play at the pump shaft. This can be done by rocking the drive sprocket on the pump shaft up and down. To do this you will need to remove the tension on the timing chain or belt as well as access the water pump.

All water pumps

35   In rare cases or on high-mileage vehicles, another sign of water pump failure may be the presence of coolant in the engine oil. This condition will adversely affect the engine in varying degrees.
Note: Finding coolant in the engine oil could indicate other serious issues besides a failed water pump, such as a blown head gasket or a cracked cylinder head or block.
36   Even a pump that exhibits no outward signs of a problem, such as noise or leakage, can still be due for replacement. Removal for close examination is the only sure way to tell. Sometimes the fins on the back of the impeller can corrode to the point that cooling efficiency is diminished significantly.

Heater system

37   Little can go wrong with a heater. If the fan motor will run at all speeds, the electrical part of the system is okay. The three basic heater problems fall into the following general categories:

a) Not enough heat
b) Heat all the time
c) No heat

38   If there's not enough heat, the control valve or door is stuck in a partially open position, the coolant coming from the engine isn't hot enough, or the heater core is restricted.

If the coolant isn't hot enough, the thermostat in the engine cooling system is stuck open, allowing coolant to pass through the engine so rapidly that it doesn't heat up quickly enough. If the vehicle is equipped with a temperature gauge instead of a warning light, watch to see if the engine temperature rises to the normal operating range after driving for a reasonable distance.
39   If there's heat all the time, the control valve or the door is stuck wide open.
40   If there's no heat, coolant is probably not reaching the heater core, or the heater core is plugged. The likely cause is a collapsed or plugged hose, core, or a frozen heater control valve. If the heater is the type that flows coolant all the time, the cause is a stuck door or a broken or kinked control cable.

Air conditioning system

41   If the cool air output is inadequate: Inspect the condenser coils and fins to make sure they're clear.

a) Check the compressor clutch for slippage.
b) Check the blower motor for proper operation.
c) Inspect the blower discharge passage for obstructions.
d) Check the system air intake filter for clogging.

42   If the system provides intermittent cooling air:

a) Check the circuit breaker, blower switch and blower motor for a malfunction.
b) Check the compressor clutch for slippage.
c) Inspect the plenum door to make sure it's operating properly.
d) Inspect the evaporator for clogging.
e) If the unit is icing up, it may be caused by excessive moisture in the system, incorrect super heat switch adjustment or low thermostat adjustment.

43   If the system provides no cooling air: Inspect the compressor drivebelt. Make sure it is not loose or broken.
Make sure the compressor clutch engages. If it doesn't, check for a blown fuse.
If the compressor clutch doesn't engage, bridge the terminals of the AC pressure switch(es) with a jumper wire; if the clutch now engages, and the system is properly charged, the pressure switch is bad.
Inspection the wiring harnesses for broken or disconnected wires.
Make sure the blower motor is not disconnected or burned out.
Make sure the compressor isn't partially or completely seized.
Inspect the refrigerant lines for leaks.
Check the components for leaks.
Inspect the receiver-drier/accumulator or expansion valve/tube for clogged screens.
44   If the system is noisy:

a) Look for loose panels in the passenger compartment.
b) Inspect the compressor drivebelt. It may be loose or worn.

c) Check the compressor mounting blots. They should be tight.
d) Listen carefully to the compressor. If may be worn out.
e) Listen to the idler pulley and bearing, and the clutch. Either may be defective.
f) The winding in the compressor clutch coil or solenoid may be defective.
g) The compressor oil level may be low.
h) The blower motor fan bushing or the motor itself may be worn out.
i) If there is an excessive charge in the system, you'll hear a rumbling noise in the high-pressure line, a thumping noise in the compressor, or see bubbles or cloudiness in the sight glass.
j) If there's a low charge in the system, you might hear hissing in the evaporator case at the expansion valve, or see bubbles or cloudiness in the sight glass.

---

3   Air conditioning and heating system - check and maintenance

---

Air conditioning system

Warning: The air conditioning system is under high pressure. Do not loosen any hose fittings or remove any components until after the system has been discharged. Air conditioning refrigerant should be properly discharged into an EPA-approved recovery/recycling unit at a dealer service department or an automotive air conditioning repair facility. Always wear eye protection when disconnecting air conditioning system fittings.
Caution: All models covered by this manual use environmentally friendly R-134a. This refrigerant (and its appropriate refrigerant oils) are not compatible with R-12 refrigerant system components and must never be mixed or the components will be damaged.
Caution: When replacing entire components, additional refrigerant oil should be added equal to the amount that is removed with the component being replaced. Be sure to read the can before adding any oil to the system, to make sure it is compatible with the R-134a system.
1   The following maintenance checks should be performed on a regular basis to ensure that the air conditioning continues to operate at peak efficiency.
Inspect the condition of the compressor drivebelt. If it is worn or deteriorated, replace it (see Chapter 1).

a) Check the drivebelt tension (see Chapter 1).
b) Inspect the system hoses. Look for cracks, bubbles, hardening and deterioration. Inspect the hoses and all fittings for oil bubbles or seepage. If there is any evidence of wear, damage or leakage, replace the hose(s).
c) Inspect the condenser fins for leaves, bugs and any other foreign material that may have embedded itself in the fins. Use a fin comb or compressed air to remove debris from the condenser.

3.9 Insert a thermometer in the center vent, turn on the air conditioning system and wait for it to cool down; depending on the humidity, the output air should be 35 to 40 degrees cooler than the ambient air temperature

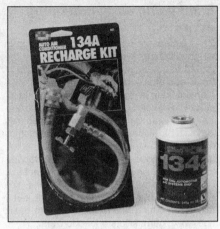

3.11 R-134a automotive air conditioning charging kit

3.13a On 2012 and earlier models, the low-side charging port is located near the brake master cylinder

3.13b On 2013 and later models, the low-side charging port is located at the right side of the engine compartment

d) *Make sure the system has the correct refrigerant charge.*

2   It's a good idea to operate the system for about ten minutes at least once a month. This is particularly important during the winter months because long term non-use can cause hardening, and subsequent failure, of the seals. Note that using the Defrost function operates the compressor.

3   If the air conditioning system is not working properly, proceed to Step 6 and perform the general checks outlined below.

4   Because of the complexity of the air conditioning system and the special equipment necessary to service it, in-depth troubleshooting and repairs beyond checking the refrigerant charge and the compressor clutch operation are not included in this manual. However, simple checks and component replacement procedures are provided in this Chapter. For more complete information on the air conditioning system, refer to the *Haynes Automotive Heating and Air Conditioning Manual*.

5   The most common cause of poor cooling is simply a low system refrigerant charge. If a noticeable drop in system cooling ability occurs, one of the following quick checks will help you determine if the refrigerant level is low.

Checking the refrigerant charge

6   Warm the engine up to normal operating temperature.

7   Place the air conditioning temperature selector at the coldest setting and put the blower at the highest setting.

8   After the system reaches operating temperature, feel the larger pipe exiting the evaporator at the firewall **(see illustration 10.4)**. The outlet pipe should be cold (the tubing that leads back to the compressor). If the evaporator outlet pipe is warm, the system probably needs a charge.

9   Insert a thermometer in the center air

distribution duct **(see illustration)** while operating the air conditioning system at its maximum setting - the temperature of the output air should be 35 to 40 degrees F below the ambient air temperature (down to approximately 40 degrees F). If the ambient (outside) air temperature is very high, say 110 degrees F, the duct air temperature may be as high as 60 degrees F, but generally the air conditioning is 30 to 40 degrees F cooler than the ambient air.

10   Further inspection or testing of the system requires special tools and techniques and is beyond the scope of the home mechanic.

Adding refrigerant

Caution: *Make sure any refrigerant, refrigerant oil or replacement component you purchase is designated as compatible with R-134a systems.*

11   Purchase an R-134a automotive charging kit at an auto parts store **(see illustration)**. A charging kit includes a can of refrigerant, a tap valve and a short section of hose that can be attached between the tap valve and the system low side service valve.

Caution: *Never add more than one can of refrigerant to the system. If more refrigerant than that is required, the system should be evacuated and leak tested.*

12   Back off the valve handle on the charging kit and screw the kit onto the refrigerant can, making sure first that the O-ring or rubber seal inside the threaded portion of the kit is in place.

Warning: *Wear protective eyewear when dealing with pressurized refrigerant cans.*

13   Remove the dust cap from the low-side charging port and attach the hose's quick-connect fitting to the port **(see illustrations)**.

Warning: *DO NOT hook the charging kit hose to the system high side! The fittings on the charging kit are designed to fit only on the low side of the system.*

14   Warm up the engine and turn On the air conditioning. Keep the charging kit hose away from the fan and other moving parts.

Note: *The charging process requires the compressor to be running. If the clutch cycles off, you can put the air conditioning switch on High and leave the car doors open to keep the clutch on and compressor working. The compressor can be kept on during the charging by removing the connector from the pressure switch and bridging it with a paper clip or jumper wire during the procedure.*

15   Turn the valve handle on the kit until the stem pierces the can, then back the handle out to release the refrigerant. You should be able to hear the rush of gas. Keep the can upright at all times, but shake it occasionally. Allow stabilization time between each addition.

Note: *The charging process will go faster if you wrap the can with a hot-water-soaked rag to keep the can from freezing up.*

16   If you have an accurate thermometer, you can place it in the center air condition-

ing duct inside the vehicle and keep track of the output air temperature. A charged system that is working properly should cool down to approximately 40 degrees F. If the ambient (outside) air temperature is very high, say 110 degrees F, the duct air temperature may be as high as 60 degrees F, but generally the air conditioning is 35 to 40 degrees F cooler than the ambient air.

17   When the can is empty, turn the valve handle to the closed position and release the connection from the low-side port. Reinstall the dust cap.

18   Remove the charging kit from the can and store the kit for future use with the piercing valve in the UP position, to prevent inadvertently piercing the can on the next use.

Heating systems

19   If the carpet under the heater core is damp, or if antifreeze vapor or steam is coming through the vents, the heater core is leaking. Remove it (see Section 10) and install a new unit (most radiator shops will not repair a leaking heater core).

20   If the air coming out of the heater vents isn't hot, the problem could stem from any of the following causes:

   a) *The thermostat is stuck open, preventing the engine coolant from warming up enough to carry heat to the heater core. Replace the thermostat (see Section 4).*
   b) *There is a blockage in the system, preventing the flow of coolant through the heater core. Feel both heater hoses at the firewall. They should be hot. If one of them is cold, there is an obstruction in one of the hoses or in the heater core, or the heater control valve is shut. Detach the hoses and back flush the heater core with a water hose. If the heater core is clear but circulation is impeded, remove the two hoses and flush them out with a water hose.*
   c) *If flushing fails to remove the blockage from the heater core, the core must be replaced (see Section 10).*

Eliminating air conditioning odors

21   Unpleasant odors that often develop in air conditioning systems are caused by the growth of a fungus, usually on the surface of the evaporator core. The warm, humid environment there is a perfect breeding ground for mildew to develop.

22   The evaporator core on most vehicles is difficult to access, and factory dealerships have a lengthy, expensive process for eliminating the fungus by opening up the evaporator case and using a powerful disinfectant and rinse on the core until the fungus is gone. You can service your own system at home, but it takes something much stronger than basic household germ-killers or deodorizers.

23   Aerosol disinfectants for automotive air conditioning systems are available in most auto parts stores, but remember when shopping for them that the most effective treatments are also the most expensive. The basic procedure for using these sprays is to start by running the system in the RECIRC mode for ten minutes with the blower on its highest speed. Use the highest heat mode to dry out the system and keep the compressor from engaging by disconnecting the wiring connector at the compressor.

24   The disinfectant can usually comes with a long spray hose. Insert the nozzle into an intake port inside the cabin, and spray according to the manufacturer's recommendations. Follow the manufacturer's recommendations for the length of spray and waiting time between applications.

Automatic heating and air conditioning systems

25   Some vehicles are equipped with an optional automatic climate control system. This system has its own computer that receives inputs from various sensors in the heating and air conditioning system. This computer, like the PCM, has self-diagnostic capabilities to help pinpoint problems or faults within the system. Vehicles equipped

with automatic heating and air conditioning systems are very complex and considered beyond the scope of the home mechanic. Vehicles equipped with automatic heating and air conditioning systems should be taken to dealer service department or other qualified facility for repair.

---

4   Thermostat - removal and installation

Warning: *Do not allow antifreeze to come in contact with your skin or painted surfaces of the vehicle. Rinse off spills immediately with plenty of water. Antifreeze is highly toxic if ingested. Never leave antifreeze lying around in an open container or in puddles on the floor; children and pets are attracted by its sweet smell and may drink it. Check with local authorities about disposing of used antifreeze. Many communities have collection centers which will see that antifreeze is disposed of safely. Never dump used antifreeze on the ground or pour it into drains.*

Warning: *Wait until the engine is completely cool before beginning this procedure.*

1   Drain the cooling system (see Chapter 1). If the coolant is relatively new, or is in good condition, save it and re-use it.

Removal

V6 engine

2   2012 and earlier models: Remove the air filter housing (see Chapter 4).

3   2013 and later models: Unbolt the coolant reservoir and set it aside.

4   Remove the upper radiator hose.

5   Remove the fan shrouds as necessary to gain easier access.

6   Disconnect the lower radiator hose and the oil cooler hose from the coolant inlet. If the hose is stuck, grasp it near the end with a pair of large adjustable pliers and twist it to break the seal, then pull it off. If the hose is old or deteriorated, cut it off and install a new one.

7   Remove the thermostat housing/thermostat assembly **(see illustration)**.

Note: *If the thermostat is defective, you'll have to replace the entire housing/thermostat assembly.*

V8 engine

8   Remove the engine cover **(see illustration)**.

9   Remove the air intake duct between the throttle body and the air filter housing (see Chapter 4).

10   Remove the thermostat housing cover mounting bolts, then separate the cover from the housing **(see illustration)**.

Note: *Leave the radiator hose attached to the housing cover unless the hose is going to be replaced.*

11   Note the position of the thermostat, then pull the thermostat out of the housing **(see**

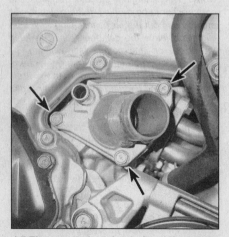

4.7 Thermostat housing bolts - V6 engines

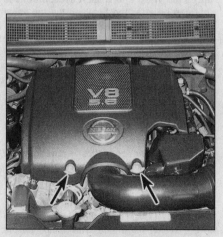

4.8 Engine cover fasteners

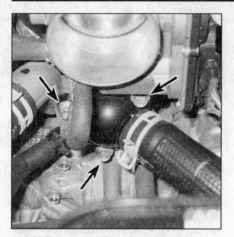

4.10 Thermostat housing cover bolts - V8 engines

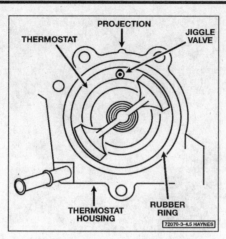

4.11 Thermostat installation details

5.5 Detach the lower shroud from the upper shroud

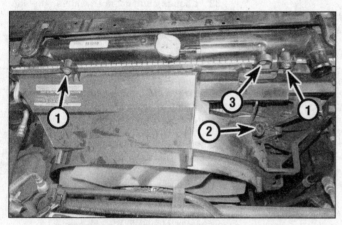

5.10a Upper fan shroud and electric fan details

5.10b Slide the fan shroud straight up

1   Upper fan shroud bolts
2   Fan electrical connector (harness already unlpugged)
3   Fan motor frame bolt

illustration). During installation, the jiggle valve must be up (matching the index in the thermostat housing.

Installation

12   Installation is the reverse of removal. Clean the mating surfaces thoroughly and always use a new gasket (V6 engines) or O-ring (V8 engines). Tighten the thermostat housing bolts to the torque listed in this Chapter's Specifications.
13   Refill the cooling system (see Chapter 1).
14   Start the engine and allow it to reach normal operating temperature, then check for leaks and proper thermostat operation.

5   Engine cooling fans -replacement

Warning: *The models covered by this manual are equipped with a Supplemental Restraint System (SRS), more commonly known as airbags. Always disarm the airbag system before working in the vicinity of any airbag system*

component to avoid the possibility of accidental deployment of the airbag, which could cause personal injury (see Chapter 12). Do not use a memory saving device to preserve the PCM's memory when working on or near airbag system components.
Warning: *Do not allow antifreeze to come in contact with your skin or painted surfaces of the vehicle. Rinse off spills immediately with plenty of water. Antifreeze is highly toxic if ingested. Never leave antifreeze lying around in an open container or in puddles on the floor; children and pets are attracted by its sweet smell and may drink it. Check with local authorities about disposing of used antifreeze. Many communities have collection centers which will see that antifreeze is disposed of safely. Never dump used antifreeze on the ground or pour it into drains.*
Warning: *The engine must be completely cool before beginning this procedure.*
1   Disconnect the cable from the negative terminal of the battery (see Chapter 5).
2   Raise the front of the vehicle and sup-

port it securely on jackstands.

2012 and earlier models

3   Remove the under-vehicle splash shield.

V6 engine

4   Drain some coolant from the radiator (to a level that's lower than the upper radiator hose) (see Chapter 1).

Electric fan

5   Detach the lower part of the fan shroud from the upper fan shroud **(see illustration).**
6   Lower the vehicle and remove the engine cover and the intake air duct (see Chapter 4).
7   Loosen the clamp and detach the upper radiator hose from the radiator.
8   Detach the coolant reservoir hose from the radiator filler neck and the fan shroud.
9   Disconnect the electrical connector from the fan motor.
10   Remove the upper fan shroud bolts and pull the shroud up and out of its lower mounts **(see illustrations).**
11   Remove the fan motor frame bolt and

5.11 Remove the fan motor frame bolt and pull the assembly up and out of the lower mounts

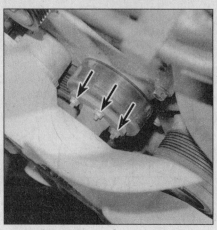

5.17 Fan clutch nuts (three of four shown)

pull the assembly straight up **(see illustration)**.

12   Installation is the reverse of the removal procedure. Make sure the fan frame and upper fan shroud lower mounts engage properly with their respective slots, and that the lower shroud properly clips into place with the upper shroud.

13   Reconnect the battery and perform the necessary re-learn procedures (see Chapter 5).

14   Refill the cooling system (see Chapter 1).

Belt-driven fan

15   Remove the fan shrouds (see Steps 1 through 10).

16   Remove the drivebelt (see Chapter 1).

17   Remove the fan clutch nuts and remove the fan and fan clutch assembly **(see illustration)**.

Note: *To prevent the pulley from turning, you can immobilize it with a strap wrench or wedge a screwdriver between one of the nuts and the shaft.*

Caution: *To prevent silicone fluid from draining from the clutch assembly into the fan drive*

bearing and ruining the lubricant, don't place the clutch/fan assembly in a position with the shaft pointing down.

18   Carefully inspect the fan blades for any damage. Replace if necessary. Inspect the fan clutch for signs of fluid leakage or roughness when rotating the assembly. Inspect the fan bracket on the engine by spinning the pulley, checking for any signs of roughness or play. Replace the fan/bracket/bearing assembly if necessary.

19   Installation is the reverse of removal. Re-install the fan blade with the "F" mark on the fan hub facing towards the front of the vehicle.

V8 engine
Electric fan

20   Remove the radiator grille (see Chapter 11).

21   Disconnect the fan motor electrical connector.

22   Remove the two mounting bolts from the top of the fan motor frame, then remove the frame and motor assembly.

23   Installation is the reverse of the removal

procedure. Reconnect the battery and perform the necessary re-learn procedures (see Chapter 5).

24   Reconnect the battery and perform the necessary re-learn procedures (see Chapter 5).

Belt-driven fan

25   Drain the engine coolant (see Chapter 1).

26   Remove the air intake duct (see Chapter 4).

27   Detach the coolant reservoir hose from the radiator filler neck and the fan shroud.

28   Detach the upper radiator hose from the radiator and move it aside.

29   Detach the lower radiator hose from the engine and set it aside.

30   Disconnect the automatic transmission fluid cooler hoses from the radiator **(see illustration)**. Plug the hoses and fittings.

31   Remove the upper shroud mounting bolts and remove the shroud.

32   Loosen, but do not remove, the fan clutch nuts **(see illustration)**.

33   Remove the drivebelt (see Chapter 1).

34   Remove the fan clutch nuts and detach the fan blade and clutch from the pulley.

Caution: *To prevent silicone fluid from draining from the clutch assembly into the fan drive bearing and ruining the lubricant, don't place the clutch/fan assembly in a position with the shaft pointing down.*

35   Carefully inspect the fan blades for any damage. Replace if necessary. Inspect the fan clutch for signs of fluid leakage or roughness when rotating the assembly. Inspect the fan bracket on the engine by spinning the pulley, checking for any signs of roughness or play in the bearing. Replace the fan bracket/bearing assembly if necessary.

36   At this point, the fan may be unbolted from the clutch, if necessary. Re-install the fan blade with the "F" mark on the fan hub facing towards the front of the vehicle.

37   Installation is the reverse of removal. Tighten the fan and clutch mounting nuts evenly and securely.

38   Refill the cooling system (see Chapter 1).

39   Reconnect the battery and perform the

5.30 Automatic transmission fluid cooler hose connections (A) and the mounting tabs for the lower shroud (B)

5.32 Fan mounting fasteners (one fastener not shown)

necessary re-learn procedures (see Chapter 5).

40   Check the automatic transmission fluid level, adding as necessary (see Chapter 1).

2013 and later models

41   Drain some coolant from the radiator (to a level that's lower than the upper radiator hose) (see Chapter 1).

42   Remove the fresh inlet duct and the air filter housing (see Chapter 4).

43   Remove the battery and the battery tray (see Chapter 5).

44   Remove the radiator support cover.

45   Detach the upper radiator hose from the radiator.

46   Disconnect the electrical connectors from the fan controller, then remove the fan controller.

47   Remove the bolts at the upper corners of the fan support, then pull it upward to detach it at the bottom. Remove the fan assembly.

48   Installation is the reverse of removal. Refill the cooling system (see Chapter 1)

49   Reconnect the battery and perform the necessary re-learn procedures (see Chapter 5).

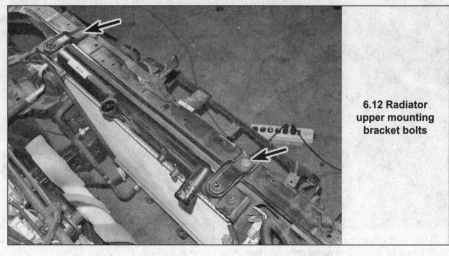

6.12 Radiator upper mounting bracket bolts

6   Radiator and coolant reservoir - removal and installation

Warning: *The models covered by this manual are equipped with a Supplemental Restraint System (SRS), more commonly known as airbags. Always disarm the airbag system before working in the vicinity of any airbag system component to avoid the possibility of accidental deployment of the airbag, which could cause personal injury (see Chapter 12). Do not use a memory saving device to preserve the PCM's memory when working on or near airbag system components.*

Warning: *Do not allow antifreeze to come in contact with your skin or painted surfaces of the vehicle. Rinse off spills immediately with plenty of water. Antifreeze is highly toxic if ingested. Never leave antifreeze lying around in an open container or in puddles on the floor; children and pets are attracted by its sweet smell and may drink it. Check with local authorities about disposing of used antifreeze. Many communities have collection centers which will see that antifreeze is disposed of safely. Never dump used antifreeze on the ground or pour it into drains.*

Warning: *Wait until the engine is completely cool before beginning this procedure.*

Radiator

1   On 2013 and later models, have the air conditioning system discharged by a licensed air conditioning technician.

2   Disconnect the cable from the negative terminal of the battery (see Chapter 5).

3   Raise the front of the vehicle and support it securely on jackstands. Remove the under-vehicle splash shield.

4   Drain the cooling system (see Chapter 1).

5   Remove the engine cover and the air

inlet duct (see Chapter 4).

6   Remove the radiator top cover.

7   Detach the upper and lower radiator hoses from the radiator.

2012 and earlier models

8   Separate the upper and lower fan shrouds from the radiator (see Section 5).

9   Disconnect the transmission fluid cooler lines from the radiator.

10   Remove the electric (V6 models) or belt-driven (V8 models) cooling fan (see Section 5).

11   Remove the radiator grille (see Chapter 11).

12   Remove the radiator upper mounting brackets **(see illustration)**.

13   Remove the condenser upper mounting bolts (from the front side).

14   Tilt the top of the radiator to the rear, pull up the condenser slightly to disengage its lower mounting tangs from the radiator, then lift the radiator up and out of the engine compartment. Take care not to spill coolant on the vehicle.

Caution: *Be careful not to damage the fins on the radiator or the condenser.*

15   Support the condenser with wire or rope while the radiator is out so the refrigerant lines are not strained.

16   Inspect the radiator for leaks and damage. If it needs repair, have a radiator shop or dealer service department perform the work, as special techniques are required.

17   Bugs and dirt can be removed from the radiator with a soft brush, followed by forcing water from a garden hose through the core from the engine side. Don't bend the cooling fins as this is done.

18   Installation is the reverse of removal. Be sure the radiator mounts are seated properly in their bushings.

19   Fill the cooling system with the proper mixture of antifreeze and water (see Chapter 1).

20   Reconnect the battery and perform the necessary re-learn procedures (see Chapter 5). Allow the engine to reach normal operating temperature, indicated by the upper radiator hose becoming hot. Recheck the coolant level and

add more if required (see Chapter 1).

21   Check and add transmission fluid as needed (see Chapter 1).

2013 and later models

22   Remove the hood latch assembly (see Chapter 11).

23   Remove the bumper cover (see Chapter 11).

24   Disconnect the electrical connectors from the horns, then remove the radiator support brace.

25   Disconnect the coolant reservoir hose from the radiator filler neck.

26   Remove the engine cooling fans (see Section 5).

27   Remove the air conditioning condenser (see Section 12).

28   Remove the upper radiator mounts and lift out the radiator, being careful not to damage the cooling fins. Take care not to spill coolant on the vehicle.

29   Support the condenser to prevent strain on the refrigerant line fittings.

Caution: *The fins on the radiator and condenser can easily become damaged. Be careful during radiator removal.*

30   Inspect the radiator for leaks and damage. If it needs repair, have a radiator shop or dealer service department perform the work, as special techniques are required.

31   Bugs and dirt can be removed from the radiator with a soft brush, followed by forcing water from a garden hose through the core from the engine side. Don't bend the cooling fins as this is done.

32   Installation is the reverse of removal. Be sure the radiator mounts are seated properly in their bushings.

33   Fill the cooling system with the proper mixture of antifreeze and water (see Chapter 1).

34   Reconnect the battery and perform the necessary re-learn procedures (see Chapter 5). Allow the engine to reach normal operating temperature, indicated by the upper radiator hose becoming hot. Recheck the coolant level and add more if required (see Chapter 1).

35   Check and add transmission fluid as needed (see Chapter 1).

6.39 Coolant reservoir mounting details (2012 and earlier models; 2013 and later models have only one fastener, accessible from the top)

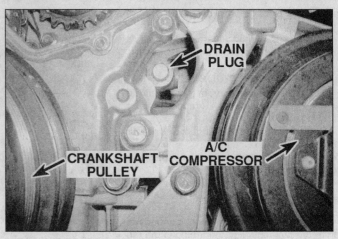

7.14 Location of the water pump drain plug

Coolant reservoir

36   On 2012 and earlier models, remove the battery (see Chapter 5).

37   On 2013 and later models, remove the radiator support cover.

38   On 2012 and earlier models, disconnect the overflow hose from the reservoir. On 2013 and later models, disconnect the hose from the radiator filler neck.

39   Unbolt the coolant reservoir and remove it from the vehicle **(see illustration)**.

40   Pour the coolant into a container. Wash out the reservoir with soapy water and a long brush to make the coolant level easier to read. Inspect the reservoir for cracks and chafing. Replace it if any damage is found.

41   Installation is the reverse of removal.

---

7   Water pump - replacement

Warning: *Do not allow antifreeze to come in contact with your skin or painted surfaces of the vehicle. Rinse off spills immediately with plenty of water. Antifreeze is highly toxic if ingested. Never leave antifreeze lying around in an open container or in puddles on the floor; children and pets are attracted by its sweet smell and may drink it. Check with local authorities about disposing of used antifreeze. Many communities have collection centers which will see that antifreeze is disposed of safely. Never dump used antifreeze on the ground or pour it into drains.*
Warning: *Wait until the engine is completely cool before beginning this procedure.*

V6 engines

Warning: *The air conditioning system is under high pressure. Do not loosen any fittings or remove any components until after the system has been discharged. Air conditioning refrigerant should be properly discharged into an EPA-approved container at a dealer service department or an automotive air conditioning repair facility. Always wear eye protection*

7.18 Remove the timing chain tensioner cover (A) and the water pump cover (B) from the timing chain cover

when disconnecting air conditioning system fittings.

1   On 2013 and later models, have the refrigerant discharged at a dealer service department or an automotive air conditioning repair facility.

2   Disconnect the cable from the negative terminal of the battery (see Chapter 5).

3   Remove the engine cover and the air inlet duct (see Chapter 4).

4   On 2013 and later models, loosen the right-front wheel lug nuts.

5   Raise the vehicle and support it securely on jackstands. Remove the under-vehicle splash shield.

6   On 2013 and later models, remove the right front wheel and the inner fender splash shield (see Chapter 11).

7   Drain the cooling system (see Chapter 1). If the coolant is relatively new, or is in good condition, save it and re-use it.

8   Set the engine to TDC on the compression stroke for cylinder no. 1 (see Chapter 2A). Make sure that the pointer is aligned with the TDC mark on the crankshaft pulley and that the engine is on the compression stroke.

9   Remove the upper radiator hose.

10   Remove the drivebelt, (see Chapter 1). On 2013 and later models, also remove the tensioner.

11   On 2013 and later models, remove the coolant reservoir (see Section 6).

12   On 2013 and later models, remove the right-side engine mount assembly and the torque rod (see Chapter 2A).

13   On 2012 and earlier models, remove the cooling fans (see Section 5).

14   On 2012 and earlier models, remove the coolant drain plug from the water pump side of the engine block **(see illustration)**. Discard the washer. A new one must be used during installation.

15   On 2013 and later models, remove the coolant drain plug from the front side of the engine block.Discard the washer. A new one must be used during installation.

Note: *Canadian models use a block heater instead of a drain plug. Note the position of the plug and connector, then disconnect the connector before removing the heater.*

16   On 2013 and later models, remove the power steering fluid pump motor and bracket (see Chapter 10).

17   On 2013 and later models, disconnect the wiring from the rear IVT control valve. Remove the rear IVT control valve cover.

18   Clean around the chain tensioner cover and the water pump cover on the engine front cover and then remove the covers **(see illustration)**.

7.19 Depress the timing chain tensioner and lock it into place by inserting a paper clip into the hole on the front of the tensioner

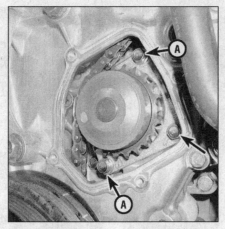

7.21 After the water pump mounting bolts have been removed, install the two M8 x 1.25 bolts into the holes designated by the letter A and tighten them evenly until the water pump is forced out of the engine block

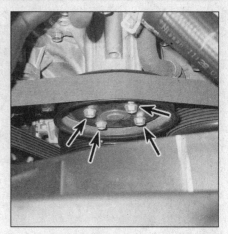

7.38 Water pump pulley mounting fasteners

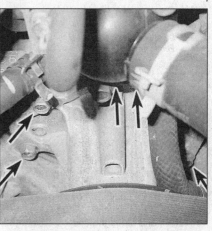

7.41 Water pump mounting bolts (some bolts not visible in this photo)

19   Push the tensioner plunger in, then lock it in the retracted position by inserting a small drill bit or similar steel rod into the hole **(see illustration)**.

20   Carefully rotate the crankshaft pulley counterclockwise until the timing chain becomes somewhat loose on the tensioner side, then remove the tensioner.

21   Remove the water pump mounting bolts **(see illustration)**.

Caution: *Don't allow the bolts to drop into the timing chain cover.*

22   Turn the crankshaft counterclockwise (no more than 20 degrees) until the chain becomes slack on the water pump sprocket.

23   Install two 8 mm bolts, about 2 inches long and of the proper thread pitch (1.25 mm), into the water pump bolt holes and tighten them equally until they bottom against the timing chain cover. It will be necessary to rotate the water pump slightly to allow the bolts to drive against the rear timing chain case cover instead of the bolt holes.

24   Remove the water pump.

25   Clean the sealant from the mating surface and discard the O-rings; new ones must be used on installation.

26   Inspect the water pump looking for cracks, rust or other visible damage. Rotate the vane shaft. It should move smoothly with no looseness. Replace the water pump assembly if damaged.

27   Install the new O-ring with the white paint mark into the groove closest to the pump flange and the second O-ring into its groove. Apply a light amount of oil to the O-rings. Make sure the timing chain and water pump sprockets are engaged, and then tighten the pump bolts to the torque listed in this Chapter's Specifications.

28   Installation is the reverse of removal. Note the following:

a) *Clean all old sealant from the water pump and timing chain tensioner covers. Apply a bead of RTV sealant to the covers.*

b) *Tighten the timing chain tensioner bolts and the tensioner cover bolts to the torque listed in the Chapter 2A Specifications.*

c) *Tighten the water pump cover bolts to the torque listed in this Chapter's Specifications.*

d) *On 2012 and earlier models, apply RTV sealant to the threads of the cylinder block drain plug and then tighten it to the torque listed in this Chapter's Specifications.*

e) *On 2013 and later models, install a new copper sealing washer and then install the cylinder block drain plug (or engine block heater on Canadian models) to the torque listed in this Chapter's Specifications.*

Note: *Timing chain noise may be apparent after performing this procedure. This noise is normal and should only last until the air has bled out of the high pressure chamber of the primary timing chain tensioner. If after several minutes the noise is still apparent, run the engine at 3,000 rpm with the transmission in Neutral or Park until the noise subsides.*

29   Refill the cooling system (see Chapter 1). Reconnect the battery and perform the necessary re-learn procedures (see Chapter 5). On 2013 and later models, have the air conditioning system recharged by the shop that discharged it.

V8 models

30   Disconnect the cable from the negative terminal of the battery (see Chapter 5).

31   Remove the engine cover **(see illustration 4.9)**.

32   Remove the air intake duct between the throttle body and the air filter housing (see Chapter 4).

33   Raise the vehicle and support it securely on jackstands. Remove the under-vehicle splash shield.

34   Drain the cooling system (see Chapter 1). If the coolant is relatively new, or is in good condition, save it and re-use it.

35   Remove the coolant reservoir (see Section 6).

36   Remove the upper radiator hose.

37   Remove the belt-driven cooling fan (see Section 5).

38   Loosen, but do not remove, the water pump pulley mounting fasteners **(see illustration)**.

39   Remove the drivebelt (see Chapter 1).

40   Remove the water pump pulley mounting fasteners, then remove the pulley.

41   Remove the water pump mounting bolts, then detach the water pump from the engine **(see illustration)**. Check the impeller on the backside for evidence of corrosion or missing fins. Rotate the impeller and verify that it turns smoothly and that there's no looseness in the shaft. Replace the water pump assembly if damaged.

42   Compare the new pump to the old one to make sure they're identical.

43   Remove all traces of the old gasket from

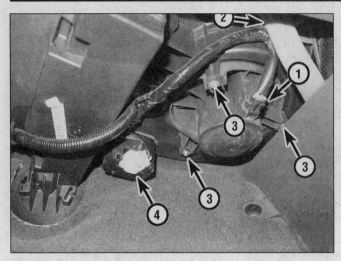

8.3 Front blower motor and resistor mounting details (2012 and earlier models shown)

8.18 Rear blower motor resistor electrical connector (A) and mounting screws (B)

1   Blower motor electrical connector
2   Harness fastener at blower motor housing
3   Blower motor mounting screws
4   Blower motor resistor electrical connector

the engine as necessary.
44   Carefully attach the pump to the engine and thread the bolts into the holes finger tight.
45   Tighten the bolts, a little at a time, to the torque listed in this Chapter's Specifications. Don't overtighten the bolts or the pump may be distorted.
46   Reinstall all parts removed for access to the pump.
47   Refill and bleed the cooling system (see Chapter 1). Run the engine and check for leaks and proper operation.
48   Check the automatic transmission fluid level, adding as necessary (see Chapter 1).

8   Blower motor - removal and installation

Warning: *The models covered by this manual are equipped with a Supplemental Restraint System (SRS), more commonly known as airbags. Always disarm the airbag system before working in the vicinity of any airbag system component to avoid the possibility of accidental deployment of the airbag, which could cause personal injury (see Chapter 12). Do not use a memory saving device to preserve the PCM's memory when working on or near airbag system components.*
1   Disconnect the cable from the negative terminal of the battery (see Chapter 5).

Front blower motor
2   Remove the glove box and the lower trim panel from the instrument panel (see Chapter 11).
3   Disconnect the blower motor electrical connector **(see illustration)**.

4   Remove the blower motor mounting screws and lower the blower motor out of the vehicle.
5   Installation is the reverse of removal.

Center blower motor (2013 and later models)
6   Remove the center console (see Chapter 11).
7   Remove the console bracket fasteners and bracket.
8   Disconnect the electrical harness connectors.
9   Remove the center blower unit mounting screws and separate the unit from the console.
10   Remove the lower case screws, then remove the case and blower motor from the housing.
11   Separate the blower motor from the case.
12   Installation is the reverse of removal.

Rear blower motor
13   Remove the rear heating/air conditioning unit (see Section 10).
14   Remove the blower motor mounting screws, then pull the blower motor out of the housing.
15   If you are replacing the motor, detach the fan and transfer it to the new motor.

Blower motor resistor - 2012 and earlier models
Note: *For some models years, the manufacturer refers to this component as a "variable blower motor control."*
Note: *On 2013 and later models, the blower motor resistor has been incorporated into the*

body control module and is not serviceable separately.
16   To remove the front resistor, remove the glove compartment and lower dash trim (see Chapter 11).
17   To remove the rear resistor, remove the lower right-rear interior trim panel in the luggage compartment (see Chapter 11).
18   Disconnect the blower motor resistor electrical connector **(front resistor, see illustration 8.3; rear resistor, see accompanying illustration)**.
19   Remove the blower motor resistor mounting screws, then carefully pull the resistor out of the housing.
20   Installation is the reverse of removal. Run the blower and check for proper operation.

9   Heater and air conditioning control assembly - removal and installation

Warning: *The models covered by this manual are equipped with a Supplemental Restraint System (SRS), more commonly known as airbags. Always disarm the airbag system before working in the vicinity of any airbag system component to avoid the possibility of accidental deployment of the airbag, which could cause personal injury (see Chapter 12). Do not use a memory saving device to preserve the PCM's memory when working on or near airbag system components.*
1   Disconnect the cable from the negative terminal of the battery (see Chapter 5).
2   On models without a navigation system, use a trim tool to pry up the liner from the storage tray, then pry out the storage tray from the

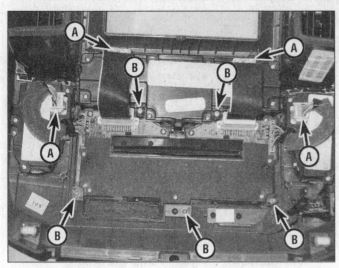

9.6 Disconnect the electrical connectors (A) then remove the mounting screws (B) and controller from the panel

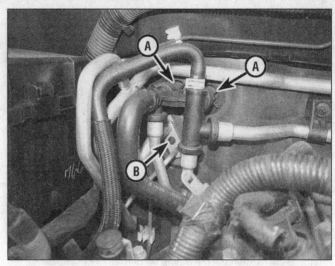

10.4 Heater hose connections (A) and refrigerant line fitting bolt (B) at the firewall (2012 and earlier models shown)

center of the instrument panel and remove the exposed screw.

3   On models with a navigation system, use a trim tool to pry up the front of the small trim panel just below the viewing screen, then remove the exposed screw.

4   Using the trim tool, pry along the edges of the control panel to disengage the clips and pull the control assembly from the instrument panel.

5   Remove the radio unit and brackets from the trim panel (see Chapter 12).

6   Disconnect the control assembly electrical connectors **(see illustration)** then remove the mounting screws and remove the control assembly from the center trim panel.

7   Installation is the reverse of removal.

10   Heater core - removal and installation

Warning: *The models covered by this manual are equipped with a Supplemental Restraint System (SRS), more commonly known as airbags. Always disarm the airbag system before working in the vicinity of any airbag system component to avoid the possibility of accidental deployment of the airbag, which could cause personal injury (see Chapter 12). Do not use a memory saving device to preserve the PCM's memory when working on or near airbag system components.*

Warning: *The air conditioning system is under high pressure. Do not loosen any fittings or remove any components until after the system has been discharged. Air conditioning refrigerant should be properly discharged into an EPA-approved container at a dealer service department or an automotive air conditioning repair facility. Always wear eye protection*

when disconnecting air conditioning system fittings.

Warning: *Wait until the engine is completely cool before beginning this procedure.*

Note: *Replacement of the heater core is a difficult procedure for the home mechanic, involving removal of the entire dashboard, console, and many wiring connectors. If you attempt it at home, keep track of the assemblies by taking notes and keeping screws and other hardware in small, marked plastic bags for reassembly.*

1   Have the air conditioning system evacuated by a properly equipped shop.

2   Disconnect the cable from the negative terminal of the battery (see Chapter 5).

3   Drain the cooling system (see Chapter 1).

Front

4   Disconnect the heater hoses from the pipes that protrude through the firewall **(see illustration)**.

5   Disconnect the air conditioning lines from the expansion valve block at the firewall. Seal all open ends to prevent contamination.

6   Remove the entire instrument panel assembly (see Chapter 11).

7   Remove the vertical instrument panel brace from the area of the accelerator pedal.

8   Remove the mounting screws for the vent tubes on the front side of the instrument panel **(see illustration)** then disconnect the vent tubes from the back side.

9   Remove the heater/evaporator case-to-crossbar fasteners **(see illustrations)** and separate the heater/evaporator unit from the

10.8 Remove the vent tube fasteners from the front side of the instrument panel

10.9a Remove the heater/evaporator housing fastener from the back side. . .

10.9b. . . then the remaining ones from the front side

10.11 Slide the seal out of the seal housing

10.12a Remove the seal housing fasteners, then. . .

10.12b. . . separate the housing from the case

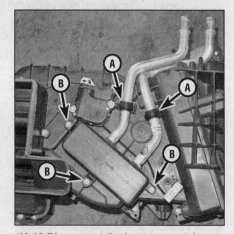

10.13 Disconnect the heater core tube-to-case clips (A) then remove the heater core cover fasteners (B)

crossbar and instrument panel assembly.
10   Disconnect the wiring from the heater unit.
11   Remove the heater case/TXV valve-to-firewall seal **(see illustration)**.
12   With the seal removed, remove the seal housing mounting screws **(see illustrations)**

and and lift the housing off of the case.
13   Disconnect the heater core tube-to-case clips then remove the heater core cover fasteners and cover **(see illustration)**.
14   Lift the heater core up and out from the case **(see illustration)**.
15   Reinstall the heater core into the heater

unit and reinstall the assembly in the reverse order of removal.
16   Refill the cooling system (see Chapter 1). Reconnect the battery and perform the necessary re-learn procedures (see Chapter 5). Check for leaks and proper system operation. Check the operation of all electrical components of the steering column and dash.
17   Have the air conditioning system recharged by the shop that discharged it.

Rear
18   Remove the liftgate kick panel and the lower and upper right-rear interior trim panels in the cargo area.
19   Disconnect the heater hoses from the heater core **(see illustration)**.
Note: *If the heater hoses are stuck to the tubes, place a small blunt tool between the tubes and hoses. Work the tool around the tubes completely to break the bond. If the hoses are old and due for replacement, simply cut them off.*
20   Detach the under-floor refrigerant lines from the assembly.
21   Detach the ducts and electrical connec-

10.14 Carefully lift the heater core out of the case making sure not to damage the cooling fins

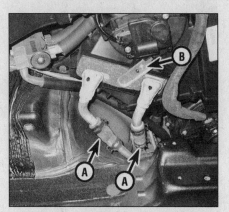

10.19 Heater core hoses (A) and retaining bracket (B) - earlier models shown, later models similar

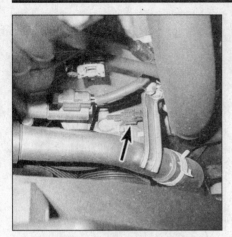

11.8 Compressor clutch electrical connector (V8 engine shown)

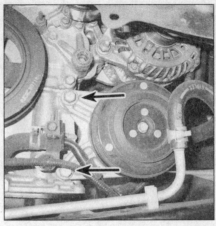

11.10a Compressor front mounting bolts (2013 and later models)

11.10b Compressor side mounting bolts (2013 and later models)

tors from the assembly.

22   Remove the fasteners and remove the heater and air conditioning unit from the vehicle.

23   Remove the heater core mounting bracket, then pull heater core out of the housing.

24   Installation is the reverse of removal.

25   Refill the cooling system (see Chapter 1), reconnect the battery and run the engine. Check for leaks and proper operation of the system. Have the air conditioning system evacuated, recharged and leak tested by the shop that discharged it.

11   Air conditioning compressor - removal and installation

Warning: *The air conditioning system is under high pressure. Do not loosen any fittings or remove any components until after the system has been discharged. Air conditioning refrigerant should be properly discharged into an EPA-approved container at a dealer service department or an automotive air conditioning repair facility. Always wear eye protection when disconnecting air conditioning system fittings.*

1   Have the refrigerant discharged at a dealer service department or an automotive air conditioning repair facility.

2   Disconnect the cable from the negative terminal of the battery (see Chapter 5). On 2012 and earlier models, loosen the left front wheel lug nuts. On 2013 and later models, loosen the right front wheel lug nuts.

3   Raise the vehicle and support it securely on jackstands. Remove the lower engine splash shield. Remove the wheel and the inner fender splash shield (see Chapter 11).

4   On 2012 and earlier models, remove the air filter housing (see Chapter 4).

5   Remove the drivebelt (see Chapter 1).

6   On V8 models, remove the power steering cooler hose bracket and move the house out of the way.

11.10c Compressor refrigerant line fitting bolts (A) and mounting fasteners (B) (2012 and earlier models [V8 shown])

7   Disconnect both refrigerant lines from the compressor and seal all openings with tape to prevent contamination.

8   Disconnect the wiring from the compressor **(see illustration)**.

9   On 2013 and later models, remove the bolts from the oil cooler line brackets, then move the lines aside.

10   Remove the compressor mounting bolts and remove the compressor from the bottom of the engine compartment **(see illustrations)**.

Note: *Keep the compressor level during handling and storage. If the compressor seized or you find metal particles in the refrigerant lines, the system must be flushed out by an air conditioning technician and the receiver-drier must be replaced (see Section 13).*

11   Prior to installation, turn the center of the clutch six times to evenly disperse any oil that has collected in the head.

12   Installation is the reverse of removal. Apply compressor oil to new O-rings and install the hoses. Tighten the compressor mounting bolts and torque listed in this Chapter's Specifications.

Caution: *Use only refrigerant oil compatible with the R-134a system in your vehicle.*

13   If you are installing a new compressor, the cycling clutch assembly may have to be transferred to the new compressor.Refer to the compressor manufacturer's instructions for adding refrigerant oil to the system.

Note: *The removal of the clutch assembly will require the use of several special tools. You may want to have the clutch assembly transferred to the new compressor by an air conditioning shop or dealer service department.*

14   Reconnect the battery and perform the necessary re-learn procedures (see Chapter 5).

15   Have the system evacuated, charged and leak tested by the shop that discharged it.

12   Air conditioning condenser - removal and installation

Warning: *The models covered by this manual are equipped with a Supplemental Restraint System (SRS), more commonly known as airbags. Always disarm the airbag system before working in the vicinity of any airbag system component to avoid the possibility of accidental deployment of the airbag, which could*

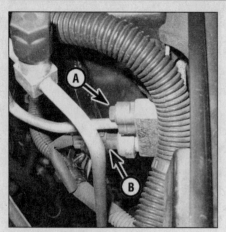

12.3a Right-side line fitting connection at the condenser (A) and pressure sensor electrical connector (B)

12.3b Left-side line fitting connection at the condenser

12.8 The air conditioning refrigerant lines attach to the condenser at this connection

cause personal injury (see Chapter 12). Do not use a memory saving device to preserve the PCM's memory when working on or near airbag system components.

Warning: *The air conditioning system is under high pressure. Do not loosen any fittings or remove any components until after the system has been discharged. Air conditioning refrigerant should be properly discharged into an EPA-approved container at a dealer service department or an automotive air conditioning repair facility. Always wear eye protection when disconnecting air conditioning system fittings.*

Warning: *Wait until the engine is completely cool before beginning this procedure.*

Removal

1   Have the refrigerant discharged at a dealer service department or an automotive air conditioning repair facility.

2012 and earlier models

2   Remove the radiator (see Section 6). Support the condenser after the radiator is removed.

3   Disconnect the refrigerant lines from the condenser and discard the O-ring seals **(see illustrations)**. Cap the fittings on the condenser and lines to prevent entry of dirt or moisture.

4   Disconnect the refrigerant pressure sensor electrical connector.

5   Carefully remove the condenser from the vehicle.

2013 and later models

6   Remove the bumper cover (see Chapter 11).

7   Disconnect the electrical connectors from the horns, then remove the hood latch and radiator support brace.

8   Remove the bolt and detach the refrigerant lines from the right (passenger's) side of the vehicle **(see illustration)**. Plug the line to prevent the entry of moisture or contaminants.

9   Disconnect the electrical connector from the pressure sensor at the left side of the condenser (on top of the receiver-drier), then unbolt the condenser upper brackets and remove the condenser.

Installation

Caution: *Use only refrigerant oil compatible with the R-134a system in your vehicle.*

10   Installation is the reverse of removal. Use new O-rings on the refrigerant line fittings. Apply refrigerant oil to the O-rings.

11   If a new condenser is installed, add 2.5 ounces (74 cc) of refrigerant oil to it.

12   Have the system evacuated, charged and leak tested by the shop that discharged it.

---

13   Air conditioning receiver-drier - removal and installation

---

Warning: *The air conditioning system is under high pressure. Do not loosen any fittings or re-*

move any components until after the system has been discharged. Air conditioning refrigerant should be properly discharged into an EPA-approved container at a dealer service department or an automotive air conditioning repair facility. Always wear eye protection when disconnecting air conditioning system fittings.

1   Have the refrigerant discharged at a dealer service department or an automotive air conditioning repair facility.

2012 and earlier models

Note: The receiver-drier on these models is an integral part of the condenser and is not serviceable separately.

2013 and later models

2   Remove the condenser (see Section 12).

3   Remove the mounting bolts and pull the receiver-drier off the condenser.

4   When installing the new receiver-drier, add 0.2 ounce (6 cc) of refrigerant oil to it.

Caution: *Use only refrigerant oil compatible with the R-134a system in your vehicle.*

5   Installation is the reverse of removal. Use new O-rings on all fittings. Apply refrigerant oil to the O-rings.

6   Have the system evacuated, charged and leak tested by the shop that discharged it.

Chapter 4
Fuel and exhaust systems

Contents

	Section		Section
Air filter housing - removal and installation	9	Fuel rail and injectors - removal and installation	11
Exhaust system servicing - general information	6	Fuel tank - removal and installation	8
Fuel lines and fittings - general information and disconnection	5	General information	1
Fuel pressure - check	4	Throttle body - removal and installation	10
Fuel pressure relief procedure	3	Troubleshooting	2
Fuel pump/fuel level sensor module - removal and installation	7		

Specifications

Fuel system pressure (approximate at idle) .... 51 psi (352 kPa)

Torque specifications
Note: *One foot-pound (ft-lb) of torque is equivalent to 12 inch-pounds (in-lbs) of torque. Torque values below approximately 15 ft-lbs are expressed in inch-pounds, since most foot-pound torque wrenches are not accurate at these smaller values.*
Throttle body mounting fasteners .... 74 in-lbs (8 Nm)

---

1 General information

Fuel system warnings

1   Gasoline is extremely flammable and repairing fuel system components can be dangerous. Consider your automotive repair knowledge and experience before attempting repairs which may be better suited for a professional mechanic.

- Don't smoke or allow open flames or bare light bulbs near the work area
- Don't work in a garage with a gas-type appliance (water heater, clothes dryer)
- Use fuel-resistant gloves. If any fuel spills on your skin, wash it off immediately with soap and water
- Clean up spills immediately
- Do not store fuel-soaked rags where they could ignite
- Prior to disconnecting any fuel line, you must relieve the fuel pressure (see Section 3)
- Wear safety glasses
- Have a proper fire extinguisher on hand

Fuel system

2   The fuel system consists of the fuel tank, electric fuel pump/fuel level sending unit (located in the fuel tank), fuel rail and fuel injectors. The fuel injection system is a multi-port system; multi-port fuel injection uses timed impulses to inject the fuel directly into the intake port of each cylinder. The Powertrain Control Module (PCM) controls the injectors. The PCM monitors various engine parameters and delivers the exact amount of fuel required into the intake ports.

3   Fuel is circulated from the fuel pump to the fuel rail through fuel lines running along the underside of the vehicle. Various sections of the fuel line are either rigid metal or nylon, or flexible fuel hose. The various sections of the fuel hose are connected either by quick-connect fittings or threaded metal fittings.

2.2a The fuel pump fuse is located in the engine compartment fuse box - on 2012 and earlier models it's the 9th fuse from the right

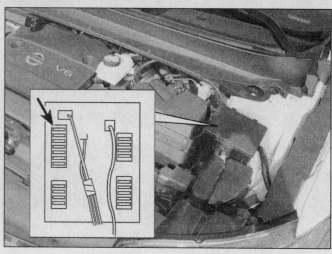

2.2b Location of the fuel pump fuse on 2013 and later models

Exhaust system

4   The exhaust system consists of the exhaust manifold(s), catalytic converter(s), muffler(s), tailpipe and all connecting pipes, flanges and clamps. The catalytic converters are an emission control device added to the exhaust system to reduce pollutants.

---

2   Troubleshooting

Fuel pump

1   The fuel pump is located inside the fuel tank. Sit inside the vehicle with the windows closed, turn the ignition key to ON (not START) and listen for the sound of the fuel pump as it's briefly activated. You will only hear the sound for a second or two, but that sound tells you that the pump is working. Alternatively, have an assistant listen at the fuel filler cap.
2   If the pump does not come on, check the fuel pump fuse **(see illustrations)**. If the

2.9 An automotive stethoscope is used to listen to the fuel injectors in operation

fuse is okay, check the wiring back to the fuel pump. If the fuse and wiring are okay, the pump might be defective. Other possibilities include a faulty fuel pump relay, which is part of the Intelligent Power Distribution Module (which is part of the underhood fuse/relay box), or a faulty Powertrain Control Module (PCM). If the pump runs continuously with the ignition key in the ON position, the Powertrain Control Module (PCM) is probably defective. Have the PCM checked by a professional mechanic.

Fuel injection system

Note: *The following procedure is based on the assumption that the fuel pump is working and the fuel pressure is adequate (see Section 4).*
3   Check all electrical connectors related to the system. Check the ground wire connections for tightness.
4   Verify that the battery is fully charged (see Chapter 1).
5   Inspect the air filter element (see Chapter 1).
6   Check all fuses related to the fuel system (see Chapter 12).
7   Check the air induction system between the throttle body and the intake manifold for air leaks. Also inspect the condition of all vacuum hoses connected to the intake manifold and to the throttle body.
8   Remove the air intake duct from the throttle body (see Section 9) and look for dirt, carbon, varnish, or other residue in the throttle body, particularly around the throttle plate. If it's dirty, clean it with carb cleaner, a toothbrush and a clean shop towel.
9   With the engine running, place an automotive stethoscope against each injector, one at a time, and listen for a clicking sound that indicates operation **(see illustration)**.
Warning: *Stay clear of the drivebelt and any rotating or hot components.*
10   If you can hear the injectors operating, but the engine is misfiring, the electrical cir-

cuits are functioning correctly, but the injectors might be dirty or clogged. Try a commercial injector cleaning product (available at auto parts stores). If cleaning the injectors doesn't help, replace the injectors.
11   If an injector is not operating (it makes no sound), disconnect the injector electrical connector and measure the resistance across the injector terminals with an ohmmeter. Compare this measurement to the other injectors. If the resistance of the non-operational injector is quite different from the other injectors, replace it.
12   If the injector is not operating, but the resistance reading is within the range of resistance of the other injectors, the PCM or the circuit between the PCM and the injector might be faulty. Have the PCM checked by a professional mechanic.

---

3   Fuel pressure relief procedure

Warning: *Gasoline is extremely flammable. See **Fuel system warnings** in Section 1.*
Note: *After the fuel pressure has been relieved, it's a good idea to lay a shop towel over any fuel connection to be disassembled, to absorb the residual fuel that may leak out when servicing the fuel system.*
1   Remove the fuel filler cap to relieve any built-up pressure in the fuel tank.
2   Remove the fuel pump fuse from the underhood fuse/relay box **(see illustrations 2.2a and 2.2b)**.
3   Start the engine and allow it to run until it stops. This should take only a few seconds. After it stalls, try cranking the engine two or three times to confirm there is no pressure.
4   Disconnect the cable from the negative terminal of the battery (see Chapter 5).
5   The fuel system pressure is now relieved. It is a good idea to surround any fuel line that will be disconnected using a shop rag to catch

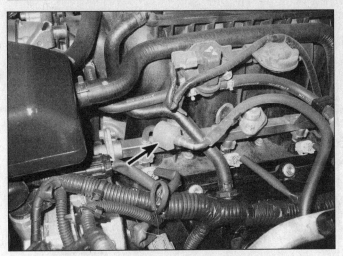

4.1a On V8 models, tee into the fuel system at this quick-connect fitting between the fuel supply line and the fuel rail

4.1b On 2012 and earlier V6 models, tee into the fuel system at this quick-connect fitting at the front of the left fuel rail. On 2013 and later models, the quick-connect fitting is located at the left (driver's) end of the engine

fuel that might spill out.

6   When you're finished working on the fuel system, install the fuel pump fuse back into the fuse panel, connect the negative cable to the battery and perform the necessary re-learn procedures (see Chapter 5).

4   Fuel pressure - check

Warning: *Gasoline is extremely flammable. See **Fuel system warnings** in Section 1.*
Note: *To perform the fuel pressure test, you will need to obtain a special fuel pressure gauge and adapter set (fuel line fittings).*

1   Relieve the fuel pressure (see Section 3). Disconnect the quick-connect fuel supply line fitting at the fuel rail **(see illustration)**. You must connect a special tee adapter in the line that incorporates a fuel pressure gauge. This special tee can be purchased or you can fabricate your own out of various fittings, hose and hose clamps **(see illustrations)**.

2   With the gauge connected and leak-tested, start the engine and allow it to idle. Note the gauge reading as soon as it stabilizes and compare it with the pressure listed in this Chapter's Specifications.

3   If the fuel pressure is far out of specification, check the following:

a) *Check for a restriction in the fuel system (kinked fuel line, plugged fuel pump inlet strainer or clogged fuel filter). If no restrictions are found, replace the fuel pump module (see Section 7).*
b) *If the fuel pressure is higher than specified, replace the fuel pump module (see Section 7).*

4   Turn off the engine. Fuel pressure should not fall more than 8 psi over five minutes. If it does, the problem could be a leaky fuel injector, fuel line leak, or faulty fuel pump module.

5   Disconnect the fuel pressure gauge. Wipe up any spilled gasoline.

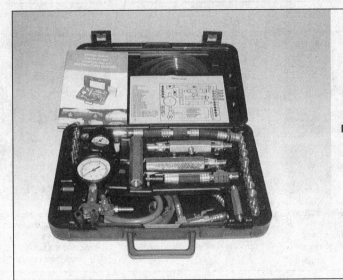

4.1c A typical fuel pressure gauge, with hoses and fittings suitable for tee-ing into the fuel delivery system

5   Fuel lines and fittings - general information and disconnection

Warning: *Gasoline is extremely flammable. See **Fuel system warnings** in Section 1.*

1   Relieve the fuel pressure before servicing fuel lines or fittings (see Section 3), then disconnect the cable from the negative battery terminal (see Chapter 5) before proceeding.

2   The fuel supply line connects the fuel pump in the fuel tank to the fuel rail on the engine. The Evaporative Emission (EVAP) system lines connect the fuel tank to the EVAP canister and connect the canister to the intake manifold.

3   Whenever you're working under the vehicle, inspect all fuel and evaporative emission lines for leaks, kinks, dents and other damage. Always replace a damaged fuel or EVAP line immediately.

4   If you find signs of dirt in the lines dur-

ing disassembly, disconnect all lines and blow them out with compressed air. Inspect the fuel strainer on the fuel pump pick-up unit for damage and deterioration.

Steel tubing

5   It is critical that the fuel lines be replaced with lines of equivalent type and specification.

6   Some steel fuel lines have threaded fittings. When loosening these fittings, hold the stationary fitting with a wrench while turning the tube nut.

Plastic tubing

7   When replacing fuel system plastic tubing, use only original equipment replacement plastic tubing.
Caution: *When removing or installing plastic fuel line tubing, be careful not to bend or twist it too much, which can damage it. Also, plastic fuel tubing is NOT heat resistant, so keep it away from excessive heat.*

Disconnecting Fuel Line Fittings

Two-tab type fitting; depress both tabs with your fingers, then pull the fuel line and the fitting apart

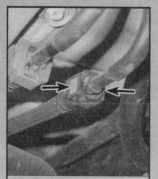

On this type of fitting, depress the two buttons on opposite sides of the fitting, then pull it off the fuel line

Threaded fuel line fitting; hold the stationary portion of the line or component (A) while loosening the tube nut (B) with a flare-nut wrench

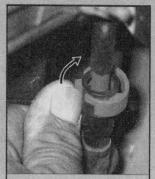

Plastic collar-type fitting; rotate the outer part of the fitting

Metal collar quick-connect fitting; pull the end of the retainer off the fuel line and disengage the other end from the female side of the fitting . . .

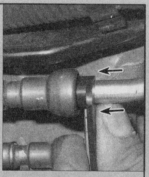

. . . insert a fuel line separator tool into the female side of the fitting, push it into the fitting and pull the fuel line off the pipe

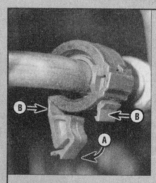

Some fittings are secured by lock tabs. Release the lock tab (A) and rotate it to the fully-opened position, squeeze the two smaller lock tabs (B) . . .

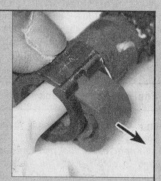

. . . then push the retainer out and pull the fuel line off the pipe

Spring-lock coupling; remove the safety cover, install a coupling release tool and close the tool around the coupling . . .

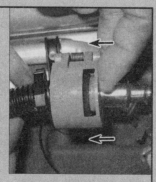

. . . push the tool into the fitting, then pull the two lines apart

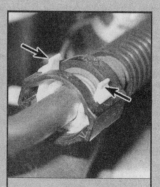

Hairpin clip type fitting: push the legs of the retainer clip together, then push the clip down all the way until it stops and pull the fuel line off the pipe

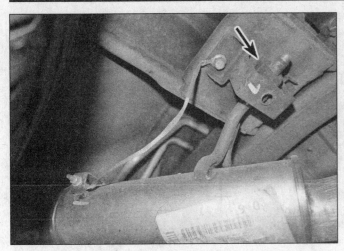

6.1 A typical exhaust system hanger. Inspect regularly and replace
at the first sign of damage or deterioration

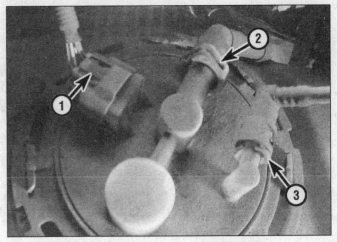

7.4 Fuel pump/fuel level sensor module:

1   *Fuel pump/level sensor electrical connector (depress the
     tab to release)*
2   *Fuel supply line quick-connect fitting*
3   *EVAP line quick-connect fitting*

Flexible hoses

8   When replacing fuel system flexible
hoses, use only original equipment replace-
ments.
9   Don't route fuel hoses (or metal lines)
within four inches of the exhaust system or
within ten inches of the catalytic converter.
Make sure that no rubber hoses are installed
directly against the vehicle, particularly in
places where there is any vibration. If allowed
to touch some vibrating part of the vehicle, a
hose can easily become chafed and it might
start leaking. A good rule of thumb is to maintain a minimum of 1/4-inch clearance around
a hose (or metal line) to prevent contact with
the vehicle underbody.

6   Exhaust system servicing -
general information

Warning: *Allow exhaust system components
to cool before inspection or repair. Also, when
working under the vehicle, make sure it is securely supported on jackstands.*
1   The exhaust system consists of the
exhaust manifolds, catalytic converter, muffler, tailpipe and all connecting pipes, flanges
and clamps. The exhaust system is isolated
from the vehicle body and from chassis components by a series of rubber hangers **(see
illustration)**. Periodically inspect these hangers for cracks or other signs of deterioration,
replacing them as necessary.
2   Conduct regular inspections of the
exhaust system to keep it safe and quiet. Look
for any damaged or bent parts, open seams,
holes, loose connections, excessive corrosion
or other defects which could allow exhaust
fumes to enter the vehicle. Do not repair deteriorated exhaust system components; replace
them with new parts.

3   If the exhaust system components are
extremely corroded, or rusted together, a
cutting torch is the most convenient tool for
removal. Consult a properly-equipped repair
shop. If a cutting torch is not available, you can
use a hacksaw, or if you have compressed air,
there are special pneumatic cutting chisels
that can also be used. Wear safety goggles to
protect your eyes from metal chips and wear
work gloves to protect your hands.
4   Here are some simple guidelines to follow when repairing the exhaust system:
a)   *Work from the back to the front when
     removing exhaust system components.*
b)   *Apply penetrating oil to the exhaust sys-
     tem component fasteners to make them
     easier to remove.*
c)   *Use new gaskets, hangers and clamps.*
d)   *Apply anti-seize compound to the
     threads of all exhaust system fasteners
     during reassembly.*
e)   *Allow sufficient clearance between the
     newly installed parts and all points on the
     underbody to avoid overheating the floor
     pan and possibly damaging the interior
     carpet and insulation. Pay particularly
     close attention to the catalytic converter
     and heat shield.*

7   Fuel pump/fuel level sensor
module - removal and installation

Warning: *Gasoline is extremely flammable.
See **Fuel system warnings** in Section 1.*
Note: *The components of the module (with the
exception of the fuel level sensor) are not replaceable individually. The entire module must
be replaced if any part of it is defective.*

Removal

1   Relieve the fuel pressure (see Section 3).

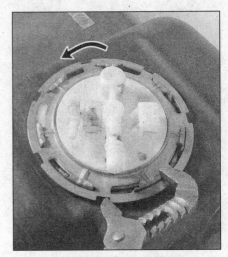

7.6 Turn the retaining ring
counterclockwise to release it

2   Disconnect the cable from the negative
terminal of the battery (see Chapter 5).

2012 and earlier models

3   Refer to Section 8 and begin to lower
the fuel tank.
4   Lower the fuel tank until the top of the
tank can be accessed. Disconnect the electrical connectors and the fuel line quick-connect
fittings **(see illustration)**.
5   Remove the fuel tank (see Section 8).
6   Mark the position of the fuel pump module in relation to the fuel tank, then unscrew
the pump module lock ring. A special tool
available at most auto parts stores can be
used to loosen the lock ring, but a large pair of
pliers will also work **(see illustration)**.
7   Carefully pull the fuel pump module out
of the tank. Angle the module as necessary

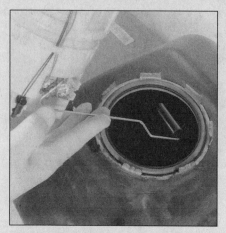

7.7 Lift the module out at an angle

7.8 Replace the O-ring with a new one

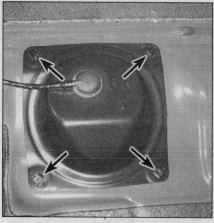

7.13 Turn the fuel pump module cover
fasteners 90 degrees to remove the cover

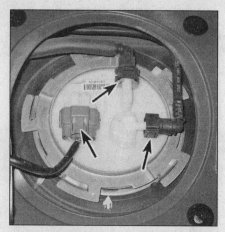

7.14 Depress the tang to disconnect the
electrical connector, then detach the fuel
and EVAP lines

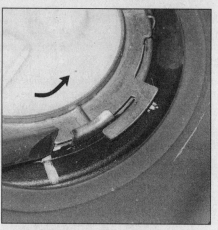

7.16 Use a brass drift and a hammer to
rotate the locking ring

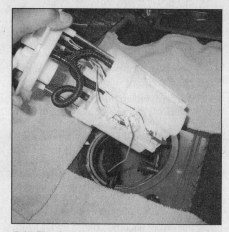

7.17 The fuel level float arm is easily bent,
so proceed carefully when lifting the fuel
pump module out

to protect the fuel level sensor float arm **(see illustration)**. On some models, you might have to detach the fuel level sensor from the pump module before you can remove the pump module from the fuel tank.

8   Remove the old O-ring, clean the mating surface on the fuel tank, then install a new O-ring **(see illustration)**.

9   To swap a fuel level sensor to another fuel pump module, trace the sensor harness to its electrical connector and disconnect it. To disengage the sensor from the pump module, depress the locks on each side of the sensor with needle-nose pliers and slide the sensor out and off. When installing the sensor module, make sure that the locks snap into place.

10   Installation is the reverse of removal.

2013 and later models

Warning: *The fuel level must be below 1/2 tank before performing this procedure. If it isn't use a siphoning kit (available at most auto parts stores) and drain the excess fuel into an approved gasoline container.*

Module removal

11   Remove the trim covers from the base of

the second row seats, then slide the seats to the fully forward position.

12   Pull back the carpet to gain access to the fuel pump inspection hole cover, the remove the center floor duct.

Note: *It's a good idea to cover the area around the access hole with plastic to prevent gasoline from damaging the carpet.*

13   Remove the fuel pump/fuel level sending unit assembly access cover **(see illustration)**.

14   Disconnect the electrical connectors from the fuel pump/fuel level sending unit **(see illustration)**.

15   Disconnect the hoses and lines from the fuel level sending unit/fuel pump assembly **(see illustration 7.14)**.

16   A special tool (#J-45747 or equivalent, available at most auto parts stores) can be used to loosen the lock ring. If the tool is not available, use a brass drift and hammer to tap the lock ring on the assembly counterclockwise **(see illustration)**. Remove the lock ring from the assembly.

17   Lift the fuel pump module from the tank. Manipulate it as you lift so you don't bend the

float arm **(see illustration)**. As you lift the module out, also note how the transfer hose is routed around the module. It must be routed the same way during installation.

18   Disconnect the transfer hose from the module **(see illustration)**.

Fuel level sensor unit replacement

19   Depress the release tabs and disconnect the fuel level sensor harness connector.

20   Release the two tangs and remove the fuel tank temperature sensor from the side of the pump assembly.

21   Squeeze the lock tab and slide the fuel level sensor up to remove it.

22   Install the new sensor unit.

Installation

23   Replace the O-ring seal **(see illustration)**.

24   Carefully lower the fuel pump module or fuel level module into the fuel tank.

25   Rotate the assembly until the alignment mark is facing the front of the vehicle and the two arrows are aligned **(see illustration)**.

26   Align the lock ring, then turn it clockwise

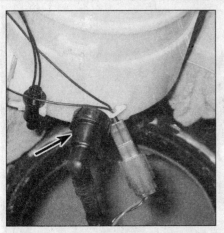

7.18 Disconnect (but do not pull) the transfer hose from the fuel pump module

7.23 Install a new O-ring seal

7.25 The alignment mark on the fuel pump module must face the front of the vehicle and align with the other arrow

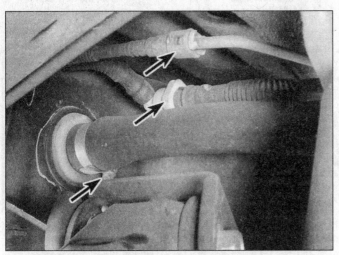

8.5 Fuel filler hose, EVAP and vent lines (2012 and earlier models shown)

8.13 Fuel tank strap bolts (2012 and earlier models; 2013 and later models have three straps)

to secure it in place.

27   Reconnect the hoses and electrical connector, then reinstall the access cover.

28   The remainder of installation is the reverse of removal.

29   Reconnect the battery and perform the necessary re-learn procedures (see Chapter 5).

8   Fuel tank - removal and installation

Warning: *Gasoline is extremely flammable. See* **Fuel system warnings** *in Section 1.*
Note: *The following procedure is much easier to perform if the fuel tank is empty. Drain the fuel into an approved fuel container using a commercially available siphoning kit (NEVER start the siphoning action by mouth), or wait until the fuel tank is nearly empty, if possible.*

1   Relieve the fuel system pressure (see Section 3).

2   Disconnect the cable from the negative terminal of the battery (see Chapter 5).

3   On 2012 and earlier models, loosen the left rear wheel lug nuts.

4   Raise the vehicle and support it securely on jackstands. On 2012 and earlier models, remove the left rear wheel.

5   Disconnect the fuel filler hose from the fuel filler pipe and the fuel tank. Disconnect the EVAP hose and the vent pipe quick connector.

6   If there is still fuel in the tank, siphon it out. Remember - NEVER start the siphoning action by mouth! Use a siphoning kit, which can be purchased at most auto parts stores.

7   On 2012 and earlier models, remove the fuel tank shield.

2013 and later models

8   Remove the fuel pump/fuel level sensor module access hole cover then disconnect the fuel line, EVAP line and electrical connector (see Section 7).

9   Remove the rear parking brake cable brackets from the tank shield.

10   Remove the outer reinforcement bar, if equipped.

11   Remove the fuel tank shields.

All models

12   Support the fuel tank with a floor jack and a plank of wood. Center the jack so as to balance the tank when the straps are removed.

13   Remove the fuel tank straps.

14   Slowly lower the tank and remove it from the vehicle.

15   Installation is the reverse of removal.

16   Reconnect the battery and perform the necessary re-learn procedures (see Chapter 5).

17   Turn the ignition key to Run and check for leaks.

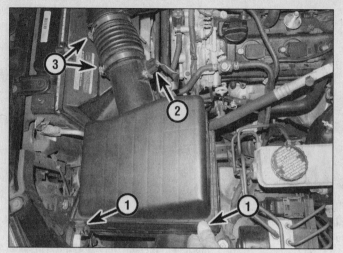

9.2a Air filter housing cover details (2012 and earlier models)

1	*Retaining clips*	3	*Air intake duct clamp*
2	*MAF sensor electrical connector*		

9.2b Air filter housing cover details (2013 and later models)

1	*Retaining clips*	3	*Air intake duct clamp*
2	*MAF sensor electrical connector*		

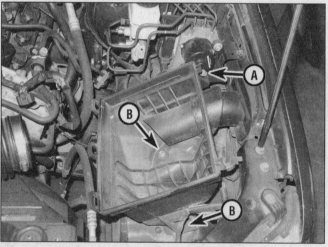

9.4 Lower housing mounting bolt (A) and grommets (B) (2012 and earlier models shown)

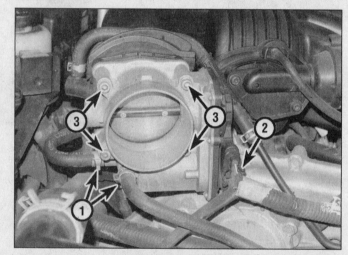

10.4 Throttle body details (2012 and earlier V6 model shown, other models similar)

1	*Coolant hoses*	3	*Mounting bolts*
2	*Electrical connector*		

9   Air filter housing - removal and installation

1   On 2013 and later models, remove the large plastic air inlet duct.

2   Loosen the air intake duct clamp and disconnect the electrical connector from the MAF/IAT sensor **(see illustrations)**.

3   Remove the lid of the air filter housing with the duct and MAF/IAT sensor attached. Remove the air filter element.

4   On V6 models, remove the mounting bolt, then pull the housing from the grommets at the bottom **(see illustration)**.

5   On V8 models, unscrew the three mounting bolts and remove the housing.

6   Installation is the reverse of removal.

10   Throttle body - removal and installation

Warning: *The engine must be completely cool before beginning this procedure.*

1   Disconnect the cable from the negative terminal of the battery (see Chapter 5).

2   On 2013 and later models, remove the cowl cover (see Chapter 11).

Note: *It isn't absolutely necessary to remove the cowl cover, but doing so will provide more working room.*

3   Remove the air filter housing cover and the air intake duct (see Section 9).

4   Clamp-off the coolant hoses to the throttle body, then disconnect them **(see illustration)**.

5   Disconnect the electrical connector from the throttle body. Label and then disconnect any remaining hoses and connectors.

6   Loosen the throttle body mounting bolts a little at a time in a criss-cross pattern to prevent distortion.

7   Remove the throttle body.

Note: *Don't try to disassemble the throttle body. If it's faulty, it must be replaced.*

8   Installation is the reverse of removal. Use a new throttle body O-ring if the old one is not in perfect condition. Tighten the bolts a little at a time in a criss-cross pattern to the torque listed in this Chapter's Specifications.

9   Check the coolant level, adding as necessary (see Chapter 1).

10   Reconnect the battery and perform the necessary re-learn procedures (see Chapter 5).

11.9 Crossover hose mounting flange bolts and fuel rail mounting bolts (right side shown, left side similar)

11.10 Fuel rail mounting bolt locations (2012 and earlier V6 models shown)

11.12a To free each injector from the fuel rail, pull off the retainer with a pair of pliers. . .

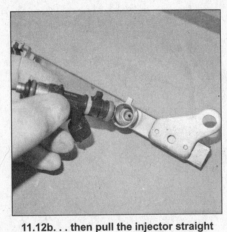

11.12b. . . then pull the injector straight out of its bore in the fuel rail

11.14 Whether you're installing new injectors or reusing the old ones, always remove the old O-rings and replace them with new ones

11 Fuel rail and injectors - removal and installation

1   Relieve the fuel system pressure (see Section 3).
2   Disconnect the cable from the negative terminal of the battery (see Chapter 5).
3   Remove the engine cover, if equipped.
4   On V8 engines, disconnect the air intake duct (see Section 9).
5   On V6 engines, remove the upper intake manifold (see Chapter 2A).
6   Disconnect the fuel supply line from the fuel rail (see Section 5).
7   Disconnect the electrical connector from each fuel injector and, on V8 engines, disconnect the EVAP canister purge control solenoid connector.
8   On 2012 and earlier V6 engines, remove the PCV hose between the valve covers.
9   On V8 engines, remove the fasteners securing the fuel rail crossover hose flanges to the left and right fuel rails **(see illustration)** and remove the fuel rail crossover.
10   Remove the fuel rail mounting bolts **(see**

illustration)**, starting with the two bolts farthest away from the fuel inlet.
11   Carefully lift the fuel rail from the engine with the injectors attached.
12   Remove the injectors from the fuel rail **(see illustrations)**, then remove and discard the O-rings.
13   If necessary, remove the fuel pressure damper. Install a new O-ring into the fuel tube flange, slide the spacer onto the damper (short side), and set the unit into the fuel tube flange.
14   Replace both O-rings on each fuel injector and lubricate them with clean engine oil prior to installation **(see illustration)**.
15   Install the injector retaining clips and push each injector into its bore in the fuel rail until the retaining clip snaps into place **(see illustration)**.
16   The remainder of installation is the reverse of removal. Tighten the fuel rail mounting bolts starting with the two closest to the fuel inlet.
17   Reconnect the battery and perform the necessary re-learn procedures (see Chapter 5).

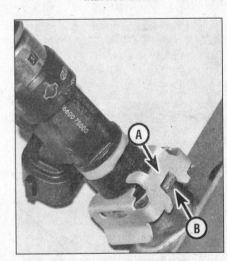

11.15 Align the slot in the clip (A) with the tab (B) on the fuel rail, then push the injector firmly into place until the clip snaps onto the ridge of the injector bore

Notes

Chapter 5
Engine electrical systems

Contents

	Section		Section
Alternator - removal and installation	7	General information and precautions	1
Battery and battery tray - removal and installation	4	Ignition coil(s) - replacement	6
Battery cables - replacement	5	Starter motor - removal and installation	8
Battery - disconnection and reconnection	3	Troubleshooting	2

1 General information and precautions

General information

Ignition system

1   The electronic ignition system consists of the Crankshaft Position (CKP) sensor, the Camshaft Position (CMP) sensor, the Knock Sensor (KS), the Powertrain Control Module (PCM), the ignition switch, the battery, the individual ignition coils or a coil pack, and the spark plugs. For more information on the CKP, CMP and KS sensors, as well as the PCM, refer to Chapter 6.

Charging system

2   The charging system includes the alternator (with an integral voltage regulator), the Powertrain Control Module (PCM), the Body Control Module (BCM), a charge indicator light on the dash, the battery, a fuse or fusible link and the wiring connecting all of these components. The charging system supplies electrical power for the ignition system, the lights, the radio, etc. The alternator is driven by a drivebelt.

Starting system

3   The starting system consists of the battery, the ignition switch, the starter relay, the Powertrain Control Module (PCM), the Body Control Module (BCM), the Transmission Range (TR) switch, the starter motor and solenoid assembly, and the wiring connecting all of the components.

Precautions

4   Always observe the following precautions when working on the electrical system:

a) Be extremely careful when servicing engine electrical components. They are easily damaged if checked, connected or handled improperly.

b) Never leave the ignition switched on for long periods of time when the engine is not running.

c) Never disconnect the battery cables while the engine is running.

d) Maintain correct polarity when connecting battery cables from another vehicle during jump starting (see Chapter 0, Section 7).

e) Always disconnect the cable from the negative battery terminal before working on the electrical system, but read the battery disconnection procedure first (see Section 3).

5   It's also a good idea to review the safety-related information regarding the engine electrical systems located in "Safety first" at the front of this manual, Section 10 before beginning any operation included in this Chapter.

2   Troubleshooting

Ignition system

1   If a malfunction occurs in the ignition system, do not immediately assume that any particular part is causing the problem. First, check the following items:

a) *Make sure that the cable clamps at the battery terminals are clean and tight.*
b) *Test the condition of the battery (see Steps 21 through 24). If if doesn't pass all the tests, replace it.*
c) *Check the ignition coil or coil pack connections.*
d) *Check any relevant fuses in the engine compartment fuse and relay box (see Chapter 12). If they're burned, determine the cause and repair the circuit.*

Check

Warning: *Because of the high voltage generated by the ignition system, use extreme care when performing a procedure involving ignition components.*

Note: *The ignition system components on these vehicles are difficult to diagnose. In the event of ignition system failure that you can't diagnose, have the vehicle tested at a dealer service department or other qualified auto repair facility.*

Note: *You'll need a spark tester for the following test. Spark testers are available at most auto supply stores.*

2   If the engine turns over but won't start, verify that there is sufficient ignition voltage to fire the spark plugs as follows.

3   On models with a coil-over-plug type ignition system, remove a coil and install the tester between the boot at the lower end of the coil and the spark plug **(see illustration)**. On models with spark plug wires, disconnect a spark plug wire from a spark plug and install the tester between the spark plug wire boot and the spark plug.

4   Crank the engine and note whether or not the tester flashes.

Caution: *Do NOT crank the engine or allow it to run for more than five seconds; running the engine for more than five seconds may set a Diagnostic Trouble Code (DTC) for a cylinder misfire.*

Models with a coil-over-plug type ignition system

5   If the tester flashes during cranking, the coil is delivering sufficient voltage to the spark plug to fire it. Repeat this test for each cylinder to verify that the other coils are OK.

6   If the tester doesn't flash, remove a coil from another cylinder and swap it for the one being tested. If the tester now flashes, you know that the original coil is bad. If the tester still doesn't flash, the PCM or wiring harness is probably defective. Have the PCM checked out by a dealer service department or other qualified repair shop (testing the PCM is beyond the scope of the do-it-yourselfer

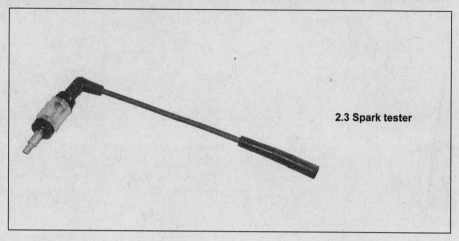

2.3 Spark tester

because it requires expensive special tools).

7   If the tester flashes during cranking but a misfire code (related to the cylinder being tested) has been stored, the spark plug could be fouled or defective.

Models with spark plug wires

8   If the tester flashes during cranking, sufficient voltage is reaching the spark plug to fire it.

9   Repeat this test on the remaining cylinders.

10   Proceed on this basis until you have verified that there's a good spark from each spark plug wire. If there is, then you have verified that the coils in the coil pack are functioning correctly and that the spark plug wires are OK.

11   If there is no spark from a spark plug wire, then either the coil is bad, the plug wire is bad or a connection at one end of the plug wire is loose. Assuming that you're using new plug wires or known good wires, then the coil is probably defective. Also inspect the coil pack electrical connector. Make sure that it's clean, tight and in good condition.

12   If all the coils are firing correctly, but the engine misfires, then one or more of the plugs might be fouled. Remove and check the spark plugs or install new ones (see Chapter 1).

13   No further testing of the ignition system is possible without special tools. If the problem persists, have the ignition system tested by a dealer service department or other qualified repair shop.

Charging system

14   If a malfunction occurs in the charging system, do not automatically assume the alternator is causing the problem. First check the following items:

a) *Check the drivebelt tension and condition (see Chapter 1). Replace it if it's worn or deteriorated.*
b) *Make sure the alternator mounting bolts are tight.*
c) *Inspect the alternator wiring harness and the connectors at the alternator and voltage regulator. They must be in good condition, tight and have no corrosion.*

d) *Check the fusible link (if equipped) or main fuse in the underhood fuse/relay box (see Chapter 12). If it is burned, determine the cause, repair the circuit and replace the link or fuse (the vehicle will not start and/or the accessories will not work if the fusible link or main fuse is blown).*
e) *Start the engine and check the alternator for abnormal noises (a shrieking or squealing sound indicates a bad bearing).*
f) *Check the battery. Make sure it's fully charged and in good condition (one bad cell in a battery can cause overcharging by the alternator).*
g) *Disconnect the battery cables (negative first, then positive). Inspect the battery posts and the cable clamps for corrosion. Clean them thoroughly if necessary (see Chapter 1). Reconnect the cables (positive first, negative last).*

Alternator - check

15   Use a voltmeter to check the battery voltage with the engine off. It should be at least 12.6 volts **(see illustration 2.21)**.

16   Start the engine and check the battery voltage again. It should now be approximately 13.5 to 15 volts.

17   If the voltage reading is more or less than the specified charging voltage, the voltage regulator is probably defective, which will require replacement of the alternator (the voltage regulator is not replaceable separately). Remove the alternator (see Section 7) and have it bench tested (most auto parts stores will do this for you).

18   The charging system (battery) light on the instrument cluster lights up when the ignition key is turned to ON, but it should go out when the engine starts.

19   If the charging system light stays on after the engine has been started, there is a problem with the charging system. Before replacing the alternator, check the battery condition, drivebelt tension and electrical cable connections.

20   If replacing the alternator doesn't restore voltage to the specified range, have the charging system tested by a dealer service department or other qualified repair shop.

2.21 To test the open circuit voltage of the battery, touch the negative probe of the voltmeter to the negative terminal and the positive probe to the positive terminal of the battery; a fully charged battery should be at least 12.6 volts

2.23 Connect a battery load tester to the battery and check the battery condition under load following the tool manufacturer's instructions

Battery - check

21   Check the battery state of charge. Visually inspect the indicator eye on the top of the battery (if equipped with one); if the indicator eye is black in color, charge the battery (see Chapter 1). Next perform an open circuit voltage test using a digital voltmeter. With the engine and all accessories Off, touch the negative probe of the voltmeter to the negative terminal of the battery and the positive probe to the positive terminal of the battery **(see illustration)**. The battery voltage should be 12.6 volts or slightly above. If the battery is less than the specified voltage, charge the battery before proceeding to the next test. Do not proceed with the battery load test unless the battery charge is correct.
Note: *The battery's surface charge must be removed before accurate voltage measurements can be made. Turn on the high beams for ten seconds, then turn them off and let the vehicle stand for two minutes.*
22   Disconnect the negative battery cable, then the positive cable from the battery.
23   Perform a battery load test. An accurate check of the battery condition can only be performed with a load tester **(see illustration)**. This test evaluates the ability of the battery to operate the starter and other accessories during periods of high current draw. Connect the load tester to the battery terminals. Load test the battery according to the tool manufacturer's instructions. This tool increases the load demand (current draw) on the battery.
24   Maintain the load on the battery for 15 seconds and observe that the battery voltage does not drop below 9.6 volts. If the battery condition is weak or defective, the tool will indicate this condition immediately.
Note: *Cold temperatures will cause the minimum voltage reading to drop slightly. Follow the chart given in the manufacturer's instructions to compensate for cold climates. Minimum load voltage for freezing temperatures*

(32 degrees F) should be approximately 9.1 volts.

Starting system

The starter rotates, but the engine doesn't

25   Remove the starter (see Section 8). Check the overrunning clutch and bench test the starter to make sure the drive mechanism extends fully for proper engagement with the flywheel ring gear. If it doesn't, replace the starter.
26   Check the flywheel ring gear for missing teeth and other damage. With the ignition turned off, rotate the flywheel so you can check the entire ring gear.

The starter is noisy

27   If the solenoid is making a chattering noise, first check the battery (see Steps 21 through 24). If the battery is okay, check the cables and connections.
28   If you hear a grinding, crashing metallic sound when you turn the key to Start, check for loose starter mounting bolts. If they're tight, remove the starter and inspect the teeth on the starter pinion gear and flywheel ring gear. Look for missing or damaged teeth.
29   If the starter sounds fine when you first turn the key to Start, but then stops rotating the engine and emits a zinging sound, the problem is probably a defective starter drive that's not staying engaged with the ring gear. Replace the starter.

The starter rotates slowly

30   Check the battery (see Steps 21 through 24).
31   If the battery is okay, verify all connections (at the battery, the starter solenoid and motor) are clean, corrosion-free and tight. Make sure the cables aren't frayed or damaged.

32   Check that the starter mounting bolts are tight so it grounds properly. Also check the pinion gear and flywheel ring gear for evidence of a mechanical bind (galling, deformed gear teeth or other damage).

The starter does not rotate at all

33   Check the battery (see Steps 21 through 24).
34   If the battery is okay, verify all connections (at the battery, the starter solenoid and motor) are clean, corrosion-free and tight. Make sure the cables aren't frayed or damaged.
35   Check all of the fuses in the underhood fuse/relay box.
36   Check that the starter mounting bolts are tight so it grounds properly.
37   Check for voltage at the starter solenoid "S" terminal when the ignition key is turned to the start position. If voltage is present, replace the starter/solenoid assembly. If no voltage is present, the problem could be the starter relay, the Transmission Range (TR) switch (see Chapter 6) or clutch start switch (see Chapter 8), or with an electrical connector somewhere in the circuit (see the wiring diagrams at the end of Chapter 12). Also, on many modern vehicles, the Powertrain Control Module (PCM) and the Body Control Module (BCM) control the voltage signal to the starter solenoid; on such vehicles a special scan tool is required for diagnosis.

---

3   Battery - disconnection and reconnection

Caution: *Always disconnect the cable from the negative battery terminal FIRST and hook it up LAST or the battery may be shorted by the tool being used to loosen the cable clamps.*
1   Some systems on the vehicle require battery power to be available at all times,

either to maintain continuous operation (alarm system, power door locks, etc.), or to maintain control unit memory (radio station presets, Powertrain Control Module and other control units). When the battery is disconnected, the power that maintains these systems is cut. So, before you disconnect the battery, please note that on a vehicle with power door locks, it's a wise precaution to remove the key from the ignition and to keep it with you, so that it does not get locked inside if the power door locks should engage accidentally when the battery is reconnected!

2   Devices known as "memory-savers" can be used to avoid some of these problems. Precise details vary according to the device used. The typical memory saver is plugged into the cigarette lighter and is connected to a spare battery. Then the vehicle battery can be disconnected from the electrical system. The memory saver will provide sufficient current to maintain audio unit security codes, PCM memory, etc. and will provide power to always hot circuits such as the clock and radio memory circuits.

Warning: *Some memory savers deliver a considerable amount of current in order to keep vehicle systems operational after the main battery is disconnected. If you're using a memory saver, make sure that the circuit concerned is actually open before servicing it.*

Warning: *If you're going to work near any of the airbag system components, the battery MUST be disconnected and a memory saver must NOT be used. If a memory saver is used, power will be supplied to the airbag, which means that it could accidentally deploy and cause serious personal injury.*

Disconnection

3   Install a memory saver device to avoid having to reprogram several of the vehicle's systems (see above).

Warning: *If you're working near any airbag system component, DO NOT use a memory saver.*

4   To disconnect the battery for service procedures requiring power to be cut from the vehicle, loosen the cable end bolt and disconnect the cable from the negative battery terminal. Isolate the cable end to prevent it from coming into accidental contact with the battery terminal.

Reconnection

5   Connect the positive battery cable first, followed by the negative cable.

6   After reconnecting the battery, several re-learn procedures must be performed. These include:

  a) *Accelerator pedal released position learning*
  b) *Throttle valve closed position learning*
  c) *Idle air volume learning*
  d) *Power window initialization and anti-pinch feature**
  e) *Sunroof memory and anti-pinch feature**
  f) *Radio presets**
  g) *Navigation system adjustment**

* *If a memory saver was used when the battery was disconnected, these functions won't*

have to be performed.

7   Refer to your owner's manual for information on resetting the radio presets and navigation system adjustment.

Accelerator pedal released position learning

8   With the accelerator pedal at rest (fully released), turn the ignition to On and wait at least two seconds.

9   Turn the ignition Off and wait at least ten seconds.

10   Turn the ignition back On again and wait at least two seconds.

11   Turn the ignition Off and wait at least ten seconds.

Throttle valve closed position learning

Note: *The engine must be cool before beginning this procedure.*

12   Start the engine when it is cool.

13   Warm the engine to normal operating temperature.

14   Open the hood.

15   With the accelerator pedal at rest (fully released), turn the ignition to On, then Off. Within a ten-second period, listen for the sound of the throttle body motor actuating, indicating that it has moved and found the closed position of the throttle plate.

Idle air volume learning

16   The engine and transmission must be at operating temperature and the charging system must be working properly for this procedure. Also make sure that the transmission is in Park or Neutral.

17   The air conditioner, headlights and defogger must be off. Point the wheels straight ahead and make sure the vehicle isn't moving. If the vehicle has daytime running lights, set the parking brake before starting the engine to turn them off.

18   Perform the accelerator pedal released position learning procedure (see Steps 8 through 11) and the throttle valve closed learning procedure (see Steps 12 and 15).

19   Start the engine and make sure it's warm and all the above conditions are satisfied.

20   Turn the engine Off and wait ten seconds or longer.

21   Ensure that the accelerator pedal is not touched. Turn the ignition On and wait three seconds.

22   Press the accelerator pedal to the floor and release it completely five times within a five second period.

23   Wait for seven seconds with the pedal fully released.

24   Press the pedal to the floor and hold it there for 20 seconds. The CHECK ENGINE light will blink during this period. When it stops blinking and stays on, release the pedal within three seconds.

25   Start the engine and let it idle for 20 seconds.

26   Rev the engine 2 or 3 times and make sure it returns to idle and runs smoothly.

Power window initialization and anti-pinch feature check

2012 and earlier models

27   Raise the glass until it is fully closed.

28   Lower the glass, holding the switch until the glass is fully open, then release the switch.

29   Make sure the switch returns to the neutral position. If it doesn't, pull it up.

30   Check the anti-pinch system by opening the window fully. Put a piece of plastic or wood such as a hammer handle into the opening.

31   Raise the window using the AUTO UP function. Make sure that the window reverses itself after it contacts the object.

2013 and later models

32   Turn the ignition to the On position.

33   Open the window completely (if it already isn't open completely).

34   Pull the power window switch up to close the window, holding the switch in the Up position for at least four seconds after the glass has closed completely.

35   Open the window completely, then place a piece of wood or other object near the top of the window frame.

Warning: *Do not use any part of your body for this check.*

36   Using the auto-up feature, close the window; confirm that the window automatically reverses direction as soon as it contacts the object.

Sunroof initialization and anti-pinch feature check

37   Turn the ignition to the On position.

38   Operate the sunroof switch in the tilt up position; hold it there until the sunroof has tilted up completely.

39   Hold the switch in the tilt up position again. The sunroof should back up after a pause; release the switch.

40   Within five seconds, push the switch to the tilt up position again and hold it there; the sunroof should move from the tilt up position to the fully open position, then back to the fully closed position. Release the switch.

41   Open the sunroof completely, then place a piece of wood or other object near the front of the sunroof opening.

Warning: *Do not use any part of your body for this check.*

42   Operate the sunroof switch with the auto-close function and verify that the sunroof automatically reverses direction as soon as it contacts the object.

---

4   Battery and battery tray - removal and installation

1   Install a memory saver device to avoid having to reprogram several of the vehicle's systems (see Section 3).

Warning: *If you're working near any airbag system component, DO NOT use a memory saver.*

4.2a Battery details (2012 and earlier models)

1   *Negative battery cable*   3   *Battery hold-down clamp*
2   *Positive battery cable*

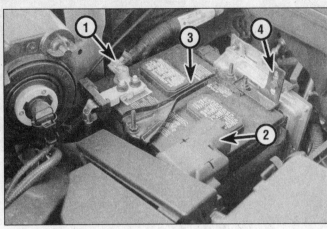

4.2b Battery details (2013 and later models)

1   *Negative battery cable*   3   *Battery hold-down clamp*
2   *Positive battery cable*   4   *PCM upper bracket*

**6.4 Ignition coil electrical connector (A)
and mounting bolt (B)**

6.5 Twist the coil, then lift it straight out

Battery

2   Disconnect the negative battery cable, then the positive battery cable, from the battery **(see illustrations)**.

Warning: *Always disconnect the negative cable first and hook it up last or the battery may be shorted by the tool being used to loosen the cable clamps.*

3   On 2013 and later models, remove the upper PCM bracket bolts and bracket.

4   Remove the battery hold-down clamp mounting nuts and remove the hold-down clamp.

5   Lift out the battery and battery cover. Special battery lifting straps that attach to the battery posts are available at auto parts stores; lifting and moving the battery is much easier if you use one.

6   Installation is the reverse of removal. Connect the positive cable first, then the negative cable. Refer to Section 3 and perform the necessary re-learn procedures.

Battery tray

7   Remove the battery (see Steps 1 through 5).

8   On 2013 models, disconnect the PCM electrical connector, remove the PCM, disconnect the Transmission Control Module (TCM) electrical connector and then remove the PCM bracket.

9   Remove the battery tray liner from the top of the battery tray.

10   Remove the battery tray mounting bolts and lift the battery tray from the battery tray support.

11   Remove the battery tray support fasteners and remove the support.

12   Installation is the reverse of removal. Connect the positive cable first, then the negative cable. Refer to Section 3 and perform the necessary re-learn procedures.

5   Battery cables - replacement

1   When removing the cables, always disconnect the cable from the negative battery terminal first and hook it up last, or you might accidentally short out the battery with the tool you're using to loosen the cable clamps. Even if you're only replacing the cable for the positive terminal, always disconnect the negative

cable from the battery first.

2   Disconnect the old cables from the battery, then trace each of them to their opposite ends and disconnect them. Note the routing of each cable before disconnecting it to ensure correct installation.

3   If you are replacing any of the old cables, take them with you when buying new cables. It is vitally important that you replace the cables with identical parts.

4   Clean the threads of the solenoid or ground connection with a wire brush to remove rust and corrosion. Apply a light coat of battery terminal corrosion inhibitor or petroleum jelly to the threads to prevent future corrosion.

5   Attach the cable to the solenoid or ground connection and tighten the mounting nut/bolt securely.

6   Before connecting a new cable to the battery, make sure that it reaches the battery post without having to be stretched.

7   Connect the cable to the positive battery terminal first, then connect the ground cable to the negative battery terminal.

6   Ignition coil(s) - replacement

1   Remove the engine cover.

2   Remove the air inlet duct and the air filter housing (see Chapter 4).

3   On V6 engines, if you're removing the coils from the right (2012 and earlier models) or rear (2013 and later models) cylinder bank, remove the upper intake manifold (see Chapter 2A).

4   Depress the release tab and disconnect the electrical connector from the coil(s) **(see illustration)**.

5   Remove the coil mounting bolt, then pull the coil straight out **(see illustration)**.

6   Installation is the reverse of removal. Before installing the ignition coils, coat the interior of the boots with silicone dielectric compound.

7.6 Alternator lower mounting bracket-to-alternator bolt (seen from the rear)

7.7 Alternator upper pivot bolt

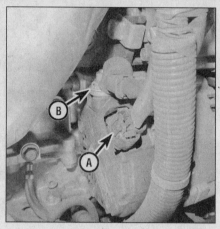

7.8 Alternator electrical connector (A) and battery cable terminal (B)

7.17 Alternator lower mounting nut/bolt (upper bolt not visible; it's accessed from the other side of the alternator)

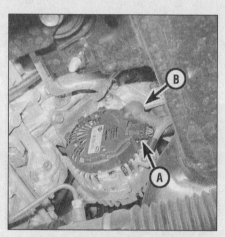

7.22 Alternator electrical connector (A) and battery cable terminal (B) (under rubber cover)

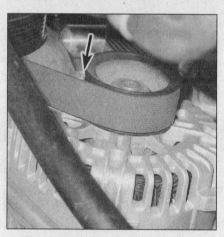

7.23 Upper and lower alternator mounting fasteners

7 Alternator - removal and installation

Warning: *The air conditioning system is under high pressure. Do not loosen any hose fittings or remove any components until after the system has been discharged. Air conditioning refrigerant should be properly discharged into an EPA-approved recovery/recycling unit at a dealer service department or an automotive air conditioning repair facility. Always wear eye protection when disconnecting air conditioning system fittings.*

Warning: *The engine must be completely cool before beginning this procedure.*

1   On 2013 and later models, have the air conditioning system evacuated by a shop with the proper equipment.

2   Disconnect the cable from the negative terminal of the battery (see Section 3).

3   Remove the engine cover.

4   Remove the drivebelt (see Chapter 1).

V6 engines
2012 and earlier models

5   Partially drain the cooling system, then remove the upper radiator hose (see Chapter 1) and the fan shroud (see Chapter 3).

6   Remove the alternator lower bracket-to-alternator bolt and loosen the bracket-to-timing chain cover bolt **(see illustration)**.

7   Remove the alternator upper pivot bolt **(see illustration)**.

8   Disconnect the electrical connector from the alternator, then remove the nut securing the battery cable to the alternator B+ terminal **(see illustration)** and remove the alternator.

2013 and later models

9   Remove the battery tray (see Section 4).

10   Loosen the right front wheel lug nuts.

11   Raise the vehicle and support it securely on jackstands, then remove the right front wheel.

12   Remove the radiator and fan shroud (see Chapter 3).

13   Remove the drivebelt tensioner (see Chapter 1).

14   Remove the access cover from the right front wheel well.

15   Remove the air filter housing and inlet duct (see Chapter 4).

16   Disconnect the wiring from the oil pressure switch and the alternator.

17   Remove the alternator mounting fasteners, then remove the alternator **(see illustration)**.

V8 engines

18   Remove the lower engine splash shield.

19   Drain the cooling system (see Chapter 1).

20   Remove the lower radiator hose and fan shrouds (see Chapter 3).

21   Disconnect the transmission cooler lines from the radiator.

22   Disconnect the electrical connector from the alternator, then remove the nut securing the battery cable to the alternator B+ terminal **(see illustration)**.

23   Remove the upper and lower alternator mounting fasteners **(see illustration)** and remove the alternator.

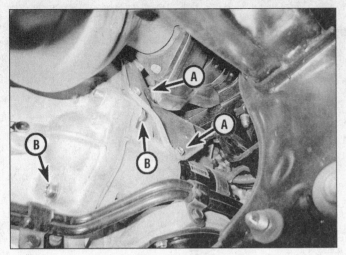

8.3 Starter motor mounting details

8.4 Starter motor electrical connector (A) and input cable (B)

A   *Starter heat shield mounting bolts*
B   *Starter motor mounting bolts*

All models

24   If you're replacing the alternator, take the old one with you when purchasing the replacement unit. Make sure that the new/rebuilt unit looks identical to the old alternator. Look at the electrical terminals on the backside of the alternator. They should be the same in number, size and location as the terminals on the old alternator.

25   Some new/rebuilt alternators DO NOT have a pulley installed, so you might have to swap the pulley from the old unit to the new/rebuilt one. When buying an alternator, find out the store's policy regarding pulley swaps. Some stores perform this service free of charge. If your local auto parts store doesn't offer this service, you'll have to purchase a puller for removing the pulley and do it yourself.

26   Installation is the reverse of removal. Tighten the alternator mounting fasteners securely.

27   Refill the cooling system (see Chapter 1).

28   Reconnect the battery and perform the necessary re-learn procedures (see Section 3).

29   If removed, tighten the wheel lug nuts to the torque listed in the Chapter 1 Specifications.

30   Check the charging voltage (see Section 1) to verify that the alternator is operating correctly.

8   Starter motor - removal and installation

1   Disconnect the cable from the negative terminal of the battery (see Section 3).

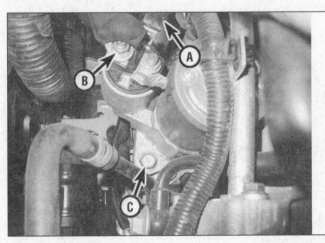

8.11 Starter motor mounting details

A   *S terminal electrical connector*
B   *B+ terminal*
C   *Lower mounting bolt (upper bolt not shown)*

V6 engines

2012 and earlier models

2   Raise the vehicle and support it securely on jackstands.

3   Remove the heat shield fasteners **(see illustration)**.

4   Disconnect the starter motor electrical connectors **(see illustration)**.

5   Remove the two mounting bolts and remove the starter.

6   Installation is the reverse of removal.

7   Reconnect the battery and perform the necessary re-learn procedures (see Section 3).

2013 and later models

8   Remove the air filter housing and duct (see Chapter 4).

9   Remove the battery tray and battery support (see Section 4).

10   Remove the CVT fill pipe fastener and pipe from the transaxle.

11   Disconnect the starter motor electrical connector **(see illustration)**.

12   Remove the two mounting bolts and remove the starter.

13   Installation is the reverse of removal.

14   Reconnect the battery and perform the necessary re-learn procedures (see Section 3).

15   Check the automatic transaxle fluid, adding as necessary (see Chapter 1).

V8 engines

16   Remove the intake manifold (see Chapter 2B).

17   Disconnect the starter motor electrical connectors.

18   Remove the starter motor mounting bolts and remove the starter motor.

19   Installation is the reverse of removal.

20   Reconnect the battery and perform the necessary re-learn procedures (see Section 3).

Notes

Chapter 6
Emissions and engine control systems

Contents

	Section
Accelerator Pedal Position (APP) sensor - replacement	4
Camshaft Position (CMP) sensor - replacement	5
Catalytic converter - replacement	15
Crankshaft Position (CKP) sensor - replacement	7
Engine Coolant Temperature (ECT) sensor - replacement	8
Evaporative Emissions Control (EVAP) system - component replacement	16
General information	1
Intake Valve Timing (IVT) control solenoid(s)/sensor(s) - replacement	6
Knock Sensor (KS) - replacement	10
Mass Air Flow/Intake Air Temperature (MAF/IAT) sensor - replacement	9

	Section
Obtaining and clearing Diagnostic Trouble Codes (DTCs)	3
On Board Diagnosis (OBD) system	2
Oxygen sensors - replacement	11
Powertrain Control Module (PCM) - replacement	14
Positive Crankcase Ventilation (PCV) valve - replacement	17
Throttle Position (TP) sensor - replacement	19
Transmission range (TR) switch - replacement and adjustment	12
Transmission speed sensors - replacement	13
Variable Induction Air System (VIAS) solenoid valves and actuators (V6 engines) - replacement	18

Specifications

Torque specifications

Note: *One foot-pound (ft-lb) of torque is equivalent to 12 inch-pounds (in-lbs) of torque. Torque values below approximately 15 ft-lbs are expressed in inch-pounds, since most foot-pound torque wrenches are not accurate at these smaller values.*

	Ft-lbs (unless otherwise indicated)	Nm
Knock sensor mounting bolt		
V6 engines	156 in-lbs	17.5
V8 engines	16	22
Oxygen sensors	37	50

1 General information

1   To prevent pollution of the atmosphere from incompletely burned and evaporating gases, and to maintain good driveability and fuel economy, a number of emission control systems are incorporated. They include the:

Catalytic converter

2   A catalytic converter is an emission control device in the exhaust system that reduces certain pollutants in the exhaust gas stream. There are two types of converters: oxidation converters and reduction converters.

3   Oxidation converters contain a monolithic substrate (a ceramic honeycomb) coated with the semi-precious metals platinum and palladium. An oxidation catalyst reduces unburned hydrocarbons (HC) and carbon monoxide (CO) by adding oxygen to the exhaust stream as it passes through the substrate, which, in the presence of high temperature and the catalyst materials, converts the HC and CO to water vapor (H_2O) and carbon dioxide (CO_2).

4   Reduction converters contain a monolithic substrate coated with platinum and rhodium. A reduction catalyst reduces oxides of nitrogen (NOx) by removing oxygen, which in the presence of high temperature and the catalyst material produces nitrogen (N) and carbon dioxide (CO_2).

5   Catalytic converters that combine both types of catalysts in one assembly are known as "three-way catalysts" or TWCs. A TWC can reduce all three pollutants.

Evaporative Emissions Control (EVAP) system

6   The Evaporative Emissions Control (EVAP) system prevents fuel system vapors (which contain unburned hydrocarbons) from escaping into the atmosphere. On warm days, vapors trapped inside the fuel tank expand until the pressure reaches a certain threshold. Then the fuel vapors are routed from the fuel tank through the fuel vapor vent valve and the fuel vapor control valve to the EVAP canister, where they're stored temporarily until the next time the vehicle is operated. When the conditions are right (engine warmed up, vehicle up to speed, moderate or heavy load on the engine, etc.) the PCM opens the canister purge valve, which allows fuel vapors to be drawn from the canister into the intake manifold. Once in the intake manifold, the fuel vapors mix with incoming air before being drawn through the intake ports into the combustion chambers where they're burned up with the rest of the air/fuel mixture. The EVAP system is complex and virtually impossible to troubleshoot without the right tools and training.

Powertrain Control Module (PCM)

7   The Powertrain Control Module (PCM) is the brain of the engine management system. It also controls a wide variety of other vehicle systems. In order to program the new PCM, the dealer needs the vehicle as well as the new PCM. If you're planning to replace the PCM with a new one, there is no point in trying to do so at home because you won't be able to program it yourself.

Positive Crankcase Ventilation (PCV) system

8   The Positive Crankcase Ventilation (PCV) system reduces hydrocarbon emissions by scavenging crankcase vapors, which are rich in unburned hydrocarbons. A PCV valve or orifice regulates the flow of gases into the intake manifold in proportion to the amount of intake vacuum available.

9   The PCV system generally consists of the fresh air inlet hose, the PCV valve or orifice and the crankcase ventilation hose (or PCV hose). The fresh air inlet hose connects the air intake duct to a pipe on the valve cover. The crankcase ventilation hose (or PCV hose) connects the PCV valve or orifice in the valve cover to the intake manifold.

Information Sensors

Accelerator Pedal Position (APP) sensor - as you press the accelerator pedal, the APP sensor alters its voltage signal to the PCM in proportion to the angle of the pedal, and the PCM commands a motor inside the throttle body to open or close the throttle plate accordingly

Camshaft Position (CMP) sensor - produces a signal that the PCM uses to identify the number 1 cylinder and to time the firing sequence of the fuel injectors

Crankshaft Position (CKP) sensor - produces a signal that the PCM uses to calculate engine speed and crankshaft position, which enables it to synchronize ignition timing with fuel injector timing, and to detect misfires

Engine Coolant Temperature (ECT) sensor - a thermistor (temperature-sensitive variable resistor) that sends a voltage signal to the PCM, which uses this data to determine the temperature of the engine coolant

Fuel tank pressure sensor - measures the fuel tank pressure and controls fuel tank pressure by signaling the EVAP system to purge the fuel tank vapors when the pressure becomes excessive

Intake Air Temperature (IAT) sensor - monitors the temperature of the air entering the engine and sends a signal to the PCM to determine injector pulse-width (the duration of each injector's on-time) and to adjust spark timing (to prevent spark knock)

Knock sensor - a piezoelectric crystal that oscillates in proportion to engine vibration which produces a voltage output that is monitored by the PCM. This retards the ignition timing when the oscillation exceeds a certain threshold

Manifold Absolute Pressure (MAP) sensor - monitors the pressure or vacuum inside the intake manifold. The PCM uses this data to determine engine load so that it can alter the ignition advance and fuel enrichment

Mass Air Flow (MAF) sensor - measures the amount of intake air drawn into the engine. It uses a hot-wire sensing element to measure the amount of air entering the engine

Oxygen sensors - generates a small variable voltage signal in proportion to the difference between the oxygen content in the exhaust stream and the oxygen content in the ambient air. The PCM uses this information to maintain the proper air/fuel ratio. A second oxygen sensor monitors the efficiency of the catalytic converter

Throttle Position (TP) sensor - a potentiometer that generates a voltage signal that varies in relation to the opening angle of the throttle plate inside the throttle body. Works with the PCM and other sensors to calculate injector pulse width (the duration of each injector's on-time)

Photos courtesy of Wells Manufacturing, except APP and MAF sensors.

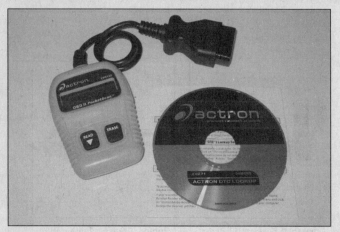

2.4a Simple code readers are an economical way to extract trouble codes when the CHECK ENGINE light comes on

2.4b Hand-held scan tools like these can extract computer codes and also perform diagnostics

2 On Board Diagnosis (OBD) system

General description

1   All models are equipped with the second generation OBD-II system. This system consists of an on-board computer known as the Powertrain Control Module (PCM), and information sensors, which monitor various functions of the engine and send data to the PCM. This system incorporates a series of diagnostic monitors that detect and identify fuel injection and emissions control system faults and store the information in the computer memory. This system also tests sensors and output actuators, diagnoses drive cycles, freezes data and clears codes.

2   The PCM is the brain of the electronically controlled fuel and emissions system. It receives data from a number of sensors and other electronic components (switches, relays, etc.). Based on the information it receives, the PCM generates output signals to control various relays, solenoids (fuel injectors) and other actuators. The PCM is specifically calibrated to optimize the emissions, fuel economy and driveability of the vehicle.

3   It isn't a good idea to attempt diagnosis or replacement of the PCM or emission control components at home while the vehicle is under warranty. Because of a federally-mandated warranty which covers the emissions system components and because any owner-induced damage to the PCM, the sensors and/or the control devices may void this warranty, take the vehicle to a dealer service department if the PCM or a system component malfunctions.

Scan tool information

4   Because extracting the Diagnostic Trouble Codes (DTCs) from an engine management system is now the first step in trouble-shooting many computer-controlled systems and components, a code reader, at the very least, will be required **(see illustration)**. More powerful scan tools can also perform many of the diagnostics once associated with expensive factory scan tools **(see illustration)**. If you're planning to obtain a generic scan tool for your vehicle, make sure that it's compatible with OBD-II systems. If you don't plan to purchase a code reader or scan tool and don't have access to one, you can have the codes extracted by a dealer service department or an independent repair shop.
Note: *Some auto parts stores even provide this service.*

3 Obtaining and clearing Diagnostic Trouble Codes (DTCs)

1   All models covered by this manual are equipped with on-board diagnostics. When the PCM recognizes a malfunction in a monitored emission or engine control system, component or circuit, it turns on the Malfunction Indicator Light (MIL) on the dash. The PCM will continue to display the MIL until the problem is fixed and the Diagnostic Trouble Code (DTC) is cleared from the PCM's memory. You'll need a scan tool to access any DTCs stored in the PCM.

2   Before outputting any DTCs stored in the PCM, thoroughly inspect ALL electrical connectors and hoses. Make sure that all electrical connections are tight, clean and free of corrosion. And make sure that all hoses are correctly connected, fit tightly and are in good condition (no cracks or tears).

Accessing the DTCs

3   The Diagnostic Trouble Codes (DTCs) can only be accessed with a code reader or scan tool. Professional scan tools are expensive, but relatively inexpensive generic code readers or scan tools **(see illustrations 2.4a and 2.4b)** are available at most auto parts stores. Simply plug the connector of the scan tool into the diagnostic connector **(see illustration)**. Then follow the instructions included with the scan tool to extract the DTCs.

4   Once you have outputted all of the stored DTCs, look them up on the accompanying DTC chart.

5   After troubleshooting the source of each DTC, make any necessary repairs or replace the defective component(s).

Clearing the DTCs

6   Clear the DTCs with the code reader or scan tool in accordance with the instructions provided by the tool's manufacturer.

Diagnostic Trouble Codes

7   The accompanying tables are a list of the Diagnostic Trouble Codes (DTCs) that can be accessed by a do-it-yourselfer working at home (there are many, many more DTCs available to professional mechanics with proprietary scan tools and software, but those codes cannot be accessed by a generic scan tool). If, after you have checked and repaired the connectors, wire harness and vacuum hoses (if applicable) for an emission-related system, component or circuit, the problem persists, have the vehicle checked by a dealer service department or other qualified repair shop.

3.3 The Data Link Connector (DLC) is located under the lower edge of the dash, to the left of the steering column

OBD-ll trouble codes

Code	Code identification
P0011	Intake valve timing control solenoid performance (bank 1)
P0014	Exhaust valve timing control solenoid performance (bank 1)
P0021	Intake camshaft position timing - over-advanced (bank 2)
P0024	Exhaust camshaft position timing - over-advanced (bank 2)
P0031	Upstream oxygen sensor heater control circuit low voltage signal (Bank 1)
P0032	Upstream oxygen sensor heater control circuit high voltage signal (Bank 1)
P0037	Downstream oxygen sensor heater control circuit low voltage signal (Bank 1)
P0038	Downstream oxygen sensor heater control circuit high voltage signal (Bank 1)
P0043	Downstream (no.3) oxygen sensor heater control circuit high voltage signal (Bank 1)
P0051	Upstream oxygen sensor heater control circuit low voltage signal (Bank 2)
P0052	Upstream oxygen sensor heater control circuit high voltage signal (Bank 2)
P0057	Downstream oxygen sensor heater control circuit low voltage signal (Bank 2)
P0058	Downstream oxygen sensor heater control circuit high voltage signal (Bank 2)
P0075	Intake valve timing control solenoid circuit (Bank 1)
P0078	Exhaust valve timing control solenoid circuit (Bank 1)
P0081	Intake valve timing control solenoid circuit (Bank 2)
P0084	Exhaust valve timing control solenoid circuit (Bank 2)
P0101	Mass Air Flow sensor circuit range or performance fault
P0102	Mass Air Flow sensor circuit low input
P0103	Mass Air Flow sensor circuit high input
P0112	Intake Air Temperature sensor circuit low input
P0113	Intake Air Temperature sensor circuit high input
P0117	Engine Coolant Temperature sensor circuit low input
P0116	Engine coolant temperature circuit range/performance problem
P0118	Engine Coolant Temperature sensor circuit high input
P0122	Throttle Position Sensor circuit low input
P0123	Throttle Position Sensor circuit high input
P0125	Engine Coolant Temperature sensor or circuit fault
P0127	Intake Air Temperature too high
P0128	Thermostat function - engine coolant does not reach correct temperature after warm-up

OBD-II trouble codes (continued)

Note: *Not all trouble codes apply to all models.*

Code	Probable cause
P0130	Upstream oxygen sensor or circuit fault (Bank 1)
P0131	Upstream oxygen sensor lean shift monitor fault (Bank 1)
P0132	Upstream oxygen sensor rich shift monitor fault (Bank 1)
P0133	O2 sensor circuit, slow response (bank 1, sensor 1)
P0134	O2 sensor circuit, no activity detected (bank 1, sensor 1)
P0137	Downstream oxygen sensor minimum voltage monitor fault
P0138	Downstream oxygen sensor maximum voltage monitor fault
P0139	Downstream oxygen sensor circuit slow response fault
P014C	Oxygen sensor 1 problem
P014D	Oxygen sensor 1 problem
P0143	O2 sensor circuit, low voltage (bank 1, sensor 3)
P0144	O2 sensor circuit, high voltage (bank 1, sensor 3)
P0145	O2 sensor circuit, slow response (bank 1, sensor 3)
P0146	O2 sensor circuit - no activity detected (bank 1, sensor 3)
P0150	Upstream oxygen sensor or circuit fault (Bank 2)
P0151	Upstream oxygen sensor lean shift monitor fault (Bank 2)
P0152	Upstream oxygen sensor rich shift monitor fault (Bank 2)
P0153	Upstream oxygen sensor circuit slow response fault (Bank 2)
P0154	Upstream oxygen sensor circuit high voltage fault (Bank 2)
P0157	Downstream oxygen sensor minimum voltage monitor fault
P0158	Downstream oxygen sensor maximum voltage monitor fault
P0159	Downstream oxygen sensor circuit slow response fault
P0171	Fuel injection system lean (Bank 1)
P0172	Fuel injection system rich (Bank 1)
P0174	System too lean (bank 2)
P0175	System too rich (bank 2)
P0181	Fuel Tank Temperature sensor circuit range or performance
P0182	Fuel Tank Temperature sensor circuit low input
P0183	Fuel Tank Temperature sensor circuit high input

Code	Probable cause
P0196	Fuel rail pressure sensor circuit, range or performance problem
P0197	Fuel rail pressure sensor circuit, low input
P0198	Fuel rail pressure sensor circuit, high input
P0222	Throttle Position Sensor circuit low input
P0223	Throttle Position Sensor circuit high input
P0300	Multiple cylinder misfire detected
P0301	Cylinder no. 1 misfire detected
P0302	Cylinder no. 2 misfire detected
P0303	Cylinder no. 3 misfire detected
P0304	Cylinder no. 4 misfire detected
P0305	Cylinder no. 5 misfire detected
P0306	Cylinder no. 6 misfire detected
P0307	Cylinder no. 7 misfire detected
P0308	Cylinder no. 8 misfire detected
P0327	Knock Sensor circuit low input
P0328	Knock Sensor circuit high input
P0322	Crankshaft Position (CKP) sensor/engine speed (RPM) sensor - no signal
P0323	Crankshaft Position (CKP) sensor/engine speed (RPM) sensor - circuit intermittent
P0332	Knock sensor no. 2 circuit, low input (bank 2)
P0333	Knock sensor no. 2 circuit, high input (bank 2)
P0335	Crankshaft Position sensor (CKP) or circuit fault
P0340	Camshaft Position sensor or circuit fault (Bank 1)
P0345	Camshaft Position sensor or circuit fault (Bank 2)
P0420	Catalyst system defective (Bank 1)
P0430	Catalyst system defective (Bank 2)
P0441	EVAP control system incorrect purge flow
P0442	EVAP system small leak (negative pressure check)
P0443	EVAP canister purge control valve circuit fault
P0444	EVAP canister purge control valve circuit open
P0445	EVAP canister purge control valve circuit shorted
P0447	EVAP canister vent control valve circuit open

OBD-II trouble codes (continued)

Note: *Not all trouble codes apply to all models.*

Code	Probable cause
P0448	EVAP canister vent control valve remains closed under certain driving conditions
P0451	EVAP system pressure sensor or circuit fault
P0452	EVAP system pressure sensor low input voltage signal
P0453	EVAP system pressure sensor high input
P0455	EVAP system gross leak
P0456	EVAP system very small leak (negative pressure check)
P0460	Fuel level sensor or circuit fault
P0461	Fuel level sensor or circuit fault
P0462	Fuel level sensor circuit low input
P0463	Fuel level sensor circuit high input
P0480	Cooling fan no. 1, control circuit malfunction
P0481	Cooling fan no. 2, control circuit malfunction
P0500	Vehicle Speed Sensor or circuit fault
P0506	Idle Air Control system signal low
P0507	Idle Air Control system signal high
P0550	Power steering pressure sensor range
P0603	PCM back-up RAM does not function properly
P0605	PCM or EEPROM fault
P0607	Control module performance
P0643	PCM detects sensor power supply low or high voltage
P0700	Transmission control system (Malfunction Indicator Light MIL) request
P0705	Transmission Range (TR) sensor, rationality
P0710	Automatic transmission fluid temperature sensor
P0717	TCM, turbine sensor circuit open or shorted
P0720	Output speed sensor circuit
P0725	Engine speed sensor circuit
P0740	Torque Converter Clutch (TCC) out of range
P0744	Torque Converter Clutch (TCC), solenoid
P0745	Line pressure solenoid, improper voltage when driving

Code	Probable cause
P0750	Shift solenoid, circuit problem
P0850	Park/Neutral position switch circuit fault in Drive and Park
P1148	Closed loop control fault
P1168	Oxygen sensors or circuit, bank 2, closed-loop function not available
P1212	Traction control system communication line fault
P1217	Engine overheating
P1225	Closed throttle position learning value low
P1226	Closed throttle position learning performance fault
P1421	Cold start control system problem
P1550	Battery current sensor problem
P1551	Battery current sensor problem
P1552	Battery current sensor problem
P1553	Battery current sensor problem
P1554	Battery current sensor problem
P1564	ASCD steering switch problem
P1572	ASCD brake switch or circuit fault
P1574	ASCD speed sensor signal performance fault
P1610-1615	NATS (alarm system), malfunction
P1700	Automatic transmission control system problem
P1706	Transmission Range (TR), circuit
P1715	Input speed sensor problem
P1716	Input speed sensor circuit problem
P1720	Vehicle speed sensor problem
P1730	Automatic transmission, interlock system problem
P1752	Automatic transmission, input clutch solenoid
P1754	Automatic transmission, input clutch solenoid
P1757	Automatic transmission, front brake solenoid circuit
P1759	Automatic transmission, front brake solenoid function
P1762	Automatic transmission, front clutch solenoid circuit
P1764	Automatic transmission, direct brake solenoid circuit
P1767	Automatic transmission, front brake solenoid circuit

OBD-II trouble codes (continued)

Note: *Not all trouble codes apply to all models.*

Code	Probable cause
P1769	Automatic transmission, High/Low reverse clutch solenoid
P1772	Automatic transmission, front brake solenoid circuit
P1774	Automatic transmission, low coast brake solenoid
P1800	VIAS control solenoid valve circuit performance fault
P1805	Brake switch or circuit fault
P2A00	Oxygen sensor 1
P2A03	Oxygen sensor 1
P2100	Throttle Control motor voltage signal is open or low voltage
P2103	Throttle Control motor relay voltage signal is shorted (ON)
P2101	Electric throttle control function problem
P2118	Throttle Control motor performance fault in circuit and/or throttle control motor
P2119	Throttle Control motor defective or stuck in position
P2122	Accelerator Pedal Position sensor 1 circuit low
P2123	Accelerator Pedal Position sensor 1 circuit high
P2127	Accelerator Pedal Position sensor 2 circuit low
P2128	Accelerator Pedal Position sensor 2 circuit high
P2135	Throttle Position Sensor circuit range or performance
P2138	Accelerator Pedal Position sensor or circuit range or performance

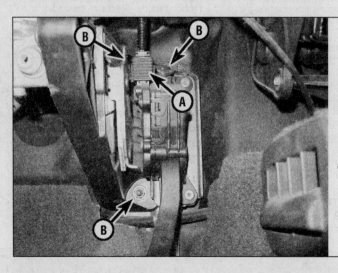

4.3 Accelerator Pedal Position (APP) sensor electrical connector (A) and mounting nuts (B, upper left nut not visible) (2012 and earlier models shown)

4   Accelerator Pedal Position (APP) sensor - replacement

1   Disconnect the cable from the negative terminal of the battery (see Chapter 5).
2   On models with an adjustable accelerator pedal, move the pedal to its most forward position to align the base of the accelerator and brake pedals.
3   Disconnect the electrical connector(s) from the sensor/pedal assembly **(see illustration)**.
4   On models with an adjustable accelerator pedal, disconnect the brake pedal cable from the accelerator pedal by releasing the locking tabs.

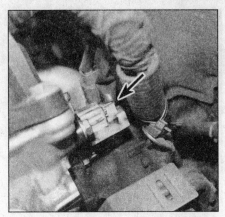

5.2a CMP sensor - left cylinder bank

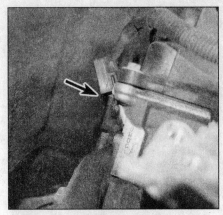

5.2b CMP sensor - right cylinder bank

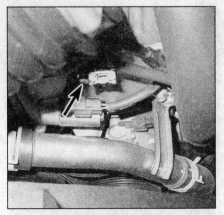

5.8 The CMP sensor is located on the front of the left (driver's side) intake camshaft timing control solenoid valve cover

5.11 The Camshaft Position (CMP) sensors are located at the left end of each valve cover

6.1a On 2012 and earlier models there are two intake valve timing control solenoids installed on top of the camshaft bearing caps

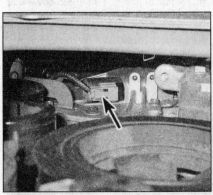

6.1b On 2013 and later models there are two intake valve timing control solenoids installed in the timing chain cover at the passenger's end of the engine (this view is from below, showing the solenoid for the rear cylinder bank)

5   Unscrew the pedal fasteners and remove the pedal.
Note: *Do not attempt to disassemble the pedal. On models with an adjustable accelerator pedal, do not disassemble the adjustment mechanism.*
6   Installation is the reverse of removal.
7   Reconnect the battery and perform the necessary re-learn procedures (see Chapter 5).

5   Camshaft Position (CMP) sensor - replacement

1   Disconnect the cable from the negative battery terminal (see Chapter 5).

2012 and earlier models
V6 engines
Note: *The CMP sensors are located on the rear end of each cylinder head.*
2   Disconnect the electrical connector from the CMP sensor **(see illustrations)**.
3   Remove the sensor mounting boltand

remove the sensor.
4   Inspect the CMP sensor O-ring for cracks, tears and other deterioration. If it's damaged, replace it.
5   When installing the CMP sensor, apply a small dab of clean engine oil to the sensor O-ring, then use a slight rocking motion to work the O-ring into the sensor mounting bore. Do NOT use a twisting motion or you could damage the O-ring.
6   Installation is otherwise the reverse of removal. Tighten the mounting bolt securely.

V8 engines
7   Remove the air intake duct (see Chapter 4).
8   Disconnect the CMP sensor electrical connector **(see illustration)**.
9   Unscrew the mounting bolt and remove the CMP sensor.
10   Installation is the reverse of removal. Replace the O-ring with a new one.

2013 and later models
11   There are two CMP sensors, located at the driver's end of each valve cover **(see illustration)**.

12   Remove the engine cover. If you're removing the sensor from the front cylinder bank, remove the air intake duct. If you're removing the sensor from the rear cylinder bank, remove the air intake duct, air filter housing (see Chapter 4) and the upper intake manifold (see Chapter 2A).
13   Disconnect the electrical connector from the sensor.
14   Remove the mounting bolt and pull out the sensor.
15   Installation is the reverse of removal. Replace the O-ring with a new one.

6   Intake Valve Timing (IVT) control solenoid(s)/sensor(s) - replacement

V6 engines
1   The IVT solenoid valves direct oil to the intake camshaft actuators in order to vary the timing of the intake camshafts **(see illustrations)**. They receive commands from the PCM.

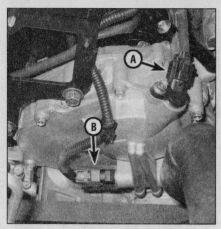

6.6 The IVT control position sensors (A) are located on top of the intake valve timing control position solenoid covers, at the front of each cylinder head. The Intake Valve Timing (IVT) solenoids (B) are below the sensors (right cylinder bank shown)

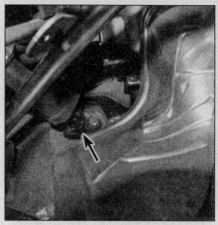

7.1a On 2012 and earlier V6 models, the Crankshaft Position (CKP) sensor is mounted in the right-hand side of the lower/rear of the engine block

7.1b On 2013 and later models, the Crankshaft Position (CKP) sensor is mounted in the oil pan on the front side of the engine, near the transmission/transaxle - this view is from under the vehicle

7.1c On V8 models, the Crankshaft Position (CKP) sensor is mounted in the transmission bellhousing

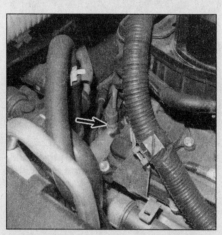

8.1 On 2012 and earlier V6 models, the ECT sensor is located on the coolant pipe at the rear of the right cylinder head

8.2 The Engine Coolant Temperature (ECT) sensor is located on the inner side of the left cylinder head, near the front upper corner - V8 models

2   Disconnect the electrical connector from the solenoid.
3   Remove the mounting bolt from the IVT solenoid, then remove the solenoid.
4   Installation is the reverse of removal. Replace the O-ring with a new one.

V8 engines

Sensors

5   If you're replacing the IVT control position sensor for the left intake cam, remove the air intake duct (see Chapter 4).
6   Disconnect the electrical connector from the sensor **(see illustration)**.
7   Unscrew the mounting bolt and remove the sensor from the IVT control solenoid valve cover.
8   Installation is the reverse of removal. Use a new O-ring on the sensor.

Solenoids

9   If you're replacing the IVT control position solenoid for the left intake cam, remove the air intake duct (see Chapter 4).
10   Disconnect the IVT control position solenoid electrical connector **(see illustration 6.6)**.
11   Remove the IVT solenoid mounting bolt and remove the solenoid.
12   Installation is the reverse of removal. Replace the O-ring with a new one.

---

7   Crankshaft Position (CKP) sensor - replacement

1   The CKP sensor is accessed from under the vehicle **(see illustrations)**.
2   Raise the vehicle and support it securely on jackstands.

3   Remove the under-vehicle splash shield.
4   Remove the sensor mounting bolt, then remove the sensor.
5   Installation is the reverse of removal. Replace the O-ring with a new one.

---

8   Engine Coolant Temperature (ECT) sensor - replacement

Warning: *Wait until the engine has completely cooled before beginning this procedure.*
1   On 2012 and earlier V6 models the ECT sensor is threaded into the coolant pipe at the rear of the right cylinder head **(see illustration)**.
2   On V8 models, the ECT sensor is located on the left-hand cylinder head **(see illustration)**.
3   On 2013 and later V6 models, the ECT

8.3 The Engine Coolant Temperature (ECT) sensor is located in the water outlet at the left (driver's side) end of the engine - 2013 and later models

9.1 The Mass Air Flow/Intake Air Temperature (MAF/IAT) sensor is installed in the air filter housing cover - 2012 and earlier V6 models shown, other models similar

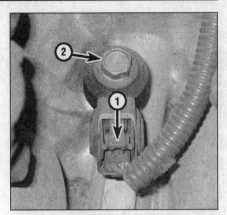

10.3 Depress the release tab (1) and disconnect the electrical connector, the remove the knock sensor retaining bolt (2)

11.2a Front cylinder bank upstream oxygen sensor (2013 and later V6 models shown, earlier models similar)

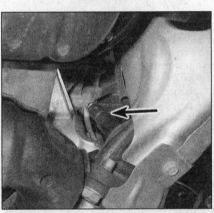

11.2b Rear cylinder bank upstream oxygen sensor (2013 and later V6 models shown, earlier models similar)

11.2c On V8 engines, the upstream oxygen sensors are located on the exhaust manifolds, directly above the catalytic converters (left upstream sensor shown from below)

sensor is mounted in the water outlet at the left end of the engine (see illustration).

4   If you're working on a V8 model or a 2013 or later model, remove the engine cover and the air intake duct (see Chapter 4).

5   Drain some engine coolant (see Chapter 1) to minimize coolant spillage.

6   Disconnect the electrical connector from the ECT sensor.

7   Unscrew the sensor from the engine and discard the sealing washer.

8   Installation is the reverse of removal. Replace the sealing washer with a new one. Refill the cooling system (see Chapter 1).

9   Mass Air Flow/Intake Air Temperature (MAF/IAT) sensor - replacement

1   The MAF/IAT sensor is mounted on the air filter housing (see illustration).

2   Disconnect the electrical connector from the MAF/IAT sensor.

3   Remove the screws and remove the sensor from the air filter housing.

4   Installation is the reverse of removal.

10   Knock Sensor (KS) - replacement

1   The knock sensors are mounted in the engine valley between the cylinder heads.

2   Remove the intake manifold (see Chapter 2A or 2B).

3   Note the direction the sensor faces and the routing of the wiring, then disconnect the knock sensor electrical connector (see illustration).

4   Remove the sensor mounting bolt, then remove the sensor.

5   Installation is the reverse of removal. Tighten the mounting bolt to the torque listed in this Chapter's Specifications.

11   Oxygen sensors - replacement

Note: *Because it is installed in the exhaust system, which contracts when cool, an oxygen sensor can be very difficult to loosen when the engine is cold. Rather than risking damage to the sensor or its mounting threads, run the engine for a minute or two, then shut it off. Be careful to avoid burns during this procedure.*

1   Be very careful when servicing an oxygen sensor:

a)   *The oxygen sensor has a permanently attached pigtail and electrical connector which should not be removed from the sensor. Damage or removal of the pigtail or electrical connector can adversely affect operation of the sensor.*

b)   *Grease, dirt and other contaminants should be kept away from the electrical connector and the louvered end of the sensor.*

c)   *Do not use cleaning solvents of any kind on the oxygen sensor.*

d)   *Do not drop or roughly handle the sensor.*

e)   *The silicone boot must be installed in the correct position to prevent the boot from being melted and to allow the sensor to operate properly.*

Replacement

Upstream oxygen sensors

2   Locate the upstream oxygen sensor electrical connector and disconnect it (see illustrations). Detach the sensor wiring harness from any clips.

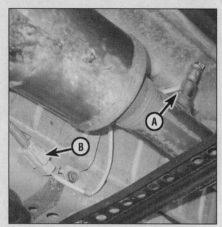

11.7 Typical downstream oxygen sensor (A), installed in the exhaust pipe after the catalytic converter, and electrical connector (B)

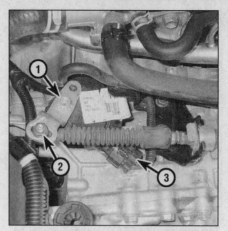

12.3 Transmission Range (TR) sensor details

1   Manual lever nut
2   Shift cable nut
3   Electrical connector

13.2a Location of the primary transmission speed sensor

13.2b Location of the secondary transmission speed sensor

3   Unscrew the sensor with an oxygen sensor socket if one is available. You may have to raise the vehicle and support it securely on jackstands to reach it.
4   If you're going to install the old sensor, apply anti-seize compound to the threads to ease future removal. If you're installing a new sensor, the threads will already have anti-seize on them.
5   Installation is the reverse of removal. Tighten the sensor to the torque listed in this Chapter's Specifications.

Downstream oxygen sensors

6   Raise the vehicle and support it securely on jackstands. The downstream oxygen sensors are accessible only from underneath.
7   Disconnect the wiring harness from the pigtail of the sensor **(see illustration)**.
8   Unscrew the sensor, using an oxygen sensor socket if one is available.
9   If you're going to install the old sensor, apply anti-seize compound to the threads to ease future removal. If you're installing a new

sensor, the threads will already have anti-seize on them.
10   Installation is the reverse of removal. Tighten the sensor to the torque listed in this Chapter's Specifications.

12   Transmission range (TR) switch - replacement and adjustment

2012 and earlier models

Note: *The Transmission Range sensor includes all of the functions of a Park/Neutral Position (PNP) switch, but the PNP switch term is still widely used amongst various manufacturers.*
1   The Transmission Range (TR) sensor prevents the engine from starting in any gear position other than PARK or NEUTRAL. The TR sensor also monitors the selector lever position and sends a signal to the Transmission Control Module (TCM). The TCM uses this information to determine the correct pressure for the electronic pressure control system of the transmission. The TR sensor is housed inside the transmission at the valve body. If diagnostic trouble codes indicate a problem with this component (or related components), it is suggested that these repairs are performed at a dealership service department or a qualified transmission repair shop.
2   If the engine will start when the shift lever is in any position other than Park or Neutral, consider shift cable adjustment (see Chapter 7A) before involving professional repair services.

2013 and later models

Replacement
3   The transmission range sensor is mounted on top of the automatic transaxle **(see illustration)**.
4   Remove the air filter housing and the air ducts (see Chapter 4). Remove the nut, then

remove the manual lever from the range sensor assembly.
5   Disconnect the electrical connector from the sensor.
6   Remove the mounting bolts and remove the range sensor.
7   Installation is the reverse of removal. Align the range sensor to its original position.
8   Verify that the engine will start only in Park or Neutral. Verify that the back-up lights come on only in Reverse. Adjust the range sensor as necessary to ensure that these conditions are met.

Adjustment
9   Set the parking brake.
10   Loosen the nut on the end of the shift cable.
11   Make sure the shift lever inside the vehicle and the manual lever on the transaxle are in Park.
12   Tighten the nut while making sure the manual lever stays in Park.
13   Check for proper operation (see Step 8).

13   Transmission speed sensors - replacement

2012 and earlier models
1   The transmission speed sensors are integral components of the valve body/Transmission Control Module (TCM) assembly, which is located inside the transmission. Replacing one of these sensors is beyond the scope of the home mechanic.

2013 and later models
2   The transmission speed sensors are mounted on top of the transaxle **(see illustrations)**. The primary speed sensor senses the speed of the primary pulley and the secondary speed sensor senses the speed of the output shaft.

Primary speed sensor

3   Disconnect the cable from the negative terminal of the battery (see Chapter 5).
4   Remove the left front wheel.
5   Raise the vehicle and support it on jackstands.
6   Disconnect the electrical connector from the sensor.
7   Remove the mounting bolt and remove the sensor. Discard the O-ring.
8   Apply some transmission fluid to the new O-ring and install it on the sensor.
9   Installation is otherwise the reverse of removal.

Secondary speed sensor

10   Remove the battery tray (see Chapter 5).
11   Remove the starter motor (see Chapter 5).
12   Disconnect the electrical connector from the sensor.
13   Remove the mounting bolt and remove the sensor. Discard the O-ring.
14   Apply some transmission fluid to the new O-ring and install it on the sensor.
15   Installation is otherwise the reverse of removal.

---

14   Powertrain Control Module (PCM) - replacement

---

1   The Powertrain Control Module (PCM) cannot be replaced at home because the new unit must be programmed with the Vehicle Identification Number (VIN) and other data. Doing so is impossible without a factory scan tool.

---

15   Catalytic converter - replacement

Warning: *The engine must be completely cool before beginning this procedure.*
Note: *Apply penetrating oil to all exhaust system fasteners before attempting to remove them.*

2012 and earlier models

V6 engine

1   Loosen the front wheel lug nuts, then raise the front of the vehicle and support it

securely on jackstands. Remove the wheels.
2   Remove the inner fender splash shield(s) (see Chapter 11).
3   Remove the exhaust manifold heat shield(s) (see Chapter 2A).
4   Remove the front portion of the exhaust system.
5   Disconnect the oxygen sensor electrical connector.
6   Remove the catalytic converter-to-exhaust manifold fasteners and detach the converter from the manifold.
7   Installation is the reverse of removal. Use new gaskets.

V8 engine

8   The catalytic converters on these models are integral with the exhaust manifolds. See Chapter 2B for the exhaust manifold removal and installation procedure.

2013 and later models

Front cylinder bank

9   Remove the air intake duct and the air filter housing (see Chapter 4).
10   Remove the battery and battery tray (see Chapter 5).
11   Loosen the front wheel lug nuts. Raise the front of the vehicle and support it securely on jackstands, then remove the wheels.
12   Remove the under-vehicle splash shield and the inner fender splash shields (see Chapter 11).
13   Remove the radiator (see Chapter 3).
14   Remove the front portion of the exhaust system (see Chapter 2A, illustration 10.19).
15   Support the engine with a hoist or an engine support fixture, then remove the front engine mount and bracket.
16   Remove the catalytic converter support bracket.
17   Remove the oxygen sensors from the exhaust manifold and catalytic converter.
18   Remove the exhaust manifold heat shield.
19   Remove the catalytic converter-to-exhaust manifold fasteners, then detach the converter from the manifold.
20   Installation is the reverse of removal. Use new gaskets.

21   Refill the cooling system (see Chapter 1).

Rear cylinder bank

22   Remove the cowl cover and lower cowl (see Chapter 11).
23   On AWD models, loosen the right front wheel lug nuts.
24   Raise the front of the vehicle and support it securely on jackstands. On AWD models, remove the right-front wheel.
25   Remove the under-vehicle splash shield. If you're working on an AWD model, remove the right inner fender splash shield (see Chapter 11).
26   Remove the front portion of the exhaust system (see Chapter 11, illustration 10.19).
27   On AWD models, remove the driveshaft and the right front driveaxle (see Chapter 8).
28   Remove the catalytic converter support bracket.
29   Remove the oxygen sensors from the exhaust manifold and catalytic converter.
30   Remove the exhaust manifold heat shield.
31   Remove the catalytic converter-to-exhaust manifold fasteners, then detach the converter from the manifold.
32   Remove the catalytic converter-to-exhaust manifold fasteners, then detach the converter from the manifold.
33   Installation is the reverse of removal. Use new gaskets.

---

16   Evaporative Emissions Control (EVAP) system - component replacement

---

EVAP purge control solenoid valve

1   Locate the purge control solenoid valve **(see illustrations)**, then detach the two hoses from the valve.
2   Disconnect the electrical connector from the solenoid valve.
3   Remove the mounting bolts, then remove the valve.
4   Installation is the reverse of removal.

16.1a On 2012 and earlier V6 models, the purge control solenoid valve is located on the left side of the timing chain cover

16.1b On 2013 and later models, the purge control solenoid valve is located at the left front corner of the intake manifold

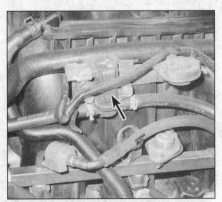

16.1c On V8 models, the purge control solenoid valve is located on the left side of the intake manifold

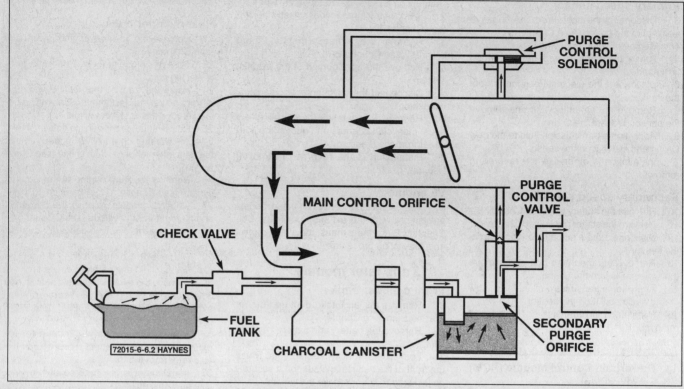

16.1d Typical schematic of the EVAP system

EVAP canister

Note: *The EVAP canister is located under the left rear of the vehicle, to the left of the spare tire.*

5   Unscrew the mounting bolt and lower the canister **(see illustrations)**.

Note: *On 2012 and earlier models, the EVAP canister is located under the vehicle in the right rear. On 2013 and later models the EVAP canister is located under the vehicle just in front of the spare tire.*

6   Disconnect the hoses and electrical connectors.

7   Remove the EVAP control system pressure sensor from the canister by pulling it out. Replace the O-ring before replacing the sensor.

8   Remove the EVAP canister vent control valve by twisting it counterclockwise. Replace the O-ring before replacing the valve.

9   Installation is the reverse of removal.

---

17   Positive Crankcase Ventilation (PCV) valve - replacement

1   Refer to Chapter 1 for information on the PCV system.

---

18   Variable Induction Air System (VIAS) solenoid valves and actuators (V6 engines) - replacement

1   This system consists of solenoid valve(s) (one on 2012 and earlier models, and two on 2013 and later models) which control vacuum to the power valve actuators **(see illustrations)**. The actuators move internal components of the intake manifold to change the lengths of the inlet passages for improved performance. The control solenoids are con-

16.5a EVAP canister mounting bolt - 2012 and earlier models

16.5b EVAP canister mounting bolt - 2013 and later models

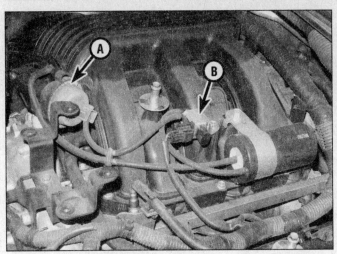

18.1a Power valve actuator (A) and solenoid (B) - 2012 and earlier models

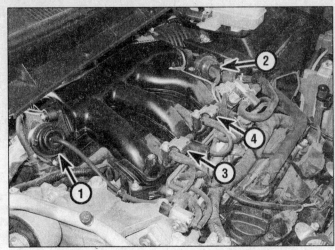

18.1b Power valve solenoid and actuator details - 2013 and later models

trolled electrically by the PCM.

2   Remove the engine cover.

Vacuum solenoid valve(s)

3   Disconnect the electrical connector from the solenoid valve.

4   Disconnect the vacuum hoses from the valve.

5   Remove the mounting bolts and remove the control solenoid valve.

6   Installation is the reverse of removal.

Actuator(s)

7   Disconnect the vacuum hose from the actuator.

8   Remove the mounting bolts and remove the actuator. Discard the gasket.

9   Installation is the reverse of removal. Replace the gasket with a new one.

19   Throttle Position (TP) sensor - replacement

1   The Throttle Position sensor on these vehicles is an integral part of the throttle body and is not serviceable separately. Refer to Chapter 4 for the throttle body replacement procedure.

Notes

Chapter 7 Part A
Automatic transmission/transaxle

Contents

	Section		Section
Automatic transmission (2012 and earlier models) - removal and installation	8	Diagnosis - general	2
Automatic transaxle (2013 and later models) - removal and installation	9	Shift cable and key interlock cable - adjustment and replacement	4
Driveaxle oil seal - replacement (2013 and later models)	6	Shifter assembly - removal and installation	3
Extension housing oil seal (2012 and earlier 2WD models) - replacement	5	Transmission Control Module (TCM) - removal and installation	10
General information	1	Transmission mount - check and replacement (2012 and earlier models)	7

Specifications

Torque specifications

	Ft-lbs	Nm

Note: *One foot-pound (ft-lb) of torque is equivalent to 12 inch-pounds (in-lbs) of torque. Torque values below approximately 15 ft-lbs are expressed in inch-pounds, since most foot-pound torque wrenches are not accurate at these smaller values.*

	Ft-lbs	Nm
Torque converter-to-driveplate bolts	38	51
Transmission mount (2012 and earlier models)		
Mount-to-transmission bolts		
V6 2WD models	36	49
V6 4WD models	65	88
V8 models	65	88
Mount-to-crossmember nuts	65	88
Transmission mounting bolts		
V6 engines	55	75
V8 engines	83	113
Transaxle-to-engine mounting bolts (2013 and later models)*		
Lower bolts (Bolts 5)	37	50
Upper bolts (Bolts 1 to 4)	55	75
Transmission pan bolts	70 in-lbs	8

*See Illustration 9.13

1 General information

1   2012 and earlier models are a body-on-frame Rear Wheel Drive (RWD) platform with a longitudinally mounted powertrain, and are equipped with an electronic-shift five-speed automatic transmission (RE5R05A). 2013 and later models are of unibody construction and a Front Wheel Drive (FWD) platform, and are equipped with a CVT (continuously variable transmission) automatic transaxle. All model years are available with All-wheel drive (AWD).

2   Because of the complexity of the automatic transmission/transaxle and the specialized equipment needed to service it, this Chapter contains only those procedures related to general diagnosis, routine maintenance, adjustment, and removal and installation.

3   If the transmission/transaxle requires major repair work, it should be taken to a dealer service department or an automotive or transmission repair shop. You can, however, save money by removing and installing the transmission/transaxle yourself, even if the repair work is done by a shop.

2 Diagnosis - general

Note: *Automatic transmission/transaxle malfunctions may be caused by five general conditions: poor engine performance, improper adjustments, hydraulic malfunctions, mechanical malfunctions or malfunctions in the computer or its signal network. Diagnosis of these problems should always begin with a check of the easily repaired items: fluid level and condition (see Chapter 1) and shift cable adjustment. Next, perform a road test to determine if the problem has been corrected or if more diagnosis is necessary. If the problem persists after the preliminary tests and corrections are completed, additional diagnosis should be done by a dealer service department or transmission repair shop. Refer to "Troubleshooting" at the front of this manual, Section 11 for information on symptoms of transaxle problems.*

Preliminary checks

1   Drive the vehicle to warm the transmission/transaxle to normal operating temperature.

2   Check the fluid level (see Chapter 1):

- *If the fluid level is unusually low, add enough fluid to bring the level within the designated area of the dipstick, then check for external leaks (see below).*
- *If the fluid level is abnormally high, drain off the excess, then check the drained fluid for contamination by coolant. The presence of engine coolant in the automatic transmission fluid indicates that a failure has occurred in the internal radiator walls that separate the coolant from the transmission fluid (see Chapter 3).*
- *If the fluid is foaming, drain it and refill the transmission/transaxle, then check for coolant in the fluid, or a high fluid level.*

3   Check for the presence of any stored diagnostic trouble codes (see Chapter 6). There are many potential transmission/transaxle-specific trouble codes that could be set, but certain engine-related problems can also affect transmission/transaxle operation.

4   Inspect the shift cable (see Section 4). Make sure that it's properly adjusted and operates smoothly.

Fluid leak diagnosis

5   Most fluid leaks are easy to locate visually. Repair usually consists of replacing a seal or gasket. If a leak is difficult to find, the following procedure may help.

6   Identify the fluid. Make sure it's transmission fluid and not engine oil or brake fluid (automatic transmission fluid [2012 and earlier models] is a deep red color, CVT transaxle fluid [2013 and later models] is a light green to amber color).

7   Try to pinpoint the source of the leak. Drive the vehicle several miles, then park it over a large sheet of cardboard. After a minute or two, you should be able to locate the leak by determining the source of the fluid dripping onto the cardboard.

8   Make a careful visual inspection of the suspected component and the area immediately around it. Pay particular attention to gasket mating surfaces. A mirror is often helpful for finding leaks in areas that are hard to see.

9   If the leak still cannot be found, clean the suspected area thoroughly with a degreaser or solvent, then dry it.

10   Drive the vehicle for several miles at normal operating temperature and varying speeds. After driving the vehicle, visually inspect the suspected component again.

11   Once the leak has been located, the cause must be determined before it can be properly repaired. If a gasket is replaced but the sealing flange is bent, the new gasket will not stop the leak. The bent flange must be straightened.

12   Before attempting to repair a leak, check to make sure that the following conditions are corrected or they may cause another leak.

Note: *Some of the following conditions cannot be fixed without highly specialized tools and expertise. Such problems must be referred to a transmission shop or a dealer service department.*

Gasket leaks

13   Check the pan periodically. Make sure the bolts are tightened to the torque listed in this Chapter's Specifications , no bolts are missing, the gasket is in good condition and the pan is flat (dents in the pan may indicate damage to the valve body inside).

14   If the pan gasket is leaking, the fluid level or the fluid pressure may be too high, the vent may be plugged, the pan bolts may be too tight, the pan sealing flange may be warped, the sealing surface of the transmission/transaxle housing may be damaged, the gasket may be damaged or the transmission/transaxle casting may be cracked or porous.

If sealant instead of gasket material has been used to form a seal between the pan and the transmission/transaxle housing, it may be the wrong sealant.

Seal leaks

15   If a transmission/transaxle seal is leaking, the fluid level or pressure may be too high, the vent may be plugged, the seal bore may be damaged, the seal itself may be damaged or improperly installed, the surface of the shaft protruding through the seal may be damaged or a loose bearing may be causing excessive shaft movement.

16   Make sure the dipstick tube seal is in good condition and the tube is properly seated. Periodically check the area around the speedometer gear or sensor for leakage. If transmission fluid is evident, check the O-ring for damage.

Case leaks

17   If the case itself appears to be leaking, the casting is porous and will have to be repaired or replaced.

18   Make sure the oil cooler hose fittings are tight and in good condition.

Fluid comes out vent pipe or fill tube

19   If this condition occurs, the transmission/transaxle is overfilled, there is coolant in the fluid, the case is porous, the dipstick is incorrect, the vent is plugged or the drain-back holes are plugged.

3 Shifter assembly - removal and installation

Warning: *The models covered by this manual are equipped with Supplemental Restraint Systems (SRS), more commonly known as airbags. Always disable the airbag system before working in the vicinity of any airbag system components to avoid the possibility of accidental deployment of the airbags, which could cause personal injury (see Chapter 12).*

1   Use a small screwdriver to pry off the shift lock override button cover **(see illustration)**.

2   Insert the small screwdriver into the opening and depress the shift lock override button **(see illustration)**. While holding the release button down, move the shift selector out of Park and into Neutral.

3   Slide the shift handle trim downwards to expose the horseshoe shaped retaining clip at the base of the shift handle. Use a small screwdriver to pry the clip outwards, then lift the handle up and off **(see illustrations)**.

4   Remove the center console (see Chapter 11).

2012 and earlier models

5   Disconnect the shifter control cable (see Section 4). Lift the key interlock cable from the housing **(see illustration)**, squeeze the slider tabs on the cable to release the interlock rod,

3.1 Using a small screwdriver pry off the button cover

3.2 Depress the shift override button and move the shifter out of park

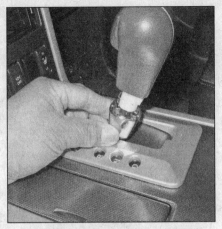

3.3a Slide the trim ring downwards from the base of the shifter. . .

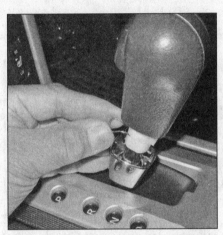

3.3b. . . then pull the horseshoe shaped retaining clip out and lift the knob off of the shifter

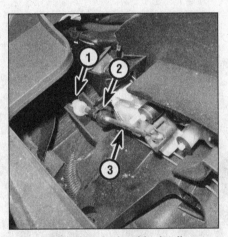

3.5 Key interlock cable details

1 Cable-to-housing connection
2 Slider
3 Interlock rod

3.7 Shifter assembly mounting bolt locations

and separate the cable from the rod.
6   Disconnect the electrical connectors and harness retainers from the shifter housing.
7   Remove the shifter assembly mounting bolts (see illustration) and lift the shifter out of the vehicle.
8   Installation is the reverse of removal. Adjust the shifter cable and key interlock cable (see Section 4).

2013 and later models

9   Remove the console ashtray mounting screws, then remove the center console side panels from the front of the console and the shift cable from the console (see Chapter 11).
10   Disconnect the wiring harness from the shifter using a flat-blade screwdriver, then release the cable from the bracket (see illustration). Also detach the cable from the pin on the shifter.

3.10 Pull out this clip to detach the cable from the shifter bracket

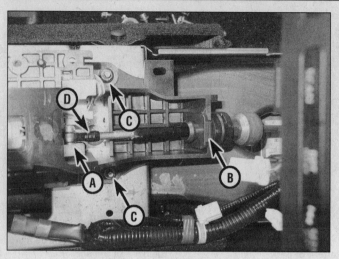

3.11a Shift cable details at the shifter

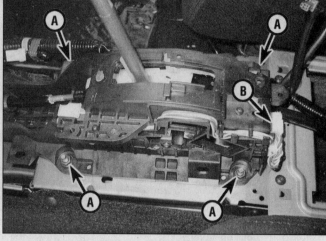

3.11b Shifter mounting nuts (A) and shift lock wiring harness connector (B)

A   Cable end retainer
B   Cable-to-bracket clip
C   Front mounting bolts
D   Serration on cable end (must face up)

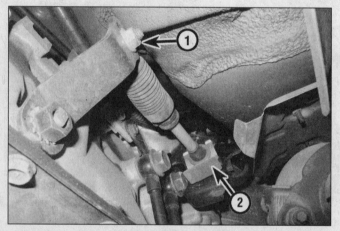

4.4a Shift cable-to-manual lever locknut (1) and cable retaining clip (2) - 2012 and earlier models

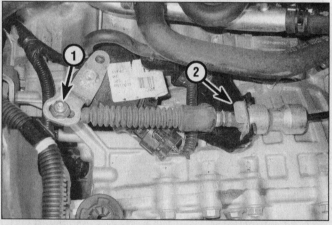

4.4b Shift cable-to-manual lever locknut (1) and cable retaining clip (2) - 2013 and later models

11   Remove the shifter assembly mounting nuts, then remove the shifter **(see illustrations)**.
12   Slide a flat-blade screwdriver under the shift lock wiring connector to detach it from the shifter. Remove the shift lock unit from the bottom of the shifter.
13   Installation is the reverse of removal. Adjust the shift cable (see Section 4).

4   Shift cable and key interlock cable - adjustment and replacement

Adjustment
Shift cable

1   On 2012 and earlier models, raise the vehicle and support it securely on jackstands.

2   On 2013 and later models, remove the air filter housing (see Chapter 4).
3   Place the shift lever in Park.
4   Loosen the shift cable-to-manual lever locknut **(see illustration)** and place the transmission/transaxle manual shift lever fully in the Park position.
5   Holding the manual lever in position, tighten the locknut.
6   Move the shift lever from "P" to "1." Make sure that it moves smoothly.

Key interlock cable (2012 and earlier models only)

7   If removed, insert the interlock rod into the adjuster holder.
8   Place the shift lever in Park, and the ignition key in the LOCK position.
9   To adjust the cable, squeeze the adjuster slider lock tabs together, and slide the inter-lock rod into the holder until the cable housing

can be inserted into place on the end of the shifter housing **(see illustration 3.5)**.

Replacement
Warning: *The models covered by this manual are equipped with Supplemental Restraint Systems (SRS), more commonly known as airbags. Always disable the airbag system before working in the vicinity of any airbag system components to avoid the possibility of accidental deployment of the airbags, which could cause personal injury (see Chapter 12).*

Shift cable
2012 and earlier models

10   Detach the cable from the shifter (see Section 3).
11   Detach the cable from the manual lever on the transmission and from the cable bracket **(see illustration 4.4a)**.

5.4 Carefully pry the old seal out of the extension housing - don't damage the splines on the output shaft or scratch the housing

5.5 Drive the new seal into place with a hammer and a seal driver or a large socket

6.5 Use care to avoid scratching the housing when prying out the driveaxle oil seals

12   Detach the grommet from the floorpan and remove the cable.

13   Installation is the reverse of removal. Adjust the cable (see Steps 1 through 6).

2013 and later models

14   Place the shifter in Park.

15   Remove the air intake duct and the air filter housing (see Chapter 4).

16   Remove the battery and the battery tray (see Chapter 5).

17   Remove the cable-to-manual lever locknut (see illustration 4.4b).

18   Remove the cable retaining clip and detach the cable from the transaxle bracket.

19   Remove the center console side panels (see Chapter 11).

20   Detach the cable from the shifter assembly (see Section 3).

21   Remove the gable grommet-to-floorpan bolts, then remove the cable from the vehicle.

22   Installation is the reverse of removal. Make sure that the ribbed surface of the cable end is up. Adjust the cable (see Steps 1 through 6).

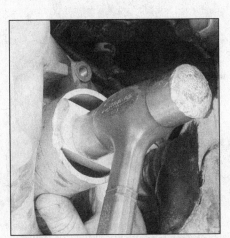

6.6 Drive in the new driveaxle oil seal until it's flush

Key interlock cable
(2012 and earlier models only)

23   Remove the center console (see Chapter 11).

24   Remove the knee bolster and steering column covers (see Chapter 11).

25   Unlock the slider by squeezing the locking tabs, then lift the end of the cable from the end of the shifter housing (see illustration 3.5) and separate the interlock rod from the cable.

26   Remove the holder from key lock cylinder and detach the cable.

27   Installation is the reverse of removal. Make sure that the cable is routed without kinks and it is snapped securely onto the shifter housing. Adjust the cable (see Steps 7 through 9).

5   Extension housing oil seal (2012 and earlier 2WD models) - replacement

1   Oil leaks frequently occur due to wear of the extension housing oil seal. Replacement of this seal is relatively easy, since it can be performed without removing the transmission from the vehicle.

2   The extension housing oil seal is located at the extreme rear of the transmission, where the driveshaft is attached. If leakage at the seal is suspected, raise the vehicle and support it securely on jackstands. If the seal is leaking, transmission lubricant will be built up on the front of the driveshaft and may be dripping from the rear of the transmission.

3   Remove the driveshaft (see Chapter 8).

4   Using a seal removal tool or a large screwdriver, carefully pry the oil seal out of the rear of the transmission **(see illustration)**. Do not damage the splines on the transmission output shaft.

5   Using a seal driver or a very large deep socket as a drift, install the new oil seal **(see illustration)**. Drive it into the bore squarely and make sure it's completely seated.

6   Lubricate the splines of the transmission output shaft and the outside of the driveshaft yoke with lightweight grease, then install the driveshaft (see Chapter 8). Be careful not to damage the lip of the new seal.

7   Check the transmission fluid level (see Chapter 1).

6   Driveaxle oil seal - replacement (2013 and later models)

1   Oil leaks can occur as a result of worn seals or O-rings. Replacement of these seals or O-rings is relatively easy, since the repairs can usually be performed without removing the transaxle from the vehicle.

2   The driveaxle oil seals are located on the sides of the transaxle or transfer case, where the inner ends of the driveaxles are splined into the differential side gears. If you suspect that a driveaxle oil seal is leaking, raise the vehicle and support it securely on jackstands. If the seal is leaking, you'll see lubricant on the side of the transaxle or transfer case, below the seal.

3   AWD models have an additional seal between the transfer case and the transaxle. If there is lubricant leaking from this seal, the transfer case must be removed in order to replace it. See Chapter 8 for more information.

4   Remove the driveaxle (see Chapter 8).

5   Using a screwdriver or seal removal tool, carefully pry the seal out of the transaxle bore **(see illustration)**.

6   Using a seal driver or a large deep socket as a drift, install the new oil seal. Drive it into the bore squarely and make sure it's properly seated **(see illustration)**.

Note: *Lubricate the lip of the new seal with multi-purpose grease.*

7   Install the driveaxle. Be careful not to damage the lip(s) of the new seal(s). Check the transaxle lubricant level and add some, if necessary, to bring it up to the required level (see Chapter 1).

7   Transmission mount - check and replacement (2012 and earlier models)

Check

1   Raise the vehicle and support it securely on jackstands.

2   Insert a large screwdriver or prybar into the space between the transmission extension housing and the crossmember and try to pry the transmission up slightly **(see illustration)**.

3   The transmission should not move much at all - if the mount is cracked or torn, replace it.

Replacement

4   Support the transmission with a floor jack. Place a block of wood on the jack head to act as a cushion.

5   Remove the mount-to-crossmember and mount-to-transmission fasteners **(see illustration)**.

6   Raise the transmission slightly with the jack and remove the mount.

7   Installation is the reverse of removal. Tighten the mount fasteners to the torque listed in this Chapter's Specifications.

8   Automatic transmission (2012 and earlier models) - removal and installation

Removal

Caution: *Remove the transmission and torque converter together as a single assembly. If you try to leave the torque converter attached to the driveplate, the driveplate will be damaged along with the pump bushing and oil seal.*

1   Disconnect the cable from the negative battery terminal (see Chapter 5).

2   Remove the engine cover **(see illustration 4.8 in Chapter 3)**.

3   Raise the vehicle and support it securely on jackstands. Remove the skid plate and skid plate crossmember, if equipped.

4   Remove the front wheels and inner fender splash shields.

5   Remove the engine splash shield from under the vehicle, if equipped.

6   Drain the transmission fluid (see Chapter 1).

7   Detach the shift cable from the manual lever and from the bracket on the transmission.

8   Mark the yokes and remove the driveshaft (see Chapter 8). On 4WD models, remove both driveshafts.

9   Remove all exhaust components which would interfere with transmission removal (see Chapter 4).

10   Remove the Crankshaft Position (CKP) sensor (see Chapter 6).

11   Follow the wiring harnesses from the top side of the transmission up to their electrical connectors, then unplug the connectors. Mark and disconnect any other electrical connectors that would interfere with transmission removal.

12   Remove the starter motor (see Chapter 5).

13   Remove the inspection cover and mark the relationship of the torque converter to the driveplate so they can be installed in the same position.

14   Remove the torque converter-to-driveplate bolts **(see illustration)**. Turn the crankshaft for access to each bolt.

Caution: *Turn the crankshaft in a clockwise direction only (as viewed from the front).*

15   Remove the fill/dipstick tube brackets and bolts and pull the tube out of the transmission. Don't lose the tube seal (it can be reused if it's still in good shape).

16   Remove the banjo-bolt fittings and detach the fluid cooler lines from the trans

mission. Discard the sealing washers that are present on either side of the fittings; new ones must be used when reconnecting the fittings.

17   On 4WD models, remove the transfer case (see Chapter 7B). If you decide to leave the transfer case attached, disconnect the electrical connectors from the transfer case speed sensors and detach the transfer case vent tube (see Chapter 7B).

Note: *If you are not planning to replace the transmission, but are removing it in order to gain access to other components such as the torque converter, it isn't really necessary to remove the transfer case. However, the transmission and transfer case are awkward and heavy when removed and installed as a single assembly; they're much easier to maneuver off and on as separate units.*

Warning: *If you decide to leave the transfer case attached to the transmission, be sure to use safety chains to help stabilize the transmission and transfer case assembly and to prevent it from falling off the jack head, which could cause serious damage to the transmission and/or transfer case and serious bodily injury to you.*

18   Support the engine with an engine hoist or support fixture from above, or with a jack placed under the oil pan. If you use a floor jack, place a block of wood on the jack head to spread the load.

19   Support the transmission with a jack - preferably a jack made for this purpose (available at most tool rental yards). Safety chains will help steady the transmission on the jack.

20   Remove the transmission mount-to-crossmember fasteners. Raise the transmission slightly and remove the crossmember.

21   Lower the engine and transmission slightly and remove the transmission-to-engine bolts. A long extension and a U-joint socket will greatly simplify this step.

Note: *Different length bolts are used - note the location of each bolt so they can be returned to their original positions when the transmission is installed.*

7.2 Insert a large screwdriver or prybar between the crossmember and the transmission and try to pry the transmission up - look at each end of the mount, it should move very little

7.5 Remove the mount-to-transmission bolts (upper two), then the mount-to-crossmember bolts

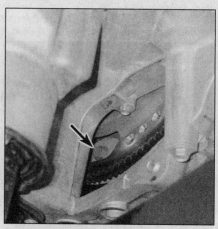

8.14 Remove one of the torque converter bolts and mark the relationship of the driveplate to the torque converter then remove the remaining bolts

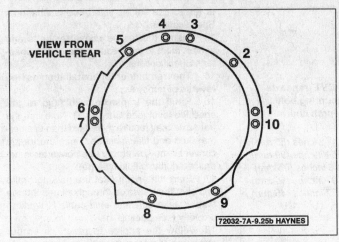

8.27a Transmission-to-engine mounting bolt tightening sequence - V6 engine models

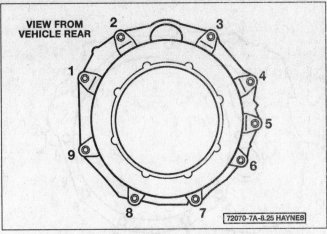

8.27b Transmission-to-engine mounting bolt tightening sequence - V8 engine models

22   Move the transmission to the rear to disengage it from the engine block dowel pins and make sure the torque converter is detached from the driveplate. Lower the transmission with the jack. Clamp a pair of locking pliers on the bellhousing case. The pliers will prevent the torque converter from falling out while you're removing the transmission.

Installation

23   Prior to installation, make sure the torque converter is securely engaged in the pump. If you've removed the converter, apply a small amount of transmission fluid on the torque converter rear hub, where the transmission front seal rides. Install the torque converter onto the front input shaft of the transmission while rotating the converter back and forth. It should engage into the transmission front pump in stages. To make sure the converter is fully engaged, lay a straightedge across the transmission-to-engine mating surface and measure the distance from the straightedge and the converter lugs. The converter lugs must be at least 0.98 inch (25 mm) for V6 models and 0.94-inch (24 mm) for V8 models below the straightedge.
24   With the transmission secured to the jack, raise it into position.
25   Turn the torque converter to line up the holes with the holes in the driveplate. The marks on the torque converter and driveplate made in Step 12 must line up.
26   Move the transmission forward carefully until the dowel pins engage with the holes in the bellhousing. Make sure the transmission mates with the engine with no gap. If there's a gap, make sure there are no wires or other objects pinched between the engine and transmission and also make sure the torque converter is completely engaged in the transmission front pump. Try to rotate the converter - if it doesn't rotate easily, it's probably not fully engaged in the pump. If necessary, lower the transmission and install the converter fully.
27   Install and tighten the transmission-to-

engine bolts, in sequence **(see illustrations)**, to the torque listed in this Chapter's Specifications. As you're tightening the bolts, make sure that the engine and transmission mate completely at all points. If not, find out why. Never try to force the engine and transmission together with the bolts or you'll break the transmission case!
28   Raise the rear of the transmission and install the transmission crossmember.
29   Remove the jacks supporting the transmission and the engine.
30   Install the torque converter-to-driveplate bolts, then tighten them to the torque listed in this Chapter's Specifications.
31   Install the transmission dipstick tube and seal into the transmission housing, then install the bolt and tighten it securely.
32   Install the torque converter inspection cover.
33   Using new sealing washers, connect the transmission fluid cooler lines to the transmission, tightening the fitting bolts securely.
34   Plug in the transmission electrical connectors.
35   Connect the shift cable (see Section 4).
36   On 4WD models, install the transfer

case, if removed (see Chapter 7B).
37   Install the driveshaft(s) (see Chapter 8).
38   Adjust the shift cable (see Section 4).
39   Install the starter motor (see Chapter 5).
40   Install any exhaust system components that were removed or disconnected (see Chapter 4).
41   Remove the jackstands and lower the vehicle.
42   Fill the transmission with the specified fluid (see Chapter 1), run the engine and check for fluid leaks.

9   Automatic transaxle (2013 and later models) - removal and installation

Removal

1   Remove the engine and transaxle assembly from the vehicle (see Chapter 2C).
2   Paint match marks on the torque converter and driveplate so they can be assembled in the same position **(see illustration)**. Remove the torque converter bolts.

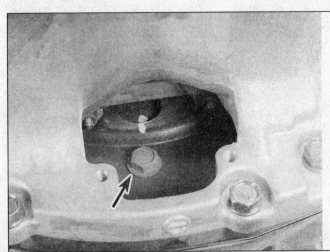

9.2 Mark the position of the torque converter to the driveplate, then remove the torque converter bolts by turning the crankshaft to bring each bolt into the opening

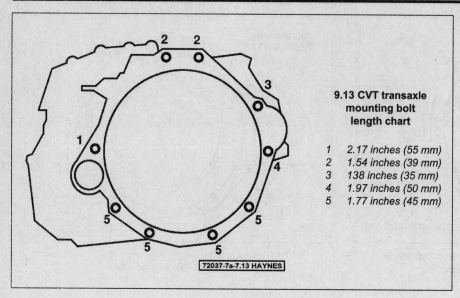

**9.13 CVT transaxle
mounting bolt
length chart**

1	2.17 inches	(55 mm)
2	1.54 inches	(39 mm)
3	138 inches	(35 mm)
4	1.97 inches	(50 mm)
5	1.77 inches	(45 mm)

72037-7a-7.13 HAYNES

3   Disconnect the wiring from the transaxle components and remove the wiring harness.

4   Remove the dipstick tube. Detach the transaxle mounts from the subframe.

5   Remove the engine-to-transaxle bolts. Keep them organized so they can be installed in the same positions.

6   Separate the transaxle from the engine and slide it away, then remove the transaxle cooler hose. Remove the torque converter and seal the open end to prevent contamination.

Installation

7   Flush the transaxle cooler and the cooler hoses and lines with solvent whenever the transaxle is removed from the vehicle. Flush the lines and fluid cooler thoroughly and make sure no solvent remains in the lines or cooler after flushing. It's a good idea to repeat the flushing procedure with clean automatic transmission fluid to ensure that no solvent remains in the lines or cooler.

8   Prior to installation, make sure that the torque converter hub is securely engaged in the pump. The front face of the torque converter must be at least 1/2-inch behind the front edge of the transaxle housing to be fully seated.

9   Maneuver the transaxle to the rear of the engine.

10   Turn the torque converter to line it up with the driveplate. The marks you made on the torque converter and the driveplate must line up.

11   Move the transaxle forward carefully until the dowel pins and the torque converter are engaged.

12   Install the transaxle mounting bolts. Make sure the bolts are installed in the proper locations.

Caution: *Don't use the bolts to force the transaxle and engine together. If the transaxle doesn't slide easily up against the engine, find out why before you tighten the bolts.*

13   Install the transaxle-to-engine bolts in their proper locations (they're different lengths) **(see illustration)**. Tighten the bolts to the torque values listed in this Chapter's Specifications.

14   Install the torque converter bolts and tighten them to the torque listed in this Chapter's Specifications.

15   The remainder of installation is the reverse of removal.

16   Refill the transaxle with fluid to the specified level (see Chapter 1). Note that the transaxle may require more fluid than in a normal fluid and filter change, since the torque converter may be empty (the converter is not drained during a fluid change).

17   Start the engine, set the parking brake and shift the transaxle through all gears three times. Make sure the shift cable is working properly (see Section 4).

18   Allow the engine to reach its proper operating temperature with the transaxle in Park or Neutral, then turn it off and check the fluid level.

19   Road test the vehicle and check for fluid leaks.

10   Transmission Control Module (TCM) - removal and installation

1   The Transmission Control Module (TCM) is a microprocessor that controls many aspects of automatic transmission or transaxle performance. On transmission models, it is located inside of the transmission at the valve body, along with the transmission fluid temperature sensor. The harness from these two electronic devices extends to a plug secured to the transmission case, sealed with an O-ring and an external lock-ring. On transaxle models, it is mounted externally in the engine compartment, in front of the battery.

2   Because of the specialized equipment and expertise required to diagnose and replace the TCM, the work should be performed at a dealership service department or a qualified transmission repair shop.

Chapter 7 Part B
Transfer case - 2012 and earlier models

Contents

	Section		Section
General information	1	Transfer case overhaul - general information	6
Oil seals - removal and installation	4	Transfer case - removal and installation	5
Shift actuator and position switch - replacement	3	Transfer Control Unit (TCU) - replacement	2

Specifications

Torque specifications

	Ft-lbs	Nm
Actuator assembly-to-transfer case bolts	16	22
Companion flange nut*	203	275
Oil drain or fill plugs	See Chapter 1	
Transfer case-to-transmission mounting bolts	27	37

*Use new fasteners on installation

1 General information

1 Four-Wheel Drive (4WD) models are equipped with an electronically-controlled transfer case ATX14B or TX15B that distributes power to both front and rear axles when the system is engaged. A switch on the instrument panel allows a choice of 2WD, 4WD High or 4WD Low.

2 Input from the switch goes to the Transfer Control Unit (TCU), which communicates with the transfer case actuator, the automatic transmission, and other devices. The actuator consists of an electric shift motor and a Transfer Case Position Switch. The motor actually does the mechanical shifting of the transfer case, when directed by the TCU. The Transfer Case Position Switch communicates the actual position of the electric shift motor to the TCU at all times.

3 We don't recommend trying to rebuild this transfer case. They're difficult to overhaul without special tools, and rebuilt units may be available that represent a savings of time and money.

Troubleshooting

Note: *This procedure applies to 2007 and earlier models only.*

4   Problems with the transfer case system will make the 4WD warning light illuminate on the instrument panel when the engine is started. Although the transfer case control system is electronic and a scan tool is the best diagnostic device, you can output a number of diagnostic codes through the 4WD warning light.

5   Begin with the engine at normal operating temperature. Turn the ignition key On and Off twice, ending with the key Off. Apply the vehicle parking brake.

6   Move the transmission shift lever to Park. With the 4WD switch turned to the 2WD position, turn the key On. The 4WD warning light should come on for a second or two, then go off, indicating the 4WD system is OK.

7   Move the transmission shifter to Reverse.

8   In sequence, turn the 4WD selector switch from 2WD to 4High and back to 2WD.

9   Move the transmission shift lever to Park and turn the shift switch from 4High to 2WD and back to 4High.

10   Move the transmission shifter to Neutral and turn the 4WD selector switch to 2WD.

11   Move the transmission shift lever to Park. You can now read the trouble codes as a series of blinks on the 4WD warning light. Two blinks would be code 2, 10 blinks would be code 10. Refer to the following chart for a list of codes.

Note: *When the light first comes on, it will be on for 2.5 seconds, then off for 1 second, then the code blinks will begin.*

TX15B transfer case

Blinks	Problem with Transfer Case control system
2	Output shaft revolution sensor signal
3	Vehicle Speed Sensor (ABS system)
4	CAN network communication error
5	Transfer Control Unit
6	4Low switch, open or short
7	Improper engine speed signal from PCM
8	Power supply voltage low
9	4WD shift switch, short circuit
10	Improper signal from wait detection switch
11	Malfunction in actuator motor
12	Actuator position switch
13	Transfer shutoff relays
14	PNP switch signal
Constant, four times per second	Memory backup power supply drained
None	PNP of 4WD switches, shorted or open

ATX14B transfer case

Blinks	Problem with transfer case control system
2	Output shaft revolution sensor signal
3	Clutch pressure solenoid signal
4	2-4WD solenoid signal
5	Transfer motor
6	Vehicle speed sensor (ABS input)

ATX14B transfer case (continued)

Blinks	Problem with transfer case control system
7	CAN communication
8	AD converter (TCU power supply problem)
9	Transfer fluid temperature
10	Neutral 4LO switch circuit
11	Clutch pressure switch circuit
12	Line pressure switch circuit
13	Engine speed signal circuit
14	Accelerator Pedal Position (APP) sensor circuit
15	Power supply for TCU low while driving
16	4WD shift switch circuit
17	ABS signal problem
18	Wait detection switch
19	Actuator motor or circuit problem
20	Actuator position switch circuit
21	Actuator circuit
22	VDC operation signal
23	TCS operation signal

2 Transfer Control Unit (TCU) - replacement

Caution: *When removing the Transfer Control Unit, the transfer case must be set to 2WD or AUTO.*

1 With the transfer case in 2WD or AUTO, turn off the engine and disconnect the cable from the negative battery terminal (see Chapter 5).
2 Remove the driver's side kick panel (see Chapter 11).
3 Disconnect the two electrical connectors at the Transfer Control Unit (TCU).
4 Unscrew the mounting bolts and remove the TCU.
5 Installation is the reverse of removal, noting the following: Check for correct positions of the transfer case system by moving the 4WD selector switch through its range. If the position on the switch does not correspond to the position of the shift actuator on the transfer case, perform the following Steps.
6 With the vehicle warmed to operating temperature, move the 4WD selector switch from 2WD to 4High to 4Low to 4High and back to 2WD. Keep the selector in each of these positions for at least two seconds.
7 Observe the 4WD shift indicator light on the instrument panel and the 4Low indicator light. The 4Low light should come on only when in 4Low, and it will flash for a few seconds while waiting for the shift actuator to complete a move to 4Low. Move the vehicle enough to ascertain that the transfer case is in 4Low when the selector switch is in that position and the dash light is on. If the 4WD indicator light or 4Low light are blinking for more than a few seconds, return to 2WD and have the relationship between the 4WD switch and the shift actuator corrected at a dealership with a scan tool.

3 Shift actuator and position switch - replacement

1 Position the 4WD selector switch to 2WD and turn off the vehicle.
2 Raise the vehicle and support it securely on jackstands.
3 Remove the front drive shaft (see Chapter 8).

ATX14B transfer case

Shift actuator

Note: *The shift actuator is mounted to the side of the transmission and has a rod that is connected to the shift lever on the transfer case.*

4 From below, disconnect the electrical connector at the shift actuator assembly. The shift position switch is an integral part of the shift actuator assembly.
5 Remove the shift actuator rod mounting bolt and nut, then separate the rod from the transfer case shift lever.
6 Disconnect the vacuum hose from the actuator, then remove the mounting bolts and pull the actuator assembly from the transmission.
7 Before reinstalling the actuator assembly, turn the flat-sided end of the shift-rod on the transfer case counterclockwise as far as it can go and make a mark on the end of the rod.

4.4 A chain wrench can be used to prevent the flange from turning while the nut is removed

4.5 A two-jaw puller will be required to remove the flange if it won't come off by hand

4.6 Use a seal removal tool or a large screwdriver to pry the seal out

4.7 Drive the new seal into place with a seal driver or a socket with an outside diameter slightly smaller than that of the seal

8   Turn the notch in the shift actuator rod to align with the mark on the rod and, with a new O-ring in place on the actuator (lubricated with petroleum jelly), install the shift actuator assembly.

9   The remainder of installation is the reverse of removal. Tighten the actuator assembly bolts to the torque listed in this Chapter's Specifications.

Transfer motor

Note: *The transfer motor is located on the rear of the transfer case and connects directly to the sub-oil pump.*

10   Disconnect the electrical connector from the motor, then remove the breather hose.

11   Remove the two mounting bolts and remove the motor.

12   Install a new O-ring in the groove on the motor (lubricated with clean automatic transmission fluid), install the motor assembly with the double-flat end of the transfer motor shaft into the slot of the sub-oil pump. Tighten the

mounting bolts securely.

13   The remainder of installation is the reverse of removal. Tighten the actuator assembly bolts to the torque listed in this Chapter's Specifications.

14   Check the transfer case fluid level (see Chapter 1). Start the engine and let it idle for one minute. Shut the engine off and recheck the fluid level.

TX15B transfer case

Note: *The shift actuator/transfer motor is mounted to the rear of the transfer case.*

15   From below, disconnect the electrical connector at the shift actuator assembly. The shift position switch is an integral part of the shift actuator assembly.

16   Disconnect the breather hose from the actuator, then remove the mounting bolts and pull the actuator assembly from the transfer case.

17   Before reinstalling the actuator assembly, turn the flat-sided end of the shift-rod on the transfer case counterclockwise as far as it can go, and make a mark on the end of the rod.

18   Turn the notch in the shift actuator rod to align with the mark on the rod and, with a new O-ring in place on the actuator (lubricated with petroleum jelly), install the shift actuator assembly.

19   The remainder of installation is the reverse of removal.

---

4   Oil seals - removal and installation

Note: *This procedure applies to both the front and rear output shaft seals.*

Note: *It may be helpful to drain some of the fluid from the transfer case. Otherwise be prepared for some spillage.*

1   Raise the vehicle and support it securely on jackstands.

2   If you're replacing the front seal, remove

the front driveshaft (see Chapter 8).

3   If you're replacing the rear seal, remove the rear driveshaft (see Chapter 8).

4   Front seal: A flange holding tool will be required to keep the companion flange from moving while the nut is loosened. A chain wrench will also work **(see illustration)**. Remove the flange nut, then make index marks matching the relationship of the shaft (that the nut was removed from) to the flange.

5   Front seal: Withdraw the flange. It may be necessary to use a two-jaw puller engaged behind the flange to draw it off **(see illustration)**. Do not attempt to pry or hammer behind the flange or hammer on the end of the shaft.

6   Pry out the old seal and discard it **(see illustration)**. On rear seals, pry the dust cover off of the case that's near the shaft to expose the seal.

7   Lubricate the lips of the new seal and the seal case with petroleum jelly, then tap it evenly into position with a seal installation tool or a large socket **(see illustration)**. Make sure it enters the housing squarely and is tapped in to its full depth.

8   Install a new dust cover with the index mark at the 12 o'clock position. Lubricate the inner circumference of the dust cover with petroleum jelly.

9   Install the companion flange by using the matchmarks made in Step 3. If necessary, tighten the nut to draw the flange into place. Do not try to hammer the flange into position. **Note:** *When installing the companion flange, use a new self-locking nut.*

10   Front seal: Apply a bead of RTV sealant to the ends of the splines visible in the center of the flange so oil will be sealed in.

11   Front seal: Install the nut and tighten it to the torque listed in this Chapter's Specifications.

12   Install the driveshaft (see Chapter 8). Check and, if necessary, add the recommended type of lubricant to bring the level up to the bottom of the filler hole (see Chapter 1).

5 Transfer case - removal and installation

Removal

Note: *Set the transfer assembly to 2WD before performing the following procedure.*

1   Position the 4WD selector switch to 2WD and turn off the vehicle. Disconnect the cable from the negative battery terminal (see Chapter 5).

2   Raise the vehicle and support it securely on jackstands. Remove the skid plate, if equipped.

3   Remove the main muffler and related exhaust pipes (see Chapter 4).

4   Disconnect the two vent tubes - one from the shift actuator and one from the transfer case.

5   Drain the transfer case lubricant (see Chapter 1).

6   Remove the front and rear driveshafts (see Chapter 8).

7   Insert a rubber plug into the rear seal after the rear driveshaft has been removed.

8   Unplug all electrical connectors and detach the vent hose from the top of the transfer case.

9   Support the transmission with a floor jack. Place a block of wood on the jack head to spread the load.

10   Support the transfer case with a jack - preferably a special jack made for this purpose. Safety chains will help steady the transfer case on the jack.

11   Remove the crossmember used to support the transmission.

12   Lower the jacks supporting the transmission and transfer case just enough for access to the upper mounting fasteners.

13   Remove the transmission-to-transfer case bolts.

Note: *On some models, there may be two different lengths of bolts securing the transfer case to the transmission. Mark their positions or keep them in order when removed so they can be returned to their proper locations.*

14   Make a final check that all wires and hoses have been disconnected from the transfer case, then move the transfer case and jack toward the rear of the vehicle until the transfer case is clear of the transmission. Keep the transfer case level as this is done. Once the input shaft is clear, lower the transfer case and remove it from under the vehicle.

Installation

15   Installation is the reverse of removal, noting the following points:

Apply anaerobic liquid gasket sealant (not RTV sealant) to the transfer case-to-transmission mating surface.

Install the transmission-to-transfer case bolts in their proper locations and tighten them to the torque listed in this Chapter's Specifications.

Refill the transfer case with the proper type and quantity of lubricant (see Chapter 1).

Check that the 4WD shift indicator corresponds to the position of the transfer case (see Section 1).

6 Transfer case overhaul - general information

1   Overhauling a transfer case is a difficult job for the do-it-yourselfer. It involves the disassembly and reassembly of many small parts. Numerous clearances must be precisely measured and, if necessary, changed with select-fit spacers and snap-rings. As a result, if transfer case problems arise, it can be removed and installed by a competent do-it-yourselfer, but overhaul should be left to a transmission repair shop. Rebuilt transfer cases may be available - check with your dealer parts department and auto parts stores. At any rate, the time and money involved in an overhaul is almost sure to exceed the cost of a rebuilt unit.

2   Nevertheless, it's not impossible for an inexperienced mechanic to rebuild a transfer case if the special tools are available and the job is done in a deliberate step-by-step manner so nothing is overlooked.

3   The tools necessary for an overhaul include internal and external snap-ring pliers, a bearing puller, a slide hammer, a set of pin punches, a dial indicator and possibly a hydraulic press. In addition, a large, sturdy workbench will be required.

4   During disassembly of the transfer case, make careful notes of how each piece comes off, where it fits in relation to other pieces and what holds it in place. Note how parts are installed when you remove them; this will make it much easier to get the transfer case back together.

5   Before taking the transfer case apart for repair, it will help if you have some idea what area of the transfer case is malfunctioning. Certain problems can be closely tied to specific areas in the transfer case, which can make component examination and replacement easier. Refer to "Troubleshooting" at the front of this manual for information regarding possible sources of trouble. Check for trouble codes for the transfer case system (see Section 1).

Notes

Chapter 7 Part C
Transfer case - 2013 and later models

Contents

	Section		Section
Control unit - removal and installation	2	Transfer case - removal and installation	1

Specifications

Torque specifications

	Ft-lbs	Nm
Transfer case-to-transaxle bolts	32	44

1 Transfer case - removal and installation

1 Loosen the front wheel lug nuts. Raise the vehicle and support it securely on jackstands. Remove the front wheels. Remove the engine under-cover and both inner fender splash shields (see Chapter 11).

2 Drain the transfer case lubricant (see Chapter 1).

3 Remove the right-side driveaxle (see Chapter 8).

4 Remove the driveshaft (see Chapter 8).

5 Remove the exhaust manifold from the rear cylinder bank (see Chapter 2A).

6 Support the transaxle with a floor jack. Place a piece of wood between the jack head and the transaxle to protect the aluminum housing.

7 Remove the steering gear (see Chapter 10).

8 Unbolt and remove the two transfer case support brackets.

9 Remove the transfer case mounting bolts and lower the transfer case from the transaxle.

10 Installation is the reverse of removal. Fill the transfer case with the recommended lubricant and check the transaxle fluid level (see Chapter 1).

2 Control unit - removal and installation

1 Disconnect the cable from the negative battery terminal (see Chapter 5).

2 Open the liftgate, then remove the storage box compartment from the floor.

3 Disconnect the electrical connectors to the control unit.

4 Remove the control unit mounting bolts and remove the control unit.

5 Installation is the reverse of removal.

Notes

Chapter 8
Driveline

Contents

	Section		Section
Differential oil seals - replacement	10	Electric controlled coupling (AWD models) - removal	
Driveaxle boot - replacement	4	and installation	12
Driveaxles - general information	2	Front differential (2012 and earlier models) - removal	
Driveaxles - removal and installation	3	and installation	11
Driveshaft(s) (2012 and earlier models) - removal		General information	1
and installation	6	Rear differential - removal and installation	9
Driveshaft (2013 and later AWD models) - removal		Universal joints - replacement	8
and installation	7		
Driveshaft(s) and universal joints - general information			
and inspection	5		

Specifications

Torque specifications	Ft-lbs	Nm
Driveaxle/hub nut		
Front		
2012 and earlier models	101	137
2013 and later models	135	183
Rear		
2012 and earlier	177	240
2013 and later	92	125
Driveaxle (right front) support bearing retainer bolts	18	24
Driveaxle (right front) support bearing bracket-to-engine block bolts	35	47
Rear		
2012 and earlier models	177	240
2013 and later models	92	125
Driveaxle flange bolts*		
Front (V8 models)	54	73.5
Rear	87	118
Driveshaft flange nuts and bolts*		
Front (2012 and earlier models)	44	60
Rear		
2012 and earlier models	77	104
2013 and later models	37	50
Driveshaft center support bearing mounting nuts	33	45
Front differential (2012 and earlier models)		
Front crossmember mounting bolt/nuts	96	130
Front differential mounting bolt/nuts	135	183
Rear differential		
Differential-to-mounting bracket bolts/nuts (rear)		
2012 and earlier models	129	175
2013 and later models	58	79
Mounting bracket-to-subframe bolts/nuts (front)		
2012 and earlier models	81	110
2013 and later models	89	121
Electric controlled coupling-to-torsion damper nuts	34	46
Electric controlled coupling-to-rear differential bolts	24	32

*Use new fasteners during installation

1 General information

1   The information in this Chapter deals with the components from the rear of the engine to the wheels, except for the transmission or transaxle and transfer case, which are dealt with in Chapters 7A and 7B or 7C.

2   Since nearly all the procedures covered in this Chapter involve working under the vehicle, make sure it's securely supported on sturdy jackstands or on a hoist where the vehicle can be easily raised and lowered.

2 Driveaxles - general information

1   On 2012 and earlier models power is transmitted from the rear differential (and front differential on 4WD models) through a pair of driveaxles. The rear driveaxles (and front driveaxles on 4WD V8 models), the inner end of each driveaxle is bolted to a stub shaft. On 4WD V6 models, the inner ends of the driveaxles are splined into the differential side gears. The outer ends of the driveaxles are splined to the axle hubs and locked in place by a large nut.

2   On 2013 and later AWD models, power is transmitted from the transfer case/transaxle (and rear differential on AWD models) to the wheels through a pair of driveaxles. The inner end of each driveaxle is splined into the differential side gears. The outer ends of the driveaxles are splined to the axle hubs and locked in place by a large nut.

3   The inner ends of the driveaxles on 2012 and earlier models are equipped with ball-and-cage type constant velocity (CV) joints. 2013 and later models are equipped with tripod-type CV joints.

4   The outer CV joints on all models are the ball-and-cage type.

5   The boots should be inspected periodically for damage and leaking lubricant. Torn CV joint boots must be replaced as soon as possible or the joints can be damaged. Boot replacement involves removal of the driveaxle (see Section 3). The most common symptom of worn or damaged CV joints, besides lubricant leaks, is a clicking noise in turns, a clunk when accelerating after coasting and vibration at highway speeds. To check for wear in the CV joints and driveaxle shafts, grasp each axle (one at a time) and rotate it in both directions while holding the CV joint housings, feeling for play indicating worn splines or sloppy CV joints.

3 Driveaxles - removal and installation

Front

2012 and earlier models (4WD)

1   Loosen the front wheel lug nuts, remove the cotter pin from the driveaxle/hub nut, and use a breaker-bar and a socket to loosen the driveaxle hub nut. Discard the cotter pin. A new one must be used during installation.

2   Raise the front of the vehicle and support it securely on jackstands. Remove the front wheel(s).

3   Remove the engine undercover.

4   Disconnect the ABS wheel sensor harness at the hub and secure it out of the way (see Chapter 9).

5   Remove the driveaxle/hub nut.

6   Remove the brake caliper and the disc (see Chapter 9). Hang the caliper out of the way on a length of wire; don't let it hang by the hose.

7   Remove the hub and bearing assembly (see Chapter 10).

8   Position a floor jack under the lower control arm and apply slight tension upward.

9   Disconnect the upper balljoint from the steering knuckle (see Chapter 10).

10   Pull the steering knuckle outward enough for the splines of the driveaxle to clear the knuckle. Support the driveaxle - don't let it hang by the inner CV joint.

V6 models

11   Use a large flat prybar to release the inner end of the driveaxle from the front differential assembly.

12   Replace the differential side seals whenever the driveaxles have been removed (see Section 10).

13   Lubricate the lip of the new seal with multi-purpose grease.

14   The remainder of installation is the reverse of removal. Keep the splines of the inner end of the driveaxle centered in the seal opening when installing the driveaxle, to avoid nicking the new seal. Drive the inner end of the driveaxle in with a hammer to seat it securely in the differential housing. Align the brake disc and wheel hub marks made during removal. Install the wheel lug nuts. Lower the vehicle and tighten the lug nuts to the torque listed in the Chapter 1 Specifications. Tighten the driveaxle/hub nut to the torque listed in this Chapter's Specifications. Install a new cotter pin.

V8 models

15   Unbolt the inner CV joint from the front differential flange.

16   Installation is the reverse of removal. Tighten the driveaxle flange bolts to the torque listed in this Chapter's Specifications. Align the brake disc and wheel hub marks made during removal. Install the wheel and lug nuts. Lower the vehicle and tighten the lug nuts to the torque listed in the Chapter 1 Specifications. Tighten the driveaxle/hub nut to the torque listed in this Chapter's Specifications. Install a new cotter pin.

2013 and later models

17   Loosen the front wheel lug nuts, raise the vehicle and support it securely on jackstands. Remove the wheel.

18   Remove the cotter pin and loosen the driveaxle/hub nut **(see illustration)**. Discard the cotter pin. A new one must be used during installation.

19   Remove the wheel speed sensor from the steering knuckle (see Chapter 9).

20   Disconnect the brake hose from the suspension strut.

21   Remove the brake caliper and the disc (see Chapter 9). Hang the caliper out of the way on a length of wire; don't let it hang by the hose.

22   Remove the strut-to-knuckle nuts and bolts and disconnect the strut from the steering knuckle.

23   Loosen the driveaxleaxle/hub nut until it is aligned with the end of the axle. Push the driveaxle out of the hub. If the driveaxle splines are frozen, free them by tapping the end of the driveaxle nut with a soft-faced hammer or a hammer and a brass punch, or use a puller to push the driveaxle from the hub.

24   Remove the driveaxle/hub nut.

25   Remove the under-vehicle splash shield. Place a drain pan underneath the transaxle to catch any lubricant that may spill out when the driveaxles are removed.

26   If you're removing the left driveaxle, carefully pry the inner CV joint out of the transaxle **(see illustration)**.

3.18 Place a prybar between two wheel studs while you loosen the driveaxle nut

3.26 If you're removing the left driveaxle, carefully pry the inner CV joint out of the transaxle

3.27 Remove the support bearing retainer bolts

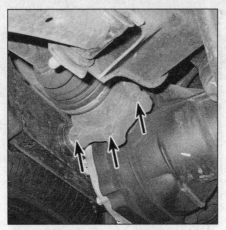

3.32 Remove the driveaxle mounting bolts and separate the driveaxle from the differential assembly - three of six bolts shown

4.2a Pry up the retaining tabs on the boot clamps. . .

27   If you're removing the right driveaxle, remove the support bearing retainer bolts, then remove the driveaxle from the transaxle **(see illustration)**.
Note: *It may be necessary to use a slide hammer to remove the driveaxle and support bearing.*
28   Install a new driveaxle oil seal (see Chapter 7A).
29   Installation is the reverse of removal. Align the brake disc and wheel hub marks made during removal. Install the wheel and lug nuts. Lower the vehicle and tighten the lug nuts to the torque listed in the Chapter 1 Specifications. Tighten the driveaxle/hub nut to the torque listed in this Chapter's Specifications. Install a new cotter pin.

Rear
2012 and earlier models
30   Loosen the rear wheel lug nuts, pry off the hub cover and remove the cotter pin from the driveaxle/hub nut, then use a breaker bar and a socket to loosen the driveaxle/hub nut. Discard the cotter pin. A new one must be used during installation. Raise the rear of the vehicle and support it securely on jackstands. Remove the rear wheel(s).
31   Remove the driveaxle/hub nut.
32   Unbolt the end of the driveaxle from the rear differential flange **(see illustration)**. Discard the bolts; new ones must be used during installation.
33   Separate the driveaxle from the hub assembly. To loosen the driveaxle from the hub splines, tap the end of the driveaxle with a hammer and brass punch. If the driveaxle is stuck in the hub splines and won't move, it may be necessary to push the driveaxle with a suitable puller.
34   Remove the driveaxle from the vehicle.
35   Installation is the reverse of removal. Install new driveaxle flange bolts and tighten them to the torque listed in this Chapter's Specifications.

36   Install the wheel and lug nuts. Lower the vehicle and tighten the lug nuts to the torque listed in the Chapter 1 Specifications. Tighten the driveaxle/hub nut to the torque listed in this Chapters Specifications. Install a new cotter pin.

2013 and later models (AWD)
37   Loosen the rear wheel lug nuts, raise the vehicle and support it securely on jackstands. Remove the wheel(s).
38   Remove the cotter pin from the rear driveaxle/hub nut, then use a breaker bar and socket to loosen the nut **(see illustration 3.20)**. Discard the cotter pin. A new one must be used during installation.
39   Remove the rear wheel speed sensor (see Chapter 9).
40   Remove the brake caliper and the disc (see Chapter 9). Hang the caliper out of the way on a length of wire; don't let it hang by the hose.
41   Loosen the hub nut until it is aligned with the end of the driveaxle, then break loose the driveaxle splines from the hub. If the driveaxle splines are frozen, free them by tapping the end of the driveaxle with a soft-faced hammer or a hammer and a brass punch, or use a puller to push the driveaxle from the hub.
42   Remove the axle nut.
43   Remove the rear hub and bearing assembly (see Chapter 10).
44   Pry the driveaxle from the rear differential, then remove the driveaxle from the vehicle.
45   Replace the rear differential oil seals (see Section 10).
46   Installation is the reverse of removal. Take care to avoid damaging the differential oil seal. Tighten the hub and bearing assembly to the torque listed in the Chapter 10 Specifications. Tighten the caliper mounting bolts to the torque listed in the Chapter 9 Specifications. Tighten the wheel lug nuts to the torque listed in the Chapter 1 Specifications. Tighten the driveaxle/hub nut to the torque listed in this

4.2b. . . then open the clamps and remove them from the boot

Chapter's Specifications. Install a new cotter pin.

---
4   Driveaxle boot - replacement

Note: *If the CV joints must be overhauled (usually due to torn boots), explore all options before beginning the job. Complete rebuilt driveaxles are available on an exchange basis, which eliminates much time and work. Whichever route you choose to take, check on the cost and availability of parts before disassembling the vehicle.*

Inner CV joint
2012 and earlier models
Disassembly
1   Remove the driveaxle (see Section 3) and mount it in a vise.
Note: Use soft inserts in the vise jaws to avoid damaging the driveaxle.
2   Remove the boot clamps **(see illustrations)**.

4.3 Pry the wire retainer ring from the CV joint housing with a small screwdriver

4.4 With the retainer removed, the outer race can be pulled off the bearing assembly

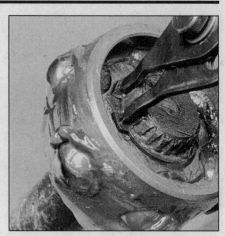

4.6 Remove the snap-ring from the end of the axleshaft

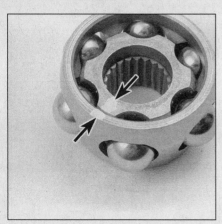

4.8 Make index marks on the inner race and cage so they'll both be facing the same direction when reassembled

4.9 Pry the balls from the cage with a screwdriver (be careful not to nick or scratch them)

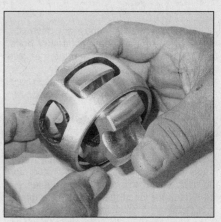

4.10 Tilt the inner race 90-degrees and rotate it out of the cage

3   Slide the boot back on the axleshaft and pry the wire ring ball retainer from the outer race **(see illustration)**.

4   Pull the outer race off the inner bearing assembly **(see illustration)**.

5   Wipe as much grease as possible off the inner bearing.

6   Remove the snap-ring from the end of the axleshaft **(see illustration)**.

7   Slide the inner bearing assembly off the axleshaft. If it won't slide off, tap it off using a hammer and brass punch placed against the inner race.

8   Mark the inner race and cage to ensure that they are reassembled with the correct sides facing out **(see illustration)**.

9   Using a screwdriver or piece of wood, pry the balls from the cage **(see illustration)**. Be careful not to scratch the inner race, the balls or the cage.

10   Rotate the inner race 90-degrees, align the inner race lands with the cage windows and rotate the race out of the cage **(see illustration)**.

Inspection

11   Clean the components with solvent to remove all traces of grease. Inspect the cage and races for pitting, score marks, cracks and other signs of wear and damage. Shiny, polished spots are normal and will not adversely affect CV joint performance **(see illustrations)**. If the outer CV joint boot is torn or damaged, now is the time to set aside the inner CV joint parts, remove the outer boot, and clean and inspect the outer CV joint.

Reassembly

12   Insert the inner race into the cage. Verify that the matchmarks are on the same side. However, it's not necessary for them to be in direct alignment with each other.

13   Press the balls into the cage windows with your thumbs **(see illustration)**.

14   Wrap the axleshaft splines with tape to avoid damaging the boot **(see illustration)**.

15   Slide the small boot clamp and boot onto the axleshaft, then remove the tape.

16   Install the inner race and cage assembly on the axleshaft with the larger diameter side, or bulge, of the cage facing the axle-

shaft end **(see illustration)**.

17   Install the snap-ring

18   Fill the boot with CV joint grease (normally included with the new boot kit).

19   Pack the inner race and cage assembly with grease, by hand, until grease is worked completely into the assembly **(see illustration)**.

20   Slide the outer race down onto the inner race and install the wire ring retainer.

21   Wipe any excess grease from the axle boot groove on the outer race. Seat the small diameter of the boot in the recessed area on the axleshaft and install the clamp. Push the other end of the boot onto the outer CV joint housing and seat it into the recessed area on the housing.

22   Position the CV joint to midway through its travel, then equalize the pressure in the boot by inserting a dull screwdriver between the boot and the outer race **(see illustration)**. Don't damage the boot with the tool.

23   Install the boot clamps **(see illustrations)**.

24   Install the driveaxle (see Section 3).

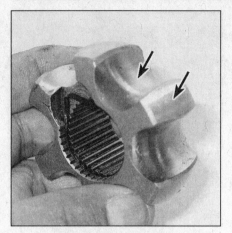

4.11a Inspect the inner race lands and grooves for pitting and score marks

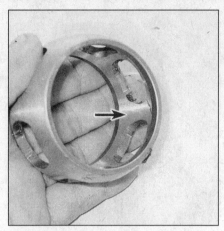

4.11b Inspect the cage for cracks, pitting and score marks (shiny spots are normal and don't affect operation)

4.13 Press the balls into the cage through the windows

4.14 Wrap the splined area of the axleshaft with tape to prevent damage to the boot(s) when installing it

4.16 Install the inner race and cage assembly with the large diameter end toward the splined end of the axleshaft

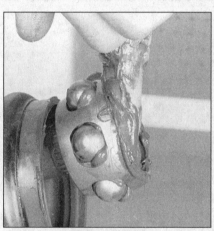

4.19 Pack grease into the bearing until it's completely full

4.22 Equalize the pressure inside the boot by inserting a small, dull screwdriver between the boot and the outer race

4.23a To install new fold-over type clamps, bend the tang down. . .

4.23b. . . then flatten the tabs to hold it in place

4.27 Pull the boot back, then pry the retaining ring from its groove

4.28 Place marks on the tripod and the driveaxle to ensure that they're properly reassembled

4.29 Remove the snap-ring from the groove in the end of the axleshaft

4.30 Drive the tripod joint from the axleshaft with a hammer and brass punch - make sure you don't damage the bearing surfaces or the splines on the shaft

4.32 Install the tripod with the chamfered (tapered) ends of the splines facing toward the axleshaft

2013 and later models

Disassembly

25   Remove the driveaxle (see Section 3) and mount it in a vise.

Note: *Use soft inserts in the vise jaws to avoid damaging the driveaxle.*

26   Remove the boot clamps **(see illustrations 4.2a and 4.2b)**.

27   Pull the boot back from the inner CV joint, remove the retaining ring, then slide off the joint housing **(see illustration)**.

28   Use paint to mark the tripod and axleshaft to ensure that they are reassembled properly. Do not scratch the surfaces to make the alignment marks **(see illustration)**.

29   Remove the snap-ring from the end of the axleshaft with a pair of snap-ring pliers **(see illustration)**.

30   Use a hammer and a brass punch to drive the tripod joint from the driveaxle **(see illustration)**. Some driveaxles are equipped

with a rubber dynamic balancer that is retained by clamps. If it is necessary to remove the balancer, be sure to first mark the location of the balancer and clamps (or measure the distance from the end of the shaft to the balancer) so they can be reinstalled in the same location.

Check

31   Clean all components with solvent to remove the grease, and check for cracks, pitting, scoring and other signs of wear.

Reassembly

32   Slide the clamps and boot onto the axleshaft. It's a good idea to wrap the axleshaft splines with tape to prevent damaging the boot **(see illustration 4.14)**. Place the tripod on the shaft **(see illustration)** and install the snap-ring. Apply grease to the tripod assembly, the inside of the joint housing and the inside of the boot.

33   Install the housing on the joint, then install the retaining ring, making sure it seats

in its groove in the housing.

34   Slide the boot into place, making sure both ends seat in their grooves.

35   Position the joint mid-way through its travel, equalize the pressure in the boot **(see illustration 4.22)**, then tighten and secure the boot clamps **(see illustrations 4.23a and 4.23b)**.

36   Install a new snap-ring on the inner CV joint stub axle.

37   Install the driveaxle (see Section 3).

Outer CV joint

38   Remove the driveaxle (see Section 3), then remove the boot clamps **(see illustrations 4.2a and 4.2b)**.

39   Refer to the accompanying illustrations and perform the outer CV joint boot replacement procedure **(see illustrations)**.

Note: *Use soft inserts in the vise jaws to avoid damaging the driveaxle.*

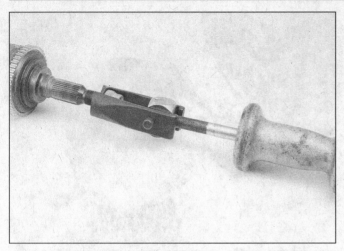

4.39a Outer CV joints can be removed with a slide hammer; you'll need an adapter and a slide hammer setup such as the one shown here

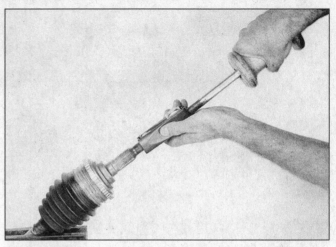

4.39b With the axleshaft firmly clamped down in a bench vise and the adapter gripping the driveaxle/hub nut, carefully extract the outer CV joint from the axleshaft. If it won't come off after five or six attempts, replace the driveaxle assembly

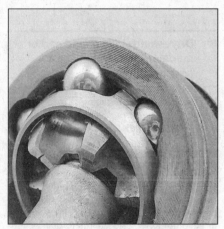

4.39c After the old grease has been rinsed away, move the inner race through its full range of motion and inspect the bearing surfaces for wear or damage

4.39d Apply CV joint grease through the splined hole, then insert a wooden dowel (slightly smaller in diameter than the hole) into the hole and push down - the dowel will force the grease into the joint. Repeat this until the joint is packed

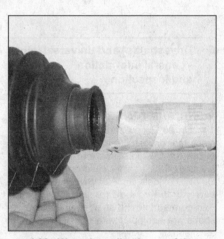

4.39e Wrap the splined area of the axleshaft with tape to prevent damage to the boot when installing it

4.39f Install the small clamp and the boot on the driveaxle and apply grease to the inside of the axle boot. . .

4.39g. . . until the level is up to the end of the axle

4.39h Install a new snap-ring into the groove at the end of the driveaxle. Position the CV joint assembly on the driveaxle, aligning the splines. . .

4.39i. . . then use a hammer and brass punch to carefully drive the joint onto the driveaxle

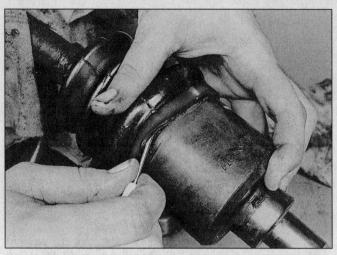

4.39j Seat the ends of the boot in their grooves, equalize the pressure inside the boot by inserting a small, dull screwdriver between the boot and the outer race, then tighten the clamps (see illustrations 4.23a and 4.23c)

5   Driveshaft(s) and universal joints - general information and inspection

General information

1   On 2012 and earlier models, a single-piece rear driveshaft employs a splined yoke at the front, which slips into the extension housing of the transfer case or transmission. On 4WD models, another driveshaft transmits power to the front differential. A slip joint is incorporated into the shaft itself. Both driveshafts are equipped with universal joints at each end.

2   On 2013 and later AWD models, the driveshafft is a pair of tubes that transmits power between the transfer case and rear differential. There are universal joints at each end of the driveshaft and a constant velocity joint in the center, supported by a bearing. The rear section of the driveshaft is equipped with a slip joint.

3   The driveshaft assembly requires very little service. The universal joints are lubricated for life. On 2012 and earlier models the universal joints are serviceable. On 2013 and llter models, the manufacturer states that the entire driveshaft must be replaced if any part of the driveshaft develops a problem. Some driveline specialty shops are capable of rebuilding these assemblies, though, so it's a good idea to call around to see if this is a viable option before purchasing a new driveshaft.

4   Since the driveshaft is a balanced unit, it's important that no undercoating or mud be allowed to stay on it. When the vehicle is raised for service, it's a good idea to clean the driveshaft and inspect it for obvious damage. Make sure that the small weights welded on to balance the driveshaft haven't been knocked off. Whenever it's removed, the driveshaft must be installed in the same position relative to the flanges on the transfer case and the differential in order to maintain the balance.

5   Problems with the driveshaft are usually indicated by a noise or vibration. A road test should verify if the problem is the driveshaft or another component. Refer to "Troubleshooting" at the front of this manual.

Inspection

6   Raise the vehicle and support it securely on jackstands. Block the wheels at the opposite end to keep it from rolling off the stands. Release the parking brake and place the transaxle in Neutral.

7   Visually inspect the driveshaft as you turn it by hand. Look for dents and cracks. If any are found, replace the driveshaft.

8   Check for leakage at the front and rear. Oil leakage here means a defective transfer case or differential seal. Also check for looseness of the joints of the rear driveaxles. Grease leakage at the CV joint boots indicates a damaged rubber boot.

9   Rotate the driveshaft and make sure the universal joints are operating properly with no binding, noise or looseness. On 2013 and later AWD models, listen for noise from the center bearing; this indicates wear or damage.

10   Grip each joint and try to twist it and wiggle it up and down. Any movement at all in the joint is a sign of considerable wear.

11   Check the driveshaft mounting bolts and nuts at each end to be sure they're tight. Finally, check the center bearing for looseness or rubber deterioration and check that the bearing bracket isn't bent.

12   If you're concerned about a possibly bent driveshaft causing a vibration, mount a dial indicator to the floor of the vehicle and check the driveshaft runout in the middle of the driveshaft (both front and rear sections on 2013 and later AWD models).

6   Driveshaft(s) (2012 and earlier models) - removal and installation

Warning: *The manufacturer recommends replacing the universal joint flange nuts and bolts whenever they are removed.*

Rear driveshaft
Removal

1   Raise the vehicle and support it securely on jackstands. Place the transmission in Neutral with the parking brake off. If necessary, remove the lower skid guards to gain access to the driveline.

2   Make reference marks on the driveshaft flange and the pinion flange in line with each other **(see illustration)**. Also mark the relationship of the front yoke to the transmission or transfer case. Use paint to make the reference marks. Do not scratch or damage the shaft or yoke surface.

3   Remove the rear universal joint nuts and bolts. Turn the driveshaft (or wheels) as necessary to bring the bolts into the most accessible position. Insert a tool into the assembly to keep it from turning as you break the nuts and bolts loose **(see illustration)**.

4   Lower the rear of the driveshaft, then slide the front yoke out of the transmission or transfer case.

5   Wrap a plastic bag over the transmission or transfer case housing and hold it in place with a rubber band. This will prevent loss of fluid and protect against contamination while the driveshaft is out.

Installation

6   Remove the plastic bag from the transmission or transfer case and wipe the area clean. Inspect the oil seal carefully. Procedures for replacement of this seal can be

6.2 Mark the relationship of the driveshaft flange to the pinion flange

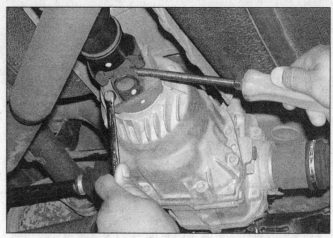

6.3 Immobilize the driveshaft by placing a large screwdriver into the U-joint while loosening the bolts

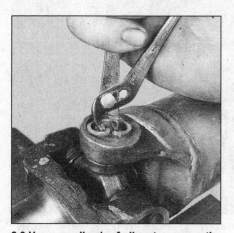

8.3 Use a small pair of pliers to remove the snap-rings from the ends of the universal joint yokes

8.4 To remove the U-joint from the driveshaft, use a vise as a press - the small socket will push the cross and bearing cap into the large socket

found in Chapter 7B.

7   Slide the front yoke of the driveshaft into the transmission or transfer case, being careful not to damage the seal in the process.

8   Raise the rear of the driveshaft into position, making sure the marks are in alignment. If not, turn the rear wheels to match the pinion flange and the driveshaft.

9   Install new bolts and nuts, tightening them to the torque listed in this Chapter's Specifications.

Front driveshaft (4WD models)

10   Raise the front of the vehicle and support it securely on jackstands. Remove the skid plate, if equipped.

11   Mark the relationship of the driveshaft to the front differential companion flange and to the transfer case companion flange. Use paint to make the reference marks. Do not scratch or damage the shaft or flange surface.

12   Remove the bolts and nuts from the flanges, then lower the shaft from the vehicle.

13   Attach the ends of the shaft to the dif-

ferential and transfer case companion flanges (line up the marks), install new bolts and nuts and tighten them to the torque listed in this this Chapter's Specifications.

14   Install the skid plate (if equipped).

7 Driveshaft (2013 and later AWD models) - removal and installation

1   Raise the rear of the vehicle and support it securely on jackstands. Block the front wheels to prevent the vehicle from rolling.

2   Turn the key On, then shift the transaxle into Neutral. Turn the key Off. Release the parking brake.

3   Mark the relationship of the driveshaft flanges to the differential and transfer case flanges (see illustration 6.2). Use paint to make the reference marks. Do not scratch or damage the shaft or flange surface.

4   Remove the heat shield, and then loosen (but don't remove) the center bearing bracket

nuts.

5   Remove the flange bolts from each end of the driveshaft. Insert a tool into the assembly to keep it from turning as you break the nuts and bolts loose (see illustration 6.3).

6   Remove the center support bearing nuts and remove the driveshaft.

7   Remove the center bearing bracket from the driveshaft.

8   Installation is the reverse of removal. Attach the center bearing bracket so that the arrow on it is facing forward and tighten the fasteners to the torque listed in this Chapter's Specifications. Align the match marks you made previously as you attach each end of the driveshaft. Tighten the nuts and bolts to the torques listed in this Chapter's Specifications.

8 Universal joints - replacement

Note: This procedure applies to 2012 and earlier models only. The universal joints on 2013 and later models are not serviceable.

Note: Always purchase a universal joint service kit for your model vehicle before beginning this procedure. Also, read through the entire procedure before beginning work.

Note: On all models, select-fit snap-rings are available to adjust the universal joint endplay, which should be 0.0008-inch (0.02 mm) or less. Check with your local auto parts store or dealer service department if the endplay is greater than specified after the joint is assembled (or if the joint is extremely tight and won't free-up).

1   Remove the driveshaft (see Section 6 or 7).

2   Place the driveshaft on a bench equipped with a vise.

3   Remove the snap-rings with a small pair of pliers (see illustration).

4   Support the cross (also called a spider) on a short piece of pipe or a large socket and use another socket to press out the cross by closing the vise (see illustration).

8.5 Locking pliers can be used to remove the bearing caps from the yoke

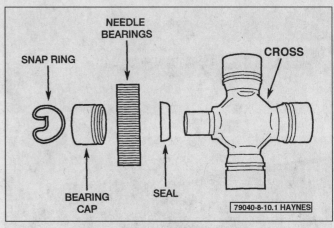

8.6 Outer snap-ring type U-joint

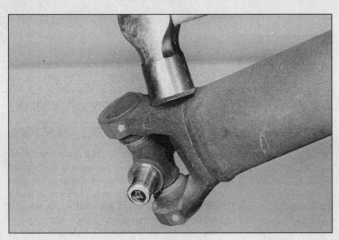

8.16 Strike the yoke sharply with a hammer to spring the yoke ears, which will free-up the joint

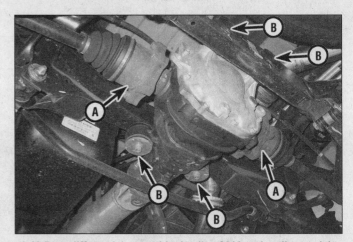

9.13 Rear differential assembly details - 2012 and earlier models

A   *Rear driveaxles and flange bolts*
B   *Rear differential mounting fasteners*

5   Press the cross through as far as possible, then grip the bearing cap with pliers and remove it **(see illustration)**.
6   A universal joint repair kit will contain a new cross, seals, bearings, caps and snap-rings **(see illustration)**.
7   Inspect the bearing cap bores in the yokes for wear and damage.
8   If the bearing cap bores in the yoke are so worn that the caps are a loose fit, the driveshaft will have to be replaced with a new one.
9   Make sure the dust seals are properly located on the cross.
10   Using a vise, press one bearing cap into the yoke approximately 1/4-inch.
11   Use chassis grease to hold the needle rollers in place in the caps.
12   Insert the cross into the partially installed bearing cap, taking care not to dislodge the needle rollers.
13   Hold the cross in correct alignment and press both caps into place by slowly and carefully closing the jaws of the vise.
14   Use a socket slightly smaller in diameter

than the caps to press them into the yoke. Press in one side, install the snap-ring, then press the other side to shift the cross assembly tight against the installed snap-ring and install the other snap-ring.
15   Repeat the operations for the remaining two bearing caps.
16   If the joint is stiff after assembly, strike the yoke sharply with a hammer **(see illustration)**. This will spring the yoke ears slightly and free up the joint.

9   Rear differential - removal and installation

1   On 2013 and later models, loosen the rear wheel lug nuts.
2   Raise the rear of the vehicle and support it securely on jackstands.
3   On 2013 and later models, remove the rear wheels.
4   Drain the differential lubricant (see Chapter 1).

5   Remove the spare tire.
6   Disconnect the driveshaft from the differential (see Section 7). Use wire to hang the rear of the driveshaft out of the way.
7   Remove the rear stabilizer bar (see Chapter 10).
8   On 2012 and earlier models, unbolt the driveaxles from the differential side gear flanges, then support them with rope or wire. On 2013 and later models, remove the rear driveaxles (see Section 3).
9   On 2012 and earlier models, remove the wheel speed sensors.
10   On 2013 and later models, disconnect the electrical connector from the electric controlled coupling, then free the harness from its bracket.
11   Note the routing of the breather hose, then detach it. On 2013 and later models, also detach the breather hose from the electric controlled coupling.
12   Support the differential with a floor jack.
13   Remove the differential mounting fasteners **(see illustration)**.
Note: *2012 and earlier models have vertical*

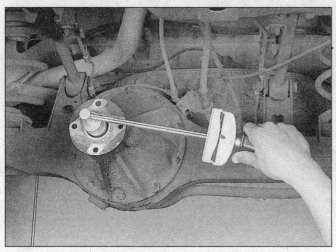

10.11 Use an inch-pound torque wrench to check the torque necessary to rotate the pinion shaft

10.12 Mark the position of the flange to the shaft and count the number of exposed threads above the nut

and horizontal mounting fasteners. On 2013 and later models the fasteners are horizontally mounted.

14   Carefully lower the differential with the jack until it can be slid out from under the vehicle.

15   Installation is the reverse of removal. Tighten the mounting fasteners to the torque listed in this Chapter's Specifications. Refill the differential with the proper lubricant (see Chapter 1).

10   Differential oil seals - replacement

Driveaxle oil seals

Note: *On 4WD models with a V8 engine, the manufacturer recommends removing the front differential assembly to replace the front drive-axle oil seals (see Section 11).*

1   Rear driveaxle oil seals: On 2012 and earlier models, unbolt the driveaxle from the differential side gear flange and support it with a length of rope or wire; on 2013 and later models, remove the driveaxle (see Section 3).

2   Front driveaxle oil seals: On V8 models, unbolt the driveaxle from the differential side gear flange and support it with a length of rope or wire; on V6 models, remove the drive-axle (see Section 3).

3   On 2012 and earlier model rear differentials, and front differentials on V8 models, use a slide hammer and flange puller adapter and pull the flange(s) out of the differential.

4   Use a seal removal tool to pull the old seals out, then clean the seal location on the differential housing. Make sure you don't damage the seal bore or the new seal may leak.

5   Use a hammer and a seal driver or a large socket of the appropriate size to drive the new seal into place.

10.13 A chain wrench is being used here to prevent the pinion flange from turning while the nut is loosened

6   Lubricate the lip of the new seal with multi-purpose grease.

7   The remainder of installation is the reverse of removal. Keep the splines of the inner end of the driveaxle or flange centered in the seal opening when installing them, to avoid nicking the new seal.

Pinion oil seal

2012 and earlier models

Note: *This procedure applies to front and rear differentials.*

8   Loosen the wheel lug nuts. Raise the front (for front differential) or rear (for rear differential) of the vehicle and support it securely on jackstands. Block the opposite set of wheels to keep the vehicle from rolling off the stands. Remove the wheels.

9   Disconnect the driveshaft from the differential companion flange and fasten it out of the way (see Section 3).

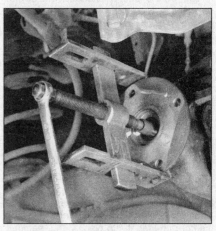

10.14 If you can't pull the pinion flange off by hand, remove it with a puller

10   Remove the rear brake discs (see Chapter 9).

11   Rotate the pinion a few times by hand. Use a beam-type or dial-type inch-pound torque wrench to check the torque required to rotate the pinion **(see illustration)**. Record it for use later.

12   Mark the relationship of the pinion flange to the shaft **(see illustration)**, then count and write down the number of exposed threads on the shaft.

13   A flange holding tool will be required to keep the companion flange from moving while the self-locking pinion nut is loosened. A chain wrench will also work **(see illustration)**.

14   Withdraw the flange. It may be necessary to use a two-jaw puller engaged behind the flange to draw it off **(see illustration)**. Do not attempt to pry or hammer behind the flange or hammer on the end of the pinion shaft.

15   Pry out the old seal and discard it.

16   Lubricate the lips of the new seal and fill the space between the seal lips with wheel bearing grease, then tap it evenly into position with a seal installation tool or a large socket **(see illustration)**. Make sure it enters the housing squarely and is tapped in to its full depth.

17   Install the pinion flange, lining up the marks made in Step 12. If necessary, tighten the pinion nut to draw the flange into place. Do not try to hammer the flange into position.

18   Apply a bead of RTV sealant to the ends of the splines visible in the center of the flange so oil will be sealed in.

19   Install a new pinion nut and pinion nut lockwasher. Do not reuse the old nut or lockwasher. Tighten the nut until the number of threads exposed in Step 12 is showing.

20   Measure the torque required to rotate the pinion and tighten the nut in small increments (no more than 5 ft-lbs) until it matches the figure recorded earlier. To compensate for the drag of the new oil seal, the nut should be tightened a little more until the rotational torque of the pinion exceeds the earlier recording by 5 in-lbs.

Note: *If the maximum nut torque is reached before the desired preload is obtained, the differential must be disassembled and a new collapsible spacer must be installed.*

21   Reinstall all components removed previously by reversing the removal Steps and tightening all fasteners to their specified torque values.

2013 and later AWD models

22   Remove the electric controlled coupling unit (see Section 12).

23   Carefully pry the seal out of the bore. Wipe the seal bore clean.

24   Lubricate the lips of the new seal with clean differential lubricant. Install the seal in the bore and tap it into place with a hammer and seal driver.

25   The remainder of installation is the reverse of removal.

11   Front differential (2012 and earlier models) - removal and installation

1   Raise the front of the vehicle and support it securely on jackstands.

2   Drain the differential lubricant (see Chapter 1).

3   Disconnect the driveshaft from the front differential (see Section 6) and support it out of the way with a length of rope or wire.

4   On V6 models, remove the driveaxles

10.16 Lubricate the lips of the new seal and seat it squarely in the bore, then drive it into the carrier with a seal driver or a large socket

(see Section 3).

5   On V8 models, unbolt the driveaxles from the flanges (see Section 3) and support them with lengths of wire or rope.

6   Remove the front crossmember (see Chapter 7A or 7B).

7   Disconnect the vent hose from the housing.

8   Support the differential/axle housing with a floor jack.

9   Remove the three front differential mounting bolts and carefully lower the differential with the jack until it can be slid out from under the vehicle.

10   Installation is the reverse of removal. Route the vent hose as it was originally and align the driveshaft flange mark with the mark on the differential flange.

11   Tighten the mounting fasteners to the torque listed in this Chapter's Specifications. Refill the differential with the proper lubricant (see Chapter 1).

12   Electric controlled coupling (AWD models) - removal and installation

Removal

1   Put the shift lever into Neutral and release the parking brake.

2   Disconnect the electrical connector from the coupling.

3   Remove the rear differential (see Section 9).

4   Remove the torsional damper-to-coupling mounting nuts. A flange wrench or a chain wrench can be used to prevent the flange from turning.

5   Remove the electrical harness bracket fasteners and bracket, then slide off the damper.

6   Remove the electric controlled coupling unit-to-differential mounting bolts and separate the coupling from the differential.

7   Remove the wave washer from the front of the differential assembly.

8   Clean all traces of old gasket material from the mating surfaces of the differential housing and the coupling.

Installation

9   Install the wave washer over the differential pinion shaft.

10   Apply RTV sealant or liquid gasket to the sealing surface of the coupling cover.

11   Install the electric controlled coupling over the spline of the drive pinion and against the differential, aligning the pin on the coupling with the groove in the differential housing.

12   Install the coupling mounting bolts and tighten them by hand only at this time.

13   Clean the torsion damper mounting surfaces with rubbing alcohol on a cotton cloth several times, then install the torsion damper.

Caution: *The damper must be installed against the coupling within seconds or before the rubbing alcohol can dry.*

14   Install the electric controlled coupling-to-torsion damper nuts, hold the damper from turning with a flange holding tool or a chain wrench, then tighten the nuts to the torque listed in this Chapter's Specifications.

15   Tighten the electric controlled coupling-to-rear differential bolts to the torque listed in this Chapter's Specifications

16   The remainder of installation is the reverse of removal.

Chapter 9
Brakes

Contents

	Section		Section
Anti-lock Brake System (ABS) - general information	3	Disc brake pads - replacement	4
Brake disc - inspection, removal and installation	6	General information	1
Brake hoses and lines - inspection and replacement	8	Master cylinder - removal and installation	7
Brake hydraulic system - bleeding	9	Parking brake - check and adjustment	11
Brake light and cruise control cancel switches - adjustment and replacement	14	Parking brake shoes - replacement	12
		Power brake booster - check, replacement and adjustment	10
Brake pedal - adjustment	13	Troubleshooting	2
Disc brake caliper - removal and installation	5		

Specifications

General
Brake fluid type... See Chapter 1

Disc brakes
Minimum pad thickness.. See Chapter 1
Brake disc minimum thickness*
    Front .... 1.024 inches (26.0 mm)
    Rear
        2012 and earlier models .... 0.630 inch (16.0 mm)
        2013 and later models .... 0.55 inch (14.0 mm)
Maximum disc runout
    Front
        2012 and earlier models .... 0.0020 inch (0.05 mm)
        2013 and later models .... 0.0016 inch (0.04 mm)
    Rear .... 0.0020 inch (0.05 mm)
Maximum disc thickness variation
    2012 and earlier models... 0.0006 inch (0.015 mm)
    2013 and later models
        Front .... 0.0003 inch (0.008 mm)
        Rear.. 0.0008 inch (0.020 mm)

If different specifications are cast into the disc, they supersede information printed here

Brake booster
Pushrod length from booster canister to center of clevis hole
    2005 models.. 4.92 inches (125 mm)
    2006 through 2012 models .... 5.91 inches (150 mm)
    2013 and later models.. 5.00 inches (127 mm)

Brake pedal
Free height from steel floor to top of pedal
    2012 and earlier models... 7.17 inches (182.1 mm)
    2013 and later models.. 8.43 to 8.82 inches (214 to 224 mm)

Parking brake

Parking brake adjustment clicks
    2012 and earlier models.. 4 to 5 clicks
    2013 and later models.. 5 to 6 clicks
Minimum lining thickness.. 0.06 inch (1.5 mm)

Brake light and cruise control cancel switches

Clearance between rubber bumper and threaded part of switch............. 0.0291 to 0.0772 inch (0.74 to 1.96 mm)

Torque specifications   Ft-lbs (unless otherwise indicated)   Nm

Note: *One foot-pound (ft-lb) of torque is equivalent to 12 inch-pounds (in-lbs) of torque. Torque values below approximately 15 foot-pounds are expressed in inch-pounds, because most foot-pound torque wrenches are not accurate at these smaller values.*

	Ft-lbs (unless otherwise indicated)	Nm
Brake caliper		
Caliper mounting bolts		
Front		
2012 and earlier models	20	27
2013 and later models	34	46
Rear		
2012 and earlier models	20	27
2013 and later models	32	43
Caliper mounting bracket bolts		
Front		
2012 and earlier models	136	184
2013 and later models	91	123
Rear		
2012 and earlier models	76	103
2013 and later models	62	84
Brake hose-to-caliper banjo bolt	156 in-lbs	17.5
Master cylinder-to-brake booster retaining nuts	18	24
Power brake booster-to-body mounting nuts		
2012 and earlier models*	18.5	25
2013 and later models	99 in-lbs	11

Use new fasteners during installation

1   General information

General

1   The vehicles covered by this manual are equipped with hydraulically operated front and rear brake systems. Both front and rear brakes are disc-type and are self-adjusting.

Hydraulic system

2   The hydraulic system consists of two separate circuits. The master cylinder has separate reservoirs for the two circuits, and, in the event of a leak or failure in one hydraulic circuit, the other circuit will remain operative and a warning indicator will light up on the instrument panel when a substantial amount of brake fluid is lost, showing that a failure has occurred.

Power brake booster

3   The power brake booster uses engine manifold vacuum to provide assistance to the brakes. It is mounted on the firewall in the engine compartment, directly behind the master cylinder.

Parking brake

4   Control cables are routed to the rear axle, where they operate small drum brake shoes that apply pressure to the inner diameter of the rear brake discs.

Service

5   After completing any operation involving disassembly of any part of the brake system, always test drive the vehicle to check for proper braking performance before resuming normal driving. When testing the brakes, perform the tests on a clean, dry, flat surface. Conditions other than these can lead to inaccurate test results.
6   Test the brakes at various speeds with both light and heavy pedal pressure. The vehicle should stop evenly without pulling to one side or the other. Under hard braking, the ABS system may engage, resulting in brake pedal pulsation. This is considered normal operation.
7   Tires, vehicle load and wheel alignment are factors which also affect braking performance.

Precautions

8   There are some general cautions and warnings involving the brake system on this vehicle:
a)   Use only brake fluid conforming to DOT 3 specifications.
b)   The brake pads and linings contain fibers which are hazardous to your health if inhaled. Whenever you work on brake system components, clean all parts with brake system cleaner. Do not allow the fine dust to become airborne. Also, wear an approved filtering mask.
c)   Safety should be paramount whenever any servicing of the brake components is performed. Do not use parts or fasteners which are not in perfect condition, and be sure that all clearances and torque specifications are adhered to. If you are at all unsure about a certain procedure, seek professional advice. Upon completion of any brake system work, test the brakes carefully in a controlled area before putting the vehicle into normal service. If a problem is suspected in the brake system, don't drive the vehicle until it's fixed.
d)   Used brake fluid is considered a hazardous waste and it must be disposed of in accordance with federal, state and local laws. DO NOT pour it down the sink, into septic tanks or storm drains, or on the ground. Clean up any spilled brake fluid immediately and then wash the area with large amounts of water. This is especially true for any finished or painted surfaces.

2   Troubleshooting

PROBABLE CAUSE	CORRECTIVE ACTION

No brakes - pedal travels to floor

1 Low fluid level	1 and 2 Low fluid level and air in the system are symptoms of another problem - a leak somewhere in the hydraulic system. Locate and repair the leak
2 Air in system	
3 Defective seals in master cylinder	3 Replace master cylinder
4 Fluid overheated and vaporized due to heavy braking	4 Bleed hydraulic system (temporary fix). Replace brake fluid (proper fix)

Brake pedal slowly travels to floor under braking or at a stop

1 Defective seals in master cylinder	1 Replace master cylinder
2 Leak in a hose, line, caliper or wheel cylinder	2 Locate and repair leak
3 Air in hydraulic system	3 Bleed the system, inspect system for a leak

Brake pedal feels spongy when depressed

1 Air in hydraulic system	1 Bleed the system, inspect system for a leak
2 Master cylinder or power booster loose	2 Tighten fasteners
3 Brake fluid overheated (beginning to boil)	3 Bleed the system (temporary fix). Replace the brake fluid (proper fix)
4 Deteriorated brake hoses (ballooning under pressure)	4 Inspect hoses, replace as necessary (it's a good idea to replace all of them if one hose shows signs of deterioration)

Troubleshooting (continued)

PROBABLE CAUSE	CORRECTIVE ACTION

Brake pedal feels hard when depressed and/or excessive effort required to stop vehicle

PROBABLE CAUSE	CORRECTIVE ACTION
1 Power booster faulty	1 Replace booster
2 Engine not producing sufficient vacuum, or hose to booster clogged, collapsed or cracked	2 Check vacuum to booster with a vacuum gauge. Replace hose if cracked or clogged, repair engine if vacuum is extremely low
3 Brake linings contaminated by grease or brake fluid	3 Locate and repair source of contamination, replace brake pads or shoes
4 Brake linings glazed	4 Replace brake pads or shoes, check discs and drums for glazing, service as necessary
5 Caliper piston(s) or wheel cylinder(s) binding or frozen	5 Replace calipers or wheel cylinders
6 Brakes wet	6 Apply pedal to boil-off water (this should only be a momentary problem)
7 Kinked, clogged or internally split brake hose or line	7 Inspect lines and hoses, replace as necessary

Excessive brake pedal travel (but will pump up)

PROBABLE CAUSE	CORRECTIVE ACTION
1 Drum brakes out of adjustment	1 Adjust brakes
2 Air in hydraulic system	2 Bleed system, inspect system for a leak

Excessive brake pedal travel (but will not pump up)

PROBABLE CAUSE	CORRECTIVE ACTION
1 Master cylinder pushrod misadjusted	1 Adjust pushrod
2 Master cylinder seals defective	2 Replace master cylinder
3 Brake linings worn out	3 Inspect brakes, replace pads and/or shoes
4 Hydraulic system leak	4 Locate and repair leak

Brake pedal doesn't return

PROBABLE CAUSE	CORRECTIVE ACTION
1 Brake pedal binding	1 Inspect pivot bushing and pushrod, repair or lubricate
2 Defective master cylinder	2 Replace master cylinder

Brake pedal pulsates during brake application

PROBABLE CAUSE	CORRECTIVE ACTION
1 Brake drums out-of-round	1 Have drums machined by an automotive machine shop
2 Excessive brake disc runout or disc surfaces out-of-parallel	2 Have discs machined by an automotive machine shop
3 Loose or worn wheel bearings	3 Adjust or replace wheel bearings
4 Loose lug nuts	4 Tighten lug nuts

Brakes slow to release

PROBABLE CAUSE	CORRECTIVE ACTION
1 Malfunctioning power booster	1 Replace booster
2 Pedal linkage binding	2 Inspect pedal pivot bushing and pushrod, repair/lubricate
3 Malfunctioning proportioning valve	3 Replace proportioning valve
4 Sticking caliper or wheel cylinder	4 Repair or replace calipers or wheel cylinders
5 Kinked or internally split brake hose	5 Locate and replace faulty brake hose

Brakes grab (one or more wheels)

PROBABLE CAUSE	CORRECTIVE ACTION
1 Grease or brake fluid on brake lining	1 Locate and repair cause of contamination, replace lining
2 Brake lining glazed	2 Replace lining, deglaze disc or drum

PROBABLE CAUSE

CORRECTIVE ACTION

Vehicle pulls to one side during braking

Probable Cause	Corrective Action
1 Grease or brake fluid on brake lining	1 Locate and repair cause of contamination, replace lining
2 Brake lining glazed	2 Deglaze or replace lining, deglaze disc or drum
3 Restricted brake line or hose	3 Repair line or replace hose
4 Tire pressures incorrect	4 Adjust tire pressures
5 Caliper or wheel cylinder sticking	5 Repair or replace calipers or wheel cylinders
6 Wheels out of alignment	6 Have wheels aligned
7 Weak suspension spring	7 Replace springs
8 Weak or broken shock absorber	8 Replace shock absorbers

Brakes drag (indicated by sluggish engine performance or wheels being very hot after driving)

Probable Cause	Corrective Action
1 Brake pedal pushrod incorrectly adjusted	1 Adjust pushrod
2 Master cylinder pushrod (between booster and master cylinder) incorrectly adjusted	2 Adjust pushrod
3 Obstructed compensating port in master cylinder	3 Replace master cylinder
4 Master cylinder piston seized in bore	4 Replace master cylinder
5 Contaminated fluid causing swollen seals throughout system	5 Flush system, replace all hydraulic components
6 Clogged brake lines or internally split brake hose(s)	6 Flush hydraulic system, replace defective hose(s)
7 Sticking caliper(s) or wheel cylinder(s)	7 Replace calipers or wheel cylinders
8 Parking brake not releasing	8 Inspect parking brake linkage and parking brake mechanism, repair as required
9 Improper shoe-to-drum clearance	9 Adjust brake shoes
10 Faulty proportioning valve	10 Replace proportioning valve

Brakes fade (due to excessive heat)

Probable Cause	Corrective Action
1 Brake linings excessively worn or glazed	1 Deglaze or replace brake pads and/or shoes
2 Excessive use of brakes	2 Downshift into a lower gear, maintain a constant slower speed (going down hills)
3 Vehicle overloaded	3 Reduce load
4 Brake drums or discs worn too thin	4 Measure drum diameter and disc thickness, replace drums or discs as required
5 Contaminated brake fluid	5 Flush system, replace fluid
6 Brakes drag	6 Repair cause of dragging brakes
7 Driver resting left foot on brake pedal	7 Don't ride the brakes

Brakes noisy (high-pitched squeal)

Probable Cause	Corrective Action
1 Glazed lining	1 Deglaze or replace lining
2 Contaminated lining (brake fluid, grease, etc.)	2 Repair source of contamination, replace linings
3 Weak or broken brake shoe hold-down or return spring	3 Replace springs
4 Rivets securing lining to shoe or backing plate loose	4 Replace shoes or pads
5 Excessive dust buildup on brake linings	5 Wash brakes off with brake system cleaner
6 Brake drums worn too thin	6 Measure diameter of drums, replace if necessary
7 Wear indicator on disc brake pads contacting disc	7 Replace brake pads
8 Anti-squeal shims missing or installed improperly	8 Install shims correctly

Troubleshooting (continued)

PROBABLE CAUSE   **CORRECTIVE ACTION**

Brakes noisy (scraping sound)

Probable Cause	Corrective Action
1 Brake pads or shoes worn out; rivets, backing plate or brake shoe metal contacting disc or drum	1 Replace linings, have discs and/or drums machined (or replace)

Brakes chatter

Probable Cause	Corrective Action
1 Worn brake lining	1 Inspect brakes, replace shoes or pads as necessary
2 Glazed or scored discs or drums	2 Deglaze discs or drums with sandpaper (if glazing is severe, machining will be required)
3 Drums or discs heat checked	3 Check discs and/or drums for hard spots, heat checking, etc. Have discs/drums machined or replace them
4 Disc runout or drum out-of-round excessive	4 Measure disc runout and/or drum out-of-round, have discs or drums machined or replace them
5 Loose or worn wheel bearings	5 Adjust or replace wheel bearings
6 Loose or bent brake backing plate (drum brakes)	6 Tighten or replace backing plate
7 Grooves worn in discs or drums	7 Have discs or drums machined, if within limits (if not, replace them)
8 Brake linings contaminated (brake fluid, grease, etc.)	8 Locate and repair source of contamination, replace pads or shoes
9 Excessive dust buildup on linings	9 Wash brakes with brake system cleaner
10 Surface finish on discs or drums too rough after machining (especially on vehicles with sliding calipers)	10 Have discs or drums properly machined
11 Brake pads or shoes glazed	11 Deglaze or replace brake pads or shoes

Brake pads or shoes click

Probable Cause	Corrective Action
1 Shoe support pads on brake backing plate grooved or excessively worn	1 Replace brake backing plate
2 Brake pads loose in caliper	2 Loose pad retainers or anti-rattle clips
3 Also see items listed under Brakes chatter	

Brakes make groaning noise at end of stop

Probable Cause	Corrective Action
1 Brake pads and/or shoes worn out	1 Replace pads and/or shoes
2 Brake linings contaminated (brake fluid, grease, etc.)	2 Locate and repair cause of contamination, replace brake pads or shoes
3 Brake linings glazed	3 Deglaze or replace brake pads or shoes
4 Excessive dust buildup on linings	4 Wash brakes with brake system cleaner
5 Scored or heat-checked discs or drums	5 Inspect discs/drums, have machined if within limits (if not, replace discs or drums)
6 Broken or missing brake shoe attaching hardware	6 Inspect drum brakes, replace missing hardware

Rear brakes lock up under light brake application

Probable Cause	Corrective Action
1 Tire pressures too high	1 Adjust tire pressures
2 Tires excessively worn	2 Replace tires
3 Defective proportioning valve	3 Replace proportioning valve

PROBABLE CAUSE   **CORRECTIVE ACTION**

Brake warning light on instrument panel comes on (or stays on)

1 Low fluid level in master cylinder reservoir (reservoirs with fluid level sensor)	1 Add fluid, inspect system for leak, check the thickness of the brake pads and shoes
2 Failure in one half of the hydraulic system	2 Inspect hydraulic system for a leak
3 Piston in pressure differential warning valve not centered	3 Center piston by bleeding one circuit or the other (close bleeder valve as soon as the light goes out)
4 Defective pressure differential valve or warning switch	4 Replace valve or switch
5 Air in the hydraulic system	5 Bleed the system, check for leaks
6 Brake pads worn out (vehicles with electric wear sensors - small probes that fit into the brake pads and ground out on the disc when the pads get thin)	6 Replace brake pads (and sensors)

Brakes do not self adjust

Disc brakes

1 Defective caliper piston seals	1 Replace calipers. Also, possible contaminated fluid causing soft or swollen seals (flush system and fill with new fluid if in doubt)
2 Corroded caliper piston(s)	2 Same as above

Drum brakes

1 Adjuster screw frozen	1 Remove adjuster, disassemble, clean and lubricate with high-temperature grease
2 Adjuster lever does not contact star wheel or is binding	2 Inspect drum brakes, assemble correctly or clean or replace parts as required
3 Adjusters mixed up (installed on wrong wheels after brake job)	3 Reassemble correctly
4 Adjuster cable broken or installed incorrectly (cable-type adjusters)	4 Install new cable or assemble correctly

Rapid brake lining wear

1 Driver resting left foot on brake pedal	1 Don't ride the brakes
2 Surface finish on discs or drums too rough	2 Have discs or drums properly machined
3 Also see Brakes drag	

3 Anti-lock Brake System (ABS) - general information

1   The Anti-lock Brake System (ABS) is designed to maintain vehicle steerability, directional stability and optimum deceleration under severe braking conditions and on most road surfaces. It does so by monitoring the rotational speed of each wheel and controlling the brake line pressure to each wheel during braking. This prevents the wheels from locking up.

Actuator assembly

2   The actuator assembly consists of an electric hydraulic pump and a pair of solenoid valves for each wheel. The electric pump provides hydraulic pressure to charge the reservoirs in the actuator, which supplies pressure to the braking system during ABS operation. The solenoid valves modulate brake line pressure during ABS operation. The body contains four valves - one for each wheel. The pump, the reservoirs and the solenoid valves are all housed in the actuator assembly (**see illustration**).

Speed sensors

3   The speed sensors, which are located at each wheel (2012 and earlier model rear wheel speed sensors are mounted inboard, on the differential cover), generate a sine wave current when the sensor rotors are turning. This analog voltage signal is monitored

3.2 The ABS actuator is mounted on either the driver's side (2012 and earlier models, shown) or passenger's side (2013 and later models) of the firewall

3.11a Front wheel speed sensor (2013 and later rear wheel speed sensor similar)

3.11b Rear wheel speed sensors - 2012 and earlier models

by the ABS control unit, which converts it to a digital signal from which it can determine wheel rotational speed.

ABS computer

4   The ABS control unit is the brain of the ABS system. The function of the control unit is to monitor and process information received from the wheel speed sensors to control the hydraulic line pressure, avoiding wheel lock up. The control unit also monitors the system for malfunctions, even when the ABS system is inactive during normal driving conditions.

5   Each time you start the engine, the system turns on the ABS warning light on the instrument cluster for about a second. As soon as the engine is running, the light should go off. The system then performs a self-test the first time the vehicle speed exceeds four mph. You may hear a mechanical noise during the test; this is normal. If the system detects a problem, the ABS light will come on and remain on. A diagnostic code will also be stored in the control unit, which indicates the problem area or component.

Wheel speed sensor - removal and installation

Note: *The rear wheel speed sensors are mounted on the steering knuckles or rear knuckles, except for the rear sensors on 2012 and earlier models; they're mounted on the differential cover.*

6   If you're replacing a front wheel speed sensor (all model years) or a rear wheel speed sensor on a 2013 or later model, loosen the wheel lug nuts.

7   Raise the vehicle and support it securely on jackstands. Remove the wheel (unless replacing a rear sensor on a 2012 or earlier model).

8   Make sure the ignition key is turned to the OFF position.

9   Trace the wiring back from the sensor, detaching all brackets and clips while noting its correct routing, then disconnect the electrical connector.

10   For front wheel sensors, it may be nec-

4.3 Always wash the brakes with brake cleaner before disassembling anything

essary to remove the inner fender splash shield (see Chapter 11) or the brake disc (see Section 6) for easier access to the sensor and the electrical connector.

Note: *For rear wheel sensors on 2012 and earlier models, removing the spare tire makes access to the electrical connectors easier.*

11   Clean the area around the bolt and sensor, and then remove the mounting bolt. Carefully pull the sensor out from its bore **(see illustrations)**.

12   Clean the wheel sensor hole and the sensor mating surface with brake cleaner.

13   Installation is the reverse of removal. Tighten the mounting fastener securely.

14   Install the wheel and lug nuts. Lower the vehicle and tighten the lug nuts to the torque listed in the Chapter 1 Specifications.

---

4   Disc brake pads - replacement

Warning: *Disc brake pads must be replaced on both front wheels at the same time - never replace the pads on only one wheel. Also, the dust created by the brake system is harmful to your health. Never blow it out with compressed*

4.5 Before removing the caliper, slowly depress the piston into the caliper bore by using a large C-clamp between the outer brake pad and the back of the caliper

air and don't inhale any of it. An approved filtering mask should be worn when working on the brakes. Do not, under any circumstances, use petroleum-based solvents to clean brake parts. Use brake system cleaner only!

1   Remove the cap from the brake fluid reservoir.

2   Loosen the front or rear wheel lug nuts, raise the front or rear of the vehicle and support it securely on jackstands. Block the wheels at the opposite end.

3   Remove the wheels. Work on one brake assembly at a time, using the assembled brake for reference if necessary. Place a drain pan under the brake assembly and thoroughly clean it with brake cleaner **(see illustration)**.

4   Inspect the brake disc carefully (see Section 6). If machining is necessary, remove the disc (see Section 6).

5   Push the piston(s) completely back into the bore(s) using a C-clamp **(see illustration)**. This is necessary to provide space for the new brake pads. When a piston is depressed to the bottom of the caliper bore, the fluid in the master cylinder will rise. Make sure that

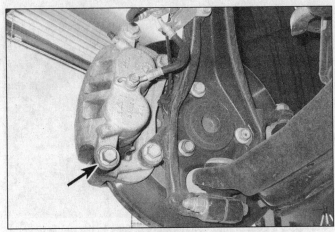

4.6a If you're working on a 2012 or earlier model, remove the lower caliper mounting bolt. If you're working on a 2013 or later model, remove the brake hose-to-strut clip and detach the hose from the strut, then remove both caliper mounting bolts and lift the caliper from the bracket

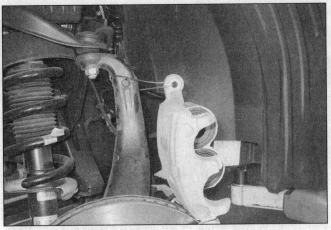

4.6b Pivot the caliper up (2012 and earlier models) or remove the caliper (2013 and later models) and secure it with wire; do not allow the caliper to hang by the brake hose. Be careful not to damage the upper guide pin boot while rotating the caliper. The brake hose banjo bolt should not be removed unless the caliper or hose requires service.

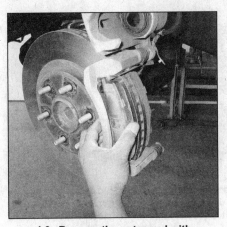

4.6c Remove the outer pad with the shim(s). . .

4.6d. . . and the inner pad with the shim(s)

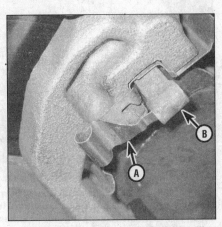

4.6e On V8 models, some designs will utilize a return spring (A) on the pad retainer that engages with the pad's wear sensor (B); on V6 models, the spring is V-shaped and the ends of the spring are seated into the backing plate of the pads

it doesn't overflow by removing more fluid as necessary.

Warning: *Brake fluid is poisonous - never siphon it by mouth. Use a suction gun or old poultry baster. If a baster is used, never again use it for the preparation of food.*

Caution: *Brake fluid will damage paint. If any fluid is spilled, wash it off immediately with plenty of clean, cold water.*

Front brake pads

6   For front pad replacement, follow **illustrations 4.6a through 4.6p** for the actual pad replacement procedure, then proceed to Step 9. Be sure to stay in order and read the caption under each illustration. Work on one brake assembly at a time using the assembled brake for reference if necessary.

4.6f Remove the upper and lower pad retainers. If they are loose or worn, replace them

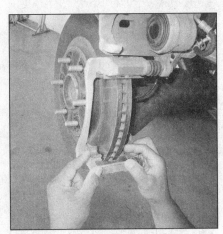

4.6g Install clean or new pad retainers

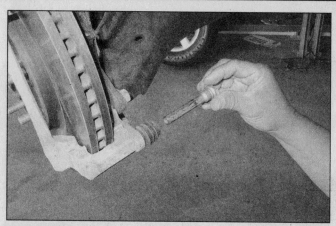

4.6h Pull out the lower guide pin; clean it and inspect it for wear or damage

4.6i Apply a coat of high-temperature grease to the guide pin and reinstall it. Seat the guide pin into the boot. Replace any guide pins or boots that are worn or damaged

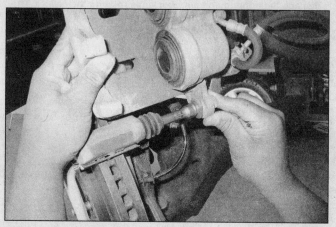

4.6j Unhook the caliper and pull it away from the mounting bracket with the upper guide pin. Be careful not to tear the guide pin boot. Clean and lubricate the upper guide pin, then place the caliper back in position. Seat the guide pin boot securely around the guide pin. Replace any guide pins or boots that are worn or damaged

4.6k Lubricate the back of each pad and related shims with high-temperature grease, or apply an anti-squeal compound. DO NOT allow any grease or anti-squeal compound to get onto the pad lining

Note: *The manufacturer recommends using new shims when replacing the brake pads. Some aftermarket brake pads may have shims that are permanently attached*

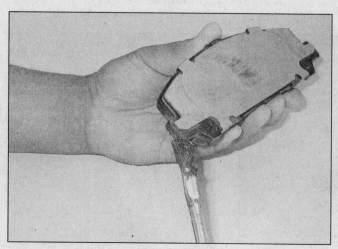

4.6l Lubricate the ends of each pad with high-temperature grease. DO NOT allow grease to get onto the pad lining

4.6m Install the inboard brake pad with the shim(s)

Note: *On some V8 models, refer to illustration 4.6e and engage the pad return spring when installing the pads.*

4.6n Install the outboard brake pad with the shim(s)

Note: *On some V8 models, refer to illustration 4.6e and engage the pad return spring when installing the pads.*
Note: *On early V6 models, install the pad return spring ends into the pads, making sure the spring is facing the correct direction.*

Rear brake pads

7   For rear pad replacement, follow **illustrations 4.7a through 4.7n** for the actual pad replacement procedure, then proceed to Step 9. Be sure to stay in order and read the caption under each illustration. Work on one brake assembly at a time using the assembled brake for reference if necessary.
Note: *If the caliper won't fit over the pads, use a C-clamp to push the piston into the caliper a little farther.*

8   When reinstalling the caliper, tighten the mounting bolts to the torque listed in this Chapter's Specifications.

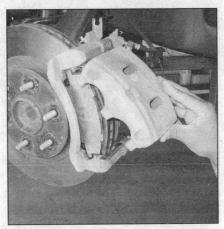

4.6o Carefully pivot the caliper down onto the mounting bracket (2012 and earlier models) or install the caliper (20123 and later models) over the new brake pads while noting the position guide pin's end in relation to the caliper

Front or rear pads

Warning: *After the job has been completed, firmly depress the brake pedal a few times to bring the pads into contact with the disc. You may not have any braking at first if this is not done.*

9   After the job has been completed, perform the following:

a) *Slowly depress the brake pedal about two-thirds of its travel a few times until the pedal is firm. This will bring the pads into contact with the brake disc.*
b) *Install the wheels and lug nuts. Lower the vehicle to the ground and tighten the*

4.6p Install the mounting bolt(s) and tighten to the torque listed in this Chapter's Specifications

lug nuts to the torque listed in this Chapter's Specifications.
c) *Check the level of the brake fluid, adding some if necessary (see Chapter 1).*
d) *In an isolated area, drive the vehicle and make a few hard stops to seat the pads to the disc. Allow the brakes to cool by driving the vehicle at least one minute in between stops.*
e) *Continue making stops until the brakes feel responsive and normal. Remember to cool the brakes in between stops.*
f) *Finally, check the operation of the brakes carefully before placing the vehicle into normal service.*

4.7a Loosen the caliper upper mounting bolt and remove the lower caliper mounting bolt (2012 and earlier models), or, if you're working on a 2013 or later model, loosen the lower mounting bolt and remove the upper mounting bolt. . .

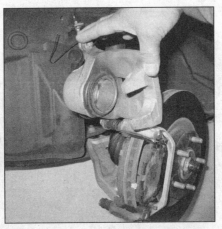

4.7b. . . and swing it away from the caliper mounting bracket; the brake hose banjo bolt shouldn't be removed unless the caliper or hose requires service

4.7c Support the caliper with a piece of wire

4.7d Remove the inner brake pad

4.7e Remove the outer brake pad

4.7f Remove the upper and lower pad retainers

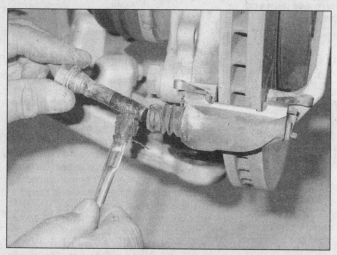

4.7g Thoroughly clean both slide pins, inspect them for corrosion and replace them if necessary; lubricate the lower. . .

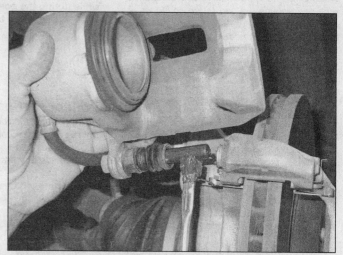

4.7h. . . and the upper pins with high-temperature brake grease

4.7i Clean the shims, then apply high-temperature brake grease or anti-squeal compound to the backs of the pads (let the compound set up for a few minutes before installing the pads)

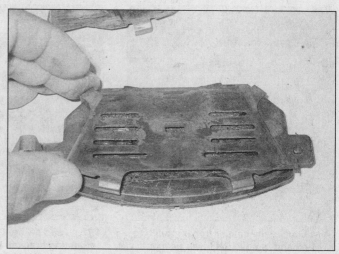

4.7j Assemble the shims to the pads in the same order in which they were originally installed

4.7k Inspect the rubber boots and replace them if necessary; reinstall the pad retainers into the caliper bracket

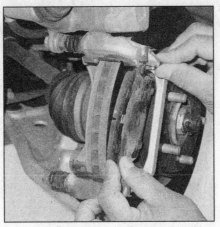

4.7l Install the outer pad

4.7m Install the inner pad

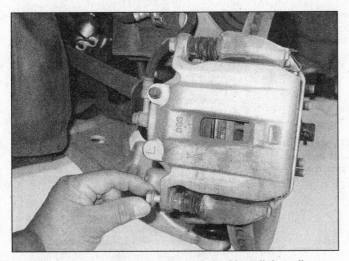

4.7n Install the caliper over the pads and install the caliper mounting bolt, tightening it to the torque listed in this Chapter's Specifications

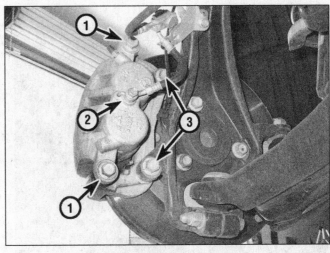

5.2a Brake caliper mounting details

1 Caliper mounting bolts	3 Caliper mounting
2 Banjo fitting bolt	bracket bolts

5   Disc brake caliper - removal and installation

Warning: *The dust created by the brake system is harmful to your health. Never blow it out with compressed air and don't inhale any of it. An approved filtering mask should be worn when working on the brakes. Do not, under any circumstances, use petroleum-based solvents to clean brake parts. Use brake system cleaner only!*

Note: *If replacement is indicated (usually because of fluid leakage), it is recommended that the calipers be replaced, not overhauled. New and factory rebuilt units are available on an exchange basis, which makes this job quite easy. Always replace the calipers in pairs - never replace just one of them.*

Removal

1   Loosen the front or rear wheel lug nuts, raise the front or rear of the vehicle and place it securely on jackstands. Block the wheels at the opposite end. Remove the front or rear wheel.

2   Remove the brake hose banjo bolt **(see illustration)**. Disconnect the brake hose from the caliper and discard the sealing washers (new ones must be used on installation). Plug the brake hose to keep contaminants out of the brake system and to prevent losing any more brake fluid than is necessary **(see illustration)**.

Note: *If you're only removing the caliper for access to other components, don't detach the hose.*

3   Remove the caliper mounting bolts and lift the caliper from its bracket.

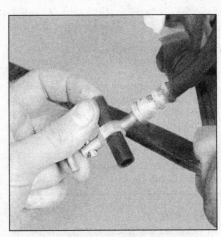

5.2b Plug the brake line with a piece of rubber hose with the same outside diameter as the inside diameter of the banjo fitting

6.3 The brake pads on this vehicle were obviously neglected, as they wore down completely and cut deep grooves into the disc - wear this severe means the disc must be replaced

6.4a To check disc runout, mount a dial indicator as shown and rotate the disc

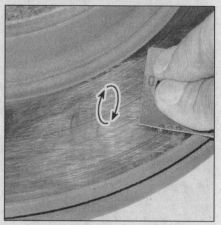

6.4b Using a swirling motion, remove the glaze from the disc surface with sandpaper or emery cloth

6.5 Use a micrometer to measure disc thickness

good idea to resurface the discs regardless of the dial indicator reading, because it will produce a smooth finish and ensure a perfectly flat surface, eliminating any brake pedal pulsation or other undesirable symptoms related to questionable discs. If you decide not to resurface the discs, at least remove the glaze from the surface with emery cloth using a swirling motion **(see illustration)**.

5   The minimum wear (or discard) thickness is cast into the disc. The disc thickness can be checked with a micrometer **(see illustration)**.

6   The disc must not be machined to a thickness less than the minimum allowable thickness listed in this Chapter's Specifications or the amount cast into the disc.

Removal

7   Remove the two caliper mounting bracket bolts **(see illustration 5.2b)** and detach the caliper mounting bracket. On rear discs, fully release the parking brake.

8   Make alignment marks on the brake disc and wheel hub. Remove the lug nuts that you installed to hold the disc in place and remove the disc from the hub.

Note: If a rear disc won't come off, remove the rubber plug from the parking brake adjuster hole. Use a small screwdriver to turn the star wheel and retract the parking brake shoes **(see illustrations 12.4a and 12.4b)**.

Installation

9   Place the disc in position over the threaded studs.

10   Install the caliper mounting bracket over the disc and tighten the bolts to the torque listed in this Chapter's Specifications.

11   Install the caliper and tighten the bolts to the torque listed in this Chapter's Specifications.

12   Install the wheel, then lower the vehicle to the ground. Tighten the lug nuts to the torque listed in the Chapter 1 Specifications.

Installation

4   Installation is the reverse of removal. Use new sealing washers for the brake hose-to-caliper banjo bolt. Tighten the banjo bolt and the caliper mounting bolts to the torque values listed in this Chapter's Specifications. Lower the vehicle and tighten the wheel lug nuts to the torque listed in the Chapter 1 Specifications.

5   Bleed the brake system (see Section 9). Make sure there are no leaks from the hose connections. Test the brakes carefully before returning the vehicle to normal service.

6   Brake disc - inspection, removal and installation

Inspection

1   Loosen the wheel lug nuts, raise the vehicle and support it securely on jackstands. Remove the wheel and install the lug nuts to hold the disc in place.

Note: If the lug nuts don't contact the disc when screwed on all the way, install washers under them.

2   Remove the brake caliper (see Section 5). It isn't necessary to disconnect the brake hose. After removing the caliper bolts, suspend the caliper out of the way with a piece of wire.

3   Visually inspect the disc surface for score marks and other damage. Light scratches and shallow grooves are normal after use and may not always be detrimental to brake operation, but deep scoring requires disc removal and refinishing by an automotive machine shop. Be sure to check both sides of the disc **(see illustration)**. If pulsating occurs during application of the brakes, suspect disc runout.

4   To check disc runout, place a dial indicator at a point about 1/2-inch from the outer edge of the disc **(see illustration)**. Set the indicator to zero and turn the disc. The indicator reading should not exceed the runout limit listed in this Chapter's Specifications. If it does, the disc should be refinished by an automotive machine shop.

Note: When replacing the brake pads, it's a

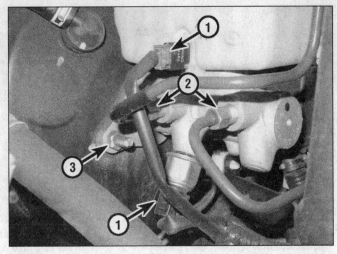

7.5 Master cylinder details (2013 and later models)

1   Hose from remote reservoir
2   Brake line fittings
3   Master cylinder mounting nuts

7.6 Master cylinder mounting details (2012 and earlier models)

1   Electrical connector
2   Brake line fittings
3   Mounting nut (other nut not visible)

Depress the brake pedal a few times to bring the brake pads into contact with the disc. Bleeding won't be necessary unless the brake hose was disconnected from the caliper. Check the operation of the brakes carefully before driving the vehicle.

7   Master cylinder - removal and installation

Caution: *Brake fluid will damage paint. If any fluid is spilled, wash it off immediately with plenty of clean, cold water.*

Removal

1   Disconnect the cable from the negative terminal of the battery (see Chapter 5).
2   On 2013 and later models, remove the air filter housing and the air intake duct (see Chapter 4).
3   Remove as much fluid as possible from the reservoir with a syringe.
4   Unplug the electrical connectors from the master cylinder.
5   On 2013 and later models, disconnect the hose that connects the remote reservoir to the master cylinder reservoir **(see illustration)**; immediately plug the hose to prevent any residual brake fluid inside the hose from dripping into the engine compartment.
6   Place rags under the brake fluid hydraulic line fittings and have caps, plugs or plastic bags to cover the ends of the lines as soon as they're disconnected. Disconnect the two brake fluid hydraulic line fittings from the master cylinder with a flare nut wrench **(see illustration)**.
7   Pull the brake lines away from the master cylinder and plug the ends to prevent contamination.

7.10 The best way to bleed the master cylinder before installing it is with a pair of bleeder tubes

8   Remove the nuts attaching the master cylinder to the power brake booster. Pull the master cylinder off the studs to remove it. Again, be careful not to spill any remaining fluid as this is done.

Installation

9   Bench bleed the new master cylinder before installing it. Mount the master cylinder in a vise, with the jaws of the vise clamping on the mounting flange.
10   Attach a pair of master cylinder bleeder tubes to the outlet ports of the master cylinder **(see illustration)**.
11   Fill the reservoir with brake fluid of the recommended type (see Chapter 1).
12   Slowly push the pistons into the master cylinder (a large Phillips screwdriver can be used for this) - air will be expelled from the pressure chambers and into the reservoir. Because the tubes are submerged in fluid, air can't be drawn back into the master cyl-

inder when you release the pistons. Repeat the procedure until no more air bubbles are present.
13   Remove the bleed tubes, one at a time, and install plugs in the open ports to prevent fluid leakage and air from entering. Install the reservoir cap.
14   Install a new O-ring seal in the groove on the end of the master cylinder and coat it with silicone grease. Also coat the bore of the power brake booster.
15   Install the master cylinder over the studs on the power brake booster and tighten the nuts only finger-tight at this time.
16   Thread the brake line fittings into the master cylinder. Since the master cylinder is still a bit loose, it can be moved slightly so the fittings thread in easily. Don't strip the threads as the fittings are tightened.
17   Tighten the mounting nuts to the torque listed in this Chapter's Specifications. Tighten the brake line fittings securely.

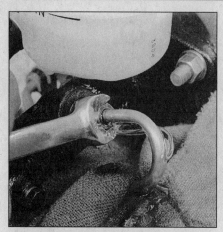

7.18 Have an assistant depress the brake pedal and hold it down, then loosen the fitting nut, allowing the air and fluid to escape; repeat this procedure on both fittings until the fluid is clear of air bubbles

8.3 Loosen the threaded fitting on the brake line; use a flare-nut wrench to protect the corners of the nut

8.4 Pull off the U-clip with a pair of pliers

18   Fill the master cylinder reservoir with fluid, bleed the lines at the master cylinder again, then bleed the remainder of the brake system (see Section 9). To bleed the lines at the master cylinder, have an assistant depress the brake pedal and hold it down. Loosen the fitting to allow air and fluid to escape **(see illustration)**. Tighten the fitting, then allow your assistant to return the pedal to its rest position. Repeat this procedure on both fittings until the fluid is free of air bubbles, then bleed the rest of the system. Check the operation of the brake system carefully before driving the vehicle.

Warning: *If you do not have a firm brake pedal at the end of the bleeding procedure, or have any doubts as to the effectiveness of the brake system, DO NOT drive the vehicle. Have it towed to a dealer service department or other qualified repair shop for diagnosis.*

19   Reconnect the battery and perform the necessary re-learn procedures (see Chapter 5).

8   Brake hoses and lines - inspection and replacement

Inspection

1   About every six months, with the vehicle raised and supported securely on jackstands, the flexible hoses which connect the steel brake lines with the front and rear brake assemblies should be inspected for cracks, chafing of the outer cover, leaks, blisters and other damage. These are important and vulnerable parts of the brake system and inspection should be complete. A light and mirror will be helpful for a thorough check. If a hose exhibits any of the above conditions, replace it with a new one.

Replacement

Brake hoses

2   Loosen the wheel lug nuts, raise the vehicle and support it securely on jackstands. Remove the wheel.

3   At the bracket, unscrew the brake line fitting from the hose **(see illustration)**. Use a flare-nut wrench to prevent rounding off the corners.

4   Remove the U-clip from the female fitting at the bracket with a pair of pliers **(see illustration)**, then pass the hose through the bracket.

5   At the caliper end of the hose, remove the banjo bolt, then separate the hose from the caliper. Note that there are two sealing washers on either side of the banjo fitting - they should be replaced with new ones during installation.

6   If you're replacing a front brake hose, remove the U-clip from the strut bracket, then detach the hose from the bracket.

7   To install the hose, pass the caliper fitting end through the strut bracket (front hose only), then connect the fitting to the caliper with the banjo bolt and new sealing washers.

8   Make sure the hose isn't twisted between the caliper and the strut bracket (or the chassis on rear brake hoses).

9   Route the hose into the frame bracket, again making sure it isn't twisted, then connect the brake line fitting, starting the threads by hand. Install the U-clip, then tighten the fitting securely.

10   Bleed the caliper (see Section 9).

11   Install the wheel and lug nuts, lower the vehicle and tighten the lug nuts to the torque listed in the Chapter 1 Specifications.

Metal brake lines

12   When replacing brake lines, be sure to use the correct parts. Don't use copper tubing for any brake system components. Purchase steel brake lines from a dealer or auto parts store.

13   Prefabricated brake line, with the tube ends already flared and fittings installed, is available at auto parts stores and dealer parts departments.

14   When installing the new line, make sure it's securely supported in the brackets and has plenty of clearance between moving or hot components.

15   After installation, check the master cylinder fluid level and add fluid as necessary. Bleed the brake system (see Section 9) and test the brakes carefully before driving the vehicle in traffic.

9   Brake hydraulic system - bleeding

Warning: *Wear eye protection when bleeding the brake system. If the fluid comes in contact with your eyes, immediately rinse them with water and seek medical attention.*

Note: *Bleeding the hydraulic system is necessary to remove any air that manages to find its way into the system when it's been opened during removal and installation of a hose, line, caliper or master cylinder.*

1   You'll probably have to bleed the system at all four brakes if air has entered it due to low fluid level, or if the brake lines have been disconnected at the master cylinder.

2   If a brake line was disconnected only at a wheel, then only that caliper or wheel cylinder must be bled.

3   If a brake line is disconnected at a fitting located between the master cylinder and any of the brakes, that part of the system served by the disconnected line must be bled.

4   Remove any residual vacuum from the brake power booster by applying the brake

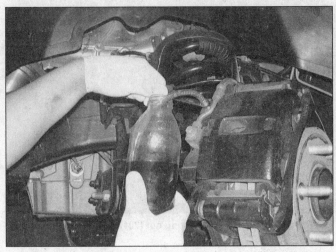

9.8 When bleeding the brakes, a hose is connected to the bleed screw at the caliper or wheel cylinder and then submerged in brake fluid - air will be seen as bubbles in the tube and container (all air must be expelled before moving to the next wheel)

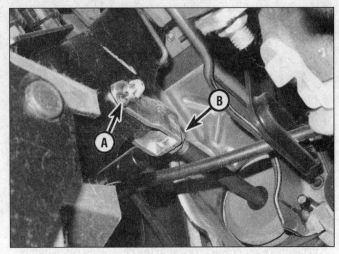

10.9 Clevis pin retaining clip (A) and pushrod locknut (B)

several times with the engine off.

5   Remove the master cylinder reservoir cover and fill the reservoir with brake fluid. Reinstall the cover. Check the fluid level often during the bleeding operation and add fluid as necessary to prevent the fluid level from falling low enough to allow air bubbles into the master cylinder.

Caution: *Turn the ignition switch off and disconnect the electrical connectors for the ABS actuator or detach the battery ground cable.*

6   Have an assistant on hand, as well as a supply of new brake fluid, a clear plastic container partially filled with clean brake fluid, a length of 3/16-inch plastic, rubber or vinyl tubing to fit over the bleeder valve and a wrench to open and close the bleeder valve.

7   Beginning at the right rear wheel, loosen the bleeder valve slightly, then tighten it to a point where it's snug but can still be loosened quickly and easily.

8   Place one end of the tubing over the bleeder valve and submerge the other end in brake fluid in the container **(see illustration)**.

9   Have the assistant pump the brakes slowly a few times to get pressure in the system, then hold the pedal down firmly.

10   While the pedal is held down, open the bleeder valve just enough to allow a flow of fluid to leave the valve. Watch for air bubbles to exit the submerged end of the tube. When the fluid flow slows after a couple of seconds, close the valve and have your assistant release the pedal.

11   Repeat Steps 9 and 10 until no more air is seen leaving the tube, then tighten the bleeder valve and proceed to the left front wheel, the left rear wheel and the right front wheel, in that order, and perform the same procedure. Check the fluid in the master cylinder reservoir frequently.

12   Never use old brake fluid. It contains moisture which will deteriorate the brake system components and could cause the fluid

to boil, which could render the brake system inoperative.

13   Refill the master cylinder with fluid at the end of the operation. If you're working on a model with ABS, be sure to reconnect the electrical connectors to the ABS actuator or reconnect the battery.

14   Check the operation of the brakes. The pedal should feel solid when depressed, with no sponginess. If necessary, repeat the entire process.

Warning: *Do not operate the vehicle if you're in doubt about the effectiveness of the brake system.*

10   Power brake booster - check, replacement and adjustment

Check

Operating check

1   Depress the brake pedal several times with the engine off and make sure there's no change in the pedal reserve distance.

2   Depress the pedal and start the engine. If the pedal goes down slightly, operation is normal.

Airtightness check

3   Start the engine and turn it off after one or two minutes. Depress the brake pedal slowly several times. If the pedal depresses less each time, the booster is airtight.

4   Depress the brake pedal while the engine is running, then stop the engine with the pedal depressed. If there's no change in the pedal reserve travel after holding the pedal for 30 seconds, the booster is airtight.

Replacement

Note: *Power brake booster units shouldn't be disassembled. They require special tools not normally found in most automotive repair*

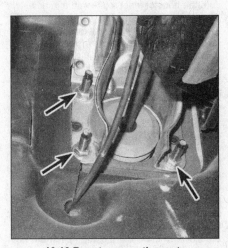

10.10 Booster mounting nuts (3 of 4 shown)

stations or shops. They're fairly complex and, because of their critical relationship to brake performance, should be replaced with a new or rebuilt one.

5   Remove the master cylinder (see Section 7), then disconnect the vacuum hose from the booster.

6   On 2012 and earlier models, remove the ABS actuator fasteners, then move the unit slightly to allow the booster to be removed.

7   Disconnect any electrical connectors.

8   On 2013 and later models, remove the cowl top panel (see Chapter 11). Remove the I-Key sensor (located on the strut tower) and move it out of the way. Remove the knee bolster trim panel (see Chapter 11).

9   Pull out the safety clip, remove the pin from the clevis and detach the pushrod from the brake pedal **(see illustration)**.

10   Remove the four mounting nuts securing the booster to the firewall, then remove the booster from the engine compartment.

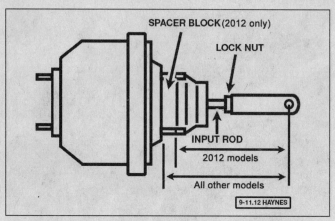

10.14 Measure the distance between the power brake booster (or spacer block on 2012 models) and the hole in the clevis and compare your measurement to the dimension listed in this Chapter's Specifications; if necessary, adjust the clevis before installing the power brake booster

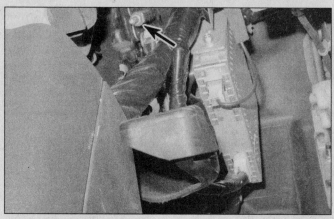

11.4 Parking brake cable adjusting nut (2012 and earlier models)

11   Before installing the new booster, measure the booster input rod length and adjust it if necessary (see Step 14).

12   Installation is the reverse of removal. Use a new gasket between the booster and the firewall. On 2012 and earlier models, use new mounting nuts.

13   Tighten the power brake booster-to-body mounting nuts to the torque listed in this Chapter's Specifications.

Adjustment

14   Measure the distance between the power brake booster and the hole in the input rod clevis **(see illustration)** and compare it to the dimension listed in this Chapter's Specifications. If necessary, loosen the adjusting nut and turn the clevis in or out to the specified length, then install the booster, connect the clevis to the brake pedal, tighten the nut securely.

11   Parking brake - check and adjustment

Check

1   The parking brake pedal, when properly adjusted, should travel the correct number of clicks when a 45 pound force is applied (see this Chapter's Specifications).

2   If the parking brake pedal travels less than the specified minimum number of clicks, it might not be releasing completely and the shoes could even be dragging against the drum. If it moves more than the specified maximum number of clicks, the parking brake may not hold adequately on an incline, allowing the car to roll.

Adjustment

3   Loosen the rear wheel lug nuts. Raise the vehicle and support it securely on jackstands. Remove the rear wheels.

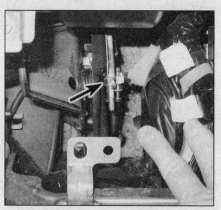

11.5 Parking brake cable adjusting nut (2013 and later models)

4   On 2012 and earlier models, remove the knee bolster trim panel (see Chapter 11, Section 24). Partially engage the parking brake for easier access to the cable adjusting nut. Loosen the cable adjusting nut, then release the parking brake.

Note: *It isn't absolutely necessary to remove the knee bolster, but doing so makes access to the adjusting nut considerably easier.*

5   On 2013 and later models, remove the fuse access cover above the parking brake pedal. Loosen the cable adjusting nut at the upper end of the parking brake pedal, then release the parking brake **(see illustration)**.

6   Install three lug nuts snugly to each rear disc to support it against the hub flange.

7   Remove the rubber adjuster hole plugs from the discs **(see illustrations 12.4a and 12.4b)**.

8   Turn the star wheel upward (2012 and earlier models) or downward (2013 and later models) until it locks the disc, then back it off five or six notches.

9   Turn the disc and make sure there is no drag. Readjust it if necessary to obtain a close adjustment with zero drag. Reinstall the hole plugs.

10   Tighten the adjusting nut (see Step 4 or 5) so you get the specified number of clicks (see this Chapter's Specifications) when you apply the parking brake pedal.

11   Release the parking brake and turn the rear discs again to verify that there is no drag. If drag exists, go over the adjustment procedure until it's correct.

12   Reinstall the wheels, lower the vehicle and tighten the lug nuts to the torque listed in the Chapter 1 Specifications.

12   Parking brake shoes - replacement

Warning: *The dust created by the brake system is harmful to your health. Never blow it out with compressed air and don't inhale any of it. An approved filtering mask should be worn when working on the brakes. Do not, under any circumstances, use petroleum-based solvents to clean brake parts. Use brake system cleaner only!*

1   Loosen the rear wheel lug nuts. Raise the vehicle and support it securely on jackstands. Remove the rear wheels.

2   Release the parking brake. Remove the discs (see Section 6).

3   Inspect the parking brake surfaces of each disc for wear or damage. Replace the discs if necessary.

4   Follow the accompanying photos **(see illustrations 12.4a through 12.4s)** for the actual parking brake shoe replacement procedure. Be sure to stay in order and read the caption under each illustration. Work on only one side at a time to avoid confusion.

Note: *The illustrations show 2013 and later models, which have the adjuster on top and the actuator in the bottom. On 2012 and earlier models, the adjuster is on the bottom of the shoes and the actuator assembly is on the top. Other than these two components, the removal and installation procedures are almost identical.*

12.4a If the disc can't be removed when the parking brake is fully released, you'll have to remove this rubber plug and use a screwdriver to turn the star wheel to retract the parking brake shoes. On 2012 and earlier models the star wheel is positioned at the bottom of the brake shoes

12.4b On 2013 and later models the star wheel is positioned at the top of the brake shoes

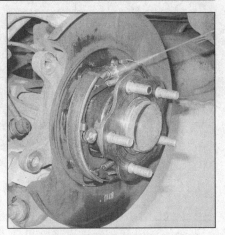

12.4c Wash the assembly with brake system cleaner; DO NOT blow off the brake dust with compressed air

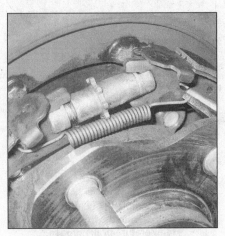

12.4d Remove the upper spring. . .

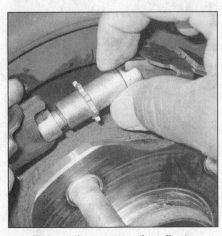

12.4e. . . then remove the adjuster

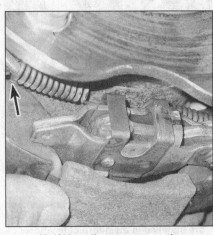

12.4f Use pliers to remove the lower spring

12.4g Turn the shoe hold-down springs to release them. . .

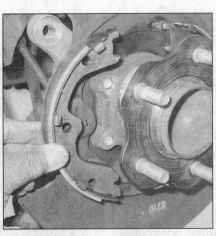

12.4h. . . then lift off the shoe

12.4i Do the same to the remaining shoe. Keep the shoes in order. If reusing the front and rear shoes, they must be installed in their original location

12.4j After cleaning the backing plates, apply brake grease to the raised contact surfaces around the perimeter

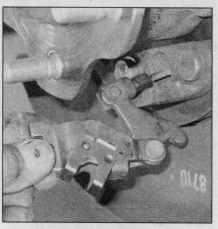

12.4k Check the actuator assembly for wear or damage

12.4l Set the actuator assembly into place

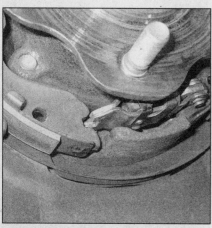

12.4m Install the new parking brake shoes and ensure that the front and rear shoes are installed in their correct location. . .

12.4n. . . and secure them with their hold-down springs

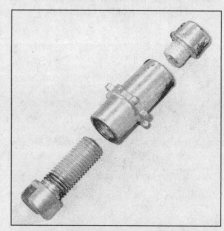

12.4o Disassemble the adjuster, clean it and lightly lubricate the threads with high-temperature brake grease

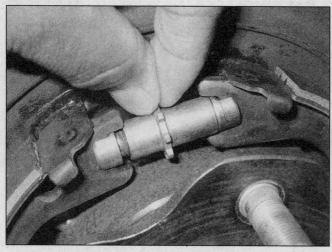

12.4p Place the adjuster between the shoes

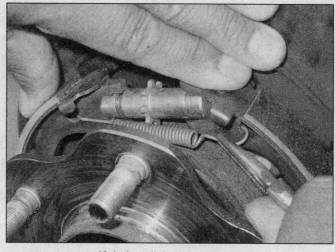

12.4q Install the top spring. . .

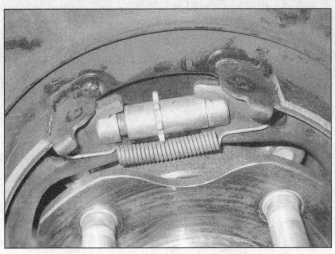

12.4r. . . so that it engages the star wheel

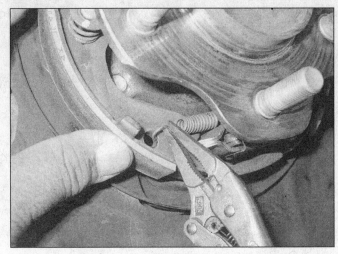

12.4s Attach the lower spring, then reinstall the disc

5   Adjust the parking brake (see Section 11).
6   When reinstalling the calipers, tighten the mounting bracket bolts and the caliper mounting bolts to the torque values listed in this Chapter's Specifications.
7   The remainder of the installation is the reverse of removal.
8   Working through the hole in the center of the brake disc (see illustrations 12.4a and 12.4b), turn the adjuster star wheel with a screwdriver until the disc is locked.
9   Turn the adjuster star wheel the other way 5 or 6 clicks. Turn the disc to verify that the parking brake shoes don't drag.
10   Install the rubber plug in the adjuster hole.
11   The parking brake pedal may need adjustment in a few weeks after the parking brake shoes become seated.

13   Brake pedal - adjustment

1   With the brake pedal fully released, measure the distance from the top of the pad to the floor with the carpet and padding pulled back. Measure at a right angle to the floor.
2   If the height is not as listed in this Chapter's Specifications, it must be adjusted.
3   Release the brake light and cruise control cancel switches by turning them counterclockwise 45-degrees.
4   Loosen the lock nut just in front of the power brake booster clevis (see illustration 10.9).
5   Turn the booster input rod until the pedal height is correct.
6   Tighten the lock nut.

7   With the threaded portion of the brake light and cruise control cancel switches contacting the bracket, turn the switches 45-degrees clockwise to lock them in place.
8   Adjust the brake light and cruise control switches if necessary (see Section 14).

14   Brake light and cruise control cancel switches - adjustment and replacement

Note: *The cruise control cancel switch is also know as the Automatic Speed Control Device (ASCD) switch.*

Adjustment

1   The brake light and cruise control cancel switches are located on a bracket near the top of the brake pedal. The switches activate the brake lights at the rear of the vehicle and cancel the cruise control operation when the pedal is depressed.
2   To check the brake light switch, note whether the brake lights come on when the pedal is depressed and go off when the pedal is released.
3   If the brake lights don't come on or the cruise control doesn't cancel when the brake pedal is depressed, make sure the brake pedal is correctly adjusted (see Section 13), then try adjusting the switch as follows.
4   Release the switch by turning it counterclockwise 45-degrees.
5   Pull the brake pedal back and hold it there, then push the switch into its bracket until the body of the switch (threaded portion) touches its stop.

14.6 The clearance between the threaded body of the switch and the pedal bracket must be as listed in the Specifications

6   Turn the switch 45-degrees clockwise to lock it in place. The distance from the pedal and the threaded part of the switch should be as listed in this Chapter's Specifications (see illustration).

Replacement

7   Unplug the electrical connector from the switch.
8   Turn the switch 45-degrees counterclockwise, pull the switch to the rear and remove it.
9   Installation is the reverse of removal.
10   Adjust the brake pedal height (see Section 13), then adjust the switch (see Steps 4 through 6).

Notes

Chapter 10
Suspension and steering

Contents

	Section		Section
Balljoints - replacement	9	Steering column - removal and installation	25
Coil springs (rear) - removal and installation	15	Steering gear - removal and installation	23
Control arm (front) (2013 and later models) - removal,		Steering gear boots - replacement	22
inspection and installation	8	Steering knuckle (2012 and earlier models) - removal	
General information	1	and installation	10
Hub and bearing assembly - removal and installation	12	Steering knuckle (2013 and later models) - removal	
Knuckle (rear) - removal and installation	14	and installation	11
Lower control arm (front) (2012 and earlier models) - removal,		Steering wheel - removal and installation	20
inspection and installation	7	Strut/coil spring assembly (front, 2013 and	
Power steering pump - removal and installation	24	later models) - removal, inspection and installation	3
Power steering system - bleeding	26	Strut/coil spring assembly (front, 2013 and	
Radius rod (2013 and later models) - removal and installation	18	later models) - replacement	4
Rear suspension control arms and rear subframe - removal		Subframe (front, 2013 and later models) - removal	
and installation	17	and installation	19
Shock absorber/coil spring assembly (front, 2012 and		Tie-rod ends - removal and installation	21
earlier models) - removal, inspection and installation	2	Upper control arm (front) (2012 and earlier models) - removal	
Shock absorbers (rear) - removal and installation	16	and installation	6
Stabilizer bar (front) - removal and installation	5	Wheel alignment - general information	28
Stabilizer bar (rear) - removal and installation	13	Wheels and tires - general information	27

Specifications

Torque specifications

Note: *One foot-pound (ft-lb) of torque is equivalent to 12 inch-pounds (in-lbs) of torque. Torque values below approximately 15-ft-lbs. are expressed in inch-pounds, since most foot-pound torque wrenches are not accurate at these smaller values.*

Front suspension	Ft-lbs (unless otherwise indicated)	Nm
2012 and earlier models		
Control arm*		
Upper control arm		
Pivot bolts	94	127
Control arm balljoint-to-steering knuckle pinch bolt/nut	58	79
Lower control arm		
Pivot bolts	100	136
Control arm balljoint-to-steering knuckle pinch bolt/nut	94	127
Hub and bearing-to-knuckle bolts*	44	60
Stabilizer bar		
Bushing clamp bolts	111	150
Link nuts	67	91
Shock absorber/coil spring assembly		
Shock absorber-to-knuckle bolts/nuts	155	210
Shock absorber upper mounting nuts	22	30
Shock absorber piston rod nut*	30	40
Wheel lug nuts	See Chapter 1	

Use new fasteners on installation

Torque specifications	Ft-lbs (unless otherwise indicated)	Nm

Note: *One foot-pound (ft-lb) of torque is equivalent to 12 inch-pounds (in-lbs) of torque. Torque values below approximately 15-ft-lbs. are expressed in inch-pounds, since most foot-pound torque wrenches are not accurate at these smaller values.*

Front suspension (continued)

2013 and later models

Control arm pivot bolts/nuts*	125	169
Control arm balljoint-to-steering knuckle pinch bolt/nut*	72	98
Hub and bearing-to-knuckle bolts	65	88
Stabilizer bar		
Bushing clamp bolts	39	53
Link nuts	62	84
Strut/coil spring assembly		
Strut-to-knuckle bolts/nuts*	122	165
Strut upper mounting bolts	26	35
Piston rod lock nut*	54	73
Subframe		
Subframe mounting bolts	114	154
Subframe brace bolts	38	52
Wheel lug nuts	See Chapter 1	

Use new fasteners on installation

Rear suspension

2012 and earlier models

Hub and bearing-to-knuckle bolts	44	60
Control arms		
Upper control arm pivot bolt nuts*	101	137
Upper control arm-to-rear knuckle pinch bolt/nut	94	127
Rear lower control arm-to-subframe pivot bolt nut*	101	137
Rear lower control arm-to-knuckle pivot bolt nut	129	175
Front lower control arm-to-knuckle pinch bolt/nut*	94	127
Front lower control arm-to-subframe nut/bolt*	101	137
Shock absorber		
Shock absorber-to-rear crossmember bolt/nut*	129	175
Shock absorber-to-lower link nut/bolt	129	175
Stabilizer bar		
Bushing clamp bolts	25	34
Link nuts	65	88
Subframe mounting bolts	148	201
Wheel lug nuts	See Chapter 1	

2013 and later models

Hub and bearing-to-knuckle bolts	65	88
Radius rod-to-subframe bolt	77	104
Radius rod-to-knuckle bolt/nut*	77	104
Control arms		
Upper control arm pivot bolt nuts*	77	104
Upper control arm-to-rear knuckle pinch bolt/nut	105	142
Rear lower control arm-to-subframe nut*	70	95
Rear lower control arm-to-knuckle bolt/nut*	70	95
Front lower control arm-to-knuckle nut/bolt*	70	95
Front lower control arm-to-subframe nut/bolt*	70	95
Shock absorber		
Shock absorber mount-to-body nuts	17	23
Shock absorber-to-knuckle bolt/nut*	70	95
Shock absorber piston rod-to-mount nut*	41	56
Stabilizer bar		
Bushing clamp nuts	44	60
Link nuts-to-rear arm	66	89
Link nuts-to-bar	76	103
Subframe		
Subframe mounting bolts	114	154
Subframe brace-to-body bolts	35	47
Subframe brace-to-subframe bolts	114	154
Wheel lug nuts	See Chapter 1	

Use new fasteners on installation

Torque specifications

	Ft-lbs (unless otherwise indicated)	Nm

Note: *One foot-pound (ft-lb) of torque is equivalent to 12 inch-pounds (in-lbs) of torque. Torque values below approximately 15-ft-lbs. are expressed in inch-pounds, since most foot-pound torque wrenches are not accurate at these smaller values.*

Steering

	Ft-lbs (unless otherwise indicated)	Nm
Airbag module bolts (2013 and later models)	82 in-lbs	9
Power steering pump rear mounting bracket-to-block bolts (2012 and earlier V6 models)	45	61
Power steering pump bracket-to-pump bolts (2012 and earlier models)	144 in-lbs	16
Power steering pump mounting bolts (2012 and earlier models)		
Long bolt	48	65
Short bolt	21	28
Power steering pump pulley nut (2012 and earlier models)	45	61
Power steering pump pressure line banjo bolt to pump (2012 and earlier models)	54	73
Power steering fluid pressure sensor (2012 and earlier models)	168 in-lbs	19
Steering gear mounting bolts/nuts		
2007 and earlier models	140	190
2008 through 2012 models	135	183
2013 and later models	125	170
Steering wheel nut	25	34
Steering shaft upper pinch bolt	33	45
Steering shaft lower pinch bolt	20	27
Steering column mounting nuts	144 in-lbs	16
Tie-rod end-to-steering knuckle nut*	37	50
Wheel lug nuts	See Chapter 1	

Use new fasteners on installation

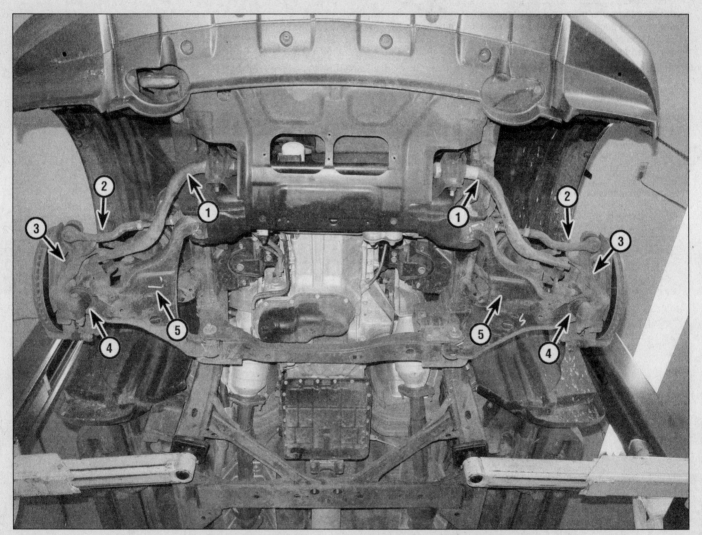

Front suspension and steering components (2012 and earlier models)

1   Stabilizer bar
2   Tie-rod ends
3   Steering knuckles

4   Lower balljoints
5   Lower control arms

Front suspension and steering component (2012 and earlier models) - side view

1	Shock absorber/coil spring	5	Steering knuckle	8	Lower balljoint
2	Stabilizer bar link	6	Lower control arm	9	Upper control arm
3	Stabilizer bar	7	Tie-rod end	10	Upper balljoint
4	Steering gear boot				

Front suspension and steering components 92013 and later models)

1	Strut/coil spring assembly	4	Control arm
2	Balljoint	5	Steering knuckle
3	Tie-rod end		

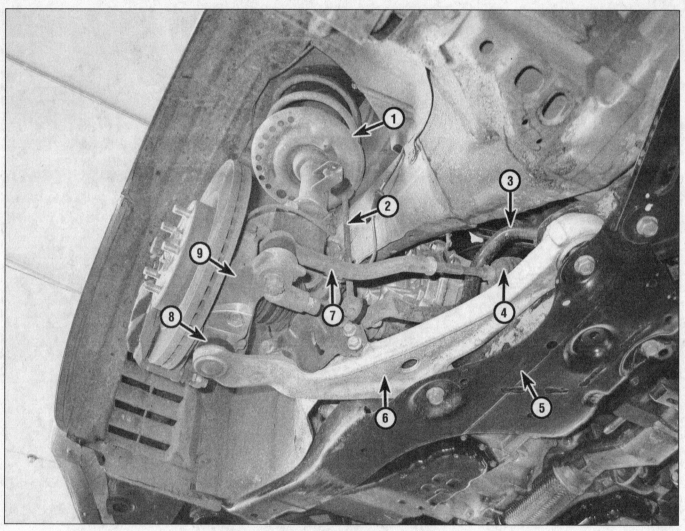

Front suspension components (2013 and later models) - side view

1	Strut/coil spring assembly	4	Steering gear boot	7	Tie-rod end
2	Stabilizer bar link	5	Subframe	8	Balljoint
3	Stabilizer bar	6	Control arm	9	Steering knuckle

Rear suspension components - 2012 and earlier models

1	Stabilizer bar	4	Rear knuckles
2	Front lower control arms	5	Rear lower control arms
3	Lower balljoints	6	Coil spring and coil spring seat

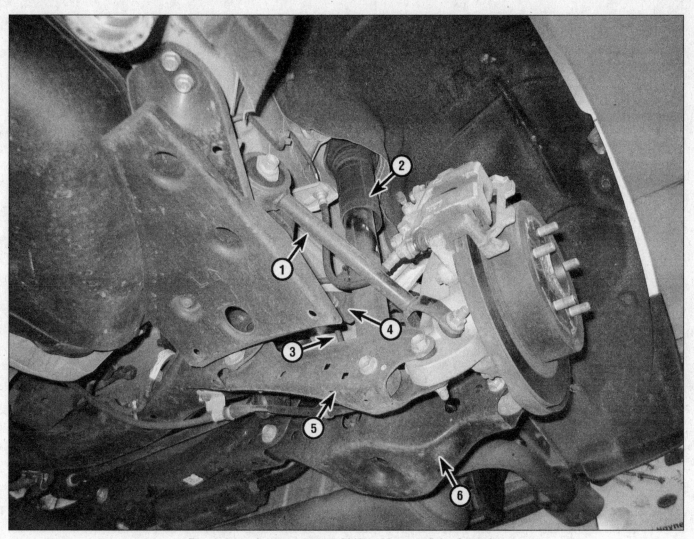

Rear suspension components 2013 and later models - front view

1	Radius rod	3	Stabilizer bar link	5	Front lower control arm
2	Shock absorber	4	Stabilizer bar	6	Rear lower control arm

Rear suspension components 2013 and later models - rear view

1	Upper control arm	3	Rear lower control arm
2	Coil spring	4	Front lower control arm

1 General information

Front suspension

2012 and earlier models

1 The front suspension (**see illustrations**) is fully independent. All models use upper and lower control arms and shock absorber/coil spring assemblies. On all models, a stabilizer bar connected to the frame and to the two lower control arms reduces body roll during cornering.

2013 and later models

2 The front suspension system (**see illustrations**) is a strut/coil spring design. The upper end of each strut is attached to the vehicle body. The lower end of the strut is connected to the upper end of the steering knuckle. The steering knuckle is attached to a balljoint mounted on the outer end of the control arm. The balljoint is an integral part of the control arm; if the balljoint is worn, the control arm must be replaced. A stabilizer bar is used on all models. The bar is attached to the subframe with a pair of clamps and to the struts with link rods.

Rear suspension

3 The rear suspension system (**see illustrations**) uses separate shock absorbers and coil springs, an upper control arm and two lower control arms (front and rear) and, on 2013 and later models, a radius rod at each side. The upper ends of the shocks are attached to the vehicle body and their lower ends are attached to the upper ends of the rear knuckles. The coil springs are positioned between the rear lower control arm and the vehicle body. The lower ends of the knuckles are attached to the outer ends of the control arms. A stabilizer bar is attached to the subframe by a pair of brackets and to the upper control arms by link rods.

4 The rack-and-pinion steering gear is bolted to the rear part of the subframe. The steering gear actuates the tie-rods, which are attached to the steering knuckles. The inner ends of the tie-rods are protected by rubber boots which should be inspected periodically for secure attachment, tears and leaking lubricant (which would indicate failed rack seals).

5 On 2012 and earlier models, the power assist system consists of a belt-driven pump and associated lines and hoses. On 2013 and later models, the power assist system consists of a electric motor-driven pump and associated lines and hoses. The fluid level in the power steering pump reservoir should be checked periodically (see Chapter 1).

6 The steering wheel operates the steering shaft, which actuates the steering gear through universal joints. Looseness in the steering can be caused by wear in the steering shaft universal joints, the steering gear, the tie-rod ends and loose retaining bolts.

7 Frequently, when working on the suspension or steering system components, you may

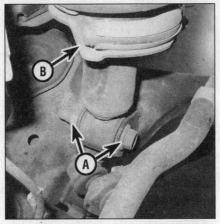

2.4 Shock absorber/coil spring assembly mounting bolt and nut (A); note that the spring end is facing outward (B)

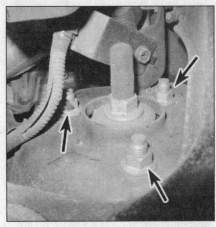

2.5 Shock absorber/coil spring assembly upper mounting nuts. DO NOT remove the nut from the piston rod (the nut in the center)

come across fasteners which seem impossible to loosen. These fasteners on the underside of the vehicle are continually subjected to water, road grime, mud, etc., and can become rusted or frozen, making them extremely difficult to remove. In order to unscrew these stubborn fasteners without damaging them (or other components), be sure to use lots of penetrating oil and allow it to soak in for a while. Using a wire brush to clean exposed threads will also ease removal of the nut or bolt and prevent damage to the threads. Sometimes a sharp blow with a hammer and punch will break the bond between a nut and bolt threads, but care must be taken to prevent the punch from slipping off the fastener and ruining the threads. Heating the stuck fastener and surrounding area with a torch sometimes helps too, but isn't recommended because of the obvious dangers associated with fire. Long breaker bars and extension, or cheater, pipes will increase leverage, but never use an extension pipe on a ratchet - the ratcheting mechanism could be damaged. Sometimes tightening the nut or bolt first will help to break it loose. Fasteners that require drastic measures to remove should always be replaced with new ones.

8 Since most of the procedures dealt with in this Chapter involve jacking up the vehicle and working underneath it, a good pair of jackstands will be needed. A hydraulic floor jack is the preferred type of jack to lift the vehicle, and it can also be used to support certain components during various operations.

Warning: *Never, under any circumstances, rely on a jack to support the vehicle while working on it. Whenever any of the suspension or steering fasteners are loosened or removed they must be inspected and, if necessary, replaced with new ones of the same part number or of original equipment quality and design. Torque Specifications must be followed for proper reassembly and component retention. Never attempt to heat or straighten any suspension or steering components. In*

stead, *replace any bent or damaged part with a new one.*

2 Shock absorber/coil spring assembly (front, 2012 and earlier models) - removal, inspection and installation

Warning: *Always replace shock absorbers in pairs - never replace just one of them.*
Note: *It is possible to replace the shocks or springs individually, but the unit will have to be disassembled by a qualified repair shop with the proper equipment. This will add considerable cost to the project. You can compare the cost of replacing the complete assemblies yourself to the cost of replacing individual components (with the help of a shop).*

Removal

1 Loosen the front wheel lug nuts. Raise the vehicle and support it securely on jackstands (see Chapter 1). Remove the front wheels.

2 Support the lower control arm with a floor jack (this will prevent the suspension from dropping when the shock absorber/coil spring assembly is removed).

3 Remove the stabilizer bar link-to-stabilizer bar bolt (see Section 5). Swing the stabilizer bar down so it is out of the way of the lower shock absorber mounting bolt.

4 Remove the shock absorber lower mounting bolt (**see illustration**).

5 Remove the fasteners that attach the upper end of the shock to the frame (**see illustration**).

6 Turn the steering knuckle outward for clearance, then remove the shock absorber.

Inspection

7 Inspect the shock absorber for leaking fluid, dents, cracks and other damage. Inspect the coil spring for chips and cracks which could cause premature failure. Inspect

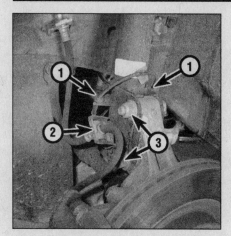

3.2 Strut lower mounting details

1   ABS wheel speed sensor
    harness brackets
2   Brake hose retaining clip
3   Strut-to-steering knuckle nuts/bolts

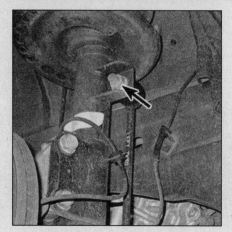

3.4 Stabilizer bar link-to-strut nut

3.8 Strut upper mounting bolts. DO NOT remove the damper shaft nut (the nut in the center)

the spring seats for hardness and general deterioration. If any of the components of the assembly are worn or damaged, have the unit serviced by a qualified repair shop or replace it.

Installation

8   Installation is the reverse of removal, making sure the spring end is facing outward **(see illustration 2.4)**. Tighten the fasteners to the torque listed in this Chapter's Specifications.
Caution: *Before tightening the lower mounting nut/bolt, raise the lower control arm with the floor jack to simulate normal ride height.*
9   Tighten the wheel lug nuts to the torque listed in the Chapter 1 Specifications.

---

3   Strut/coil spring assembly (front, 2013 and later models) - removal, inspection and installation

---

Removal

1   Loosen the front wheel lug nuts, raise the front of the vehicle and support it securely on jackstands. Remove the wheels.
2   Remove the wheel speed sensor **(see illustration)**.
3   Detach the brake hose from the bracket on the strut.
4   Disconnect the stabilizer bar link from the strut **(see illustration)**.
5   Remove the strut-to-knuckle nuts and knock the bolts out with a hammer and punch.
6   Separate the strut from the steering knuckle. Be careful not to overextend the inner CV joint and don't let the knuckle fall outward, as this could damage the brake hose and the ABS speed sensor wiring (if equipped).
7   Remove the cowl cover for access to the top of the struts (see Chapter 11).

8   Support the strut and spring assembly with one hand and remove the three strut upper mounting bolts **(see illustration)**. Remove the assembly out from the fenderwell.

Inspection

9   Check the strut body for leaking fluid, dents, cracks and other obvious damage which would warrant repair or replacement.
10   Check the coil spring for chips or cracks in the spring coating (this will cause premature spring failure due to corrosion). Inspect the spring seat for cuts, hardness and general deterioration.
11   If any undesirable conditions exist, proceed to the strut disassembly procedure (see Section 4).

Installation

12   Guide the strut assembly up into the fenderwell and install the upper mounting bolts, tightening them to the torque listed in this Chapter's Specifications. This is most easily accomplished with the help of an assistant, as the strut is quite heavy and awkward.
Note: *There is a protruding tab on the top insulator that must point outward.*
13   Slide the steering knuckle into the strut flange and insert the bolts. Install the nuts and tighten them to the torque listed in this Chapter's Specifications.
14   The remainder of installation is the reverse of removal. Tighten the stabilizer bar link nut to the torque listed in this Chapter's Specifications. Tighten the wheel lug nuts to the torque listed in the Chapter 1 Specifications.
15   Have the front end alignment checked and, if necessary, adjusted.

---

4   Strut/coil spring assembly (front, 2013 and later models) - replacement

---

1   If the struts or coil springs exhibit the telltale signs of wear (leaking fluid, loss of damp-

ing capability, chipped, sagging or cracked coil springs) explore all options before beginning any work. Strut assemblies complete with springs may be available on an exchange basis, which eliminates much time and work. Whichever route you choose to take, check on the cost and availability of parts before disassembling your vehicle.
Warning: *Disassembling a strut is potentially dangerous. Use only a high-quality spring compressor and carefully follow the manufacturer's instructions furnished with the tool. After removing the coil spring from the strut assembly, set it aside in a safe, isolated area.*
Warning: *To prevent handling irregularities, always replace the struts or coil springs in pairs - never replace just one of them.*

Disassembly

2   Remove the strut and spring assembly (see Section 3). Mount the strut assembly in a vise. Line the vise jaws with wood or rags to prevent damage to the unit and don't tighten the vise excessively. Loosen the rod nut to the end of the threaded portion but DO NOT remove it.
3   Following the tool manufacturer's instructions, install the spring compressor (which can be obtained at most auto parts stores or equipment yards on a daily rental basis) on the spring and compress it sufficiently to relieve all pressure from the upper spring seat **(see illustration)**. This can be verified by wiggling the spring.
4   Remove the piston rod nut **(see illustration)**. Discard the nut. A new one must be used during reassembly.
5   Remove the upper suspension support **(see illustration)**. Inspect the bearing in the suspension support for smooth operation. If it does not turn smoothly, replace the suspension support. Check the rubber portion of the suspension support for cracking and general deterioration. If there is any separation of the rubber, replace it.
6   Lift the spring seat and upper insulator from the piston rod. Check the rubber spring

4.3 Install the spring compressor according to the tool manufacturer's instructions and compress the spring until all pressure is relieved from the upper spring seat

4.4 Remove the piston rod nut

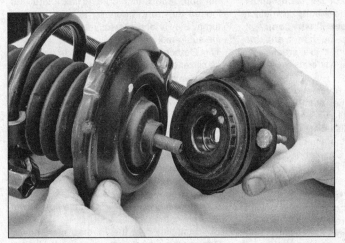

4.5 Remove the upper suspension support mount and spring seat

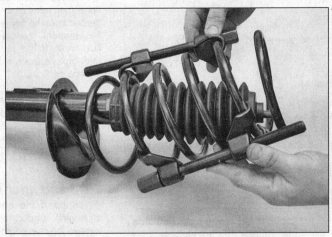

4.7 Remove the compressed spring assembly. Warning: Keep the ends of the spring pointed away from your body

seat for cracking and hardness, replacing it if necessary.

7   Carefully lift the compressed spring from the assembly **(see illustration)** and set it in a safe place.

Warning: *Carry the spring carefully and never place any part of your body near the end of the spring!*

8   Slide the dust boot off the piston rod.

9   Check the lower insulator (if equipped) for wear, cracking and hardness and replace it if necessary.

Reassembly

10   If the lower insulator is being replaced, set it into position with the dropped portion seated in the lowest part of the seat. Extend the damper rod to its full length and install the dust boot.

11   Place the coil spring onto the lower insulator, with the end of the spring resting in the lowest part of the insulator **(see illustration)**. The pin on the insulator will line up with the hole on the strut.

4.11 When installing the spring, make sure the end fits into the recessed portion of the lower seat

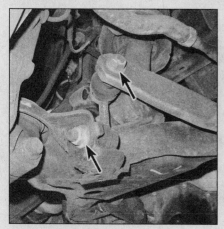

5.3 Stabilizer bar link nuts

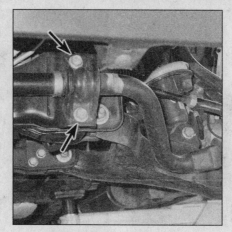

5.4 Stabilizer bar clamp bolts

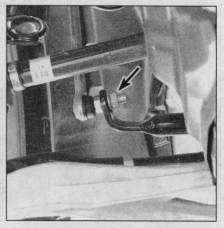

5.17 Remove the nuts securing the stabilizer bar links to the stabilizer bar

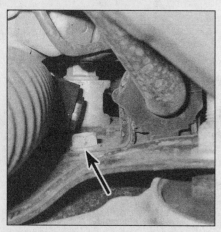

5.18 Stabilizer bar clamp bolts (left side shown, rear bolt not visible)

12   Install the upper insulator and the spring seat. Make sure the marks or arrow on the spring seat and mount insulator are facing out (away from the vehicle), in line with the strut-to-knuckle flange.

13   Install the dust seal and suspension support to the piston rod.

14   Install the piston nut and tighten it to the torque listed in this Chapter's Specifications.

15   Install the strut/coil spring assembly (see Section 3).

---

5   Stabilizer bar (front) - removal and installation

---

1   Loosen the front wheel lug nuts, raise the front of the vehicle and support it securely on jackstands, then remove the wheels.

2   Remove the under-vehicle splash shield and, if equipped, the skid plate.

2012 and earlier models

3   Detach the stabilizer bar links from the stabilizer bar (see illustration).

4   Loosen the stabilizer bar clamp upper bolts, then remove the lower bolts and detach the bar from the frame (see illustration).

5   Inspect the clamp bushings and the link ends. If the bushings are cracked or torn, replace them. If the link ends are loose, replace the links.

6   Installation is the reverse of removal. Replace the stabilizer bar clamp bolts with new ones and tighten all suspension fasteners to the torque values listed in this Chapter's Specifications. Tighten the wheel lug nuts to the torque listed in the Chapter 1 Specifications.

2013 and later models

7   Support the engine from above with an engine support fixture. On 2WD models, remove the rear engine mount bracket.

8   Remove the front section of exhaust pipe (see Chapter 2A , illustration 10.19).

9   On AWD models, remove the driveshaft (see Chapter 8).

10   Separate the control arm balljoint from the steering knuckle (see Section 8).

11   Detach the tie-rod ends from the steering knuckles (see Section 21).

12   Disconnect the electrical connector from the power steering pressure switch.

13   Remove the pinch bolt from the lower steering column (see illustration 23.7) , then separate the shaft from the steering gear. Keep the steering wheel pointed straight ahead and keep the steering gear centered in its travel.

Caution: *Don't allow the steering wheel to turn after the shaft has been disconnected; the airbag spiral cable could become damaged.*

14   Remove the front engine mount upper mounting nut and the rear engine mount through-bolt (this will allow the subframe to be lowered).

15   Free any hoses from clips securing them to the subframe.

16   Mark the position of the subframe to the chassis. Support the subframe with two floor jacks (one positioned on each side). Remove the subframe rear mounting fasteners and loosen the front mounting fasteners a few turns. Slowly and carefully lower the rear of the subframe.

17   Detach the links from the ends of the stabilizer bar (see illustration).

18   Remove the bolts from the stabilizer bar clamps (see illustration).

19   Remove the stabilizer bar from the left side of the vehicle.

20   Inspect the clamp bushings and the link ends. If the bushings are cracked or torn, replace them. If the link ends are loose, replace the links.

Note: *The slit in the bushing should face the front of the vehicle. Install the clamps in the original positions, with the notched hole facing the front of the vehicle.*

21   Installation is the reverse of removal. Replace the subframe fasteners and stabilizer bar clamp bolts with new ones and tighten all suspension and steering fasteners to the torque values listed in this Chapter's Specifications. Tighten the wheel lug nuts to the torque listed in the Chapter 1 Specifications.

---

6   Upper control arm (front) (2012 and earlier models) - removal and installation

---

Note: *The manufacturer recommends using new locknuts on the control arm pivot bolts during installation.*

Removal

1   Loosen the wheel lug nuts, then raise the front of the vehicle and support it securely on jackstands (see Chapter 1). Remove the wheel.

2   Place a jack under the lower control arm and raise it slightly to put tension on the suspension. On the left hand side, remove the pinch bolt from the lower steering gear shaft and position the shaft out of the way (see Section 23).

6.3 The upper balljoint with a puller tool installed

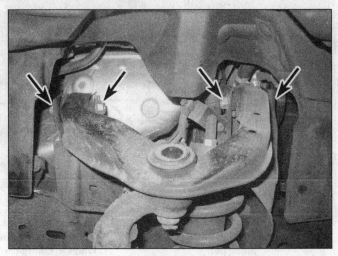

6.4 Upper control arm pivot bolts and nuts 7.5 Lower control arm balljoint pinch bolt/nut (A) and pivot fasteners (B)

3   To disconnect the upper control arm from the steering knuckle, remove the cotter pin, loosen the upper balljoint nut a few turns (don't remove it), install a balljoint separator and break the balljoint loose from the knuckle **(see illustration)**. Remove the nut.

Note: *If you don't have a press-type balljoint removal tool, a picklefork type balljoint separator can be used, but keep in mind that this type of tool will probably destroy the balljoint boot*

Note: *It's a good idea to secure the steering knuckle with wire so that it does not fall outward and cause damage to the brake lines or other components.*

4   Remove the upper control arm pivot fasteners, noting which way the bolts are installed **(see illustration)**. Remove the control arm.

Installation

5   Position the arm in the frame brackets and install the bolts and nuts, but don't tighten them yet.

6   Attach the balljoint to the steering knuckle and tighten the ballstud nut to the torque listed in this Chapter's Specifications. Install a new cotter pin.

Caution: *If necessary, tighten the nut a little more to align the slots in the nut with the hole in the ballstud; don't loosen the nut to insert the cotter pin.*

7   Tighten the control arm pivot bolts/nuts to the torque listed in this Chapter's Specifications.

Caution: *Raise the lower control arm with a floor jack to simulate normal ride height before tightening the upper control arm mounting fasteners.*

8   Reconnect the steering shaft to the steering gear. Tighten the pinch bolt to the torque listed in this Chapter's Specifications.

9   The remainder of installation is the reverse of removal. Tighten the wheel lug nuts to the torque listed in the Chapter 1 Specifications.

10   Have the front end alignment checked and, if necessary, adjusted.

7.5 Lower control arm balljoint pinch bolt/ nut (a) and pivot fasteners (B)

7   Lower control arm (front) (2012 and earlier models) - removal, inspection and installation

Note: *The manufacturer recommends using new locknuts on the control arm pivot bolts and the balljoint pinch bolt during installation.*

Removal

1   Loosen the wheel lug nuts, raise the vehicle and support it securely on jackstands. Remove the wheel.

2   On 4WD models, remove the driveaxle (see Chapter 8).

3   Detach the stabilizer bar link from the lower control arm (see Section 5).

4   Remove the shock absorber lower mounting bolt (see Section 2).

5   Remove the pinch-bolt securing the lower balljoint **(see illustration)** , then use a small puller, or equivalent, to push the ballstud out of the control arm. It's also possible to pry the control arm from the steering knuckle to

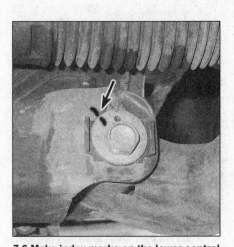

7.6 Make index marks on the lower control arm pivot/adjuster bolts and frame

separate them.

6   Mark the positions of the lower control arm pivot fasteners on both sides relative to the frame, then hold the bolts and remove and discard the locknuts **(see illustration 7.5 and the accompanying illustration)**.

Note: *In most cases, the pivot bolts are cam adjuster type bolts and marking helps preserve the alignment angle during installation. In some cases, vehicles are equipped with non-adjustable bolts and washers. It is recommended that these non-adjustable items be replaced with adjustable ones so camber and caster can be adjusted for proper alignment.*

Inspection

7   Inspect the control arm bushings for hardening, excessive wear and cracks. If they appear to be worn or deteriorated, replace the control arm.

Note: *It may be possible to have the bushing pressed out of the arm by an automotive machine shop or a repair shop that specializes in suspension work. A replacement part may be*

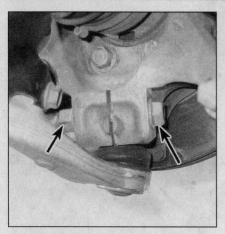

8.2 Remove the nut and balljoint pinch bolt

8.3 Pry the balljoint out of the steering knuckle, taking care to avoid damaging the rubber boot

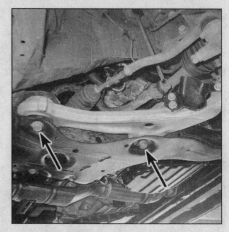

8.4 Control arm bushing bolts

available as an aftermarket (non-OEM) part, but this could not be confirmed at the time of this manual's writing.

Installation

8   Installation is the reverse of removal.
9   Use new locknuts for the balljoint pinch-bolt and the control arm pivot bolts.
10   Align the marks made during removal, then tighten all fasteners to the torque listed in this Chapter's Specifications.
Caution: *Raise the lower control arm with a floor jack to simulate normal ride height before tightening the control arm pivot fasteners.*
11   Tighten the wheel lug nuts to the torque listed in the Chapter 1 Specifications.
12   Have the front wheel alignment checked and, if necessary, adjusted.

8   Control arm (front) (2013 and later models) - removal, inspection and installation

Removal

1   Loosen the front wheel lug nuts, raise the front of the vehicle, support it securely on jackstands and remove the wheel.
Note: *It may be necessary to disconnect the strut from the knuckle (see Section 3) to allow the arm to be separated from the balljoint.*
2   Remove the balljoint pinch bolt **(see illustration)**.
3   Use a prybar to separate the balljoint stud from the steering knuckle **(see illustration)**.
4   Remove the control arm bushing nuts and bolts **(see illustration)**. Remove the control arm. Discard the nuts and bolts. New ones must be used during installation.

Inspection

5   Inspect the front and rear bushings for cracks and tears. If either bushing is damaged

or worn, replace the control arm; the bushings are not replaceable.
6   Inspect the control arm for straightness. If it's bent, replace it. Do not attempt to straighten a bent control arm.

Installation

7   Installation is the reverse of removal. Install new fasteners and tighten them to the torque listed in this Chapter's Specifications.
8   Install the wheel and lug nuts, lower the vehicle and tighten the lug nuts to the torque listed in the Chapter 1 Specifications.

9   Balljoints - replacement

2012 and earlier models

1   The manufacturer states that the balljoint is part of the control arm and the entire control arm must be replaced in the event of a worn balljoint. However, aftermarket balljoints are available. To replace them requires removing the control arm, removing the snap-ring, then using a press to remove the old balljoint out and press the new one in.
Note: *Many auto parts stores will loan or rent special tools such as balljoint presses. Some of these tools allow the repair to be performed on the vehicle by simply disconnecting the balljoint from the steering knuckle for access (the lower control arm must be supported by a floor jack while performing this procedure).*
2   The rear upper control arm balljoint is also a press-fit in the control arm and is retained by a snap-ring, but as of the time of writing, no aftermarket part information is available. Check with your auto parts supplier for availability.

2013 and later models

3   The balljoints are integral parts of the control arms. If they're worn or damaged, the control arm must be replaced (see Section 8).

10   Steering knuckle (2012 and earlier models) - removal and installation

Warning: *Dust created by the brake system is harmful to your health. Never blow it out with compressed air and don't inhale any of it. Do not, under any circumstances, use petroleum-based solvents to clean brake parts. Use brake system cleaner only.*
1   Loosen the wheel lug nuts, raise the vehicle and support it securely on jackstands and remove the wheel.
2   Remove the wheel speed sensor, brake caliper and brake disc (see Chapter 9). Don't disconnect the brake hose. Hang the caliper out of the way with a piece of wire.
3   Remove the hub and bearing assembly (see Section 12).
4   Disconnect the tie-rod end from the steering knuckle (see Section 21).
5   Disconnect the balljoints from the steering knuckle (see Section 6 or 7) and remove the steering knuckle.
6   Installation is the reverse of removal. Note the following:

 a) *Tighten the balljoint and tie-rod end fasteners to the torque values listed in this Chapter's Specifications and use new cotter pins.*
 b) *Tighten the caliper mounting bracket bolts and caliper mounting bolts to the torque values listed in the Chapter 9 Specifications.*
 c) *On 4WD models, tighten the driveaxle hub nut to the torque values listed in the Chapter 8 Specifications and use a new cotter pin.*
 d) *Tighten the wheel lug nuts to the torque listed in the Chapter 1 Specifications.*

Note: *When installing a cotter pin, tighten the nut a little more to align the slots in the nut with the hole in the ballstud; don't loosen the nut to insert the cotter pin.*

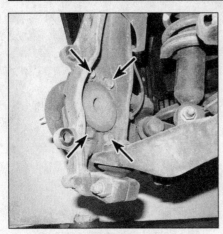

12.4a Hub and bearing assembly mounting bolts - 2012 and earlier models (2WD shown)

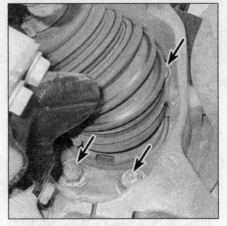

12.4b Front hub and bearing mounting bolts (fourth bolt not visible in this photo) - 2013 and later models

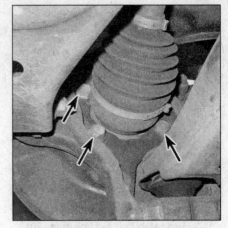

12.10a Rear hub and bearing mounting bolts (fourth bolt not visible in this photo) - 2012 and earlier models

11 Steering knuckle (2013 and later models) - removal and installation

Warning: *Dust created by the brake system is harmful to your health. Never blow it out with compressed air and don't inhale any of it. Do not, under any circumstances, use petroleum-based solvents to clean brake parts. Use brake system cleaner only.*

Removal

1 Loosen the wheel lug nuts, raise the vehicle and support it securely on jackstands. Remove the wheel.
2 Remove the cotter pin, then remove the driveaxle/hub nut (see Chapter 8).
3 Remove the brake disc (see Chapter 9).
4 Remove the wheel speed sensor from the knuckle (see Chapter 9).
5 Separate the tie-rod end from the steering knuckle (see Section 21).
6 Remove the strut-to-steering knuckle nuts, but don't remove the bolts yet (see Section 3).
7 Separate the control arm balljoint from the steering knuckle (see Section 8).
8 Separate the driveaxle from the steering knuckle (see Chapter 8). Support the end of the driveaxle with a length of wire so the CV joints aren't overextended.
9 Remove the strut-to-knuckle bolts and separate the knuckle from the strut.
10 Remove the hub-to-steering knuckle bolts (see Section 12), then detach the two components and remove the brake disc splash shield.

Installation

11 Assemble the hub, knuckle and splash shield. Tighten the bolts to the torque listed in this Chapter's Specifications.
12 Lubricate the splines of the driveaxle with multi-purpose grease. Guide the knuckle and hub assembly into position, inserting the driveaxle into the hub.

13 Push the knuckle into the strut flange and install the bolts and nuts, but don't tighten them yet.
14 Attach the control arm balljoint to the steering knuckle (see Section 8).
15 Attach the tie-rod end to the steering knuckle arm (see Section 21). Tighten the tie-rod end nut and the strut-to-knuckle nuts to the torque listed in this Chapter's Specifications. Install a new cotter pin through the tie-rod end ballstud.
Note: *When installing a cotter pin, tighten the nut a little more to align the slots in the nut with the hole in the ballstud; don't loosen the nut to insert the cotter pin.*
16 Place the brake disc on the hub and install the caliper (see Chapter 9).
17 Install the driveaxle/hub nut and tighten it to the torque listed in the Chapter 8 Specifications.
18 Install the wheel and lug nuts. Lower the vehicle and tighten the lug nuts to the torque listed in the Chapter 1 Specifications.

12 Hub and bearing assembly - removal and installation

Front

1 Loosen the wheel lug nuts, raise the front of the vehicle and support it securely on jackstands. Remove the wheel, then loosen the driveaxle/hub nut (see Chapter 8).
2 Remove the brake disc (see Chapter 9). Do not disconnect the brake hose. Support the brake caliper with wire so there's no tension on the hose. Detach the wheel speed sensor from the steering knuckle (see Chapter 9).
3 Break loose the driveaxle from the hub (see Chapter 8).
4 Remove the hub/bearing assembly mounting bolts from the rear of the steering knuckle **(see illustrations)**.
5 Remove the hub/bearing assembly from the steering knuckle.

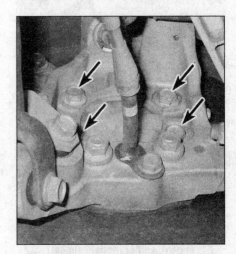

12.10b Rear hub and bearing mounting bolts - 2013 and later models (FWD model shown)

Note: *If the driveaxle splines stick in the hub, push the driveaxle out of the hub with a two-jaw puller. Once the driveaxle has been freed from the hub, support it with a length of wire to prevent over-extension of the inner CV joint.*
6 Installation is the reverse of removal. Tighten the fasteners to the torque listed in this Chapter's Specifications.

Rear

7 Loosen the wheel lug nuts, raise the rear of the vehicle and support it securely on jackstands (see Chapter 0). Remove the wheel.
8 On 4WD/AWD models, remove the cotter pin then loosen, but do not remove, the driveaxle/hub nut (see Chapter 8).
9 Remove the brake disc (see Chapter 9). Do not disconnect the brake lines. Support the brake caliper with wire so there's no tension on the brake lines. Detach the wheel speed sensor from the rear knuckle (see Chapter 9).
10 Remove the hub and bearing assembly mounting bolts **(see illustrations)**.

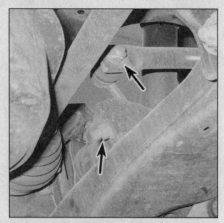

13.2a Rear stabilizer bar link nuts - 2012 and earlier models

13.2b Rear stabilizer bar link nuts - 2013 and later models

13.3 Rear stabilizer bar clamp bolts

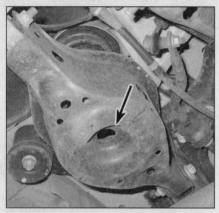

14.5 Support the rear lower control arm with a floor jack positioned under the spring pocket (2013 and later models shown, earlier models similar)

15.3 Mark the position of the cam to the subframe before loosening the bolt - set it in the same position when you assemble it

15.4 Rear lower control arm-to-knuckle fasteners (A) and arm-to-subframe fasteners (B)

11   Remove the hub and bearing assembly. **Note:** *If the driveaxle splines stick in the hub, push the driveaxle out of the hub with a two-jaw puller. Once the driveaxle has been freed from the hub, support it with a length of wire to prevent over-extension of the inner CV joint.*
12   Installation is the reverse of removal. Tighten the fasteners to the torque listed in this Chapter's Specifications.

13   Stabilizer bar (rear) - removal and installation

1   Raise the vehicle and support it securely on jackstands.
2   Remove the nuts from the link rods at the stabilizer bar ends **(see illustrations)**.
3   Remove the bushing clamp bolts **(see illustration)**, then remove the stabilizer bar.
4   Inspect all clamp bushings. If they're cracked or torn, replace them.
5   Installation is the reverse of removal. Tighten all fasteners to the torques listed in this Chapter's Specifications.

14   Knuckle (rear) - removal and installation

1   Loosen the rear wheel lug nuts. Raise the rear of the vehicle and support it securely on jackstands. Block the front wheels to prevent the vehicle from rolling. Remove the wheel.
2   Remove the brake caliper and disc (see Chapter 9).
3   Remove the hub and bearing assembly (see Section 12).
4   Remove the brake backing plate.
5   Support the rear lower control arm with a floor jack positioned under the coil spring pocket **(see illustration)**.
Warning: *The jack must remain in this position throughout the entire procedure.*
6   On 2013 and later models, detach the radius rod from the knuckle (see Section 18).
7   Disconnect the front and rear lower control arms from the knuckle (see Section 17).
8   Disconnect the upper control arm from the knuckle (see Section 17).
9   Remove the knuckle from the vehicle.
10   Installation is the reverse of removal. Tighten all fasteners to the torque listed in this

Chapter's Specifications.
Caution: *Before tightening the radius arm fasteners, the lower control arm-to-knuckle fasteners and the shock absorber lower mounting fasteners, raise the rear lower control arm with the floor jack to simulate normal ride height.*

15   Coil springs (rear) - removal and installation

Warning: *To prevent handling irregularities, always replace the coil springs in pairs - never replace just one of them.*
1   Loosen the rear wheel lug nuts, raise the rear of the vehicle, support it securely on jackstands and remove the wheels.
2   Position a floor jack under the rear lower control arm and raise the arm slightly **(see illustration 14.5)**.
3   Mark the relationship of the adjusting cam to the subframe **(see illustration)**, then loosen the bolt for the rear lower control arm at the subframe. Also mark the position of the coil spring to the subframe.
4   Detach the rear lower control arm from the knuckle **(see illustration)**.

15.6 Slowly lower the rear lower control arm until the spring is no longer compressed

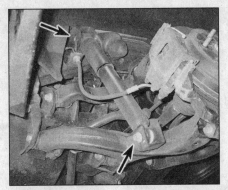

16.4 Rear shock absorber mounting fasteners - 2012 and earlier models

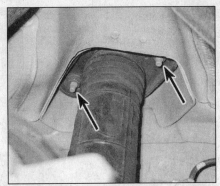

16.5a On 2013 and later models, remove these nuts from the top of the rear shock absorber...

16.5b... then remove the lower mounting bolt

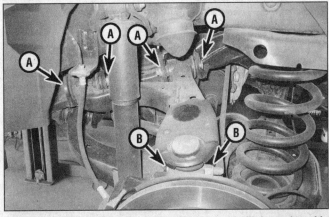

17.4 Upper control arm pivot fasteners (A) and balljoint-to-knuckle fasteners (B)

5   Slowly lower the floor jack until the coil spring is fully extended.

6   Remove the coil spring, the rubber mount and the rubber seal (see illustration).

7   Installation is the reverse of removal, noting the following points:

a) *Raise the rear lower control arm with a floor jack until it is at normal right height, then tighten the control arm bolt/nuts to the torque listed in this Chapter's Specifications. Align the marks on the adjusting cam and the subframe before tightening the fasteners.*

b) *Tighten the wheel lug nuts to the torque listed in the Chapter 1 Specifications.*

16   Shock absorbers (rear) - removal and installation

Warning: *Always replace the shock absorbers in pairs - never replace just one of them.*

1   Loosen the rear wheel lug nuts. Raise the rear of the vehicle and support it securely on jackstands. Block the front wheels to prevent the vehicle from rolling.

2   Remove the rear wheel.

3   On 2012 and earlier models, support the front lower control arm with a floor jack placed near the outer end. On 2013 and later models, support the rear lower control arm with a floor jack placed under the coil spring pocket.

Warning: *The jack must remain in this position until the shock absorber is reinstalled.*

4   On 2012 and earlier models, remove the upper and lower mounting bolts, then remove the shock absorber (see illustration).

5   On 2013 and later models, remove the shock absorber upper mounting nuts and the lower mounting bolt, then remove the shock absorber (see illustrations).

6   Installation is the reverse of removal, noting the following points:

a) *Raise the lower control arm with the jack to simulate normal ride height, then tighten the mounting fasteners to the torque listed in this Chapter's Specifications.*

b) *Tighten the wheel lug nuts to the torque listed in the Chapter 1 Specifications.*

17   Rear suspension control arms and rear subframe - removal and installation

Rear suspension control arms - 2012 and earlier models

1   Loosen the wheel lug nuts, raise the rear of the vehicle and support it securely on jackstands. Remove the wheel.

Upper control arm

2   Support the front lower control arm with a floor jack.

Warning: *The jack must stay in this position throughout the entire procedure.*

3   Remove the shock absorber (see Section 16). Also detach the stabilizer bar link from the arm.

Note: *Depending on your selection of tools, it isn't absolutely necessary to remove the shock absorber. With the right socket and extension combination or a flex-head socket wrench, the upper control arm pivot bolt heads heads can be held stationary while the nuts are loosened, and there is clearance for the bolts to be removed.*

4   Remove the upper control arm balljoint-to-knuckle fasteners (see illustration). Pry the ballstud from the knuckle until it is loose. Be careful not to damage the balljoint boot if the arm is to be reused.

5   Remove the upper control arm pivot fasteners and detach the arm from the subframe.

6   Installation is the reverse of removal. Tighten the upper control arm pivot fasteners and the balljoint-to-knuckle fasteners to the torque listed in this Chapter's Specifications.

17.9 Front lower control arm pivot fasteners (A) and balljoint-to-knuckle fasteners (B)

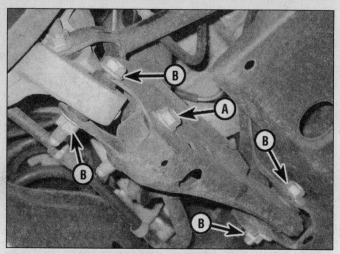

17.23 Shock absorber lower mounting bolt (A) and front lower control arm fasteners (B)

17.29 Upper control arm balljoint pinch bolt/nut

Rear suspension control arms - 2013 and later models

17   Loosen the rear wheel lug nuts. Raise the rear of the vehicle and support it securely on jackstands. Remove the wheel.

Rear lower control arm

18   Remove the coil spring (see Section 15).
19   Remove the adjusting cam bolt and nut, then remove the arm.
20   Installation is the reverse of removal, noting the following points:

a) *Raise the rear lower suspension link with a floor jack until it is at normal ride height, then tighten the suspension link bolt/nuts to the torque listed in this Chapter's Specifications.*
b) *Tighten the wheel lug nuts to the torque listed in the Chapter 1 Specifications.*
c) *Have the wheel alignment checked and, if necessary, adjusted.*

Front lower control arm

21   Support the rear lower control arm with a floor jack placed under the coil spring pocket.
Warning: *The jack must remain in this position until the arm is reinstalled.*
22   Mark the relationship of the adjusting cam to the subframe **(see illustration 15.3)**.
23   Remove the shock absorber lower mounting bolt **(see illustration)**.
24   . Remove the front lower control arm-to-subframe mounting bolt/nut and the arm-to-knuckle mounting bolt/nut, then remove the arm.
25   Installation is the reverse of removal, noting the following points:

a) *Raise the rear lower control arm with the floor jack until it is at normal ride height, then tighten the control arm bolt/nuts and the shock absorber bolt to the torque listed in this Chapter's Specifications. Align the marks on the adjusting cam and the subframe before tightening the nut.*

Tighten the wheel lug nuts to the torque listed in the Chapter 1 Specifications. Have the wheel alignment checked and, if necessary, adjusted.
Caution: *Raise the lower control arm with the floor jack to simulate normal ride height before tightening the link's mounting fasteners.*

Front lower control arm

7   Support the rear lower control arm with a floor jack placed under the spring pocket.
Warning: *The jack must stay in this position throughout the entire procedure.*
8   Remove the shock absorber lower mounting bolt and detach the shock from the control arm (see Section 16).
9   Remove the front lower control arm balljoint-to-knuckle fasteners **(see illustration)**.
10   Mark the relationship of the control arm's adjusting cam bolt to the subframe **(see illustration 15.3)**.
11   Remove the control arm's mounting fasteners and remove the arm. Use a soft hammer or prybar to separate the arm from the rear knuckle. Be careful not to damage the balljoint boot.
12   Installation is the reverse of removal.

Place the adjusting cam bolt back in the same position to restore the rear alignment to its original setting. Tighten the mounting fasteners to the torque listed in this Chapter's Specifications. Tighten the wheel lug nuts to the torque listed in the Chapter 1 Specifications. Have the wheel alignment checked and, if necessary, adjusted.
Note: *Raise the lower control arm with a floor jack to simulate normal ride height before tightening the link's mounting fasteners.*

Rear lower control arm

13   Remove the coil spring (see Section 15).
14   Remove the adjusting cam bolt and nut, then remove the arm.
15   Installation is the reverse of removal.
16   Tighten the mounting fasteners to the torque listed in this Chapter's Specifications. Tighten the wheel lug nuts to the torque listed in the Chapter 1 Specifications. Have the wheel alignment checked and, if necessary, adjusted.
Note: *Raise the lower link with a floor jack to simulate normal ride height before tightening the link's mounting fasteners.*

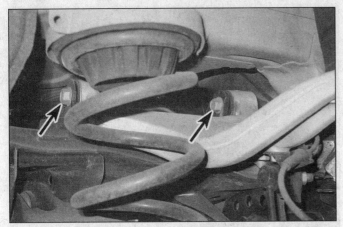

17.30 Upper control arm pivot bolts

18.2 Rear radius rod pivot bolts and nut

b) *Tighten the wheel lug nuts to the torque listed in the Chapter 1 Specifications.*

c) *Have the wheel alignment checked and, if necessary, adjusted.*

Upper control arm

26　Support the rear lower control arm with a floor jack placed under the coil spring pocket.

27　Detach the wheel speed sensor wiring harness from the control arm.

28　Detach the stabilizer bar link from the bracket on the arm (see Section 13).

29　Remove the nut and pivot bolt securing the control arm balljoint to the rear knuckle **(see illustration)**, then pry the balljoint out of the knuckle.

Warning: *Discard the nut; a new one must be used during installation.*

Caution: *Be careful not to damage the balljoint boot.*

Caution: *Don't allow the knuckle to swing outward, as this could strain the wheel speed sensor harness.*

30　Remove the control pivot bolts/nuts, then remove the link **(see illustration)**.

Warning: *Discard the nuts; new ones must be used during installation.*

31　Installation is the reverse of removal. Tighten the control arm fasteners to the torque values listed in this Chapter's Specifications. Tighten the wheel lug nuts to the torque listed in the Chapter 1 Specifications.

Caution: *Raise the lower control arm with a floor jack to simulate normal ride height before tightening the control arm pivot fasteners.*

Rear suspension subframe

32　Loosen the rear wheel lug nuts, then raise the rear of the vehicle and support it securely on jackstands. Remove the wheels.

33　Remove the spare tire.

34　Remove the brake calipers without disconnecting the hoses, then hang them out of the way with a piece of wire so the brake hoses aren't stressed (see Chapter 9).

35　Remove the rear portion of the exhaust system.

36　Remove the rear wheel speed sensors and the wiring harnesses (see Chapter 9).

37　Remove the rear stabilizer bar (see Section 13).

38　On RWD/AWD models, remove the rear differential (see Chapter 8).

39　On 2012 and earlier models, remove the bolts that connect the seat belt latch anchor to the floor pan (near the right front side of the differential housing.

40　Disconnect the parking brake cables from the rear subframe.

41　Remove the coil springs and the rear lower control arms (see Sections 16 and 18).

42　Unbolt the lower ends of the shock absorbers from the front lower suspension arms (see Section 16).

43　Support the rear suspension subframe with two floor jacks (one on each side).

44　Remove the subframe front corner braces.

45　Remove the remaining subframe-to-chassis braces. Carefully lower the jacks until the subframe and the attached suspension components are clear of the body.

Note: *On 2012 and earlier models, slowly lower the jack supporting the rear subframe until the fuel filler tube bracket fasteners can be accessed, then remove the fasteners and disconnect the fuel filler tube bracket from the subframe.*

46　The suspension arms can now be removed if necessary.

47　Installation is the reverse of removal, noting the following points:

a) *When raising the rear subframe, use the locating pins to align the rear subframe to the vehicle body.*

b) *With the rear suspension supported by jackstands, raise the lower suspension arm with a floor jack until it is at normal ride height, then tighten the pivot bolt nuts to the torque listed in this Chapter's Specifications.*

c) *Tighten all other fasteners to the torques listed in this Chapter's Specifications.*

d) *Tighten the brake fasteners to the torque listed in the Chapter 9 Specifications.*

e) *Tighten the wheel lug nuts to the torque listed in the Chapter 1 Specifications.*

18 Radius rod (2013 and later models) - removal and installation

1　Loosen the rear wheel lug nuts. Raise the rear of the vehicle and support it securely on jackstands. Block the front wheels to prevent the vehicle from rolling. Remove the wheel.

2　Remove the radius rod-to-subframe mounting bolt and the radius rod-to-knuckle mounting bolt/nut **(see illustration)**.

3　Remove the radius rod from the vehicle.

4　Installation is the reverse of removal, noting the following points:

a) *Raise the rear lower control arm with a floor jack until it is at normal ride height, then tighten the radius rod fasteners to the torque listed in this Chapter's Specifications.*

b) *Tighten the wheel lug nuts to the torque listed in the Chapter 1 Specifications.*

19 Subframe (front, 2013 and later models) - removal and installation

Note: *The subframe can be removed with other components still attached. Parts such as the control arms and the stabilizer bar can be left attached to the subframe if they are first detached from the steering knuckles and stabilizer bar links.*

1　Disconnect the cable from the negative terminal of the battery (see Chapter 5).

2　Loosen the front wheel lug nuts. Raise the vehicle and support it securely on jackstands. Be sure that it's low enough to get an engine hoist over the engine compartment yet high enough to work comfortably under the vehicle. Remove the front wheels.

Note: *The jackstands must be placed away from the subframe and the suspension components to allow the subframe to be lowered.*

3　Attach an engine support fixture to the engine or attach an engine hoist to support

19.11 Typical front subframe mounting bolts and rear braces - 2013 and later models only

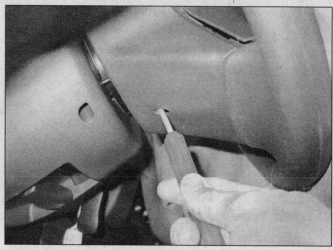

20.3 Use a blunt tool (like a punch), inserted into the hole in the bottom of the steering wheel to push the airbag retaining clip up

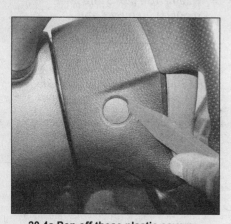

20.4a Pop off these plastic covers...

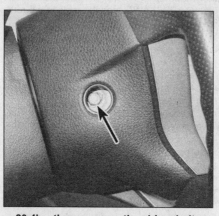

20.4b... then unscrew the airbag bolts

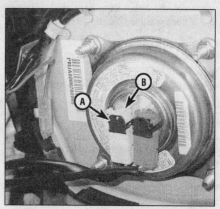

20.5 Pry up the locking clip (A), then detach the electrical connector (B) from each terminal

the engine and transaxle (see Chapter 2C).

4   Remove the air duct and any lower engine splash shields from the bottom of the vehicle.

5   Raise the engine slightly with the hoist or support fixture to take weight from the mounts, then disconnect the engine mounts from the subframe.

6   Disconnect the steering shaft from the steering gear (see Section 23). Don't turn the steering wheel or the steering components, or the steering wheel and steering gear will have to be centered.

7   Remove the front portion of the exhaust system.

8   Disconnect the fluid lines from the power steering gear.

9   Detach the stabilizer bar links from the stabilizer bar (see Section 5).

10   Detach the lower control arms from the steering knuckles (see Section 8).

11   Remove the two rear corner subframe braces **(see illustration)**.

12   Verify that all necessary components are disconnected from the subframe. Make sure that the subframe isn't supporting the weight of the engine or any other components.

13   Place two jacks under the subframe to support it. Remove the subframe mounting bolts, then carefully lower the subframe to the ground.

14   Installation is the reverse of removal.

15   Reconnect the battery and perform the necessary re-learn procedures (see Chapter 5).

16   Have the front wheel alignment checked and, if necessary, adjusted.

20   Steering wheel - removal and installation

Warning: *The models covered by this manual are equipped with Supplemental Restraint Systems (SRS), more commonly known as airbags. Always disarm the airbag system before working in the vicinity of any airbag system component to avoid the possibility of accidental deployment of the airbag, which could cause personal injury (see Chapter 12). Do not use a memory saving device to preserve the PCM's memory when working on or near airbag system components.*

Removal

1   The front wheels must be in the straight-ahead position, and the key removed before beginning the procedure.

2   Disconnect the cable from the negative terminal of the battery (see Chapter 5).

3   On 2012 and earlier models, push in the airbag retaining clip, using a blunt tool going straight up in the hole in the underside of the steering **(see illustration)**.

4   On 2013 and later models, pry off the steering wheel side covers, then remove the airbag bolts **(see illustrations)**.

Warning: *The manufacturer recommends replacing these bolts with new ones (of original part number) whenever they are removed.*

5   Remove the airbag module and disconnect the electrical connectors **(see illustration)**. Note how the wiring is routed, any wiring clips and the direction of all of the electrical connectors.

Note: *Use a small screwdriver to lift the lock button on each connector before trying to disconnect them.*

20.7 If your vehicle doesn't have steering wheel alignment marks like these, make your own

20.10 Use a steering wheel puller to break it loose from the steering shaft

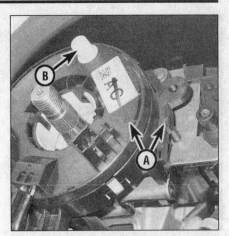

20.11 These two arrows (A) on the spiral cable housing will be aligned when it's centered; the white locating pin (B) must be at the top (2012 and earlier models shown, later models similar, but the arrows are located at the 8 o'clock position)

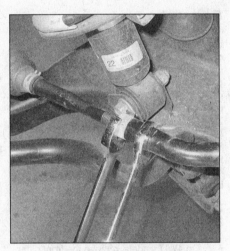

21.2a Loosen the jam nut...

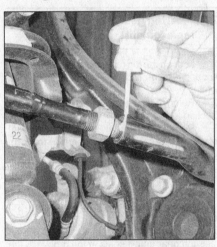

21.2b... then mark the position of the tie-rod end on the threaded part of the tie-rod

6   Set the airbag module out of the way. **Warning:** *Handle the airbag module with care, carry the module with the trim cover side facing away from your body and store it in a safe location with the trim side facing up. See the precautions in Chapter 12.*

7   Remove the steering wheel retaining nut, then mark the relationship of the steering wheel to the steering shaft (if there are no factory alignment marks) **(see illustration)**.

8   On 2012 and earlier models, disconnect the electrical connectors for the steering wheel switches and heated steering wheel, if equipped.

9   On 2013 and later models, remove the steering wheel switches.

10   Use a steering wheel puller to separate the steering wheel from the steering shaft **(see illustration)**. When removing the wheel, make sure the electrical leads for the airbag module and the cruise control system don't snag on the wheel.

Warning: *Do not turn the steering shaft while the steering wheel is removed.*
Caution: *Do not hammer on the steering wheel or shaft to break it loose.*

Installation

11   Verify that the front wheels are pointing straight ahead. If the spiral cable for the airbag has been removed and/or its center position lost, turn the spiral cable clockwise by hand until it becomes hard to turn (don't apply too much force), then rotate it about two turns counterclockwise until the marks align and the location pin is straight up at the 12 o'clock position **(see illustration)**.

12   Pull the electrical leads for the airbag module and the cruise control system through the steering wheel and install the wheel, aligning the marks as you do so. Make sure the spiral cable pin is properly engaged with the corresponding hole in the back of the steering wheel.

13   On 2012 and earlier models, reconnect the steering wheel switches and the heated steering wheel connector.

14   On 2013 and later models, reinstall the steering wheel switches.

15   Install the steering wheel retaining nut and tighten it to the torque listed in this Chapter's Specifications.

16   On 2012 and earlier models, connect the airbag connectors, push in their locking tabs, then push the airbag module onto the steering wheel until the mounting clips lock it in place. The wiring must be installed exactly as noted during removal.

17   On 2013 and later models, install the airbag module, tightening the bolts to the torque listed in this Chapter's Specifications. The wiring must be installed exactly as noted during removal. Install the covers.

18   Reconnect the battery and perform the necessary re-learn procedures (see Chapter 5).

19   Verify that the airbag circuit is operational by turning the ignition key to the On or Start position. The AIR BAG warning light should illuminate for a few seconds, then turn off.

21   Tie-rod ends - removal and installation

Removal

1   Loosen the wheel lug nuts. Raise the front of the vehicle, support it securely on jackstands, then remove the front wheel.

2   Loosen the jam nut enough to mark the position of the tie-rod end in relation to the threads **(see illustrations)**.

3   Remove the cotter pin and loosen, but don't remove, the nut on the tie-rod end stud.

4   Disconnect the tie-rod end from the

21.4 Install a small puller to separate the tie-rod end from the steering knuckle

22.3 The outer end of the boot is secured by a spring clamp (A) that can be slid off by pinching the ends together; the inner end of the boot is retained by a clamp (B) that must be cut off and discarded

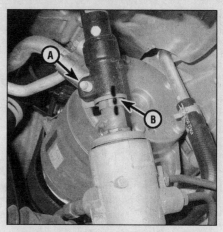

23.7 Steering shaft lower pinch bolt (A) and index marks (B)

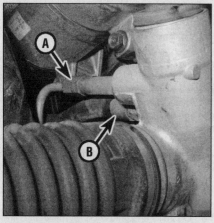

23.8 Power steering gear pressure line (A) and return hose (B)

steering knuckle arm with a puller (see illustration). Remove the nut and separate the tie-rod.

5   Unscrew the tie-rod end from the steering rod.

Installation

6   Thread the tie-rod end on to the marked position and insert the tie-rod stud into the steering knuckle arm. Tighten the jam nut securely.

7   Install the nut on the ballstud and tighten it to the torque listed in this Chapter's Specifications. Install a new cotter pin.

Caution: *If necessary, tighten the nut a little more to align the slots in the nut with the hole in the ballstud; don't loosen the nut to insert the cotter pin.*

8   Install the wheel and lug nuts. Lower the vehicle and tighten the lug nuts to the torque listed in Chapter 1 Specifications.

9   Have the wheel alignment checked, and if necessary, adjusted.

22   Steering gear boots - replacement

1   Loosen the lug nuts, raise the vehicle and support it securely on jackstands. Remove the wheel.

2   Remove the tie-rod end and jam nut (see Section 21).

3   Remove the outer steering gear boot clamp with a pair of pliers (see illustration). Cut off the inner boot clamp with a pair of diagonal cutters. Slide off the boot.

4   Before installing the new boot, wrap the threads on the end of the steering rod with tape so the small end of the new boot isn't damaged.

5   Slide the new boot into position on the steering gear until it seats in the groove in the steering rod and install new clamps.

6   Remove the tape and install the tie-rod end (see Section 21).

7   Install the wheel and lug nuts. Lower the vehicle and tighten the lug nuts to the torque listed in the Chapter 1 Specifications.

8   Have the wheel alignment checked, and if necessary, adjusted by a dealer service department or an alignment shop.

23   Steering gear - removal and installation

Warning: *The models covered by this manual are equipped with Supplemental Restraint Systems (SRS), more commonly known as airbags. Always disarm the airbag system before working in the vicinity of any airbag system component to avoid the possibility of accidental deployment of the airbag, which could cause personal injury (see Chapter 12). Do not use a memory saving device to preserve the PCM's memory when working on or near airbag system components.*

Removal

1   Loosen the front wheel lug nuts, raise the front of the vehicle and support it securely on jackstands. Make sure the wheels are pointed straight ahead, then use the seat belt or some rope to tie the steering wheel in this position. Apply the parking brake and remove the wheels.

2   Remove the inner fender splash shields (see Chapter 11).

3   Drain the power steering fluid (see Chapter 1).

4   Separate the tie-rod ends from the steering knuckle arms (see Section 21).

2012 and earlier models

5   Remove the engine splash shield from under the vehicle.

6   On 4WD models, remove the front differential assembly (see Chapter 8).

7   Mark the relationship of the steering shaft to the steering gear input shaft, then remove the pinch-bolt (see illustration).

Warning: *Do not turn the steering wheel while the steering gear is removed. If the steering wheel is inadvertently turned, remove the steering wheel and center the spiral cable (see Section 20). To prevent the steering wheel from turning, loop the seat belt through the steering wheel and fasten it into its latch.*

Caution: *Do not disturb the small plastic cap on the steering gear input shaft.*

8   Place a drain pan under the steering gear. Using a flare-nut wrench, disconnect the pressure and return fluid lines at the steering gear and allow the fluid to drain (see illustration).

9   On 2WD models, remove the front stabilizer bar brackets and lower the bar for clearance (see Section 5).

10   Remove the steering gear mounting fasteners, then remove the steering gear (see illustration).

23.10 Steering gear mounting fasteners

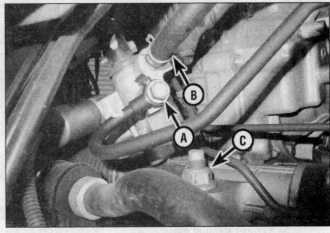

23.11 Disconnect the high pressure line (A) and the return hose (B) - (C) is the left mounting bolt and nut

2013 and later models

11   Place a drain pan under the steering gear, then disconnect the fluid lines **(see illustration)**. Plug the ends to prevent contamination.

12   Remove the rear engine mount support bracket. On AWD models, the complete rear engine mount must be removed (see Chapter 2A).

13   Remove the front portion of the exhaust system (see Chapter 2A, illustration 10.19).

14   On AWD models, remove the driveshaft (see Chapter 8).

15   Mark the relationship of the steering shaft to the steering gear. Remove the pinch bolt from the lower steering shaft **(see illustration)**, then separate the shaft from the steering gear. Keep the steering wheel pointed straight ahead.

Warning: *Do not turn the steering wheel while the steering gear is removed. If the steering wheel is inadvertently turned, remove the steering wheel and center the spiral cable (see Section 20). To prevent the steering wheel from turning, loop the seat belt through the steering wheel and fasten it into its latch.*

16   Remove the stabilizer bar (see Section 5).

17   On AWD models, all hydraulic lines must be removed from the steering gear to allow for enough clearance between the gear and the subframe.

18   Remove the steering gear mounting bolts and maneuver the steering gear out from the left-side wheelwell.

Installation

Note: *Make sure the steering gear is centered from side to side before installing it.*

19   Installation is the reverse of removal. Note the following:

a) *Install the bolts and tighten them to the torque listed in this Chapter's Specifications.*

b) *Connect the tie-rod ends to the steering knuckle arms (see Section 21).*

23.15 Remove the pinch bolt from the lower steering shaft U-joint

c) *Install the steering column pinch bolt and tighten it to the torque listed in this Chapter's Specifications.*

d) *Connect the power steering pressure and return hoses to the steering gear and fill the power steering pump reservoir with the recommended fluid (see Chapter 1).*

e) *Install the wheels and lug nuts, then lower the vehicle and tighten the lug nuts to the torque listed in the Chapter 1 Specifications.*

f) *Bleed the steering system (see Section 26).*

g) *Have the wheel alignment checked, and if necessary, adjusted.*

24   Power steering pump - removal and installation

Warning: *The air conditioning system is under high pressure. Do not loosen any fittings or remove any components until after the system has been discharged. Air conditioning refrigerant should be properly discharged into an EPA-approved container at a dealer service department or an automotive air conditioning repair facility. Always wear eye protection*

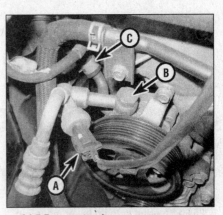

24.7 Power steering pressure sensor electrical connector (A), pressure line fitting (B), and feed hose clamp (C)

when disconnecting air conditioning system fittings.

Warning: *Perform this procedure when the engine is cool. The pump will be hot while running and after driving.*

Removal

1   On 2013 and later models, have the refrigerant discharged at a dealer service department or an automotive air conditioning repair facility.

2   Disconnect the cable from the negative terminal of the battery (see Chapter 5).

3   Using a large syringe or suction gun, suck as much fluid out of the power steering fluid reservoir as possible. Place a drain pan under the vehicle to catch any fluid that spills out when the hoses are disconnected.

2012 and earlier models

4   Remove the air intake duct (see Chapter 4).

5   Remove the drivebelt (see Chapter 1).

6   Remove the cooling fan (see Chapter 3).

7   Disconnect the pressure sensor electrical connector **(see illustration)**.

8   Detach the pressure line and feed hose from the pump. Discard the sealing washers

24.9 Power steering pump mounting fasteners

25.8 Index marks on the intermediate shaft coupler and the steering column shaft (A) and the pinch bolt and nut (B)

25.9a Steering column upper mounting fasteners

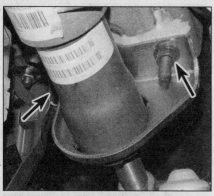

25.9b Steering column lower mounting fastener locations

used on the pressure line fitting (new ones should be used during installation). Plug the hoses.

9   Unscrew the mounting fasteners and remove the pump from the vehicle, taking care not to spill fluid on the painted surfaces **(see illustration)**.

2013 and later models

10   Lift up on the power steering pump cover to disengage the clips and remove the cover.

11   Remove the upper torque rod mounting bolts and remove the torque rod.

12   Remove the right hand upper engine mount insulator nuts (see Chapter 2A).

13   Disconnect the air conditioning lines at the expansion valve at the firewall and cap the openings.

14   Disconnect the electrical connectors from the pump, open the harness clamps and move the harness out of the way.

15   Disconnect the fluid feed hose and reservoir hose from the pump.

16   Remove the pump mounting bolts, then remove the pump from the vehicle.

Installation

17   On 2013 and later models, when installing air conditioning lines to the expansion valve,

use new O-rings on the refrigerant line fittings. Have the system evacuated, charged and leak tested by the shop that discharged it.

18   Installation is the reverse of removal. Note the following.

  a) *Tighten the power steering pump mounting bolts to the torque listed in this Chapter's Specifications.*

  b) *If the power steering pump fluid pressure sensor was removed, install a new sealing washer and tighten the sensor to the torque listed in this Chapter's Specifications*

  c) *On 2012 and earlier models, use new sealing washers and tighten the banjo bolts to the torque listed in this Chapter's Specifications.*

  d) *Reconnect the battery and perform the necessary re-learn procedures (see Chapter 5).*

  e) *Top up the fluid level in the reservoir (see Chapter 1).*

  f) *Bleed the system (see Section 26).*

25   Steering column - removal and installation

Warning: *The models covered by this manual are equipped with Supplemental Restraint Systems (SRS), more commonly known as airbags. Always disable the airbag system before working in the vicinity of any airbag system components to avoid the possibility of accidental deployment of the airbag(s), which could cause personal injury (see Chapter 12).*
Note: *According to the manufacturer, models equipped with Vehicle Dynamic Control will require steering angle sensor calibration after this procedure. Special tools are necessary; refer to a dealership service department or a qualified repair location.*

Removal

1   Park the vehicle with the wheels pointing straight ahead. Disconnect the cable from the negative battery terminal (see Chapter 5).

Disable the airbag system (see Chapter 12).

2   Remove the steering wheel (see Section 20), and the combination switch housing (see Chapter 12). Turn the ignition key to the LOCK position to prevent the steering shaft from turning.
Caution: *If the steering column is not locked, the airbag clockspring could be damaged.*

3   Remove the knee bolster and the reinforcement behind it (see Chapter 11).

4   Remove the steering column covers (see Chapter 11).

5   On 2013 and later models, remove the steering angle sensor (if equipped), and disconnect the electrical connectors to the tilt and telescopic motor.

6   Disconnect the shift cable from the column shift lever and the key interlock cable from the steering column, if equipped (see Chapter 7A).

7   Disconnect the electrical connectors for the steering column and detach the harness from the column.

8   Mark the relationship of the intermediate shaft coupler to the steering column shaft. Remove the shaft coupler nut and bolt **(see illustration)**. Discard the nut.

9   Remove the steering column mounting fasteners **(see illustrations)**, lower the column and pull it to the rear, making sure nothing is still connected. Separate the intermediate shaft from the steering shaft and remove the column.

Installation

10   Guide the steering column into position, connect the intermediate shaft coupler, then install the mounting fasteners, but don't tighten them yet.

11   Install the pinch bolt with a new nut and tighten it to the torque listed in this Chapter's Specifications.

12   Tighten the column mounting fasteners to the torque listed in this Chapter's Specifications.

13   The remainder of installation is the reverse of removal.

26 Power steering system - bleeding

1 Following any operation in which the power steering fluid lines have been disconnected, the power steering system must be bled to remove all air and obtain proper steering performance.

2 With the front wheels in the straight ahead position, check the power steering fluid level and, if low, add fluid (see Chapter 1).

3 Turn the steering wheel from lock to lock several times with the engine Off. Do this several times until no bubbles are seen in the reservoir. Don't let the fluid level drop below the MIN mark.

4 Start the engine, then hold the steering wheel against each lock for no more than three seconds. Repeat this until air has been removed from the system and bubbles stop appearing in the reservoir. Do this several times until no bubbles are seen in the reservoir. Don't let the fluid level drop below the MIN mark.

5 Recheck the fluid level and add more if necessary to reach the MAX mark on the reservoir.

6 When the air is worked out of the system, return the wheels to the straight ahead position and leave the vehicle running for several more minutes before shutting it off.

7 Road test the vehicle to be sure the steering system is functioning normally and quietly.

8 Recheck the fluid level to be sure it is up to the HOT mark while the engine is at normal operating temperature. Add fluid if necessary (see Chapter 1).

27 Wheels and tires - general information

1 All vehicles covered by this manual are equipped with metric-sized steel belted radial tires **(see illustration)**. Use of other size or type of tires may affect the ride and handling of the vehicle. Don't mix different types of tires, such as radials and bias belted, on the same vehicle as handling may be seriously affected. It's recommended that tires be replaced in pairs on the same axle, but if only one tire is being replaced, be sure it's the same size, structure and tread design as the other.

2 Because tire pressure has a substantial effect on handling and wear, the pressure on all tires should be checked at least once a month or before any extended trips (see Chapter 1).

3 Wheels must be replaced if they are bent, dented, leak air, have elongated bolt holes, are heavily rusted, out of vertical symmetry or if the lug nuts won't stay tight. Wheel repairs that use welding or peening are not recommended.

4 Tire and wheel balance is important in the overall handling, braking and performance of the vehicle. Unbalanced wheels can

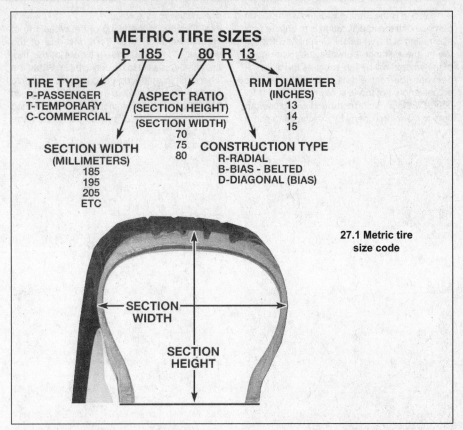

METRIC TIRE SIZES
P 185 / 80 R 13

TIRE TYPE
P-PASSENGER
T-TEMPORARY
C-COMMERCIAL

ASPECT RATIO
(SECTION HEIGHT)
―――――――――――
(SECTION WIDTH)
70
75
80

RIM DIAMETER
(INCHES)
13
14
15

SECTION WIDTH
(MILLIMETERS)
185
195
205
ETC

CONSTRUCTION TYPE
R-RADIAL
B-BIAS - BELTED
D-DIAGONAL (BIAS)

SECTION WIDTH

SECTION HEIGHT

27.1 Metric tire size code

adversely affect handling and ride characteristics as well as tire life. Whenever a tire is installed on a wheel, the tire and wheel should be balanced by a shop with the proper equipment.

28 Wheel alignment - general information

1 A wheel alignment refers to the adjustments made to the wheels so they are in proper angular relationship to the suspension and the ground. Wheels that are out of proper alignment not only affect vehicle control, but also increase tire wear. The front end angles normally measured are camber, caster and toe-in **(see illustration)**. On 2012 and earlier models, camber, caster and toe-in are adjustable. On 2013 and later models, camber and caster are preset at the factory; toe-in is the only adjustable angle on these vehicles (however, camber and caster are usually measured to check for bent or worn suspension parts). Toe-in and camber are both adjustable at the rear.

2 Getting the proper wheel alignment is an exacting process, one in which complicated and expensive machines are necessary to perform the job properly. Because of this, you should have a technician with the proper equipment perform these tasks. We will, however, use this space to give you a basic idea of what is involved with a wheel alignment so you can better understand the process and deal intelligently with the shop that does the work.

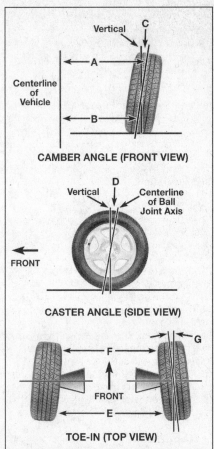

CAMBER ANGLE (FRONT VIEW)

CASTER ANGLE (SIDE VIEW)

TOE-IN (TOP VIEW)

28.1 Camber, caster and toe-in angles

3   Toe-in is the turning in of the wheels. The purpose of a toe specification is to ensure parallel rolling of the wheels. In a vehicle with zero toe-in, the distance between the front edges of the wheels will be the same as the distance between the rear edges of the wheels. The actual amount of toe-in is normally only a fraction of an inch. Incorrect toe-in will cause the tires to wear improperly by making them scrub against the road surface.

4   Camber is the tilting of the wheels from vertical when viewed from one end of the vehicle. When the wheels tilt out at the top, the camber is said to be positive (+). When the wheels tilt in at the top the camber is negative (-). The amount of tilt is measured in degrees from vertical and this measurement is called the camber angle. This angle affects the amount of tire tread which contacts the road and compensates for changes in the suspension geometry when the vehicle is cornering or traveling over an undulating surface.

5   Caster is the tilting of the front steering axis from the vertical. A tilt toward the rear is positive caster and a tilt toward the front is negative caster.

Chapter 11
Body

Contents

	Section
Body repair - major damage	4
Body repair - minor damage	3
Bumper covers - removal and installation	20
Center console - removal and installation	22
Cowl cover - removal and installation	26
Dashboard trim panels - removal and installation	24
Door latch, key lock cylinder and handles - removal and installation	16
Door - removal, installation and adjustment	15
Door trim panels - removal and installation	14
Door window glass - removal and installation	17
Door window glass regulator - removal and installation	18
Fastener and trim removal	5
Fender (front) - removal and installation	19
General information	1
Hinges and locks - maintenance	7

	Section
Hood - removal, installation and adjustment	9
Hood release latch and cable - removal and installation	10
Instrument panel - removal and installation	25
Liftgate - removal, installation and adjustment	12
Liftgate latch - removal and installation	13
Mirrors - removal and installation	21
Radiator grille - removal and installation	11
Rear quarter trim panels - removal and installation	28
Rear spoiler - removal and installation (2013 and later models)	29
Repairing minor paint scratches	2
Seats - removal and installation	27
Steering column covers - removal and installation	23
Upholstery, carpets and vinyl trim - maintenance	6
Windshield and fixed glass - replacement	8

1   General information

Warning: *The models covered by this manual are equipped with Supplemental Restraint Systems (SRS), more commonly known as airbags. Always disable the airbag system before working in the vicinity of any airbag system components to avoid the possibility of accidental deployment of the airbags, which could cause personal injury (see Chapter 12).*

1   Certain body components are particularly vulnerable to accident damage and can be unbolted and repaired or replaced. Among these parts are the hood, doors, tailgate, liftgate, bumpers and front fenders.

2   Only general body maintenance practices and body panel repair procedures within the scope of the do-it-yourselfer are included in this Chapter.

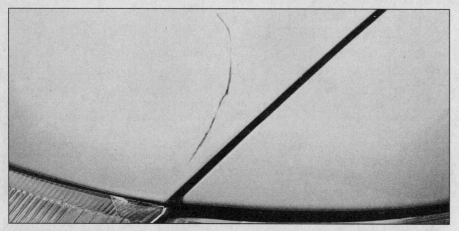

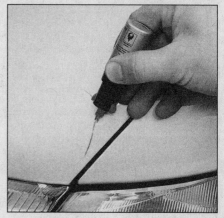

Make sure the damaged area is perfectly clean and rust free. If the touch-up kit has a wire brush, use it to clean the scratch or chip. Or use fine steel wool wrapped around the end of a pencil. Clean the scratched or chipped surface only, not the good paint surrounding it. Rinse the area with water and allow it to dry thoroughly

Thoroughly mix the paint, then apply a small amount with the touch-up kit brush or a very fine artist's brush. Brush in one direction as you fill the scratch area. Do not build up the paint higher than the surrounding paint

2   Repairing minor paint scratches

No matter how hard you try to keep your vehicle looking like new, it will inevitably be scratched, chipped or dented at some point. If the metal is actually dented, seek the advice of a professional. But you can fix minor scratches and chips yourself. Buy a touch-up paint kit from a dealer parts department or an auto parts store. To ensure that you get the right color, you'll need to have the specific make, model and year of your vehicle and, ideally, the paint code, which is located on a special metal plate under the hood or in the door jamb.

3   Body repair - minor damage

Plastic body panels

1   The following repair procedures are for minor scratches and gouges. Repair of more serious damage should be left to a dealer service department or qualified auto body shop. Below is a list of the equipment and materials necessary to perform the following repair procedures on plastic body panels.

Wax, grease and silicone removing solvent
Cloth-backed body tape
Sanding discs
Drill motor with three-inch disc holder
Hand sanding block
Rubber squeegees
Sandpaper
Non-porous mixing palette
Wood paddle or putty knife
Wood paddle or putty knife
Curved-tooth body file
Flexible parts repair material

Flexible panels (bumper trim)

2   Remove the damaged panel, if necessary or desirable. In most cases, repairs can be carried out with the panel installed.

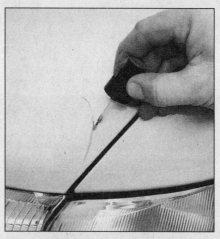

If the vehicle has a two-coat finish, apply the clear coat after the color coat has dried

3   Clean the area(s) to be repaired with a wax, grease and silicone removing solvent applied with a water-dampened cloth.
4   If the damage is structural, that is, if it extends through the panel, clean the backside of the panel area to be repaired as well. Wipe dry.
5   Sand the rear surface about 1-1/2 inches beyond the break.
6   Cut two pieces of fiberglass cloth large enough to overlap the break by about 1-1/2 inches. Cut only to the required length.
7   Mix the adhesive from the repair kit according to the instructions included with the kit, and apply a layer of the mixture approximately 1/8-inch thick on the backside of the panel. Overlap the break by at least 1-1/2 inches.
8   Apply one piece of fiberglass cloth to the adhesive and cover the cloth with additional adhesive. Apply a second piece of fiberglass cloth to the adhesive and immediately cover the cloth with additional adhesive in sufficient quantity to fill the weave.

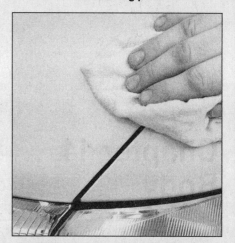

Wait a few days for the paint to dry thoroughly, then rub out the repainted area with a polishing compound to blend the new paint with the surrounding area. When you're happy with your work, wash and polish the area

9   Allow the repair to cure for 20 to 30 minutes at 60-degrees to 80-degrees F.
10   If necessary, trim the excess repair material at the edge.
11   Remove all of the paint film over and around the area(s) to be repaired. The repair material should not overlap the painted surface.
12   With a drill motor and a sanding disc (or a rotary file), cut a "V" along the break line approximately 1/2-inch wide. Remove all dust and loose particles from the repair area.
13   Mix and apply the repair material. Apply a light coat first over the damaged area; then continue applying material until it reaches a level slightly higher than the surrounding finish.
14   Cure the mixture for 20 to 30 minutes at 60-degrees to 80-degrees F.
15   Roughly establish the contour of the area being repaired with a body file. If low areas or

pits remain, mix and apply additional adhesive.

16   Block sand the damaged area with sandpaper to establish the actual contour of the surrounding surface.

17   If desired, the repaired area can be temporarily protected with several light coats of primer. Because of the special paints and techniques required for flexible body panels, it is recommended that the vehicle be taken to a paint shop for completion of the body repair.

Steel body panels

Repairing simple dents

18   When repairing dents, the first job is to pull the dent out until the affected area is as close as possible to its original shape. There is no point in trying to restore the original shape completely as the metal in the damaged area will have stretched on impact and cannot be restored to its original contours. It is better to bring the level of the dent up to a point that is about 1/8-inch below the level of the surrounding metal. In cases where the dent is very shallow, it is not worth trying to pull it out at all.

19   If the backside of the dent is accessible, it can be hammered out gently from behind using a soft-face hammer. While doing this, hold a block of wood firmly against the opposite side of the metal to absorb the hammer blows and prevent the metal from being stretched.

20   If the dent is in a section of the body which has double layers, or some other factor makes it inaccessible from behind, a different technique is required. Drill several small holes through the metal inside the damaged area, particularly in the deeper sections. Screw long, self-tapping screws into the holes just enough for them to get a good grip in the metal. Now pulling on the protruding heads of the screws with locking pliers can pull out the dent.

21   The next stage of repair is the removal of paint from the damaged area and from an inch or so of the surrounding metal. This is easily done with a wire brush or sanding disk in a drill motor, although it can be done just as effectively by hand with sandpaper. To complete the preparation for filling, score the surface of the bare metal with a screwdriver or the tang of a file or drill small holes in the affected area. This will provide a good grip for the filler material. To complete the repair, see the Section on filling and painting.

Repair of rust holes or gashes

22   Remove all paint from the affected area and from an inch or so of the surrounding metal using a sanding disk or wire brush mounted in a drill motor. If these are not available, a few sheets of sandpaper will do the job just as effectively.

23   With the paint removed, you will be able to determine the severity of the corrosion and decide whether to replace the whole panel, if possible, or repair the affected area. New body panels are not as expensive as most people think and it is often quicker to install a new panel than to repair large areas of rust.

24   Remove all trim pieces from the affected area except those which will act as a guide to the original shape of the damaged body, such as headlight shells, etc. Using metal snips or a hacksaw blade, remove all loose metal and any other metal that is badly affected by rust. Hammer the edges of the hole in to create a slight depression for the filler material.

25   Wire-brush the affected area to remove the powdery rust from the surface of the metal. If the back of the rusted area is accessible, treat it with rust inhibiting paint.

26   Before filling is done, block the hole in some way. This can be done with sheet metal riveted or screwed into place, or by stuffing the hole with wire mesh.

27   Once the hole is blocked off, the affected area can be filled and painted. See the following subsection on filling and painting.

Filling and painting

28   Many types of body fillers are available, but generally speaking, body repair kits which contain filler paste and a tube of resin hardener are best for this type of repair work. A wide, flexible plastic or nylon applicator will be necessary for imparting a smooth and contoured finish to the surface of the filler material. Mix up a small amount of filler on a clean piece of wood or cardboard (use the hardener sparingly). Follow the manufacturer's instructions on the package, otherwise the filler will set incorrectly.

29   Using the applicator, apply the filler paste to the prepared area. Draw the applicator across the surface of the filler to achieve the desired contour and to level the filler surface. As soon as a contour that approximates the original one is achieved, stop working the paste. If you continue, the paste will begin to stick to the applicator. Continue to add thin layers of paste at 20-minute intervals until the level of the filler is just above the surrounding metal.

30   Once the filler has hardened, the excess can be removed with a body file. From then on, progressively finer grades of sandpaper should be used, starting with a 180-grit paper and finishing with 600-grit wet-or-dry paper. Always wrap the sandpaper around a flat rubber or wooden block, otherwise the surface of the filler will not be completely flat. During the sanding of the filler surface, the wet-or-dry paper should be periodically rinsed in water. This will ensure that a very smooth finish is produced in the final stage.

31   At this point, the repair area should be surrounded by a ring of bare metal, which in turn should be encircled by the finely feathered edge of good paint. Rinse the repair area with clean water until all of the dust produced by the sanding operation is gone.

32   Spray the entire area with a light coat of primer. This will reveal any imperfections in the surface of the filler. Repair the imperfections with fresh filler paste or glaze filler and once more smooth the surface with sandpaper. Repeat this spray-and-repair procedure until you are satisfied that the surface of the filler and the feathered edge of the paint are perfect. Rinse the area with clean water and allow it to dry completely.

33   The repair area is now ready for painting. Spray painting must be carried out in a warm, dry, windless and dust free atmosphere. These conditions can be created if you have access to a large indoor work area, but if you are forced to work in the open, you will have to pick the day very carefully. If you are working indoors, dousing the floor in the work area with water will help settle the dust that would otherwise be in the air. If the repair area is confined to one body panel, mask off the surrounding panels. This will help minimize the effects of a slight mismatch in paint color. Trim pieces such as chrome strips, door handles, etc., will also need to be masked off or removed. Use masking tape and several thickness of newspaper for the masking operations.

34   Before spraying, shake the paint can thoroughly, then spray a test area until the spray painting technique is mastered. Cover the repair area with a thick coat of primer. The thickness should be built up using several thin layers of primer rather than one thick one. Using 600-grit wet-or-dry sandpaper, rub down the surface of the primer until it is very smooth. While doing this, the work area should be thoroughly rinsed with water and the wet-or-dry sandpaper periodically rinsed as well. Allow the primer to dry before spraying additional coats.

35   Spray on the top coat, again building up the thickness by using several thin layers of paint. Begin spraying in the center of the repair area and then, using a circular motion, work out until the whole repair area and about two inches of the surrounding original paint is covered. Remove all masking material 10 to 15 minutes after spraying on the final coat of paint. Allow the new paint at least two weeks to harden, then use a very fine rubbing compound to blend the edges of the new paint into the existing paint. Finally, apply a coat of wax

4   Body repair - major damage

1   Major damage must be repaired by an auto body shop specifically equipped to perform body and frame repairs. These shops have the specialized equipment required to do the job properly.

2   If the damage is extensive, the frame must be checked for proper alignment or the vehicle's handling characteristics may be adversely affected and other components may wear at an accelerated rate.

3   Due to the fact that all of the major body components (hood, fenders, etc.) are separate and replaceable units, any seriously damaged components should be replaced rather than repaired. Sometimes the components can be found in a wrecking yard that specializes in used vehicle components, often at considerable savings over the cost of new parts.

These photos illustrate a method of repairing simple dents. They are intended to supplement *Body repair - minor damage* in this Chapter and should not be used as the sole instructions for body repair on these vehicles.

1 If you can't access the backside of the body panel to hammer out the dent, pull it out with a slide-hammer-type dent puller. Tap with a hammer near the edge of the dent to help 'pop' the metal back to its original shape, about 1/8-inch below the surface of the surrounding metal

2 Using coarse-grit sandpaper, remove the paint down to the bare metal. Clean the repair area with wax/silicone remover.

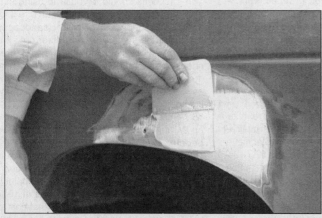

3 Following label instructions, mix up a batch of plastic filler and hardener, then quickly press it into the metal with a plastic applicator. Work the filler until it matches the original contour and is slightly above the surrounding metal

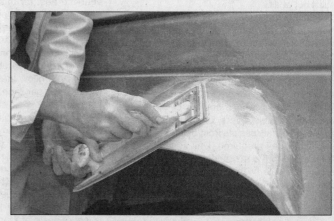

4 Let the filler harden until you can just dent it with your fingernail. File, then sand the filler down until it's smooth and even. Work down to finer grits of sandpaper - always using a board or block - ending up with 360 or 400 grit

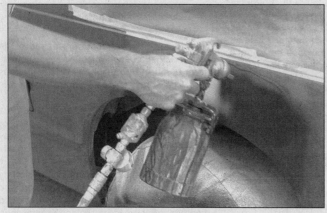

5 When the area is smooth to the touch, clean the area and mask around it. Apply several layers of primer to the area. A professional-type spray gun is being used here, but aerosol spray primer works fine

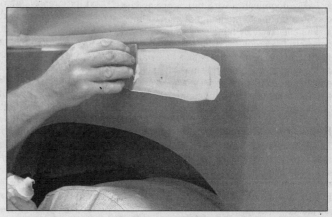

6 Fill imperfections or scratches with glazing compound. Sand with 360 or 400-grit and re-spray. Finish sand the primer with 600 grit, clean thoroughly, then apply the finish coat. Don't attempt to rub out or wax the repair area until the paint has dried completely (at least two weeks)

5 Fastener and trim removal

1 There is a variety of plastic fasteners used to hold trim panels, splash shields and other parts in place in addition to typical screws, nuts and bolts. Once you are familiar with them, they can usually be removed without too much difficulty.

2 The proper tools and approach can prevent added time and expense to a project by minimizing the number of broken fasteners and/or parts.

3 The illustrations below show various types of fasteners that are typically used on most vehicles and how to remove and install them. Replacement fasteners are commonly found at most auto parts stores, if necessary.

4 Trim panels are typically made of plastic and their flexibility can help during removal. The key to their removal is to use a tool to pry the panel near its retainers to release it without damaging surrounding areas or breaking-off any retainers. The retainers will usually snap out of their designated slot or hole after force is applied to them. Stiff plastic tools designed for prying on trim panels are available at most auto parts stores **(see illustration)**. Tools that are tapered and wrapped in protective tape, such as a screwdriver or small pry tool, are also very effective when used with care.

6 Upholstery, carpets and vinyl trim - maintenance

Upholstery and carpets

1 Every three months remove the floormats and clean the interior of the vehicle (more frequently if necessary). Use a stiff whiskbroom to brush the carpeting and loosen dirt and dust, then vacuum the upholstery and carpets thoroughly, especially along seams and crevices.

2 Dirt and stains can be removed from carpeting with basic household or automotive carpet shampoos available in spray cans. Follow the directions and vacuum again, then use a stiff brush to bring back the nap of the carpet.

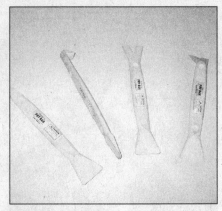

5.4 These small plastic pry tools are ideal for prying off trim panels

Fasteners

This tool is designed to remove special fasteners. A small pry tool used for removing nails will also work well in place of this tool

A Phillips head screwdriver can be used to release the center portion, but light pressure must be used because the plastic is easily damaged. Once the center is up, the fastener can easily be pried from its hole

Here is a view with the center portion fully released. Install the fastener as shown, then press the center in to set it

This fastener is used for exterior panels and shields. The center portion must be pried up to release the fastener. Install the fastener with the center up, then press the center in to set it

This type of fastener is used commonly for interior panels. Use a small blunt tool to press the small pin at the center in to release it . . .

. . . the pin will stay with the fastener in the released position

Reset the fastener for installation by moving the pin out. Install the fastener, then press the pin flush with the fastener to set it

This fastener is used for exterior and interior panels. It has no moving parts. Simply pry the fastener from its hole like the claw of a hammer removes a nail. Without a tool that can get under the top of the fastener, it can be very difficult to remove

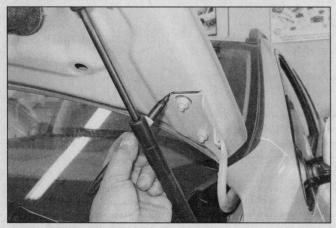

9.2 Before removing the hood, draw a line around the hinge plates

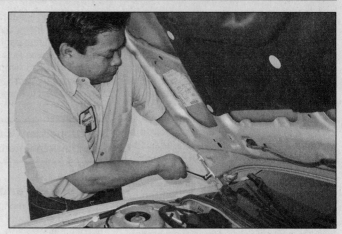

9.5 Support the hood with your shoulder while removing the hinge-to-hood nuts

9.11 Twist the hood bumpers in or out to make fine adjustments to the hood closed height

3   Most interiors have cloth or vinyl upholstery, either of which can be cleaned and maintained with a number of material-specific cleaners or shampoos available in auto supply stores. Follow the directions on the product for usage, and always spot-test any upholstery cleaner on an inconspicuous area (bottom edge of a backseat cushion) to ensure that it doesn't cause a color shift in the material.
4   After cleaning, vinyl upholstery should be treated with a protectant.
Caution: *Do not use protectant on vinyl-covered steering wheels.*
Note: *Make sure the protectant container indicates the product can be used on seats - some products may make a seat too slippery.*
5   Leather upholstery requires special care. It should be cleaned regularly with saddle-soap or leather cleaner. Never use alcohol, gasoline, nail polish remover or thinner to clean leather upholstery.
6   After cleaning, regularly treat leather upholstery with a leather conditioner, rubbed in with a soft cotton cloth. Never use car wax on leather upholstery.
7   In areas where the interior of the vehicle is subject to bright sunlight, cover leather seating areas of the seats with a sheet if the

vehicle is to be left out for any length of time.

Vinyl trim

8   Don't clean vinyl trim with detergents, caustic soap or petroleum-based cleaners. Plain soap and water works just fine, with a soft brush to clean dirt that may be ingrained. Wash the vinyl as frequently as the rest of the vehicle.
9   After cleaning, application of a high-quality rubber and vinyl protectant will help prevent oxidation and cracks. The protectant can also be applied to weather-stripping, vacuum lines and rubber hoses, which often fail as a result of chemical degradation, and to the tires.

7   Hinges and locks - maintenance

Once every 3000 miles, or every three months, the hinges and latch assemblies on the doors, hood and trunk should be given a few drops of light oil or lock lubricant. The door latch strikers should also be lubricated with a thin coat of grease to reduce wear and ensure free movement. Lubricate the door and trunk locks with spray-on graphite lubricant.

8   Windshield and fixed glass - replacement

Replacement of the windshield and fixed glass requires the use of special fast-setting adhesive/caulk materials and some specialized tools. It is recommended that these operations be left to a dealer or a shop specializing in glass work.

9   Hood - removal, installation and adjustment

Note: *The hood is heavy and somewhat awkward to remove and install - at least two people should perform this procedure.*

Removal and installation

1   Use blankets or pads to cover the cowl area of the body and fenders. This will protect the body and paint as the hood is lifted off.
2   Make marks or scribe a line around the hood hinge to ensure proper alignment during installation **(see illustration)**.
3   Disconnect any cables or wires that will interfere with removal.
4   Place a prop under the hood to hold it open after the support strut is detached.
5   Have assistant support one side of the hood. Take turns removing the hinge-to-hood nuts and lift off the the hood **(see illustration)**.
Caution: *Do NOT try to remove the hood by yourself; it's heavy, and you could injure yourself and/or scratch or damage something.*
6   Installation is the reverse of removal.

Adjustment

7   Adjust the hood fore-and-aft and side-to-side by moving the hinge plate slot after loosening the nuts.
8   Scribe a line around the entire hinge plate so you can determine the amount of movement.
9   Loosen the nuts and move the hood into correct alignment. Move it only a little at a time. Tighten the hinge nuts and carefully lower the hood to check the position.
10   If necessary after installation, the entire hood latch assembly can be adjusted up-and-down as well as from side-to-side on the radiator support so the hood closes securely and flush with the fenders. To make the adjustment, scribe a line or mark around the hood latch mounting bolts to provide a reference point, then loosen them and reposition the latch assembly, as necessary (see Section 10). Following adjustment, retighten the mounting bolts.
11   Finally, adjust the hood bumpers on the hood by turning them in or out **(see illustration)**, so when closed, is flush with the fenders.
12   Periodically, lubricate the hood latch assembly, as well as the hinges, with white, lithium-base grease to prevent binding and wear.

10.2 Scribe a line around the hood latch before removing the three mounting bolts

10.7 The hood release cable is secured along its length with clips

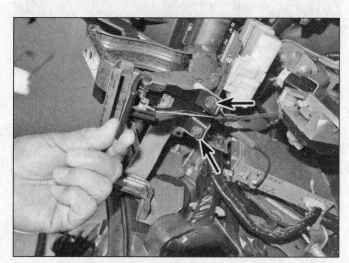

10.9 Remove the release handle fasteners

11.1 Remove the fasteners along the top of the grille

10 Hood release latch and cable - removal and installation

Latch

1   On 2012 and earlier models, remove the radiator grille (see Section 11). On 2013 and later models, remove the radiator core cover clips and remove the cover.

2   Scribe a line around the latch to aid alignment when installing. Remove the latch retaining bolts (see illustration) and remove the latch.

3   Flip the hood latch assembly over and disengage the hood release cable from the latch.

4   Installation is the reverse of removal.

Note: *Adjust the latch so the hood engages securely when closed and the hood bumpers are slightly compressed. The hood should close under its own weight when dropped from approximately 8 inches (200 mm). Do not drop the hood from more than 11 inches (300 mm).*

Cable

5   Unbolt the hood release latch and disconnect the hood release cable from the latch (see Steps 1 through 3).

6   Remove driver's side headlight housing (see Chapter 12) and the left inner fender splash shield (see Section 19).

7   Detach the cable from the clips along its length (see illustration).

8   Remove the knee bolster (see Section 24).

9   Remove the mounting fasteners securing the hood release handle to the underside of the instrument panel (see illustration), then detach the cable from the handle.

10   Pull the cable grommet into the passenger compartment, then pull the cable through the hole.

11   Installation is the reverse of removal.

Note: *Push on the grommet with your fingers from the passenger compartment to seat the grommet snugly in the firewall.*

11 Radiator grille - removal and installation

Warning: *The models covered by this manual are equipped with a Supplemental Restraint System (SRS), more commonly known as airbags. Always disarm the airbag system before working in the vicinity of any airbag system component to avoid the possibility of accidental deployment of the airbag, which could cause personal injury (see Chapter 12). Do not use a memory saving device to preserve the PCM's memory when working on or near airbag system components.*

2012 and earlier models

1   Open the hood and remove the grille-to-radiator support fasteners (see illustration).

11.2 Use a screwdriver to release the side clips - left side shown right side identical

11.3 Working from the top of the grille, locate the lower fastener and remove it

11.7 Pinch these retainers to release them

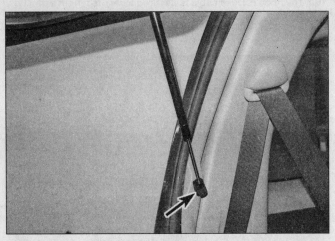

12.5 Make sure that the liftgate is securely supported before you pry out the retainers and detach the struts from the liftgate

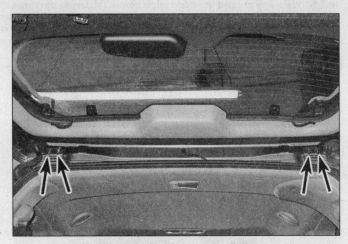

12.6 Remove the liftgate mounting nuts

2   Disengage the left and right side clips by twisting the clips through the grille **(see illustration)**.

3   Remove the lower grille fastener-to-bumper cover **(see illustration)** from above and remove the grille from the vehicle.

4   Installation is the reverse of removal.

2013 and later models

5   Open the hood, remove the radiator cover fasteners and remove the cover.

6   Disconnect the electrical connector to the camera, if equipped.

7   Use pliers to disengage the mounting tabs from the inside of the grille at each end near the headlights **(see illustration)**.

8   Carefully pry loose the six lower grille clips, then remove the grille.

9   Installation is the reverse of removal.

12   Liftgate - removal, installation and adjustment

Note: *The liftgate is heavy and somewhat awkward to remove and install - at least two people should perform this procedure.*

Removal and installation

1   Open the liftgate and cover the edges of the open rear compartment with pads or cloths to protect the painted surfaces when the liftgate is removed.

2   Remove the trim panels from the liftgate (see Section 14).

3   Working through the access hole in the upper part of the liftgate, disconnect the electrical connectors for all harnesses routed between the liftgate and the vehicle body. Disconnect the washer line, then pull the harnesses and the washer line out of the liftgate.

4   Support the liftgate securely with a hood prop or a broom handle; whatever you use must be strong enough to support the considerable weight of the liftgate when the support struts are removed.

5   Use a small flat-blade screwdriver to release the steel clip at the liftgate end of each support strut **(see illustration)**. Detach the struts from the liftgate and allow it to rest against the prop.

6   Outline the exact positions of the liftgate hinges prior to removal. Have an assistant

help you as you carefully remove the liftgate mounting nuts from the hinges **(see illustration)**.

7   Installation is the reverse of removal. Align the lid-to-hinge bolts with the marks made during removal.

Adjustment

8   Fore-and-aft and side-to-side adjustments of the liftgate are accomplished by moving the liftgate in relation to the hinge after loosening the bolts or nuts.

9   Scribe a line around the entire hinge plate so you can determine the amount of movement.

10   Loosen the bolts or nuts and move the liftgate into correct alignment. Move it only a little at a time. Tighten the hinge bolts or nuts and carefully lower the liftgate to check the alignment.

11   If necessary after installation, the entire liftgate striker assembly can be adjusted up and down as well as from side to side on the liftgate, so the lid closes securely and is flush with the quarter panels. To do this, scribe a line around the liftgate striker assembly to provide a reference point. Loosen the bolts and

13.4a Remove the mounting bolts from the end of the latch...

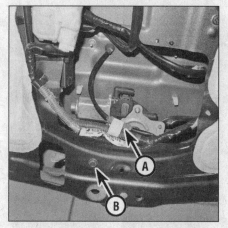

13.4b... then disconnect the electrical connector (A) and the remaining latch fastener (B) - 2012 and earlier models shown, later models similar

13.9 Remove the glass latch mounting bolts

14.2a Carefully pry off the handle cover

14.2b Pull the handle forward and pry off the remaining cover

14.3 Carefully pry up the switch panel - release each clip, starting at the rear

14.4 Pry up the armrest, carefully releasing each clip

reposition the striker as necessary. Following adjustment, retighten the mounting bolts.

12 The liftgate latch assembly, as well as the hinges, should be periodically lubricated with white lithium-base grease to prevent sticking and wear.

13 Liftgate latch - removal and installation

Latch

1   Remove the liftgate inner trim panel (see Section 14).
2   Disconnect the electrical connector from the lock.
3   Scribe a line around the latch assembly for a reference point to aid the installation procedure.
4   Remove the mounting bolts and remove the latch (see illustrations).
5   Installation is the reverse of removal.

Glass latch - 2012 and earlier models

6   Remove the liftgate trim panel (see Section 14).
7   Disconnect the release cable from the glass latch.
8   Disconnect the electrical connectors

from the latch.
9   Remove the glass latch mounting bolts (see illustration) and remove the latch.
10   Installation is the reverse of removal.

14 Door trim panels - removal and installation

Side doors

1   Open the window all the way.
2   Carefully pry off the inside handle trim covers to expose the mounting fastener under the trim (see illustrations).
3   Carefully pry up the power window switch trim panel, disengaging the clips as you go (see illustration). Pull out the switch, disconnect the electrical connectors and remove the switch panel.
4   On 2012 and earlier models, carefully pry up the arm rest pad, disengaging the clips as you go (see illustration).
5   On 2013 and later models, pry out the

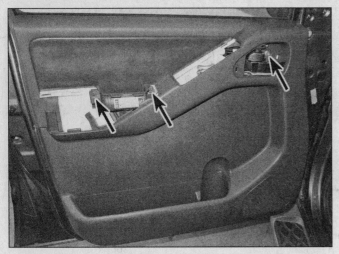

14.7 Door panel mounting screw locations - 2012 and earlier models shown, later models similar

14.8 Start at the bottom, then work your way around the rear, lower and front edges of the trim panel

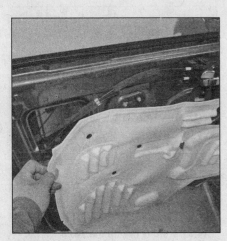

14.14 Carefully pull the water shield off of the door

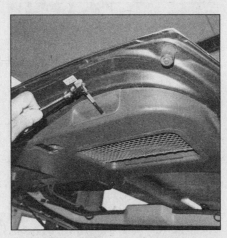

14.16a Remove the screw from the center of the handle...

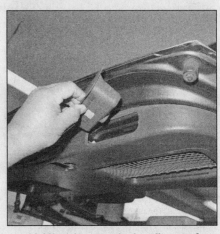

14.16b... then pry the handle out of the liftgate

14.17 Remove the mounting screws - 2008 model shown, other models similar

armrest cover to expose the mounting bolt.

6   Carefully pry off the door lamp lens, if equipped, then disconnect the electrical connector.

7   Remove the door panel mounting screws **(see illustration)**.

8   Starting at the bottom of the door trim panel, carefully pry loose the panel retaining clips **(see illustration)**. Work around the edge until the panel is loose.

Caution: *Pry next to the clips only. Prying between the clips can damage the door panel.*

9   When all the clips are disengaged, lift the panel UP to disengage the channel along the upper edge of the trim panel from the ridge running along the top of the door window opening.

10   On 2012 and earlier model driver doors, disconnect the memory seat connector, if equipped.

11   On 2012 and earlier model rear doors,

disconnect the tweeter electrical connectors.

12   On 2013 and later models, disconnect the door lock and door handle cables and the wiring harness bracket from the panel.

13   Remove the door trim panel.

14   Remove the water shield from the door **(see illustration)**.

15   Installation is the reverse of removal.

Note: *The manufacturer recommends installing new door handle trim any time it is removed.*

Liftgate

2012 and earlier models

16   Open the liftgate and remove the handle grip fastener, then pry the grip out of the liftgate **(see illustrations)**.

17   Remove the panel mounting screws **(see illustration)**.

18   Insert a trim removal tool between the lower edge of the lower trim panel and the

14.18 Pry off the liftgate trim panel starting from the bottom, then working around the perimeter of the panel, being careful to avoid damaging the clips

14.20 Pry off the liftgate trim panel starting from the top, working around the perimeter of the panel, being careful to avoid damaging the clips

15.5 Unbolt the door check strut

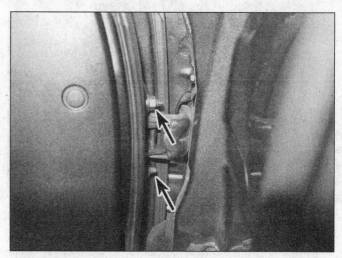

15.7 Remove the lower hinge then the upper hinge - unbolt the lower hinge first and allow the door to rest on its support while removing the upper nuts

liftgate. Work the tool along the edges of the trim panel, releasing the clips as you go, then remove the lower liftgate trim panel **(see illustration)**.

19   Support the liftgate, then detach the support struts (see Section 12). Insert a trim tool between the window glass trim and the liftgate.

20   Work along the perimeter of the panel, releasing the clips as you go **(see illustration)**, then remove the window trim panel.

21   Installation is the reverse of removal.

2013 and later models

22   Open the liftgate and carefully pry off the handle grip panel.

23   Insert the trim removal tool between the upper edge of the trim panel and the glass, then pull down to release the clips along the top edge.

24   Remove the three trim pieces from around the glass.

25   Release the push-pin clips along the bottom of the trim panel.

26   If equipped, pry off the lenses of the cargo area lights, disconnect the electrical connectors and remove the lights.

27   Release the steel clips at each upper corner of the trim panel.

28   Work the tool along the other three edges of the trim panel, releasing the clips as you go, then remove the liftgate trim panel.

29   Installation is the reverse of removal.

---

15   Door - removal, installation and adjustment

Note: *The doors are heavy and somewhat awkward to remove and install - at least two people should perform this procedure.*

Removal and installation

1   Lower the window completely in the door. Disconnect the cable from the negative terminal of the battery (see Chapter 5).

2   Open the door all the way and support it on jacks or blocks covered with rags to prevent damaging the paint.

3   It's easiest to remove the door trim panel and watershield at this time (see Section 14).

4   Pull the grommet and wiring harness out of the front door jamb until the connectors are exposed, then disconnect the electrical connectors.

5   Unbolt the door stop **(see illustration)**.

6   Mark around the door hinges with a pen or a scribe to facilitate realignment during reassembly.

7   With an assistant holding the door, remove the hinge-to-door nuts **(see illustration)** and lift off the door.

15.12 Adjust the door lock striker by loosening the mounting screws and gently tapping the striker in the desired direction

16.2a Remove the inside door handle retaining screw

16.2b Remove the handle from the door and disengage the latch and lock cables from the inside door handle

16.8 Remove this plug from the rear edge of the door to access the Torx bolt that secures the key lock cylinder

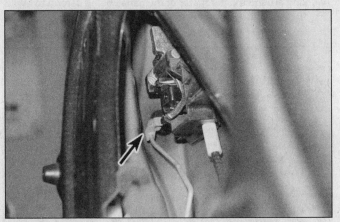

16.10 To disconnect either end of the actuator rod, pop off the slotted part of the clip that wraps around the rod, then push the end of the rod out of the clip

8   Installation is the reverse of removal. Reconnect the battery and perform the necessary re-learn procedures (see Chapter 5).

Adjustment

9   Having proper door-to-body alignment is a critical part of a well-functioning door assembly. Check the door hinge pins for excessive play. Fully open the door and lift up and down on the door without lifting the body. If a door has 1/16-inch or more excessive play, the hinges should be replaced.

10   Door-to-body alignment adjustments are made by loosening the hinge-to-body bolts or hinge-to-door bolts and moving the door. Proper body alignment is achieved when the top of the doors are parallel with the roof section, the front door is flush with the fender, the rear door is flush with the rear quarter panel and the bottom of the doors are aligned with the lower rocker panel. If these goals can't be reached by adjusting the hinge-to-body or hinge-to-door bolts, body alignment shims may have to be purchased and inserted behind the hinges to achieve correct alignment.

11   To adjust the door closed position, scribe

a line or mark around the striker plate to provide a reference point, then check that the door latch is contacting the center of the latch striker. If not, adjust the up and down position first.

12   Finally, adjust the latch striker sideways position, so that the door panel is flush with the center pillar or rear quarter panel and provides positive engagement with the latch mechanism **(see illustration)**.

---

16   Door latch, key lock cylinder and handles - removal and installation

---

Inside door handle

1   Remove the door trim panel (see Section 14).

2   On 2012 and earlier models, remove the handle mounting screw **(see illustration)**, detach the handle from the door, then disconnect the cable from the handle **(see illustration)**.

3   On 2013 and later models, disconnect the actuator cable from the handle, remove

the handle mounting screws and detach the handle from the backside of the door trim panel.

4   Installation is the reverse of removal.

Key lock cylinder and outside door handle

5   Remove the door trim panel and watershield (see Section 14).

6   On 2012 and earlier models, remove the window regulator (see Section 18).

7   On 2013 and later models, disconnect the electrical connectors attached to the outside handle and separate the wires from the wire clamps.

8   Remove the rubber plug from the rear edge of the door **(see illustration)**.

Caution: *Don't try to remove the Torx bolt completely; just back it out until it stops.*

9   Loosen but do not remove the Torx bolt that secures the door lock cylinder (driver's door) or the handle trim (passenger's door).

10   Disconnect the actuator rod that connects the key lock cylinder to the door latch assembly **(see illustration)**. If you're removing the outside door handle, disconnect the upper end of the rod; if you're removing the

16.11 Pull the door handle out and remove the lock cylinder assembly

16.12 To remove the outside handle, pull it out, then slide it to the rear

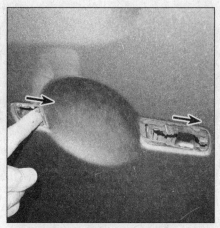

16.13a To remove the outside door handle mounting bracket, slide it to the rear

16:13b To disengage the actuator cable, push the cable ferrule out of its slot, then align the cable with the slot and slide out the cable end plug

16.18 To detach the latch from the door, remove these three Torx bolts

latch assembly, disconnect the lower end of the rod. The rod is secured to the actuator arms on both the key lock cylinder and the latch by small nylon clips. To disconnect either end of the rod, pop the part of the clip that wraps around the rod free of the rod, then push the end of the rod out of the nylon clip.

11   Pull the outside door handle, then remove the lock cylinder assembly (see illustration) (driver's side) or the outside handle trim cap (passenger's side).

12   Pull out the lock cylinder end of the outside handle and slide it to the rear to remove it (see illustration).

13   To remove the outside door handle mounting bracket, slide it toward the rear of the vehicle (see illustration) and pull it out of the door. Then flip it over and disconnect the actuator cable (see illustration).

14   Remove the door handle gaskets if necessary.

15   Installation is the reverse of removal.

Door latch

16   Remove the door trim panel (see Section 14).

17   Raise the door window glass completely.

18   Remove the Torx bolts from the rear edge of the door (see illustration) and pull the latch assembly out of the door. Discard the Torx bolts. New ones must be used during installation.

19   Disconnect the electrical connector and the actuator cable from the door latch (see illustration) and remove the latch assembly.

20   Installation is the reverse of removal. Install new Torx bolts.

---

17   Door window glass - removal and installation

Removal and installation

1   Lower the window.

2   Remove the door trim panel (see Section 14).

3   Carefully pry up and remove the inner seal that runs along the bottom of the window opening.

4   If removing the rear window, remove the glass run from the partition glass.

16.19 Disconnect the electrical connector from the latch assembly

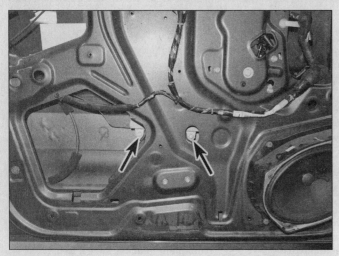

17.5 Door window glass bolts - 2012 and earlier models shown

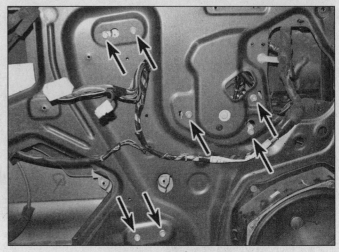

18.4 Window regulator bolt locations (2012 and earlier models shown)

18.5 Remove the regulator assembly through the opening in the door panel

5   Temporarily connect the power window switch, then move the window to align the glass mounting bolts with the access holes **(see illustration)**.

6   Remove the glass mounting bolts.

Note: *On 2013 and later models, the glass mounting bolts are located towards the outer edges of the glass instead of the middle of the glass as shown on earlier models.*

7   Pull the rear of the glass up and tilt it to the outside of the door as you remove it.

8   If removing the rear glass on 2012 and earlier models, remove the partition glass sash bolts and remove the sash.

9   Installation is the reverse of removal. Check the alignment of the glass and adjust the regulator or guide rails if necessary.

10   Initialize the system (see Steps 11 through 16).

System initialization

Note: *This procedure must be done whenever any window component has been removed or when an electrical component of the system has been removed or disconnected. These*

parts include the battery, switches, glass, regulator, etc.

2012 and earlier models

11   Raise the glass until it is fully closed.

12   Lower the glass, holding the switch until the glass is fully open, then release the switch.

13   Make sure the switch returns to the neutral position. If it doesn't, pull it up.

14   Check the anti-pinch system by opening the window fully. Put a piece of plastic or wood such as a hammer handle into the opening.

15   Raise the window using the AUTO UP function. Make sure that the window reverses itself after it contacts the object.

2013 and later models

16   Disconnect the battery (see Chapter 5), wait for one minute, then reconnect the battery.

17   Turn the ignition switch to ON.

18   Open the window completely.

19   Select AUTO UP and close the window, then hold the switch for at least four more

seconds with the window fully closed.

20   Check the anti-pinch system by opening the window fully. Put a piece of plastic or wood such as a hammer handle into the opening.

21   Raise the window using the AUTO UP function. Make sure that the window reverses itself after it contacts the object.

18 Door window glass regulator - removal and installation

1   Remove the door trim panel (see Section 14).

2   Remove the window glass assembly (see Section 17).

Note: *The glass need not be removed completely. It can be held in the top position and out of the way with tape.*

3   Disconnect the electrical connector from the window regulator motor.

4   Remove the bolts/nuts securing the regulator and power window motor to the door **(see illustration)**.

Note: *On 2013 and later models, the regulator assembly uses only nuts to mount the assembly to the door. The regulator consists of two run channels joined by a pair of drive cables.*

5   Remove the regulator assembly from the door **(see illustration)**.

6   Installation is the reverse of removal. Apply light grease to all moving parts.

7   See Section 17 for the initialization procedure.

19 Fender (front) - removal and installation

1   Loosen the front wheel lug nuts. Raise the vehicle and support it securely on jackstands. Remove the front wheel.

2   Remove the mudguards, then remove

19.2a Mudguard fasteners

19.2b Inner fender splash shield fasteners

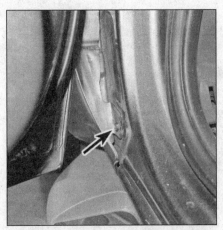

19.6a Open the door to remove the lower rear fender bolt...

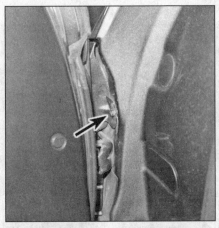

19.6b... and the upper rear fender bolt

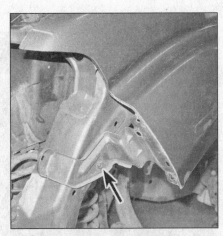

19.6c Fender front mounting bolt location

the inner fender splash shield **(see illustrations)**.

3   Remove the headlight housing (see Chapter 12).

4   On 2012 and earlier models, remove the front bumper cover (see Section 20).

5   On 2013 and later models, remove the plastic trim panel fasteners along the upper edge of the fender and remove the panels to access the upper mounting bolts.

6   Remove the fender mounting bolts **(see illustrations)** and remove the fender.

Caution: *The fender is glued to the body with foam adhesive. The foam can be peeled off a little at a time until it's removed. Use care when separating the fender from the body to avoid bending the fender.*

Note: *When removing the driver's side fender on 2012 and earlier models, the hood support rod will have to be removed. Support the hood with another hood prop before removing the upper fender mounting bolts.*

7   Installation is the reverse of removal. Adjust the hood (see Section 9) and doors (see Section 15) if necessary.

20   Bumper covers - removal and installation

Warning: *The models covered by this manual are equipped with a Supplemental Restraint System (SRS), more commonly known as air-bags. Always disarm the airbag system before working in the vicinity of any airbag system component to avoid the possibility of accidental deployment of the airbag, which could cause personal injury (see Chapter 12). Do not use a memory saving device to preserve the PCM's memory when working on or near airbag system components.*

Front bumper cover

1   Disconnect the cable from the negative terminal of the battery (see Chapter 5).

2   Apply the parking brake, raise the front of the vehicle and support it securely on jackstands.

3   Remove the radiator grille (see Section 11).

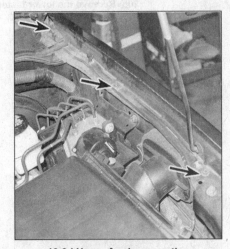

19.6d Upper fender mounting bolt locations

20.5a Remove the lower center valance fasteners...

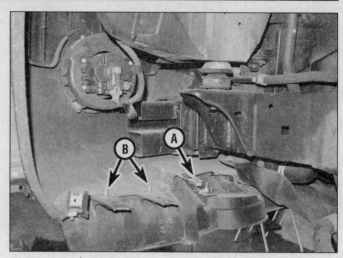

20.5b... then remove the left and right lower valance mounting screw (A) and nuts (B) - left side shown, right side identical

20.6 Remove the lower fasteners

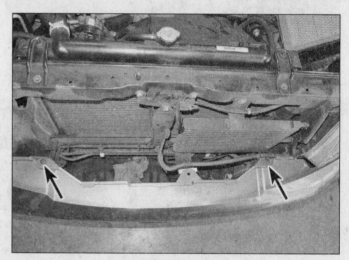

20.8 With the grille removed, remove these two fasteners

20.9 These screws secure the upper rear part of the bumper cover to the fender

2012 and earlier models

4   Remove the inner fender splash shield (see Section 19).

5   Remove the three lower valance fasteners **(see illustrations)** then remove the valances from the bottom of the bumper cover.

6   Remove the bumper cover-to-lower splash shield fasteners **(see illustration)**.

7   Disconnect the electrical connectors from the fog lights, if equipped.

8   Remove the plastic fasteners along the top edge of the bumper cover **(see illustration)**.

9   Working inside the bumper cover, remove the screws from the upper rear corners of the bumper cover where it's attached to the fenders **(see illustration)**.

10   Grasp each end of the bumper cover and pull it outward to separate its clips from the fenders, and remove the bumper cover.

Note: *You might need an assistant to help with the final removal of the bumper cover.*

11   Installation is the reverse of removal.

2013 and later models

Note: *On models equipped with a front camera, a calibration must be performed after removing/replacing the camera. This should be done by a Nissan repair facility.*

12   Remove the fasteners from the upper edge of the bumper cover.

13   Remove the two splash shields from the lower rear part of the bumper cover.

14   Working inside the bumper cover, remove the screws from the upper rear corners of the bumper cover where it's attached to the fenders.

15   Disconnect the electrical connectors from the fog lights, if equipped.

16   Grasp each end of the bumper cover and pull it outward to separate its clips from

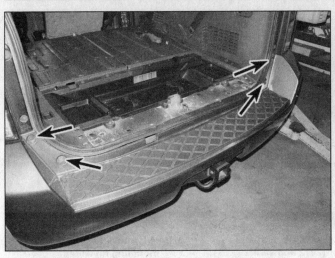

20.22 After the taillight assemblies are removed, remove the screws located under each taillight housing area

20.23 Mudguard fastener locations

the fenders, then remove it.

Note: *Having an assistant makes bumper cover removal easier.*

17　Installation is the reverse of removal.

Rear bumper cover

Note: *The illustrations in this Section show 2012 and earlier models. On later models, the sequence is the identical but the component locations are slightly different.*

18　Apply the parking brake.

19　Raise the rear of the vehicle and support it securely on jackstands.

20　Open the rear liftgate.

21　Remove the taillight assemblies (see Chapter 12).

22　Remove the bumper cover screws under each taillight (**see illustration**).

23　Remove the rear mudguard fasteners (**see illustration**), and remove the guards from both rear wheel wells (if equipped).

24　Remove the inner fender splash shield fasteners (**see illustration**) and the shield.

25　Working inside the bumper cover, remove the screw from the upper rear corners of the bumper cover where it's attached to the body (**see illustration**).

26　Remove the fasteners from the lower edge of the bumper cover (**see illustration**).

27　On 2012 and earlier models, remove the bumper cover support strut lower bolt from each side.

28　On 2012 and earlier models, remove the draft duct from the lower side of the left quarter panel.

29　Disconnect any electrical connectors.

30　Pull the bumper cover carefully to release the clips at the side brackets, then remove the bumper cover.

31　Installation is the reverse of removal.

20.24 Inner fender splash shield locations

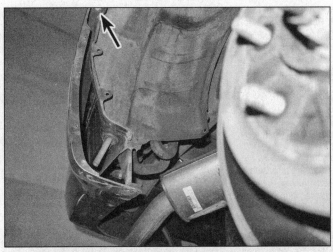

20.25 Upper rear bumper cover-to-body screw

20.26 Lower rear bumper cover fastener locations

21.2a Remove the trim panel plastic fasteners...

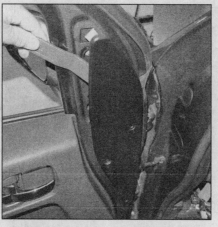

21.2b... then carefully pry off the mirror trim panel from the door (2012 and earlier models shown)

21.4 Remove the mirror mounting fasteners

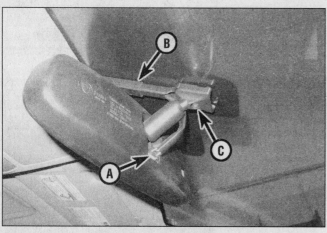

21.6 Inside mirror electrical connector (A), harness trim cover (B) and set screw (C) (2012 and earlier models shown)

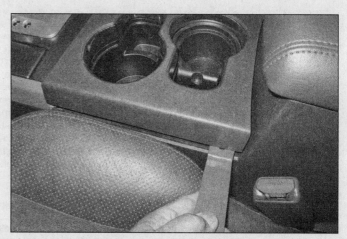

22.3 Pry out the cup holder trim panel

21   Mirrors - removal and installation

Outside mirrors

1   On 2013 and later models, remove the door trim panel (see Section 14).

2   Remove the trim panel plastic fasteners, if equipped, then pry off the mirror trim panel **(see illustrations)**.

3   Disconnect the mirror electrical connector, if equipped.

4   Remove the mirror mounting nuts **(see illustration)** and detach the mirror from the door.

5   Installation is the reverse of removal.

Inside mirror

6   Disconnect the electrical connector from the mirror **(see illustration)**.

7   On 2012 and earlier models, remove the trim cover from over the wiring harness.

8   Loosen the set screw and slide the mir-

ror up and off its base.

9   If the mirror base has come off the windshield, adhesive kits are available at auto parts stores to re-secure it. Follow the instructions included with the kit.

10   Installation is the reverse of removal.

22   Center console - removal and installation

Warning: *The models covered by this manual are equipped with a Supplemental Restraint System (SRS), more commonly known as airbags. Always disarm the airbag system before working in the vicinity of any airbag system component to avoid the possibility of accidental deployment of the airbag, which could cause personal injury (see Chapter 12). Do not use a memory saving device to preserve the PCM's memory when working on or near airbag system components.*

1   Disconnect the cable from the negative

terminal of the battery (see Chapter 5) and set the parking brake.

2012 and earlier models

2   Remove the knee bolster, center trim panel, glove box and lower passenger's side instrument panel (see Section 24).

3   Pry up the cup holder trim panel **(see illustration)**.

4   Remove the knob from the shift lever (see Chapter 7A).

5   Remove the shift indicator panel then disconnect the electrical connectors from the panel **(see illustrations)**.

6   Remove the fasteners from the rear section of the console, remove the fasteners from the front of the rear section, and unhook the console rear section from the console front section **(see illustrations)**.

7   Lift up the rear section and disconnect all electrical connectors, then remove the rear section of the console.

8   Remove the console-to-instrument

22.5a Use a trim tool to pry up the shift indicator panel...

22.5b... then disconnect the electrical connectors from the panel

22.6a Remove the screws from both lower corners of the rear section...

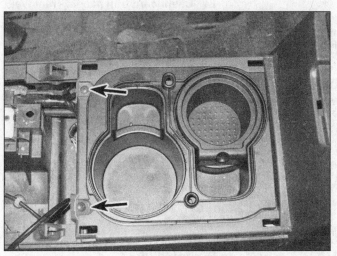

22.6b... then remove the screws from the top

22.6c Unhook the rear section from the front section

panel mounting screws (**see illustration**) and maneuver the front section of the console out of the vehicle.

9   Remove the center console from the vehicle.

10   Installation is the reverse of removal.

2013 and later models

11   Using a trim tool, carefully pry the left and right side trim panels out from the front sides of the console.

12   Working at the top front of the console, remove the mat from the front tray, then remove the fasteners below. Use a trim tool to disengage the clips, and lift the tray up enough to disconnect the electrical connectors and remove the tray.

13   Place the shifter in neutral.

14   Slide the cover under the shift knob down, then pry back and remove the knob retaining clip with a small screwdriver or an awl (see Chapter 7A). Remove the knob.

22.8 Remove the console-to-instrument panel retaining screws

23.3 Lower cover mounting screw locations

23.4 Disengage the clips along the perimeter and lift off the upper cover

24.1 Pull up on the kick panel to dislodge the retaining clips

15   Use a plastic trim removal tool or a screwdriver wrapped with tape to carefully pry up around the edges of the shift lever trim panel, releasing the clips as you go. There are two plastic claws at the front that must also be disengaged.

16   Lift the trim panel up, disconnect the electrical connectors from the underside and remove the panel.

17   Open the center arm rest, carefully pry out the trim just below the hinge, and remove the four mounting screws.

18   Use a plastic trim removal tool or a screwdriver wrapped with tape to carefully pry the trim panel from the rear of the console, then disconnect the electrical connectors from the panel.

19   Remove the console mounting screws around the perimeter. Pull up the rear, then slide it rearward to remove the console. Carefully lift it out of the vehicle.

20   Installation is the reverse of removal.

---

23   Steering column covers - removal and installation

Warning: *The models covered by this manual are equipped with a Supplemental Restraint System (SRS), more commonly known as airbags. Always disarm the airbag system before working in the vicinity of any airbag system component to avoid the possibility of accidental deployment of the airbag, which could cause personal injury (see Chapter 12). Do not use a memory saving device to preserve the PCM's memory when working on or near airbag system components.*

1   Disconnect the cable from the negative terminal of the battery (see Chapter 5).

2   Remove the knee bolster trim panel (see Section 24).

2012 and earlier models

3   Remove the screws from the lower half of the steering column cover **(see illustration)**.

4   Pull the upper cover straight up and off **(see illustration)**.

5   Detach the lower half of the steering column cover from the column.

6   Installation is the reverse of removal. Reconnect the battery (see Chapter 5).

2013 and later models

7   Remove the three steering column cover screws. There is one screw in the lower cover and there are two that connect the upper cover to the lower cover, behind the steering wheel. To access each of the upper screws, turn the steering wheel slightly to expose each screw cover. Pry out the covers and remove the screws.

8   The upper and lower covers are secured by four mounting tabs located in the upper half of the cover (two on each side). Grasp the upper and lower column cover halves firmly and pull them apart.

9   Carefully work the upper cover, then the lower cover off the steering column. Make sure that you don't scratch or damage anything.

10   Installation is the reverse of removal. Reconnect the battery and perform the necessary re-learn procedures (see Chapter 5).

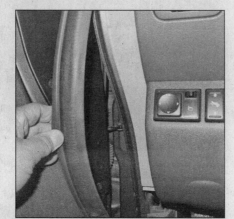

24.3 Pull the weatherstripping back from the edge of the opening

---

24   Dashboard trim panels - removal and installation

Warning: *The models covered by this manual are equipped with a Supplemental Restraint System (SRS), more commonly known as airbags. Always disarm the airbag system before working in the vicinity of any airbag system component to avoid the possibility of accidental deployment of the airbag, which could cause personal injury (see Chapter 12). Do not use a memory saving device to preserve the PCM's memory when working on or near airbag system components.*

Caution: *Use plastic trim removal tools on all procedures in this Section to avoid damage to the soft plastic dashboard trim panels (see Section 6).*

Kick panels

1   Pull up and dislodge the kick panel **(see illustration)**, or if necessary, pry up the kick panel using a trim tool.

2   To install, align the clips with their corresponding holes in the floor, then push the panel firmly until the clips snap into place.

Instrument panel end trim and caps

2012 and earlier models

Note: *The accompanying photo depicts the removal of the left end cap, but this procedure applies to either end cap.*

3   Remove the kick panel (see Step 1) then carefully pull the weatherstripping back from the opening **(see illustration)**.

4   Use a plastic trim tool or a screwdriver wrapped with tape to pry out either end cap **(see illustration)**.

5   To install an end cap, align the clips with their corresponding holes in the dash and push the cap firmly onto the dash until the clips snap into place.

24.4 Pry off the instrument panel end caps with a plastic trim tool

24.10 Knee bolster mounting screw locations

24.11 Work your way around the perimeter of the panel to disengage the clips

24.21 Twist the trim ring out of the panel

24.22 Instrument cluster bezel screws

2013 and later models

6   Using a trim tool, pry the end cap from the end of the instrument panel.

7   Installation is the reverse of removal.

Knee bolster trim panel

2012 and earlier models

8   Remove the kick panel (see Step 1).

9   Remove the left instrument panel end trim (see Steps 3 and 4).

10   Remove the knee bolster mounting screws (see illustration).

11   Working your way around the perimeter of the panel, use a trim tool to disengage the clips securing the knee bolster trim panel (see illustration). Grasp the panel firmly and pull it off. Detach the data link connector and all wiring and ducting attached to the backside of the panel, and remove the panel.

12   Installation is the reverse of removal.

2013 and later models

13   Remove the left instrument panel end cap (see Step 6).

14   Remove the knee bolster mounting screw.

15   Remove the hood lock release handle fasteners and remove the handle from the panel.

16   Remove the data link connector fasteners and remove the connector from the panel.

17   Working your way around the perimeter of the panel, use a trim tool to disengage the clips securing the knee bolster trim panel, and remove the panel.

18   Installation is the reverse of removal.

Instrument cluster trim bezel

2012 and earlier models

19   Remove the driver's side A-pillar trim (see Steps 29 through 33).

20   Remove the knee bolster trim panel (see Steps 8 through 11).

21   Remove the ignition switch trim ring (see illustration).

22   Remove the instrument cluster bezel fasteners (see illustration).

23   Carefully pry off the instrument cluster

24.23 Carefully pry off the instrument cluster trim bezel

bezel (see illustration). Detach any wiring harnesses attached to the backside of the bezel and remove it.

24   Installation is the reverse of removal.

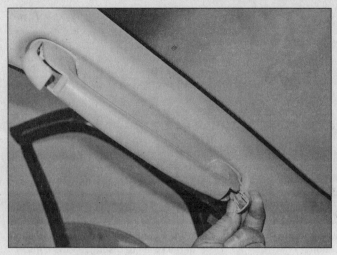

24.29a Pry open the screw trim covers...

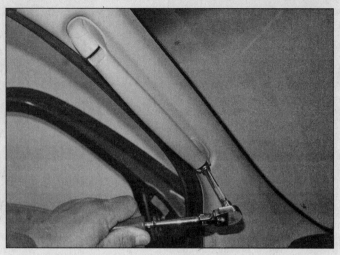

24.29b... then remove the handle mounting screws

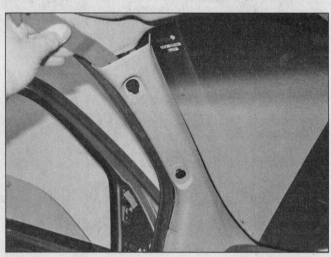

24.31 Disengage the two clips tvhat secure the trim to the A-pillar

24.38 Glove box outer screws

2013 and later models

25   Remove the end caps (see Step 6).
26   Remove the knee bolster trim panel (see Steps 13 through 17).
27   Carefully pry off the instrument cluster bezel. Detach any wiring harnesses attached to the backside of the bezel and remove it.
28   Installation is the reverse of removal.

A-pillar (windshield pillar) trim

29   On 2012 and earlier models, open the screw covers from the handles on the A-pillars, then remove the fasteners and handles **(see illustrations)**.
30   On 2013 and later models, partially remove the door weatherstrip.
31   Use a plastic trim tool or a screwdriver wrapped with tape to carefully pry loose the two mounting clips under the trim **(see illustration)**.
32   On 2013 and later models, pull the trim piece out just enough to reach behind and cut the tether clip located in the approximate cen-

ter of the trim piece.
33   Pull the trim up to disengage the lower locator tabs from the instrument panel, then remove the trim. On 2013 and later models, disconnect the electrical connectors, if equipped.
34   To install the A-pillar trim, align the locator tabs on the lower end of the trim with their corresponding slots in the instrument panel. On 2013 and later models, install a new tether clip and ensure it is properly installed before finishing installation.
35   Push the trim down against the instrument panel until it seats, then push the trim against the A-pillar until the two clips snap into place.

Glove box

2012 and earlier models

Lower glove box

36   Remove the A-pillar trim (see Steps 29 through 33).

37   Remove the kick panel (see Step 1), then remove the end trim (see Steps 3 and 4).
38   Remove the screws from the bottom of the glove box **(see illustration)**.
39   Open the glove box, then remove the screws from the top edge and interior of the glove box **(see illustration)**.
40   Remove the glove box along with the lower right side trim panel.
41   Installation is the reverse of removal.

Upper glove box

42   Remove the lower glove box (see Steps 36 through 40).
43   Open the upper glove box lid.
44   Remove the mounting screws **(see illustration)**.
45   Remove the glove box from the instrument panel.
46   Installation is the reverse of removal.

2013 and later models

47   Remove the end caps (see Step 6).
48   Remove the lower mounting screws.

24.39 Remove the glove box mounting screws

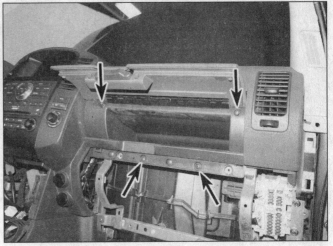

24.44 Upper glove box mounting screws

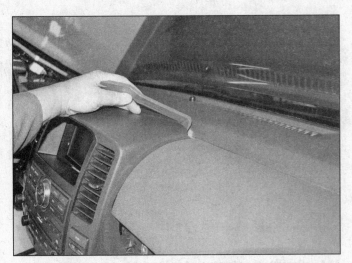

24.56 Carefully pry out the upper center trim panel with a trim tool

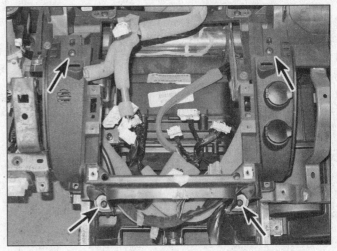

24.67 Lower center trim panel fastener locations

49   Open the glove box lid and remove the three mounting screws along the upper edge of the opening.
50   Slide the glove box outwards, disconnect the electrical connectors, and remove the glove box.
51   Installation is the reverse of removal.

Upper center trim panel

2012 and earlier models
52   Remove the shift indicator panel (**see illustrations 22.5a and 22.5b**).
53   On models with a standard audio system, remove the storage tray, then remove the exposed screw.
54   On models with a display unit, remove the center bin screws and remove the center bin. Remove the two lower screws (see Chapter 12 , illustration 12.6).
55   Remove the knee bolster, instrument cluster bezel and lower glove box as described in this Section.
56   Use a trim tool to carefully pry along the

perimeter of the panel (**see illustration**), and pull the trim panel and audio unit away from the instrument panel as an assembly.
57   Disconnect the electrical connectors to the audio and air conditioning control units, then remove the assembly.
58   If you're replacing the trim panel, remove the audio unit bracket mounting screws and remove the audio unit. Remove the air conditioning and heater control unit mounting screws, and separate the unit from the panel.
59   Installation is the reverse of removal.

2013 and later models
60   Remove the lower center trim panel (see Steps 70 through 72).
61   Remove the mounting screws just below the vents on the trim panel.
62   Working your way around the perimeter of the panel, use a trim tool to disengage the clips securing the upper center trim panel, and remove the panel.
Note: *Once the panel is out, if the vents need to be replaced, depress the tabs on the sides*

of the vent(s) and pull the vent(s) out of the panel.
63   Installation is the reverse of removal.

Lower center trim panel

2012 and earlier models
64   Remove the center console (see Section 22).
65   Remove the knee bolster, instrument cluster bezel and lower glove box as described in this Section.
66   Remove the upper center trim panel as described in this Section.
67   Remove the mounting screws from the panel (**see illustration**). Slide the panel forward and disconnect the electrical connectors.
68   Remove the trim panel from the vehicle.
69   Installation is the reverse of removal.

2013 and later models
70   Use a trim tool to disengage the clips securing the lower trim panel under the air

25.15a Remove the fuse box mounting bolts and maneuver the box off of the instrument panel

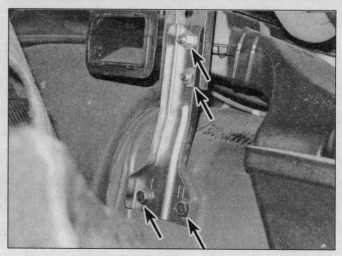

25.15b Remove the instrument panel left side center support fasteners

25.15c Remove the right side center support fasteners and support

25.15d Remove the plastic caps in the door openings then remove the mounting bolts from each side - 2012 and earlier models shown

conditioning and heater control unit, and remove the panel.

71   Use trim tool to pry up the small panel just below the screen, then remove the fastener now exposed.

72   Use a trim tool to pry the lower center trim panel out of the instrument panel. Remove the air conditioning and heater control unit mounting screws and separate the unit from the panel.

73   Installation is the reverse of removal.

25 Instrument panel - removal and installation

Warning: *The models covered by this manual are equipped with a Supplemental Restraint System (SRS), more commonly known as airbags. Always disarm the airbag system before working in the vicinity of any airbag system component to avoid the possibility of accidental deployment of the airbag, which could*

cause personal injury (see Chapter 12). Do not use a memory saving device to preserve the PCM's memory when working on or near airbag system components.

Caution: *This is definitely a two-man job. Even stripped of all its components, the instrument panel, or dashboard, is fairly heavy. Do NOT attempt to lift it out of the vehicle by yourself.*

1   Disconnect the cable from the negative terminal of the battery (see Chapter 5).

2   Remove the instrument panel trim end caps (see Section 24).

3   Move the front seats as far back as they will go. Removing the seats will give you more working room (see Section 27)

4   Remove the center console (see Section 22).

5   Remove the steering wheel (see Chapter 10), the steering column covers (see Section 23) and all of the dashboard trim panels (see Section 24).

6   Remove all dashboard-mounted speakers (see Chapter 12).

Note: *On 2013 and later models, once the dashboard speakers are removed, locate the instrument panel mounting bolt in the corners of the speaker openings and remove the bolts.*

7   Remove the instrument cluster (see Chapter 12).

8   Remove the heater and air conditioning control unit (see Chapter 3).

9   Remove the audio unit (see Chapter 12).

10   Remove the A-pillar trim handles and trim panel (see Section 24).

11   If equipped, remove the display screen from behind the center vent unit (see Chapter 12).

12   Remove the glove box (see Section 24).

13   Disconnect the wiring from the passenger's airbag module, then remove the module's mounting bolt.

Note: *All electrical connectors for airbag harnesses are bright yellow.*

14   Clearly label, then disconnect, all electrical connectors in the dashboard area and

26.2 Use a small screwdriver to remove the plastic fasteners

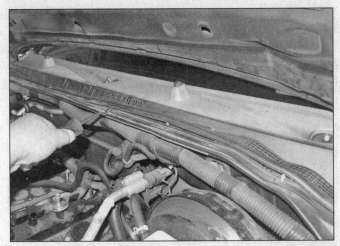

26.3 Use a trim tool to pry up the seal

26.4 Lift the cowl cover up, then disconnect the washer line

3   Remove the cowl cover seal along the front edge of the panel **(see illustration)**.
4   Lift the cowl cover up, disconnect the washer line from the washer nozzles **(see illustration)** and remove the cowl cover.
5   Remove the cowl extension fasteners and remove the extensions from both sides.
6   Installation is the reverse of removal.

2013 and later models
Cowl cover
7   Remove the cowl cover seal fasteners along the front edge of the panel and remove the seal.
8   Disengage the clips and hooks along the hood-to-cowl trim panels and remove the panels from each corner.
9   Disconnect the windshield washer line at the splice connector in the engine compartment.
10   Remove the fasteners from the plastic trim pieces from the left and right lower corners of the windshield, then remove the trim pieces.
11   Remove the cowl cover fasteners, then pull the cowl forward to remove it.
12   Installation is the reverse of removal.

Lower cowl
13   Disconnect the cable from the negative terminal of the battery (see Chapter 5).
14   Remove the wiper motor (see Chapter 12).
15   Remove the brake fluid reservoir bracket nuts, release the brake level sensor harness clips, then move the brake fluid reservoir out of the way. Keep the reservoir upright to prevent fluid spills.
16   Remove the fuse and relay box mounting nuts and secure the fuse and relay box out of the way.
17   Remove the lower cowl mounting bolts, then remove the cowl.
18   Installation is the reverse of removal.
19   Reconnect the battery and perform the

27.2 Slide off the plastic trim covers, then remove the rear mounting bolts

necessary relearn procedures (see Chapter 5).

---

27   Seats - removal and installation

Warning: *The models covered by this manual are equipped with a Supplemental Restraint System (SRS), more commonly known as airbags. Always disarm the airbag system before working in the vicinity of any airbag system component to avoid the possibility of accidental deployment of the airbag, which could cause personal injury (see Chapter 12). Do not use a memory saving device to preserve the PCM's memory when working on or near airbag system components.*

Front seat
1   Position the seat as far forward as possible to access the rear mounting bolts.
2   Remove the trim covers from the seat bolts, then unscrew the bolts **(see illustration)**.
3   Move the seat as far rearward as possible to access the front mounting bolts.

---

detach all wiring harnesses from the dash.
Note: *You might not be able to reach every harness clip; keep this in mind while pulling out the dash.*
15   Remove all the instrument panel mounting screws **(see illustrations)**.
16   With the help of an assistant, lift the instrument panel back just far enough to access and disconnect any remaining wiring harnesses or other components.
17   Carefully remove the instrument panel through the passenger's door opening.
18   Installation is the reverse of removal. Reconnect the battery and perform the necessary re-learn procedures (see Chapter 5).

---

26   Cowl cover - removal and installation

1   Remove the windshield wiper arms (see Chapter 12).

2012 and earlier models
2   Remove the fasteners from both corners of the cowl **(see illustration)**.

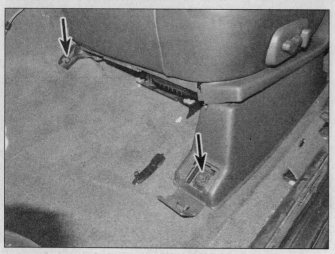

27.4 Slide the seat to the rear and remove the plastic trim covers and front mounting bolts

27.9 Second row seat mounting bolt locations

27.26 Remove the seat bolts from the front

27.28 Remove the bolts from the back side of the seats

4   Remove the trim covers from the seat bolts, then unscrew the bolts **(see illustration)**.

5   Disconnect the cable from the negative terminal of the battery, then disconnect the positive cable (see Chapter 5). Wait at least 10 minutes before proceeding.

6   Tilt the seat fully forward and disconnect the airbag wiring harness and any other wiring attached to the seat. Detach the wiring harness clips, then carefully lift the seat out.

7   Installation is the reverse of removal. Reconnect the battery and perform the necessary re-learn procedures (see Chapter 5).

Rear seat

Second row seats

2012 and earlier models

8   Release the seat and tilt it forward.

9   Remove the seat mounting bolts **(see illustration)**.

10   Lower the seat then tilt the seatback forward.

11   On the outboard seat, remove the seat trim covers from the front side of the seat at the base, then remove the seat mounting nuts and remove the seat.

12   Remove the center seat cushion mounting bolts and remove the cushion.

13   Installation is the reverse of removal.

2013 and later models

14   Use a trim tool to pry out the rear kick plate, disengaging the clips.

15   Remove the headrests from the seats.

16   Slide the seats as far back as possible, then remove the bolt trim covers.

17   Pull up on the front edge of the seat to release it from the locking pawls. Place a special tool (J-51030 cross brace with bolts) over the track alignment holes, then use the two left-hand threaded bolts through the brace into the track, and tighten the bolts.

18   Disconnect the harness connector, if equipped, and remove the harness from the seat frame.

19   Remove the seat bolts from the front side of the seat.

20   Slide the seat fully forward.

21   Remove the trim covers and pull up on the rear edge to release the locking pawls.

22   Place the special tool (J-51030 cross brace with bolts) over the track alignment holes, then use the four left-hand threaded bolts through the brace into the track, and tighten the bolts.

23   Remove the seat bolts from the rear side of the seat.

24   Place the seatback in the flat position, then remove the seat from the vehicle.

25   Installation is the reverse of removal.

Third row seats

2012 and earlier models

26   Remove the trim cover from the front side of the seats, then remove the mounting bolts **(see illustration)**.

27   Lower the seatbacks into the cargo floor position storage position.

28   Remove the rear mounting bolts **(see illustration)** and remove the seats.

2013 and later models

29   Remove the trim covers from the front side of the seats then remove the mounting bolts.

30   Pull the seat back release lever and fold down the seat backs.

31   Open the storage compartment lid then remove the storage box fasteners and box from the rear of the vehicle.

32   Remove the jack and jack bracket mounting bolts, then remove the jack.

33   Remove the trim cover side trim from each side.

34   Remove the seatbelt mounting bolts, then remove the seat bolts from the back side of the seats.

35   Remove the seats from the vehicle.

36   Installation is the reverse of removal.

28.5 Mounting bolt locations - right side shown, left side similar

28   Rear quarter trim panels - removal and installation

1   Remove the second and third row seats (see Section 27).

2   Pry off the covers and remove the bolts from the second and third row seat belt upper anchors.

2012 and earlier models

3   Pry off the rear kick panels.

4   Remove the plastic trim fasteners around the window trim, then carefully pry the trim from around the window.

5   Remove the rear quarter trim panel mounting bolts **(see illustration)**.

6   Remove the plastic trim fasteners along the upper edge of the panel.

7   Use a trim tool to carefully pry along the edges of the quarter trim panel to release the

remaining clips, then remove the panel from the vehicle.

8   To remove the liftgate kick plate, slide a trim tool under the edge and work the clips loose.

9   Installation is the reverse of removal.

2013 and later models

10   Open the storage box then remove the fasteners and lift out the box.

11   Remove the trim covers to access the mounting bolts, then remove the mounting bolts.

12   Remove the plastic trim fasteners around the perimeter.

13   Using a trim tool, carefully pry around the edges of the panel until all the fasteners are released, then remove the panel from the vehicle.

14   To remove the liftgate kick plate, release the steel clips at each corner, then work a trim

tool around the edge to release the trim clips.

15   Installation is the reverse of removal.

29   Rear spoiler - removal and installation (2013 and later models)

1   Remove the liftgate trim panels (see Section 14).

2   From inside the liftgate, remove the spoiler mounting nuts.

3   Disconnect the electrical connector from the high-mount brake light.

4   Disconnect and plug the rear washer tube.

5   Use a plastic trim removal tool to pry along the upper edge of the spoiler to disengage the mounting clips, then lift the spoiler up and off.

6   Installation is the reverse of removal.

Notes

Chapter 12
Chassis electrical system

Contents

	Section		Section
Airbag system - general information	25	Horn - replacement	19
Audio antenna - removal and installation	14	Instrument cluster - removal and installation	11
Body Control Module (BCM) - general information	8	Intelligent Power Distribution Module (IPDM) - description,	
Bulb replacement	18	check and replacement	26
Circuit breakers - general information	4	Power door lock system - general information	23
Cruise control system - description and check	21	Power window system - general information	22
Dashboard switches - replacement	10	Radio and speakers - removal and installation	12
Electrical connectors - general information	6	Rear window defogger - check and repair	13
Electrical troubleshooting - general information	2	Relays - general information	5
Fuses and fusible links - general information	3	Remote keyless entry fob - battery replacement	7
General information	1	Steering column switches - replacement	9
Headlights adjustment	17	Sunroof - general information	24
Headlight bulb - replacement	16	Wiper arms and motors - removal and installation	20
Headlight housing - removal and installation	15	Wiring diagrams - general information	27

1   General information

1   The electrical system is a 12-volt, negative ground type. Power for the lights and all electrical accessories is supplied by a lead/acid-type battery that is charged by the alternator.

2   This Chapter covers repair and service procedures for the various electrical components not associated with the engine. Information on the battery, alternator, ignition system and starter motor can be found in Chapter 5.

3   It should be noted that when portions of the electrical system are serviced, the negative cable should be disconnected from the battery (see Chapter 5) to prevent electrical shorts and/or fires.

2   Electrical troubleshooting - general information

1   A typical electrical circuit consists of an electrical component, any switches, relays, motors, fuses, fusible links or circuit breakers related to that component and the wiring and connectors that link the component to both the battery and the chassis. To help you pinpoint an electrical circuit problem, wiring diagrams are included at the end of this Chapter.

2   Before tackling any troublesome electrical circuit, first study the appropriate wiring diagrams to get a complete understanding of what makes up that individual circuit.

Trouble spots, for instance, can often be narrowed down by noting if other components related to the circuit are operating properly. If several components or circuits fail at one time, chances are the problem is in a fuse or ground connection, because several circuits are often routed through the same fuse and ground connections.

3   Electrical problems usually stem from simple causes, such as loose or corroded connections, a blown fuse, a melted fusible link or a failed relay. Visually inspect the condition of all fuses, wires and connections in a problem circuit before troubleshooting the circuit.

4   If test equipment and instruments are going to be utilized, use the diagrams to plan ahead of time where you will make the necessary connections in order to accurately pinpoint the trouble spot.

5   The basic tools needed for electrical troubleshooting include a circuit tester or voltmeter (a 12-volt bulb with a set of test leads can also be used), a continuity tester, which includes a bulb, battery and set of test leads, and a jumper wire, preferably with a circuit breaker incorporated, which can be used to bypass electrical components (see illustrations). Before attempting to locate a problem with test instruments, use the wiring diagram(s) to decide where to make the connections.

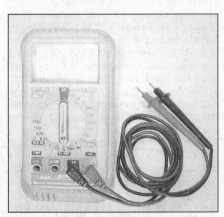

2.5a The most useful tool for electrical troubleshooting is a digital multimeter that can check volts, amps, and test continuity

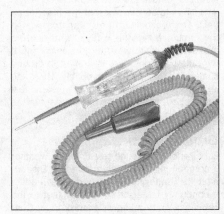

2.5b A test light is a very handy tool for checking voltage

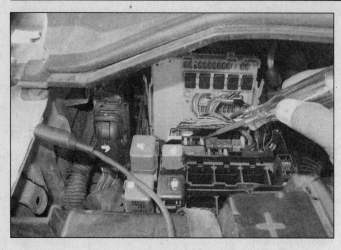

2.6 In use, a basic test light's lead is clipped to a known good ground, then the pointed probe can test connectors, wires or electrical sockets - if the bulb lights, the part being tested has battery voltage

2.9 With a multimeter set to the ohms scale, resistance can be checked across two terminals - when checking for continuity, a low reading indicates continuity, a high reading indicates lack of continuity

Voltage checks

6   Voltage checks should be performed if a circuit is not functioning properly. Connect one lead of a circuit tester to either the negative battery terminal or a known good ground. Connect the other lead to a connector in the circuit being tested, preferably nearest to the battery or fuse **(see illustration)**. If the bulb of the tester lights, voltage is present, which means that the part of the circuit between the connector and the battery is problem free. Continue checking the rest of the circuit in the same fashion. When you reach a point at which no voltage is present, the problem lies between that point and the last test point with voltage. Most of the time the problem can be traced to a loose connection.
Note: *Keep in mind that some circuits receive voltage only when the ignition key is in the Accessory or Run position.*

Finding a short

7   One method of finding shorts in a circuit is to remove the fuse and connect a test light or voltmeter in place of the fuse terminals. There should be no voltage present in the circuit. Move the wiring harness from side-to-side while watching the test light. If the bulb goes on, there is a short to ground somewhere in that area, probably where the insulation has rubbed through. The same test can be performed on each component in the circuit, even a switch.

Ground check

8   Perform a ground test to check whether a component is properly grounded. Disconnect the battery and connect one lead of a continuity tester or multimeter (set to the ohms scale), to a known good ground. Connect the other lead to the wire or ground connection being tested. If the resistance is low (less than 5 ohms), the ground is good. If the

bulb on a self-powered test light does not go on, the ground is not good.

Continuity check

9   A continuity check is done to determine if there are any breaks in a circuit - if it is passing electricity properly. With the circuit off (no power in the circuit), a self-powered continuity tester or multimeter can be used to check the circuit. Connect the test leads to both ends of the circuit (or to the power end and a good ground), and if the test light comes on the circuit is passing current properly **(see illustration)**. If the resistance is low (less than 5 ohms), there is continuity; if the reading is 10,000 ohms or higher, there is a break somewhere in the circuit. The same procedure can be used to test a switch, by connecting the continuity tester to the switch terminals. With the switch turned On, the test light should come on (or low resistance should be indicated on a meter).

Finding an open circuit

10   When diagnosing for possible open circuits, it is often difficult to locate them by sight because the connectors hide oxidation or terminal misalignment. Merely wiggling a connector on a sensor or in the wiring harness may correct the open circuit condition. Remember this when an open circuit is indicated when troubleshooting a circuit. Intermittent problems may also be caused by oxidized or loose connections.
11   Electrical troubleshooting is simple if you keep in mind that all electrical circuits are basically electricity running from the battery, through the wires, switches, relays, fuses and fusible links to each electrical component (light bulb, motor, etc.) and to ground, from which it is passed back to the battery. Any electrical problem is an interruption in the flow of electricity to and from the battery.

3   Fuses and fusible links - general information

Fuses

1   The electrical circuits of the vehicle are protected by a combination of fuses, circuit breakers and fusible links. The main fuse/relay panels are in the engine compartment, while the interior fuse/relay panel is located inside the passenger compartment **(see illustrations)**. Each of the fuses is designed to protect a specific circuit, and the various circuits are identified on the fuse panel itself.
2   Several sizes of fuses are employed in the fuse blocks. There are small, medium and large sizes of the same design, all with the same blade terminal design. The medium and large fuses can be removed with your fingers, but the small fuses require the use of pliers or the small plastic fuse-puller tool found in most fuse boxes.
3   If an electrical component fails, always check the fuse first. The best way to check the fuses is with a test light. Check for power at the exposed terminal tips of each fuse. If power is present at one side of the fuse but not the other, the fuse is blown. A blown fuse can also be identified by visually inspecting it **(see illustration)**.
4   Be sure to replace blown fuses with the correct type. Fuses (of the same physical size) of different ratings may be physically interchangeable, but only fuses of the proper rating should be used. Replacing a fuse with one of a higher or lower value than specified is not recommended. Each electrical circuit needs a specific amount of protection. The amperage value of each fuse is molded into the top of the fuse body.
5   If the replacement fuse immediately fails, don't replace it again until the cause of the problem is isolated and corrected. In most

3.1a On 2012 and earlier models, the interior fuse box is located at the right side of the instrument panel, behind the glove box door and the fuse panel cover

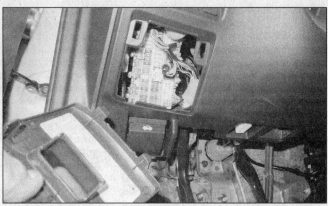

3.1b On 2013 and later models, the interior fuse box is located at the left side of the instrument panel, behind the fuse panel cover

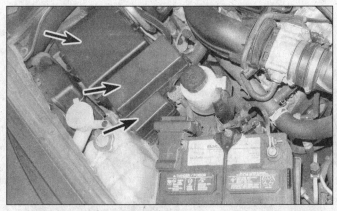

3.1c On 2012 and earlier models, the engine compartment fuse/relay boxes are located along the right side of the engine compartment

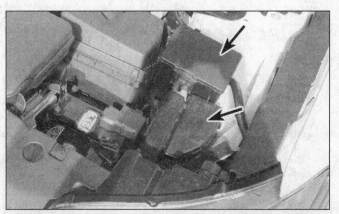

3.1d On 2013 and later models, the engine compartment fuse/relay boxes are located along the left side of the engine compartment

cases, this will be a short circuit in the wiring caused by a broken or deteriorated wire.

Fusible links

6   Some circuits are protected by fusible links. The links are used in circuits which are not ordinarily fused, or which carry high current, such as the circuit between the alternator and the starter motor. Cartridge-type fusible links are located in the engine compartment fuse/relay box and are similar to a large fuse. After disconnecting the negative battery cable, simply unplug the fusible link and replace it with a fusible link of the same amperage. If you have to replace a blown fusible link, make sure that you replace it with one of the same rating. If the replacement fusible link blows in the same circuit, make sure that you troubleshoot the circuit in which the fusible link melted BEFORE installing another fusible link.

4   Circuit breakers - general information

1   Circuit breakers protect certain circuits, such as the power windows or heated seats.

Depending on the vehicle's accessories, there may be one or two circuit breakers, located in the fuse/relay box in the engine compartment.
2   Because the circuit breakers reset automatically, an electrical overload in a circuit breaker-protected system will cause the circuit to fail momentarily, then come back on. If the circuit does not come back on, check it immediately.
3   For a basic check, pull the circuit breaker up out of its socket on the fuse panel, but just far enough to probe with a voltmeter. The breaker should still contact the sockets. With the voltmeter negative lead on a good chassis ground, touch each end prong of the circuit breaker with the positive meter probe. There should be battery voltage at each end. If there is battery voltage only at one end, the circuit breaker must be replaced.
4   Some circuit breakers must be reset manually.

5   Relays - general information

1   Several electrical accessories in the vehicle, such as the fuel injection system, horns,

starter, and fog lamps use relays to transmit the electrical signal to the component. Relays use a low-current circuit (the control circuit) to open and close a high-current circuit (the power circuit). If the relay is defective, that component will not operate properly. Most relays are mounted in the engine compartment and interior fuse/relay boxes **(see illustrations 3.1a, 3.1b, 3.1c and 3.1d)**.

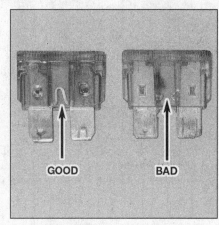

3.3 When a fuse blows, the element between the terminals melts

6   Electrical connectors - general information

1   Most electrical connections on these vehicles are made with multiwire plastic connectors. The mating halves of many connectors are secured with locking clips molded into the plastic connector shells. The mating halves of some large connectors, such as some of those under the instrument panel, are held together by a bolt through the center of the connector.

2   To separate a connector with locking clips, use a small screwdriver to pry the clips apart carefully, then separate the connector halves. Pull only on the shell, never pull on the wiring harness as you may damage the individual wires and terminals inside the connectors. Look at the connector closely before trying to separate the halves. Often the locking clips are engaged in a way that is not immediately clear. Additionally, many connectors have more than one set of clips.

3   Each pair of connector terminals has a male half and a female half. When you look at the end view of a connector in a diagram, be sure to understand whether the view shows the harness side or the component side of the connector. Connector halves are mirror images of each other, and a terminal shown on the right side end-view of one half will be on the left side end-view of the other half.

4   It is often necessary to take circuit voltage measurements with a connector connected. Whenever possible, carefully insert a small straight pin (not your meter probe) into the rear of the connector shell to contact the terminal inside, then clip your meter lead to the pin. This kind of connection is called "backprobing." When inserting a test probe into a terminal, be careful not to distort the terminal opening. Doing so can lead to a poor connection and corrosion at that terminal later. Using the small straight pin instead of a meter probe results in less chance of deforming the terminal connector.

Electrical connectors

Most electrical connectors have a single release tab that you depress to release the connector

Some electrical connectors have a retaining tab which must be pried up to free the connector

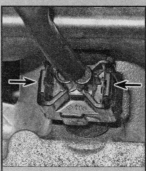

Some connectors have two release tabs that you must squeeze to release the connector

Some connectors use wire retainers that you squeeze to release the connector

Critical connectors often employ a sliding lock (1) that you must pull out before you can depress the release tab (2)

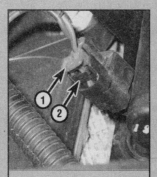

Here's another sliding-lock style connector, with the lock (1) and the release tab (2) on the side of the connector

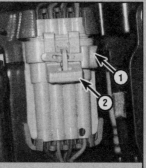

On some connectors the lock (1) must be pulled out to the side and removed before you can lift the release tab (2)

Some critical connectors, like the multi-pin connectors at the Powertrain Control Module employ pivoting locks that must be flipped open

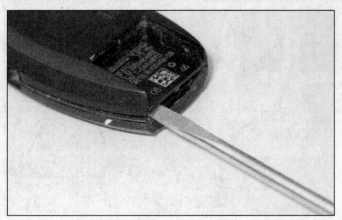

7.1 Remove the key and pry apart the fob

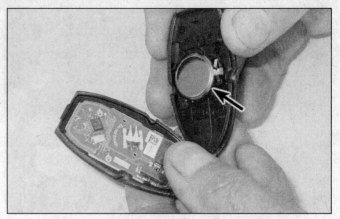

7.2 Carefully remove the battery without touching any other components

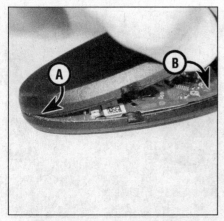

7.3 Engage the lip of the back half of the cover (A) into the end of the other half of the fob, then swing the other end down and snap it into place (B)

8.2a On 2012 and earlier models, the BCM is located under the left side of the instrument panel, mounted to a bracket above the accelerator pedal

8.2b On 2013 and later models, the BCM is located behind the instrument cluster

7   Remote keyless entry fob - battery replacement

1   Remove the key from the fob, then carefully pry open the keyless entry fob by inserting a small screwdriver into the notch in the body of the transmitter **(see illustration)**.
2   Carefully pry out the old battery with a small screwdriver **(see illustration)**.
Caution: *Do not touch the circuit board or battery terminal contacts inside the key fob.*
3   Install the new battery, making sure the positive (+) terminal faces the bottom of the case, then reassemble the two halves **(see illustration)**.
Caution: *Handle the battery by its edges only; holding it like a coin (touching both sides) can reduce the battery's life by partially discharging it.*

8   Body Control Module (BCM) - general information

1   The Body Control Module (BCM) receives inputs from various switches and sensors and sends commands, some in the form of multiplex voltage signals, to corresponding components to operate them. Some circuits are controlled by the BCM in conjunction with the Intelligent Power Distribution Module (IPDM) (see Section 26) and/or the Powertrain Control Module (PCM) (see Chapter 6). The circuits under BCM control include the:

Combination switch system
Signal buffer system
Power consumption control system
Auto light system
*Turn signal and hazard warning
  light system*
Headlight system
Fog light system
Daytime running lights system
Interior illumination system
*Interior illumination battery
  saver system*
Windshield wiper/washer system
Warning chime system
Power door lock system
Power window system
Air conditioning compressor clutch

Nissan Anti-Theft System (NATS)
Vehicle security system
Rear window defogger system
Remote keyless entry system
Intelligent Key system
Ignition push switch system
Electronic steering column lock
Tire pressure monitor system (TPMS)
*Retained accessory power
  (RAP) system*

2   On 2012 and earlier models, the BCM is located at the driver's side of the instrument panel just above the accelerator pedal; on 2013 and later models, it is located behind the instrument cluster **(see illustrations)**. Removal and installation of the BCM is not covered in this manual because special equipment is required to diagnose it and the systems it controls. Additionally, if the BCM requires replacement, it must be programmed with the same special equipment before it will work. So, diagnosis and replacement of the BCM must be performed at a dealer service department or other qualified repair shop equipped with the necessary tool.

9.3 Squeeze the two clips to release the switch from the column (turn/headlight switch shown; wiper/washer switch similar)

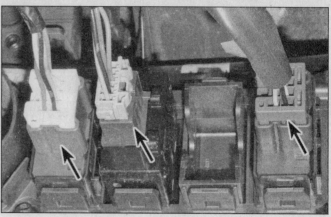

10.4 Disconnect the electrical connector

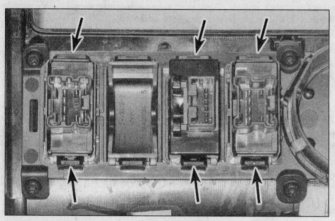

10.5 To remove the switch, release the clips

11.3a Instrument cluster mounting screws - 2012 and earlier models

9   Steering column switches - replacement

Warning: *The models covered by this manual are equipped with Supplemental Restraint Systems (SRS), more commonly known as airbags. Always disable the airbag system before working in the vicinity of any airbag system components to avoid the possibility of accidental deployment of the airbags, which could cause personal injury (see Section 25).*

1   Disconnect the cable from the negative terminal of the battery (see Chapter 5).
2   Remove the steering column covers (see Chapter 11).

2012 and earlier models

Note: *Each switch can be replaced independently of the other.*
3   Press in the two clips and pull out the switch **(see illustration)**.
4   Installation is the reverse of removal.

2013 and later models

Note: *The lighting and turn signal switch as well as the wiper/washer switch are integrated into the combination switch and must be re-*

placed as an assembly.
5   Remove the steering wheel (see Chapter 10).
6   Remove the combination switch mounting screws.
7   Disconnect the electrical connector from the combination switch and remove the switch.
8   Installation is the reverse of removal.

10   Dashboard switches - replacement

Warning: *The models covered by this manual are equipped with Supplemental Restraint Systems (SRS), more commonly known as airbags. Always disable the airbag system before working in the vicinity of any airbag system components to avoid the possibility of accidental deployment of the airbags, which could cause personal injury (see Section 25).*

1   Disconnect the cable from the negative terminal of the battery (see Chapter 5).
2   For lower driver's side switches, remove the driver's knee bolster (see Chapter 11).
3   For center dash switches, remove the center trim panel (see Chapter 11).

4   Disconnect the electrical connector from the switch being replaced **(see illustration)**.
5   Use a small screwdriver to release the clips **(see illustration)** and pull out the switch.
6   Installation is the reverse of removal. Reconnect the battery and perform the necessary re-learn procedures (see Chapter 5).

11   Instrument cluster - removal and installation

Warning: *The models covered by this manual are equipped with Supplemental Restraint Systems (SRS), more commonly known as airbags. Always disable the airbag system before working in the vicinity of any airbag system components to avoid the possibility of accidental deployment of the airbags, which could cause personal injury (see Section 25).*

1   Disconnect the cable from the negative terminal of the battery (see Chapter 5).
2   Remove the instrument cluster bezel (see Chapter 11).
3   Remove the mounting screws from the instrument cluster and pull out the cluster **(see illustrations)**.

11.3b Instrument cluster mounting screws - 2013 and later models

12.6 Radio bracket-to-instrument panel bolt locations

12.7 Disconnect the electrical connectors from the back of the radio unit

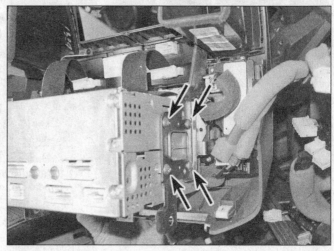

12.8 Remove the radio bracket screws from each side of the radio

4   Unplug the electrical connectors and remove the cluster from the vehicle.

5   Installation is the reverse of removal. Reconnect the battery and perform the necessary re-learn procedures (see Chapter 5).

12   Radio and speakers - removal and installation

Warning: *The models covered by this manual are equipped with Supplemental Restraint Systems (SRS), more commonly known as airbags. Always disable the airbag system before working in the vicinity of any airbag system components to avoid the possibility of accidental deployment of the airbags, which could cause personal injury (see Section 25).*

1   Disconnect the cable from the negative terminal of the battery (see Chapter 5).

Radio

Base unit

2   Remove the upper center trim panel (see Chapter 11).

3   Remove the radio mounting screws and detach the radio from the trim panel.

4   Remove the radio bracket screws and remove the brackets from the unit, if necessary.

5   Installation is the reverse of removal. Reconnect the battery and perform the necessary re-learn procedures (see Chapter 5).

Mid level and higher units

Note: *The accompanying photos show 2012 and earlier models; 2013 and later models are similar.*

Note: *The radio unit is mounted to the instrument panel center trim panel.*

6   Remove the center console (see Chap-

ter 11) to access the radio unit bracket-to-instrument panel bolts **(see illustration)**.

7   Remove the small trim panel below the radio then remove the center trim panel (see Chapter 11) and pull the center trim panel out enough to disconnect the electrical connectors from the radio unit **(see illustration)**.

8   Remove the bracket mounting screws **(see illustration)** and separate the radio unit from the center trim panel.

9   Installation is the reverse of removal.

A/C and Radio switch unit

10   Remove the radio (see earlier in this Section).

11   Remove the A/C and radio switch unit mounting screws, then remove the unit from the center trim panel.

12   Installation is the reverse of removal.

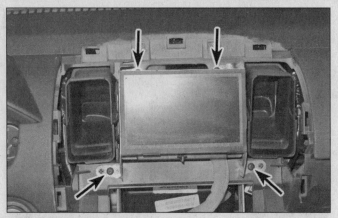

12.14 Display unit bracket mounting screw locations - 2012 and earlier models shown, later models similar

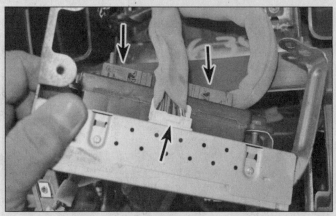

12.15 Disconnect the electrical connectors from the back of the display unit

12.19 Using a trim tool, pry up the speaker grille

12.20 Remove the instrument panel speaker mounting screws

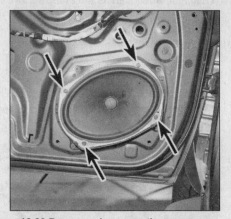

12.23 Door speaker mounting screws - front door shown, rear door similar

Display unit

13   Remove the upper and lower center trim panels (see Chapter 11).
14   Remove the display unit mounting bracket screws **(see illustration)**.
15   Pull out the display unit, disconnect the electrical connectors **(see illustration)** and remove the unit.
16   If you are replacing the display unit, remove the unit-to-bracket mounting screws and separate the bracket from the display.
17   Installation is the reverse of removal.

Speakers

Instrument panel speakers

18   Disconnect the cable from the negative terminal of the battery (see Chapter 5).
19   Carefully pry up the speaker grille **(see illustration)**.
20   Remove the speaker mounting screws, then disconnect the electrical connector and remove the speaker **(see illustration)**.
21   Installation is the reverse of removal. Reconnect the battery and perform the necessary re-learn procedures (see Chapter 5).

Door speakers

Note: *On models equipped with rear door*

tweeters, the removal and installation procedures are the same as the door speakers.
22   Remove the door trim panel (see Chapter 11).
23   Remove the speaker mounting screws, disconnect the electrical connector and remove the speaker **(see illustration)**.
24   Installation is the reverse of removal.

Front tweeter speakers

25   Remove the windshield A-pillar trim panels (see Chapter 11).
26   Remove the speaker mounting screws, disconnect the electrical connector and remove the speakers.
27   Installation is the reverse of removal.

Rear speakers - 2013 and later models

28   Remove the rear quarter trim panels (see Chapter 11).
29   Working from the back side of the panel, remove the grille and speaker assembly-to-trim panel fasteners and separate the unit.
30   Remove the speaker mounting screws, disconnect the electrical connector and remove the speakers from the grille.
31   Installation is the reverse of removal.

Subwoofer

2012 and earlier models

32   Remove the driver's side rear quarter trim panel (see Chapter 11).
33   Remove the subwoofer mounting fasteners.
34   Lift the subwoofer off its mounting tabs and remove it enough to disconnect the electrical connector.
35   Remove the subwoofer.
36   Installation is the reverse of removal.

2013 and later models

37   Remove the spare tire.
38   Raise the subwoofer enough to disconnect the electrical connector.
39   Remove the subwoofer.
40   Installation is the reverse of removal.

---

13   Rear window defogger - check and repair

1   The rear window defogger consists of a number of horizontal heating elements baked onto the inside surface of the glass. Power is supplied through two fuses and a relay in the IPDM relay box in the engine compartment. A defogger switch on the instrument panel con-

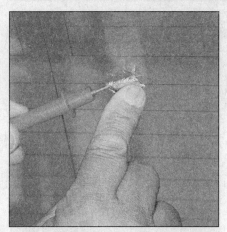

13.5 When measuring the voltage at the rear window defogger grid, wrap a piece of aluminum foil around the negative probe of the voltmeter and press the foil against the wire with your finger

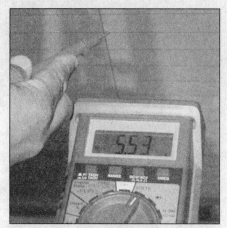

13.6 To determine if a heating element has broken, check the voltage at the center of each element - if the voltage is 6-volts, the element is unbroken

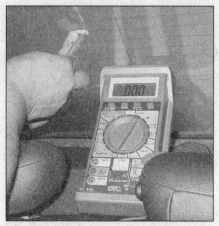

13.8 To find the break, place the voltmeter negative lead against the defogger ground terminal, place the voltmeter positive lead with the foil strip against the heat wire at the positive terminal end and slide it toward the negative terminal end. The point at which the voltmeter deflects from several volts to zero volts is the point at which the wire is broken

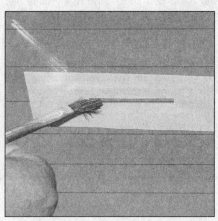

13.14 To use a defogger repair kit, apply masking tape to the inside of the window at the damaged area, then brush on the special conductive coating

trols the defogger grid.
2   Small breaks in the element can be repaired without removing the rear window.

Check

3   Turn the ignition and defogger switches to the ON position.
4   Using a voltmeter, place the positive probe against the defogger grid positive side and the negative probe against the ground side. If battery voltage is not indicated, check that the ignition switch is On and that the feed and ground wires are properly connected. Check the two fuses, defogger switch, defogger relay and related wiring. A dealer can scan the body control module if necessary. If voltage is indicated, but all or part of the defogger doesn't heat, proceed with the following tests.
5   When measuring voltage during the next two tests, wrap a piece of aluminum foil around the tip of the voltmeter positive probe and press the foil against the heating element

with your finger **(see illustration)**. Place the negative probe on the defogger grid ground terminal.
6   Check the voltage at the center of each heating element **(see illustration)**. If the voltage is 5 to 6 volts, the element is okay (there is no break). If the voltage is 0 volts, the element is broken between the center of the element and the positive end. If the voltage is 10 to 12 volts, the element is broken between the center of the element and the ground side. Check each heating element.
7   If none of the elements are broken, connect the negative probe to a good chassis ground. The voltage reading should stay the same; if it doesn't, the ground connection is bad.
8   To find the break, place the voltmeter negative probe against the defogger ground terminal. Place the voltmeter positive probe with the foil strip against the heating element at the positive side and slide it toward the negative side. The point at which the voltmeter deflects from several volts to zero is the point where the heating element is broken **(see illustration)**.

Repair

9   Repair the break in the element using a repair kit specifically for this purpose, such as DuPont paste No. 4817 (or equivalent). The kit includes conductive plastic epoxy.
10   Before repairing a break, turn off the system and allow it to cool for a few minutes.
11   Lightly buff the element area with fine steel wool, then clean it thoroughly with rubbing alcohol.
12   Use masking tape to mask off the area being repaired.
13   Thoroughly mix the epoxy, following the kit instructions.
14   Apply the epoxy material to the slit in the masking tape, overlapping the undamaged area about 3/4-inch on either end **(see illus-**

tration).
15   Allow the repair to cure for 24 hours before removing the tape and using the system.

14   Audio antenna - removal and installation

2012 and earlier models

1   The antenna on these models is incorporated into the glass of the rear quarter windows. The antenna wiring is routed up the passenger's side windshield post along to the rear of the vehicle to the quarter windows. Because the headliner must be removed for access to the wiring and the quarter windows to replace the antenna, it is recommended that the antenna be serviced at a dealership or an automotive glass shop.

2013 and later models

Antenna mast

2   Unscrew the mast from the antenna base to remove it.
3   Installation is the reverse of removal.

Antenna base

4   The rear section of the headliner must be detached and carefully pulled down for access to the inside of the antenna base. It is usually best to have this done by an experienced auto upholstery shop. If you attempt it at home, refer to Chapter 11 for general information about removing plastic interior trim panels.
5   With the rear of the headliner lowered, disconnect the antenna cable from the extension cable at the right rear corner of the roof.
6   Remove the antenna base nut, then pull

15.4a Remove the headlight housing side mounting bolt

15.4b Remove the top and lower mounting bolts and pull the housing straight out - 2012 and earlier models shown, later models similar

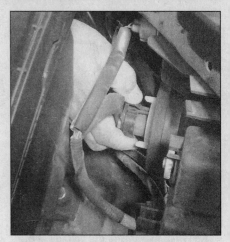

16.3a Depress the tab and disconnect the electrical connector. . .

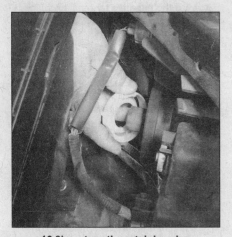

16.3b. . . turn the retaining ring counterclockwise and remove it. . .

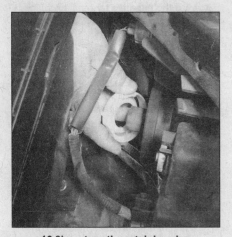

16.3c. . . then remove the bulb from the housing

ages produced by this system can be fatal in the event of a shock. Also, the voltage can remain in the circuit even after the headlight switch has been turned to OFF and the ignition key has been removed. Therefore, for your safety, we don't recommend that you try to remove the headlight housing(s) on a vehicle equipped with xenon bulbs. Instead, have this service performed by a dealer service department or other qualified repair shop.

16   Headlight bulb - replacement

Models equipped with halogen bulbs

Warning: *Halogen gas-filled bulbs, which are under pressure, may shatter if the surface is scratched or the bulb is dropped. Wear eye protection and handle the bulbs carefully, grasping only the base whenever possible. Do not touch the surface of the bulb with your fingers because the oil from your skin could cause it to overheat and fail prematurely. If you do touch the bulb surface, clean it with rubbing alcohol.*

1   If you're replacing a right-side bulb on a 2012 or earlier model, remove the battery for access (see Chapter 5).

2   If you're replacing a low-beam bulb on a 2013 or later model, remove the inner fender plastic trim panel (in the engine compartment) to access the the bulb (this isn't necessary for high-beam bulb replacement).

Note: *On some models it might be easier to unplug the connector after the bulb holder has been removed from the housing.*

3   On 2012 and earlier models, unplug the electrical connector, rotate the retaining ring counterclockwise and remove it, then pull the bulb from the housing **(see illustrations)**.

4   On 2013 and later models, unplug the electrical connector, twist the bulb holder counterclockwise and pull it out.

5   Installation is the reverse of removal.

---

the antenna base and cable out from the roof of the vehicle.

7   Installation is the reverse of removal.

Note: *Tighten the base nut to 58 in-lbs. Any more torque may dent the roof and less will result in poor radio reception.*

15   Headlight housing - removal and installation

Warning: *The models covered by this manual are equipped with Supplemental Restraint Systems (SRS), more commonly known as airbags. Always disable the airbag system before working in the vicinity of any airbag system components to avoid the possibility of accidental deployment of the airbags, which could cause personal injury (see Section 25).*

Models equipped with halogen bulbs

1   Remove the fasteners from the front section of the inner fender splash shield (see

Chapter 11).

2   Remove the front bumper cover (see Chapter 11).

3   On 2013 and later models, when removing the passenger's side housing, disconnect the electrical connectors and hoses from the base of the washer fluid reservoir, remove the reservoir mounting bolts and remove the reservoir.

4   Remove the mounting bolts from the headlight housing **(see illustrations)**.

5   Detach the wiring harness clips from the assembly, then slide the headlight unit forward to remove it. Disconnect the electrical connector as you lift it out.

6   Installation is the reverse of removal.

Models equipped with Xenon bulbs

Warning: *Some models use Xenon bulbs (also known as High Intensity Discharge [HID] bulbs) instead of halogen bulbs. These can be identified by the high-voltage warning sticker on the headlight housing or under the hood. According to the manufacturer, the high volt-*

17.1 Headlight housing adjustment screw (2012 andearlier models)

Models equipped with Xenon bulbs

Warning: *Some models use Xenon bulbs (also known as High Intensity Discharge [HID] bulbs) instead of halogen bulbs. These can be identified by the high-voltage warning sticker on the headlight housing or under the hood. According to the manufacturer, the high voltages produced by this system can be fatal in the event of a shock. Also, the voltage can remain in the circuit even after the headlight switch has been turned to OFF and the ignition key has been removed. Therefore, for your safety, we don't recommend that you try to replace one of these bulbs yourself. Instead, have this service performed by a dealer service department or other qualified repair shop.*

17 Headlights adjustment

Note: *It is important that the headlights are aimed correctly. If adjusted incorrectly they could blind the driver of an oncoming vehicle and cause a serious accident or seriously reduce your ability to see the road. The headlights should be checked for proper aim every 12 months and any time a new headlight is installed or front end body work is performed. It should be emphasized that the following procedure is only an interim step that will provide temporary adjustment until the headlights can be adjusted by a properly equipped shop.*

Note: *Turn off the fog lights, if equipped, during headlight adjustment.*

1 All models are equipped with one adjustment screw in each headlight housing (**see illustration**). The headlights are only adjustable vertically.

2 This method requires a blank wall, masking tape and a level floor.

3 Position masking tape vertically on the wall in reference to the vehicle centerline and the centerlines of both headlights.

4 Position a horizontal tape line in reference to the centerline of all the headlights.

Note: *It may be easier to position the tape*

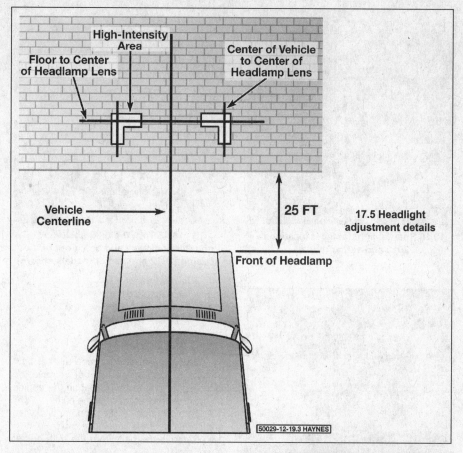

17.5 Headlight adjustment details

on the wall with the vehicle parked only a few inches away.

5 Adjustment should be made with the vehicle parked 25 feet from the wall, sitting level, the gas tank half-full and no unusually heavy load in the vehicle (**see illustration**).

6 Starting with the low beam adjustment, position the high intensity zone so it is two inches below the horizontal line and two inches to the side of the headlight vertical line away from oncoming traffic.

Note: *Adjustment is easier if the light opposite the one being adjusted is covered with a towel.*

7 With the high beams on, the high intensity zone should be vertically centered with the exact center just below the horizontal line.

Note: *It may not be possible to position the headlight aim exactly for both high and low beams. If a compromise must be made, keep in mind that the low beams are the most used and have the greatest effect on safety.*

8 Have the headlights adjusted by a dealer service department or service station at the earliest opportunity.

18 Bulb replacement

Warning: *Wear eye protection and handle the bulbs carefully, grasping only the base whenever possible. Do not touch the surface of the bulb with your fingers because the oil from your skin could cause it to overheat and fail prematurely. If you do touch the bulb surface, clean it with rubbing alcohol.*

18.2 Healight housing bulb details (2012 and earlier models)

1 Headlight bulb
2 Parking/turn signal light
3 Side marker light

Front parking and turn signal lights

2012 and earlier models

1 If you're removing a right-side parking/turn signal bulb, remove the battery for access (see Chapter 5).

2 Turn the bulb socket counterclockwise and pull it out of the housing (**see illustration**).

3 Twist the bulb holder counterclockwise and remove it from the housing.

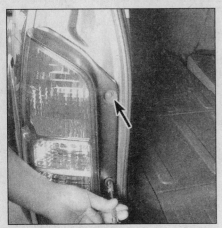

18.16 Rear taillight fastener locations - 2012 and earlier models

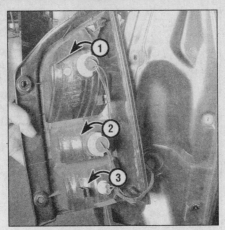

18.18 Turn the bulb socket counterclockwise and pull it out of the housing (2012 and earlier models shown)

1   Tail/brake light bulb
2   Turn signal bulb
3   Back-up light bulb

18.21 Disconnect the electrical connector from the bulb

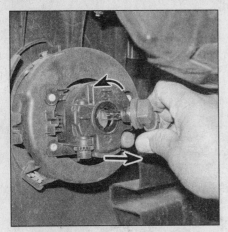

18.22 Rotate the bulb counterclockwise and remove it from the housing

4   Remove the bulb from the bulb holder (see Step 45).
5   Installation is the reverse of removal.

2013 and later models

Note: *The turn signal light is vertically mounted in the underside of the headlight housing. The parking light is mounted directly below the high-beam headlight.*

6   If you're replacing a left-side turn signal bulb, remove the battery (see Chapter 5). If you're replacing a right-side turn signal bulb, remove the windshield washer fluid reservoir. Access to the bulb on either side is by reaching underneath the housing.
7   Twist the bulb holder counterclockwise and remove it from the housing.
8   Remove the bulb from the bulb holder (see Step 45).
9   Installation is the reverse of removal.

Front side marker lights

10   If you're removing a right-side marker light bulb on a 2012 or earlier model, remove the battery for access (see Chapter 5).

11   If you're removing a side marker light bulb on a 2013 or later model, remove the inner fender plastic trim panel (in the engine compartment) to access the the bulb.
12   Turn the bulb socket counterclockwise and pull it out of the housing.
13   Remove the bulb from the bulb holder (see Step 45).
14   Installation is the reverse of removal.

Tail/brake and rear turn signal lights

15   Open the liftgate.
16   On 2012 and earlier models, remove the rear taillight housing fasteners **(see illustration)** and remove the housing.
17   On 2013 and later models, remove the taillight trim panel with a trim tool to expose the housing fasteners. Remove the taillight assembly mounting screws and remove the assembly.
18   Twist the bulb holder counterclockwise and pull it from the housing **(see illustration)**. Remove the bulb from the bulb holder (see Step 45).
19   Installation is the reverse of removal.

Fog lights

20   Detach the inner fender splash shield at the front edge, then pull the liner back to access the bulb (see Chapter 11).
21   Disconnect the electrical connector from the bulb **(see illustration)**.
22   Turn the bulb counterclockwise and pull it out of the housing **(see illustration)**.
23   Without touching the glass with your fingers, insert the new bulb assembly into the fog light housing and rotate the bulb clockwise to lock it into place.
24   Installation is the reverse of removal.

License plate light

25   Remove the liftgate trim panel (see Chapter 11).
26   Twist the bulb socket counterclockwise and pull it out of the license plate light housing.
27   Remove the bulb from the bulb holder (see Step 45).
28   Installation is the reverse of removal.

High-mounted stop light

Note: *This light uses LEDs instead of bulbs. If it doesn't light, the entire unit must be replaced.*

2012 and earlier models

29   To replace the unit, pry off the liftgate trim panel (see Chapter 11). Disconnect the wiring, remove the mounting nuts **(see illustration)** and remove the brake light.
30   Installation is the reverse of removal.

2013 and later models

31   Remove the rear spoiler (see Chapter 11).
32   Disconnect the electrical connector, then remove the high-mounted stop light mounting nuts and remove the unit.
33   Installation is the reverse of removal.

Back-up lights

2012 and earlier models

34   The back-up lights are located in the taillight housing. Remove the housing to access the bulbs (see Steps 15 through 19).

2013 and later models

35   Remove the liftgate lower trim panel (see Chapter 11).
36   Remove the mounting nuts and the clip from the back-up light housing.
37   Pull the back-up light housing from the liftgate.
38   Turn the bulb holder counterclockwise and pull it out of the housing. Remove the bulb from the bulb holder (see Step 45).
39   Installation is the reverse of removal.

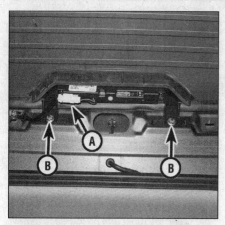

18.29 Disconnect the wiring (A), then remove the mounting nuts (B)

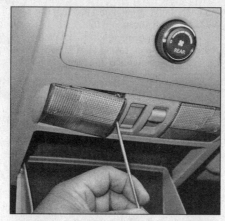

18.40 Use a small screwdriver to carefully pry off the lenses of the interior lights - the bulbs can then be pulled out of the housing

release the tab on the side of the lens, then pivot the lens open. The bulb can then be replaced as above.

Instrument cluster illumination

44   Instrument cluster illumination is contained within the cluster. Replace the cluster (see Section 11) as a complete unit if there is a problem with any of its individual components.

19   Horn - replacement

Note: *On 2005 models and 2013 and later models, the horns are located in front of the radiator. On 2006 through 2012 models, the horns are located behind the driver's side headlight housing.*

1   If you're working on a 2005 model or a 2013 or later model, remove the radiator grille (see Chapter 11).

2   Disconnect the horn electrical connectors and remove the bracket bolt **(see illustration)**, then remove the horns.

3   Installation is the reverse of removal.

Interior lights

40   All interior light bulbs are replaced in the same general way. Use a small screwdriver or trim tool to carefully pry off the lens **(see illustration)**.

41   Pull the bulb straight out of its socket to remove it.

42   Replace the bulb, then snap the lens back in place.

43   To replace the cargo area light bulb,

Bulb removal

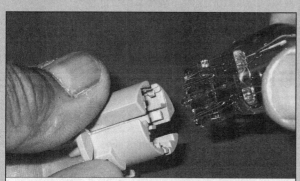

To remove many modern exterior bulbs from their holders, simply pull them out

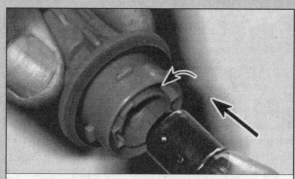

On bulbs with a cylindrical base ("bayonet" bulbs), the socket is spring-loaded; a pair of small posts on the side of the base hold the bulb in place against spring pressure. To remove this type of bulb, push it into the holder, rotate it 1/4-turn counterclockwise, then pull it out

If a bayonet bulb has dual filaments, the posts are staggered, so the bulb can only be installed one way

To remove most overhead interior light bulbs, simply unclip them

20   Wiper arms and motors - removal and installation

1   Turn the wiper ON then OFF, making sure that the blades are in the proper park position.

Removal

Windshield wiper

2   Mark the positions of the blades on the windshield with tape so they can be installed in the same alignment.
3   Pry off the wiper arm pivot caps, then remove the nuts **(see illustration)**.
4   Remove the wiper arms from the drive studs. Wiggle the ends of the arms up and down to release them.
5   Remove the upper cowl cover (see Chapter 11).
6   Disconnect the electrical connector from the wiper motor.
7   Remove the windshield wiper module

mounting bolts, then lift out the wiper assembly **(see illustration)**.
8   Remove the linkage arm from the windshield wiper motor, taking care to avoid damaging the plastic parts of the joints. Unbolt the motor from the frame and remove it.

Rear wiper

9   Lift the cover and remove the wiper arm nut **(see illustration)**.
10   Remove the wiper arm from the drive stud. Wiggle the end of the arm up and down to release it.

2012 and earlier models

11   From the outside of the liftgate glass, remove the drive stud cover, then remove the wiper motor nut.
12   From inside the liftgate glass, pry off the wiper motor cover **(see illustration)**, then remove the motor mounting nut and separate the motor and base from the glass **(see illustration)**.
13   If necessary, remove the screws and

separate the base trim cover from the motor base.

2013 and later models

14   Remove the liftgate trim panel (see Chapter 11). Remove the three mounting bolts and remove the motor.

Installation

15   Installation is reverse of removal. Note the following.

a)   *When installing the wiper motor assembly, connect the electrical connector to the motor, then turn it ON then OFF to place the unit in the PARK position before attaching the wiper arms.*
b)   *Clean the wiper arm pivot area to remove any dirt, rust or other debris.*
c)   *On the rear wiper motor, replace the drive stud seal, if damaged.*
d)   *Align the front wiper arms with the tape marks made during removal. Rest the rear wiper arm against the stopper.*

19.2 Disconnect the electrical connectors (A, connector for other horn not visible) and remove the bracket bolt (B) (2006 through 2012 models shown)

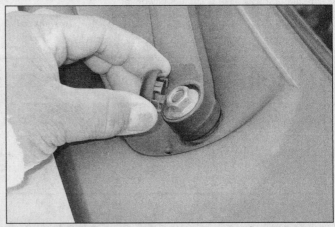

20.3 Pry up the wiper arm pivot caps, then remove the nuts

20.7 Disconnect the wiper motor electrical connector (A), then remove the windshield wiper module mounting bolts (B)

20.9 Remove the wiper arm nut

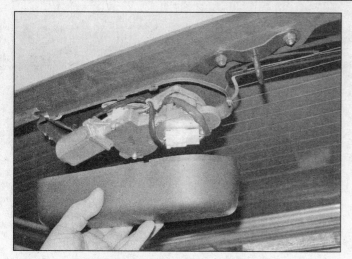

20.12a Pull off or carefully pry off the wiper motor cover

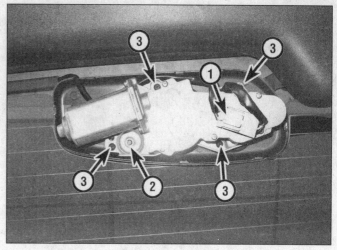

20.12b Rear wiper motor details (2012 and earlier models)

1   *Electrical connector*
2   *Wiper motor mounting nut*
3   *Wiper motor base-to-trim cover screws*

21   Cruise control system - description and check

1   All models have an electronically controlled throttle body - there is no accelerator cable (or cruise control cable). When you select the speed that you want to maintain, the PCM controls vehicle speed by opening and closing the throttle plate by means of a computer-controlled solenoid (motor) inside the throttle body.

2   The diagnostic procedures for troubleshooting the cruise control system are beyond the scope of this manual, but if the system can't be set, or the set speed doesn't cancel when the brake pedal is depressed, check the fuses. Start with the fuses in the engine compartment fuse and relay box, then check the fuses in the under-dash fuse and relay box. If the set speed doesn't cancel when the CANCEL button is depressed, check the fuse for that circuit.

3   Other than checking fuses, the diagnostic procedures for troubleshooting the cruise control system on these models are beyond the scope of this manual. A dealer service department should handle any further testing.

22   Power window system - general information

1   The power window system operates electric motors, mounted on the doors, which lower and raise the windows. The system consists of the control switches, the motors, regulators, glass mechanisms, the Body Control Module (BCM) and associated wiring.

2   The power windows can be lowered and raised from the master control switch by the driver or by the switch located at the passenger window. Each window has a separate motor that is reversible. The position of the control switch determines the polarity and therefore the direction of operation.

3   The circuit is protected by fuses and a circuit breaker. Check the fuses in the fuse panel. Each motor is equipped with an internal circuit breaker; this prevents one stuck window from disabling the whole system. Refer to the wiring diagrams at the end of this Chapter. Problems within this system can only be diagnosed with a factory scan tool. If you have eliminated the obvious causes of a problem, have the vehicle checked at a dealership service department or other properly equipped repair shop.

23   Power door lock system - general information

1   The power door lock system operates the power door motors, which are integral components of the door latch units in each door. The system consists of a fuse (in the engine compartment fuse and relay box), the Body Control Module (BCM), the control switches (in each of the front doors), the power door motors and the electrical wiring harnesses connecting all of these components.

2   The lock mechanisms in the door latch units are actuated by a reversible electric motor in each door. When you push the door lock switch to LOCK, the motor operates one way and locks the latch mechanism. When you push the door lock switch the other way,

to the UNLOCK position, the motor operates in the other direction, unlocking the latch mechanism. Because the motors and lock mechanisms are an integral part of the door latch units, they cannot be repaired. If a door lock motor or lock mechanism fails, replace the door latch unit (see Chapter 11).

3   Some vehicles have an optional Intelligent Key system that allows you to lock and unlock the doors from outside the vehicle. The intelligent key system consists of the transmitter (the electronic push-button "key") and a remote keyless entry receiver mounted behind the glove box.

4   Some features of the door lock system on these vehicles rely on resources that they share with other electronic modules through the Programmable Communications Interface (PCI) data bus network. Professional diagnosis of these modules and the PCI data bus network requires the use of a CONSULT-III (proprietary factory) scan tool and factory diagnostic information. At-home repairs are therefore limited to inspecting the wiring for bad connections and for minor faults that can be easily repaired. If you are unable to locate the trouble using the following general steps, consult your dealer service department.

5   Always check the circuit fuses first. Refer to the wiring diagrams. Problems within this system can only be diagnosed with a factory scan tool. If you have eliminated the obvious causes of a problem, have the vehicle checked at a dealership service department or other properly equipped repair shop.

Note: *It is not uncommon for wires to break in the harness between the body and the door because repeatedly opening and closing the door fatigues and eventually breaks the wires.*

25.3a On 2012 and earlier models, the front crash zone sensor is mounted to the front of the radiator lower support

25.3b On 2013 and earlier models, the front crash zone sensor is located on the rear of the radiator support

24 Sunroof - general information

1   The sunroof is powered by a single motor located in the roof.

2   The sunroof switch (tilt and slide) sends an operation signal to the sunroof motor CPU encoder when the switches are pressed. Power is supplied to the motor from the Body Control Module (BCM) located under the instrument panel. The front door switch detects the open/close condition and sends an operating signal to the BCM. The sunroof will retain power for 45 seconds after the key has been turned off to operate the system. The retained power can be cancelled by opening the front door, turning the ignition switch to ON again or allowing the 45 seconds to elapse.

3   With the ignition On but the engine Off, operate the sunroof control switch through the tilt and slide functions.

4   Listen carefully for the sound of the sunroof motor running in the roof.

5   If the motor can be heard but the sunroof glass doesn't move, there's probably a problem with the drive mechanism.

6   If the sunroof does not operate and no sound comes from the motor, check the fuses (in the interior fuse panel and in the engine compartment power distribution center).

7   If there's voltage at the switch, disconnect it. Check the switch for continuity in all its operating positions. If the switch does not have continuity, replace it. If you have eliminated the obvious causes of a problem, have the vehicle checked at a dealership service department or other properly equipped repair shop.

25 Airbag system - general information

1   These models are equipped with a Supplemental Restraint System (SRS), more

commonly known as airbags, designed to protect the driver and the passenger from serious injury in the event of a head-on collision. Some models are also equipped with side impact airbags in the front seats and along the roof rail. All models have a diagnostic control unit, located on the floor under the center console.

Note: *If your vehicle is ever involved in a flood, or the interior carpeting is soaked for any reason, disconnect the battery and do not start the vehicle until the airbag system can be checked by a dealer service department or other repair facility equipped with the proper tool. If the SRS system is subjected to flooding, the airbags could go off upon starting the vehicle, even without an accident taking place.*

Airbag modules

2   The airbag modules consist of a housing incorporating the cushion (airbag) and inflator unit. The inflator assembly is mounted on the back of the housing over a hole through which gas is expelled, inflating the bag almost instantaneously when an electrical signal is sent from the system. The specially wound wire on the driver's side that carries this signal to the module is called a spiral cable. The spiral cable is a flat, ribbon-like electrically conductive tape that is wound many times so that it can transmit an electrical signal regardless of steering wheel position. Airbag modules are located in the steering wheel and on the passenger's side above the glove box. Some models are equipped with side-impact airbags located in the seat backs, and head-level airbags located along the roof rails (side curtain airbags).

Control unit and sensors

3   The diagnosis/sensor unit contains an on-board microprocessor which monitors the operation of the system, and also contains a crash sensor. It checks this system every time

the vehicle is started, causing the "AIRBAG" light to go on then off, if the system is operating properly. If there is a fault in the system, the light will go on and stay on and the unit will store fault codes indicating the nature of the fault. If the AIRBAG light goes on and stays on, the vehicle should be taken to your dealer immediately for service. The diagnosis/ sensor unit is located under the center console. The crash zone sensor is located on the radiator support **(see illustrations)** and the side airbag sensor (satellite crash sensor) is in each door "B" pillar.

Operation

4   For the airbag(s) to deploy, the impact sensor(s) must be activated. When this condition occurs, the circuit to the airbag inflator is closed and the airbag inflates.

Self-diagnosis system

5   A self-diagnosis circuit in the SRS unit displays a light on the instrument panel when the ignition switch is turned to the On position. If the system is operating normally, the light should go out after about five seconds. If the light doesn't come on, or doesn't go out after a short time, or if it comes on while you're driving the vehicle, or if it blinks at any time, there's a malfunction in the SRS system. Have it inspected and repaired as soon as possible. Do not attempt to troubleshoot or service the SRS system yourself. Even a small mistake could cause the SRS system to malfunction when you need it.

Servicing components near the SRS system

6   There are times when you need to remove the steering wheel, radio or service other components on or near the dashboard. At these times, you'll be working around components and wire harnesses for the SRS system.

Note: *Do not use electrical test equipment on airbag system wires; it could cause the airbag(s) to deploy. ALWAYS DISABLE THE SRS SYSTEM BEFORE WORKING NEAR THE SRS SYSTEM COMPONENTS OR RELATED WIRING.*

Disabling the SRS system

Warning: *Any time you are working in the vicinity of airbag wiring or components, DISABLE THE SRS SYSTEM.*

Warning: *An auxiliary voltage input device (memory saver) must not be used when working on or near airbag system components.*

7   To disable the airbag system, perform the following steps:

Turn the steering wheel to the straight-ahead position and turn the ignition switch to the Lock position, then remove the key.

Disconnect the battery negative cable, then the positive cable, then wait ten minutes before proceeding with any work.

Before touching any airbag system component, ground yourself to a metal part of the vehicle to discharge any static electricity built up in your body.

Enabling the system

8   After you've disabled the airbag and performed the necessary service, reconnect the two-pin airbag connector into the two-pin spiral cable connector (driver's side), the SRS main harness (passenger's side) or the side-impact airbag. Reinstall the trim to the underside of the steering wheel or reinstall the glove box/trim panel or upper trim panels.

9   To enable the airbag system, perform the following steps:

a) Turn the ignition switch to the On position.
b) Make sure nobody is inside the vehicle.
c) Connect the battery cables.
d) Turn the ignition to the Off position, then with your body out of the path of the airbag, turn the ignition switch to the On position. Confirm that the airbag warning light is functioning properly.
e) Perform the necessary re-learn procedures (see Chapter 5).
f) Take the vehicle to a dealer service department or other qualified repair facility and have the airbag system checked and the warning light canceled if it remains lit.

Removal and installation

Warning: *The bolts used throughout the airbag system to mount the airbag modules, diagnosis sensor unit, crash zone sensor and satellite sensors have a special coating. These bolts are designed to be used once. Replace them with new factory bolts, and never use a substitute fastener.*

Driver's side airbag and spiral cable

10   Refer to Chapter 10, Section 20 for removal and installation of the driver's side airbag and steering wheel (which will give you access to the spiral cable).

Note: *When installing the spiral cable, be sure to follow the centering instructions carefully.*

Passenger's side airbag and other airbag modules

11   Even if you have to remove the instrument panel, it's not necessary to remove the passenger airbag module to do so; it can simply remain installed in the instrument panel. We don't recommend removing any of the other airbag modules either. These jobs are best left to a professional.

Impact seat belt retractors

12   All models are equipped with pyrotechnic (explosive) units in the front seat belt retracting mechanisms for both the lap and shoulder belts. During an impact that would trigger the airbag system, the airbag control unit also triggers the seat belt retractors. When the pyrotechnic charges go off, they accelerate the retractors to instantly take up any slack in the seat belt system to more fully prepare the driver and front seat passenger for impact. The airbag system should be disabled any time work is done on or around the seats.

Note: *Never strike the pillars or floor pan with a hammer or use an impact-driver tool in these areas unless the system is disabled.*

---

26   Intelligent Power Distribution Module (IPDM) - description, check and replacement

---

Description

1   The Intelligent Power Distribution Module (IPDM) is a solid state device that controls various relays and circuits when commands are received from the Powertrain Control Module (PCM) and/or the Body Control Module (BCM). The circuits under its control are:

Headlights
Parking and side marker lights
Tail lights/license plate lights
Fog lights
Windshield wipers
Electronic steering column lock
Air conditioning compressor clutch
Starter relay
Fuel pump relay
Cooling fan relay
Horn relay
Rear window defogger relay

Check

2   Although the IPDM is usually very reliable, it must always be factored in to any diagnosis of the circuits under its control. Thorough testing of the unit requires a proprietary Nissan scan tool, but a simple test, called the Auto Active Test, can help you determine the possible source of a problem with some of the

circuits under its control. The circuits checked in this test include the:

Front windshield wiper circuit
Tail/parking/license plate/side marker light circuits
Fog light circuit
Headlight circuit
Air conditioning compressor clutch circuit
Engine cooling fan circuit
Oil pressure warning light

3   Lift the windshield wipers from the windshield and close the right front door. Make sure the ignition switch is in the Off position.

Note: *If you must keep the hood open during the test, leave the wipers down and spray some water on the glass to prevent scratching.*

4   To initiate the Auto Active Test, turn the ignition switch to the On position and depress the left front door switch 10 times within 20 seconds, then turn the ignition switch to the Off position.

5   Within 10 seconds, turn the ignition switch back to the On position. The horn should beep once, signifying the start of the test.

6   On 2012 and earlier models, when the test begins, the following sequence of events should happen (and the sequence of events should repeat three times):

a) The oil pressure light should blink continuously for the duration of the test.
b) The rear window defogger should come on for 10 seconds.
c) The windshield wiper should operate on low speed for 5 seconds, then high speed for 5 seconds
d) The parking lights/taillights/license plate lights/fog lights should come on for 10 seconds
e) The headlights should turn on to low-beams for 10 seconds and then to the high-beam for 5 seconds.
f) The air conditioning compressor clutch should engage (click on and off) 5 times
g) The engine cooling fan should come on for 10 seconds.

7   On 2013 and later models, when the test begins, the following sequence of events should happen (and the sequence of events should repeat three times):

a) The front wipers should come on at low speed for 3 seconds, then high speed for 3 seconds.
b) The fog lights/parking lights/side marker lights/taillights/license plate lights should come on for 10 seconds.
c) Daytime running lights, if equipped, should come on for 10 seconds.
d) Headlights should cycle from low to high 5 times
e) The A/C compressor should turn on/off 5 times.
f) The engine cooling fan should come on at low speed for 5 seconds, then high speed for 5 seconds.

26.17a Depress the cover locking tab and lift off the cover

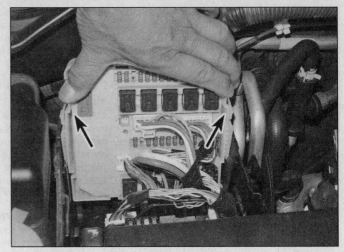

26.17b Depress the tabs on each side of the IPDM and slide it out of the case

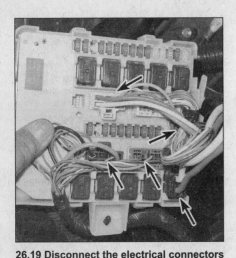

26.19 Disconnect the electrical connectors from the Intelligent Power Distribution Module (IPDM) in the engine compartment - 2012 and earlier models shown, later models similar

Diagnosis

Wipers, parking lights/daytime running lights (if equipped)/tail lights/license plate lights/fog lights

8   If any of these systems do not operate during the Auto Active Test, the problem could be caused by:

   a) *Wiper motor, or the circuit between the IPDM and wiper motor faulty*
   b) *Wiper motor ground problem*
   c) *Light bulb, or the circuit between the IPDM and light faulty*
   d) *Light bulb/housing ground problem*
   e) *Faulty IPDM*

9   If the system in question does operate during the Auto Active Test but doesn't operate under normal conditions, the problem could be a faulty switch, a faulty Body Control Module (BCM), or the circuit between the two.

Air conditioning compressor clutch

10   If the compressor clutch doesn't operate during the Auto Active Test, the problem could be caused by:

   a) *Compressor clutch or the circuit between the IPDM and compressor clutch faulty*
   b) *Faulty IPDM*

11   If the compressor clutch does operate during the Auto Active Test but doesn't operate under normal conditions, the problem could be a faulty switch, a faulty Body Control Module (BCM), a faulty PCM, a fault in the circuit between the PCM and the BCM, or a fault in the circuit between the PCM and the IPDM.

Electric engine cooling fan

12   If the engine cooling fan doesn't operate during the Auto Active Test, the problem could be caused by:

   a) *Cooling fan motor, relay or the circuit between the cooling fan motor and IPDM faulty*
   b) *Faulty IPDM*

13   If the engine cooling fan does operate during the Auto Active Test but doesn't operate under normal conditions, the problem could be a faulty PCM, a faulty coolant temperature sensor, the circuit between the coolant temperature sensor and the PCM, or the circuit between the PCM and the IPDM.

Oil pressure warning light

14   If the oil pressure warning light doesn't blink during the Auto Active Test, the problem could be caused by:

   a) *Problem in the CAN communication circuit between the BCM and the IPDM*
   b) *Problem in the CAN communication circuit between the BCM and the IPDM*
   c) *Problem in the CAN communication circuit between the BCM and the instrument cluster*
   d) *Faulty instrument cluster*

15   If the oil pressure warning light does blink during the Auto Active Test but doesn't

operate when it should (during the bulb check when the ignition is turned On), the problem could be a faulty oil pressure sending unit, a faulty IPDM, or the circuit between the two.

Replacement

Note: *The IPDM is located in either the right rear corner (2012 and earlier models) or the left rear corner (2013 and later models) of the engine compartment. It is part of the main fuse/relay panel.*

16   Disconnect the cable from the negative terminal of the battery (see Chapter 5).

17   On 2012 and earlier models, remove the cover, then depress the tabs and slide the IPDM out of the case **(see illustrations)**.

18   On 2013 and later models, depress the locking tabs on the outside edges of the IPDM to release it from the case.

19   Lift the IPDM from the case, disconnect the electrical connectors from the IPDM **(see illustration)** and remove it from the vehicle.

20   Installation is the reverse of removal.

27   Wiring diagrams - general information

1   Since it isn't possible to include all wiring diagrams for every year and model covered by this manual, the following diagrams are those that are typical and most commonly needed.

2   Prior to troubleshooting any circuits, check the fuses and circuit breakers (if equipped) to make sure they are in good condition. Make sure the battery is properly charged and has clean, tight cable connections (see Chapter 1).

3   When checking the wiring system, make sure that all electrical connectors are clean, with no broken or loose pins. When unplugging an electrical connector, do not pull on the wires, only on the connector housings themselves.

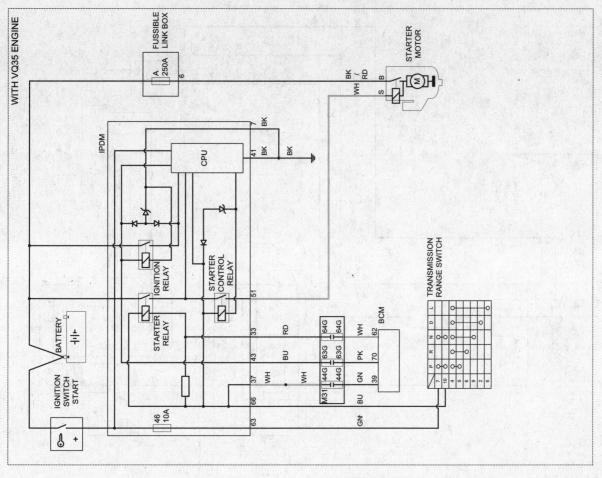

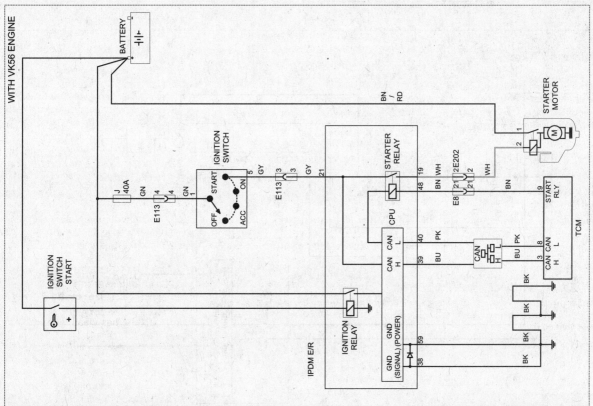

Starting system

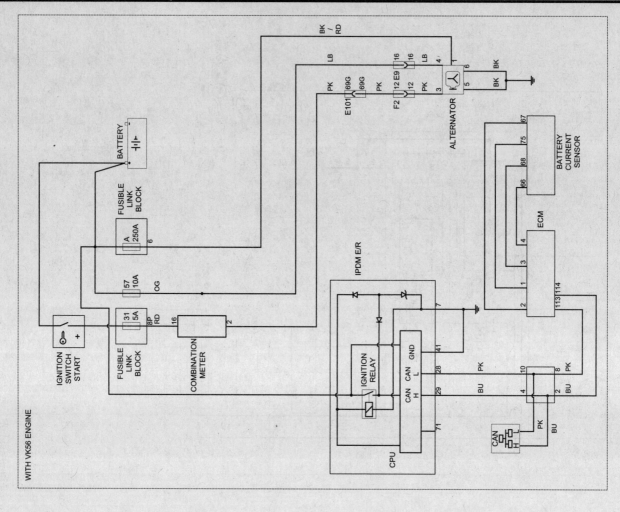

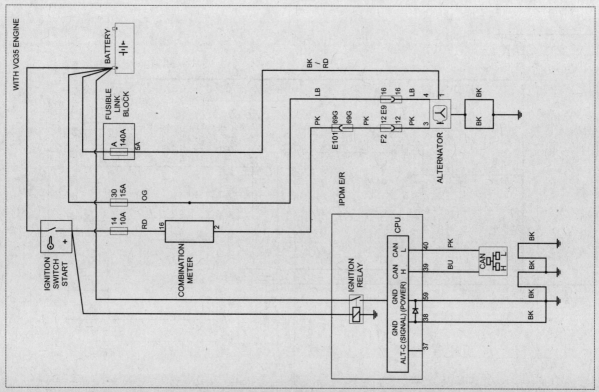

Charging system

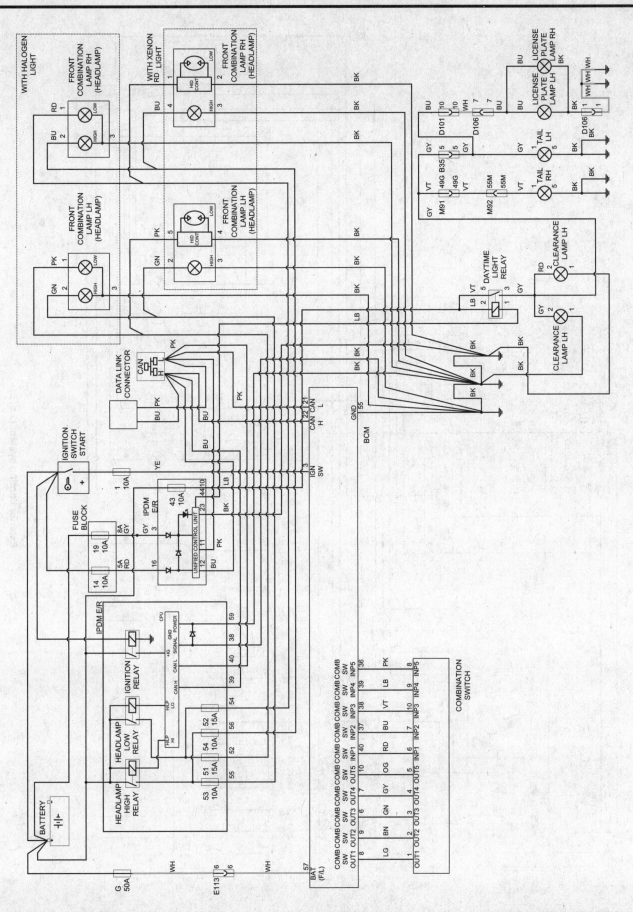

Exterior lighting system (1 of 2)

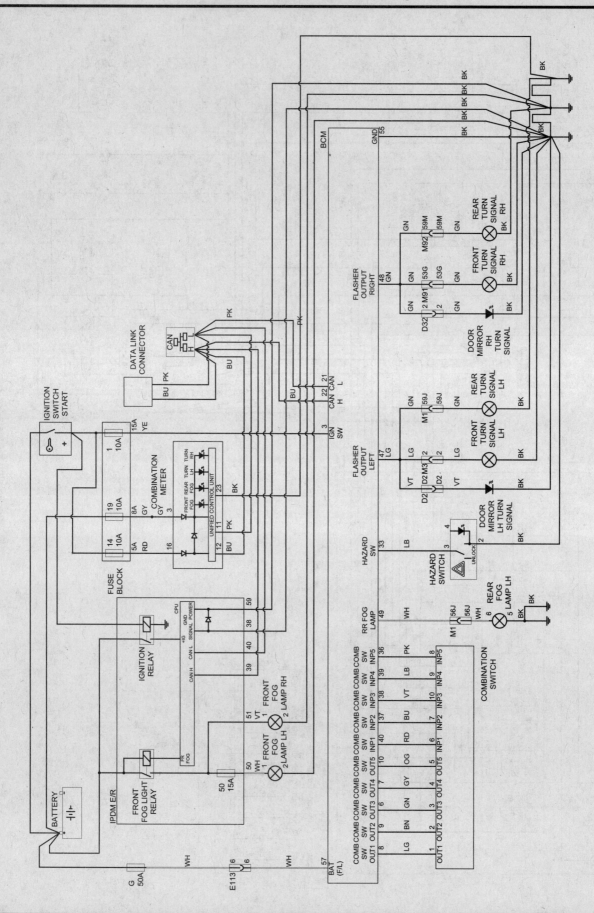

Exterior lighting system (2 of 2)

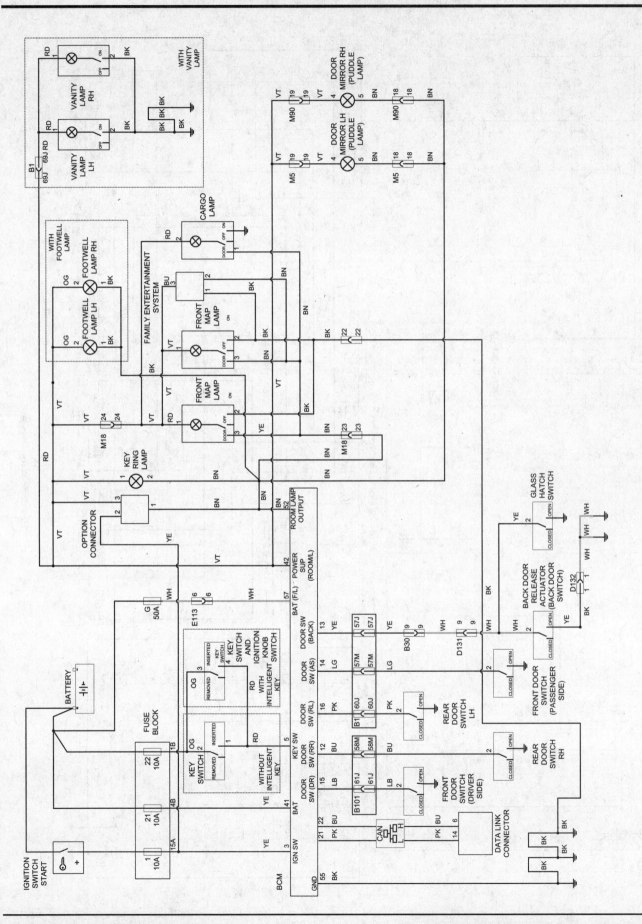

Interior lighting system

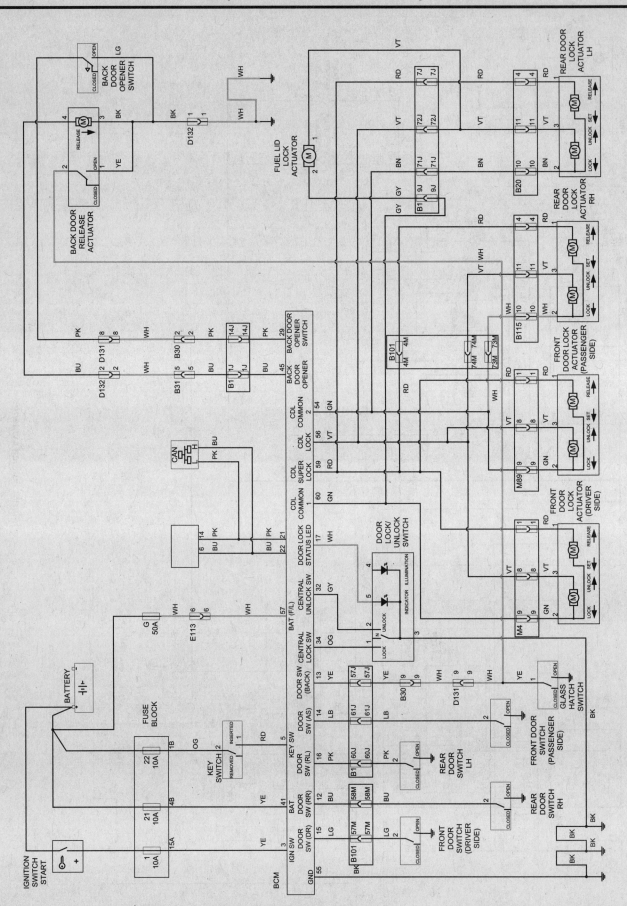

Power door lock system

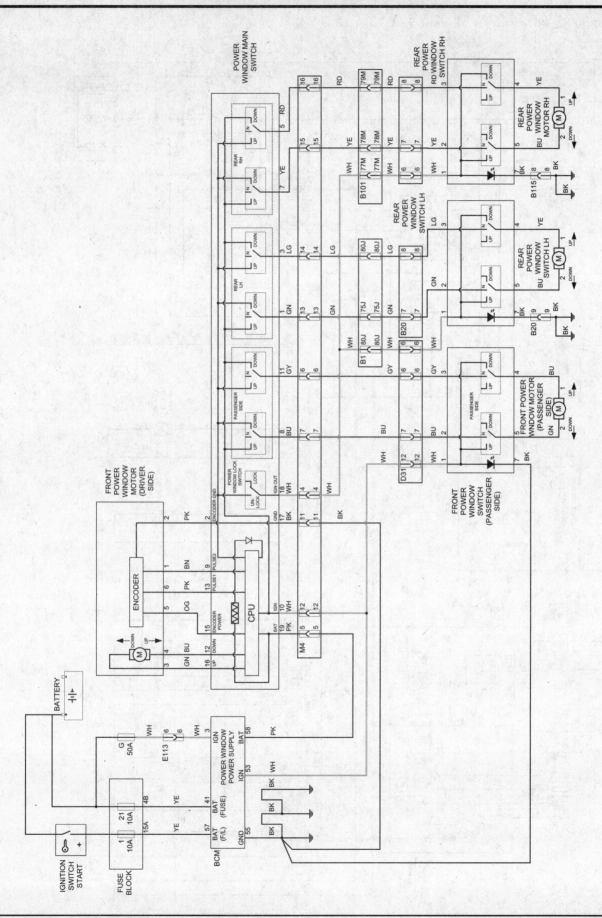

Power window system

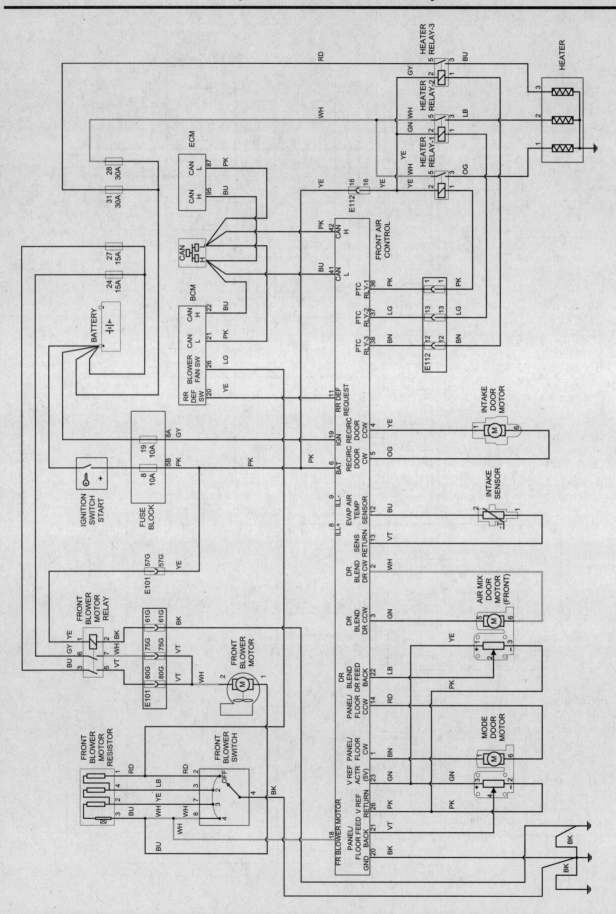

Heating and air conditioning system (manual)

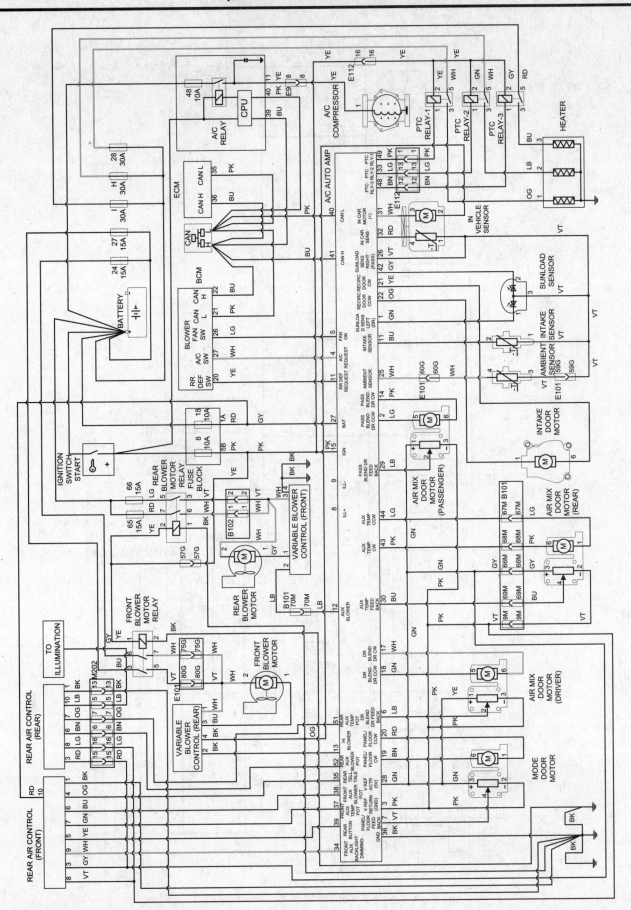

Heating and air conditioning system (automatic)

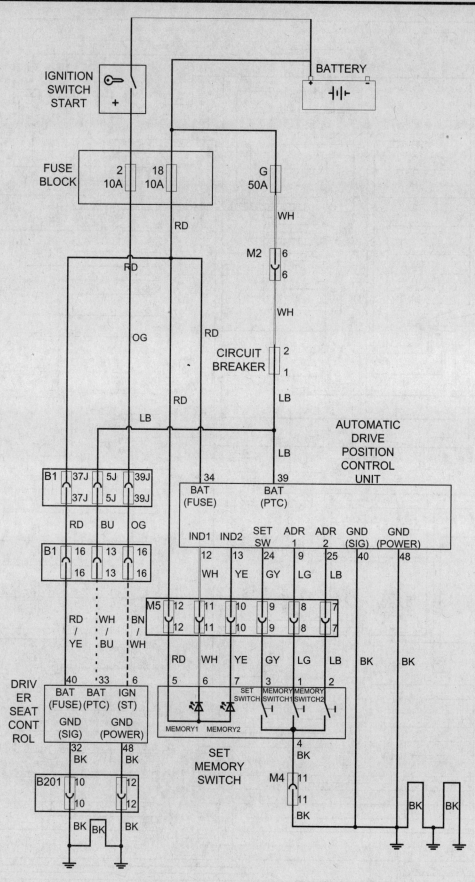

Cruise control system

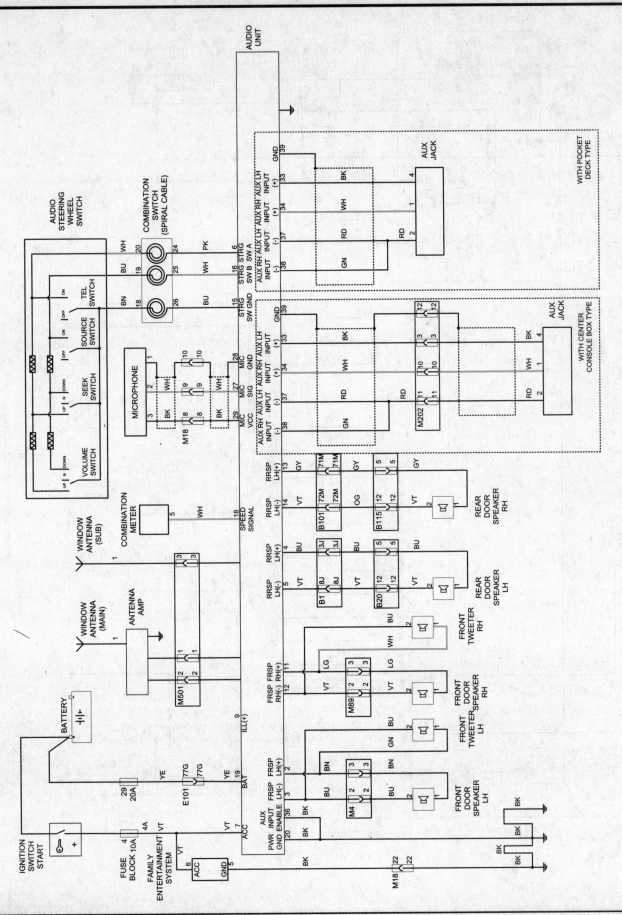

Audio system

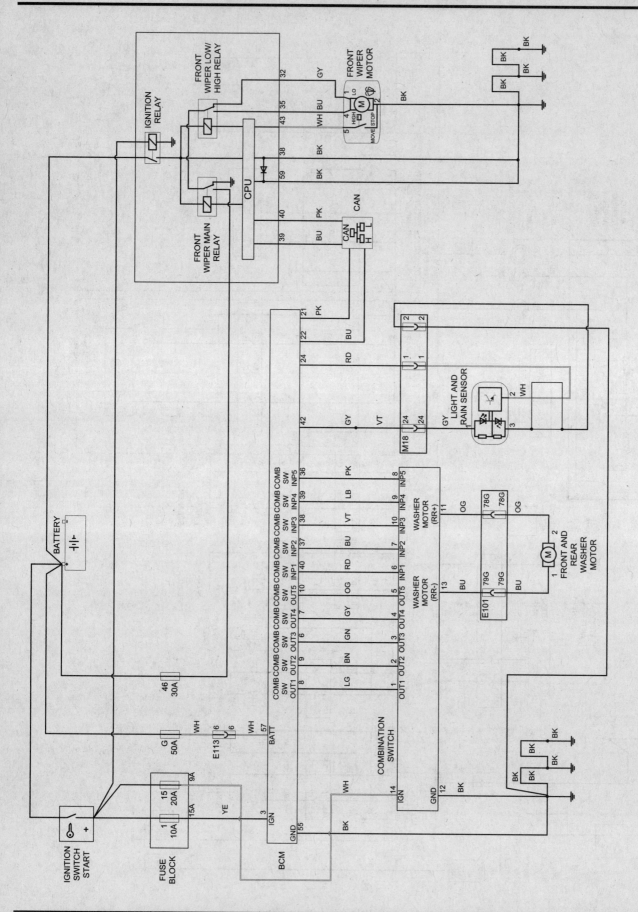

Windshield wiper and washer system

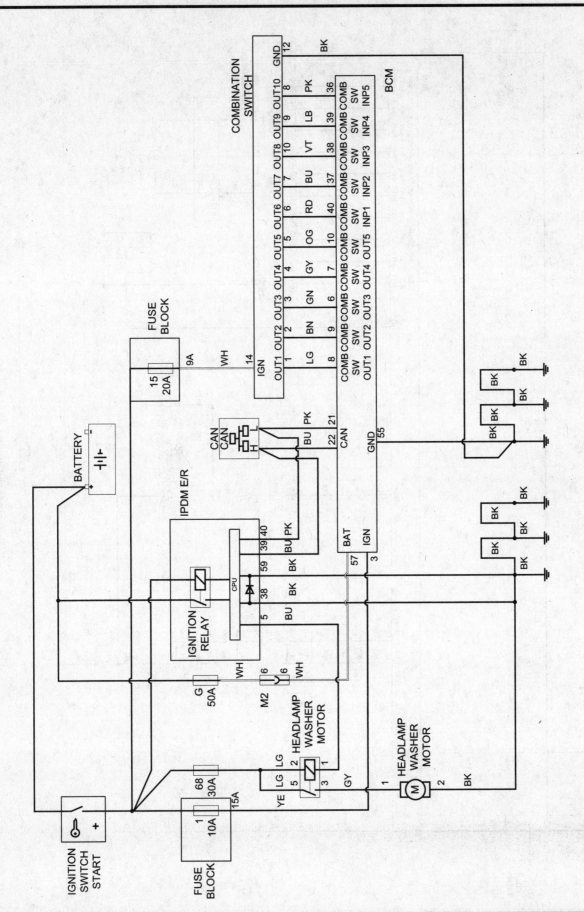

Headlight wiper and washer system

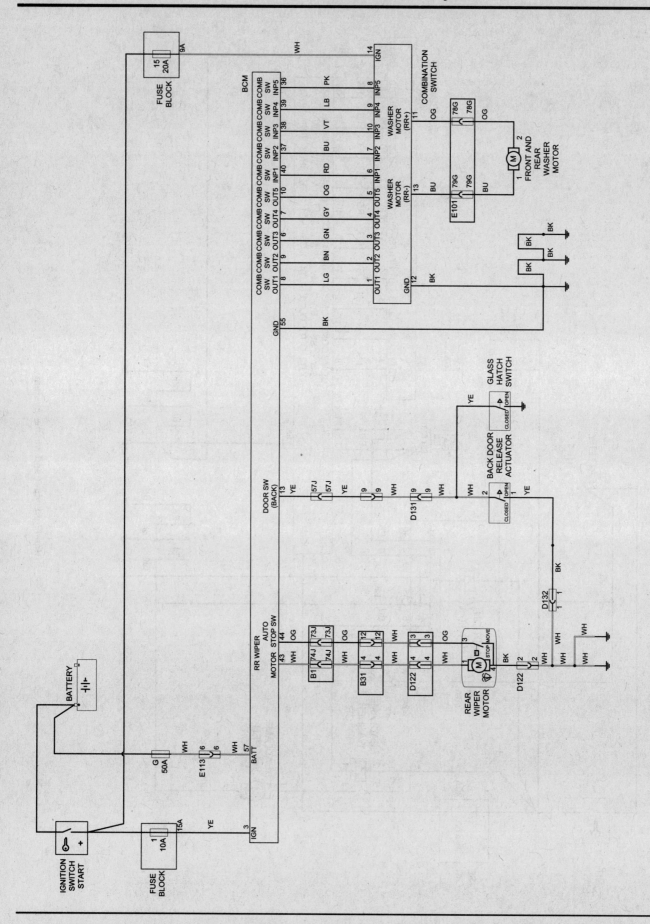

Rear wiper and washer system

Notes

Notes

Index

A

About this manual, 0-5
Accelerator Pedal Position (APP) sensor - replacement, 6-10
Air conditioning and heating system - check and maintenance, 3-4
Air conditioning compressor - removal and installation, 3-15
Air conditioning condenser - removal and installation, 3-15
Air conditioning receiver-drier - removal and installation, 3-16
Air filter check and replacement, 1-22
Air filter housing - removal and installation, 4-8
Airbag system - general information, 12-16
Alternator - removal and installation, 5-6
Anti-lock Brake System (ABS) - general information, 9-7
Audio antenna - removal and installation, 12-9
Automatic transaxle (2013 and later models) - removal and installation, 7A-7
Automatic transmission (2012 and earlier models) - removal and installation, 7A-6
Automatic transmission/transaxle fluid change, 1-26
Automatic transmission/transaxle fluid level check, 1-12
Automotive chemicals and lubricants, 0-20

B

Balljoints - replacement, 10-16
Battery - disconnection and reconnection, 5-3
Battery and battery tray - removal and installation, 5-4
Battery cables - replacement, 5-5
Battery check, maintenance and charging, 1-15
Blower motor - removal and installation, 3-12
Body Control Module (BCM) - general information, 12-5
Body repair - major damage, 11-3
Body repair - minor damage, 11-2
Body, 11-1
    Body repair - major damage, 11-3
    Body repair - minor damage, 11-2
    Bumper covers - removal and installation, 11-15
    Center console - removal and installation, 11-18
    Cowl cover - removal and installation, 11-25
    Dashboard trim panels - removal and installation, 11-20
    Door - removal, installation and adjustment, 11-11
    Door latch, key lock cylinder and handles - removal and installation, 11-12
    Door trim panels - removal and installation, 11-9
    Door window glass - removal and installation, 11-13
    Door window glass regulator - removal and installation, 11-14
    Fastener and trim removal, 11-5
    Fender (front) - removal and installation, 11-14
    General information, 11-1
    Hinges and locks - maintenance, 11-6
    Hood - removal, installation and adjustment, 11-6
    Hood release latch and cable - removal and installation, 11-7
    Instrument panel - removal and installation, 11-24
    Liftgate - removal, installation and adjustment, 11-8
    Liftgate latch - removal and installation, 11-9
    Mirrors - removal and installation, 11-18
    Radiator grille - removal and installation, 11-7
    Rear quarter trim panels - removal and installation, 11-27
    Rear spoiler - removal and installation (2013 and later models), 11-27
    Repairing minor paint scratches, 11-2
    Seats - removal and installation, 11-25
    Steering column covers - removal and installation, 11-20
    Upholstery, carpets and vinyl trim - maintenance, 11-5
    Windshield and fixed glass - replacement, 11-6
Booster battery (jump) starting, 0-19
Brake check, 1-20
Brake disc - inspection, removal and installation, 9-14
Brake hoses and lines - inspection and replacement, 9-16
Brake hydraulic system - bleeding, 9-16
Brake light and cruise control cancel switches - adjustment and replacement, 9-21
Brake pedal - adjustment, 9-21
Brakes, 9-1
    Anti-lock Brake System (ABS) - general information, 9-7
    Brake disc - inspection, removal and installation, 9-14
    Brake hoses and lines - inspection and replacement, 9-16
    Brake hydraulic system - bleeding, 9-16
    Brake light and cruise control cancel switches - adjustment and replacement, 9-21
    Brake pedal - adjustment, 9-21
    Disc brake caliper - removal and installation, 9-13
    Disc brake pads - replacement, 9-8
    General information, 9-3
    Master cylinder - removal and installation, 9-15
    Parking brake - check and adjustment, 9-18
    Parking brake shoes - replacement, 9-18
    Power brake booster - check, replacement and adjustment, 9-17
    Troubleshooting, 9-3
Bulb replacement, 12-11
Bumper covers - removal and installation, 11-15
Buying parts, 0-10

C

Cabin air filter replacement, 1-21
Camshaft Position (CMP) sensor - replacement, 6-11
Camshafts and lifters - removal, inspection and installation, 2A-12
Camshafts and lifters - removal, inspection and installation, 2B-9
Catalytic converter - replacement, 6-15
Center console - removal and installation, 11-18
Chassis electrical system, 12-1
    Airbag system - general information, 12-16
    Audio antenna - removal and installation, 12-9
    Body Control Module (BCM) - general information, 12-5
    Bulb replacement, 12-11
    Circuit breakers - general information, 12-3
    Cruise control system - description and check, 12-15
    Dashboard switches - replacement, 12-6
    Electrical connectors - general information, 12-4
    Electrical troubleshooting - general information, 12-1
    Fuses and fusible links - general information, 12-2
    General information, 12-1
    Headlights adjustment, 12-11
    Headlight bulb - replacement, 12-10
    Headlight housing - removal and installation, 12-10
    Horn - replacement, 12-13
    Instrument cluster - removal and installation, 12-6
    Intelligent Power Distribution Module (IPDM) - description, check and replacement, 12-17
    Power door lock system - general information, 12-15
    Power window system - general information, 12-15
    Radio and speakers - removal and installation, 12-7
    Rear window defogger - check and repair, 12-8
    Relays - general information, 12-3
    Remote keyless entry fob - battery replacement, 12-5
    Steering column switches - replacement, 12-6
    Sunroof - general information, 12-16
    Wiper arms and motors - removal and installation, 12-14
    Wiring diagrams ñ general information, 12-18
Circuit breakers - general information, 12-3
Coil springs (rear) - removal and installation, 10-18
Control arm (front) (2013 and later models) - removal, inspection and installation, 10-16
Control unit - removal and installation, 7C-1
Conversion factors, 0-21
Cooling system check, 1-19
Cooling system servicing (draining, flushing and refilling), 1-25
Cooling, heating and air conditioning systems, 3-1
    Air conditioning compressor - removal and installation, 3-15
    Air conditioning condenser - removal and installation, 3-15
    Air conditioning and heating system - check and maintenance, 3-4
    Air conditioning receiver-drier - removal and installation, 3-16
    Blower motor - removal and installation, 3-12
    Engine cooling fans - replacement, 3-7
    General information, 3-2
    Heater and air conditioning control assembly - removal and installation, 3-12
    Heater core - removal and installation, 3-13
    Radiator and coolant reservoir - removal and installation, 3-9
    Thermostat - removal and installation, 3-6
    Troubleshooting, 3-2
    Water pump - replacement, 3-10
Cowl cover - removal and installation, 11-25
Crankshaft - removal and installation, 2C-14
Crankshaft front oil seal - replacement, 2A-18
Crankshaft front oil seal - replacement, 2B-13
Crankshaft Position (CKP) sensor - replacement, 6-7
Crankshaft pulley - removal and installation, 2A-18
Crankshaft pulley - removal and installation, 2B-13
Cruise control system - description and check, 12-15
Cylinder compression check, 2C-4
Cylinder head - removal and installation, 2A-16
Cylinder head - removal and installation, 2B-12

D

Dashboard switches - replacement, 12-6
Dashboard trim panels - removal and installation, 11-20
Diagnosis - general, 7A-2
Differential lubricant change, 1-27
Differential oil seals ñ replacement, 8-11
Disc brake caliper - removal and installation, 9-13
Disc brake pads - replacement, 9-8
Door - removal, installation and adjustment, 11-11
Door latch, key lock cylinder and handles - removal and installation, 11-12
Door trim panels - removal and installation, 11-9
Door window glass - removal and installation, 11-13
Door window glass regulator - removal and installation, 11-14
Driveaxle boot - replacement, 8-3
Driveaxle boot check, 1-23
Driveaxle oil seal - replacement (2013 and later models), 7A-5
Driveaxles - general information, 8-2
Driveaxles - removal and installation, 8-2
Drivebelt check and replacement, 1-17
Driveline, 8-1
    Differential oil seals ñ replacement, 8-11
    Driveaxle boot - replacement, 8-3
    Driveaxles - general information, 8-2
    Driveaxles - removal and installation, 8-2
    Driveshaft(s) (2012 and earlier models) - removal and installation, 8-8
    Driveshaft (2013 and later AWD models) - removal and installation, 8-9
    Driveshaft(s) and universal joints - general information and inspection, 8-8
    Electric controlled coupling (AWD models) - removal and installation, 8-12
    Front differential (2012 and earlier models) - removal and installation, 8-12
    General information, 8-2
    Rear differential - removal and installation, 8-10
    Universal joints - replacement, 8-9
Driveplate - removal and installation, 2A-22
Driveplate - removal and installation, 2B-16
Driveshaft (2013 and later AWD models) - removal and installation, 8-9
Driveshaft(s) (2012 and earlier models) - removal and installation, 8-8
Driveshaft(s) and universal joints - general information and inspection, 8-8

E

Electric controlled coupling (AWD models) - removal and installation, 8-12

Electrical connectors - general information, 12-4

Electrical troubleshooting - general information, 12-1

Emissions and engine control systems, 6-1

Accelerator Pedal Position (APP) sensor ñ replacement, 6-10

Camshaft Position (CMP) sensor - replacement, 6-11

Catalytic converter - replacement, 6-15

Crankshaft Position (CKP) sensor - replacement, 6-7

Engine Coolant Temperature (ECT) sensor - replacement, 6-7

Evaporative Emissions Control (EVAP) system - component replacement, 6-15

General information, 6-2

Intake Valve Timing (IVT) control solenoid(s)/sensor(s) - replacement, 6-11

Knock Sensor (KS) - replacement, 6-13

Mass Air Flow/Intake Air Temperature (MAF/IAT) sensor - replacement, 6-13

Obtaining and clearing Diagnostic Trouble Codes (DTCs), 6-4

On Board Diagnosis (OBD) system, 6-4

Oxygen sensors - replacement, 6-13

Powertrain Control Module (PCM) - replacement, 6-15

Positive Crankcase Ventilation (PCV) valve - replacement, 6-16

Throttle Position (TP) sensor - replacement, 6-17

Transmission range (TR) switch - replacement and adjustment, 6-14

Transmission speed sensors - replacement, 6-14

Variable Induction Air System (VIAS) solenoid valves and actuators (V6 engines) - replacement, 6-16

Engine - removal and installation, 2C-7

Engine – in-vehicle repair procedures

V6 engines, 2A-1

Camshafts and lifters - removal, inspection and installation, 2A-12

Crankshaft front oil seal - replacement, 2A-18

Crankshaft pulley - removal and installation, 2A-18

Cylinder head - removal and installation, 2A-16

Driveplate - removal and installation, 2A-22

Engine mounts - check and replacement, 2A-23

Engine oil cooler and oil filter adapter - general information and replacement, 2A-22

Exhaust manifold - removal, inspection and installation, 2A-15

General information, 2A-4

Intake manifold - removal and installation, 2A-14

Oil pans - removal and installation, 2A-19

Oil pump - removal, inspection and installation, 2A-20

Rear main oil seal - replacement, 2A-23

Repair operations possible with the engine in the vehicle, 2A-4

Timing chain and sprockets - removal, inspection and installation, 2A-8

Top Dead Center (TDC) for number one piston - locating, 2A-4

Valve clearance check and adjustment, 2A-5

Valve covers - removal and installation, 2A-4

Valve springs, retainers and seals - replacement, 2A-6

V8 engine, 2B-1

Camshafts and lifters - removal, inspection and installation, 2B-9

Crankshaft front oil seal - replacement, 2B-13

Crankshaft pulley - removal and installation, 2B-13

Cylinder head - removal and installation, 2B-12

Driveplate - removal and installation, 2B-16

Engine mounts - check and replacement, 2B-17

Engine oil cooler - general information, removal and installation, 2B-16

Exhaust manifolds - removal and installation, 2B-12

General information, 2B-3

Intake manifold - removal and installation, 2B-11

Oil pans - removal and installation, 2B-14

Oil pump - removal, inspection and installation, 2B-15

Rear main oil seal - replacement, 2B-16

Repair operations possible with the engine in the vehicle, 2B-3

Timing chains and sprockets - removal, inspection and installation, 2B-7

Top Dead Center (TDC) for number one piston - locating, 2B-3

Valve clearance - check and adjustment, 2B-4

Valve covers - removal and installation, 2B-3

Valve springs, retainers and seals - replacement, 2B-6

Engine Coolant Temperature (ECT) sensor - replacement, 6-7

Engine cooling fans - replacement, 3-7

Engine electrical systems, 5-1

Alternator - removal and installation, 5-6

Battery and battery tray - removal and installation, 5-4

Battery cables - replacement, 5-5

Battery - disconnection and reconnection, 5-3

General information and precautions, 5-1

Ignition coil(s) - replacement, 5-5

Starter motor - removal and installation, 5-7

Troubleshooting, 5-2

Engine mounts - check and replacement, 2A-23

Engine mounts - check and replacement, 2B-17

Engine oil and oil filter change, 1-13

Engine oil cooler - general information, removal and installation, 2B-16

Engine oil cooler and oil filter adapter - general information and replacement, 2A-22

Engine overhaul - disassembly sequence, 2C-8

Engine overhaul - reassembly sequence, 2C-17

Engine rebuilding alternatives, 2C-5

Engine removal - methods and precautions, 2C-6

Evaporative Emissions Control (EVAP) system - component replacement, 6-15

Evaporative emissions control system check, 1-26

Exhaust manifold - removal, inspection and installation, 2A-15

Exhaust manifolds - removal and installation, 2B-12

Exhaust system check, 1-23

Exhaust system servicing - general information, 4-5

Extension housing oil seal (2012 and earlier 2WD models) - replacement, 7A-5

F

Fastener and trim removal, 11-5
Fender (front) - removal and installation, 11-14
Fluid level checks, 1-9
Fraction/decimal/millimeter equivalents, 0-22
Front differential (2012 and earlier models) - removal and
    installation, 8-12
Front differential lubricant level check, 1-20
Fuel and exhaust systems, 4-1
    Air filter housing - removal and installation, 4-8
    Exhaust system servicing - general information, 4-5
    Fuel lines and fittings - general information and
        disconnection, 4-3
    Fuel pressure - check, 4-3
    Fuel pressure relief procedure, 4-2
    Fuel pump/fuel level sensor module - removal and
        installation, 4-5
    Fuel rail and injectors - removal and installation, 4-9
    Fuel tank - removal and installation, 4-7
    General information, 4-1
    Throttle body - removal and installation, 4-8
    Troubleshooting, 4-2
Fuel lines and fittings - general information and
    disconnection, 4-3
Fuel pressure - check, 4-3
Fuel pressure relief procedure, 4-2
Fuel pump/fuel level sensor module - removal and
    installation, 4-5
Fuel rail and injectors - removal and installation, 4-9
Fuel system check, 1-22
Fuel tank - removal and installation, 4-7
Fuses and fusible links - general information, 12-2

G

General engine overhaul procedures, 2C-1
    Crankshaft - removal and installation, 2C-14
    Cylinder compression check, 2C-4
    Engine - removal and installation, 2C-7
    Engine overhaul - disassembly sequence, 2C-8
    Engine overhaul - reassembly sequence, 2C-17
    Engine rebuilding alternatives, 2C-5
    Engine removal - methods and precautions, 2C-6
    General information - engine overhaul, 2C-2
    Initial start-up and break-in after overhaul, 2C-17
    Oil pressure check, 2C-4
    Pistons and connecting rods - removal and installation, 2C-9
    Vacuum gauge diagnostic checks, 2C-5

H

Headlight bulb - replacement, 12-10
Headlight housing - removal and installation, 12-10
Headlights adjustment, 12-11
Heater and air conditioning control assembly - removal
    and installation, 3-12
Heater core - removal and installation, 3-13
Hinges and locks - maintenance, 11-6
Hood - removal, installation and adjustment, 11-6
Hood release latch and cable - removal and installation, 11-7
Horn - replacement, 12-13
Hub and bearing assembly - removal and installation, 10-17

I

Ignition coil(s) - replacement, 5-5
Initial start-up and break-in after overhaul, 2C-17
Instrument cluster - removal and installation, 12-6
Instrument panel - removal and installation, 11-24
Intake manifold - removal and installation, 2A-14
Intake manifold - removal and installation, 2B-11
Intake Valve Timing (IVT) control solenoid(s)/sensor(s) -
    replacement, 6-11
Intelligent Power Distribution Module (IPDM) - description,
    check and replacement, 12-17
Introduction, 0-5
Introduction, 1-9

J

Jacking and towing, 0-18

K

Knock Sensor (KS) - replacement, 6-13
Knuckle (rear) - removal and installation, 10-18

L

Liftgate - removal, installation and adjustment, 11-8
Liftgate latch - removal and installation, 11-9
Lower control arm (front) (2012 and earlier models) -
    removal, inspection and installation, 10-15

M

Maintenance reminder indicator resetting procedure, 1-28
Maintenance schedule, 1-8
Maintenance techniques, tools and working facilities, 0-11
Manual transaxle, 7A-1
    Automatic transmission (2012 and earlier models) - removal
        and installation, 7A-6
    Automatic transaxle (2013 and later models) - removal
        and installation, 7A-7
    Driveaxle oil seal - replacement (2013 and later models), 7A-5
    Extension housing oil seal (2012 and earlier 2WD models) -
        replacement, 7A-5
    General information, 7A-2
    Diagnosis - general, 7A-2
    Shift cable and key interlock cable - adjustment and
        replacement, 7A-4
    Shifter assembly - removal and installation, 7A-2
    Transmission Control Module (TCM) - removal and
        installation, 7A-8
    Transmission mount - check and replacement (2012 and
        earlier models), 7A-6

Mass Air Flow/Intake Air Temperature (MAF/IAT) sensor - replacement, 6-13
Master cylinder - removal and installation, 9-15
Mirrors - removal and installation, 11-18

O

Obtaining and clearing Diagnostic Trouble Codes (DTCs), 6-4
Oil pans - removal and installation, 2A-19
Oil pans - removal and installation, 2B-14
Oil pressure check, 2C-4
Oil pump - removal, inspection and installation, 2A-20
Oil pump - removal, inspection and installation, 2B-15
Oil seals - removal and installation, 7B-4
On Board Diagnosis (OBD) system, 6-4
Oxygen sensors - replacement, 6-13

P

Parking brake - check and adjustment, 9-18
Parking brake shoes - replacement, 9-18
Pistons and connecting rods - removal and installation, 2C-9
Positive Crankcase Ventilation (PCV) valve - replacement, 6-16
Positive Crankcase Ventilation (PCV) valve check and replacement, 1-27
Power brake booster - check, replacement and adjustment, 9-17
Power door lock system - general information, 12-15
Power steering fluid level check, 1-12
Power steering pump - removal and installation, 10-25
Power steering system - bleeding, 10-27
Power window system - general information, 12-15
Powertrain Control Module (PCM) - replacement, 6-15

R

Radiator and coolant reservoir - removal and installation, 3-9
Radiator grille - removal and installation, 11-7
Radio and speakers - removal and installation, 12-7
Radius rod (2013 and later models) - removal and installation, 10-21
Rear differential - removal and installation, 8-10
Rear differential lubricant level check, 1-20
Rear main oil seal - replacement, 2A-23
Rear main oil seal - replacement, 2B-16
Rear quarter trim panels - removal and installation, 11-27
Rear spoiler - removal and installation (2013 and later models), 11-27
Rear suspension control arms and rear subframe - removal and installation, 10-19
Rear window defogger - check and repair, 12-8
Recall information, 0-7
Relays - general information, 12-3
Remote keyless entry fob - battery replacement, 12-5
Repair operations possible with the engine in the vehicle
    V6 engines, 2A-4
    V8 engine, 2B-3
Repairing minor paint scratches, 11-2

S

Safety first!, 0-23
Seats - removal and installation, 11-25
Shift actuator and position switch - replacement, 7B-3
Shift cable and key interlock cable - adjustment and replacement, 7A-4
Shifter assembly - removal and installation, 7A-2
Shock absorber/coil spring assembly (front, 2012 and earlier models) - removal, inspection and installation, 10-11
Shock absorbers (rear) - removal and installation, 10-19
Spark plug check and replacement, 1-24
Stabilizer bar (front) - removal and installation, 10-14
Stabilizer bar (rear) - removal and installation, 10-18
Starter motor - removal and installation, 5-7
Steering and suspension check, 1-22
Steering column - removal and installation, 10-26
Steering column covers - removal and installation, 11-20
Steering column switches - replacement, 12-6
Steering gear - removal and installation, 10-24
Steering gear boots - replacement, 10-24
Steering knuckle (2012 and earlier models) - removal and installation, 10-16
Steering knuckle (2013 and later models) - removal and installation, 10-17
Steering wheel - removal and installation, 10-22
Strut/coil spring assembly (front, 2013 and later models) - removal, inspection and installation, 10-12
Strut/coil spring assembly (front, 2013 and later models) - replacement, 10-12
Subframe (front, 2013 and later models) - removal and installation, 10-21
Sunroof - general information, 12-16
Suspension and steering, 10-1
    Balljoints ñ replacement, 10-16
    Coil springs (rear) - removal and installation, 10-18
    Control arm (front) (2013 and later models) - removal, inspection and installation, 10-16
    General information, 10-11
    Hub and bearing assembly - removal and installation, 10-17
    Knuckle (rear) - removal and installation, 10-18
    Lower control arm (front) (2012 and earlier models) - removal, inspection and installation, 10-15
    Power steering pump - removal and installation, 10-25
    Power steering system - bleeding, 10-27
    Radius rod (2013 and later models) - removal and installation, 10-21
    Rear suspension control arms and rear subframe - removal and installation, 10-19
    Shock absorber/coil spring assembly (front, 2012 and earlier models) - removal, inspection and installation, 10-11
    Shock absorbers (rear) - removal and installation, 10-19
    Stabilizer bar (front) - removal and installation, 10-14
    Stabilizer bar (rear) - removal and installation, 10-18
    Steering column - removal and installation, 10-26
    Steering gear - removal and installation, 10-24
    Steering gear boots - replacement, 10-24
    Steering knuckle (2012 and earlier models) - removal and installation, 10-16
    Steering knuckle (2013 and later models) - removal and installation, 10-17

Steering wheel - removal and installation, 10-22
Strut/coil spring assembly (front, 2013 and later models) - removal, inspection and installation, 10-12
Strut/coil spring assembly (front, 2013 and later models) - replacement, 10-12
Subframe (front, 2013 and later models) - removal and installation, 10-21
Tie-rod ends - removal and installation, 10-23
Upper control arm (front) (2012 and earlier models) - removal and installation, 10-14
Wheel alignment - general information, 10-27
Wheels and tires - general information, 10-27

T

Thermostat - removal and installation, 3-6
Throttle body - removal and installation, 4-8
Throttle Position (TP) sensor - replacement, 6-17
Tie-rod ends - removal and installation, 10-23
Timing chain and sprockets - removal, inspection and installation, 2A-8
Timing chains and sprockets - removal, inspection and installation, 2B-7
Tire and tire pressure checks, 1-11
Tire rotation, 1-19
Top Dead Center (TDC) for number one piston - locating, 2A-4
Top Dead Center (TDC) for number one piston - locating, 2B-3
Transfer case - 2012 and earlier models, 7B-1
General information, 7B-1
Oil seals - removal and installation, 7B-4
Shift actuator and position switch - replacement, 7B-3
Transfer case overhaul - general information, 7B-4
Transfer case - removal and installation, 7B-4
Transfer Control Unit (TCU) - replacement, 7B-3
Transfer case - 2013 and later models, 7C-1
Control unit - removal and installation, 7C-1
Transfer case - removal and installation, 7C-1
Transfer case - removal and installation, 7B-4
Transfer case - removal and installation, 7C-1
Transfer case lubricant change, 1-28
Transfer case lubricant level check, 1-20
Transfer case overhaul - general information, 7B-4
Transfer Control Unit (TCU) - replacement, 7B-3
Transmission Control Module (TCM) - removal and installation, 7A-8
Transmission mount - check and replacement (2012 and earlier models), 7A-6
Transmission range (TR) switch - replacement and adjustment, 6-14
Transmission speed sensors - replacement, 6-14
Troubleshooting, 0-24
Tune-up and routine maintenance, 1-1
Air filter check and replacement, 1-22
Automatic transmission/transaxle fluid change, 1-26
Automatic transmission/transaxle fluid level check, 1-12
Battery check, maintenance and charging, 1-15
Brake check, 1-20
Cabin air filter replacement, 1-21
Cooling system check, 1-19
Cooling system servicing (draining, flushing and refilling), 1-25
Differential lubricant change, 1-27
Driveaxle boot check, 1-23
Drivebelt check and replacement, 1-17
Engine oil and oil filter change, 1-13
Evaporative emissions control system check, 1-26
Exhaust system check, 1-23
Fluid level checks, 1-9
Front differential lubricant level check, 1-20
Fuel system check, 1-22
Introduction, 1-9
Maintenance reminder indicator resetting procedure, 1-28
Maintenance schedule, 1-8
Positive Crankcase Ventilation (PCV) valve check and replacement, 1-27
Power steering fluid level check, 1-12
Rear differential lubricant level check, 1-20
Spark plug check and replacement, 1-24
Steering and suspension check, 1-22
Tire and tire pressure checks, 1-11
Tire rotation, 1-19
Tune-up general information, 1-9
Transfer case lubricant change, 1-28
Transfer case lubricant level check, 1-20
Underhood hose check and replacement, 1-18
Windshield wiper blade inspection and replacement, 1-14
Tune-up general information, 1-9

U

Underhood hose check and replacement, 1-18
Universal joints - replacement, 8-9
Upholstery, carpets and vinyl trim - maintenance, 11-5
Upper control arm (front) (2012 and earlier models) - removal and installation, 10-14

V

V6 engines, 2A-1
V8 engine, 2B-1
Vacuum gauge diagnostic checks, 2C-5
Valve clearance - check and adjustment, 2B-4
Valve clearance check and adjustment, 2A-5
Valve covers - removal and installation, 2A-4
Valve covers - removal and installation, 2B-3
Valve springs, retainers and seals - replacement, 2A-6
Valve springs, retainers and seals - replacement, 2B-6
Variable Induction Air System (VIAS) solenoid valves and actuators (V6 engines) - replacement, 6-16
Vehicle identification numbers, 0-6

W

Water pump - replacement, 3-10
Wheel alignment - general information, 10-27
Wheels and tires - general information, 10-27
Windshield and fixed glass - replacement, 11-6
Windshield wiper blade inspection and replacement, 1-14
Wiper arms and motors - removal and installation, 12-14
Wiring diagrams - general information, 12-18

Haynes Automotive Manuals

ACURA
- 12020 **Integra** '86 thru '89 & **Legend** '86 thru '90
- 12021 **Integra** '90 thru '93 & **Legend** '91 thru '95
  Integra '94 thru '00 - *see HONDA Civic (42025)*
  MDX '01 thru '07 - *see HONDA Pilot (42037)*
- 12050 **Acura TL** all models '99 thru '08

AMC
- **Jeep CJ** - *see JEEP (50020)*
- 14020 **Mid-size models** '70 thru '83
- 14025 **(Renault) Alliance & Encore** '83 thru '87

AUDI
- 15020 **4000** all models '80 thru '87
- 15025 **5000** all models '77 thru '83
- 15026 **5000** all models '84 thru '88
  Audi A4 '96 thru '01 - *see VW Passat (96023)*
- 15030 **Audi A4** '02 thru '08

AUSTIN-HEALEY
- **Sprite** - *see MG Midget (66015)*

BMW
- 18020 **3/5 Series** '82 thru '92
- 18021 **3-Series** incl. Z3 models '92 thru '98
- 18022 **3-Series** incl. Z4 models '99 thru '05
- 18023 **3-Series** '06 thru '10
- 18025 **320i** all 4 cyl models '75 thru '83
- 18050 **1500 thru 2002** except Turbo '59 thru '77

BUICK
- 19010 **Buick Century** '97 thru '05
  Century (front-wheel drive) - *see GM (38005)*
- 19020 **Buick, Oldsmobile & Pontiac Full-size**
  (Front-wheel drive) '85 thru '05
  Buick Electra, LeSabre and Park Avenue;
  Oldsmobile Delta 88 Royale, Ninety Eight
  and Regency; **Pontiac** Bonneville
- 19025 **Buick, Oldsmobile & Pontiac Full-size**
  (Rear wheel drive) '70 thru '90
  Buick Estate, Electra, LeSabre, Limited,
  Oldsmobile Custom Cruiser, Delta 88,
  Ninety-eight, **Pontiac** Bonneville,
  Catalina, Grandville, Parisienne
- 19030 **Mid-size Regal & Century** all rear-drive
  models with V6, V8 and Turbo '74 thru '87
  Regal - *see GENERAL MOTORS (38010)*
  Riviera - *see GENERAL MOTORS (38030)*
  Roadmaster - *see CHEVROLET (24046)*
  Skyhawk - *see GENERAL MOTORS (38015)*
  Skylark - *see GM (38020, 38025)*
  Somerset - *see GENERAL MOTORS (38025)*

CADILLAC
- 21015 **CTS & CTS-V** '03 thru '12
- 21030 **Cadillac Rear Wheel Drive** '70 thru '93
  Cimarron - *see GENERAL MOTORS (38015)*
  DeVille - *see GM (38031 & 38032)*
  Eldorado - *see GM (38030 & 38031)*
  Fleetwood - *see GM (38031)*
  Seville - *see GM (38030, 38031 & 38032)*

CHEVROLET
- 10305 **Chevrolet Engine Overhaul Manual**
- 24010 **Astro & GMC Safari Mini-vans** '85 thru '05
- 24015 **Camaro V8** all models '70 thru '81
- 24016 **Camaro** all models '82 thru '92
- 24017 **Camaro & Firebird** '93 thru '02
  Cavalier - *see GENERAL MOTORS (38016)*
  Celebrity - *see GENERAL MOTORS (38005)*
- 24020 **Chevelle, Malibu & El Camino** '69 thru '87
- 24024 **Chevette & Pontiac T1000** '76 thru '87
  Citation - *see GENERAL MOTORS (38020)*
- 24027 **Colorado & GMC Canyon** '04 thru '10
- 24032 **Corsica/Beretta** all models '87 thru '96
- 24040 **Corvette** all V8 models '68 thru '82
- 24041 **Corvette** all models '84 thru '96
- 24045 **Full-size Sedans** Caprice, Impala, Biscayne,
  Bel Air & Wagons '69 thru '90
- 24046 **Impala SS & Caprice and Buick Roadmaster**
  '91 thru '96
  Impala '00 thru '05 - *see LUMINA (24048)*
- 24047 **Impala & Monte Carlo** all models '06 thru '11
  Lumina '90 thru '94 - *see GM (38010)*
- 24048 **Lumina & Monte Carlo** '95 thru '05
  Lumina APV - *see GM (38035)*
- 24050 **Luv Pick-up** all 2WD & 4WD '72 thru '82
  Malibu '00 thru '04 - *see GM (38026)*
- 24055 **Monte Carlo** all models '70 thru '88
  Monte Carlo '95 thru '01 - *see LUMINA (24048)*
- 24059 **Nova** all V8 models '69 thru '79
- 24060 **Nova and Geo Prizm** '85 thru '92
- 24064 **Pick-ups** '67 thru '87 - Chevrolet & GMC
- 24065 **Pick-ups** '88 thru '98 - Chevrolet & GMC

- 24066 **Pick-ups** '99 thru '06 - Chevrolet & GMC
- 24067 **Chevrolet Silverado & GMC Sierra** '07 thru '12
- 24070 **S-10 & S-15 Pick-ups** '82 thru '93,
  Blazer & Jimmy '83 thru '94,
- 24071 **S-10 & Sonoma Pick-ups** '94 thru '04, including **Blazer, Jimmy & Hombre**
- 24072 **Chevrolet TrailBlazer, GMC Envoy &**
  Oldsmobile Bravada '02 thru '09
- 24075 **Sprint** '85 thru '88 & **Geo Metro** '89 thru '01
- 24080 **Vans - Chevrolet & GMC** '68 thru '96
- 24081 **Chevrolet Express & GMC Savana**
  Full-size Vans '96 thru '10

CHRYSLER
- 10310 **Chrysler Engine Overhaul Manual**
- 25015 **Chrysler Cirrus, Dodge Stratus,**
  Plymouth Breeze '95 thru '00
- 25020 **Full-size Front-Wheel Drive** '88 thru '93
  K-Cars - *see DODGE Aries (30008)*
  Laser - *see DODGE Daytona (30030)*
- 25025 **Chrysler LHS, Concorde, New Yorker,**
  Dodge Intrepid, **Eagle** Vision, '93 thru '97
- 25026 **Chrysler LHS, Concorde, 300M,**
  Dodge Intrepid, '98 thru '04
- 25027 **Chrysler 300, Dodge Charger &**
  Magnum '05 thru '09
- 25030 **Chrysler & Plymouth Mid-size**
  front wheel drive '82 thru '95
  Rear-wheel Drive - *see Dodge (30050)*
- 25035 **PT Cruiser** all models '01 thru '10
- 25040 **Chrysler Sebring** '95 thru '06, **Dodge** Stratus
  '01 thru '06, **Dodge** Avenger '95 thru '00

DATSUN
- 28005 **200SX** all models '80 thru '83
- 28007 **B-210** all models '73 thru '78
- 28009 **210** all models '79 thru '82
- 28012 **240Z, 260Z & 280Z** Coupe '70 thru '78
- 28014 **280ZX** Coupe & 2+2 '79 thru '83
  300ZX - *see NISSAN (72010)*
- 28018 **510 & PL521 Pick-up** '68 thru '73
- 28020 **510** all models '78 thru '81
- 28022 **620 Series Pick-up** all models '73 thru '79
  720 Series Pick-up - *see NISSAN (72030)*
- 28025 **810/Maxima** all gasoline models '77 thru '84

DODGE
- **400 & 600** - *see CHRYSLER (25030)*
- 30008 **Aries & Plymouth Reliant** '81 thru '89
- 30010 **Caravan & Plymouth Voyager** '84 thru '95
- 30011 **Caravan & Plymouth Voyager** '96 thru '02
- 30012 **Challenger/Plymouth Saporro** '78 thru '83
- 30013 **Caravan, Chrysler Voyager, Town &**
  Country '03 thru '07
- 30016 **Colt & Plymouth Champ** '78 thru '87
- 30020 **Dakota Pick-ups** all models '87 thru '96
- 30021 **Durango** '98 & '99, **Dakota** '97 thru '99
- 30022 **Durango** '00 thru '03 **Dakota** '00 thru '04
- 30023 **Durango** '04 thru '09, **Dakota** '05 thru '11
- 30025 **Dart, Demon, Plymouth Barracuda,**
  Duster & Valiant 6 cyl models '67 thru '76
- 30030 **Daytona & Chrysler Laser** '84 thru '89
  Intrepid - *see CHRYSLER (25025, 25026)*
- 30034 **Neon** all models '95 thru '99
- 30035 **Omni & Plymouth Horizon** '78 thru '90
- 30036 **Dodge and Plymouth Neon** '00 thru '05
- 30040 **Pick-ups** all full-size models '74 thru '93
- 30041 **Pick-ups** all full-size models '94 thru '01
- 30042 **Pick-ups** full-size models '02 thru '08
- 30045 **Ram 50/D50 Pick-ups & Raider and**
  Plymouth Arrow Pick-ups '79 thru '93
- 30050 **Dodge/Plymouth/Chrysler RWD** '71 thru '89
- 30055 **Shadow & Plymouth Sundance** '87 thru '94
- 30060 **Spirit & Plymouth Acclaim** '89 thru '95
- 30065 **Vans - Dodge & Plymouth** '71 thru '03

EAGLE
- **Talon** - *see MITSUBISHI (68030, 68031)*
- **Vision** - *see CHRYSLER (25025)*

FIAT
- 34010 **124 Sport Coupe & Spider** '68 thru '78
- 34025 **X1/9** all models '74 thru '80

FORD
- 10320 **Ford Engine Overhaul Manual**
- 10355 **Ford Automatic Transmission Overhaul**
- 11500 **Mustang** '64-1/2 thru '70 Restoration Guide
- 36004 **Aerostar Mini-vans** all models '86 thru '97
- 36006 **Contour & Mercury Mystique** '95 thru '00
- 36008 **Courier Pick-up** all models '72 thru '82
- 36012 **Crown Victoria & Mercury Grand**
  Marquis '88 thru '10
- 36016 **Escort/Mercury Lynx** all models '81 thru '90
- 36020 **Escort/Mercury Tracer** '91 thru '02

- 36022 **Escape & Mazda Tribute** '01 thru '11
- 36024 **Explorer & Mazda Navajo** '91 thru '01
- 36025 **Explorer/Mercury Mountaineer** '02 thru '10
- 36028 **Fairmont & Mercury Zephyr** '78 thru '83
- 36030 **Festiva & Aspire** '88 thru '97
- 36032 **Fiesta** all models '77 thru '80
- 36034 **Focus** all models '00 thru '11
- 36036 **Ford & Mercury Full-size** '75 thru '87
- 36044 **Ford & Mercury Mid-size** '75 thru '86
- 36045 **Fusion & Mercury Milan** '06 thru '10
- 36048 **Mustang V8** all models '64-1/2 thru '73
- 36049 **Mustang II** 4 cyl, V6 & V8 models '74 thru '78
- 36050 **Mustang & Mercury Capri** '79 thru '93
- 36051 **Mustang** all models '94 thru '04
- 36052 **Mustang** '05 thru '10
- 36054 **Pick-ups & Bronco** '73 thru '79
- 36058 **Pick-ups & Bronco** '80 thru '96
- 36059 **F-150 & Expedition** '97 thru '09, **F-250** '97
  thru '99 & **Lincoln Navigator** '98 thru '09
- 36060 **Super Duty Pick-ups, Excursion** '99 thru '10
- 36061 **F-150** full-size '04 thru '10
- 36062 **Pinto & Mercury Bobcat** '75 thru '80
- 36066 **Probe** all models '89 thru '92
  Probe '93 thru '97 - *see MAZDA 626 (61042)*
- 36070 **Ranger/Bronco II** gasoline models '83 thru '92
- 36071 **Ranger** '93 thru '10 & **Mazda Pick-ups** '94 thru '09
- 36074 **Taurus & Mercury Sable** '86 thru '95
- 36075 **Taurus & Mercury Sable** '96 thru '05
- 36078 **Tempo & Mercury Topaz** '84 thru '94
- 36082 **Thunderbird/Mercury Cougar** '83 thru '88
- 36086 **Thunderbird/Mercury Cougar** '89 thru '97
- 36090 **Vans** all V8 Econoline models '69 thru '91
- 36094 **Vans** full size '92 thru '10
- 36097 **Windstar Mini-van** '95 thru '07

GENERAL MOTORS
- 10360 **GM Automatic Transmission Overhaul**
- 38005 **Buick Century, Chevrolet Celebrity,**
  Oldsmobile Cutlass Ciera & Pontiac 6000
  all models '82 thru '96
- 38010 **Buick Regal, Chevrolet Lumina,**
  Oldsmobile Cutlass Supreme &
  Pontiac Grand Prix (FWD) '88 thru '07
- 38015 **Buick Skyhawk, Cadillac Cimarron,**
  Chevrolet Cavalier, Oldsmobile Firenza &
  Pontiac J-2000 & Sunbird '82 thru '94
- 38016 **Chevrolet Cavalier &**
  Pontiac Sunfire '95 thru '05
- 38017 **Chevrolet Cobalt & Pontiac G5** '05 thru '11
- 38020 **Buick Skylark, Chevrolet Citation,**
  Olds Omega, Pontiac Phoenix '80 thru '85
- 38025 **Buick Skylark & Somerset,**
  Oldsmobile Achieva & Calais and
  Pontiac Grand Am all models '85 thru '98
- 38026 **Chevrolet Malibu, Olds Alero & Cutlass,**
  Pontiac Grand Am '97 thru '03
- 38027 **Chevrolet Malibu** '04 thru '10
- 38030 **Cadillac Eldorado, Seville, Oldsmobile**
  Toronado, Buick Riviera '71 thru '85
- 38031 **Cadillac Eldorado & Seville, DeVille, Fleetwood**
  & Olds Toronado, Buick Riviera '86 thru '93
- 38032 **Cadillac DeVille** '94 thru '05 & **Seville** '92 thru '04
  Cadillac DTS '06 thru '10
- 38035 **Chevrolet Lumina APV, Olds Silhouette**
  & Pontiac Trans Sport all models '90 thru '96
- 38036 **Chevrolet Venture, Olds Silhouette,**
  Pontiac Trans Sport & Montana '97 thru '05
  General Motors Full-size
  Rear-wheel Drive - *see BUICK (19025)*
- 38040 **Chevrolet Equinox** '05 thru '09 **Pontiac**
  Torrent '06 thru '09
- 38070 **Chevrolet HHR** '06 thru '11

GEO
- **Metro** - *see CHEVROLET Sprint (24075)*
  Prizm - '85 thru '92 see CHEVY (24060),
  '93 thru '02 see TOYOTA Corolla (92036),
- 40030 **Storm** all models '90 thru '93
  Tracker - *see SUZUKI Samurai (90010)*

GMC
- **Vans & Pick-ups** - *see CHEVROLET*

HONDA
- 42010 **Accord CVCC** all models '76 thru '83
- 42011 **Accord** all models '84 thru '89
- 42012 **Accord** all models '90 thru '93
- 42013 **Accord** all models '94 thru '97
- 42014 **Accord** all models '98 thru '02
- 42015 **Accord** '03 thru '07
- 42020 **Civic 1200** all models '73 thru '79
- 42021 **Civic 1300 & 1500 CVCC** '80 thru '83
- 42022 **Civic 1500 CVCC** all models '75 thru '79

(Continued on other side)

Haynes North America, Inc., 861 Lawrence Drive, Newbury Park, CA 91320-1514 • (805) 498-6703 • http://www.haynes.com

Haynes Automotive Manuals (continued)

NOTE: If you do not see a listing for your vehicle, consult your local Haynes dealer for the latest product information.

42023 **Civic** all models '84 thru '91
42024 **Civic & del Sol** '92 thru '95
42025 **Civic** '96 thru '00, **CR-V** '97 thru '01,
      Acura Integra '94 thru '00
42026 **Civic** '01 thru '10, **CR-V** '02 thru '09
42035 **Odyssey** all models '99 thru '10
      Passport - *see ISUZU Rodeo (47017)*
42037 **Honda Pilot** '03 thru '07, **Acura MDX** '01 thru '07
42040 **Prelude CVCC** all models '79 thru '89

HYUNDAI
43010 **Elantra** all models '96 thru '10
43015 **Excel & Accent** all models '86 thru '09
43050 **Santa Fe** all models '01 thru '06
43055 **Sonata** all models '99 thru '08

INFINITI
      G35 '03 thru '08 - *see NISSAN 350Z (72011)*

ISUZU
      Hombre - *see CHEVROLET S-10 (24071)*
47017 **Rodeo, Amigo & Honda Passport** '89 thru '02
47020 **Trooper & Pick-up** '81 thru '93

JAGUAR
49010 **XJ6** all 6 cyl models '68 thru '86
49011 **XJ6** all models '88 thru '94
49015 **XJ12 & XJS** all 12 cyl models '72 thru '85

JEEP
50010 **Cherokee, Comanche & Wagoneer Limited**
      all models '84 thru '01
50020 **CJ** all models '49 thru '86
50025 **Grand Cherokee** all models '93 thru '04
50026 **Grand Cherokee** '05 thru '09
50029 **Grand Wagoneer & Pick-up** '72 thru '91
      Grand Wagoneer '84 thru '91, Cherokee &
      Wagoneer '72 thru '83, Pick-up '72 thru '88
50030 **Wrangler** all models '87 thru '11
50035 **Liberty** '02 thru '07

KIA
54050 **Optima** '01 thru '10
54070 **Sephia** '94 thru '01, **Spectra** '00 thru '09,
      Sportage '05 thru '10

LEXUS
      ES 300/330 - *see TOYOTA Camry (92007) (92008)*
      RX 330 - *see TOYOTA Highlander (92095)*

LINCOLN
      Navigator - *see FORD Pick-up (36059)*
59010 **Rear-Wheel Drive** all models '70 thru '10

MAZDA
61010 **GLC Hatchback** (rear-wheel drive) '77 thru '83
61011 **GLC** (front-wheel drive) '81 thru '85
61012 **Mazda3** '04 thru '11
61015 **323 & Protegé** '90 thru '03
61016 **MX-5 Miata** '90 thru '09
61020 **MPV** all models '89 thru '98
      Navajo - *see Ford Explorer (36024)*
61030 **Pick-ups** '72 thru '93
      Pick-ups '94 thru '00 - *see Ford Ranger (36071)*
61035 **RX-7** all models '79 thru '85
61036 **RX-7** all models '86 thru '91
61040 **626** (rear-wheel drive) all models '79 thru '82
61041 **626/MX-6** (front-wheel drive) '83 thru '92
61042 **626, MX-6/Ford Probe** '93 thru '02
61043 **Mazda6** '03 thru '11

MERCEDES-BENZ
63012 **123 Series Diesel** '76 thru '85
63015 **190 Series** four-cyl gas models, '84 thru '88
63020 **230/250/280** 6 cyl sohc models '68 thru '72
63025 **280 123 Series** gasoline models '77 thru '81
63030 **350 & 450** all models '71 thru '80
63040 **C-Class:** C230/C240/C280/C320/C350 '01 thru '07

MERCURY
64200 **Villager & Nissan Quest** '93 thru '01
      All other titles, see FORD Listing.

MG
66010 **MGB** Roadster & GT Coupe '62 thru '80
66015 **MG Midget, Austin Healey Sprite** '58 thru '80

MINI
67020 **Mini** '02 thru '11

MITSUBISHI
68020 **Cordia, Tredia, Galant, Precis &**
      Mirage '83 thru '93
68030 **Eclipse, Eagle Talon & Ply. Laser** '90 thru '94
68031 **Eclipse** '95 thru '05, **Eagle Talon** '95 thru '98
68035 **Galant** '94 thru '10
68040 **Pick-up** '83 thru '96 & **Montero** '83 thru '93

NISSAN
72010 **300ZX** all models including Turbo '84 thru '89
72011 **350Z & Infiniti G35** all models '03 thru '08
72015 **Altima** all models '93 thru '06
72016 **Altima** '07 thru '10
72020 **Maxima** all models '85 thru '92
72021 **Maxima** all models '93 thru '04
72025 **Murano** '03 thru '10
72030 **Pick-ups** '80 thru '97 **Pathfinder** '87 thru '95
72031 **Frontier Pick-up, Xterra, Pathfinder** '96 thru '04
72032 **Frontier & Xterra** '05 thru '11
72040 **Pulsar** all models '83 thru '86
      Quest - *see MERCURY Villager (64200)*
72050 **Sentra** all models '82 thru '94
72051 **Sentra & 200SX** all models '95 thru '06
72060 **Stanza** all models '82 thru '90
72070 **Titan pick-ups** '04 thru '10 **Armada** '05 thru '10

OLDSMOBILE
73015 **Cutlass** V6 & V8 gas models '74 thru '88
      For other OLDSMOBILE titles, see BUICK,
      CHEVROLET or GENERAL MOTORS listing.

PLYMOUTH
      For PLYMOUTH titles, see DODGE listing.

PONTIAC
79008 **Fiero** all models '84 thru '88
79018 **Firebird** V8 models except Turbo '70 thru '81
79019 **Firebird** all models '82 thru '92
79025 **G6** all models '05 thru '09
79040 **Mid-size Rear-wheel Drive** '70 thru '87
      Vibe '03 thru '11 - *see TOYOTA Matrix (92060)*
      For other PONTIAC titles, see BUICK,
      CHEVROLET or GENERAL MOTORS listing.

PORSCHE
80020 **911** except Turbo & Carrera 4 '65 thru '89
80025 **914** all 4 cyl models '69 thru '76
80030 **924** all models including Turbo '76 thru '82
80035 **944** all models including Turbo '83 thru '89

RENAULT
      Alliance & Encore - *see AMC (14020)*

SAAB
84010 **900** all models including Turbo '79 thru '88

SATURN
87010 **Saturn** all S-series models '91 thru '02
87011 **Saturn Ion** '03 thru '07
87020 **Saturn** all L-series models '00 thru '04
87040 **Saturn VUE** '02 thru '07

SUBARU
89002 **1100, 1300, 1400 & 1600** '71 thru '79
89003 **1600 & 1800** 2WD & 4WD '80 thru '94
89100 **Legacy** all models '90 thru '99
89101 **Legacy & Forester** '00 thru '06

SUZUKI
90010 **Samurai/Sidekick & Geo Tracker** '86 thru '01

TOYOTA
92005 **Camry** all models '83 thru '91
92006 **Camry** all models '92 thru '96
92007 **Camry, Avalon, Solara, Lexus ES 300** '97 thru '01
92008 **Toyota Camry, Avalon and Solara and**
      Lexus ES 300/330 all models '02 thru '06
92009 **Camry** '07 thru '11
92015 **Celica Rear Wheel Drive** '71 thru '85
92020 **Celica Front Wheel Drive** '86 thru '99
92025 **Celica Supra** all models '79 thru '92
92030 **Corolla** all models '75 thru '79
92032 **Corolla** all rear wheel drive models '80 thru '87
92035 **Corolla** all front wheel drive models '84 thru '92
92036 **Corolla & Geo Prizm** '93 thru '02
92037 **Corolla** models '03 thru '11
92040 **Corolla Tercel** all models '80 thru '82
92045 **Corona** all models '74 thru '82
92050 **Cressida** all models '78 thru '82
92055 **Land Cruiser** FJ40, 43, 45, 55 '68 thru '82
92056 **Land Cruiser** FJ60, 62, 80, FZJ80 '80 thru '96
92060 **Matrix & Pontiac Vibe** '03 thru '11
92065 **MR2** all models '85 thru '87
92070 **Pick-up** all models '69 thru '78
92075 **Pick-up** all models '79 thru '95
92076 **Tacoma, 4Runner, & T100** '93 thru '04
92077 **Tacoma** all models '05 thru '09
92078 **Tundra** '00 thru '06 & **Sequoia** '01 thru '07
92079 **4Runner** all models '03 thru '09
92080 **Previa** all models '91 thru '95
92081 **Prius** all models '01 thru '08
92082 **RAV4** all models '96 thru '10
92085 **Tercel** all models '87 thru '94
92090 **Sienna** all models '98 thru '09
92095 **Highlander & Lexus RX-330** '99 thru '07

TRIUMPH
94007 **Spitfire** all models '62 thru '81
94010 **TR7** all models '75 thru '81

VW
96008 **Beetle & Karmann Ghia** '54 thru '79
96009 **New Beetle** '98 thru '11
96016 **Rabbit, Jetta, Scirocco & Pick-up** gas
      models '75 thru '92 & Convertible '80 thru '92
96017 **Golf, GTI & Jetta** '93 thru '98, **Cabrio** '95 thru '02
96018 **Golf, GTI, Jetta** '99 thru '05
96019 **Jetta, Rabbit, GTI & Golf** '05 thru '11
96020 **Rabbit, Jetta & Pick-up** diesel '77 thru '84
96023 **Passat** '98 thru '05, **Audi A4** '96 thru '01
96030 **Transporter 1600** all models '68 thru '79
96035 **Transporter 1700, 1800 & 2000** '72 thru '79
96040 **Type 3 1500 & 1600** all models '63 thru '73
96045 **Vanagon** all air-cooled models '80 thru '83

VOLVO
97010 **120, 130 Series & 1800 Sports** '61 thru '73
97015 **140 Series** all models '66 thru '74
97020 **240 Series** all models '76 thru '93
97040 **740 & 760 Series** all models '82 thru '88
97050 **850 Series** all models '93 thru '97

TECHBOOK MANUALS
10205 **Automotive Computer Codes**
10206 **OBD-II & Electronic Engine Management**
10210 **Automotive Emissions Control Manual**
10215 **Fuel Injection Manual** '78 thru '85
10220 **Fuel Injection Manual** '86 thru '99
10225 **Holley Carburetor Manual**
10230 **Rochester Carburetor Manual**
10240 **Weber/Zenith/Stromberg/SU Carburetors**
10305 **Chevrolet Engine Overhaul Manual**
10310 **Chrysler Engine Overhaul Manual**
10320 **Ford Engine Overhaul Manual**
10330 **GM and Ford Diesel Engine Repair Manual**
10333 **Engine Performance Manual**
10340 **Small Engine Repair Manual, 5 HP & Less**
10341 **Small Engine Repair Manual, 5.5 - 20 HP**
10345 **Suspension, Steering & Driveline Manual**
10355 **Ford Automatic Transmission Overhaul**
10360 **GM Automatic Transmission Overhaul**
10405 **Automotive Body Repair & Painting**
10410 **Automotive Brake Manual**
10411 **Automotive Anti-lock Brake (ABS) Systems**
10415 **Automotive Detailing Manual**
10420 **Automotive Electrical Manual**
10425 **Automotive Heating & Air Conditioning**
10430 **Automotive Reference Manual & Dictionary**
10435 **Automotive Tools Manual**
10440 **Used Car Buying Guide**
10445 **Welding Manual**
10450 **ATV Basics**
10452 **Scooters 50cc to 250cc**

SPANISH MANUALS
98903 **Reparación de Carrocería & Pintura**
98904 **Manual de Carburador Modelos**
      Holley & Rochester
98905 **Códigos Automotrices de la Computadora**
98906 **OBD-II & Sistemas de Control Electrónico**
      del Motor
98910 **Frenos Automotriz**
98913 **Electricidad Automotriz**
98915 **Inyección de Combustible** '86 al '99
99040 **Chevrolet & GMC Camionetas** '67 al '87
99041 **Chevrolet & GMC Camionetas** '88 al '98
99042 **Chevrolet & GMC Camionetas**
      Cerradas '68 al '95
99043 **Chevrolet/GMC Camionetas** '94 al '04
99048 **Chevrolet/GMC Camionetas** '99 al '06
99055 **Dodge Caravan & Plymouth Voyager** '84 al '95
99075 **Ford Camionetas y Bronco** '80 al '94
99076 **Ford F-150** '97 al '09
99077 **Ford Camionetas Cerradas** '69 al '91
99088 **Ford Modelos de Tamaño Mediano** '75 al '86
99089 **Ford Camionetas Ranger** '93 al '10
99091 **Ford Taurus & Mercury Sable** '86 al '95
99095 **GM Modelos de Tamaño Grande** '70 al '90
99100 **GM Modelos de Tamaño Mediano** '70 al '88
99106 **Jeep Cherokee, Wagoneer & Comanche**
      '84 al '00
99110 **Nissan Camioneta** '80 al '96, **Pathfinder** '87 al '95
99118 **Nissan Sentra** '82 al '94
99125 **Toyota Camionetas y 4Runner** '79 al '95

Over 100 Haynes
motorcycle manuals
also available

7-12